Centerville Library
Washington DISCARD blic Library
Centerville, Ohio

D0076016

Great Women Mystery Writers

Great Women Mystery Writers

Second Edition

Elizabeth Blakesley Lindsay

GREENWOOD PRESS
Westport, Connecticut • London

Library of Congress Cataloging-in-Publication Data

Lindsay, Elizabeth Blakesley.
  Great women mystery writers. — 2nd ed. / by Elizabeth Blakesley
Lindsay.
      p. cm.
  Updated ed. of: Great women mystery writers : classic to contemporary
/ edited by Kathleen Gregory Klein. 1994.
  Includes bibliographical references and indexes.
  ISBN 0–313–33428–5 (alk. paper)
  1. Detective and mystery stories, English—Bio-bibliography. 2.
Detective and mystery stories, American—Bio-bibliography. 3.
Detective and mystery stories, English—Stories, plots, etc. 4.
Detective and mystery stories, American—Stories, plots, etc. 5.
English fiction—Women authors—Bio-bibliography. 6. American fiction—
Women authors—Bio-bibliography. 7. Women authors, English—
Biography—Dictionaries. 8. Women authors, American—Biography—
Dictionaries. I. Great women mystery writers. II. Title.

  PR830.D4G74   2007
  823'.0872099287—dc22   2006026202

British Library Cataloguing in Publication Data is available.

Copyright © 2007 by Elizabeth Blakesley Lindsay

All rights reserved. No portion of this book may be
reproduced, by any process or technique, without the
express written consent of the publisher.

Library of Congress Catalog Card Number: 2006026202
ISBN: 0–313–33428–5

First published in 2007

Greenwood Press, 88 Post Road West, Westport, CT 06881
An imprint of Greenwood Publishing Group, Inc.
www.greenwood.com

Printed in the United States of America

The paper used in this book complies with the
Permanent Paper Standard issued by the National
Information Standards Organization (Z39.48–1984).

10 9 8 7 6 5 4 3 2 1

In memory of my grandparents

Chauncey Creighton Blakesley
1922–1993
Eldora Louise Morton Blakesley
1924–1996
Lawrence Lark Lutes
1924–1996
Helen Duncan Beaudette Lutes
1927–1983

Contents

Preface

This work was originally envisioned as a bio-bibliographic guide for new women mystery writers. Having the proposal accepted as the second edition of *Great Women Mystery Writers* changed that initial focus. This volume includes entries on 90 English-speaking women writers. Selections were made based on their status as award winners or nominees, their commercial success, and excellent critical acclaim. Each entry provides biographical information, discusses her works and major themes, offers an overview of critical reception and, if applicable, scholarly treatments, and lists primary and secondary works.

This volume contains entries on many writers who were new to the field or not even writing at the time of Kathleen Gregory Klein's first edition. It also provides updated entries for many women writers who have continued to publish and flourish since 1994. Writers who were already deceased at the time of the first edition are not included here. Writers who have died since 1994, but whose first edition entries remain complete, also do not have updated entries; see Appendix E for a listing of these writers and their dates of death. Some writers have not published new works since the time of the first edition; updated entries are not included to provide space for coverage of new writers.

In addition to the appendix noted previously, there are also indexes by character name, setting, type of detective, and other fields. Information about major American and British awards is provided, with lists of women award nominees and winners. A final appendix provides information about the Sisters in Crime organization.

Acknowledgments

I appreciate the support of the Washington State University (WSU) Libraries in the form of weekly professional activity time and a two-week research leave that helped me complete this work. I want to thank our former director Ginny Steel and our interim director Cindy Kaag for their support for this project. Thanks are also due to our Access Services department. This project could not have been completed without their work in procuring materials for me via interlibrary loan and consortial borrowing partners. Recognition is also due to the student workers who reshelved all those bound copies of *Publishers Weekly* and *Booklist* that I used.

I appreciate the support of Greenwood editor George Butler who inherited this project from another editor. He was always prompt, helpful, and encouraging with his feedback.

I am extremely lucky to have so many wonderful colleagues and friends at WSU. I wish I had space to insert our entire employee list. Lorena O'English, Carol Robinson, Cheryl Gunselman, and Sarah McCord, along with Lara Cummings, Jane Scales, and Corey Johnson, among many others, have all been extremely supportive and interested in this project and its progress.

Since the late 1990s, I have found many wonderful fellow mystery readers online. I want to mention two particularly wonderful groups: femmystery and ARM Readers, which are both hosted at Yahoo!. Since moving to Washington State, I have also relied on the Internet to trade mystery recommendations with former coworker and friend Mary Adams. My mother-in-law, Jessica Onstrom, is another mystery fan who always has a good recommendation for me. I must also mention two friends from long ago, Michelle Baughman Clark and Cynthia Rincón. They always told me I would write a book someday, and it turns out they were right.

All my love to my husband, Shawn, and to my parents, William and Linda Blakesley. Shawn has been a source of constant encouragement and support and has done more than his share of the dishes these past two years. My mother read to me before I was even born, and my parents encouraged my love of reading and of mysteries, from my days of Encyclopedia Brown and Nancy Drew onward. I could not have done any of this without you.

Introduction

In her introduction to the first edition of *Great Women Mystery Writers,* Kathleen Gregory Klein provided a history of women's contributions to the mystery genre. As this volume takes up where Klein's left off, the introduction to this second edition focuses on the continued development of women in the mystery field and the questions of genre and feminism that have attracted the attention of many scholars.

Maureen T. Reddy noted that 207 new mystery series by women writers were begun in the 1980s, proving her point that readers who sought new mystery fiction beyond Nancy Drew had a much wider selection in 1989 than when the Drew series began in 1929 (1062). She also stated that the growth in mystery fiction by women was continuing in the 1990s, and she was certainly right. For example, reviews of the industry for *Publishers Weekly* by Carolyn Anthony (1990) and Robert A. Carter (1991) both indicated strong growth in the mystery field, among women writers in particular. One editor credited the work of Sisters in Crime, which is discussed here in Appendix M, for helping boost the publicity for women's mystery writing (Anthony 28). Another editor noted that women writers were "really coming into their own" and that "two out of four books feature female detectives these days" (Carter 18).

Priscilla L. Walton and Manina Jones confirm Reddy's claim with data. Their work shows that there were four novels featuring a female professional investigator published during 1961–65, and that during 1991–95, the number of such books published grew to 366 (Walton 29). Further evidence comes with consulting the third edition of Willetta L. Heising's *Detecting Women* and tallying the numbers of series that she indicates debuted in the 1990s. This exercise shows that 538 new mystery series were begun by women writers. Of those, 60 were in the private investigator genre, 92 featured police or other law enforcement agency professionals, and 386 featured amateur sleuths from a variety of professions or situations. Of the 60 private investigator series, 55 of them have a woman as the main character, four have a male protagonist, and one series (S. J. Rozan's) features a male-female P.I. team. Of the 92 series in the police genre, 59 have a woman protagonist, with many featuring a male detective partner, and 33 feature a male lead. The amateur sleuth category features 335 series with a female lead, 8 with a male-female pair, and 43 with a male protagonist. It is safe to say that the trend is continuing: of the 90 authors included here, 12 began writing since Heising's third edition, which was published in 2000.

Although there has been growth in the P.I. and police procedural genres, a great deal of the explosion in mystery publishing is in the amateur sleuth realm. Since the early 1990s, readers have been able to find not just an increasing number of women detectives to read about, but books about women sleuths who are interested in the same activities they are interested in. For example, a number of mystery series feature caterers. Examples include Diane Mott Davidson's series that features a woman named Goldy Bear. The series debuted in 1990 and the novels include descriptions of her work and recipes. Tamar Myers's series about Mennonite inn owner Magdalena Yoder, which began in 1994, also includes recipes. In 1997, Phyllis Richman began a series about a restaurant critic, which included her solving crimes involving restaurant owners, chefs, and other newspaper writers. Joanne Fluke launched a series in 2000 about a bakery manager, and Jerrilyn Farmer's Madeline Bean series features a caterer and party planner in Hollywood.

Another area of emphasis in amateur sleuth mysteries is arts and crafts. For example, Monica Ferris began a series about a woman who inherits her sister's yarn store, takes over management of the store, even though she knows nothing of needlecrafts, and solves her sister's murder. These novels include details of techniques and supplies, and each has a pattern in the back for a project. Maggie Sefton began a series that follows a young woman who returns to her hometown when her yarn-store owning aunt is killed. She solves the murder, learns how to knit, and stays in her hometown with her new friends and colleagues. Laura Childs's new series is set in a scrapbooking store in New Orleans; the first novel in the series was *Keepsake Crimes* (2003).

An increasing number of amateur sleuth series feature characters with unusual jobs. The new amateur sleuths have moved way beyond the typical personae of retired ladies, stay-at-home moms, and lawyers to include greeting card writers, tea shop owners, film editors, and more. Donna Andrews's Meg Langslow is an ornamental blacksmith, and Janet Evanovich's Stephanie Plum takes on bounty hunting after losing her job at the lingerie factory. Barbara Block introduced a pet store owner in her series, and Laurien Berenson introduced a teacher posing as a dog breeder in hers. Sujata Massey's Rei Shimura and Sharon Fiffer's Jane Wheel are both freelancers in the antiques business; Taffy Cannon writes a series featuring a former police officer who has become a tour guide. Susan Wittig Albert writes about China Bayles, who owns an herb store, and her friend Ruby Wilcox, who runs a New Age store; Denise Osborne's sleuth is a Feng Shui practitioner. Amateur sleuths in the great outdoors also became popular in the 1990s, with Nevada Barr beginning her series about National Park Service ranger Anna Pigeon in 1993, Skye Kathleen Moody introducing Fish and Wildlife agent Venus Diamond in 1996, and Jessica Speart introducing her Fish and Wildlife agent, Rachel Porter, in 1997.

Another trend among amateur sleuths involves unusual abilities. Christine T. Jorgensen's *Stella the Stargazer* series was one of the first to offer a psychic sleuth. Martha C. Lawrence's series follows Elizabeth Chase, an investigator who has a Ph.D. in paranormal psychology and her own talents in that area. Nancy Atherton's Aunt Dimity series features a ghost as the main character. Charlaine Harris has given readers two protagonists with unusual abilities. Sookie Stackhouse works as a waitress in a small town in Louisiana. Her life is miserable because she is able to read people's minds, but her abilities do not extend to the town's new citizens, who are vampires. In a new series, Harris writes about Harper Connelly, who was left with the ability to locate dead people after being struck by lightning. Both become involved in crime-solving endeavors.

Marilyn Stasio links the growth of amateur sleuth novels with the advice she heard a major editor give to aspiring authors, which was "to retool their unsold novels as mysteries" (14). Stasio examined several women who write what she calls "chick-lit mysteries," noting the formulaic approach taken regarding sidekick characters, personality quirks, use of humor, and prevalence of sex (14–15). Stasio does credit writers like Janet Evanovich for her "mastery of the structural mechanics of classic farce" and Kate White for her strong sense of satire and ability to use humor effectively beyond just the characterization of her series protagonist (15).

All types of detective fiction, not just the recent trend of "chick-lit mysteries," remain subject to critique and being limited by those who perceive the genre as less important or less valuable. These types of criticisms have even been raised by writers who are often classified as mystery writers. Patricia Highsmith reportedly disliked being labeled as a mystery and suspense writer, although she wrote in 1966, perhaps ironically, that one of her greatest achievements was being labeled by the *Times Literary Supplement* as "the crime writer who comes closest to giving crime writing a good name" (viii). More recently, Sharyn McCrumb has been clear about her intentions and preference to be considered as a writer, not a mystery writer. McCrumb has stated clearly that she writes novels that should not labeled with any genre classifications, and that above all, she sees herself as a storyteller (Silet 1995:370, 380).

Other mystery writers believe that the genre does not limit them and some, like Liza Cody, emphasize that the genre allows for their attention to character development. As Cody told Charles L. P. Silet, the knowledge that a mystery novel must end, and in a certain way, allows her characters to emerge (1999:27). Margaret Maron is another who takes great pride in the genre. Maron believes "the mystery genre is just as respectable as books generally labeled 'literary,' and thinks that mysteries 'have the added benefit of being well-plotted and entertaining'" (Nicholson). She further notes that she hates that mystery fiction "has been shunted over into a separate genre," and she resents that it is often viewed as "less valid," emphasizing that "there's nothing you can't say in a mystery" (Nicholson). P. D. James chose to write in the genre for pragmatic reasons, but she believed that detective fiction was "challenging," with its "inner tensions between plot and character and atmosphere" (Joyner 108), and critics find that her works certainly offer quality and depth on a par with other literary authors.

The continued issues with the image of detective fiction and the increased number of amateur sleuth characters have led to persistent concerns among some feminist scholars. Others, including editors, have also weighed in on the issue over the years. For example, one editor criticized the quality of some of the works seen during the surge in women's mystery writing, noting that "with all of the female sensibility, a lot of these women seem to be rewriting *The Maltese Falcon* but missing the point" (Anthony 28).

Sally R. Munt and Walton and Jones trace the development of women characters in the hard-boiled private investigator genre. The early contributions to the genre from male writers such as Raymond Chandler and Dashiell Hammett did not feature strong, independent women characters. Placing a woman into the key role of this style of novel has been viewed as an unsatisfactory substitution by many critics. The violence and sexual behavior of the early women private investigators, such as is seen in the early novels by Sue Grafton, for example, can be viewed as yet another negative portrayal of women and even as antifeminist. Munt also explores the works of Ruth Rendell through a similar lens, pointing out Rendell's negative portrayals of feminism and lesbianism in the Inspector Wexford series (20–22).

As Marilyn Rye notes, Kathleen Gregory Klein and others "have concluded that genre conventions inevitably lead authors to subvert or sabotage female heroines" (105). Klein has stated that early works of detective fiction that featured women characters showed the women as failing in their work or as weak in other ways, positing that the woman is as outside of the status quo as the criminal in the story and that showing her as "an incompetent detective or an inadequate woman" allows for a second catharsis for readers (1995:4–5). Klein further argues that even when the woman character in detection fiction is a feminist or portrayed through a feminist lens, the work still "winds up supporting the existing system which oppresses women when she reestablishes the ordered status quo" by solving the crime and bringing order and justice (1995:200–201). According to Klein, feminist writers who use the formula of the genre are trapped (1995:201).

As Patricia Johnson points out, though, Maureen Reddy and Jane Bakerman, among others, view feminist crime fiction as transformative and valuable and as rewriting the genre or working beyond the genre (98). Sue Turnbull argues that arguments put forth by critics like Klein and Janice Radway, whose 1984 work *Reading the Romance: Women, Patriarchy and Popular Literature* studied romance fiction through a feminist lens, fail to consider the "possibility that there might be pleasure to be derived from the formula without a commitment to the ideologies it expresses" (71). The growth in the number of women being published, as well as the growth in the number of online chat groups and email lists devoted to the mystery genre, seem to bear out Turnbull's point, that many women will read—and perhaps even write—mystery fiction for the enjoyment that the genre provides.

Klein's *The Woman Detective* examines five writers who she sees as "attempt[ing] to resist the contradiction" between feminist ideology and hard-boiled detective actions (1995:202). However, Klein's exploration of the writings of Grafton, Paretsky, Muller, M. F. Beal and Susan Steiner does not lead to a tidy conclusion. Klein leaves us with questions about the clash of feminist ideology and the genre, noting that substitution of a female character into the hard-boiled formula is ineffective. Klein notes that the "genre must be completely remade, stripped of some of its most characteristic elements and reinforced by a new ideology and awareness" (1995:220). She is concerned, though, whether the resulting works could really be "either detective fiction or feminist" (1995:220).

In the second edition of *The Woman Detective,* Klein notes in the new afterword that after the first edition appeared, there was a notable increase in the publication of private investigator novels with a female protagonist. She also points out a shift in outlook that marked many of the new series that appeared between 1988 and 1995: "rather than catching a killer by becoming like a killer, many of these characters choose instead to avenge a victim by caring about the victim" (Klein 1995:233).

This sentiment carries over into other subgenres of detective fiction that Klein omits from her analysis. Most of the amateur sleuth novels that have accounted for much of the growth in the genre feature women characters who become involved in solving the crime because of their personal connection or general compassion for the victim. Although the protagonists of many of those novels could not be seen as feminist—and in many cases would not be concerned about that—it is certainly true that women have moved beyond being just contenders in the genre. The growth of opportunities for women to publish in the field can certainly be counted as a victory for feminism, particularly for those writers who formed Sisters in Crime and who have worked to increase the visibility and status of women writers in the mystery and detective fiction arena.

BIBLIOGRAPHY

Anthony, Carolyn. "Crime Marches On." *Publishers Weekly* 13 April 1990: 24–29.
Carter, Robert A. "Scene of the Crime." *Publishers Weekly* 29 March 1991: 18–21.
Della Cava, Frances A. and Madeline H. Engel. "The Magnifying Glass Becomes the Mirror: How the Character and Her Context Have Grown." *Female Detectives in American Novels: A Bibliography and Analysis of Serialized Female Sleuths.* New York: Garland, 1993. 3–54.
Heising, Willetta L. *Detecting Women.* 3rd ed. Dearborn, MI: Purple Moon Press, 2000.
Highsmith, Patricia. *Plotting and Writing Suspense Fiction.* New York: Writers Inc., 1966.
Jackson, Christine A. *Myth and Ritual in Women's Detective Fiction.* Jefferson, NC: McFarland, 2002.
Johnson, Patricia E. "Sex and Betrayal in the Detective Fiction of Sue Grafton and Sara Paretsky." *Journal of Popular Culture* 27.4 (1994): 97–106.

Joyner, Nancy Carol. "P. D. James." *10 Women of Mystery.* Ed. Earl F. Bargainnier. Bowling Green: Bowling Green State U P, 1981. 107–23.

Klein, Kathleen Gregory. "Introduction." *Great Women Mystery Writers.* Westport: Greenwood, 1994. 1–9.

———. "Habeas Corpus: Feminism and Detective Fiction." *Feminism in Women's Detective Fiction.* Ed. Glenwood Irons. Toronto: U Toronto P, 1995. 171–89.

———. *The Woman Detective: Gender and Genre.* 2nd ed. Urbana: U Illinois P, 1995.

Mizejewski, Linda. *Hardboiled and High Heeled: The Woman Detective in Popular Culture.* New York: Routledge, 2004.

Munt, Sally R. *Murder by the Book? Feminism and the Crime Novel.* London: Routledge, 1994.

Nicholson, Scott. "Margaret Maron: Bootlegger Belle." N.d. Accessed May 22, 2005. http://www.hauntedcomputer.com/ghostwr28.htm.

Reddy, Maureen T. *Sisters in Crime: Feminism and the Crime Novel.* New York: Continuum, 1988.

———. "The Female Detective: From Nancy Drew to Sue Grafton." *Mystery and Suspense Writers: The Literature of Crime, Detection, and Espionage.* Eds. Robin W. Winks and Maureen Corrigan. New York: Scribners, 1998. 1047–67.

Rye, Marilyn. "Changing Gender Conventions and the Detective Formula: J. A. Jance's Beaumont and Brady Series." *Journal of Popular Culture* 37.1 (2003): 105–19.

Silet, Charles L. P. "She Walks These Hills: An Interview with Sharyn McCrumb." *Armchair Detective* 28.4 (1995): 368–80.

———. "Anna Lee, Eva Wylie, and the Contemporary Crime Novel." *Talking Murder: Interviews with 20 Mystery Writers.* Princeton: Ontario Review Press, 1999. 24–38.

Stasio, Marilyn. "A Girl's Guide to Killing." *New York Times Book Review* 21 August 2005: 14–15.

Turnbull, Sue. "'Nice Dress, Take It Off:' Crime, Romance and the Pleasure of the Text." *International Journal of Cultural Studies* 5.1 (2002): 67–82.

Walton, Priscilla L. and Manina Jones. *Detective Agency: Women Rewriting the Hard-Boiled Tradition.* Berkeley: U California P, 1999.

Susan Wittig Albert (1940–)

BIOGRAPHY

Susan Wittig Albert was born January 2, 1940, in Maywood, Illinois, to John H. and Lucille Franklin Webber. She attended college at the University of Illinois and earned a bachelor's degree in 1967. In 1972, Albert earned a Ph.D. in English from the University of California, Berkeley. She was married and had three children, Robert, Robin, and Michael.

She taught at the University of Texas, Austin, from 1972 to 1979, serving as assistant and associate professor and as associate dean of the graduate school. She left Texas for a dean's position at Sophie Newcomb College in New Orleans and also served as vice president for academic affairs at Southwest Texas State University from 1982 to 1986. She left academia to pursue writing on a full-time basis in 1987. Other changes were taking place in her life during this time. Her first marriage ended in divorce and she remarried William Albert, a writer, in 1986.

Before turning to mystery fiction, Albert wrote children's books. In addition to working solo, the Alberts collaborated on numerous books for young adult readers. She has noted that she was "thoroughly fed up with academic politics," but that leaving academia was a hard decision and required a period of adjusting to a different, less structured schedule and new career (homepage). She finds that she has "more intellectual challenges outside the university" and that she enjoys being able to do research in a number of areas, not just her official specialization (White). Albert has thought of herself as a writer ever "since I could hold a pencil and make letters," and she has enjoyed all the genres and styles of writing she has worked in (Susan 16). She has a variety of projects planned, including fiction and nonfiction works and notes that "the world is full of things to write about. I'll never run out of projects" (Susan 16).

MAJOR WORKS AND THEMES

Albert's first mystery series features a lawyer named China Bayles, who leaves her profession, moves to a small town, and opens an herb shop. This theme is important to Albert, as someone who left a career to pursue her writing and who also wrote a book about women leaving the career track to pursue other interests. In the first novel, Bayles is unable to accept that a friend's death was suicide, and along with her friend, Ruby Wilcox, she investigates the case to uncover the truth. Throughout the series, the flamboyant Wilcox serves as a

Also writing as Robin Paige

sidekick to the more staid Bayles, who initially clashes and eventually falls in love with the local homicide detective, Mike McQuaid. Albert's portrayal of the relationship Bayles has with McQuaid's son is realistic and positive.

Each novel features a particular herb, and Albert provides recipes and historical lore about the herbs. The information about the herbs can be extensive, but it avoids "bogging down the plot" (Cogdill 3) and has been described as "soothing and fascinating" (DeCandido 1346). For example, *Chile Death* centers on a murder at a chili cook-off, and *Dilly of a Death* finds Bayles and her cohorts solving the murder of the woman who owned a local pickle factory.

Most of the series takes place in the fictitious setting of Pecan Springs, Texas, but *Bloodroot* finds Bayles investigating her own family history along with a mystery in her hometown in Mississippi. The mystery plotting is solid, but the plot line involving Bayles's discoveries of her family's slave-holding past is deeply interesting.

A second series co-written with her husband under the name Robin Paige features a pair of sleuths in Victorian England. Kate Ardleigh, a young American, goes to England to care for her aunt. Ardleigh is sympathetic to the suffrage movement and other precursors of feminism, and she has a hidden profession, writing mystery and suspense stories under a male pseudonym. In the first novel she is drawn into investigating a case and meets Lord Charles Sheridan, who is an early expert in forensic investigative techniques. The two join forces to solve crimes and also fall in love. Each novel connects with real historical events and includes real people as characters. The series has portrayed Beatrix Potter, the Victorian-era Prince of Wales, automobile makers Henry Rolls and Charles Royce, Jennie Churchill and her son Winston, Lillian Langtry, Jack London, and Arthur Conan Doyle, along with other members of the royalty. Albert notes that they chose the period because many forensic techniques were emerging at that time (White). The Alberts travel to England each year to do research for the series.

Albert also has begun a second historical mystery featuring writer Beatrix Potter, who, as noted previously, debuted in *Death at Gallows Green*. This series will appeal to both children and adult readers, with its mix of historical fiction, gentle mysteries, and Potter's menagerie of animals. A prolific writer, Albert also is author or co-author of several composition textbooks and more than 60 children's books. In addition, she published a guide for writers and the previously mentioned work about changing one's career path, *Work of Her Own: A Woman's Guide to Success off the Career Track*. She also maintains an online journal, available at http://susanalbert.blogspot.com/.

CRITICAL RECEPTION

Thyme of Death garnered nominations for Agatha and Anthony awards for best first mystery, but reviews were mixed, with some reviewers posting quite critical reviews of the book. Other reviewers cited by *Contemporary Authors,* however, saw great potential for the character and the series and noted that Albert was "a name to watch" based on the "lively and engaging tale" (Susan 15). As the Bayles series has progressed, critical reception has remained positive.

A review of *Love Lies Bleeding* spoke of its "charming heroine, snappy plot and batch of appealing folksy characters," calling it the "best yet in an appealing series that just keeps getting better" (Melton 456). Peter Cannon praised *Bloodroot,* noting that "what in lesser hands could have become a caricature of a family saga is saved by Albert's clear love of her subject matter, smooth styling and rich marbling of past and present" (2001a:72). In a review of *Indigo Dying,* Jeff Zaleski noted that "Albert does a nice job of placing believable red herrings in Bayles's way, and she adds colorful details about herbal medicine and the dye business" (42). Further, he stated that "the heart of the book is the detailed depiction of small-town life, which separates the novel from genre fodder by providing a rich context for the mystery" (Zaleski 42).

Mary Campbell wrote that some amateur sleuth novels turn out better than others, and she rated Albert's *Dilly of a Death* as one of the best (2). In addition to providing a good plot, strong characters, and interesting herb lore, Campbell praised Albert for not making the "mistake" many writers make of having the heroine rush into a dangerous situation alone, only to escape by transforming into a "superwoman" (2).

The Victorian mystery series has also earned praise for its rich historical details. In a review of *Death at Epsom Downs,* Barbara Bibel noted that the plot offers "enough danger and intrigue to keep readers turning the pages, which are filled with vivid historical details" (1231), and Peter Cannon called it "another clever, richly detailed whodunit" (2001b:72).

BIBLIOGRAPHY

Works by Susan Wittig Albert

China Bayles Series

Thyme of Death. New York: Scribner, 1992.
Witches' Bane. New York: Scribner, 1993.
Hangman's Root. New York: Scribner, 1994.
Rosemary Remembered. New York: Berkley, 1995.
Rueful Death. New York: Berkley, 1996.
Love Lies Bleeding. New York: Berkley, 1997.
Chile Death. New York: Berkley, 1998.
Lavender Lies. New York: Berkley, 1999.
Mistletoe Man. New York: Berkley, 2000.
Bloodroot. New York: Berkley, 2001.
Indigo Dying. New York: Berkley, 2002.
An Unthymely Death and Other Garden Mysteries. New York: Berkley, 2003.
A Dilly of a Death. New York: Berkley, 2004.
Dead Man's Bones. New York: Berkley, 2005.
Bleeding Hearts. New York: Berkley, 2006.

Beatrix Potter Series

The Tale of Hill Top Farm. New York: Berkley, 2004.
The Tale of Holly How. New York: Berkley, 2005.
The Tale of Cuckoo Brow Wood. New York: Berkley, 2006.

Other Works

Work of Her Own: A Woman's Guide to Success off the Career Track. New York: Putnam, 1994.
Writing from Life: Telling Your Soul's Story. New York: Putnam, 1997.

Works Written as Robin Paige

Kate Ardleigh and Charles Sheridan Series

Death at Bishop's Keep. New York: Berkley, 1994.
Death at Gallow's Green. New York: Berkley, 1995.
Death at Daisy's Folly. New York: Berkley, 1997.
Death at Devil's Bridge. New York: Berkley, 1998.
Death at Rottingdean. New York: Berkley, 1999.
Death at Whitechapel. New York: Berkley, 2000.
Death at Epsom Downs. New York: Berkley, 2001.
Death at Dartmoor. New York: Berkley, 2002.
Death at Glamis Castle. New York: Berkley, 2003.

Death in Hyde Park. New York: Berkley, 2004.
Death at Blenheim Palace. New York: Berkley, 2005.
Death on the Lizard. New York: Berkley, 2006.

Works about Susan Wittig Albert

Bibel, Barbara. "*Death at Epsom Downs.*" *Booklist* 1 March 2001: 1231.
Campbell, Mary. "'Dilly' of a Murder Mystery Heroine." *Chicago Tribune* 12 March 2004: 2.
Cannon, Peter. "*Bloodroot.*" *Publishers Weekly* 24 September 2001a: 72.
———. "Death at Epsom Downs." *Publishers Weekly* 5 February 2001b: 72.
Cogdill, Oline H. "Herb Shop, Wedding and Murder Mystery Make a Tasty Stew." *Chicago Tribune* 28 October 1999: 3.
DeCandido, GraceAnne A. "*Dead Man's Bones.*" *Booklist* 1 April 2005: 1346.
Melton, Emily. "*Love Lies Bleeding.*" *Booklist* 1 November 1997: 456.
Partners in Crime HQ: Susan Wittig Albert and Bill Albert. Homepage. 2005. 22 May 2005. http://www.mysterypartners.com/
"Susan Wittig Albert." *Contemporary Authors.* Vol. 101, New Revision Series. Ed. Scot Peacock. Detroit: Gale, 2002. 12–17.
White, Claire E. "A Conversation with Susan Wittig Albert." *Internet Writing Journal* July 1999. 22 May 2005. http://www.writerswrite.com/journal/jul99/albert.htm
Zaleski, Jeff. "*Indigo Dying.*" *Publishers Weekly* 13 January 2003: 41–42.

Donna Andrews

BIOGRAPHY

Donna Andrews was born in Yorktown, Virginia, to Jay Donald Andrews, a marine biologist, and Mary Stuart Hornsby Andrews; she grew up there with one brother. She studied English and drama at the University of Virginia. Although she did not initially pursue a career in fiction writing, she did work as a business writer on the communications team of a financial organization in Washington, D.C. (Press).

She was an avid reader of science fiction as a child, and she developed an interest in mystery fiction during college (Press). She always wanted to write, noting that she began writing stories while in elementary school (McBride). Before her success with the mystery genre, she had written two novels that were never published. The first, written during college, was in the fantasy genre; later she wrote a novel about a young woman who wants to be an actress (McBride). She submitted the manuscript for her first mystery novel to the Malice Domestic contest sponsored by St. Martin's Press and won.

According to her Web site, Andrews recently completed a course designed for private investigators. Although she does not plan to actively work as an investigator, the knowledge gained about the profession will be put to good use in her fiction (homepage).

She resides in Reston, Virginia.

MAJOR WORKS AND THEMES

Andrews has produced two very different mystery series. Her first series features Meg Langslow, an ornamental blacksmith. In the first novel, Langslow is slated to be the bridesmaid in three different weddings. She is coerced into helping with planning the events as well, and returns to her hometown for the summer. When murder interrupts the events, Langslow's father begins snooping for clues, and Langslow becomes involved as well. In the second novel, Langslow and her new boyfriend, Michael Waterston, take a trip to Monhegan Island, Maine, only to find that the cottage they planned to stay in is already occupied by an assortment of her relatives. When a local resident with ties to her family is found murdered, Langslow begins investigating, no easy feat given that practically everyone on the island has a motive. The third novel finds the characters back in Yorktown, gearing up for the annual colonial crafts fair. When a participant is found dead, Langslow solves the case. In *Crouching Buzzard, Leaping Loon*, Langslow is working temporarily at her brother's software company. The crime in this novel involves a murder at the office. In *Owl's Well That Ends Well*, Langslow and Waterston buy an old mansion filled with antique furnishings and collectibles. They also discover a body, and Langslow again puts her sleuthing skills to the test. This series is noted for its humorous dialogue and the amusing array of secondary characters among Langslow's quirky extended family. All the novels also feature a bird-related theme, as seen in the titles.

Her second series is unique in that the main character, Turing Hopper, is not a real person. Hopper is an artificial intelligence personality (AIP) who works at Universal Library outside Washington, D.C. The AIPs perform the duties similar to reference librarians, but they are, as Hopper describes them in the first novel, faster, able to handle multiple clients, and "never busy when you call" (2002:8). Hopper has abilities beyond her peers, but she hides her sentience so that the programmers will not be alarmed. She enlists the assistance of human colleagues Tim Pincoski and Maude Graham in solving cases. Andrews calls Hopper a "twenty-first century Nero Wolfe" who relies on human colleagues to do the legwork outside (McBride). The first case involves investigating the disappearance of Hopper's programmer. Other cases involve solving the murder of a computer programmer and looking into a computer company that may be involved in identity theft.

CRITICAL RECEPTION

Critical reception has been quite strong for Andrews's works. In addition to winning the St. Martin's contest, her first novel won several major awards, including the Agatha and Anthony awards, and also Barry and Lefty awards. She won another Agatha for *You've Got Murder*.

In her review of *Murder for Puffins*, Jenny McLarin noted that "the author's dry humor and offbeat characters are much more entertaining than her mystery plots," but praised it as "an enjoyable flight of fancy" (2000:1610). *Revenge of the Wrought Iron Flamingos* was called "a lighthearted gem" that features Andrews's "trademark witty dialogue and fine sense of the ridiculous" (Cannon 2001:58). Another reviewer noted that the novel's "fearless protagonist, remarkable supporting characters, lively action, and a keen wit put this at the top of the list" (Klett 238). A review of *Crouching Buzzard, Leaping Loon* praised "the crackling dialogue [that] propels the plot" (Cannon 2003:60). The most recent in the Langslow series was heralded as "another laugh-out-loud lark that will leave readers singing Andrews' praises" (McLarin 2005:1268).

Her first novel featuring Turing Hopper was praised as "a unique effort executed with great skill" (Cannon 2002:80). The review also noted that "the high-tech investigation, Turing's plan for herself and her ruminations about becoming almost human are sure to engage computer buffs everywhere" (Cannon 2002:80). A reviewer of the second novel noted that many technical terms are explained, but that those who are computer literate will especially "appreciate the author's talent for blending information-age details with an enjoyable crime puzzle" (Cannon 2003:42). The third novel in the series was praised for its "expert plotting and a highly original heroine" whose "wry, witty musings on human-computer relations that make this 'technocozy' series a true standout" (Access 26). The "quirky, engrossing" *Delete All Suspects* was acclaimed for being "full of surprising twists and turns" (Delete 66).

Ethelle S. Bean's article on the use of technology in detective fiction discusses the Turing Hopper novels, comparing Andrews's use of technology with that of other mystery writers.

BIBLIOGRAPHY

Works by Donna Andrews

Meg Langslow Series

Murder with Peacocks. New York: Thomas Dunne Books, 1999.
Murder with Puffins. New York: Thomas Dunne Books, 2000.
Revenge of the Wrought-Iron Flamingos. New York: Thomas Dunne Books, 2001.
Crouching Buzzard, Leaping Loon. New York: Thomas Dunne Books, 2003.
We'll Always Have Parrots. New York: Thomas Dunne Books, 2004.
Owl's Well That Ends Well. New York: Thomas Dunne Books, 2005.
No Nest for the Wicket. New York: St. Martin's Minotaur, 2006.

Turing Hopper Series

You've Got Murder. New York: Berkley Prime Crime, 2002.
Click Here for Murder. New York: Berkley Prime Crime, 2003.
Access Denied. New York: Berkley Prime Crime, 2004.
Delete All Suspects. New York: Berkley Prime Crime, 2005.

Works about Donna Andrews

"Access Denied." *Publishers Weekly* 29 November 2004: 26–27.
Bean, Estelle S. "Technology and Detective Fiction." *Clues* 24.1 (2005): 27–34.
Cannon, Peter. "*Revenge of the Wrought Iron Flamingos.*" *Publishers Weekly* 17 September 2001: 58.
———. "*You've Got Murder.*" *Publishers Weekly* 18 March 2002: 80.
———. "*Click Here for Murder.*" *Publishers Weekly* 21 April 2003: 42.
———. "*Crouching Buzzard, Leaping Loon.*" *Publishers Weekly* 20 January 2003: 60.
"*Delete All Suspects.*" *Publishers Weekly* 26 September 2005: 66.
Donna Andrews. Homepage. n.d. 31 December 2005. http://www.donnaandrews.com
"Donna Andrews." *Contemporary Authors.* Literature Resource Center (online database). 2005. 16 December 2005.
Klett, Rex E. "Revenge of the Wrought Iron Flamingos." *Library Journal* 1 September 2001: 238.
McBride, Susan. "Flying High: An Interview with Award-Winning Author Donna Andrews." *Charlotte Austin Review* 2000. 15 December 2005. http://charlotteaustinreviewltd.com
McLarin, Jenny. "*Murder for Puffins.*" *Booklist* 1 May 2000: 1610.
———. "*Owl's Well That Ends Well.*" *Booklist* 15 March 2005: 1268.
Press Kit. Donna Andrews.com. n.d. 31 December 2005. http://www.donnaandrews.com/presskit.shtml

Jo Bannister (1951–)

BIOGRAPHY

Jo Bannister was born in Rochdale, England on July 31, 1951, to Alan and Marjorie Ashcroft Bannister. She attended school in Birmingham and Nottingham before her family moved to Bangor, Northern Ireland.

She left school at age 16 and began working as an office clerk for the *County Down Spectator* in Bangor. She soon moved into journalism itself, having been offered the chance to become a reporter for the *County Down Spectator*. She worked as a reporter from 1969 to 1974 and then became deputy editor. She also served as editor of the paper from 1983 to 1987. During this time she also was affiliated with other papers as a feature writer. She won several professional awards for her work in journalism.

In the early 1980s, she published several science fiction novels, and after leaving the editorship of the paper, she turned to fiction writing as her full-time career. Since then, she has written numerous mystery and suspense novels. She resides in Northern Ireland.

MAJOR WORKS AND THEMES

Bannister has written several crime fiction series and also a number of stand-alone suspense novels. Her first few books were science fiction and after moving to the crime and suspense genre, she has published novels including *The Lazarus Hotel,* which features six people who find themselves brought together and subjected to a sinister plot, and *Unlawful Entry,* which focuses on a woman who learns she has a half-brother only when he has been killed and becomes embroiled in international intrigue as she attempts to learn more about his life and death. In addition to the stand-alone novels are several series.

Her first crime fiction series is set in Castlemere and features several police detectives there. In the first novel, the beloved leader of the unit has suddenly died and a replacement named Liz Graham has been sent. In addition to dealing with a staff consumed with grief, Graham faces scrutiny not only as a replacement boss but as a female superior officer. One of the detectives, Cal Donovan, cannot accept the death of his mentor and ends up uncovering the fact that the chief was murdered. In subsequent novels, Graham, Donovan, and a third detective named Frank Shapiro work together to solve cases. They face a variety of villains; Bannister often includes elements of psychological suspense. One notable entry in the series is *The Hireling's Tale,* which features the village in panic after a series of consumer products are tampered with and cause illness.

Bannister has written two novels about Primrose Hammond, a retired pathologist who begins writing an advice column for the local paper. She becomes embroiled in solving crimes. These novels are notable for their combination of a light tone and dark mystery elements. She also wrote three novels featuring a physician who writes mystery novels, Clio Rees, and a chief inspector named Harry Marsh. In the first novel, Rees does not accept that a friend's death is a suicide, and investigates the case. In addition to proving herself a useful sleuth, Rees and Marsh join forces personally and professionally in subsequent books. Bannister has also tried her hand at political intrigue, with a pair of suspense novels featuring a photojournalist named Mickey Flynn who becomes embroiled in cases involving international espionage.

In the Brodie Farrell series, Bannister writes about another amateur sleuth. Farrell opens an agency called "Looking for Something" to help people find things, such as collectible glassware or antique books. One of her first clients asks her to track down a person, and Farrell completes the task, finding herself more talented at investigation than she imagined. She soon learns, though, that the people seeking Daniel Hood had nefarious intent, and that she also located the wrong Daniel Hood for them. To make amends, she befriends Hood and sets out to locate those who did him harm. Subsequent books in the series have Farrell and Hood continuing their friendship, with Hood occasionally assisting Farrell or providing the link to a new mystery to be solved. As in many amateur sleuth novels, there is a police detective who is alternately irritated and helped by the sleuth. Inspector Jack Deacon also becomes a love interest for Farrell. Although the series certainly follows well-recognized formulaic elements, Bannister's characters have unique qualities and never seem clichéd.

CRITICAL RECEPTION

One of Bannnister's early stand-alone thrillers won praise for being "tautly written and deftly plotted," with the potential to leave the reader "breathless" (Steinberg 51). A review of a later stand-alone novel noted that Bannister has often "demonstrat[ed] a gift for precise and evocative language" (Brainard 1997: 47). The reviewer found the plot of *The Lazarus Hotel* an "ambitious" take on the locked-room mystery, and concluded that Bannister "superbly develops this tale's understated menace" (Brainard 1997: 47).

Her first Castlemere novel was praised for its "well-developed" plotting and for how Bannister "nicely integrates women into the standard British procedural genre" (Miller 1993: 120). A review of another Castlemere novel noted the "appealing police trio" and the "diverse strengths and weaknesses" as they tackle "deeply suspenseful situations" (Brainard 1996: 48). A third Castlemere series review heralded her "craft and subtlety" in building the tension in a "brilliantly plotted" novel (Zaleksi 70).

The first novel featuring Rose Hammond was quite a departure for Bannister, although a successful one. As one reviewer wrote, she "transforms this improbable, even slightly ridiculous, plot into a coherent, believable whole that is both very funny and very entertaining," praising the novel as a "most surprising and enjoyable mystery from one of the best" (Miller 1998:1204). Another reviewer felt that the novel, although "intriguing," suffered from a slow start (Brainard 1998:207).

Reviews of the Brodie Farrell series also recognize Bannister's accomplishments. In a review of the first novel in this series, Peter Cannon states that Bannister once again "skillfully juxtaposes a complex puzzle with insightful character studies" (2001:51). Cannon has also noted that Bannister "skillfully moves her characters through an intriguing tale of tragedy and death," with Farrell as a "refreshingly realistic sleuth" (2002:45).

BIBLIOGRAPHY
Works by Jo Bannister
Castlemere Series

A Bleeding of Innocents. New York: St. Martin's, 1993.
Charisma. New York: St. Martin's, 1994. Also published as *Sins of the Heart* (London: Macmillan, 1994).
A Taste for Burning. New York: St. Martin's, 1995.
No Birds Sing. New York: St. Martin's, 1996.
Broken Lines. New York: St. Martin's, 1999.
The Hireling's Tale. New York: St. Martin's, 1999.
Changelings. New York: St. Martin's, 2000.

Primrose Holland Series

The Primrose Convention. New York: St. Martin's, 1998.
The Primrose Switchback. London: Severn House, 2000.

Clio Rees and Harry Marsh Series

Striving with Gods. Garden City: Doubleday, 1984. Also published as *Uncertain Death* (London: Severn House, 1997).
Gilgamesh. Garden City: Doubleday, 1989.
The Going Down of the Sun. Garden City: Doubleday, 1989.
The Fifth Cataract. London: Severn House, 2005.

Mickey Flynn Series

Shards. Garden City: Doubleday, 1990. Also published as *Critical Angle* (London: Severn House, 1999).
Death and Other Lovers. New York: Doubleday, 1991.

Brodie Farrell Series

Echoes of Lies. New York: St. Martin's Minotaur, 2001.
True Witness. New York: St. Martin's Minotaur, 2002.
Reflections. New York: St. Martin's Minotaur, 2003.
The Depths of Solitude. New York: St. Martin's Minotaur, 2004.
Breaking Faith. New York: St. Martin's Minotaur, 2005.
Requiem for a Dealer. New York: St. Martin's Minotaur, 2006.

Other Novels

The Matrix. London: R. Hale, 1981.
The Winter Plain. London: R. Hale, 1982.
A Cactus Garden. London: R. Hale, 1983.
Mosaic. Garden City: Doubleday, 1987.
The Mason Codex. Garden City: Doubleday, 1988. Also published as *Unlawful Entry* (London: Severn House, 1988).
The Lazarus Hotel. New York: St. Martin's, 1997.

Works about Jo Bannister

Brainard, Dulcy. "*No Birds Sing.*" *Publishers Weekly* 24 June 1996: 48.
———. "*The Lazarus Hotel.*" *Publishers Weekly* 16 June 1997: 47.
———. "*The Primrose Convention.*" *Publishers Weekly* 16 February 1998: 207.
Cannon, Peter. "*Echoes of Lies.*" *Publishers Weekly* 19 November 2001: 51.
———. "*True Witness.*" *Publishers Weekly* 18 November 2002: 44–5.
"Jo Bannister." *Contemporary Authors.* New Revision Vol. 96. Ed. Scot Peacock. Detroit: Gale, 2001. 11–12.
Miller, Stuart. "*The Bleeding of Innocents.*" *Booklist* 15 September 1993: 130.
———. "*The Primrose Convention.*" *Booklist* 15 March 1998: 1204.
Steinberg, Sybil. "*Mosaic.*" *Publishers Weekly* 14 November 1986: 51.
Zaleski, Jeff. "*Broken Lines.*" *Publishers Weekly* 22 February 1999: 70.

Linda Barnes (1949–)

BIOGRAPHY

Born Linda Joyce Appelblatt on December 6, 1949, in Detroit, she is the daughter of Irving and Hilda Grodman Appelblatt. Her father was a mechanical engineer, and her mother was a teacher; she grew up in the suburbs of Detroit with an older sister and younger brother (Hogan). Appelblatt married Richard Allen Barnes in 1970 and earned her B.F.A. in theatre from Boston University in 1971. She and her husband have one son, Samuel, and live in Brookline, Massachusetts.

Barnes had an interest and a talent for writing at a young age. She won a writing award from the National Council of Teachers of English Writing at age 17 but decided "any skill so simple it could be mastered at 17 wasn't worth much" (Conversation). She turned her attention to pursuing a career as a Shakespearean actress, but after college, she "chickened out" and did not go to New York as planned (Conversation). From 1971 to 1978, Barnes taught drama in high schools in Chelmsford and Lexington, Massachusetts. She wrote a play called "Wings" for her students, which led to a number of award-winning performances for her cast, and the play was soon published. When she turned to writing full-time, she chose the mystery genre over playwriting because she liked reading mysteries and wanted to work alone without the aspects of dealing with actors and directors; she also notes she wanted to address unsolved mysteries she had experienced, including a shooting in her childhood neighborhood and the suicide of a friend (Conversation).

MAJOR WORKS AND THEMES

Her first mystery series featured an actor and amateur sleuth named Michael Spraggue, who solves crimes with the assistance of his aunt. She has called the Spraggue series her "apprentice work" (Semple 50), and notes that she "learned a lot" from writing the Spraggue novels, namely that she would prefer writing in the first person and having a character who was not an amateur detective (Anable 68). Barnes noted that her amateur sleuth was becoming involved only when harm came to his friends and relatives and that the character became "so depressed that [she] just couldn't write him anymore" (Jacobson D3). She initially wanted to write about a woman character but was told such works wouldn't sell (Kenney 11).

She first wrote about Carlotta Carlyle, a private investigator who was formerly a police officer, in a short story called "Lucky Penny." The story was accepted by several magazines, all of which went out of business before printing her work (Kenney 11). It finally reached print in 1985 and won a number of awards, including an Anthony, which meant that her publisher "suddenly showed almost as much interest in acquiring a Carlotta novel as [Barnes] had in writing one" (Cohen 42). Since 1987, Barnes has focused on Carlyle in her novels.

Along with her previous stint as a police officer, Carlyle worked as a cab driver and continues her affiliation with the company as a cover. At six feet tall, with red hair, Carlyle is not inconspicuous undercover. The series features a wide array of well-developed secondary characters, including a police detective named Mooney; Gloria, the manager of the cab company; and Carlyle's on-again off-again boyfriend, Sam Giannelli, who comes from a Mafia family. As the series progresses, Paolina, a girl Carlyle first meets in the Big Sisters program, and her tenant Roz, who is a computer whiz and helps Carlyle in return for breaks on rent, become more prominent.

Her first case involves a search for an elderly man who is missing. The case becomes more than she initially expects, with connections to the IRA. In *The Snake Tattoo,* Carlyle works to help clear Mooney's name after he is wrongly accused of brutality, and in *Coyote,* Carlyle becomes embroiled in a case involving illegal aliens and human trafficking.

Several of Carlyle's cases also have aspects related to music. Carlyle's love of the blues and her guitar is often discussed in the series, and in *Steel Guitar* readers learn more of Carlyle's earlier marriage to a musician, which ended when he left her for her best friend, a blues singer. The singer returns to Boston after 15 years and persuades Carlyle to assist her in finding a missing person.

Snapshot addresses issues of medical malpractice; *Hardware* finds Carlyle and Giannelli in danger from an unknown assailant. The plot involves computer technology issues, but the case eventually reveals connections to Giannelli's years in Vietnam. *Cold Case* has a literary theme involving a young woman who published a novel at age 14, but was dead by age 15, an apparent suicide. Twenty-four years later, Carlyle is hired to find out who has written a new manuscript that appears to be in the young woman's handwriting. She delves into the author's life and death, uncovering a long-held secret involving a powerful political family. *Flashpoint* finds Carlyle working to clear the name of an acquaintance, while uncovering the real murderer and the motive, which is tied to the victim's past.

The Big Dig used as a backdrop the massive construction project that no one ever thought would be completed. Carlyle is hired to investigate possible fraud with one of the construction companies and goes undercover as a secretary. Barnes did a good deal of research at the sites, including talking with many workers and contractors, although she also noted that wearing a hardhat and carrying a clipboard provided her with anonymity (Kenney 11). *Deep Pockets* looks at issues of class and race, when an African American professor from Harvard hires Carlyle because he's being blackmailed about his affair with an undergraduate student.

CRITICAL RECEPTION

Sybil Steinberg praised the Spraggue novels, finding them "engaging" and noting that in *Cities of the Dead,* Spraggue uses his acting skills in "apt and interesting" ways while working undercover (1986:44). Steinberg found the first novel in the Carlyle series to be equally strong, noting that "Carlotta is the sort of storyteller capable of enlisting readers' sympathies" from the start (1987:63). The first Carlyle novel, *A Trouble of Fools,* was nominated for all four major mystery awards. Steinberg also praised *The Snake Tattoo* as a "rivetingly well-told story" (1989:94).

Steel Guitar was viewed as a "cleverly plotted and zestfully related adventure" and heralded as a "characteristically gripping tale, packed with taut, energy-charged images"(Steinberg 1991:45). Novelist Susan Isaacs also reviewed the novel, calling Carlyle "a woman of wit and gravity, compassion and toughness" and "a heroine worth spending time with" (19). Another reviewer was struck by the blend of toughness and humor in the novel, noting that "Barnes manages to overcome the too-tough tendencies of her detective with salvos of self-deprecating wit," such as when Carlyle veers off from following a suspect to check out a shoe sale (Robertson 2077).

In a review of *Snapshot,* Dulcy Brainard called Carlyle a "standout" in an "ever-increasing crowd" of women private investigators and noted that the novel featured plot lines that are "adroitly connected" in an ending with a "nifty final turn" (1993:53).

Hardware was praised for its "good plotting" and "exciting, unsentimental finish" (Lukowsky 992). Another review noted that the plot's "puzzle works well, but it's mainly Carlotta and her interactions with the well-drawn folks around her that make the story hum" (Brainard 1995:440).

Cold Case was called a "a riveting read that is at once poignant, funny, sad, suspenseful and hopeful," with the author heralded as a "master storyteller" (Melton 1997:1392). Another review found the writing "confident" and the characters "engrossing," with Carlyle's "wry voice a bracing counterpoint to the lifestyles of the rich and famous" who are at the center of the plot (Brainard 1997:213). *Flashpoint* was seen as the latest in Barnes's "string of intelligent mysteries," praised for its "smart finish" (Cygnar 146). Another review noted that the Carlyle character is "a breath of fresh air in a subgenre that has begun to develop its own clichés. Three cheers for this solidly entertaining series, and three cheers for the savvy and sassy Carlotta" (Melton 1999:2032).

The *Big Dig* was seen as a "shrewd piece of writing, well researched and smartly told" (Stasio 22). Another review found the "taut" novel to showcase "writing that's vivid, economical and fun" (Cannon 2002:67), and *Deep Pockets* was called an "intricate web with a pleasingly poisonous spider at its middle," featuring "superb use" by Barnes of "town-gown tensions" (Cannon 2004:54).

Her works have also been widely studied by various literary scholars, often in comparison with Grafton and Paretsky. Margaret Kinsman has two works about Barnes. Both essays examine the role of feminism in crime fiction. One focuses on Barnes and Paretsky and their treatment of women's friendships (2000); her other work compares Paretsky, Barnes, and Barbara Wilson, specifically exploring approaches to teaching their novels (1999). Louise Conley Jones wrote about issues of feminism as related to the crime novels of Barnes, Paretsky, and Grafton (1995); and Frederic Svoboda looked at Barnes, Paretsky, and Grafton in connection with Robert B. Parker's Spenser novels (1995). Barnes herself has contributed to the scholarship about Carlotta Carlyle, with a short piece about the influence of Nancy Drew on women writers and the differences between the characters and motivations of Carlyle and Drew.

BIBLIOGRAPHY

Works by Linda Barnes

Michael Spraggue Series

Blood Will Have Blood. New York: Avon, 1982.
Bitter Finish. New York: St. Martin's, 1983.
Dead Heat. New York: St. Martin's, 1984.
Cities of the Dead. New York: St. Martin's, 1986.

Carlotta Carlyle Series

A Trouble of Fools. New York: St. Martin's, 1987.
The Snake Tattoo. New York: St. Martin's, 1989.
Coyote. New York: Delacorte, 1990.
Steel Guitar. New York: Delacorte, 1991.
Snapshot. New York: Delacorte, 1993.
Hardware. New York: Delacorte, 1995.
Cold Case. New York: Delacorte, 1997.
Flashpoint. New York: Hyperion, 1999.
The Big Dig. New York: St. Martin's, 2002.
Deep Pockets. New York: St. Martin's, 2004.
Heart of the World. New York: St. Martin's, 2006.

Works about Linda Barnes

Anable, Stephen. "PW Talks with Linda Barnes: Dirt Beneath the Big Dig." *Publishers Weekly* 14 October 2002: 68.

Barnes, Linda. "Nancy and Carlotta: Lives Together, Worlds Apart." *Rediscovering Nancy Drew*. Eds. Carolyn Stewart Dyer and Nancy Tillman Romalov. Iowa City: U of Iowa P, 1995. 212–14.

Brainard, Dulcy. "*Snapshot*." *Publishers Weekly* 19 April 1993: 53.

———. "*Hardware*." *Publishers Weekly* 16 January 1995: 440.

———. "*Cold Case*." *Publishers Weekly* 17 February 1997: 213.

Cannon, Peter. "*The Big Dig*." *Publishers Weekly* 14 October 2002: 66–67.

———. "*Deep Pockets*." *Publishers Weekly* 23 February 2004: 54–55.

Cohen, Leslie. "An Interview with Linda Barnes." *Mystery Scene* 66 (2000): 42.

"A Conversation with Linda Barnes." 2001. 8 January 2006. http://www.lindabarnes.com/conversation3.htm

Cygnar, Cecilia R. "*Flashpoint*." *Library Journal* August 1999: 146.

Hogan, Ron. "Beatrice Interview: Linda Barnes." Beatrice.com. 1997. 7 January 2006. http://www.beatrice.com/interviews/barnes

Jacobson, David. "Linda Barnes' Female Size-11 Gumshoe is a Stand-Up Hit." *Detroit News* 10 August 1994: D3.

Jones, Louise Conley. "Feminism and the PI Code: Or, Is a Hard-Boiled Warshawski Unsuitable to Be Called a Feminist?" *Clues* 16.1 (1995): 77–87.

Kenney, Michael. "Another Case, and She's Digging Around For Ideas." *Boston Globe* 13 October 2002: 11.

Kinsman, Margaret. "'Different and Yet the Same': Women's Worlds/Women's Lives and the Classroom." *Diversity and Detective Fiction*. Ed. Kathleen Gregory Klein. Bowling Green: Bowling Green State U P, 1999. 5–21.

———. "A Band of Sisters." *The Art of Detective Fiction*. Eds. Martin Swales and Robert Vilain. New York: St. Martin's, 2000. 153–69.

"Linda Joyce Barnes." *Contemporary Authors*. New Revision Series, Vol. 162. Eds. Daniel Jones and John D. Jorgenson. Detroit: Gale, 1998. 21–22.

Lukowsky, Wes. "*Hardware*." *Booklist* 1 February 1995: 992.

Melton, Emily. "*Cold Case*." *Booklist* 15 April 1997: 1392.

———. "*Flashpoint*." *Booklist* August 1999: 2031–32.

Robertson, Peter. "*Steel Guitar*." *Booklist* August 1991: 2077.

Sempel, Linda and Ted Hertel. "Linda Barnes." *St. James Guide to Crime & Mystery Writers*. 4th ed. Ed. Jay P. Pederson. Detroit: St. James Press, 1996. 49–51.

Stasio, Marilyn. "Crime." *New York Times Book Review* 3 November 2002: 22.

Steinberg, Sybil. "*Cities of the Dead*." *Publishers Weekly* 3 January 1986: 44.

———. "*A Trouble of Fools*." *Publishers Weekly* 6 November 1987: 63.

———. "*The Snake Tattoo*." *Publishers Weekly* 6 January 1989: 94.

———. "*Steel Guitar*." *Publishers Weekly* 27 September 1991: 45.

Svoboda, Frederic. "Hard-Boiled Feminist Detectives and Their Families: Reimaging a Form." *Gender in Popular Culture: Images of Men and Women in Literature, Visual Media and Material Culture*. Ed. Jane S. Bakerman. Cleveland: Ridgemont, 1995. 247–72.

Nevada Barr (1952–)

BIOGRAPHY

Born March 1, 1952, in Yerington, Nevada, Nevada Barr grew up with parents who were both pilots. Her mother, Mary Barr, transported airplanes during World War II, and both Mary and Dave Barr flew for the Forest Service as firefighters during their careers (Shindler 1995:308). The family, including her sister Molly, who became a commercial pilot, later moved to Susanville, California, when her parents found work. In addition to their mother, the Barr daughters grew up with several other strong women role models in the family, including an aunt who taught in the New York public schools and a Quaker grandmother who traveled the world. As Barr puts it, "these women did not come in at the second act to fluff up the pillows and leave" (qtd in Davison 145).

Barr earned a bachelor's degree in communication and a master's of fine arts degree in acting. She lived in New York and worked irregularly as an actress for six years. She moved to Minneapolis to try her luck in the theater and was surprised to find a great deal of work in industrial films. She notes that she looked like "the quintessential yuppie" and was hired to play roles in business training films (Shindler 1995:309). Her first husband was also an actor and a director. In 1989, as a result of their involvement in issues related to the environmental movement, they both joined the National Park Service. Barr worked as a law enforcement ranger in the Guadalupe Mountains in Texas, Mesa Verde in Colorado, Michigan's Isle Royale, and Idaho's Horsefly Fire Camp. Her last posting began in 1993 at the Natchez Trail Parkway in Mississippi.

Barr and her second husband, Richard Jones, who was the district ranger at Natchez Trail, are both now retired from the National Park Service and reside in Clinton, Mississippi, in a house with numerous unique decorations reflecting the natural world Barr loves and respects (Christensen D5).

MAJOR WORKS AND THEMES

Barr began her writing career in 1984 with a historical novel entitled *Bittersweet.* Set in the American West during the frontier times, the story features two women who begin a relationship and leave Pennsylvania to live in Nevada. Barr has called it a "neo-Gothic lesbian western" (Rowen 1462). She wrote four other novels in the 1980s; all remain unpublished. One of the novels tells the story of her parents' work for the Forest Service; another is a historical novel about a 1913 coal strike in Colorado (Shindler 2003: 230).

In 1993, her first mystery novel, *Track of the Cat,* was published. The series features Anna Pigeon, who was married to an actor but widowed in her thirties, who has joined the National Park Service. Pigeon works in all the places Barr herself was posted, which gives the novels great authentic detail about the work of a ranger and the settings. Sydonie Benet points out that "by having Anna relocate to another National Park for each new adventure, Barr keeps her settings fresh and exciting" (52). Barr notes that the parks are characters in her novels, "sometimes a good character, sometimes an evil character, but always there" (How I Write 66). She also notes that instead of note-taking or journaling as background to the novels, she does the physical activities Pigeon will do, "absorb[ing] everything on a visceral level ... what it does to me emotionally and physically" (66).

Firestorm begins with Pigeon having been assigned to a firefighting crew working during a wildfire in California. When a flash fire threatens them, they take shelter in their fireproof emergency tents. After 12 minutes, which seem to last an eternity, in a passage crafted so well that the reader feels s/he is present, the fire passes over them. As they reassemble, one of the crew members is found dead in his tent, but not of natural causes or from the effects of the fire. One of the other crew members has certainly put the knife in his back, and Pigeon is trapped on the mountain with a murderer as they await a rescue mission. As a trained law enforcement officer, Pigeon cannot help but investigate the case, and she uses fleeting moments of contact with an FBI agent over a satellite phone to relay and receive further information for her case.

Pigeon is physically active and often finds herself solving crimes under stressful situations, such as in the middle of a wildfire or while exploring underground caves. The mysteries often have connections to social issues. In *Deep South,* Pigeon uncovers the tragic truth about the death of two white girls. *Ill Wind* deals with the theft of Anasazi Indian relics and practices of construction and expansion in sacred areas. *Flashback* includes a parallel story of the wife of an officer at a Civil War era prison and a mystery plot that involves the alleged collaborators of John Wilkes Booth. In addition to her historical plot elements, environmental protection and endangered species are also recurrent themes throughout the series.

The recent entry in the series, *Hard Truth,* finds Pigeon in Colorado tackling a case that involves religious fundamentalism and sexual abuse. Pigeon meets a former ice climber who was paralyzed in a fall, and they both are drawn into a case when two young girls arrive at the park, on the run from a religious retreat.

Pigeon is a loner, and Barr portrays Pigeon's relationships with others in realistic detail. Pigeon's prime confidant is her sister Molly, a psychiatrist living in New York, whom Pigeon most often talks with over the phone. Pigeon's few romantic relationships are often difficult and are not sustained. In the professional arena, Pigeon's personality often leads to altercations with the bureaucracy of the federal agency, and she also faces sexism in many of the books. Benet notes that during the time Barr was still an active ranger, she was criticized by some for her portrayal of the National Parks bureaucracy, but that others applauded her "frank portrayal" of the agency's structure and actions (52).

In addition to her works of fiction, Barr has written a book about spirituality. An account of her own personal spiritual quest, the book is composed of short chapters on topics such as love, death, friendship, and grief. Barr notes that it "isn't meant as a guide to living. It's meant to evoke discussion" (Shindler 2003: 230). With titles such as "On Getting into Heaven," "Guilt," "Humility," "Sex," and "Flip-Flops, Girlfriends and Levi Jackets," Barr's humor and direct style will surely succeed in that. In addition to these works, Barr has published many pieces in magazines such as *National Geographic Traveler* and *Southern Living.*

CRITICAL RECEPTION

Barr's first work of historical fiction received mixed reactions, but even the negative reviews addressed her strengths in character development and her skills in writing powerful scenes. Her first Anna Pigeon novel garnered strong positive reactions in major newspapers. A review also appeared in the more scholarly *Women's Review of Books,* which examined the work within the lens of ecofeminism (Wesson 23). In addition, it was nominated for several awards and won both the Agatha and Anthony awards for best first novel. Barr has noted that it was amusing to win a "Best First Novel" award for what was really her fifth book (Rowen 1462).

Firestorm was particularly well received by the critics as an "ingenious resurrect[ion]" of the locked-room style of mystery (Corrigan WBK6). Additional reviewer comments likened Barr's writing to Norman Maclean's *Young Men and Fire* (Corrigan WBK6) and proclaimed the forest fire scenes so authentic and "chilling" that readers "can smell the smoke and taste the ashes" (Lochte 11).

A review of *Hunting Season* noted that Barr shines in crafting "suspenseful, atmospheric scenes" (Pate 3), and in a review of *High Country,* Barr is hailed as having "a true gift" for nature writing and for "nail-biting" suspense (Cannon 40). A review of *Hard Truth* noted that Barr is known "for her precise plotting and atmospheric descriptions of nature" and in this novel "again proves her skill in putting believable characters in peril against a backdrop of breathtaking scenery" ("*Hard Truth*" 57).

BIBLIOGRAPHY

Works by Nevada Barr

Bittersweet. New York: St. Martin's, 1984.
Track of the Cat. New York: Putnam, 1993.
A Superior Death. New York: Putnam, 1994.
Ill Wind. New York: Putnam, 1995.
Firestorm. New York: Putnam, 1996.
Endangered Species. New York: Putnam, 1997.
Blind Descent. New York: Putnam, 1998.
Liberty Falling. New York: Putnam, 1999.
Deep South. New York: Putnam, 2000.
Blood Lure. New York: Putnam, 2001.
Hunting Season. New York: Putnam, 2002.
Seeking Enlightenment—Hat by Hat: A Skeptic's Path to Religion. New York: Putnam, 2003.
Flashback. New York: Putnam, 2003.
High Country. New York: Putnam, 2004.
"How I Write." *The Writer* June 2004: 66.
Hard Truth. New York: Putnam, 2005.

Works about Nevada Barr

Benet, Sydonie. "Nevada Barr." *St. James Guide to Crime & Mystery Writers.* 4th ed. Ed. Jay P. Pederson. Detroit: St. James Press, 1996. 51–52.
Cannon, Peter. "*High Country.*" *Publishers Weekly* 12 January 2004: 40.
Christensen, Susan G. "Author's House Is Her Own Wild Kingdom: Nature Rules Barr's Abode." *USA Today* 23 Jan. 2004: D5.
Corrigan, Maureen. "Mysteries." *The Washington Post* 21 April 1996: WBK6.
"*Hard Truth.*" *Publishers Weekly* 14 February 2005: 57.
Lochte, Dick. "Criminal Pursuits." *Los Angeles Times* 28 April 1996: 11.
"Nevada Barr." Ed. Scot Peacock. *Contemporary Authors.* New Revision Series, Vol. 95. Detroit: Gale, 2001. 47–51.
Nevada Barr. 2004. 11 October 2004. http://www.nevadabarr.com/
Pate, Nancy. "Suspense Caught in the Cross Hairs." *Chicago Tribune* 11 March 2002: 3.
Reynolds, Moira Davison. "Nevada Barr." *Women Authors of Detective Series: Twenty- One American and British Writers, 1900–2000.* Jefferson, NC: McFarland, 2001. 145–48.
Rowen, John. "The Booklist Interview: Nevada Barr." *Booklist* 15 April 1995: 1462–63.
Shindler, Dorman T. "The Law of Nature: An Interview with Nevada Barr." *The Armchair Detective* 28.3 (1995): 308–11.
———. "Nevada Barr: Taking on History's Mysteries." *Publishers Weekly* 27 January 2003: 230.
Silet, Charles L.P. "Nevada Barr." *Mystery Scene* 53 (1996): 38+.
Wesson, Mimi. "When the Criminal is Political." *Women's Review of Books* 12.4 (January 1995): 22–23.

Cara Black (1951–)

BIOGRAPHY

Cara Black was born on November 14, 1951, in Chicago, Illinois. She attended Cañada College in California and Sophia University in Tokyo, and she earned bachelor's and master's degrees in education from San Francisco State University. She previously worked as a preschool teacher and preschool director.

Throughout her life, Black has spent a great deal of time in Paris, where she sets her mystery series. She has also lived in Switzerland and Japan and has traveled extensively in Europe, North Africa, and India. She lives with her husband Jun Ishimuro and their son in San Francisco.

MAJOR WORKS AND THEMES

Black's series is set in Paris and features Aimée Leduc, the daughter of a Frenchman and an American woman. Her mother left when she was young, and her father, a police detective, raised her alone. Leduc becomes a private investigator, specializing in corporate security. The first novel is set in 1993, as Leduc is still struggling to get over the death of her father at the hands of a terrorist bomb and also with her dwindling business as a result of new European Union trade regulations that have lost her several business contracts. Her business partner, René Friant, is a computer expert.

Given the firm's financial problems, she accepts a lucrative assignment from an old friend of her father's. What begins as a simple task of breaking an encryption code turns into a case involving murder and Nazis, both during World War II and in present-day politics. Leduc is a master of disguise and goes undercover with a neo-Nazi group to track down the killer.

Black was inspired to write the novel after visiting Paris in 1984. She had been there many times but had never visited the Marais. A friend, the daughter of a Holocaust survivor, recounted for Black the history of the neighborhood during the Nazi occupation (Cara 58). Black was particularly haunted by the story of her friend's mother who returned from school one day to find her family gone, taken by the Nazis (Cara 58), and she writes this event for one of her characters in *Murder in the Marais.*

Black enjoys researching the historical aspects of her novels and strives to "do more than write an intriguing crime novel," by offering information on French culture and history and providing social commentary (Jones H1). In her other novels, she has written about the problems faced by Algerian immigrants and the clashes between upper class French and the Vietnamese immigrants who are moving into the neighborhood. In *Murder in the Sentier,* Leduc is lured into trouble by the promise of contact with her mother, and ends up in a case involving a group of radicals. In *Murder in the Bastille,* Leduc is attacked and temporarily blinded. Assuming she was the victim of mistaken identity, Leduc discovers there is more to her case than she originally thought, and she must rely on Friant more than ever to find her way to the solution.

CRITICAL RECEPTION

In addition to critical acclaim, Black has received Anthony Award nominations for *Murder in the Marais* and *Murder in the Sentier.* Her first novel, *Murder in the Marais,* was noted as "an extremely good example of what a mystery novel can do" (McGarrahan 8). The reviewer also felt that as Black explores the motives for the crimes, she "deals with the passions, cowardice and courage of the people she writes about, which means she is tackling no less a subject than life itself" (McGarrahan 8). Another review heralded the "literate prose, intricate plotting, and multifaceted and unusual characters" of the "excellent first mystery" (Klett 1999:140). It was also called a "first-rate debut" that "deftly combines fascinating anecdotes from the city's war years with classic images" of Paris (Zaleski 77).

Rex Klett described *Murder in the Sentier* as "not just good suspense but an affecting and realistic psychological study of a daughter's coming to terms with an absent parent" (2002:146). *Murder in the Bastille* was called "absorbing" and was praised for a complex plot and offering "the rich ambiance of Paris, as well as a realistic and moving account of Aimee's coming to terms" with her temporary disability (Cannon 239).

   Murder in Clichy was labeled as an entry in a "consistently satisfying series" in which Black "seamlessly integrates fascinating historical material about both Paris itself and the immigrant groups in the story" (Ott 944). Another reviewer noted that the "plot is inevitably complex, but it is beautifully—and thrillingly—rendered" (Hoffert 78). This novel was seen as consistent with Black's earlier works in how she "renders the city in dazzling detail" and "scores again" with her "weaving [of] culture, history and suspense" (*Murder in Clichy* 39).

BIBLIOGRAPHY

Works by Cara Black

Aimée Leduc Series

Murder in the Marais. New York: Soho Press, 1999.
Murder in Belleville. New York: Soho Press, 2000.
Murder in the Sentier. New York: Soho Press, 2002.
Murder in the Bastille. New York: Soho Press, 2003.
Murder in Clichy. New York: Soho Press, 2004.
Murder in Montmartre. New York: Soho Press, 2006.

Works about Cara Black

Cannon, Peter. "*Murder in the Bastille.*" *Publishers Weekly* 27 January 2003: 239.
Cara Black. Homepage. 2005. 16 June 2005. http://www.carablack.com
"Cara Black." *Contemporary Authors.* Vol. 190. Ed. Scot Peacock. Detroit: Gale, 2001. 57–59.
Heising, Willetta L. "Black, Cara." *Detecting Women.* 3rd ed. Dearborn: Purple Moon Press, 2000. 34.
Hoffert, Barbara. "*Murder in Clichy.*" *Library Journal* 15 March 2005: 78.
Jones, Kelly. "Author Clears Up the Mystery: Cara Black Tells How She Weaves History Lessons into Plots with Parisian Detective Aimée Leduc." *Modesto Bee* 22 May 2005: H1.
Klett, Rex E. "Murder in the Marais." *Library Journal* July 1999: 140.
———. *Murder in the Sentier. Library Journal* 1 April 2002: 146.
McGarrahan, Ellen. "Sinister Paris, Spooky Seance s and Obsession." *San Francisco Chronicle* 8 August 1999: 8.
"*Murder in Clichy.*" *Publishers Weekly* 20 December 2004: 39.
Ott, Bill. "*Murder in Clichy.*" *Booklist* 1 February 2005: 944.
Zaleski, Jeff. "*Murder in the Marais.*" *Publishers Weekly* 7 June 1999: 77.

Eleanor Taylor Bland (1944–)

BIOGRAPHY

Eleanor Taylor Bland is credited with writing the first mystery series to feature an African American female professional detective. She was born on December 21, 1944, in Boston, to Leroy and Mildred Gershefski Taylor. Her father, an African American, worked as a cab driver. Her mother was white, and her parents separated when she was young (Portnoy

18L). Bland married at age 14. Her husband was in the U.S. Navy and after years of regular relocations, his final posting was in the Great Lakes area. After he retired, they remained in that region. They have two sons, Kevin and Todd.

In her early thirties, she received a GED and began courses at a community college (Portnoy 18L). She then attended Southern Illinois University, earning a bachelor's degree in accounting and education. She worked as a cost accountant for Abbott Laboratories from 1981 to 1999. Divorced in 1989, she lives in Waukegan, Illinois, where she is active in a number of civic and social programs, including women's shelters, the public library, and arts groups.

MAJOR WORKS AND THEMES

The series is set in a fictionalized area of northern Chicago called Lincoln Heights, which is closely modeled on Waukegan, where Bland lives. The series features police detective Marti MacAlister and her children and extended family. MacAlister is a widowed, former police officer in Chicago. She moved with her two children, Theo and Joanna, to the suburbs after her husband, also a police officer, is killed. In the first few books, she shares a house with her friend Sharon, who is also a single mother. At work, she is partnered with a white male detective, Matthew "Vik" Jessenovik, and the two of them tackle cases that involve various social issues and problems. In her writing, Bland strives to "give voice" to the homeless, the mentally ill, the elderly, and children, groups who do not often have their own voice or who cannot make their voices heard (Curtright). She has stated that she does not specifically set out to change readers' minds, but that if people "no longer look at the world exactly the way" they did before reading her works, then she has succeeded (Benson 20).

Bland has written about a number of social issues throughout the series. In the first novel, MacAlister and Jessenovik solve a case involving the murder of a mentally ill woman. *Gone Quiet* addresses the murder of a man who is discovered to have been a pedophile, and *Keep Still* explores issues of both child abuse and elder abuse. In *See No Evil,* MacAlister tries to find the killer of an unidentified young woman, as well as a missing homeless man, unaware that she and her family are being stalked. *Tell No Tales* combines a cold case with a new one, raising connections that threaten to divide MacAlister and her partner. *Fatal Remains* also combines history with fresh mystery, but in this novel, Bland explores the plight of the Potawotami Indians and the history of the Underground Railroad. In addition to the social issues, Bland also delves into the personal lives of her characters, presenting a number of subplots about challenges they face with their children, families, and spouses as they cope with their professional concerns.

CRITICAL RECEPTION

Some reviewers of her first novels found Bland's writing "subdued" and "detached," but they praised her interesting characters and attention to important social issues (Klett 1992:129; Brainard 1995:58). One reviewer called the debut "auspicious," and mentioned the "evolving relationship" between MacAlister and Jessenovik as "handled with sensitivity and humor" (Brainard 1992:66). The reviewer later noted that "the understated Marti is a strong, quiet presence" with a story that "resonates" (Brainard 1995:58). Others had no concerns with the style, praising the debut novel as "a well-paced, cleverly plotted procedural with fully developed engaging characters" (Miller 1993:39).

Reviewers often discuss Bland's skill in portraying the important social issues that surround her plots. *Dead Time* was noted for "evoking with chilling reality the plight" of the mentally ill and of children at risk (Brainard 1992:66). A review of *Keep Still* described how a shocking link between two unrelated cases emerges and noted that Bland "pulls no punches" in her portrayal of child abuse (Brainard 1996:69).

As the series has progressed, reviews have praised the growing depth in plotting and characters. *Tell No Tales* was heralded as showing "her most complicated plotline yet," and the reviewer noted that Bland "delivers it with verve" (Miller 1999:836). A review of *Scream in Silence* called it a "generously layered novel, with the best parts peripheral to the mystery" (Zaleski 47).

Bland has received some notice from literary scholars, particularly those who are looking at issues of race in the genre. Priscilla L. Walton and Manina Jones looked at Bland in comparison with other African American women crime writers, particularly noting that in other series, it is typical for the African American woman to have left the police force to become a private investigator. Walton and Jones noted that MacAlister stays on the police force in spite of the issues related to her race and gender, perhaps because it is a position of power (203). Even when others may try to undermine her authority as an officer because she is an African American woman, she can assert her status and power if necessary (Walton and Jones 110–111).

Maureen T. Reddy voiced concern that Bland's treatment of racism is "more tractable" than other writers (61). Reddy noted that Jessenovik's racism and sexism are "portrayed as simple ignorance," and that he is changed "fairly easily" merely by coming to know McAlister (61). Reddy found this at odds with Bland's plotting, which she views as clearly addressing the racism and sexism inherent in society and the justice system (61).

BIBLIOGRAPHY

Works by Eleanor Taylor Bland

Dead Time. New York: St. Martin's Press, 1992.
Slow Burn. New York: St. Martin's Press, 1993.
Gone Quiet. New York: St. Martin's Press, 1994.
Done Wrong. New York: St. Martin's Press, 1995.
Keep Still. New York: St. Martin's Press, 1996.
See No Evil. New York: St. Martin's Press, 1998.
Tell No Tales. New York: St. Martin's Press, 1999.
Scream in Silence. New York: St. Martin's Press, 2000.
Whispers in the Dark. New York: St. Martin's Press, 2001.
Windy City Dying. New York: St. Martin's Press, 2002.
Fatal Remains. New York: St. Martin's Press, 2003.
A Cold and Silent Dying. New York: St. Martin's Press, 2004.
A Dark and Deadly Deception. New York: St. Martin's Press, 2005.

Works about Eleanor Taylor Bland

Benson, Christopher. "Local Heroes: Murder, She Wrote." *Chicago* February 1999: 20.
Brainard, Dulcy. "*Dead Time.*" *Publishers Weekly* 3 February 1992: 66.
———. "Done Wrong." *Publishers Weekly* 15 May 1995: 58.
———. "Keep Still." *Publishers Weekly* 27 May 1996: 69.
Curtright, Lauren. "Eleanor Taylor Bland." *VG: Voices from the Gaps: Women Artists and Writers of Color.*. 11 August 2004. 15 June 2005. http://voices.cla.umn.edu/vg/Bios/entries/bland_eleanor_taylor.html

"Eleanor Taylor Bland." *Contemporary Authors.* Vol. 116, New Revision Series. Ed. Scot Peacock. Detroit: Gale, 2003. 33–36.

Heising, Willetta L. "Bland, Eleanor Taylor." *Detecting Women.* 3rd ed. Dearborn: Purple Moon Press, 2000. 35.

Jordan, Jon. "Interview with Eleanor Taylor Bland." MysteryOne. November 2001. 16 June 2005. http://www.mysteryone.com/EleanorTaylorBlandInterview.htm

Klett, Rex E. "*Dead Time.*" *Library Journal* 1 February 1992: 129.

Miller, Stuart. "*Slow Burn.*" *Booklist* 1 September 1993: 39.

———. "*Tell No Tales.*" *Booklist* January 1999: 836.

Portnoy, Marsha. "Murder at Home: Waukegan Sets Scene for a Mystery Writer." *Chicago Tribune* 23 August 1992:18L.

Reddy, Maureen T. *Traces, Codes and Clues: Reading Race in Crime Fiction.* New Brunswick: Rutgers U P, 2003.

Walton, Priscilla L. and Manina Jones. *Detective Agency: Women Rewriting the Hard-Boiled Tradition.* Berkeley: U California P, 1999.

Zaleski, Jeff. "*Scream in Silence.*" *Publishers Weekly* 17 January 2000: 47.

Rhys Bowen (1941–)

BIOGRAPHY

Janet Quin-Harkin was born September 24, 1941, and was raised in Bath, England. Her father, Frank Newcombe, was an engineer and her mother, Margery Rees Lee Newcombe, was a school teacher. Her mother was Welsh, and she spent many of her childhood summers visiting their relatives in Wales. She studied at the University of London and also did graduate study in Freiburg and Kiel.

After finishing her degree at the University of London in 1963, she worked as a studio manager in the drama department of the British Broadcasting Corporation, where she produced and also wrote radio plays. Because of the "bloody awful" weather, she moved to Australia, where she met her husband, John Quin-Harkin (Frisbee). He had planned to immigrate to the United States, and they have lived in San Francisco since 1966. They have four children, Clare, Anne, Jane, and Dominic.

Bowen uses her Welsh grandfather's name as her pseudonym for her mystery novels. In addition to the works published as Rhys Bowen, she published more than 100 children's and young adult books under her real name. She began writing children's books when she could not find broadcasting work in the United States (Frisbee). She won awards for her early works and was approached to write for various teen series (Janet 357). She also wrote historical romances before turning to the mystery genre. She notes that her prolific work with writing for young adult series put her four children through college (Frisbee), but she turned to mystery writing after realizing she felt that she was on a "teenage treadmill" (White). She decided to write what she liked to read—"mysteries, with a strong sense of place"—and notes that she has not regretted her decision (Janet 360).

MAJOR WORKS AND THEMES

Bowen writes two mystery series. Her first is set in Llanfair, Wales, a fictionalized village in the Mt. Snowdon area, and features police constable Evan Evans. As if his name weren't confusing enough, Llanfair is filled with people named Evans, whom Bowen distinguishes by trade. Residents do not confuse Evans-the-Law with, for example, Evans-the-Meat, their butcher. Constable Evans tackles a number of crimes, including the death of hikers, a murder connected to the plans for a theme park, and murder during a musical festival. The series is noted for its cast of eccentric characters and portrayal of life in the village.

Her second series features Molly Murphy, a private investigator in New York. This series is set in the early 1900s and begins in Ireland, where Murphy is on the run, having killed a man in self-defense. Knowing that she has no chance for justice, as the dead man was the son of the landowner her family works for, she flees to England. She meets a woman who has a ticket for America, but the woman is dying of tuberculosis and knows she will be denied entry. She asks Murphy to take her children to the United States to join their father. On the ship, a man Murphy had argued with is murdered, and she finds herself at the center of an investigation. After proving her innocence and starting her new life in New York, she becomes an apprentice investigator and soon is on her own after her mentor is murdered. She solves that case and takes on others throughout the series while dealing with sexism and class discrimination.

Bowen imbues the Murphy novels with details of historical and cultural events from the first years of the twentieth century, including the experiences of Irish immigrants, the assassination of President McKinley, and the typhoid epidemic of 1902, among other events and themes. A reviewer noted that Bowen "avoids the temptation to give cameos to every famous figure of the day, but those she does work in—like New York's first 'lady policeman'—are wonderfully chosen" (*Oh Danny Boy* 40).

CRITICAL RECEPTION

Bowen won an Agatha Award for *Murphy's Law* and has been nominated for Anthony, Agatha, and Mary Higgins Clark awards for other works. She won an Anthony Award for one of her short stories. Critical response has also been positive.

Her first Evans novel was noted for its "straightforward plotting, tempered with unique characterization and subtle humor" (Klett 159). The second novel was praised for Bowen's "quiet humor and her appreciation for rural village life," which "make this a jewel of a story" (Brainard 52). The third entry in the "charming series" was critiqued for its lack of suspense, but the reviewer noted that Bowen's "keen sense of small-town politics and gossip that will keep her fans turning pages" (Zaleski 1999:226). Another reviewer was more uniformly positive, stating that "along with vivid descriptions of the quaint village, Bowen also provides a valuable lesson in cultural history, describing in detail the region's various customs" (McLarin 1999:1466).

The plot of *Evan and Elle* was not seen as the strongest, but reviewers found the novel to be "a light confection of a mystery, sweetened with the author's obvious affection for her characters, as well as for all things Welsh" (Zaleski 2000:48) and having a "high charm quotient" (McLarin 1999:759). *Evan's Gate* is noted for "deliver[ing] an enchanting portrait of Wales with genuine, flawed characters, a modicum of humor and plenty of red herrings to keep the detective constable and the reader guessing" (Cannon 42). In *Evan Blessed,* Bowen is praised for "keep[ing] the suspense slowly building to a satisfying and tidy conclusion" (Evan 42).

Murphy's Law was "enhanced by an appealing, spunky and quite believable heroine" and an "authentic sense of the life of Irish immigrants in turn-of-the-century New York City" (Cogdill 13G). Another review praised how Bowen "vividly portrays the vicissitudes of immigration at the turn of the 20th Century and offers an engrossing and entertaining read" (New 32). *For the Love of Mike* was acclaimed as "engaging" (*For the Love of Mike* 57), and *In Like Flynn* was heralded as an "absorbing, well-plotted" novel (*In Like Flynn* 45). *Oh Danny Boy* was called "entertaining" with praise for Bowen's "recreation of early 20th-century New York" (*Oh Danny Boy* 40).

BIBLIOGRAPHY

Works by Rhys Bowen

Evan Evans Series

Evan Help Us. New York: St. Martin's Press, 1998.
Evanly Choirs. New York: St. Martin's Press, 1999.
Evan and Elle. New York: St. Martin's Press, 2000.
Evan Can Wait. New York: St. Martin's Press, 2001.
Evans to Betsy. New York: St. Martin's Press, 2002.
Evan's Gate. New York: St. Martin's Press, 2004.
Evan Blessed. New York: St. Martin's Press, 2005.
Evanly Bodies. New York: St. Martin's Press, 2006.

Molly Murphy Series

Murphy's Law. New York: St. Martin's Press, 2001.
Death of Riley. New York: St. Martin's Press, 2002.
For the Love of Mike. New York: St. Martin's Press, 2003.
In Like Flynn. New York: St. Martin's Press, 2005.
Oh Danny Boy. New York: St. Martin's Press, 2006.

Works about Rhys Bowen

Bowen, Rhys. Homepage. 2005. 30 January 2006. http://www.rhysbowen.com/
Brainard, Dulcy. "*Evan Help Us.*" *Publishers Weekly* 17 August 1998: 52.
Cannon, Peter. "*Evan's Gate.*" *Publishers Weekly* 29 March 2004: 42.
Cogdill, Oline H. "Irish Immigrant Tackles New York." *South Florida Sun-Sentinel* 11 November 2001: 13G.
"*Evan Blessed.*" *Publishers Weekly* 30 May 2005: 42.
"*For the Love of Mike.*" *Publishers Weekly* 3 November 2003: 57.
Frisbee, Suzanne and Jean Marie Ward. "Rhys Bowen: A Little Slice of Evan." *Crescent Blues* 4.1 (2001). 30 January 2006. http://www.crescentblues.com/4_1issue/bowen.shtml
"*In Like Flynn.*" *Publishers Weekly* 28 February 2005: 45.
"Janet Quin-Harkin." *Contemporary Authors.* New Revision Series, Vol., 104. Ed. Sot Peacock. Detroit: Gale, 2002. 354–61.
Klett, Rex E. "*Evans Above.*" *Library Journal* December 1997: 159.
McLarin, Jenny. "*Evan and Elle.*" *Booklist* 15 December 1999: 759.
———. "*Evanly Choirs.*" *Booklist* 15 April 1999: 1466.
"New U.S. Book Releases: A Sampling of New and Recently Released Books of Interest to Boston Irish Americans." *Boston Irish Reporter* 31 October 2001: 32.
"*Oh Danny Boy.*" *Publishers Weekly* 16 January 2006: 40.
White, Claire E. "A Conversation With Rhys Bowen." *Writers Write: The Internet Writing Journal.* Feb 2001. 30 January 2006. http://www.writerswrite.com/journal/feb01/bowen.htm
Zaleski, Jeff. "*Evanly Choirs.*" *Publishers Weekly* 5 April 1999: 226.
———. "*Evan and Elle.*" *Publishers Weekly* 10 January 2000: 48.

Edna Buchanan (1939–)

BIOGRAPHY

Several mystery writers began as journalists, but Edna Buchanan is the only one who won a Pulitzer Prize for her work. Born Edna Rydzik on March 16, 1939, near Paterson, New Jersey, she was one of four daughters of a Polish factory worker. Her mother is described in various sources as a Ukrainian émigré factory worker or as a respiratory therapist; another profile describes her mother as a woman deemed by her family, particularly her Daughters of the American Revolution grandmother, to have married beneath her (Reynolds 119; Weaver M1; Trillin 44). When she was young, her father purchased a tavern, and for various reasons, her parents eventually divorced.

Buchanan was a voracious reader, but she did not enjoy school. She also began writing stories at a young age and was encouraged by one teacher in particular. Throughout her childhood, her mother worked several jobs to support the family. She herself began working summer jobs at age 12. After a childhood and adolescence of working part-time to help the family, Buchanan and her mother both obtained full-time work at Western Electric and were able to gain more financial security for the family (Reynolds 121).

In 1961, she and her mother took a vacation to Miami Beach. Buchanan fell in love with the locale and moved there soon after. She enrolled in a creative writing class and got a position at the *Miami Beach Daily Sun,* beginning with the society pages and also learning about printing practices. She married a fellow student from her writing class, James Buchanan, who was also working as a reporter for the *Daily Sun.* They divorced in 1965. She later married and divorced Emmitt Miller, a police officer in Miami.

In 1965, Buchanan applied to work for the *Miami Herald* but was turned down because she did not have formal education in journalism and had only brief experience at the *Daily Sun.* The *Herald* editor told her to work for five years and then come back. The *Daily Sun* was under new management at that time, and when the new editor asked her if she had a degree in journalism, she feared for that job, too. His response was positive, though, glad that they "wouldn't have to unteach" Buchanan ("Edna Buchanan" 56).

After gaining five years of experience at the *Daily Sun,* Buchanan wrote to the editor of the *Miami Herald* and reminded him of his earlier words. He offered her a position and she began writing for the larger newspaper in 1970, focusing on political topics, ranging from local issues to international news. This work led to court reporting and then to the police beat. One of the few women to cover the police beat at that time, Buchanan found her calling in this area. In addition to solid reporting and a tenacious attitude, she became well known for her strong, catchy leads. Buchanan has said that her idea of a successful lead is one that will cause a person reading the paper over breakfast to "spit out his coffee, clutch his chest, and say, 'My God, Martha! Did you read this?'" (qtd in Trillin 40). An example of a lead that caught Calvin Trillin's eye was for a story Buchanan wrote about a drunken man who became angry because a fast food restaurant had run out of the item he desired. The incident escalated into the man's being shot and killed by a security guard. Buchanan's lead was: "Gary Robinson died hungry" (Trillin 39).

She won several awards from national and regional associations during the 1970s and, after her reporting of numerous cases, included a racially charged police brutality case, Buchanan won the Pulitzer Prize for general reporting in 1986. Her 1988 leave of absence from the *Herald* became permanent, and Buchanan has been writing fiction full-time since then while continuing to reside in Miami.

MAJOR WORKS AND THEMES

Before turning to fiction, Buchanan wrote a true crime book and a book about her work as a crime reporter. Her first novel, *Nobody Lives Forever,* was nominated for an Edgar Award. With her second novel, she began her popular Britt Montero series. Montero, like Buchanan, is a crime reporter in Miami. Through her reporting, Montero is often involved with solving the cases she writes about. Throughout the series, the Cuban-American Montero faces a number of issues reflecting life and crime in Miami. The first Montero book, *Contents Under Pressure,* focuses on an African American sports star who dies at the hands of the police. Other works in the series focus on an old unsolved case whose prime suspect is now running for governor, serial killers, and a case that provides new information about the death of her father, who was killed when Montero was three years old. One of the best-reviewed books in the series, *You Only Die Twice,* features a case where a woman's body washes up on shore. The problem is that she had been declared dead 10 years before and her husband was awaiting execution for the crime. *Suitable for Framing* tackles what Buchanan calls the "total failure of the juvenile justice system" (Virgin C1).

Buchanan's work also addresses the issues facing a woman journalist in crime reporting. As Sarah D. Fogle points out, tensions arise in many of the novels because Montero "feels pressured to remain professional at all times and to refrain from showing what would be deemed feminine emotions" (75). Montero, as Buchanan did, deals with sensitive topics within the male-dominated fields of journalism and policing. Further, as Margaret Kinsman noted, Montero's dedication to her work plays an important role in the novels, allowing them to address a number of issues that women may face in any profession (2001:85).

More recently, Buchanan began a new series with a novel entitled *Cold Case Squad.* As the title implies, this series focuses on a group of police detectives in Miami who reexamine unsolved cases and look for possible solutions based on new technology, additional information, and fresh ideas. The leader of the department is K. C. Riley, who appears in several of the Montero series. The group returns in *Shadows,* which takes on several cold cases, including the unsolved murders of one of the detective's parents.

A number of Montero's cases also involve reopening unsolved or wrongly resolved cases, an effective theme in the mystery genre. Although cold cases are popular topics for reality-based and fictional television shows, Buchanan wrote about cold cases during much of her career, and "developed a deep understanding of them" (Weinberg 2004:F13). Margaret Kinsman noted that Buchanan "has said she writes crime fiction so she can 'make it right,' something she has not always been able to do as a newspaper reporter" (1996:124).

CRITICAL RECEPTION

Although critics have not always been completely positive in their reviews of Buchanan's work, there is widespread notice of her skill in plotting, dialogue, and detail. Her works were nominated for Edgar Awards in 1990 and 1994. Her work as a journalist honed her skills in taut writing and also provides her novels with a high level of authenticity. Steve Weinberg noted that the level of authenticity in *You Only Die Twice* "might make [it] a good textbook" for new journalists (2001:F1). Another reviewer stated that "Buchanan's Pulitzer Prize-winning reporter's eye doesn't miss much in Miami," working from knowledge of "its poshest precincts, its poorest projects and the troubles lurking in both" (Brainard 57).

Montero's enthusiasm for her work was clear to Erica Noonan, who described Montero as "never happier than when she's waist-deep in a juicy story" (D2). Noonan also praised *You Only Die Twice* for offering "more detail and insight into Britt's relationship with her mother," noting that if any reader was concerned "that there's nothing left to learn about South Florida's best breaking news reporter, Buchanan manages to pull out a surprise" (D2).

Even when a reviewer quibbled with character development, he admitted that the plotting leads to the success of the work (Weinberg 2004:F13), and as a Kirkus Reviews piece noted, "even on deadline, Buchanan couldn't write a boring page" ("Edna Buchanan" 56).

BIBLIOGRAPHY

Works by Edna Buchanan

Britt Montero Series

Contents Under Pressure. New York: Hyperion, 1992.
Miami, It's Murder. New York: Hyperion, 1994.
Suitable for Framing. New York: Hyperion, 1995.
Act of Betrayal. New York: Hyperion, 1996.
Margin of Error. New York: Hyperion, 1997.
Garden of Evil. New York: Avon, 1999.
You Only Die Twice. New York: William Morrow, 2001.
The Ice Maiden. New York: William Morrow, 2002.

Cold Case Squad Series

Cold Case Squad. New York: Simon & Schuster, 2004.
Shadows. New York: Simon & Schuster, 2005.

Other Works

Carr: Five Years of Rape and Murder from the Personal Account of Robert Frederick Carr III. New York: Dutton, 1979.
The Corpse Had a Familiar Face: Covering Miami, America's Hottest Beat. New York: Random House, 1987.
Nobody Lives Forever. New York: Random House, 1990.
Never Let Them See You Cry: More from Miami, America's Hottest Beat. New York: Random House, 1992.
Pulse. New York: Avon, 1998.

Works about Edna Buchanan

Brainard, Dulcy. "*Margin of Error.*" *Publishers Weekly* 2 June 1997: 57.
"Edna (Rydzik) Buchanan." Ed. Scot Peacock. *Contemporary Authors.* New Revision Series, Vol. 111. Detroit: Gale, 1999. 53–58.
Fogle, Sarah D. "Miami Noir: The Woman's Vantage Point." Eds. Steve Glassman and Maurice O'Sullivan. *Crime Fiction and Film in the Sunshine State.* Bowling Green: Bowling Green State U P, 1997. 65–83.
Kinsman, Margaret. "Edna Buchanan." *St. James Guide to Crime & Mystery Writers.* 4th ed. Ed. Jay P. Pederson. Detroit: St. James Press, 1996. 123–24.
———. "Investigative Journalist Britt Montero." *Clues: A Journal of Detection* 22.2 (2001): 83–93.
Noonan, Erica. "New Love, Mystery for Buchanan's Sleuth." *Boston Globe* 17 May 2001: D2.
Reynolds, Moira Davison. "Edna Buchanan." *Women Authors of Detective Series: Twenty-One American and British Writers, 1900–2000.* Jefferson, NC: McFarland, 2001. 119–27.
Silet, Charles L. P. "Edna Buchanan." *Mystery Scene* 62 (1999): 54–59.
Trillin, Calvin. "Covering the Cops." *The New Yorker* 17 February 1986: 39–57.
Virgin, Bill. "Edna Buchanan Is in Her Element with Fiction, Too." *Seattle Post-Intelligencer* 16 February 1995: C1.
Weaver, Teresa K. "Miami's Murder Mistress Makes a Confession." *Atlanta Journal-Constitution* 21 December 2003: M1.

Weinberg, Steve. "Dead Again." *Denver Post* 22 April 2001: F1.
————. "Buchanan Has Topic Down Cold." *Denver Post* 20 June 2004: F13.

Jan Burke (1953–)

BIOGRAPHY

Jan Fischer Burke was born August 1, 1953, in Houston, Texas. Her father John was a metallurgist and in 1960, the family, including her mother Velda and three siblings, moved to southern California. She grew up in a family "where service to one's community was important," and this molded her into someone who would be "actively involved in the world" (Parker).

She earned a degree in history from California State University, Long Beach in 1978 and pursued a graduate degree in the field. She decided not to finish the graduate degree and went to work in manufacturing, serving as a plant manager for almost 13 years before beginning her writing career. She married Tim Burke, a musician, and they have remained residents of southern California. She occasionally teaches writing classes for the UCLA Extension Program.

Although Burke recounts an early triumph of having one of her poems put up on the bulletin board in second grade (White) and tells of her first novel about Micronesia that was begun in the eighth grade, but was slow to progress because she "knew nothing of Micronesia" (Kelly 7D), she notes that her decision to write fiction is tied to her graduate work in history (Lanham 9). Burke was interviewing women who had worked in aircraft manufacturing during World War II for an oral history project and, struck by the regrets the women voiced, pledged to never let herself become bitter (Lanham 9). When that moment arrived, as Burke puts it, with her "hating to put [her] shoes on in the morning," she began writing her first novel about Irene Kelly (qtd in Lanham 9). After the unsolicited manuscript was sold, she began writing full time.

She enjoys the research for her books to such an extent that she attended a seminar at the Armed Forces Institute of Pathology and has taken other forensic science courses (Lanham 9; Gillespie). She has stated that doing research is one of her "favorite parts of writing books" and that she approaches the research process "with excitement" (White). She notes that perhaps 2 percent of all the research material she compiles winds up in the novels, but that the remaining 98 percent helps her situate the characters "in a more realistic world and to allow them to see what might be in front of them in a real situation" (Jordan). She also put these interests into action in founding the Crime Lab Project, which is a public action group designed to raise awareness of issues, particularly of limited funding, that forensic laboratories face (homepage).

MAJOR WORKS AND THEMES

In the first four books in the series, investigative reporter Irene Kelly tackles cases of corruption and murder. In the first outing, *Goodnight Irene*, Kelly must solve the murder of her mentor, who was working a cold case. *Sweet Dreams, Irene* finds Kelly taking on dirty politicians and Satanists; in *Remember Me, Irene* a former professor contacts her for help but is killed before she can meet him; in *Dear Irene* Kelly receives letters from a serial killer.

With *Hocus*, Burke moved beyond the structure of the first four Irene Kelly novels. The change in the titling of the book was also an indication that a different style was being presented. Burke feels that she is rooted in the traditions of mystery writing and appreciates the masters, including Christie, Chandler, and Hammett, but also wants to "bring something fresh" to the readers "without alienating them from the story" (Parker). In *Hocus,* Kelly faces a team of young kidnappers who have taken her husband hostage in hopes of using him to uncover a police officer they think is responsible for their fathers' deaths. In *Liar,* readers learn more about Irene's family history. When an estranged aunt is killed in a hit and run that looks deliberate, and Kelly inherits everything from her, the police suspect her. Kelly investigates to clear her own name and to solve the case. With *Bones,* Burke makes clear her serious interest in forensic research; the novel features realistic portrayals of searches with cadaver dogs in the hunt for a serial killer.

Flight is a unique entry in the series. Irene's husband, police detective Frank Harriman, is the main character and narrator, with Irene on the sidelines. She had been interested in featuring him because of his different role as a homicide investigator and also because she had always found him to be "an interesting character ... more closed off ... quieter, more tightly wrapped" (Gillespie). In this novel, Harriman reopens a case when new evidence shows that a police detective suspected of murder may have been innocent.

Burke's most recent work is even more complex, covering several decades and several cases. In *Bloodlines,* readers meet Irene's mentor, Conn O'Connor, who is dead as the series begins but plays an important role and has a notable presence throughout the novels. The book covers O'Connor's rise in the journalism business, and through extensive flashbacks, describes his initial work as a newspaper boy at age 8. O'Connor's older sister is abducted and murdered in 1950, and he also investigates a complicated case of kidnapping and murder in 1958; both cases remain unsolved. In 1978, when Irene is beginning her career, she has the opportunity to reinvestigate the matter with O'Connor, and the novel resolves in 1998, when all threads finally tie together.

Most of Burke's work focuses on Irene Kelly, but *Nine,* her ninth novel, was a stand-alone thriller about a police detective's fight against "an exclusive club of deranged boys" led by a disturbed young man who killed his serial killer stepfather (Zaleski 52). The group is taking justice into is own hands and killing murderers who are on the FBI's "most wanted" list. *Eighteen* is a collection of short stories that range widely in theme and style, including "ghost stories, romantic suspense, a whodunit, a tale of revenge and a humorous intrigue" with narrators "as disparate as an abused wife and an aristocratic gentleman, and, at one point, even a non-human narrator" (Yamashita 43).

CRITICAL RECEPTION

Goodnight, Irene was well received by critics and attracted extra attention when President Clinton mentioned it during one of his first interviews after the inauguration (Lanham 9; Gillespie). Burke won the Edgar Award for *Bones* in 2000 and has won Agatha and Macavity awards for three of her short stories, which are reprinted in *Eighteen.* Most of her books have been nominated for at least one award.

Reviews of the first few books praised Burke for "good pacing, fast action and appealing characters" (Melton 1994:1188) and for "exciting action, clever dialogue, solid writing, and smart, likable heroine" (Melton 1996:993). Critical reception has been positive throughout the series, although some reviews have been mixed. One reviewer felt *Bones* had strong characters but too many red herrings (Zaleski 1999:51), but others heralded it as "deviously plotted" and "full of screw-tightening suspense" (Melton 1999:2032). Peter Cannon felt *Flight* took too long to resolve, lessening the suspense, but he did praise Burke for her strong "understanding of personal relationships and motivation, plus the memorable characters she creates, notably the murderer, who is so crazy he passes for sane" (68).

In reviewing *Nine,* Jeff Zaleski noted that the novel was a departure "from her Irene Kelly series to test the waters of stand-alone mainstream thrillers, and [she] proves she can swim with the sharks in this tale of vigilante justice" with its "absorbing and inventive plot "(52). *Bloodlines* has been well received by critics. Michael Harris stated that the novel is "marvelously crafted" with numerous plot lines (E22). He further noted that "when the tumblers finally fall and the rusty lock on the truth springs open, we feel an old- fashioned pleasure" (E22).

BIBLIOGRAPHY

Works by Jan Burke

Irene Kelly Series

Goodnight, Irene. New York: Simon & Schuster, 1993.
Sweet Dreams, Irene. New York: Simon & Schuster, 1994.
Dear Irene. New York: Simon & Schuster, 1995.
Remember Me, Irene. New York: Simon & Schuster, 1996.
Hocus. New York: Simon & Schuster, 1997.
Liar. New York: Simon & Schuster, 1998.
Bones. New York: Simon & Schuster, 1999.
Flight. New York: Simon & Schuster, 2001.
Bloodlines. New York: Simon & Schuster, 2005.
Kidnapped. New York: Simon & Schuster, 2006.

Other Works

Nine. New York: Simon & Schuster, 2002.
Eighteen. New York: Pocket, 2003.

Works about Jan Burke

Cannon, Peter. "*Flight.*" *Publishers Weekly* 29 January 2001: 68.
Gillespie, Larrian. Jan Burke Interview. *Larrian's Loft/The Goddess Diet.* 2002. 17 November 2004. http://goddessdiet.com/burke.htm
Harris, Michael. "Nostalgia That's Swashbuckling." *Los Angeles Times* 4 March 2005: E22.
"Jan Burke." *Contemporary Authors.* Vol. 87, New Revision Series. Ed. Scot Peacock. Detroit: Gale, 2000. 62–63.
Jan Burke. 2004. 17 November 2004. http://www.janburke.com
Jordan, Jon. "Interview with Jan Burke." *Mystery One.* 26 December 1999. 17 November 2004. http://www.mysteryone.com/JanBurke.htm
Kelly, Katy. "Mysterious Start to Burke's Career." *USA Today* 7 May 1998: 7D.
Lanham, Fritz. "No I-wish-I-hads for Her: Jan Burke Came to Writing to Escape a Dull Business Career." *Houston Chronicle* 25 March 2001: 9.
Melton, Emily. "*Sweet Dreams, Irene.*" *Booklist* 1 March 1994: 1188.
———. "*Remember Me, Irene.*" *Booklist* 15 February 1996: 993.
———. "*Bones.*" *Booklist* August 1999: 2032.
Parker, T. Jefferson. "At Home Online: Jan Burke." *Mystery Readers International.* 17 November 2004. http://www.mysteryreaders.org/athomeburke.html
White, Claire E. "A Conversation with Jan Burke." *Writers Write: The Internet Writing Journal.* July 1998. 17 November 2004. http://www.writerswrite.com/journal/ju98/burke.htm
Yamashita, Brianna. "*Eighteen.*" *Publishers Weekly* 22 December 2003: 43.
Zaleski, Jeff. "*Bones.*" *Publishers Weekly* 23 August 1999: 51.
———. "*Nine.*" *Publishers Weekly* 7 October 2002: 52.

Sarah Caudwell (1939–2000)

BIOGRAPHY

Born Sarah Cockburn on May 27, 1939, in London, her parents were well known in the arts. Claud Cockburn was a writer, best known as a Communist journalist, and her mother, Jean Ross, was an actress and writer. Ross was "widely acknowledged as Christopher Isherwood's model for Sally Bowles, the central figure in *I Am a Camera* and *Cabaret*" (Dyer 38).

Caudwell studied at Aberdeen University and St. Anne's College, Oxford. She worked to change the status of women in the college; at the time she was a student there, women were barred from participating in various activities or using certain facilities. One particular venue that did not welcome women was the Oxford Union debating club, and Caudwell caused a stir by attending dressed a man (Batten E14).

She practiced law throughout her career, serving as a barrister in London, as well as a lecturer in law at University College of Wales. Later in her career she was a member of the legal department of Lloyd's Bank's trust division.

She was an avid pipe smoker and keen crossword puzzle fan, having often placed in the finals of a crossword competition sponsored by *The Times* (Edwards 50). She died of cancer on January 28, 2000.

MAJOR WORKS AND THEMES

Caudwell's fictional works feature Hilary Tamar, a pipe-smoking professor of law who assists a group of four young barristers named Julia Larwood, Selena Jardine, Michael Cantrip, and Desmond Ragwort. Another barrister named Timothy Shepherd was included in the first novel but did not appear in subsequent ones. The team has been described as being able to "out-Rumpole Rumpole" (Ripley 49). Tamar, whom Caudwell never clearly identified as male or female, solves the cases with a wide knowledge of arcane elements of the law. Simon Brett calls the fact that readers can never clearly determine Tamar's gender as "a typical Caudwell joke" (56). According to Lucinda Dyer, Caudwell never told her agents, publishers, or editors either, and quotes Caudwell's agent as saying that she "loved puzzles. That's why she fell in love with mystery fiction" (38). Caudwell herself noted that "Hilary's voice was in [her] head before any of the plots," and that Tamar was destined to be an Oxford don of "equivocal sex and even more equivocal age, resembling that precise, donnish kind of individual who starts being elderly at the age of 22" (Edwards 50).

Caudwell's books share several elements, including plots related to tricky legal or financial matters rather than gory violent crimes, along with exotic settings, the use of letters to share information among the group, and no shortage of dry humor, often likened to Barbara Pym. In the first novel, Larwood has gone to Venice on an art tour and ends up embroiled in a case of murder for financial gain. The second novel also takes place outside of Britain, with the group traveling to Corfu in hopes of solving the case surrounding a mysterious will, although, as Simon Brett noted, "most of the action takes place over plentiful bottles in the Corkscrew wine bar" or their favorite Italian restaurant (56). *The Sirens Sang of Murder* follows the group from the Cayman Islands to Monaco, as Tamar helps the barristers locate missing beneficiaries of a trust that has lost many of its beneficiaries to accidents. The final novel involves an arcane tax matter that leads to crimes ranging from insider trading to murder.

CRITICAL RECEPTION

Caudwell's works were well received by critics and readers, and she won an Anthony Award for *The Sirens Sang of Murder*. A review of her second novel noted that the plotting was traditional, but that "it's all in the telling" and likened Caudwell's use of language to Oscar Wilde, proclaiming it to be "utterly delightful" with "polished, stylized prose" (Callendar 17). A review of *The Sirens Sang of Murder* noted the presence of "astringently British witticisms" (Steinberg 41), and another reviewer described Caudwell's style as "largely elegant and literate," with "delights of prose and humor" available to the stalwart reader (Klett 122).

Her final novel was published posthumously and also garnered praise. According to Marilyn Stasio, "the wit, erudition and stylistic elegance" of Caudwell's earlier works are "abundantly at play" in the final novel (28). Stasio found this novel to include elements of the English village mystery and eighteenth-century epistolary novels, with Caudwell "ransacking the literary forms that amuse her" (28). Caudwell was often praised for her use of humor, well described by one critic as "by turns charming and acidic, though never mean"(Ripley 49). Another reviewer heralded the final entry of the "engaging series" as "narrated in [a]delightfully understated manner … a literate and leisurely sendup of the traditional English village mystery, complete with pubs and poison" (Pate 3).

Sharon A. Russell wrote an essay about Caudwell for Kathleen Gregory Klein's *Women Times Three*. This essay explores the issues of gender in detective fiction and the impact of Caudwell's character being unclearly defined, as well as the treatment of gender and sexuality throughout the novels.

BIBLIOGRAPHY

Works by Sarah Caudwell

Thus Was Adonis Murdered. New York: Scribner, 1981.
The Shortest Way to Hades. London: Collins, 1984; New York: Scribner, 1985.
The Sirens Sang of Murder. New York: Scribner, 1989.
The Sibyl in Her Grave. New York: Delacorte Press, 2000.

Works about Sarah Caudwell

Batten, Jack. "The Secret's in Her Grave." *Toronto Star* 27 August 2000: E14.
Brett, Simon. "Dark Deeds and Donnish Debate." *Daily Mail* 10 May 2002: 56.
Callendar, Newgate. "Crime." *New York Times Book Review* 19 January 1986: 17.
Dyer, Lucinda. "Is He or Isn't She?" *Publishers Weekly* 9 April 2001: 38.
Edwards, Martin. "Sarah Caudwell: A Most Ingenious Legal Mind." *Mystery Scene* 87 (2004): 50–51.
Klett, Rex E. "*The Sirens Sang of Murder*." *Library Journal* 1 October 1989: 122.
Pate, Nancy. "Caudwell Series Swan Song Full of Ravens, Vultures, and Wit." *Chicago Tribune* 4 August 2000: 3.
Ripley, Mike. "Mike Ripley's Crime File." *Birmingham Post* 31 August 2002: 49.
Russell, Sharon A. "Gender and Voice in the Novels of Sarah Caudwell." *Women Times Three*. Ed. Kathleen Gregory Klein. Bowling Green: Bowling Green State UP, 1995. 43–52.
"Sarah Caudwell (Obituary)." *Daily Telegraph* 10 February 2000: 33.
"Sarah Cockburn." *Contemporary Authors*. Vol. 199. Ed. Scot Peacock. Detroit: Gale, 2002. 55–57.
Stasio, Marilyn. "Crime." *New York Times Book Review* 9 July 2000: 28
Steinberg, Sybil. "*The Sirens Sang of Murder*." *Publishers Weekly* 22 September 1989: 41.

Jill Churchill (1943–)

BIOGRAPHY

Born Janice Young Brooks on January 11, 1943, in Kansas City, Missouri, Churchill's parents were J. W. and Louise Jones Young. Her father was a surgeon. She earned a bachelor's degree in education at the University of Kansas in 1965 and also pursued graduate study at the University of Missouri-Kansas City during 1965–1967. She taught elementary school for a number of years. After a hiatus from teaching, she became the book reviewer for the Kansas City Star, a position she held from 1978 to 1992. Divorced, she lives in Kansas. She has a son and daughter and two grandchildren.

MAJOR WORKS AND THEMES

Before turning to the mystery genre, Churchill published a number of works of historical fiction under her real name. She describes these novels as family sagas with multiple generations and "realistic characters and situations, lots of subplots and local flavor … exactly the sort of book [she] most loves to read" (Janice 63).

In 1989, she introduced Jane Jeffry, a widow with three children in suburban Chicago, who constantly finds herself mixed up with murder cases. With her best friend and neighbor, Shelley Nowack, as a sidekick, Jeffry solves crimes and assists or, depending on who is defining her role, meddles in the work of Mel VanDyne, the police detective she meets in the first novel, who becomes her love interest. The titles of the novels are puns based on the titles of well-known classic and contemporary literary works to reflect the cozy, domestic themes of the novels. Examples are *Grime and Punishment* and *Mulch Ado about Nothing*. In between taking care of her children and numerous domestic duties and volunteer positions, Jeffry solves the crimes that come to her neighborhood with great aplomb.

In 1999, Churchill began a new mystery series, set during the Great Depression. The series features a brother and sister, Robert and Lily Brewster, who have lost their family fortune in the crash and are adjusting to a new lifestyle. While trying to make ends meet in New York, they become active as amateur sleuths. Later in the series, they inherit a house in upstate New York from an uncle. After solving the mystery surrounding their uncle's death, they open their new home as a guest house to earn a living. They become involved in a variety of cases, sometimes involving their boarders and sometimes linked to events of the day.

CRITICAL RECEPTION

Churchill won the Agatha and Macavity awards for the first novel in the Jane Jeffry series. A review of *A Farewell to Yarns* noted that Jeffry was an "appealing heroine" with a "fully drawn" supporting cast (Kaganoff 47). *Silence of the Hams* was noted for its "complicated" plot twists and being "seasoned with wit" (Simson 81).

In *War and Peas*, Jeffry and Nowack investigate a "slew of suspects—smarmy, lecherous, devious and greedy, but never dull," in a novel with a "cozy setting, beguiling plot and three-dimensional characters" (Brainard 1996:59). In a review of *Fear of Frying*, Churchill is again praised for creating strong characters, with the reviewer noting that the entire secondary cast are "all well-drawn, distinctive characters in Churchill's hands" (Brainard 1997:56). Another reviewer found this novel a "pleasant, hard-to-solve mystery, with evocative autumnal atmosphere (a good Halloween read), lively writing, and often humorous dialogue " (Rowen 309).

A review of *Groom with a View* noted that "with calm efficiency and occasional grace, Jane Jeffry, who last year solved a murder while doing the Christmas baking," again solves a case involving family secrets that arise during a wedding (DeCandido 71). Jeffry is praised as "companionable, smart, and down to earth" (DeCandido 71). Another reviewer noted that "the identity of the killer will come as no great surprise," but praised Churchill for "deliver[ing] a satisfying plot laced with subtle humor and some enjoyable gothic flourishes" (Zaleski 50). *A Midsummer Night's Scream* was lauded as an effective mix of "a more than serviceable plot with a nice combination of romance, domesticity and sleuthing" (Cannon 2004:51).

A review of *Anything Goes* praised Churchill for "adeptly captur[ing] the spirit of this early twentieth-century Hudson Valley community, insulated from the rest of the world," further noting that "its various twists and false leads to the murderer" makes the novel a "pleasant diversion" (Rotella 64). A review of *Love for Sale* praised Churchill for "bring[ing] the Depression era to appealing life in her latest well-plotted cozy" (Cannon 2003:52).

BIBLIOGRAPHY

Works by Jill Churchill

Jane Jeffry Series

Grime and Punishment. New York: Bantam, 1989.
A Farewell to Yarns. New York: Avon, 1991.
A Quiche before Dying. New York: Avon, 1993.
The Class Menagerie. New York: Avon, 1994.
A Knife to Remember. New York: Avon, 1994.
From Here to Paternity. New York: Avon, 1995.
Silence of the Hams. New York: Avon, 1996.
War and Peas. New York: Avon, 1996.
Fear of Frying. New York: Avon, 1997.
The Merchant of Menace. New York: Avon, 1998.
A Groom with a View. New York: Avon, 1999.
Mulch Ado about Nothing. New York: Morrow, 2000.
The House of Seven Mables. New York: Morrow, 2002.
Bell, Book and Scandal. New York: Morrow, 2003.
A Midsummer Night's Scream. New York: Morrow, 2004.

Grace and Favor Series

Anything Goes. New York: Avon, 1999.
In the Still of the Night. New York: Avon, 2000.
Someone to Watch over Me. New York: Avon, 2001.
Love for Sale. New York: Morrow, 2003.
It Had to Be You. New York: Morrow, 2004.
Who's Sorry Now? New York: Morrow, 2005.

Other Fiction

As Amanda Singer. *Ozark Legacy.* New York: Avalon, 1975.
As Janice Young Brooks. *Forbidden Fires.* New York: Playboy Press, 1977.
As Janice Young Brooks. *Seventrees.* New York: New American Library, 1980.
As Valerie Vayle. *Lady of Fire.* New York: Dell, 1980.
As Valerie Vayle. *Seaflame.* New York: Dell, 1980.
As Valerie Vayle. *Oriana.* New York: Dell, 1981.

As Janice Young Brooks. *Still the Mighty Waters.* New York: Dell, 1983.
As Janice Young Brooks. *Our Lives, Our Fortunes.* New York: Dell, 1984.
As Janice Young Brooks. *Glory.* New York: Dell, 1985.
As Janice Young Brooks. *The Circling Years.* New York: New American Library, 1986.
As Janice Young Brooks. *Crown Sable.* New York: New American Library, 1987.
As Janice Young Brooks. *Cinnamon Wharf.* New York: New American Library, 1988.
As Janice Young Brooks. *Guests of the Emperor.* New York: Ballantine, 1990.
As Janice Young Brooks. *The Herron Heritage.* London: Headline, 1992.

Nonfiction by Janice Young Brooks

Kings and Queens: The Plantagenets of England. Nashville: Thomas Nelson, 1975.

Works about Jill Churchill

Brainard, Dulcy. "*War and Peas.*" *Publishers Weekly* 23 September 1996: 59.
———. "*Fear of Frying.*" *Publishers Weekly* 27 October 1997: 56.
Cannon, Peter. "*Love for Sale.*" *Publishers Weekly* 26 May 2003: 52.
———. "*A Midsummer Night's Scream.*" *Publishers Weekly* 18 October 2004: 51.
DeCandido, Graceanne A. "*A Groom with a View.*" *Booklist* 1 September 1999: 71.
"Janice Young Brooks." *Contemporary Authors.* New Revision Series, Vol. 104. Ed. Scot Peacock. Detroit: Gale, 2002. 62–64.
Jill Churchill. Homepage. 2005. 6 February 2006. http://www.jillchurchill.com
Kaganoff, Penny. "*A Farewell to Yarns.*" *Publishers Weekly* 22 November 1991: 47.
Rotella, Mark. "*Anything Goes.*" *Publishers Weekly* 10 May 1999: 64.
Rowen, John. "*Fear of Frying.*" *Booklist* 1 October 1997: 309.
Simson, Maria. "*Silence of the Hams.*" *Publishers Weekly* 3 June 1996: 81.
Zaleski, Jeff. "*A Groom with a View.*" *Publishers Weekly* 23 August 1999: 50.

Mary Higgins Clark (1929–)

BIOGRAPHY

Mary Eleanor Higgins was born December 24, 1929, in New York. Her father, Luke Joseph Higgins, was a first-generation Irish immigrant who owned a restaurant; her mother, Nora Durkin Higgins, worked as a department store buyer before they started their family. Higgins grew up in the Bronx, which she describes as being rural at that time (Kelly 102), with her two brothers. She began writing at age 7, with output ranging from poems that her mother had her recite to visitors, to plays and skits that she coerced her brothers into performing with her (Arant 68). She also began keeping diaries at that time, and she still has all of them (Hirschhorn 75).

Her father died when she was 10 years old, and the family's lives changed drastically. In addition, her brother Joseph died of spinal meningitis when she was 15. She has noted that these losses drove her to give up a college scholarship to attend secretarial school for financial security and to help her mother (Arant 68–69). After secretarial school, she worked as an advertising assistant. She also worked briefly as a flight attendant for Pan American during 1949–1950. She married Warren Clark, a family friend and airline executive, on December 26, 1949. She and her husband had five children, Marilyn, Warren, David,

Carol, and Patricia. Warren Clark died of a heart attack in 1964, leaving Higgins with five young children.

Long before becoming a novelist, Clark had been writing short stories. Her first attempt to become published was at age 16. She sent a story to *True Confessions,* expecting acceptance "on the basis that everything they published was so lousy that they'd be sure to take" her work, but the rejection letter admonished her that her characters were "too upscale" (Weich). Her first publication came in 1956, and she also took creative writing courses at New York University. She had several more stories published, mostly in women's magazines, but after the death of her husband, she turned more seriously to writing, finding full-time work as a radio scriptwriter and later as a producer of radio programming, from 1965 to 1980.

After the success of her first novel in 1975, she decided she could finally pursue her college degree. She earned her bachelor's degree in philosophy at Fordham University in 1979. In 1980, she was financially able to leave her work in radio and concentrate on writing full-time. She was briefly married to a lawyer in 1978, but her marriage to retired businessman John Conheeney has lasted since 1996. Conheeney has four children from a previous marriage, and they have many grandchildren between them. They have homes in Manhattan, Cape Cod, and New Jersey.

MAJOR WORKS AND THEMES

Her first novel, *Aspire to the Heavens,* was published in 1969, and although it was critically acclaimed and won an award, it was not a commercial success. Clark has joked that the novel was remaindered as it came off the press (Arant 69). The novel, which was about George and Martha Washington, was republished in 2002 as *Mount Vernon Love Story.* She enjoyed reading mystery novels and decided to turn her attention to that genre. Her first suspense novel, *Where Are the Children?* was rejected by two publishers, because of the subject matter of kidnapped children (Arant 70). Simon and Schuster bought it in 1974, and they have published all her works since.

Her first few novels were inspired by current events or issues. The first was written at a time when child abductions were on the rise, and her second novel dealt with a boy who had witnessed his mother's murder and on a broader level was an exploration of the death penalty. *The Cradle Will Fall* dealt with medical issues and was written after the first test-tube baby was born. She continued this with many of her novels, drawing on current events or social issues. Clark has stated that "a good suspense novel can and should hold a mirror up to society and make a social comment" (qtd in Arant 74).

In addition to novels like *Moonlight Becomes You* that explored conditions at nursing homes and *Loves Music, Loves to Dance,* which looked at the dangers of personal ads, other novels deal with what happens to people when the unexpected occurs. In *I'll Be Seeing You,* a young woman's world is shattered when he father dies in a car accident, but when the body is never recovered from the Hudson River and she meets someone who could be her twin sister, she has to investigate her own family's past.

Recent novels have taken on a variety of plots and themes. *On the Street Where You Live* combined a new mystery with a historical one, with a particular house tied to both. *Daddy's Little Girl* tells the story of a young woman whose sister was murdered years before and her investigation into the crime after the alleged killer, still proclaiming his innocence, is released. *The Second Time Around* features a reporter looking into a medical research firm, and *No Place Like Home* finds a woman with a secret past thrust back into her childhood hometown.

She has edited several volumes of stories, and in 1996, she launched the *Mary Higgins Clark Mystery Magazine*, which publishes mystery and suspense short stories. In 2002, she published her memoir, *Kitchen Privileges,* which recounts her youth and family, her early days as a writer, and her successes since 1975.

CRITICAL RECEPTION

Clark has won a number of awards and honors, and was inducted as a Grand Master by the Mystery Writers Association in 2000. In addition, her work inspired the creation of a new award for mystery writers. The Mary Higgins Clark Award is sponsored by Simon and Schuster and is awarded by the Mystery Writers of America for a novel that best emulates Clark's model. Since breaking into the mystery and suspense arena, Clark has been a best-selling author and has also received decent critical reception over the years.

Many reviewers praise various aspects of her work, while often finding her character development thin and plots and villains predictable. For example, a review of *While My Pretty One Sleeps* praised the final clue as "so subtly placed that the finale is an absolute marvel of invention," but also noted that this solid ending raised "the impact of the some-what shallow story" (Steinberg 1989:46). Another example is found in a review of *All Around the Town*, which is praised for its "swift and slickly managed" plotting, but the reviewer warned that readers seeking "nuance, flavor and shading" will be "unsatisfied" (Steinberg 1992:91). Another review of *All Around the Town* noted that the novel has "moments of sheer terror," but also "stretches of sheer boredom" (Donavin 1483).

A review of *Loves Music, Loves to Dance* stated that Clark "deserves her reputation for creating splendid suspense fiction" and also noted that the "thoroughly engaging" plot "more than makes up for [the] flaw" of her "simple" characters (Cohen 16). Another review of this novel praised the "great potential for terror" while critiquing the "surfeit of insignificant minor characters and one too many red herring" (Steinberg 1991:138). Yet another review characterized her work as solid but not "dazzling," though her novel is called "entertainingly absorbing" with "neatly paced plot and colorful, sympathetic characters" (Hooper 1602).

Recently, she has enjoyed more positive critical response, gaining recognition for her recent plot twists and fresh ideas. *Daddy's Little Girl* was noted for its use of first-person narration, and one reviewer praised the novel for "its textured plot, well-sketched secondary characters, strong pacing and appealing heroine," calling it "Clark at her most winning" (Zaleski 2002:44). One review of *No Place Like Home* praised Clark's "clever use of a bit of New Jersey real estate code"(*No Place Like Home* 56). A review of *Second Time Around* stated that Clark "knows how to spin an intriguing tale, and this time she's created a convincing heroine in Carley" (Wilkens 1538); another reviewer noted that "what the novel lacks in suspense it makes up for in grace, charm and solid storytelling" (Zaleski 2003:47).

The lack of entirely positive critical response has never bothered Clark, though. As Wendi Arant noted, if her readers are entertained, then Clark is satisfied with the quality of her work (70).

BIBLIOGRAPHY

Works by Mary Higgins Clark

Aspire to the Heavens. New York: Meredith Press, 1969. Republished as *Mount Vernon Love Story.* New York: Simon & Schuster, 2002.

Where Are the Children? New York: Simon & Schuster, 1975.
A Stranger Is Watching. New York: Simon & Schuster, 1978.
The Cradle Will Fall. New York: Simon & Schuster, 1980.
A Cry in the Night. New York: Simon & Schuster, 1982.
Stillwatch. New York: Simon & Schuster, 1984.
While My Pretty One Sleeps. New York: Simon & Schuster, 1989.
The Anastasia Syndrome and Other Stories. New York: Simon & Schuster, 1989.
Loves Music, Loves to Dance. New York: Simon & Schuster, 1991.
All around the Town. New York: Simon & Schuster, 1992.
I'll Be Seeing You. New York: Simon & Schuster, 1993.
Remember Me. New York: Simon & Schuster, 1994.
Silent Night: A Novel. New York: Simon & Schuster, 1995.
Let Me Call You Sweetheart. New York: Simon & Schuster, 1995.
Moonlight Becomes You. New York: Simon & Schuster, 1996.
My Gal Sunday. New York: Simon & Schuster, 1996.
Pretend You Don't See Her. New York, Simon & Schuster, 1997.
You Belong to Me. New York: Simon & Schuster, 1998.
We'll Meet Again. New York: Simon & Schuster, 1999.
Before I Say Goodbye. New York: Simon & Schuster, 2000.
On the Street Where You Live. New York: Simon & Schuster, 2001.
Daddy's Little Girl. New York: Simon & Schuster, 2002.
The Second Time Around. New York: Simon & Schuster, 2003.
Nighttime Is My Time. New York: Simon & Schuster, 2004.
No Place Like Home. New York: Simon & Schuster, 2005.
Two Little Girls in Blue. New York: Simon & Schuster, 2006.

Alvirah and Willy Meehan Series

Weep No More, My Lady. New York: Simon & Schuster, 1987.
Death on the Cape and Other Short Stories. New York: Simon & Schuster, 1993.
The Lottery Winner: Alvirah and Willy Stories. New York: Simon & Schuster, 1994.
All through the Night. New York: Simon & Schuster, 1998.
With Carol Higgins Clark. *Deck the Halls.* New York: Simon & Schuster, 2000.
With Carol Higgins Clark. *He Sees You When You're Sleeping.* New York: Simon & Schuster, 2001.
Memoir/autobiography *Kitchen Privileges.* New York: Simon & Schuster, 2002.

Works about Mary Higgins Clark

Arant, Wendi. "Mary Higgins Clark." *Dictionary of Literary Biography*, Vol. 306:
American Mystery and Detective Writers. Ed. George Parker Anderson. Detroit: Gale, 2005.
    66–75.
Cohen, Joyce. "*Loves Music, Loves to Dance.*" *New York Times Book Review* 16 June 1991: 16.
Donavin, Denise Perry. "*All around the Town.*" *Booklist* 15 April 1992: 1483.
Hirschhorn, Joel. "PW Talks with Mary Higgins Clark: Novel(ist's) Advice: Write What You Know."
    Publishers Weekly 4 November 2002: 75.
Hooper, Brad. "*Loves Music, Loves to Dance.*" *Booklist* 15 April 1991: 1602.
Kelly, Mary Pat. "Mary Higgins Clark: Queen of Suspense." *Irish America* 30 November 2000: 102.
"Mary Higgins Clark." *Contemporary Authors. New Revision Series*, Vol. 133. Ed. Tracey L. Matthews.
    Detroit: Gale, 2005. 146–51.
"*No Place Like Home.*" *Publishers Weekly* 28 March 2005: 56.
Steinberg, Sybil. "*While My Pretty One Sleeps.*" *Publishers Weekly* 31 March 1989: 46.
———. "*Loves Music, Loves to Dance.*" *Publishers Weekly* 5 April 1991: 138.
———. "*All Around the Town.*" *Publishers Weekly* 30 March 1992: 91.

Weich, Dave. Interview with Mary Higgins Clark. Powells.com. 13 May 1999. 31 January 2006. http://www.powells.com/authors/higginsclark.html
Wilkens, Mary Frances. "*The Second Time Around.*" *Booklist* 1 May 2003: 1538.
Zaleski, Jeff. "*Daddy's Little Girl.*" *Publishers Weekly* 15 April 2002: 43–44.
———. "*The Second Time Around.*" *Publishers Weekly* 7 April 2003: 47.

Barbara Cleverly

BIOGRAPHY

Before turning to writing full-time, Barbara Cleverly taught French, English, and Latin. She was born in Yorkshire and attended the University in Durham, where she earned degrees in French and Latin. She lives in Suffolk, where her late husband, Peter, was an architect.

She has revealed that she began writing stories about India to entertain her husband as he was dying (Knight 7; Hix 23). One of her husband's great-uncles had served in India, and he had a good deal of memorabilia that had been passed down through the family. His interest in that era, coupled with her noticing a contest sponsored by the Crime Writers Association for new writers, led her to write the first version of *The Last Kashmiri Rose.* Although she did not win the contest, she was one of the finalists and attracted the notice of an agent.

MAJOR WORKS AND THEMES

Cleverly's first mystery series features a Scotland Yard inspector named Joe Sandilands, with characteristics based on her husband's relative, Harold Sandilands. The series begins in 1922, with Sandilands being sent to India to solve a string of unexplained deaths of officers' wives in Bengal. Subsequent cases take place against the backdrop of British colonialism and political intrigue near the end of the Empire.

On her homepage, Cleverly describes Sandilands as "good looking, sexy, socially at ease wherever he finds himself" and notes that he "does not bring with him the dire baggage of personal problems" often found in modern crime fiction. She provides a "guarantee that this hero has no Drinking Problem, Complaining Wife, Troublesome Teenage Daughter or Boss Who's Out To Get Him" (homepage).

She is planning a new series, also set in the 1920s, with an archaeologist named Laetitia Talbot, whom Cleverly describes as "a bluestocking but a free-thinking bohemian" (Hix 24). In the first novel, tentatively titled *The Corn Maiden,* Talbot travels to France to solve the murder of her godfather.

CRITICAL RESPONSE

Cleverly's first novel won the Crime Writers Association's Debut Dagger, and she also won the Ellis Peters Historical Dagger for *The Damascened Blade.* Critical acclaim has been strong.

The Last Kashmiri Rose was praised as an "impressive debut," a "well-written fairplay mystery" with a "satisfying ending" (Cannon 2002:57). Another reviewer found it to be a "spellbinding debut," with a classic whodunit formula that is "embellished by the vivid colonial setting" (Stasio 54). It also gained praise for being "deftly plotted and filled with unexpected twists," as well as "effectively captur[ing] the sights and sounds of 1920s India and provides a fascinating look at the social and political climate of the time" (Melton 1929–30).

Her second novel, *Ragtime in Simla,* was noted for its "fully developed characters and a convincing portrayal of time and place," and the "murderer's identity comes as a nice and logical surprise" (*Ragtime in Simla* 57). Another reviewer praised Cleverly's "great plot, exotic Indian surrounds, and historical ambiance" in addition to her "very sympathetic protagonist" (Klett 120). Cleverly was also acclaimed for "deftly transport[ing] readers to an exotic locale filled with intrigue, suspense, and characters skilled in the art of deception" in a novel called "perfect armchair travel for historical mystery fans" (Bibel 2003:67).

The Damascened Blade was said to "evoke, and in some ways surpass" Agatha Christie's work, with Cleverly praised for "a masterful job of combining traditional puzzle elements, including false endings and subtle fair-play clues, with convincing period atmosphere and characters with more complexity and sophistication than Christie typically provided" (Cannon 2004:46–47). Another reviewer called it an "excellent historical mystery" and praised Cleverly for introducing "several strong feminist characters who prove that they are more than capable of surviving in the harsh frontier environment" (Bibel 2004:1823).

The Palace Tiger placed Cleverly "in the first rank of historical mystery writers," owing to her "increasingly impressive ability to depict a convincing, three-dimensional colonial India through the perspective of her rugged, insightful sleuth" (Palace). The review also praised her "trademark twisty plotting" and noted that "while the clues are all hidden in plain sight, even veteran mystery readers may find it a considerable challenge to arrive at the correct solution" (Palace). Another reviewer noted that "as always, Cleverly draws readers into the British raj with colorful historical details, a complex plot, and fascinating characters" (Bibel 2005:1904).

BIBLIOGRAPHY

Works by Barbara Cleverly

Joe Sandilands Series

The Last Kashmiri Rose. New York: Carroll & Graf, 2002.
Ragtime in Simla. New York: Carroll & Graf, 2003.
The Damascened Blade. New York: Carroll & Graf, 2004.
The Palace Tiger. New York: Carroll & Graf, 2005.
The Bee's Kiss. New York: Carroll & Graf, 2006.

Other Fiction

An Old Magic. Suffolk: Suffolk Press, 2003.

Works about Barbara Cleverly

Barbara Cleverly. Homepage. n.d. 16 March 2006. http://www.barbaracleverly.com
Bibel, Barbara. "*Ragtime in Simla.*" *Booklist* 1 September 2003: 67.
———. "*The Damascened Blade.*" *Booklist* July 2004: 1823.
———. "*The Palace Tiger.*" *Booklist* July 2005: 1904.
Cannon, Peter. "*The Last Kashmiri Rose.*" *Publishers Weekly* 15 July 2002: 57.
———. "*The Damascened Blade.*" *Publishers Weekly* 14 June 2004: 46–47.
Hix, Charles. "Making the Historical Fictional." *Publishers Weekly* 22 November 2004: 23–24.

Klett, Rex E. "*Ragtime in Simla.*" *Library Journal* 1 October 2003: 120.

Knight, Virginia R. "Barbara Cleverly: Inspired by History, Memories and Political Storms." *Mystery News* August/September 2005: 6–7.

Melton, Emily. "*The Last Kashmiri Rose.*" *Booklist* August 2002: 1929–30.

"*The Palace Tiger.*" *Publishers Weekly* 8 August 2005. 18 March 2006. < http://reviews.publishersweekly.com/bd.aspx?isbn = 0786715723&pub = pw

"*Ragtime in Simla.*" *Publishers Weekly* 4 August 2003: 57.

Stasio, Marilyn. "Crime." *New York Times Book Review* 17 November 2002: 54.

Liza Cody (1944–)

BIOGRAPHY

Liza Cody was the first to introduce a female British detective in the hard-boiled style. Born Liza Nassim on April 11, 1944, she attended the City and Guilds of London Art School, studying painting, sculpture, etching, and engraving, and was then awarded a place in the Royal Academy School of Art (Rahn 71). In addition to her work as a writer, she has been a painter, a studio technician at Madame Tussauds Wax Museum, and a graphic designer. She married a sculptor and had a daughter in 1966 (Rahn 72). Cody lives in England.

Writing is something that Cody came to "by accident," as she left school early, a dyslexic in the days when dyslexia was not recognized or addressed (Silet 25). While on vacation in Italy with several families, she began telling the children elaborate bedtime stories. Her husband encouraged her to write children's books, but she found herself drawn to writing for adults, particularly in the mystery genre. She notes that writing mysteries, where the story has to end, allowed her to control part of the process, while allowing the characters to emerge (Silet 27).

MAJOR WORKS AND THEMES

Cody writes two very different series. The first series features Anna Lee, a former police detective who joins a firm of private investigators. In the first two novels, she handles routine cases for the agency, such as investigating a car accident and surveillance work, that turn into more than she bargained for. In *Stalker* and *Hard Case* she works on two different missing person cases. Cody's work is often viewed as feminist detective fiction, although Cody says Lee would never think of herself as a feminist (Silet 28). Also, Lee is different from other female private investigators like V. I. Warshawski or Kinsey Millhone in that she does not have as much power over her working life; rather than a solo investigator, Lee is merely an employee in a firm filled with sexist co-workers who don't appreciate her.

Cody's second series features a much different type of heroine in works that Susan Allen Ford calls "anti-detective novels" (53). Eva Wylie is a down-on-her-luck type who holds odd jobs such as guarding a junkyard and working as a bodyguard for prostitutes. She also wrestles under the name London Lassassin. Wylie is a large, angry, asexual person who assumes she will be taken advantage of if she lets anyone near. She had a difficult childhood with a negligent mother and has suffered at the hands of others throughout her life for being unattractive and unfeminine. She goes further than most investigators, not just bending the laws, but clearly breaking them. For example, Wylie steals money to survive.

Wylie and Lee join forces in *Bucket Net,* with Lee playing a cameo role in solving the mystery. In *Musclebound,* her family plays a large role in the plot. When Wylie comes into a large sum of money, her mother concocts a scheme to have her boyfriend kidnap Wylie's beloved sister to collect ransom money from Wylie. Cody notes that while writing this character she realized that "books try to make something reasonable of life" and that she did not "believe that life is very reasonable" (Silet 37). With Wylie as an unreliable narrator, Cody was able to portray the character as insensitive and unintelligent without "authorial superiority" intruding (Silet 38).

Two stand-alone novels mark Cody's work in the suspense genre. *Rift* is based on her travels in Africa in the 1970s, when she was caught up in the revolution in Ethiopia (Rahn 72). Anna Wilson describes it as a "chronicle [of] a young woman's geographical and psychological journey of discovery" (111). Although the plot "provides the pleasures of a thriller," with the protagonist being in a foreign country while a civil war erupts, Cody focuses on the narrator's quest to "develop and protect her own independent identity" (Wilson 112).

The other stand-alone novel, *Gimme More,* tells the story of Birdie, the aging widow of a rock star. When people start searching for tapes he left behind, she takes matters into her own hands. Isobel Montgomery noted that "rock and roll doesn't usually transfer well to the page, but this thriller is carried by the ultra-cynical voice of Birdie and Cody's ability to create fictional lyrics, gigs and bands that won't make you wince" (11).

CRITICAL RECEPTION

Cody was recognized by critics from the start. Her first novel won the John Creasey Award from the Crime Writers Association. A review of *Bad Company* praised her "crackling, intense story" that includes an "interpretation of the kidnappers [that] can raise the hairs on the back of the neck, perfectly capturing their cruelty and stupidity" (Moxley 107).

Eva Wylie was called "one of the most unusual, and strangely fascinating, new characters in crime fiction" (Wood 5C). This review of *Musclebound* also noted that "all the threads of this novel's complex plot are expertly woven into a compelling yarn by Cody, who is, I think, the cleverest of current British mystery writers" (Wood 5C).

Several scholars have addressed Cody's writing. Susan Allen Ford explored the Eva Wylie series, looking at the Wylie character through the lens of Sandra Gilbert and Susan Gubar's feminist theory and discussing her use of Cody's works in the courses she teaches about the Gothic in literature. Glenwood Irons and Joan Warthling Roberts trace the development of the female sleuth in British fiction, comparing Anna Lee to Agatha Christie's Miss Marple. Mary Hadley also analyzed Cody's work as literature, exploring the two models of detective fiction Cody has used in the Lee and Wylie series. Another area Hadley explored is Cody's depiction of violence, given the differences in gun laws and attitudes about guns between the United States and Britain.

BIBLIOGRAPHY

Works by Liza Cody

Anna Lee Series

Dupe. New York: Scribner, 1981.
Bad Company. New York: Scribner, 1982.

Stalker. New York: Scribner, 1984.
Head Case. New York: Scribner, 1986.
Under Contract. New York: Scribner, 1987.
Backhand. New York: Doubleday, 1992.

Eva Wylie Series

Bucket Nut. New York: Doubleday, 1993.
Monkey Wrench. New York: Mysterious Press, 1994.
Musclebound. New York: Mysterious Press, 1997.

Other Works

Rift. New York: Scribner, 1988.
Gimme More. London: Bloomsbury, 2000.
Lucky Dip and Other Stories. Norfolk: Crippen and Landru, 2003.

Works about Liza Cody

Bakerman, Jane S. "Liza Cody." *St. James Guide to Crime & Mystery Writers.* 4th ed. Ed. Jay P. Pederson. Detroit: St. James Press, 1996. 205–206.
Ford, Susan Allen. "Detecting (and Teaching) the Gothic." *Studies in Popular Culture* 24.1 (October 2001): 47–57.
Hadley, Mary. "Liza Cody." *British Women Mystery Writers: Authors of Detective Fiction with Female Sleuths.* Jefferson, NC: McFarland, 2002. 56–76.
Irons, Glenwood and Joan Warthling Roberts. "From Spinster to Hipster: The 'Suitability' of Miss Marple and Anna Lee." *Feminism in Women's Detective Fiction.* Ed. Glenwood Irons. Toronto: U Toronto P, 1995. 64–73.
"Liza Cody." *Contemporary Authors.* Vol. 71, New Revision Series. Eds. Daniel Jones and John D. Jorgensen. Detroit: Gale, 1999. 162–64.
Montgomery, Isobel. "Saturday Review: Books." *The Guardian* 7 April 2001: 11.
Moxley, Melody A. "*Bad* Company." *Library Journal* 15 October1997: 107.
Rahn, B. J. "Liza Cody." *Great Women Mystery Writers.* Ed. Kathleen Gregory Klein. Westport: Greenwood, 1994. 71–75.
Silet, Charles L. P. "Anna Lee, Eva Wylie, and the Contemporary Crime Novel."
Talking Murder: Interviews with 20 Mystery Writers. Princeton: Ontario Review Press, 1999. 24–38.
Wilson, Anna. "Liza Cody." Dictionary of Literary Biography, Vol. 276: *British Mystery and Thriller Writers Since 1960.* Ed. Gina Macdonald. Detroit: Gale, 2003. 109–113.
Wood, Sue Ann. "Liza Cody's Wrestler in Class by Herself: Clever Tale Follows 'London Lassassin.'" *St. Louis Post-Dispatch* 7 September 1997: 5C.

Margaret Coel (1937–)

BIOGRAPHY

Margaret Speas Coel was born October 11, 1937, in Denver, Colorado, to Samuel and Margaret McCloskey Speas. Her father worked as a railroad engineer, and her family has been in Colorado since 1865. Except for attending college in Milwaukee and spending two years stationed in Alaska when her husband was serving in the Air Force, she has always lived in Colorado herself. She graduated from Marquette University in 1960 with a degree in journalism, and after graduation, returned to Colorado and began working as a reporter at the *Westminster Journal.* She married George W. Coel, a dentist, on July 22, 1962. They have two daughters, Kristin and Lisa, and one son, who is deceased.

In 1972, she returned to work as a features writer for the *Boulder Daily Camera,* and then did freelance work for them from 1975 to 1990. She also worked as a writing instructor at the University of Colorado, Boulder, from 1985 to 1990. In addition to her mystery novels, she has a number of nonfiction books about Native Americans and western U.S. history to her credit and has been a frequent contributor to newspapers across the United States. She and her husband live in Boulder.

MAJOR WORKS AND THEMES

Coel's mystery series is set at the Wind River reservation in Wyoming. The series centers on recovering alcoholic priest John O'Malley who is sent to the reservation as a punishment of sorts; it is not considered a plum assignment by the Church. However, O'Malley fights his addiction and finds his niche there serving the Arapaho Catholics, and he fights to stay in this assignment in several subsequent novels. In the first novel, he becomes involved in a murder case and begins his partnership with local attorney Vicki Holden. Holden left the reservation to attend college and law school and initially a career in the city, but she has returned to the area to serve her own people.

The plots of the novels are inspired by real events that Coel learned about through historical research, such as the role of the ledger books, pictographic histories written by Plains Indians, which are a key plot element in *The Story Teller.* The plot for her first mystery was based on research she had done about the disenfranchisement of the Arapahoes for her nonfiction book *Chief Left Hand* (Kaczmarek). *The Spirit Woman* includes the story of Sacajawea; the plot of *The Shadow Dancer* involves Wovoka, the prophet of the Ghost Dance religion. Coel has also dealt with issues including the forced adoption of babies off the reservation and the effects of a casino. Coel notes that she "is fascinated by the way past injustices percolate into the present and must be dealt with on new terms" (homepage).

Character development is a strong feature in the series. Shelle Rosenfeld noted that "Father John is an appealing character, a baseball aficionado as well as a spiritual advisor, who finds unexpected fulfillment in righting wrongs while preserving tradition and opportunities for youth" (1608). Coel wanted a character who was an outsider, so that readers could learn the culture along with him (Walker O3). The unconsummated love between Holden and O'Malley represents a plot device Lynn Kazcmarek typically dislikes, but "in Coel's deft hands, this is subtly managed and does not detract from the stories" (Kaczmarek). Although she is "not quite ready to say it adds to them," she finds that the "friendship that has arisen between the pair and their genuine love for each other is quite appealing" (Kaczmarek).

CRITICAL RECEPTION

Coel made an impression on critics from the start. Common themes in reviews are her strong character development, vivid settings, and interesting, sensitive portrayals of Native Americans and their issues. "Murder, romance, a nuclear storage facility and Indian lore blend appealingly in" *The Dream Stalker,* with the reviewer continuing that "the nicely drawn Wyoming backdrop, capable plotting and engaging characters all add up to another coup for Coel" (Brainard 1997:67–68).

Dulcy Brainard also reviewed *The Story Teller,* which she described as having "all the strengths of this fine series: Coel's knowledge of and respect for western history, a solid mystery with a credible premise in Indian lore and the struggles of Holden and O'Malley with their powerful, but so far unconsummated, attraction to each other" (1998: 78). John Rowen called *The Story Teller* "one of the best of the year," featuring "vivid western landscapes, intriguing history, compelling characters, and quick, tight writing that is a joy to read. The mystery looks easy, but Coel offers many twists and surprises" (202).

Leslie Doran noted that "one of Coel's many talents is creating characters with messy and interesting lives…. Her secondary characters are forceful personalities in their own right" (EE2). Doran summed up that with *The Shadow Dancer,* Coel "continues her winning combination of great atmosphere, interesting and complex characters, and fascinating and intriguing settings that involve visions, murder and mystery" (EE2). Peter Cannon also praised the novel, noting that "even minor characters are real and human" and that "the poignant ending will catch even the most astute mystery aficionado by surprise" (2002:70).

The "superbly crafted" *Killing Raven* kept readers "sweating, guessing and turning the pages" ("Killing" 61). Another reviewer proclaimed that Coel "surpasses her own high standard" with *The Wife of Moon,* which "masterfully blend[s] authentic history with an ingenious plot" (Cannon 2004:234).

BIBLIOGRAPHY

Works by Margaret Coel

Father John O'Malley and Vicki Holden Series

The Eagle Catcher. Boulder: U of Colorado P, 1995.
The Ghost Walker. New York: Berkley, 1996.
The Dream Stalker. New York: Berkley, 1997.
The Story Teller. New York: Berkley, 1998.
The Lost Bird. New York: Berkley, 1999.
The Spirit Woman. New York: Berkley, 2000.
The Thunder Keeper. New York: Berkley, 2001.
The Shadow Dancer. New York: Berkley, 2002.
Killing Raven. New York: Berkley, 2003.
Wife of Moon. New York: Berkley, 2004.
Eye of the Wolf. New York: Berkley, 2005.
The Drowning Man. New York: Berkley, 2006.

Works about Margaret Coel

Brainard, Dulcy. "*The Dream Stalker.*" *Publishers Weekly* 14 July 1997: 67–68.
———. "The Story Teller." *Publishers Weekly* 3 August 1998: 77–78.
Cannon, Peter. "*The Shadow Dancer.*" *Publishers Weekly* 19 August 2002: 70.
———. "Wife of Moon." *Publishers Weekly* 9 August 2004: 234.
Doran, Leslie. "Visionary Makes Waves in Coel's Latest." *Denver Post* 23 March 2003: EE2.

Foxwell, Elizabeth. "Mysteries Among the Arapahos." *Mystery Scene* 73 (2001): 12–13.

Kaczmarek, Lynn. "Hana je nahadina: An Interview with Margaret Coel." n.d. 17 November 2004. http://www.margaretcoel.com/about_interviews2.html

"*Killing Raven.*" *Publishers Weekly* 18 August 2003: 61.

"Margaret Coel." *Contemporary Authors.* Vol. 222. Ed. Lisa Kumar. Detroit: Gale, 2004. 51–68.

Margaret Coel. Homepage. 2004. 17 November 2004. http://www.margaretcoel.com

Rosenfeld, Shelle. "*The Eagle Catcher.*" *Booklist* 1 May 2000: 1608.

Rowen, John. "*The Story Teller.*" *Booklist* 15 September 1998: 202.

Walker, Tom. "From the Reservation to the Big City: Coel's *Story Teller* Plays Out in Denver." *Denver Post* 4 October 1998: O3.

Patricia Cornwell (1956–)

BIOGRAPHY

Patricia Daniels Cornwell was born June 9, 1956, in Miami, Florida. Her father, Sam Daniels, was an attorney, and her mother, Marilyn Zenner Daniels, was a secretary who had worked as an airline attendant. Her parents divorced when she was five, and her mother took her and her two brothers to live in North Carolina.

After a tumultuous childhood and adolescence, including being placed in foster care and suffering from anorexia nervosa, she attended Davidson College in North Carolina on a tennis scholarship, earning a bachelor's degree in 1979. She married Charles Cornwell, a professor at Davidson College, on June 14, 1980. They were divorced in 1990.

After graduation, she worked as a police reporter for the *Charlotte Observer,* and when she moved with her husband to Virginia where he was attending divinity school, she found work as a computer analyst and technical writer for the Office of the Chief Medical Examiner in Richmond from 1985 to 1991. Her interest in crime reporting and solving had not waned, and she was able to observe autopsies and learn about the forensic techniques being used.

During that time she began writing fiction and wrote three novels that remain unpublished. Kay Scarpetta was a minor character in those works, and, on the advice of an editor, she wrote another novel featuring Scarpetta as the main protagonist (Etheridge 77; Duncan 47). That work, *Postmortem,* was published in 1990, and she turned to writing full-time soon after.

MAJOR WORKS AND THEMES

Cornwell was the first writer to bring forensic techniques to the center of her novels, leading the way for other writers, like Kathy Reichs and Karin Slaughter, and for the explosion of television shows and films that feature forensic science and crime solving. The bulk of Cornwell's work is comprised of the Kay Scarpetta series. Scarpetta, who holds both law and medical degrees, is the chief medical examiner for Virginia, where the series is set. Although this office is the same place Cornwell worked, she is careful to note that Scarpetta is "not similar to anyone" (Duncan 46). Through her involvement with finding and recording forensic evidence in murder cases, Scarpetta helps solve many crimes. At the time she began writing *Postmortem*, there was a series of deaths in Richmond, with women being strangled in their homes. She used this as the basis for *Postmortem*, with a colleague of Scarpetta's as one of the victims. In *Body of Evidence*, Scarpetta solves the murder of a woman, again fighting to understand the women and fight for justice for the dead women.

In the first few books, Scarpetta is involved in several different cases, where she partners with Pete Marino, a homicide detective. In *Cruel and Unusual* she begins dealing with a recurring nemesis named Temple Gault, and the plots become more elaborate. *The Body Farm* finds Scarpetta branching into federal cases, again involving Gault. This novel also introduces Benton Wesley, a profiler for the FBI, with whom Scarpetta begins a romantic relationship. At this point in the series, Scarpetta's niece, Lucy Farinelli, has grown from a nerdy child into a technologically savvy FBI intern. The four characters compose a crime-fighting team for several novels.

Before Scarpetta can vanquish Gault's evil partner, Carrie Grethen, Wesley is killed at the end of *Point of Origin*. In *Black Notice*, Cornwell's characters deal with the aftermath. Cornwell has told interviewers that when she began writing *Black Notice* "her feelings of anger and pain were so intense she had to quit after twenty pages" and write a Judy Hammer novel instead (Terrazas Y1). Although there is a mystery plot in *Black Notice*, which involves Scarpetta's being targeted by an international crime family and its son, known as "The Werewolf," who is afflicted with hypertrichosis, the novel is mostly about grief and how Scarpetta deals with the loss of Wesley.

The Last Precinct features Scarpetta, Marino, and Farinelli taking on cases no one else will touch, creating a "last resort" detective agency. *Blow Fly* marks intense changes for the series in several ways. In terms of plot, Cornwell requires more suspension of disbelief than ever before, when she reveals that Wesley is alive and part of a witness protection program. In addition, Marino's personality has undergone odd changes, and Farinelli has become a renegade mercenary killer. Stylistically, Cornwell abandons the first-person point of view that had been used in all the Scarpetta novels, using instead third-person omniscient and making Scarpetta seem more distant to the readers.

Cornwell has also written three novels about a woman police chief named Judy Hammer and a police reporter named Andy Brazil. This series is set in Charlotte, North Carolina, and is much lighter in tone. The crimes they investigate are serious, but there is a good deal of humor in this series, even veering into the slapstick or zany realm of Carl Hiaasen or Joan Hess's Maggody books.

In May 2001, Cornwell became interested in the Jack the Ripper case when she visited Scotland Yard. When she learned that no one had applied modern forensic techniques to the Ripper case, she decided to treat it as a cold case and open an investigation. She notes that she originally intended it as research for a Scarpetta novel, but that her "hair began to stand on end as [she] began to look into Walter Sickert" (Zaleski 53); Sickert is one of several suspects favored by a faction of those who follow the case, known as Ripperologists. Cornwell spent $6 million on researching the case and having various tests conducted on pieces of 114-year-old evidence. Her findings were published in 2002 as *Portrait of a Killer: Jack the Ripper—Case Closed*. Although most believe the Ripper case to still be open, her contribution to the case and its history is substantial.

Scarpetta was "less like a would-be Wonder Woman and more like the intensely serious medical examiner she was in early books" (Wood 1997:5C). The reviewer echoes that praise in her coverage of *Point of Origin,* noting that Cornwell "seems to have recovered from her infatuation with the FBI and computer technology that had dominated" recent plots and "returned to the forensic detection methods featured in her early novels." (Wood 1998:D5). Not all reviewers agreed. Another review found *Point of Origin* to be "stalled" and "sluggish," with a "haphazardly conceived" plot (Cogdill 3). Reviews of the Judy Hammer series have been mixed as well. Many critics generally lambasted it for its unflattering portrayal of the South and its citizens, but others found the humor and characters to be a welcome change of pace from the Scarpetta series.

Cornwell's works have been addressed by literary scholars as well. Christiana Gregoriou compared *Southern Cross* to works by James Patterson and Michael Connelly, discussing the narrative techniques these writers use to tell parts of the story from the criminal's point of view. Rose Lucas takes a psychoanalytic approach in examining cycles of repetition and anxiety in the Scarpetta novels. Lucas analyzes fear, death, and the representation of the body in Cornwell's work. Peter Messent explores why readers are attracted to crime fiction, using Cornwell as one example, looking at readers' desires for justice and reactions to violence. Gerard Collins addresses two key themes in Cornwell's works, technology and disease, in his exploration of the villains she creates and their impact on her plots.

BIBLIOGRAPHY

Works by Patricia Cornwell

Kay Scarpetta Series

Postmortem. New York: Scribner, 1990.
Body of Evidence. New York: Scribner, 1991.
All That Remains. New York: Scribner, 1992.
Cruel and Unusual. New York: Scribner, 1993.
The Body Farm. New York: Scribner, 1994.
From Potter's Field. New York: Scribner, 1995.
Cause of Death. New York: Putnam, 1996.
Unnatural Exposure. New York: Putnam, 1997.
Point of Origin. New York: Putnam, 1998.
Black Notice. New York: Putnam, 1999.
The Last Precinct. New York: Putnam, 2000.
Blow Fly. New York: Putnam, 2003.
Trace. New York: Putnam, 2004.
Predator. New York: Putnam, 2005.

Judy Hammer Series

Hornet's Nest. New York: Putnam, 1997.
Southern Cross. New York: Putnam, 1998.
Isle of Dogs. Boston: Little, Brown, 2001.

Other Works by Patricia Cornwell

A Time for Remembering: The Story of Ruth Bell Graham. San Francisco: Harper & Row, 1983.
Scarpetta's Winter Table. Charleston: Wyrick, 1998.
Life's Little Fable. Illus. Barbara Leonard Gibson. New York: Putnam, 1999.
Food to Die For: Secrets from Kay Scarpetta's Kitchen. New York: Putnam, 2001.
Portrait of a Killer: Jack the Ripper—Case Closed. New York: Putnam, 2002.
At Risk. New York: Putnam, 2006.

Works about Patricia Cornwell

Beahm, George. *The Unofficial Patricia Cornwell Companion*. New York: St. Martin's Minotaur, 2002.
Bleiler, Ellen. "Patricia Cornwell." *Mystery and Suspense Writers: The Literature of Crime, Detection and Espionage*. Eds. Maureen Corrigan and Robin Winks. New York: Scribner's, 1998. 243–50.
Champlin, Charles. "Bloody Sunday." *Los Angeles Times Book Review* 11 February 1990: 5.
Cogdill, Oline H. "Patricia Cornwell Plays Fast and Loose with Her Plot." *Chicago Tribune* 28 July 1998: 3.
Collins, Gerard. "Contagion and Technology in Patricia Cornwell's Scarpetta Novels." *The Devil Himself: Villainy in Detective Fiction and Film*. Eds. Stacy Gillis and Philippa Gates. Westport: Greenwood, 2002. 159–69.
Corrigan, Maureen . "Mysteries." *Washington Post Book World* 20 August 1995: 11.
Duncan, Paul. "Patricia Cornwell: Verbal Evidence." *Mystery Scene* 57 (1997): 45–49.
Earle, Peggy Deans. "Cornwell's Creep Takes Slice of out Big Apple." Virginian—Pilot 20 August 1995: J2.
———. "Scarpetta Back on the Case, This Time in Hampton Roads." Virginian—Pilot 18 July 1996: E1.
Etheridge Jr., Charles L. "Patricia Cornwell." *Dictionary of Literary Biography*, Vol. 306: American Mystery and Detective Writers. Ed. George Parker Anderson. Detroit: Gale, 2005. 76–86.
Ford, Susan Allen. "Tracing the Other in Patricia D. Cornwell: Costs and Other Accommodations." *Clues* 20.2 (1999): 27–34.
Gregoriou, Christiana. "Criminally Minded: The Stylistics of Justification in Contemporary American Crime Fiction." *Style* 37.2 (2003): 144–59.
Harvey, Duston. "Four Years into Her Career, Patricia Cornwell." *Seattle Post Intelligencer* 19 September 1992: D1.
Holt, Patricia. "A Woman Warrior Against Crime." *San Francisco Chronicle*, Sunday Review 30 June 1996: 1.
Lucas, Rose. "Anxiety and Its Antidotes: Patricia Cornwell and the Forensic Body." *Literature Interpretation Theory* 15 (2004): 207–22.
Melton, Emily. "From Potter's Field." *Booklist* 1 May 1995: 1531.
Messent, Peter. "Authority, Social Anxiety and the Body in Crime Fiction: Patricia Cornwell's Unnatural Exposure." *The Art of Detective Fiction*. Eds. Warren Chernaik, Martin Swales and Robert Vilain. London: Macmillan and New York: St. Martin's, 2000. 124–37.
"Patricia Cornwell." *Contemporary Authors*. Vol. 131, New Revision Series. Ed. Tracey Watson. Detroit: Gale, 2005. 74–78.
Robbins, Joan Hamerman. "Living Dangerously." *Women's Review of Books* 7 July 1991: 219–20.
Terrazas, Beatriz. "Characters in Pursuit of Author." *The Record (Bergen County)* 17 August 1999: Y1.
White, Jean M. "The Luong Goodbye." *Washington Post* 21 January 1990: O6.
———. "Anatomy of a Murder." *Washington Post* 17 February 1991: K10.
Wood, Sue Ann. "Scarpetta is on Trail and Back on Track." *St. Louis Post Dispatch* 13 July 1997: 5C.
———. "Cornwell Turns Back to Forensic Detection." *St. Louis Post Dispatch* 5 July 1998: D5.
Zaleski, Jeff. "PW Talks with Patricia Cornwell: On the Trail of Jack the Ripper." *Publishers Weekly* 11 November 2002: 53.

Deborah Crombie (1952–)

BIOGRAPHY

Born on June 5, 1952 in Dallas, Texas, to Charles and Mary Dozier Darden, Deborah Crombie grew up in McKinney, Texas. She attended Austin College, earning a bachelor's degree in biology while also studying medieval literature. Before becoming a full-time writer, she worked for a family business and also in newspaper advertising. She lived in England and Scotland for several years with her first husband before returning to the United States in 1981 (Dingus 26). She told one interviewer that she always wanted to write about what she loved, and she had "been an Anglophile ever since reading *Winnie the Pooh*" (qtd in Dingus 26). She travels to England frequently for research, but is "never completely happy [in] either place," feeling homesick for Texas when she's in England and missing England when she's home in Texas (Dingus 26). Crombie lives with her second husband, daughter, and a menagerie of pets in McKinney, Texas.

MAJOR WORKS AND THEMES

Crombie's series focuses on two Scotland Yard colleagues, Gemma James and Duncan Kincaid, who begin a personal relationship in the series. In the first novel, *A Share in Death*, Kincaid encounters a murder case while on vacation; in the second novel, he suspects foul play in the death of his neighbor. Throughout the first four novels, Kincaid and James collaborate on various cases and become closer personally. Crombie tackles the problems of workplace relationships and also sensitively portrays issues related to blended families. As Anne Dingus noted, Crombie's characters are "blessedly unwacky" and her plots avoid overused themes, focusing on the psychological aspects of the crimes and criminals (26).

The arts and academia play a part in *Dreaming of the Bones*, which features Kincaid's ex-wife, an English literature professor. When she uncovers evidence that a poet she is researching was murdered and did not commit suicide, she contacts Kincaid for assistance. This set off a chain of events that leads to another murder, and the poetry of the earlier victim provides the key to the solution. This novel was much more complex than the earlier entries in the series, and Crombie notes that she had an "absolute terrifying doubt whether or not [she] could pull it off," especially since she would have to write "hopefully passable" poetry for the text (Kaczmarek 1). The poet in question is a fictional descendant of Rupert Brooke, and excerpts from his works are used as chapter headings. Given the number of awards it garnered, Crombie indeed pulled it off.

Historical research is a passion of Crombie's, who notes that "the trick is not getting carried away, not losing sight of the story in a muddle of detail" ("Deborah" 79). In *Kissed a Sad Goodbye*, Crombie deals with a case that has roots in World War II and the effects of the Blitz on London. While researching the material, Crombie notes that she became overwhelmed and kept expanding her research interests into all areas and aspects of the war (Kaczmarek 3). This book also ties in the history of the tea trade, another area Crombie enjoyed researching.

In *Now May You Weep*, Crombie moves the action to Scotland, where James goes on vacation to visit her close friend Hazel Cavendish, who has retreated to her family's home during a personal crisis. While there, a murder occurs and James, although she has no official standing, is compelled to help investigate. Although Crombie had lived in Edinburgh, her research for this novel gave her opportunities to explore the Highlands and the distillery industry (HarperCollins). *In a Dark House* features a gritty, realistic portrayal of an arson case. While dealing with a custody battle, James and Kincaid uncover connections between their cases and must race to solve a complex arson, kidnapping, and murder case in time to save a kidnapped child.

CRITICAL RECEPTION

A Share in Death was nominated for Agatha and Macavity Awards for best first novel, and *Dreaming of the Bones* was nominated for an Edgar Award. The latter was also chosen by the Independent Mystery Booksellers of America for the 100 Best Crime Novels of the Century list.

In addition to its nominations, her debut novel was well received by critics, one of whom noted that the "polished" novel seemed to be the work of "a seasoned genre master" (Brainard 1992:42). One reviewer praised its "great continuity, clever plotting and hidden agendas" (Klett 1993:169); another review called it a "thoroughly entertaining mystery with a cleverly constructed and well-executed plot," further praising its humor and the "likable, intelligent" Kincaid (Melton 881).

Stuart Miller noted that the second in the series, *All Shall Be Well,* "respects all the conventions of the police procedural" while being "fresh and lively" (902), and *Leave the Grave Green* offered "lucid prose, a well-focused plot and all the trappings of a cosy British mystery" (Klett 1995:140). Another reviewer found the novel's pacing to be "immaculate," making for a "superbly engrossing whodunit" (Hooper 992). Another reviewer noted that *Mourn Not Your Dead* features a "meticulously, affectionately drawn cast" (Brainard 1996:52).

Dreaming of the Bones was certainly heralded as a turning point for the series. Its complexity and range made it a standout in an already acclaimed series. One reviewer noted that Crombie "excels at investing her mysteries with rich characterization and a sophisticated wash of illuminating feminism" (Brainard 1997:69). Shirley E. Havens called it a "powerful and complex story with a terrible secret stretching back over three decades" and recommended it for fans of P. D. James, Ruth Rendell and Elizabeth George (164). Marilyn Stasio found Crombie's work as transcending mysteries where romantic ties "smother the mystery," praising Crombie for a "multi-layered novel" and for "making the tangled love relationships the very heart of her mystery by linking them with questions about our responsibilities to the ones we love" (29).

And Justice There Is None has Kincaid and James at odds over a possible serial killer case. Peter Cannon praised Crombie's plotting and pacing, noting that the two detectives' investigations "become linked in startling, unexpected ways, culminating in an exciting denouement with serious undercurrents" (2002:55). Cannon also reviewed *A Finer End,* calling it a "finely nuanced novel replete with multilayered characters" (2001:47). Although he found the ending "too traditional," Cannon praised Crombie's sustained "sharp sense of a magical history bleeding into the present" (47).

Now May You Weep was cited for its "vivid settings, well-developed characters and a finely tuned mystery" ("*Now May You Weep*" 87). Calling Crombie "a master storyteller," the reviewer praised her ability to "weave together" the historical and present-day plot lines into "a fabric as rich and history-laden as a tartan plaid" ("*Now May You Weep*" 87).

BIBLIOGRAPHY

Works by Deborah Crombie

Gemma James and Duncan Kincaid Series

A Share in Death. New York: Scribner, 1993.
All Shall Be Well. New York: Scribner, 1994.
Leave the Grave Green. New York: Scribner, 1995.
Mourn Not Your Dead. New York: Scribner, 1996.
Dreaming of the Bones. New York: Scribner, 1997.
Kissed a Sad Goodbye. New York: Bantam, 1999.
A Finer End. New York: Bantam, 2001.
And Justice There Is None. New York: Bantam, 2002.
Now You May Weep. New York: Morrow, 2003.
In a Dark House. New York: Morrow, 2004.
Water Like a Stone. New York: Morrow, 2006.

Works about Deborah Crombie

Brainard, Dulcy. "*A Share in Death.*" *Publishers Weekly* 14 December 1992: 42–43.
———. "*Mourn Not Your Dead.*" *Publishers Weekly* 15 April 1996: 52.
———. "*Dreaming of the Bones.*" *Publishers Weekly* 4 August 1997: 69.
Cannon, Peter. "*A Finer End.*" *Publishers Weekly* 16 April 2001: 47.
———. "*And Justice There Is None.*" *Publishers Weekly* 5 August 2002: 55.
"Deborah Crombie." *Contemporary Authors.* Vol. 187. Ed. Scot Peacock. Detroit: Gale, 2000. 78–80.
Dingus, Anne. "Briterature." *Texas Monthly* November 1997: 26.
Graff, M. K. "Deborah Crombie: The Yellow Rose of Mystery." *Mystery Scene* 87 (2004): 18–19.
HarperCollins.com. "Author Interview: Deborah Crombie." 2005. 4 May 2005. http://www.harpercollins.ca/global_scripts/product_catalog/book_xml.asp?isbn =0060525231&tc = ai
Havens, Shirley E. "Secrets from the Past." *Library Journal* July 1998: 164.
Hooper, Brad. "*Leave the Grave Green.*" *Booklist* 1 February 1995: 992.
Kaczmarek, Lynn. "Deborah Crombie, the British Stylist from Texas." *Mystery News* 17.2 (April/May 1999): 1–3.
Klett, Rex E. "*A Share in Death.*" *Library Journal* January 1993: 169.
———. "*Leave the Grave Green.*" *Library Journal* January 1995: 140.
Melton, Emily. "*A Share in Death.*" *Booklist* 15 January 1993: 880–81.
Miller, Stuart. "*All Shall Be Well.*" *Booklist* 15 January 1994: 902.
"Now May You Weep." *Publishers Weekly* 22 September 2003: 87.
Stasio, Marilyn. "Crime." *New York Times Book Review* 9 November 1997: 29.

Amanda Cross (1926–2003)

BIOGRAPHY

When Carolyn G. Heilbrun began writing mysteries in the early 1960s, she was an untenured faculty member at Columbia University and chose the name Amanda Cross as her pseudonym to protect her identity from her colleagues. Heilbrun was born January 13, 1926, in East Orange, New Jersey, to Archibald and Estelle Roemer Gold. Her father was an accountant who had come to the United States from Latvia as a child. Her mother was born in New York to parents who were Austrian immigrants. Her parents were Jewish but rejected their religious heritage (Kress 27–28). Their daughter did so as well, but she "later came to realize that the veiled anti-Semitism she experienced in her younger years contributed to the development of her feminist thinking" (Etheridge 88).

Heilbrun and her family moved to New York when she was six years old and she grew up across from Central Park. She became interested in biographies at a young age and once recounted that she read through all the biographies in the St. Agnes branch of the New York Public Library in alphabetical order, even dreaming of the experience later in life, dreaming about having to "deny [herself] an attractive book in R because [she] had reached only G" (Kress 1).

In 1945, while she was attending college, she married James Heilbrun, an economics professor. They had three children, Emily, Margaret, and Robert. She graduated Phi Beta Kappa from Wellesley College in 1947 and continued on with her graduate studies in English at Columbia University, earning a master's degree in 1951 and her Ph.D. in 1959. After teaching for one year at Brooklyn College, she returned to Columbia and was a faculty member in the English department from 1960 to 1993.

Throughout her academic career, Heilbrun won a number of awards for teaching and service, was awarded many honorary degrees, was active in key academic associations, and since the 1970s had served on the editorial boards of two key academic journals, *Twentieth Century Literature* and *Signs*. Heilbrun's papers from 1946 through 1979 are collected at Smith College in Northampton, Massachusetts. The remaining papers will remain sealed until 2015 (Etheridge 97).

Heilbrun made her views on suicide clear throughout her life, often stating her plan to die by age 70. Her unexpected enjoyment of later life led her to write *The Last Gift of Time: Life Beyond Sixty.* She committed suicide at age 77, on October 9, 2003, in New York.

MAJOR WORKS AND THEMES

Heilbrun noted on many occasions that she began writing mystery novels because she could not find any new detective fiction she enjoyed reading (Kress 71; Stein 31; Cleveland 259). A fan of Dorothy L. Sayers, Heilbrun wanted to read "literary mysteries" that featured conversation and women characters that were "more than decoration and appendages, domestic machinery or sex objects" (Kress 71). Although Kate Fansler was an English professor at a prestigious New York university like Heilbrun, the similarities between the character and the writer ended there. Fansler was from an upper-class Protestant family, was beautiful and stylish, and although married to lawyer Reed Amhearst, remained childless by choice. Through Fansler, Heilbrun was able to create mystery fiction that met her criteria and that allowed her "to express the full complexity and irony of her social vision" (Carter 270).

The first two novels are classic mysteries, "carefully plotted with all questions of motive, means, and opportunity meticulously detailed" (Yarbrough 94). *In the Last Analysis* finds Fansler solving the murder of a student, who was killed in the office of a psychoanalyst, who is also a friend of Fansler's. In the second novel, *The James Joyce Murder,* Fansler is asked to edit letters from Joyce to a publisher and, while visiting the Berkshires to do so, becomes embroiled in a case. With *Poetic Justice,* she returns to the city and becomes involved in a case involving student protests and turmoil among the university administration. Fansler takes a temporary appointment at the private school she attended and uncovers the truth about a murder in *The Theban Mysteries;* in *The Question of Max* she helps a friend and colleague who is accused of murder. Her approach to the genre changed over the years, though, with the inclusion of crime-less novels in the series, and her increased usage of women's journals or memoirs within the plots of the novels (Yarbrough 94).

The next novel, *Death in a Tenured Position,* is often referred to as the best of the series. It features Fansler solving the murder of the first woman to become tenured in the English Department at Harvard. In *Sweet Death, Kind Death* Fansler looks into a suspected suicide of a woman professor and uncovers a murder. *No Word from Winifred* is notable in its lack of a murder. Fansler instead investigates the disappearance of a woman by researching her writings and journals. In *A Trap for Fools,* Fansler again looks into two murders that take place on campus, finding herself an initial suspect in the first. This novel raises a number of issues, including racism, police misconduct, blackmail, and corruption. In *The Players Come Again* there is again a mystery with no murder. While researching material for a biography of a writer, Fansler uncovers information about the woman's past and her circle of friends.

The last four books in the series were published during 1995–2002. In *An Imperfect Spy,* Fansler and her husband are both visiting professors, where Fansler becomes involved in investigating the murder of a professor there. After an assessment of their marriage in *An Imperfect Spy,* Fansler is faced with her husband's kidnapping in *The Puzzled Heart,* and *Honest Doubt* has Fansler playing a secondary role to a private investigator named Estelle Woodhaven. In *The Edge of Doom,* which turned out to be the last book in the series, Fansler must face the fact that her mother had an affair and that her father is not the man she grew up with, turning upside down her ideas about her heritage and her role in her family. The novel focuses on Fansler's quest to decide whether genetics trumps the way she was raised, while looking into the man claiming to be her real father and solving a crime connected to him.

Through the Cross novels, Heilbrun "skewered" academia and its "concern for reputation" ("Carolyn" 176), portraying homicides among an atmosphere that was most famous for "murdering the spirit" (Lipez X10). In addition, Heilbrun also provided a cross section of all the people typically found there, making the professors, administrators, students, and scholars all "believable as types and often as individuals" (Cleveland 260). As Susan Kress noted, the Cross novels "are open to the larger events and movements of history," with Fansler investigating various cases set against the backdrop of the Vietnam War, student protests, the women's movement, and Watergate (5).

CRITICAL RECEPTION

The first Cross novel was nominated for an Edgar Award. She later confessed that this recognition was problematic for her, because if she had won, it would have "blown her cover" (Boken 63). She later won a Nero for *Death in a Tenured Position,* which came long after she had earned tenure and disclosed her identity.

Throughout the series, reviewers have acclaimed the novels as literate, intelligent, elegant and witty. As Marilyn Stasio put it, "even in crisis, Kate is quotable" (20). Although some reviews critique plotting and character development, other critics chose to attack Heilbrun for flaws in the accounting of Fansler's career and research. Julia B. Boken described a review of *The Question of Max* by J. M. Purcell, in which he was "incensed" at Heilbrun's characterization of Oxbridge and criticized the fact that Fansler seems to be working on research topics that mirrored Heilbrun's own work, asking why Fansler was "professionally such a blank," in addition to desiring an accounting of Fansler's own books and articles and the projects of the students she advised (81).

Reviews of the last few books praised the qualities of Fansler and the elegance of the writing. For example, a review of *The Puzzled Heart* praised her "virtuosity, wit and keen intelligence" (R. A. Carter 27); *The Edge of Doom* was viewed as "very satisfying on both an intellectual and an emotional level" (DeCandido 579). Although *The Edge of Doom* was viewed as slowly paced, another reviewer noted that the "literary wit and classy conversation" would be "reason enough to celebrate" for many readers (Cannon 53).

Heilbrun's status as a major second-wave feminist and literary critic through her scholarly works perhaps has led many scholars to explore Heilbrun's fictional works through similar critical lenses. Numerous literary scholars have addressed her work published as Cross. Kress's biography, *Feminist in a Tenured Position,* includes a great deal of analysis of the Cross novels and the issues within them, with connections to Heilbrun's life. In another essay, Thomas Stein compared *Death in a Tenured Position* to Dorothy L. Sayers' *Gaudy Night,* an apt comparison given that Sayers was a direct influence on Heilbrun's mystery writing.

A recent issue of *Clues,* with contributions mainly from librarians, explored the use of research techniques in detective fiction. Mariana Regalado described Fansler's techniques of detection and analyzed her effectiveness using the Association of College and Research Libraries' standards for information literacy competency.

Steven R. Carter outlined her effective use of comic techniques and her building of suspense through thematic red herrings in his essay on her novels. Although her works are widely acclaimed, Carter noted her stereotypical and negative portrayals of homosexuals in her early works (275–76) and in her exploration of feminism in the writings of Cross and others. Maureen T. Reddy pointed to Heilbrun's uncritical presentation of Fansler's elitism and racist attitudes, a criticism often leveled at second-wave feminists (185). The representations of these issues changed over the years; although Fansler aged little during the series, Heilbrun wrote the novels over several decades (Yarbrough 96). On the other hand, Susanne M. Maier defends Heilbrun against Camille Paglia's criticism of her, showing the growth in Fansler's feminism as parallel to Heilbrun's own intellectual journey.

BIBLIOGRAPHY

Works by Amanda Cross

In the Last Analysis. New York: Macmillan, 1964.
The James Joyce Murder. New York: Macmillan, 1967.
Poetic Justice. New York: Knopf, 1970.
The Theban Mysteries. New York: Knopf, 1971.
The Question of Max. New York: Knopf, 1976.
Death in a Tenured Position. New York: Dutton, 1981. (Also published as *A Death in the Faculty.* London: Gollancz, 1981.)
Sweet Death, Kind Death. New York: Dutton, 1984.
No Word from Winifred. New York: Dutton, 1986.
A Trap for Fools. New York: Dutton, 1989.
An Imperfect Spy. New York: Ballantine, 1995.
The Collected Stories of Amanda Cross. New York: Ballantine, 1997.
The Puzzled Heart. New York: Ballantine, 1998.

Honest Doubt. New York: Ballantine, 2000.
The Edge of Doom. New York: Ballantine, 2002.

Nonfiction works by Carolyn G. Heilbrun

The Garnett Family. New York: Macmillan, 1961.
Christopher Isherwood. New York: Columbia UP, 1970.
Toward a Recognition of Androgyny: Aspects of Male and Female in Literature. New York: Knopf, 1973.
Reinventing Womanhood. New York: Norton, 1979.
Writing a Woman's Life. New York: Norton, 1988.
Hamlet's Mother and Other Women. 1990. New York: Columbia UP, 2002.
The Education of a Woman: The Life of Gloria Steinem. New York: Dial, 1995.
The Last Gift of Time: Life Beyond Sixty. New York: Dial, 1997.
Women's Lives: The View from the Threshold. Toronto: U Toronto P, 1999.
When Men Were the Only Models We Had: My Teachers Barzun, Fadiman, Trilling. Philadelphia: U Pennsylvania P, 2001.

Works about Amanda Cross

Boken, Julia. *Carolyn G. Heilbrun.* New York: Twayne, 1996.
Cannon, Peter. "*The Edge of Doom.*" *Publishers Weekly* 30 September 2002: 53.
"Carolyn Heilbrun." *Contemporary Authors.* Vol. 94, New Revision Series. Ed. Scot Peacock. Detroit: Gale, 2001. 174–78.
Carter, Robert A. "Academic Murder Makes Classic Reading." *Houston Chronicle* 1 March 1998: 27.
Carter, Steven R. "Amanda Cross." Ed. Earl F. Bargainnier. *10 Women of Mystery.* Bowling Green: Bowling Green State UP, 1981. 270–96.
Cleveland, Carol. "Amanda Cross." *St. James Guide to Crime & Mystery Writers.* 4th ed. Ed. Jay P. Pederson. Detroit: St. James Press, 1996. 259–60.
DeCandido, GraceAnne A. "*The Edge of Doom.*" *Booklist* 15 November 2002: 579.
Etheridge Jr., Charles L. "Amanda Cross." *Dictionary of Literary Biography,* Vol. 306: *American Mystery and Detective Writers.* Ed. George Parker Anderson. Detroit: Gale, 2005. 87–97.
Kress, Susan. *Carolyn G. Heilbrun: Feminist in a Tenured Position.* Charlottesville: U P of Virginia, 1997.
Lipez, Richard. "A Harvest of New Titles from Tried and True Purveyors of Deadly Intrigue." *Washington Post* 26 November 2000: X10.
Maier, Susanne M. "The Scholar as Detective: The Literary Life of Carolyn G. Heilbrun as Amanda Cross's Kate Fansler." *The Great Good Place? A Collection of Essays on American and British College Mystery Novels.* Ed. Peter Nover. Frankfurt: Peter Lang, 1999. 95–113.
Marchino, Lois A. "The Female Sleuth in Academe." *Journal of Popular Culture* 23.3 (1989): 89–100.
Reddy, Maureen T. "The Feminist Counter-Tradition in Crime: Cross, Grafton, Paretsky, and Wilson." *The Cunning Craft: Original Essays on Detective Fiction and Contemporary Literary Theory.* Eds. Ronald G. Walker and June M. Frazer. Macomb: Western Illinois U P, 1990. 174–87.
Regalado, Mariana. "The Excitement of the Chase: Information Literacy in the Kate Fansler Novels by Amanda Cross." *Clues* 24.1 (2005): 44–53.
Stasio, Marilyn. "Crime." *New York Times Book Review* 25 January 1998: 20.
Stein, Thomas. "University Fiction Now and Then: Dorothy L. Sayers's *Gaudy Night* and Amanda Cross's *Death in a Tenured Position.*" *VII* 10 (1993): 31–42.
Yarbrough, Trisha. "The Achievement of Amanda Cross." *Clues* 15.1 (1994): 93–104.

Barbara D'Amato (1938–)

BIOGRAPHY

D'Amato was born Barbara Steketee on April 10, 1938, in Grand Rapids, Michigan, to Harold and Yvonne Watson Steketee. Her father was a department store owner. She began college at Cornell University in 1956 and left school to marry Anthony D'Amato in 1958. He became a law school professor, and she later finished her bachelor's degree in 1971 at Northwestern. She also earned a master's degree there in 1972. They have two sons, Brian and Paul, and live in Chicago.

Before turning to writing full-time in 1973, she worked in a number of positions including carpentry and legal research. Her first works were plays co-written with her husband. She tried various genres, but the first novel accepted for publication was a mystery work (Silet 72) .

She won Agatha and Anthony awards for her nonfiction work, *The Doctor, the Murder, the Mystery: The True Story of the Dr. John Branion Murder Case.* This work was based on a case that her husband was asked to consult on in 1984. Branion had been convicted of killing his ex-wife in 1968, and years later his second wife hired Anthony D'Amato to get the case reopened. D'Amato worked on the necessary research, and her findings served as the foundation for the habeas corpus brief. Branion was eventually pardoned and released, although he died shortly after gaining his freedom (Silet 75).

MAJOR WORKS AND THEMES

D'Amato has written a number of novels in several series, as well as stand-alone works. Her first series featured a psychologist named Gerrit de Graaf. He appeared in only two novels; the first was a locked-room style mystery featuring a seemingly impossible murder during a bridge game; the second found de Graaf visiting his grandmother in the Southwest. Concerned about her safety in her retirement home, de Graaf arrives and becomes involved in solving a murder. She also wrote a stand-alone suspense novel under the pseudonym Malacai Black before introducing her longest running series character, Cat Marsala, in 1990.

Marsala is an investigative reporter in Chicago, who finds herself serving as an amateur sleuth when her research leads her into more complex cases. The novels often feature replications of maps, charts, drawings, and other tools Marsala creates and uses to assist her in solving the crimes. In addition to interesting plots, the novels feature a cast of solid supporting characters, including her Shakespeare-quoting pet parrot and her police detective friend Harold McCoo. Marsala's first case involves drug legalization. While interviewing a proponent for legalization, a bomb explodes, killing the woman and leading Marsala into solving the crime. *Hard Tack* is a locked room style mystery set on a yacht. Caught in a storm on the Great Lakes while conducting an interview of the yacht's owner, Marsala puts her sleuthing skills to work when murder occurs. *Hard Women* explores the lives of prostitutes, and health care reform is in focus in *Hard Case,* which deals with a murder of a doctor in a trauma unit. In *Hard Christmas,* Marsala travels north to research a feature story on Christmas tree farming and finds herself solving a murder. *Hard Bargain* addresses police brutality, *Hard Evidence* finds Marsala accidentally discovering evidence of a murder, and *Hard Road* takes place during a fictional Wizard of Oz festival.

She also has written two novels featuring Chicago police officers Suze Figueroa and Norm Bennis, along with a number of stand-alone thrillers that deal with child abduction, serial killers, and autistic children. As noted, most of her works deal with a social issue. D'Amato believes that issues-related crime fiction is natural, as most "controversial social issues generate violence" (Silet 83). Chicago is also a key element of her works. D'Amato is keenly concerned with the richness and accuracy of her settings. She knows Chicago well and states that she "walks her mysteries," checking out locations and considering the space and what would be realistic for the characters given those spaces (Fletcher 1522).

CRITICAL RECEPTION

D'Amato's first Marsala novel was well reviewed as an "informative" mystery that "introduces a gutsy, fast-thinking heroine" (Steinberg 1989:51). The reviewer particularly praised the "sense of terror and claustrophobia" that D'Amato "adeptly creates" during a tense scene (Steinberg 51). D'Amato's following novel, *Hard Tack,* was seen as an "inventive approach to a classic mystery form," with its locked room style plot set on a yacht (Swanson 1935). The reviewer further noted that "the setting may be wet, but the humor is dry and the writing excellent" (Swanson 1935). The "descriptions of state lottery problems and procedures [in *Hard Luck*] are factual and fascinating, and her characters are lively and believable" (Carroll 1665). Another review of *Hard Luck* praised the character development, which gives "the tough, street-smart reporter a distinctive, warmly human quality"(Brainard 1992:40).

In *Hard Women,* Marsala is seen as an "appealing and good-humored sleuth" in a "suspense-filled" and "thought-provoking" story (Melton 1993:1413). The "riveting read" *Hard Case* is seen as a successful entry in a "hardhitting, gritty, witty and wise" series (Melton 1994:116). *Hard Christmas* was noted for "the pleasures of Cat's company" and for "her appealing, often funny, first-person voice" (Brainard 1995:77). The novel also was also praised as featuring the "perfect female sleuth—tough, feisty, smart and fearless but also kind, gentle, and highly principled," with D'Amato offering "fine writing, clever plot twists, and quick wit" (Melton 1995:387).

Hard Bargain offered "unexpected twists, a devious plot, and action aplenty" with Marsala's "usual sardonic but intelligent approach" (Melton 1997:63). Another review praised its "distinctly Chicago atmosphere," with writing that is "edgy, surprising and spiced with rich characterizations" (Brainard 1997:69–70). *Hard Evidence* featured a "vivid supporting cast, sprightly yet controlled wit and some fine cooking advice" from the "ever-reliable" D'Amato (Zaleski 1999:73).

Good Cop, Bad Cop was heralded as a "page-turner of a procedural that will leave readers limp but satisfied" (Melton 1997:685). Another stand-alone, *Help Me Please,* was noted for its contrast of the "plodding, shoe-leather approach" with the "dazzle of computerized crime-solving" in a "slick, suspenseful and fast-paced" mystery (Melton 1999:71). Another reviewer found "all of D'Amato's storytelling skills" present in *Help Me Please,* including a "lightning-fast plot, engaging characters, deftly dropped clues, and an earthy Chicago atmosphere" (Steinberg 1999:41–2). The review of *Authorized Personnel Only* warned readers not to "read this book with your back to the cellar door," noting that readers would "find it easy—no, mandatory—to stay up all night to finish the book" (Zaleski 2000:49). *Authorized Personnel Only* won the first Mary Higgins Clark Award in 2000. D'Amato's latest stand-alone novel, *Death of a Thousand Cuts,* was praised for its "wry humor and characters with real depth" (Cannon 37).

BIBLIOGRAPHY

Works by Barbara D'Amato

Cat Marsala Series

Hardball. New York: Scribner, 1990.
Hard Tack. New York: Scribner, 1991.
Hard Luck. New York: Scribner, 1992.
Hard Women. New York: Scribner, 1993
Hard Case. New York: Scribner, 1994.
Hard Christmas. New York: Scribner, 1995.
Hard Bargain. New York: Scribner, 1997.
Hard Evidence. New York: Scribner, 1999.
Hard Road. New York: Scribner, 2001.

Suze Figueroa and Norm Bennis Series

Killer.app. New York: Forge, 1996.
Authorized Personnel Only. New York: Forge, 2000.

Dr. Gerrit De Graaf Series

Hands of Healing Murder. New York: Diamond, 1980.
Eyes on Utopia Murders. New York: Ace, 1981.

Other Mystery Novels

As Malacai Black. *On My Honor.* New York: Pinnacle, 1989.
Good Cop, Bad Cop. New York: Forge, 1997.
Help Me Please. New York: Forge, 1999.
White Male Infant. New York: Tor, 2002.
Death of a Thousand Cuts. New York: Forge, 2004.

Works about Barbara D'Amato

"Barbara D'Amato." *Contemporary Authors.* New Revision Series, Vol. 104. Ed. Scot Peacock. Detroit: Gale, 2002. 113–15.
Brainard, Dulcy. "*Hard Luck.*" *Publishers Weekly* 20 April 1992: 40.
———. "*Hard Christmas.*" *Publishers Weekly* 11 September 1995: 77.
———. "*Hard Bargain.*" *Publishers Weekly* 30 June 1997: 69–70.
Cannon, Peter. "*Death of a Thousand Cuts.*" *Publishers Weekly* 17 May 2004: 37.
Carroll, Mary. "*Hard Luck.*" *Booklist* 15 May 1992: 1665.
Fletcher, Connie. "The Booklist Interview: Barbara D'Amato." *Booklist* 1 May 2003: 1522.
Koch, Pat. "PW Talks with Barbara D'Amato." *Publishers Weekly* 20 November 2000: 50.
Melton, Emily. "*Hard Women.*" *Booklist* 1 April 1993: 1413.
———. "*Hard Case.*" *Booklist* 15 September 1994: 116.
———. "*Hard Christmas.*" *Booklist* 15 October 1995: 387.
———. "*Good Cop, Bad Cop.*" *Booklist* 15 December 1997: 685.
———. "*Hard Bargain.*" *Booklist* 1 September 1997: 63.
———. "*Help Me Please.*" *Booklist* 1 September 1999: 71.
Silet, Charles L. P. "Hard Talk and Mean Streets: Barbara D'Amato." *Talking Murder: Interviews with 20 Mystery Writers.* New York: Norton, 1999. 71–86.
Steinberg, Sybil. "*Hardball.*" *Publishers Weekly* 1 December 1989: 51.
———. "*Help Me Please.*" *Publishers Weekly* 23 August 1999: 41–42.
Swanson, Elliott. "*Hard Tack.*" *Booklist* 15 June 1991: 1935.
Zaleski, Jeff. "*Hard Evidence.*" *Publishers Weekly* 22 March 1999: 73.
———. "Authorized Personnel Only." *Publishers Weekly* 20 November 2000: 49.

Lindsey Davis (1949–)

BIOGRAPHY

Lindsey Davis was born and raised in Birmingham, England. She studied English at Oxford, although she notes she considered history and archeology. After completing her studies, she went to work for the civil service, because she "believed they were fair to women" (Lindzey). She worked for the Ministry of Works, which had been renamed the Property Services Agency, for 13 years. After she realized that her department "was not fair to its women, and not worth fighting," she left the agency and began pursuing writing full-time (Lindzey). Her first works were serialized romance stories, but she soon turned to conducting research into the history of first-century Europe to write historical fiction (Official). She notes that she was interested in writing and began writing at an early age, but she "didn't know it was something you could do as your proper job" until later in her life (Marks 190).

MAJOR WORKS AND THEMES

While researching the Roman Empire for her writing, she became interested in how Rome "reminded her of the big, dangerous metropolitan cities" that are often associated with "the gumshoe stories," which were another interest of hers (Marks 191). Davis decided to combine her research and knowledge of Rome with the mystery genre. Her series is set in first-century Rome and features a detective named Marcus Didius Falco. Falco, born in 41 A.D., served in the army in Britain and returned to Rome. He serves as an investigator for the Emperor Vespasian, often working undercover. Falco, born a plebian, also strives to improve his social standing, mostly so that he can legitimize his relationship with the woman he loves, who is of a higher class, the daughter of a Senator.

In the first novel, *Silver Pigs,* Falco is sent undercover to Britain to investigate possible fraud in a silver mine. In *Venus in Copper,* he is asked to investigate a woman who has been a widow three times and may be planning to murder her fourth husband. Along with other cases in Rome and Britain that have links to politics and corruption, he is sent to Spain in *A Dying Light on Corduba* to investigate problems with the olive oil business. *Two for the Lions* finds him back in Rome, investigating tax evaders for the Emperor. Davis's writing is marked by her use of humor, and reviewers often call Falco an ancient predecessor of modern detectives ranging from Sam Spade and Philip Marlowe to Columbo and Travis McGee. Like many other contemporary sleuths, Falco's extended family plays a large role in the novels.

In addition to the Falco novels, she has published *Course of Honour,* a novel that deals with the life of Vespasian and his mistress, Antonia Caenis, who was a former slave.

CRITICAL RECEPTION

Davis has won two awards from the Crime Writers Association, an Ellis Peters Dagger and a Dagger in the Library, along with other prizes for her works. *Silver Pigs* was lauded as a "creative twist on classic hard-boiled detective novels" with an "appealing, wisecracking, self-deprecating detective (in a toga rather than a fedora) whose bravado conceals both a tender heart and an intolerance for injustice" (Rosenfeld 1608). A review in *History Today* noted that "Los Angeles comes to ancient Rome and makes a hit" in Davis's "delightful thriller" (Evans 4). *Publishers Weekly* found the novel to have an "intriguing premise" with "depth of characterization" and historical detail (Steinberg 86–7).

The second novel, *Shadows in Bronze,* was praised for its "well-etched characters," "wonderful wit" and "delightful evocation of ancient Rome's sights, sounds and smells" (Altner 114). Another reviewer noted that Davis "again melds hard-nosed procedural basics with a solid and atmospheric background of not-so-glorious Rome" (Brosnahan 1320). *Venus in Copper* offered "period details, humor and Falco's modern sensibility" that made the novel a "sterling performance" for one reviewer (Brainard 1992:90), and another reviewer called Falco a "treasure" with kudos to Davis for being a "genuine master of the smart-ass one liner" (Robertson 1339). A reviewer found that *Poseidon's Gold* "couldn't be wittier or more vivid and charming" (Seaman 241).

A Dying Light in Corduba was heralded as a "fast-moving narrative that makes ancient Rome feel as real as the streets of New York or L.A."(Brainard 1997:59), and another reviewer noted that "it takes skill to write of scrolls, slaves, Jove and togas without absurdity," and Davis has the skill to accomplish that, along with "insert[ing] modern slang and preoccupations into her narrative without making them seem anachronistic" in a "highly readable, funny and colourful novel that works" (Cooper 1996:24).

Two for the Lions won praise for Davis for being "surefooted" with her characters and "playful" with her readers (Beard 28). *Three Hands in the Fountain* was seen to offer "scintillating suspense, laugh-out-loud humor, devilishly clever plotting, and a cast of wonderfully eccentric characters" (Melton 1471). Another reviewer concurred, that "once again, Davis weaves an intricate, irreverent plot filled with wittily imagined characters" (Zaleski 74). *A Body in the Bath House* offered "clever dialogue and quick-paced encounters between sophisticated Romans ... and sullen locals," with Davis "leav[ing] us laughing at how little life has changed over the millennia" (Cannon 2002:280). Another reviewer found that Davis "conjures up the ancient world with confidence and contrives a plot as interesting as the best of modern detective fiction"(Warshaw 24).

In the "thoroughly entertaining" *Jupiter Myth,* Davis "skillfully braids references to Britain's future into her story of its past without ever diminishing the thrust of Falco's adventures" ("*The Jupiter Myth*" 261). In *The Accusers,* noted one reviewer, "the convoluted case, which involves a wealthy, fractious family and tricky questions of inheritance, gives Davis the opportunity to explore the vagaries of Roman law, which she approaches with her usual mix of respect and sarcasm" (Cannon 2004:154). Another review noted that Davis has "particular skill in creating a believable society" of the ancient world, while also "cast[ing] many sly looks at 21st century society through her characters and their ideas" (Cooper 2003:27).

BIBLIOGRAPHY

Works by Lindsey Davis

Marcus Didius Falco Series

The Silver Pigs. New York: Crown, 1989.
Shadows in Bronze. New York: Crown, 1990.
Venus in Copper. New York: Crown, 1991.
The Iron Hand of Mars. New York: Crown, 1992.
Poseidon's Gold. New York: Crown, 1993.
Last Act in Palmyra. New York: Mysterious Press, 1994.

Time to Depart. New York: Mysterious Press, 1997.
A Dying Light in Corduba. New York: Mysterious Press, 1998.
Three Hands in the Fountain. New York: Mysterious Press, 1999.
Two for the Lions. New York: Mysterious Press, 1999.
One Virgin Too Many. New York: Mysterious Press, 2000.
Ode to a Banker. New York: Mysterious Press, 2001.
A Body in the Bath House. New York: Mysterious Press, 2002.
The Jupiter Myth. New York: Mysterious Press, 2003.
The Accusers. New York: Mysterious Press, 2004.
Scandal Takes a Holiday. New York: Mysterious Press, 2004.
See Delphi and Die. New York: St. Martin's, 2006.

Other Fiction

The Course of Honor. New York: Mysterious Press, 1998.

Works about Lindsey Davis

Altner, Patricia. " *Shadows in Bronze.*" *Library Journal* 15 March 1991: 114.
Beard, Mary. "Gladitorial Gossip." *Times Literary Supplement* 18 September 1998: 28.
Brainard, Dulcy. "*Venus in Copper.*" *Publishers Weekly* 27 January 1992: 90.
———. "*A Dying Light in Corduba.*" *Publishers Weekly* 10 November 1997: 58–9.
Brosnahan, John. "*Shadows in Bronze.*" *Booklist* 1 March 1991: 1320
Cannon, Peter. "*A Body in the Bath House.*" *Publishers Weekly* 12 August 2002: 280.
———. "*The Accusers.*" *Publishers Weekly* 16 February 2004: 154.
Cooper, Natasha. "*The Accusers.*" *Times Literary Supplement* 19–26 December 2003: 27.
———. "A Dying Light in Corduba." *Times Literary Supplement* 23 August 1996: 24.
Evans, Sarah Jane. "Sam Spade in Ancient Rome." *History Today* 39.4 (July 1989): 4–5.
"The Jupiter Myth." *Publishers Weekly* 11 August 2003: 261.
"Lindsey Davis." *Contemporary Authors.* New Revision Series, Vol. 103. Ed. Scot Peacock. Detroit: Gale, 2002. 86–88.
Lindzey, Ginny. "Lindsey Davis: An Interview with the Author of *Silver Pigs.*" *Texas Classics in Action.* Winter 1993. 22 January 2006. http://www.txclassics.org/exrpts3.htm
Marks, Jeffrey. "When in Rome … Lindsey Davis and Her Mysteries of the Ancient World." *Armchair Detective* 30.2 (1997): 190–94.
Melton, Emily. "*Three Hands in the Fountain.*" *Booklist* 15 April 1999: 1471.
Official Website of Lindsey Davis. n.d. 22 January 2006. http://www.lindseydavis.co.uk/
Robertson, Peter. "*Venus in Copper.*" *Booklist* 15 March 1992: 1339.
Rosenfeld, Shelle. "*Silver Pigs.*" *Booklist* 1 May 2000: 1608.
Seaman, Donna. "*Poseidon's Gold.*" *Booklist* 1 October 1994: 241.
Steinberg, Sybil. "*Silver Pigs.*" *Publishers Weekly* 30 June 1989: 86–7.
Warshaw, Justin. "The Revenge of Anacrites." *Times Literary Supplement* 29 June 2001: 24.
Zaleski, Jeff. "*Three Hands in the Fountain.*" *Publishers Weekly* 22 March 1999: 74.

Marele Day (1947–)

BIOGRAPHY

Marele Day was born May 4, 1947, in Sydney, Australia. She and her younger sister grew up in an industrial suburban area called Pagewood. Her father had a clerk position and her mother worked as a bookbinder (Waldren). She attended Sydney Girls High School and later earned certification from Sydney Teachers' College in 1965. She also earned a bachelor's degree with honors from Sydney University in 1976.

She has worked as a patent searcher and also held researcher positions in academia. She taught elementary school in the 1980s and has also taught English as a second language. Since 1988, she has worked as a freelance editor and writer. She has published mainstream novels, crime fiction, guides for aspiring writers, and short stories in numerous anthologies.

She lives in Sydney when she is not traveling the globe.

MAJOR WORKS AND THEMES

Her mystery series features a private investigator named Claudia Valentine. Her debut case, *The Life and Crimes of Harry Lavender,* finds Valentine assisting a friend in determining whather his brother's death was truly from natural causes. In *The Case of the Chinese Boxes,* Valentine is hired to locate a missing item for a Chinese woman, and she finds herself embroiled in a case involving the Chinatown Triad. The third novel finds Valentine investigating the death of a dancer named Delores Delgado. The police believe the death was from natural causes, but Valentine uncovers the links to a corrupt land development deal that cost Delgado her life. In the fourth novel, Valentine has been hired to track down a teenager. Valentine's mother divulges information about her father, and she also embarks on a journey to track down information about him.

Her breakthrough novel was a departure from her crime series. Entitled *Lambs of God,* it features three cloistered nuns who are the last living members of their order. Located on a remote island, they live in total isolation with their sheep until an emissary from the Bishop arrives. When they learn that he has plans to sell the island to developers, they must spring to action to save their home and way of life. The novel has been often described as a mixture of magic realism, surrealism, folklore, and theology, with a great sense of humor.

Day has also published a collection of short stories about an aspiring amateur sleuth named Mavis Levack and her reluctant sidekick, husband Eddy. As the book jacket states, "a lack of clients is not enough to thwart Mavis."

CRITICAL RECEPTION

In addition to various awards in Australia, Day won the Shamus Award in 1993 for the first novel in the Claudia Valentine series. A review of *The Last Tango of Dolores Delgado* noted that the novel was "as tough and outrageous as the characters who populate it" (Kaganoff 70). Day was praised for her creation of a "realistic setting with vivid descriptions of Sydney suburbs and the use of colloquial expressions" (Klett 108). Also noted were Day's characterization of Valentine, with "wry humor and gutsy behavior" (Klett 109). Her collection of short stories about Mavis Levack was called "quirky," with praise given to Day's "cleverness" and "deft handling"(*Paperbacks* 34).

Day's mystery writing has also attracted attention from scholars. Alison Littler examined Day's work in light of feminist theory and the placement of a feminist detective within the hard-boiled private investigator genre. Karen Lynch looked at *The Case of the Chinese Boxes* in her study of images of Chinatown in mystery novels and films.

BIBLIOGRAPHY

Works by Marele Day

Claudia Valentine Series

The Life and Crimes of Harry Lavender. Sydney: Allen & Unwin, 1988.
The Case of the Chinese Boxes. Sydney:Allen & Unwin, 1990.
The Last Tango of Dolores Delgado. Sydney: Allen & Unwin, 1992.
The Disappearances of Madalena Grimaldi. Sydney: Allen & Unwin, 1994; New York: Walker, 1996.

Other Fiction

Shirley's Song. London: Harvester Press, 1984.
Lambs of God. New York: Riverhead Books, 1998.
Mavis Levack, P.I. Sydney: Allen & Unwin, 2000.

Nonfiction Works

The Art of Self-Promotion for Writers. Sydney: Allen & Unwin, 1993.
How to Write Crime. Ed. Marele Day. Sydney: Allen & Unwin, 1996.

Works about Marele Day

Kaganoff, Penny. "The Last Targo of Dolores Delgado." *Publishers Weekly* 5 April 1993: 70.
Kleh, Rex E. "The Dissapearances of Madalena Grimaldi." *Library Journal* 1 March 1996: 108–9.
Littler, Alison. "Marele Day's 'Cold Hard Bitch': The Masculist Imperatives of the Private-Eye Genre." *Journal of Narrative Technique* 21.1 (1991): 121–35.
Lynch, Karen. "Orientation via Orientalism: Chinatown in Detective Narratives." *Popular Culture Review* 11.1 (2000): 13–29.
"Marele Day." *Contemporary Authors.* Vol. 173. Ed. Scot Peacock. Detroit: Gale, 1999. 111–13.
"Paperbacks." *Southland Times* 27 January 2001: 34.
Waldren, Murray. "Day's Break: Praise the Lord and Pass the Royalties." *The Australian* 5–6 July 1997. 11 November 2005. http://members.optusnet.com.au/~waldrenm/day.html

Joanne Dobson (1942–)

BIOGRAPHY

Joanne Dobson was born March 27, 1942, in New York City, the daughter of Charles and Mildred McKinley Abele. She married David Eugene Dobson in July 1963. They have three children. She earned her bachelor's degree in English in 1963 from King's College in Briarcliff Manor, NY. She returned to graduate studies later, earning a master's degree from the University of New York at Albany in 1977 and her Ph.D. from the University of Massachusetts at Amherst in 1985. She taught at Amherst College and Tufts University before taking a tenure-track position at Fordham University. She was assistant professor there from 1987 to 1992 and has been associate professor since 1992. She founded a scholarly society devoted to Emily Dickinson and was a founding editor of *Legacy: Journal of American Women Writers.* She lives in Brewster, New York.

MAJOR WORKS AND THEMES

Dobson's series features Karen Pelletier, an English professor at Enfield College in Enfield, Massachusetts, a fictionalized version of Amherst and its colleges. Pelletier grew up in a working-class family in Lowell and was the first of her family to attend college. Her path toward academia was made even more difficult by the fact she became pregnant during her senior year in high school, kept the baby and attended college and graduate school as a single mother, on her own, estranged from her family. The relationships between Pelletier and her daughter and between Pelletier and her own mother and sisters are strikingly different and provide insights into the characters. Pelletier finds herself drawn into cases involving manuscripts, writers, and others in academia. She often works in concert with the local police, particularly detective Charlie Piotrowski, although he often prefers that she not meddle in his cases. Pelletier and Piotrowski develop a personal relationship throughout the series as well.

In two of the novels, Dobson deals with real authors, Emily Dickinson, her academic specialty, and Edgar Allan Poe. In *The Maltese Manuscript,* she is hosting a literary conference focusing on mysteries when murder occurs. Peter Cannon noted that her "obvious knowledge of, and respect for, mystery and detective fiction is immense" (58). The other two novels in the series, along with the one focused on Poe, involve fictional writers created by Dobson. Elaine Showalter wrote that this is "what makes this series so fascinating and entertaining for the academic reader," namely Dobson's "ability to concoct the lost imaginary texts" (B12). Showalter found Dobson more similar to A. S. Byatt's work in *Possession* in "weaving past literary genres into modern whodunits" than to Carolyn Heilbrun's Amanda Cross novels (B12). In *The Raven and the Nightingale,* documents found in the manuscripts of a female poet indicate Poe may have plagiarized work. In *The Northbury Papers,* Dobson creates Serena Northbury, a nineteenth-century writer of "sentimental" fiction whose archives hold a mystery. In *Cold and Pure and Very Dead,* a cranky Pelletier names a *Peyton Place*-style potboiler in response to a newspaper reporter's question about the best novel ever. This rejuvenates interest in the book and its reclusive author, and Pelletier finds herself in the middle of another crime-solving adventure. Andy Plonka noted that "prestige and stature" replace the typical motives of love and money in academic mysteries (Plonka), and those are indeed the key issues at stake in the cases Pelletier solves. Her knowledge and understanding of academia and its concerns allow her to seek the truth more effectively than the local police.

CRITICAL RECEPTION

Although some critics have given mixed reviews on development of secondary characters and the mystery elements in the plots, critics all agree that Dobson nails the academic setting. As Shirley E. Havens noted in one review, readers "will appreciate the academic hijinks and lowlifes" that Dobson portrays (132). Marilyn Stasio was particularly enchanted with the subject matter of *The Maltese Manuscript,* noting that Dobson "sends up academic archness" with "manic wit" (17). Tom and Enid Schantz wrote that "comparisons with Amanda Cross are inevitable, but academia was never so lively in her mysteries as it is in Dobson's" series (G2). Another reviewer noted that "although the series features an amateur sleuth Dobson does not fall prey to many of the usual failings of novels of this type. Coincidence does not play a significant role and the police vs. amateur sleuth relationships are well handled" (Plonka). Francine Fialkoff discussed how "Pelletier manages to survive the culture wars in her own elite New England college and discover the murderer, too. A wonderful send up of the old vs. new college guard and a decent mystery as well" (139).

Katja Hawlitschka looked at the series in terms of Pelletier's personal and professional interests in literature and how she works with both literary and popular works. L. Timmel Duchamp explored issues of class and gender in the series. In addition to the reviewers who perceived Dobson's writing as more lively than Cross's, Dobson's work also differs in its class consciousness. Whereas Cross's sleuth Kate Fansler was wealthy and privileged, Pelletier has fought her way up from a more disadvantaged background. This, Duchamp argued, gives Pelletier a "moral and ethical grounding [that] not only grants her a moral certainty and ease with her feminist perspective that was denied to her fictional feminist predecessors" but also gives her the freedom to "express ideas and ask questions" (Duchamp). She is also on "firmer, steadier, and far less lonely ground than [Kate Fansler] when she battles the sometimes dangerous outrages of sexist offenses against women" (Duchamp).

BIBLIOGRAPHY

Works by Joanne Dobson

Karen Pelletier Series

Quieter than Sleep: A Modern Mystery of Emily Dickinson. New York: Doubleday, 1997.
The Northbury Papers. New York: Doubleday, 1998.
The Raven and the Nightingale: A Modern Mystery of Edgar Allan Poe. New York: Doubleday, 1999.
Cold and Pure and Very Dead. New York: Doubleday, 2000.
The Maltese Manuscript. New York: Poisoned Pen Press, 2003.

Other Works

Dickinson and the Strategies of Reticence: The Woman Writer in Nineteenth-Century America. Bloomington: Indiana U P, 1989.

Works about Joanne Dobson

Cannon, Peter. "The Maltese Manuscript." *Publishers Weekly* 3 February 2003: 58.
Duchamp, L. Timmel. "What's the Story? Reading Joanne Dobson's *Cold and Pure and Very Dead*." 2002. 22 May 2005. http://ltimmel.home.mindspring.com/dobson.html
Fialkoff, Francine. "*The Northbury Papers*." *Library Journal* August 1998: 139.
Havens, Shirley E. "Of Manuscripts and Murder." *Library Journal* 15 June 1999: 132.
Hawlitschka, Katja. "Detection, Deconstruction and Academic Death Sentences: Female Scholars Reading the Mysteries of High and Low Culture." *Clues* 25.3 (2005): 15–29.
"Joanne Dobson." *Contemporary Authors*. Vol. 104, New Revision Series. Ed. Scot Peacock. Detroit: Gale, 2002. 128–30.
Plonka, Andy. "*Cold and Pure and Very Dead*." The Mystery Reader. n.d. 22 May 2005. http://www.themysteryreader.com/dogson-cold.html
Schantz, Tom and Enid. "Missing Manuscript at Center of Campus Plot." *Denver Post* 8 November 1999: G2.
Showalter, Elaine. "Academic Predators, Poseurs, and Heroes in Three New Academic Novels." *The Chronicle of Higher Education* 16 February 2001: B11-B13.
Stasio, Marilyn. "Crime." *New York Times Book Review* 9 February 2003: 17.

Sarah Dunant (1950–)

BIOGRAPHY

Born August 8, 1950, Sarah Dunant was raised in London. Her father, David Dunant, was a manager with an airline, and her mother, Estelle Joseph Dunant, was a teacher. After attending Goldophin and Latymer School in Hammersmith, she earned a degree in history at Cambridge in 1972. She worked as a producer for BBC Radio in the mid-1970s. Since 1977, she has been a freelance broadcaster and writer, continuing to work on many BBC programs, including the television program "The Late Show" and Radio 3's "NightWaves." Divorced with two teenage daughters, she lives in London and Florence.

MAJOR WORKS AND THEMES

In addition to a variety of stand-alone novels, Dunant has written a series featuring a private investigator named Hannah Wolfe. Wolfe is introduced in *Birth Marks,* where she solves a case involving a missing woman who was serving as a surrogate mother. She returns in *Fatlands,* where the case revolves around a violent animal rights activist group. Her third appearance is in *Under My Skin,* in which she investigates suspicious events at a spa. Dunant has said that she wanted to create a female detective that was a "real woman with whom women readers could identify," while also giving women readers "a piece of the action" and "good lines," empowering women within a genre often dominated by males (Davies 420).

Her first two novels were written in collaboration with Peter Busby and are best described as being in the thriller genre. *Exterminating Angels* deals with a vigilante group, and *Intensive Care* is a political thriller. Her first solo novel was also published in the 1980s. *Snow Storms in a Hot Climate* focuses on a literature professor who becomes involved in a murder case while trying to help a friend escape from a drug-addicted, abusive boyfriend.

She has also published two other novels that moved into the realm of psychological thrillers. *Transgressions* tells the story of a woman translator who is working on an extremely violent Czech novel. A series of unusual events leads her to question her sanity until she comes to realize that someone is preying on her. The novel explores the relationship between the victim and predator. *Mapping the Edges* explores the disappearance of a journalist who left her daughter in the care of friends while traveling in Italy. Dunant explores two possible explanations for her disappearance: that she left by choice or that she has been kidnapped by a sadistic killer. Dunant alternates between the two parallel narratives. She has recently completed screenplays for both of these novels (Dukes).

Her most recent novels are combinations of thrillers and historical fiction. *The Birth of Venus* takes place during the 1500s in Florence, with characters affected by the political and cultural upheavals that took place during the era. Dunant notes that during the first summer she spent in Florence, she learned a great deal about art and history, but came to realize that women were mostly omitted (Larson). She created the main character of Alessandra in response to her own questions of what life was like for women in that era (Larson). *In the Company of the Courtesan* deals with the same time period, telling the story of a couple and their adventures amidst the world of political intrigue of sixteenth-century Italy.

Dunant has also edited two books of cultural criticism. One, *The War of the Words,* consists of a collection of essays about the political correctness debate, and the other, *The Age of Anxiety,* includes essays about issues around the new millennium.

CRITICAL RECEPTION

Dunant won a Silver Dagger Award from the Crime Writers' Association in 1993 for *Fatlands*. Critical response to her works has been favorable.

Birth Marks was heralded as "exceptionally astute and entertaining" (Craig 1991:19), and another reviewer called Wolfe "smart, self-aware, witty, tough and sexy" (Lukowsky 125). The second novel featuring Wolfe, the award-winning *Fatlands* was viewed as "strong and stylish" and an "engrossing thriller" (Craig 1993:18). Another reviewer stated that many authors have dealt with animal rights activism in their plots, but that Dunant "claims the territory for her own" (Klett 115). The novel was also praised for "smooth, polished, funny and sophisticated" writing, with an "inventive plot and sharp-edged commentary about the ethics" of business and science (Melton 1994:480). Although Emily Melton found *Fatlands* to be a stronger novel, she praised *Under My Skin* as an "entertaining and educational read" that offered a "keep-'em-guessing plot and dry wit" (1995:142).

Her works have also attracted the attention of literary scholars. Tracy Johnson looked at the role of the gothic and treatment of femininity in Dunant's *Transgressions* as compared to a novel called *The Blindfold* by Siri Hustvedt.

BIBLIOGRAPHY

Works by Sarah Dunant

With Peter Busby as Peter Dunant. *Exterminating Angels*. London: Deutsch, 1983.
With Peter Busby as Peter Dunant. *Intensive Care*. London: Deutsch, 1986.
Snow Storms in a Hot Climate. New York: Random House, 1988.
Transgressions. London: Virago, 1997; New York: Regan Books, 1998.
Mapping the Edge. London: Virago, 1999; New York: Random House, 2001.
The Birth of Venus. London: Little, Brown, 2003; New York: Random House, 2004.
In the Company of the Courtesan. London: Little, Brown, 2005.

Hannah Wolfe Series

Birth Marks. London: M. Joseph, 1991; New York: Doubleday, 1992.
Fatlands. New York: O. Penzler Books, 1994.
Under My Skin. New York: Scribner, 1995.

Nonfiction Works

Dunant, Sarah, ed. *The War of the Words: The Political Correctness Debate*. London: Virago, 1995.
Dunant, Sarah and Roy Porter, eds. *The Age of Anxiety*. London: Virago, 2006.

Works about Sarah Dunant

Craig, Patricia. "Criminal Proceedings." *Times Literary Supplement* 12 April 1991: 19.
———. "*Fatlands*." *Times Literary Supplement* 13 August 1993: 18.
Davies, David. "The Female Eye: An Interview with Sarah Dunant." *Armchair Detective* 27.4 (1994): 418–21.
Dukes, Jessica. "Meet the Writers: Sarah Dunant." Barnes and Noble.com. 2004. 31 December 2005. http://www.barnesandnoble.com/writers/writerdetails.asp?userid = m72cRcdCXw&cid =1037180# interview
Johnson, Tracy. "The Fear Industry: Women, Gothic, and Contemporary Crime Narrative." *Gothic Studies* 4.1 (2002): 44–62.

Klett, Rex E. "*Fatlands.*" *Library Journal* 1 November 1994: 115.

Larson, Kate. "Book Club Interview with Sarah Dunant." BookPassage.com. n.d. 31 December 2005. http://www.bookpassage.com/bookclubs/dunantSarah.shtml

Lukowsky, Wes. "*Birth Marks.*" *Booklist* 15 September 1992: 125.

Melton, Emily. "*Fatlands.*" *Booklist* 1 November 1994: 480.

———. "*Under My Skin.*" *Booklist* 15 September 1995: 142.

"Sarah Dunant." *Contemporary Authors.* New Revision Series, Vol. 91. Ed. Scot Peacock. Detroit: Gale, 2000. 108–10.

"Sarah Dunant." Contemporary Writers British Council—Arts. n.d. 31 December 2005. http://www. contemporarywriters.com/authors/?p = auth32

Steinberg, Sybil. "Sarah Dunant: Fact and Fiction in Florence." *Publishers Weekly* 8 March 2004: 43–44.

Janet Evanovich (1943–)

BIOGRAPHY

Born in 1943, Janet Evanovich grew up in South River, New Jersey, in a Danish-American family. She was the first in her family to attend college, and she studied art at Douglass College, graduating in 1965. She then married Peter Evanovich, her high school sweetheart, who later earned a doctorate in mathematics from Rutgers.

In the 1980s, she began writing stories and novels, but all of them were rejected. She gave up on writing, went to work as a secretary, and four months later, received word that the last manuscript she had sent out for review had been accepted. She turned out 12 romance novels in the next five years. She has said that she was writing them so quickly she had to keep the characters' names taped to the computer screen (Kaczmarek 2). When she tired of the romance genre, she decided to learn about law enforcement and related issues so that she could turn to writing mystery novels. Part of her training regimen to improve her writing of dialogue was to read Robert B. Parker novels and to do improvisation routines at comedy clubs (Kaczmarek 2). The first novel in her Stephanie Plum series was published in 1994.

She and her husband moved to Hanover, New Hampshire in 1995. Her husband serves as her business manager, her son Peter is her financial manager, and her daughter Alex maintains her Web site and creates promotional materials.

MAJOR WORKS AND THEMES

The bulk of Evanovich's work is composed of the Stephanie Plum series, but she began a second mystery series in 2004, which features a character named Alexandra Barnaby. Also, one of her earlier romance novels was reworked with a new co-author, Charlotte Hughes, and published in 2003. She and Hughes have continued to collaboratively publish additional romance novels.

At the beginning of the first series, which is set in Trenton, New Jersey, Stephanie Plum has lost her job at the lingerie factory and has few prospects. To earn some quick money, she convinces her sleazy cousin, Vinnie the bail bondsman, to hire her. Bounty hunting turns out to be more difficult than she imagined, but it does become her new career. Throughout the series, Plum attempts to apprehend people who have failed to appear in court and, while fumbling through those assignments, stumbles into larger cases. Plum usually manages to destroy at least one car per novel.

The series is known for its humor and its cast of zany secondary characters, including Lula, a former prostitute who works for Vinnie as a file clerk; Grandma Mazur, who attends funerals as a social diversion; a rival from high school who also works as a bounty hunter; her long-suffering father; her perfect sister Valerie; and a host of others. Plum also has two love interests throughout most of the series: Joe Morelli, a police detective who was a boyfriend during school, and Ranger, a mysterious, professional bounty hunter who saves Plum on more than one occasion. *High Five* closes with a cliffhanger regarding which man she'll choose, but even with the initial resolution in *Hot Six,* Evanovich keeps the sexual tension between the characters high in subsequent books. Each novel brings in more madcap characters, and with the help of all of these people, but mostly Morelli and Ranger, Plum somehow manages to solve the cases she finds herself caught up in.

In 2004, Evanovich published the first novel in her second mystery series, which was entitled *Metro Girl.* Featuring a Baltimore mechanic's daughter named Alexandra Barnaby, called Barney, it is in the same vein as the Plum novels, offering humorous capers, snappy dialogue, and romance. In the first outing, Barney goes to Florida to find her missing brother, and she joins forces with a NASCAR driver to solve the case.

CRITICAL RECEPTION

Evanovich's works have received awards in both the United States and the United Kingdom. She has won three awards from the Crime Writers Association: a John Creasey Memorial Award, a Last Laugh award, and a Silver Dagger. At home, her work has been awarded a Dilys, an award given by the Independent Booksellers Association. *One for the Money* was nominated for Agatha, Anthony, Edgar, and Shamus awards.

The first two Plum novels received strong reviews, with *Library Journal* praising it as a "witty, well-written and gutsy debut" featuring a "wonderful sense of humor, an eye for detail and a self-deprecating narrative" (Klett 132). Another reviewer called Plum "one of the funniest, most appealing new heroines" to appear in a "long while," and praised Evanovich for her "breezy, bright, and witty" dialogue and an "ingenious and fresh" plot (Melton 1994:27).

One reviewer noted that in *Three to Get Deadly,* "Stephanie muddles through another case full of snappy one-liners as well as corpses," and with both the help and hindrance of "her charmingly clueless family and various cohorts," solves the mystery (Brainard 1996:59). The same reviewer examined *Four to Score,* stating that "with her brash exterior and high emotionality, Stephanie Plum is a welcome antidote to suave professional PIs" (Brainard 1998:62).

Emily Melton reviewed Plum's "fifth madcap adventure," noting "that she's lived long enough to have five adventures is amazing enough, considering that Stephanie has near-death experiences (bombings, shootings, kidnappings) like normal people have breakfast" (1999:1558). Melton continued that "the combination of hilarious dialogue, oddball characters, and eye-popping action is hard to beat on its own, but the heroine, a righteous babe if ever there was one, is what sets the over-the-top series apart from all the competition in the comic mystery field" (1999:1558). Another review hailed the return of "Jersey girl and bounty hunter extraordinaire" in *High Five,* praising Evanovich's ability to "tell her fast-paced and furiously funny story expertly. The action never stops, the dialogue is snappy and the characters are more than memorable" (Zaleski 1999:60–61). A British reviewer found that "with its robust approach, high quota of suspense, gusto and extravagance, *High Five* expands the private-eye genre to incorporate aplomb and merriment" (Craig 33).

Jeff Zaleski noted that in *Hot Six* "determination and contacts (she's grown up with half the cops and crooks in Trenton) compensate for Steph's poor aim with a gun, bad luck with cars and soft-hearted approach to her job (one bail jumper evades her four times)" (2000:52). Oline H. Cogdill described the novel as having the "superb silliness of Lucille Ball and the broad pratfalls of the Three Stooges," noting that "in the hands of a lesser talent, the humor could fall flat. But Evanovich is one of the few mystery writers who can make what should be a serious scene into something raucously funny" (2000:9D).

Seven Up received mixed reviews. Reviewers still enjoyed the characters and their antics, but noted that this was her "most uneven outing [with] humor that seems forced and formulaic" (Cogdill 2001:9D) and that it "doesn't quite hit the high marks of her last two" (Cannon 2001:228). But *Hard Eight* pleased the reviewers, with a critic of the seventh novel noting that in the eight "Evanovich does it again, delivering an even more suspenseful and more outrageous turn with the unstoppable Stephanie" (Cannon 2002:50).

For one reviewer, *To the Nines* "features Evanovich's trademark broad humor, outlandish characters and bizarre characters with a plotline that could basically be summed up as bad things happen in Trenton, N.J." (Cogdill 2003:13D). The reviewer noted that "the formula holds steady, but … her zigzagging between two men is getting a bit wearisome" (Cogdill 2003:13D). Another reviewer viewed the novel as "clever, sexy and funny" but found the road trip to Las Vegas plot line unsatisfying (Martin EE2). Aside from that "mistake," the reviewer found *To the Nines* to be "the edgiest of the Stephanie Plum books," noting that "as Stephanie searches for the psycho who keeps murdering witnesses … the plot gets as tight as a weighted noose" (Martin EE2).

Peter Cannon found that Evanovich was "at her best" in *Ten Big Ones,* which he noted "reads like the screenplay for a 1930s screwball comedy: fast, funny and furious" (2004:35). He concluded that "the rollicking plot, replete with car chases, family squabbles, massive doughnut consumption and a frantic, wacky finale, keeps the reader breathless" (Cannon 2004:36).

BIBLIOGRAPHY

Works by Janet Evanovich

Stephanie Plum Series

One for the Money. New York: Scribner, 1994.
Two for the Dough. New York: Scribner, 1996.
Three to Get Deadly. New York: Scribner, 1997.
Four to Score. New York: St. Martin's, 1998.
High Five. New York: St. Martin's, 1999.
Hot Six. New York: St. Martin's, 2000.
Seven Up. New York: St. Martin's, 2001.
Hard Eight. New York: St. Martin's, 2002.
Visions of Sugar Plums. New York: St. Martin's, 2002.
To the Nines. New York: St. Martin's, 2003.
Ten Big Ones. New York: St. Martin's, 2004.

Eleven on Top. New York: St. Martin's, 2005.
Twelve Sharp. New York: St. Martin's, 2006.

Alexandra Barnaby Series

Metro Girl. New York: HarperCollins, 2004.
Motor Mouth. New York: HarperCollins, 2006.

Other Novels

As Steffie Hall. *Hero at Large.* New York: Second Chance at Love, 1987.
The Grand Finale. New York: Bantam, 1988.
Thanksgiving. New York: Bantam, 1988.
Manhunt. New York: Bantam, 1988.
As Steffie Hall. *Full House.* New York: Second Chance at Love, 1989.
As Steffie Hall. *Foul Play.* New York: Second Chance at Love, 1989.
Ivan Takes a Wife. New York: Bantam, 1989.
Back to the Bedroom. New York: Bantam, 1989.
Wife for Hire. New York: Bantam, 1990.
Smitten. New York: Bantam, 1990.
The Rocky Road to Romance. New York: Bantam, 1991.
Naughty Neighbor. New York: Bantam, 1992.
With Charlotte Hughes. *Full Tilt.* New York: St. Martin's Press, 2003.
With Charlotte Hughes. *Full Speed.* New York: St. Martin's Press, 2003.
With Charlotte Hughes. *Full Blast.* New York: St. Martin's Press, 2004.
With Charlotte Hughes. *Full Bloom.* New York: St. Martin's Press, 2005.
With Charlotte Hughes. *Full Scoop.* New York: St. Martin's Press, 2006.

Works about Janet Evanovich

Brainard, Dulcy. "*Three to Get Deadly.*" *Publishers Weekly* 25 November 1996: 59.
———. "*Four to Score.*" *Publishers Weekly* 6 April 1998: 62.
Cannon, Peter. "*Seven Up.*" *Publishers Weekly* 7 May 2001: 227–28.
———. "*Hard Eight.*" *Publishers Weekly* 20 May 2002: 50.
———. "*Ten Big Ones.*" *Publishers Weekly* 7 June 2004: 35–36.
Cogdill, Oline H. "Slapstick Sleuth is Still Hot Stuff." *South Florida Sun Sentinel* 25 June 2000: 9D.
———. "Numbers Sleuth Zeros in on a Niche." *South Florida Sun Sentinel* 8 July 2001: 9D.
———. "Klutzy Bounty Hunter's Still Hilarious." *South Florida Sun Sentinel* 6 July 2003: 13D.
Craig, Patricia. "*High Five.*" *Times Literary Supplement* 5 November 1996: 33.
Janet Evanovich. Homepage. 2005. 27 May 2005. http://www.evanovich.com/
"Janet Evanovich." *Contemporary Authors.* Vol. 115, New Revision Series. Ed. Scot Peacock. Detroit: Gale, 2003. 135–37.
Kaczmarek, Lynn. "You're Damn Skippy! An Interview with Janet Evanovich." *Mystery News* 16.3 (1998): 1–3.
Klett, Rex. "*One for the Money.*" *Library Journal* July 1994: 132.
Lanham, Fritz. "'Plum' Author Evanovich Didn't Enjoy Overnight Success." *Daily Breeze* 7 September 2003: B2.
Martin, Claire. "Stephanie Plum Hits the Road: Vegas Only Drawback in Edgy *To the Nines.*" *Denver Post* 17 August 2003: EE2.
Melton, Emily. "*One for the Money.*" *Booklist* 1 September 1994: 27.
———. "*High Five.*" *Booklist* 1 May 1999: 1558.
Zaleski, Jeff. "*High Five.*" *Publishers Weekly* 21 June 1999: 60–61.
———. "*Hot Six.*" *Publishers Weekly* 1 May 2000: 52.

Linda Fairstein (1947–)

BIOGRAPHY

Linda Fairstein was born May 5, 1947 in Mt. Vernon, New York. Her father, Samuel Johnson Fairstein, was a physician and her mother, Alice Atwell Fairstein, was a registered nurse. She has one brother, who is a corporate lawyer.

Fairstein earned a bachelor's degree in English literature in 1969 from Vassar College and went to the University of Virginia for law school, earning her J.D. in 1972. She went to work for the New York County District Attorney's Office after graduation and was appointed the chief of the sex crimes prosecution unit in 1976, a posting she held until 2002. She also served as the deputy chief of the trial division from 1981 to 2002. Fairstein was responsible for a number of innovations, particularly in extending the status of investigator held by assistant district attorneys in murder cases to the sex crimes unit and in following a Wisconsin prosecutor's lead and instituting a program of indicting DNA profiles of unknown rapists. She was a visible figure as an assistant district attorney, having served as prosecutor in several high-profile cases during the 1980s, including the "Preppy Murderer" case and the 1989 Central Park Jogger case. She has received a number of awards for her legal work and public service. Fairstein remains active as a consultant and speaker on legal issues and continues to work on selected cases on a pro bono basis.

She married lawyer Justin N. Feldman on May 2, 1987; he had three children from a previous marriage. They live in Manhattan and Martha's Vineyard.

MAJOR WORKS AND THEMES

Fairstein's mystery series features a character who shares Fairstein's professional training, expertise, and position. Alexandra Cooper is an assistant district attorney in Manhattan who heads up the sex crimes unit. The similarities end there, according to Fairstein, who calls Cooper "younger, blonder, thinner, and much richer" (McGlone). Cooper's personal history involves having independent wealth from her father's invention of an artificial heart valve and having tragically lost her fiancé in a car accident while he was on his way to the wedding. Cooper works closely with two police detectives, Mike Chapman and Mercer Wallace. The three share a close personal friendship, as well as a professional camaraderie. Character quirks include the fact that they have a standing bet for the final question on the "Jeopardy!" game show.

Although the novels all deal with some type of rape or assault case, the plots are complex and often include a historical or cultural aspect. For example, in *The Deadhouse,* a scientist is killed. Cooper had been working with her on a case against her abusive ex-husband, so suspicion falls to him early on. The case is much more complex though, stemming from the woman's research into infectious diseases. To solve the case, Cooper must learn about the past uses of quarantine facilities on Roosevelt Island and present-day research controversies. In *The Bone Vault,* Cooper, Chapman, and Wallace are pulled into investigating the world of art and museums when a curator is assaulted and killed in a museum. *Entombed* involves their investigation of a rape and murder victim and possible connections to another case of a body being found in the walls during the demolition of a house where Edgar Allan Poe once lived.

CRITICAL RECEPTION

Critical reception to her first book, a nonfiction work about sex crimes and prosecuting rape in the United States was positive, particularly among academic reviewers. Reviews of her first novel, though, were mixed. Many reviewers found her expertise flawless and thought it made for solid plotting, with one noting that even a description of a typical day in Cooper's life would keep "most readers fascinated" but that Fairstein "pitches the plot at high intensity right away" (Brainard 1996:50). The same reviewer, though, felt disappointed that Cooper rushed foolishly into jeopardy and also deemed the dialogue to be "as wooden as a judge's gavel" (Brainard 1996:50). Another reviewer predicted that this "thriller, which will keep readers asking questions and turning pages" would be quite successful (Michaud 121). A third review was much harsher, complaining of an "amateurish plot, unnecessary digressions, poor characterizations and silly attempts at plot twists" (Holt D10).

Likely to Die found reviewers again critiquing the slow plotting and problems with characterization and dialogue (Gorman 1997:138; Steinberg 57–58), but reviews of *Cold Hit* show that Fairstein was hitting her stride. Molly Gorman noted that in *Cold Hit,* "Alex is relentlessly likeable… but it is her empathy for victims of violence and unswerving determination to collar the scumbag that truly endear her to readers" (1999:146). The review mentioned that "the author's frequent explanations of police procedures are jarring" but summed up that the book was "fascinating and fast-paced" (Gorman 1999:146). Another review of *Cold Hit* noted that "Fairstein's rough-and-tumble courthouse scenes ring true, as do her descriptions of the mundane police work," continuing that Cooper "remains a shining protagonist, comfortable in the upper echelons of New York society but eager to roll up her sleeves at work, her heart aching for her staff and the victims they defend" (Zaleski 346).

One reviewer of *The Deadhouse,* which won a Nero award, praised her ability to "weave present and past woes to good effect" and noted that "her focus on Roosevelt Island will intrigue New Yorkers who know little about its shameful former uses" (Cannon 67). Carol Memmott wrote that Fairstein "get[s] her story off to a rollicking start" and noted that there are "no lulls, no lagging scenes" and that "the characters, even the minor ones, are realistically and revealingly wrought" (Memmott D9). Calling it "a fine blend of legal thriller and police procedural," Oline H. Cogdill found that although some dialogue about the museum's bureaucracy "feels leaden," "the suspense and fascinating characterizations keep *The Bone Vault* moving at a fast pace" (9D). Cogdill also praised the "intense rivalries among museums, out-of-control egos, questionable ethics and a secret storage room" that all "add texture to the complex story" (9D).

A *Publishers Weekly* review of *The Kills* noted that "Fairstein's style and skills have matured over the years, making this a consistently dependable series with a likable and intelligent heroine" ("*The Kills*" 54). In reviewing *Entombed,* a reviewer stated that "it's a tribute to Fairstein's integrity and her clear, measured prose that the novel never tips into prurience. Her methodical presentation of authentic detail engages reader interest more than narrative flourish or cheap thrills," concluding that "she's the real deal" (36–37).

BIBLIOGRAPHY

Works by Linda Fairstein

Alexandra Cooper series

Final Jeopardy. New York: Scribner, 1996.
Likely to Die. New York: Scribner, 1997.
Cold Hit. New York: Scribner, 1999.

The Deadhouse. New York: Scribner, 2001.
The Bone Vault. New York: Scribner, 2003.
The Kills. New York: Scribner, 2004.
Entombed. New York: Scribner, 2005.
Death Dance. New York: Scribner, 2006.

Other Works

Sexual Violence: Our War against Rape. New York: Morrow, 1993.

Works about Linda Fairstein

Brainard, Dulcy. "*Final Jeopardy.*" *Publishers Weekly* 1 April 1996: 50.
BookEnds Interview: Linda Fairstein. n.d. 27 May 2005. http://www.thebookplace.com/bookends/be_interviews_fairstein.asp
Browning, Pat. "Spotlight Profile: Linda Fairstein." Sisters in Crime Internet Chapter. December 2001. 27 May 2005. http://www.sinc-ic.org/spot1201.shtml
Cannon, Peter. "*The Deadhouse.*" *Publishers Weekly* 3 September 2001: 67.
Cogdill, Oline H. "Past and Present Are Intertwined on Dry Tortugas; Murder in a Museum." *Sun-Sentinel* 9 February 2003: 9D.
Di Maio, Dina. "An Interview with Linda Fairstein." *The Square Table.* 2003. 27 May 2005. http://www.thesquaretable.com/Spring03/linda.htm
"*Entombed.*" *Publishers Weekly* 22 November 2004: 36–37.
Gorman, Molly." *Likely To Die.*" *Library Journal* 1 May 1997: 138–39.
Gorman, Molly. "*Cold Hit.*" *Library Journal* August 1999: 146.
Holt, Patricia. "Behind the Sex Crimes Scene." *San Francisco Chronicle* 7 June 1996: D10.
"*The Kills.*" *Publishers Weekly* 13 October 2003: 54.
Kornbluth, Jesse. "Interview with Linda Fairstein." Bookreporter.com. 6 January 2004. 27 May 2005. http://aolsvc.bookreporter.aol.com/authors/au-fairstein-linda.asp
"Linda Fairstein." *Contemporary Authors.* Vol. 127, New Revision Series. Ed. Tracey Watson. Detroit: Gale, 2004. 117–20.
McGlone, Jackie. "Lore and Order." *The Scotsman* 22 January 2005. 27 May 2005. http://news.scotsman.com/features.cfm?id = 65142005
Memmott, Carol. "Skilled Writers Put Strong Women in Charge." *USA Today* 4 October 2001: D9.
Michaud, Charles. "*Final Jeopardy.*" *Library Journal* 15 April 1996: 121.
Steinberg, Sybil S. "*Likely to Die.*" *Publishers Weekly* 12 May 1997: 57–58.
Zaleski, Jeff. "*Cold Hit.*" *Publishers Weekly* 9 August 1999: 346.

Jerrilyn Farmer

BIOGRAPHY

Born and raised in Lincolnwood, Illinois, Jerrilyn Farmer earned a degree in English and theatre from Northern Illinois University. After working in theatre in Chicago, she moved to California to pursue more opportunities in acting. She was a contestant on a game show and then found work as a writer for game shows, including "Jeopardy!" and "Supermarket Sweep" (Smith). She also wrote for "Saturday Night Live" before turning to mystery fiction (White). She took a class on mystery writing at UCLA Extension, which led to her first novel. In 2005, she began teaching that mystery writing workshop for UCLA Extension. She resides in southern California with her husband and two sons.

MAJOR WORKS AND THEMES

Her mystery series features Madeline Bean, a caterer and event planner in Hollywood. Bean's company is called Mad Beans, and her work takes her into many areas of the Hollywood scene. The novels feature a mix of humor and crime, with Bean and her friends and colleagues providing much comic relief. Bean deals with various crimes that occur during events she caters or plans, including murder. The novels include many details about the food, but as her reviewers have noted, she balances the humor and culinary features with the more serious aspects of the mysteries to be solved.

CRITICAL RECEPTION

Her novels have received many nominations for Agatha, Anthony, and Macavity awards; she won the Macavity Award for her first novel. She has also won several Lefty Awards, which are given at the Left Coast Crime Convention each year for best humorous mystery.

A review of *Mumbo Gumbo* noted that Farmer "provides a fascinating insider's peek at a supposedly glamorous world," while "dish[ing] up zany yet convincing characters and a sturdy plot. Unlike many culinary-themed mysteries, [this] is no puff piece" (Pate). *Perfect Sax* "smoothly blends all the right ingredients: Beverly Hills money mania, tart humor, romance and, of course, murder" (Zaleski 50). Another reviewer noted that Farmer "again proves her flair for original storytelling augmented by a good sense of humor" (Cogdill 2004:6). In *The Flaming Luau of Death,* Farmer showed she "knows how to balance humor with a serious tone and appealing characters" (Cogdill 2005). The reviewer also noted that the plot is light, but that "the story is not lightweight as Farmer ponders the ramifications of friendship, obsession and wealth" (Cogdill 2005).

BIBLIOGRAPHY

Works by Jerrilyn Farmer

Madeline Bean Series

Sympathy for the Devil. New York: Avon, 1998.
Immaculate Reception. New York: Avon, 1999.
Killer Wedding. New York: Avon, 2000.
Dim Sum Dead. New York: Avon, 2001.
Mumbo Gumbo. New York: Morrow, 2003.
Perfect Sax. New York: Morrow, 2004.
The Flaming Luau of Death. New York: Morrow, 2005.

Works about Jerrilyn Farmer

Cogdill, Oline H. "*Sax* a Professional Job in Amateur Sleuthing." *Chicago Tribune* 5 February 2004: 6.
———. "*The Flaming Luau of Death.*" *Knight Ridder Tribune News Service* 8 June 2005. March 10, 2006. Washington State University Libraries. ProQuest Direct.
Jerrilyn Farmer. Homepage. 2006. 16 March 2006. http://home.earthlink.net/~jerrilyn/
Pate, Nancy. "*Mumbo Gumbo.*" *Knight Ridder Tribune News Service* 4 June 2003.
Smith, Teri. "Jerrilyn Farmer: Mystery Does Hollywood." *Crescent Blues* 4.2 (2001). 16 March 2006. http://www.crescentblues.com/4_2issue/int_jerrilyn_farmer.shtml
White, Claire E. "A Conversation with Jerrilyn Farmer." *Writers Write: The Internet Writing Journal.* April 2001. 16 March 2006. http://www.writerswrite.com/journal/apr01/farmer.htm
Zaleski, Jeff. "*Perfect Sax.*" *Publishers Weekly* 8 December 2003: 50.

Earlene Fowler (1954–)

BIOGRAPHY

Earlene Fowler was born August 23, 1954, in Lynwood, California, to Earl and Mary Worley. He father was a machinist, and her mother had worked as a secretary. She grew up in the Los Angeles area, in La Puente, with her three sisters. After graduating from La Puente High School, she went to work in an office in downtown Los Angeles. In September 1973, she married her high school sweetheart, Allen Fowler, who is an engineer. In addition to various jobs, she also worked in the children's department of the Huntington Beach Library from 1987 to 1992.

From the late 1970s, she took creative writing classes at various community colleges and wrote short fiction without any success in publishing. She worked on a novel in the late 1980s, and in 1989, took her novel to another writing course at a local college. The instructor was the novelist Jo-Ann Mapson, who found Fowler's work promising and connected Fowler with her own agent, who quickly secured Fowler a publishing deal (McLellan 2; Goldsmith; Dudick D1).

She and her husband reside in Orange County, California.

MAJOR WORKS AND THEMES

Except for one nonseries novel, Fowler's work features Albenia "Benni" Harper, a young widow who leaves ranch life to become the director of a folk art museum. The series is set in a fictionalized version of San Luis Obispo called San Celina. Harper was raised by her grandmother, Dove, who along with her father and other relatives, plays an important role in her life and in the series. In the first novel, she discovers one of the local artists murdered, and is particularly concerned because she saw her cousin's car driving away from the murder scene. Harper is compelled to try to clear her cousin, and in doing so, clashes with the town's new police chief, Gabriel Ortiz. As in many mystery series, animosity turns to love, and Harper and Ortiz join forces romantically and also to solve the mystery.

Throughout the series, Fowler links history and culture with crimes that Harper becomes involved with solving, under the protests from Ortiz. *Irish Chain* touches on the history of Japanese internment during World War II, and *Delectable Mountains* features a crime linked to the theft of an antique violin. *Broken Dishes* and *Seven Sisters* explore themes of family secrets and class conflicts. In *Sunshine and Shadow,* Harper is pulled into a case that leads to her uncovering the truth about her first husband's death. Most novels are set against the backdrop of quilt shows, storytelling contests, photography exhibits, or other events taking place at the museum, allowing Fowler to weave in details of arts and culture. All of the book titles are named for quilt patterns, which often tie into the novels in some way.

Her recent work, *The Saddlemaker's Wife,* is a departure from the Harper series. The novel tells the story of a recent widow who learns she has inherited part of a ranch from her husband. When she goes to visit the area, she discovers relatives her husband had claimed were dead, and she delves into the family history to discover more about her husband and his life.

CRITICAL RECEPTION

Fowler won an Agatha Award for *Mariner's Compass* in 1999. Critical response to her work has been strong throughout her career, although some reviews of her first novel were a bit mixed. One review found *Fool's Puzzle* to offer "well-paced action combined with humor, pathos and romance" with an "original and spirited heroine" (Havens 112), with another reviewer calling it "the start of a promising new series" (Klett 142). A strongly positive review noted that the "expertly written debut mystery is vibrant, witty and captivating" (Patterson G5). Another review critiqued the character development and budding relationship with police chief Ortiz to be "dangerously close to cliché," although the summation called it a "very promising first novel" (Miller 1666–67).

A *Publishers Weekly* reviewer found the first novel to be "predictable," with Harper acting in a "foolhardy" fashion (Brainard 1994:86), but *Irish Chain* changed that reviewer's mind. In her review of the second novel, Harper is noted for her "charming personality" and the novel is praised for "intricately blend[ing] social history and modern mystery" (Brainard 1995:67). Another review of *Irish Chain* noted that Fowler "weaves a tight plot focusing on racism, history and revenge while developing a strong heroine" (Cogdill 11D).

Goose in the Pond was praised for its "engaging" dialogue and effective use of "local California color" (DeCandido 1403). *Dove in the Window* was acclaimed for how Fowler "writes beautifully about the picturesque Central Coast, ranching, and local cuisine" with "sympathetic, witty characters of all ages and backgrounds" adding to the appealing "mix of history-laden story, engaging and individualistic female sleuths, and vivid settings" (Rowen 1998:1382).

The award-winning *Mariner's Compass* was positively reviewed. John Rowen noted that "Fowler continues to deepen her characters—eccentric and sympathetic Californians and transplanted southerners" and praised her plot as "tighter and better organized" with "surprising and funny moments" found in the novel (1999:1472). Another reviewer found it "captivating," praising the plot and character development in this "excellent addition to a notable series" (Zaleski 1999:65).

Rowen compared *Seven Sisters* to Ross MacDonald's works, while noting that "the tantalizing subplot about Benni's amusing, poignant relationship with her husband's first wife is as intriguing as the mystery" (2000:1332). Another review pointed to Harper's sleuthing as unlocking a past secret that "relates to the present tragedy, provid[ing] the stunning climax to a compelling story" (Zaleski 2000:65).

Steps to the Altar was praised as "delicious reading, with plenty of passion, snappy dialogue and a whiz-bang plot" (Cannon 2002:45). *Delectable Mountains* was noted for a "heart-hammering hostage situation [that] leads to a highly unexpected ending" (Cannon 2005:47). In addition, Fowler's works were explored in a recent master's thesis on the theological aspects of mystery fiction (Bulock).

BIBLIOGRAPHY

Works by Earlene Fowler

Benni Harper Series

Fool's Puzzle. New York: Berkley, 1994.
Irish Chain. New York: Berkley, 1995.
Kansas Troubles. New York: Berkley, 1996.
Goose in the Pond. New York: Berkley, 1997.
Dove in the Window. New York: Berkley, 1998.
Mariner's Compass. New York: Berkley, 1999.
Seven Sisters. New York: Berkley, 2000.
Arkansas Traveler. New York: Berkley, 2001.

Steps to the Altar. New York: Berkley, 2002.
Sunshine and Shadow. New York: Berkley, 2003
Broken Dishes. New York: Berkley, 2004.
Delectable Mountains. New York: Berkley, 2005.

Other Fiction

The Saddlemaker's Wife. New York: Berkley, 2006.

Works about Earlene Fowler

Brainard, Dulcy. "*Fool's Puzzle*." *Publishers Weekly* 28 March 1994: 86.
———. "*Irish Chain*." *Publishers Weekly* 13 February 1995: 67.
Bulock, Lynn. "Thou Shall Not Kill: Theological Aspects of the Traditional Mystery Novel." M.A. thesis. California State University, Dominguez Hills. 2004.
Cannon, Peter. "*Steps to the Altar*." *Publishers Weekly* 25 March 2002: 45.
———. "*Delectable Mountains*." *Publishers Weekly* 18 April 2005: 46–47.
Cogdill, Oline H. "*Irish Chain* Links Characters, History." *Sun Sentinel* 7 May 1995: 11D.
DeCandido, Graceanne A. "*Goose in the Pond*." *Booklist* 15 April 1997: 1403.
Dudick, J. Mark. "A Patchwork of Mysteries." *Anchorage Daily News* 19 August 2001: D1.
"Earlene Fowler." *Contemporary Authors*. New Revision Series, Vol. 96. Ed. Scot Peacock. Detroit: Gale, 2001. 118–19.
Goldsmith, Dawn. "Earlene Fowler: Down-home Murder." *Crescent Blues* 3.6 (1998). 6 February 2006. http://www.crescentblues.com/3_6issue/fowler.shtml
Havens, Shirley E. "Coastal Intrigue." *Library Journal* 15 October 1994: 112.
James, Dean. "Earlene Fowler." *Mystery Scene* 61 (1998): 58–62.
Klett, Rex E. "*Fool's Puzzle*." *Library Journal* 1 May 1994: 142.
McLellan, Dennis. "Student Gets Extra Credit: A Woman in a Writing Workshop at Orange Coast College Sells Her First Novel." *Los Angeles Times* 17 December 1992: 2.
Miller, Stuart. "*Fool's Puzzle*." *Booklist* 15 May 1994: 1666–67.
Patterson, Michelle. "Mysteries Have Right Ingredients." *Tulsa World* 26 May 1996: G5.
Rowen, John. "*Dove in the Window*." *Booklist* 15 April 1998: 1382.
———. "*Mariner's Compass*." *Booklist* 15 April 1999: 1472.
———. "*Seven Sisters*." *Booklist* 15 March 2000: 1332.
Zaleski, Jeff. "*Mariner's Compass*." *Publishers Weekly* 19 April 1999: 65.
———. "*Seven Sisters*." *Publishers Weekly* 13 March 2000: 65.

Frances Fyfield (1948–)

BIOGRAPHY

Frances Hegarty was born November 18, 1948, in Derbyshire, England to Andrew George and Winifred Fyfield Hegarty. In the biography on her homepage, she notes that her father, a doctor, and her mother, a nurse, met in Egypt during World War II. She grew up with an older sister and two younger brothers. She has noted that her father was an alcoholic, and that her parents, who had both been raised in urban settings, had difficulties with living in the country. Although there were some problems, she notes that was "very lucky to have parents like them. He made me read and she made me write" (homepage).

She attended the University of Newcastle upon Tyne and studied English and law. These areas were chosen because, as she puts it, she "was not sure what to do. So many careers start by accident" (homepage). In 1975, she moved to London to begin work as a solicitor with the Crown Prosecution Service. She worked on a wide range of cases for 15 years, including numerous homicide cases, "before the bureaucracy sent [her] stark, staring mad" (homepage).

During the 1970s, she began writing romantic stories for women's magazines. She was married briefly, but it did not last, and even though she believed she wasn't suited for marriage, she felt "bitterly ashamed" after the breakup and "hid indoors" (homepage). During that time, she began writing her first novel and as she puts it, "discovered [her] vocation" (homepage).

MAJOR WORKS AND THEMES

She has published several novels under her real name of Frances Hegarty, but the bulk of her mystery and suspense novels are published under the name of Frances Fyfield. She writes two series that feature women attorneys. One series follows the cases of Crown Prosecutor Helen West and her partner Detective Superintendent Geoffrey Bailey. Fyfield's other series focuses on an attorney named Sarah Fortune.

The West and Bailey series combines aspects of the courtroom drama with police procedurals, showing the investigation and prosecution phrases of cases involving murder, domestic abuse, and other issues. In *A Question of Guilt,* a murder-for-hire scheme is more than it initially appears, and in *Without Consent,* a colleague and friend of Bailey's is accused of serial rape. *Deep Sleep* features a case of possible suicide that looks suspicious to West. West and Bailey navigate their professional ties in solving and prosecuting cases while developing a personal relationship. Relationships are never easy in Fyfield novels. As Gary J. McCallum points out, Fyfield's characters are "almost invariably widowed, divorced or unhappily married" with unfaithful spouses, disturbed children and dysfunctional families (290). Her portrayal of West and Bailey's relationship is less negative, and as McCallum noted, is the only functional relationship in her fictional works (290).

The Fortune novels are even darker and more suspenseful. The first two novels feature Fortune's tracking of a psychotic man who violently abused his wife and later targets Fortune, and the third novel has Fortune involved in a dangerous case involving twin brothers, one of whom is a (perhaps) reformed bomb-maker. Fear of dentists and, more generally, disfigurement play a role in this novel, as it also does in *Blind Date.* Along with the case, the plot "explores the nature of true love and natural virtue" (O'Donoghue 1999:23).

In addition to dealing with sordid cases, Fortune has a remarkable sideline in addition to her work as a lawyer. Recovering from a nasty marriage, Fortune chooses to serve as a prostitute of sorts for men whom she feels she will be able to help emotionally (James 390). Heather O'Donoghue called Fortune "a tart with a heart, sleeping with several different men more from kindness than passion" (1999:23). Ensuing relationships with her select companions are not surprisingly fraught with problems. Fyfield, who calls Fortune her favorite character, notes that Fortune enters prostitution to escape a job she hates but continues because "she's just naturally promiscuous" (homepage).

Other stand-alone novels published by Fyfield echo the themes of the Fortune series, with violence against women being a common motif. In *Blind Date,* Elisabeth Kennedy, a police detective on a disability retirement due to an acid attack that left her disfigured, solves her half-sister's murder, but the culprit is released on a legal technicality. He later kills himself, but doubts arise about whether he was the killer. Fyfield weaves together plot lines involving women who come to harm after signing up for a dating service and Kennedy's relationships with her nephew and neighbor. Heather O'Donoghue called it "a fable about the collision between the enduring dream of one-to-one romance and the contemporary reality of knowing scarcely the first thing about your potential soulmate" (1998:22).

In *Undercurrents* a man comes to England to search for a long-lost love, only to find she has been imprisoned for killing her child. He cannot reconcile this with his memories of her, and having gotten some strange reactions from townspeople and her family, he begins to investigate the case on his own in what one reviewer called "a grim, tense story about regret, loneliness and leaving well enough alone" (Zaleski 2001:64).

CRITICAL RECEPTION

Fyfield's first novel, *A Question of Guilt*, was nominated for an Edgar Award for best novel and an Agatha Award for best first novel. She was awarded the Crime Writers Association Silver Dagger Award in 1991 for *Deep Sleep*, another of the West and Bailey novels.

One review praised Fyfield for taking on issues of domestic assault in *A Clear Conscience* without treating the subject in a "movie of the week" style, but rather offering a "subtle and nuanced" exploration with "vividly drawn" characters and a literary style ("Notes" 132). In *Without Consent*, Fyfield's portrayal of the victimized women caught Marilyn Stasio's attention. Stasio noted that Fyfield's "unflinching characterizations … bristle with wounding insights into the pathology of women who conspire in their own manipulation" and that her portrayal of West's reactions to sexual issues are an example of the "human complication that gives the edge to Fyfield's smart novels" (44).

Fyfield is credited with "a knack for creating twisted characters" and in *Staring at the Light* her "Dickensian cast gratifies" as she "elaborate[s] themes of dependency and revenge" (Zaleski 2000: 48). Heather O'Donoghue applauded the suspense in the novel, where characters are "tantalizingly unaware" of a key link and "are constantly within a hair's breadth of making a connection which would alert them to danger" (1999:23).

Elsa Pendleton noted that *Without Consent* was an excellent police procedural, but that *Blind Date* is even better. She continued: "Fyfield goes beyond the mystery genre" to take her place among the women suspense writers like Ruth Rendell and Minette Walters "who are unafraid to create characters all too aware of their shortcomings" (Pendleton 131). David Pitt concurred that *Blind Date* was a "unique and fascinating psychological thriller" with a protagonist who is most often viewed through other characters' eyes, "as if she's so afraid that she resists appearing in her own novel" (1975).

BIBLIOGRAPHY

Works by Frances Fyfield

Helen West & Geoffrey Bailey Series

A Question of Guilt. New York: Pocket, 1989.
Not That Kind of Place. New York: Pocket, 1990. (Also published as *Trial by Fire*)
Deep Sleep. New York: Pocket, 1991.
Shadow Play. New York: Pantheon, 1993.
A Clear Conscience. New York: Pantheon, 1995.
Without Consent. New York: Viking, 1997.

Sarah Fortune Series

Shadows on the Mirror. New York: Pocket, 1991.
Perfectly Pure and Good. New York: Pantheon, 1994.

Staring at the Light. New York: Viking, 2000.
Looking Down. London: Little, Brown, 2004.
Safer Than Houses. London: Little, Brown, 2005.

Other Novels

Blind Date. New York: Penguin, 2000.
Undercurrents. New York: Viking, 2001.
The Art of Drowning. London: Little, Brown, 2006.

Works Published as Frances Hegarty

The Playroom. New York: Pocket, 1991.
Half Light. New York: Pocket, 1992.
Let's Dance. London: Viking, 1995.

Works about Frances Fyfield

Frances Fyfield. Home page. http://www.figuresdestyle.com/fyfield/index_en.htm 26 April 2005.

"Frances Hegarty." *Contemporary Authors.* Vol. 84, New Revision Series. Ed. Scot Peacock. Detroit: Gale, 2000. 204–206.

James, Dean. "Frances Fyfield." *St. James Guide to Crime & Mystery Writers.* 4th ed. Ed. Jay P. Pederson. Detroit: St. James Press, 1996. 389–90.

McCallum, Gary J. "A Promiscuous Sympathy: Some Notes on the Novels of Frances Fyfield." *The Armchair Detective* 28.3 (1995): 288–91.

"Notes on Current Books: *A Clear Conscience.*" *Virginia Quarterly Review* 71.4 (1995): 132.

O'Donoghue, Heather. "*Blind Date.*" *Times Literary Supplement* 30 January 1998: 22.

———. "Fortune and Her Follies." *Times Literary Supplement* 5 February 1999: 23.

Pendleton, Elsa. "*Blind Date.*" *Library Journal* August 1998: 131.

Pitt, David. "*Blind Date.*" *Booklist* August 1998: 1975.

Stasio, Marilyn. "Crime." *New York Times Book Review* 23 November 1997: 44.

Zaleski, Jeff. "*Staring at the Light.*" *Publishers Weekly* 10 January 2000: 48.

———. "*Undercurrents.*" *Publishers Weekly* 5 March 2001: 64.

Carolina García-Aguilera (1949–)

BIOGRAPHY

Born on July 13, 1949, in Havana, Cuba, Carolina García-Aguilera came to the United States in 1959 with her parents, Carlos García-Beltran, an agricultural engineer, and Lourdes Aguilera de García, and her siblings. They lived in Palm Beach for several years before moving to New York.

From an early age, she loved detective fiction, from Nancy Drew and beyond. She has reported that she was one of the youngest members of the Sherlock Holmes Society (Newcomb B2). Although she had always dreamed of writing mysteries, she earned a bachelor's degree in history and political science from Rollins College in 1971 and was working on a master's degree in linguistics at Georgetown when she married. She lived abroad with her husband in Hong Kong, Tokyo, and Beijing. They spent eight years in Beijing, and her two older daughters, Sara and Antonia, were born there.

They returned to the United States in 1981, and she studied finance at the University of South Florida, earning an MBA degree in 1983. When her first marriage ended, she moved to Miami to be close to family and worked in hospital administration. She remarried and had her youngest daughter, Gabriella.

Her interest in writing mysteries continued to outweigh her other interests, and she decided to become a private investigator to learn about the field so she could write effective fiction about detectives. After completing training, she was licensed as a private investigator and later managed her own firm, C & J Investigations in Miami. Ten years of experience working as an investigator gave her the background she desired to begin writing a mystery series, and her first novel was published in 1996. She lives with her family in Miami Beach.

MAJOR WORKS AND THEMES

Most of García-Aguilera's work is in the Lupe Solano series. Solano, like García-Aguilera, comes from a family of Cuban exiles. Her father keeps up a boat expressly for the purpose of being able to return to Cuba as soon as Castro falls. Solano runs a private investigation firm, with her cousin serving as assistant. Throughout the series, several cases bring Solano into conflicts involving the Cuban community in Miami, and people who are involved in the pro- and anti-Castro movements. Issues regarding her family and conflicts between traditional and contemporary mores also play a large role in the novels. Although she runs her own business, Solano often sleeps at her parents' house. Although she wears religious medals pinned to her bra, she is sexually liberated. Although she is tough in her work as a private investigator, she adores designer clothes and other luxury items.

Her first few cases involve illegal adoptions, finding the truth behind the self-defense claim of a jeweler who killed a burglar, and solving a case surrounding stolen family fortunes. *Miracle in Paradise* finds Solano investigating a case involving a group of nuns who are predicting a miracle. In *Havana Heat,* Solano takes a case involving art left behind by Cuban exiles and risks everything to sneak back into Cuba to interview a source. In *Bitter Sugar,* Solano helps a family friend find out what happened to his family's land in Cuba while also solving the death of the man's nephew.

In addition to the Solano series, García-Aguilera has written two stand-alone novels. *One Hot Summer* features a successful Cuban-American lawyer, Margarita Santos Silva, who risks her marriage by rekindling a relationship with an American she knew in college. Santos Silva also deals with having to choose between her legal career and staying at home with her young son. The second novel, *Luck of the Draw,* turns back toward the mystery genre, but this time with an amateur sleuth. In this novel, Esmeralda Navarro Montoya must search for her missing sister in Las Vegas. She joins forces with a retired police detective to solve the case.

CRITICAL RECEPTION

García-Aguilera's first novel was deemed a "great success" in its use of "standard mystery formula" with "subtle twists" (Klett 1996:102), but another reviewer found it to be "more melodrama than mystery" (Brainard 1996b: 61). These reviewers again split in their assessments of the second novel in the series, with one calling it "an essential purchase" with its "colorful characters" and "upbeat, witty, and engaging plot" (Klett 1997:110) and the other criticizing the plot and lamenting that Solano, "rather than evolving into a complex character, is morphing into a banal admirer of luxury consumer goods" (Brainard 1996a:58).

A review of the third novel posited that her experience as a private investigator set her work above others, noting that "surveillance scenes are well-drafted, making even the most mundane routine sound interesting" but that it was García-Aguilera's "detailed attention to her heritage that puts the unique spin on this series" (Cogdill 1998:11D). Another reviewer praised García-Aguilera for works that are "fast-paced and brimming with energy" and that "are energized by the cultural fetishes inherent in Latinos, as well as the realistic characters" she portrays (Ponce 44).

Miracle in Paradise was heralded as a "memorable tale of Cuban-American life" that "boasts an engaging plot and a fiery heroine armed with sharp insights into Cuban and Catholic ways that will lead readers happily into the sultry heat of Little Havana" (Zaleski 79). *Havana Heat,* which won a Shamus Award, was praised for its combination of "a clever plot and an endearing protagonist with a fascinating portrayal of Cuba's turbulent history and vibrant culture" (McLarin 2119). Another reviewer also recommended this novel for its "stunning mixture of art history, Cubans-in-exile politics, a uniquely classy Miami heroine, and riveting plot" (Klett 2000:254).

Oline H. Cogdill noted in her review of *Bitter Sugar* that "the vagaries of culture, identity and tropical politics are skillfully woven into" García-Aguilera's writing, and cited a particularly moving scene in which Solano realizes that only one photograph of her family made the journey with them from Cuba (2001:11G). Another reviewer noted that "Lupe cracks the case with style and a sense of humor and teaches readers a bit about Cuba in the process" (Bissey 301).

BIBLIOGRAPHY

Works by Carolina García-Aguilera

Lupe Solano Series

Bloody Waters. New York: Putnam, 1996.
Bloody Shame. New York: Putnam, 1997.
Bloody Secrets. New York: Putnam, 1998.
A Miracle in Paradise. New York: Putnam, 1999.
Havana Heat. New York: Morrow, 2000.
Bitter Sugar. New York: Morrow, 2001.

Other Novels

One Hot Summer. New York: Rayo, 2002.
Luck of the Draw. New York: Rayo, 2003.

Works about Carolina García-Aguilera

Bissey, Carrie. "*Bitter Sugar.*" *Booklist* 1 October 2001: 301.
Brainard, Dulcy. "*Bloody Shame.*" *Publishers Weekly* 30 December 1996a: 58.
———. "*Bloody Waters.*" *Publishers Weekly* 8 January 1996b: 61.
Carolina García-Aguilera. Homepage. 2001. 15 June 2005. http://www.carolinaontheweb.com
Cogdill, Oline H. "Justice in Exile: Loyalties Blur when a Cuban-American Sleuth is Asked to Right a Decades Old Wrong." *Sun Sentinel* 1 February 1998: 11D.
———. "Exploring Cuban Exiles' Lost Heritage." *South Florida Sun Sentinel* 28 October 2001: 11G.
Klett, Rex E. "*Bloody Waters.*" *Publishers Weekly* 1 February 1996: 102.

———. "*Bloody Shame.*" *Publishers Weekly* 1 February 1997: 110.
———. "*Havana Heat.*" *Library Journal* 1 September 2000: 254.
McLarin, Jenny. "*Havana Heat.*" *Booklist* August 2000: 2119.
Newcomb, Amelia. "Miami Private Investigator Is Now on Her Own as Author." *Christian Science Monitor* 25 July 1996: B2.
Ponce, Mary Helen. "Latino Sleuths: Hispanic Mystery Writers Make Crime Pay." *Hispanic* May 1998: 44.
Sutton, Molly. "Carolina García-Aguilera." *VG: Voices from the Gaps: Women Artists and Writers of Color.* 2002. 13 June 2005. http://voices.cla.umn.edu/vg/Bios/entries/garciaaguilera_carolina.html
Zaleski, Jeff. "*Miracle in Paradise.*" *Publishers Weekly* 20 September 1999: 78–79.

Anne George (d. 2001)

BIOGRAPHY

Anne Carroll George was a native of Alabama, and before starting her mystery series, she was known in other writing circles as a Pulitzer Prize-nominated poet. She was a graduate of Samford University, and she also had a master's degree in English. In addition to her writing career, she had taught high school English. With Jerri Beck, she founded Druid Press in the early 1980s, with the intention of increasing readers' access to poetry and literature. She won numerous awards for her poetry and was extremely proud of having been named the Samford University Alumna of the Year (Bell).

She and her husband Earl had a son and a daughter. She died on March 14, 2001, during heart surgery.

MAJOR WORKS AND THEMES

George wrote a series of mysteries featuring two sisters, Patricia Anne "Mouse" Hollowell and Mary Alice "Sister" Crane. The two live in Birmingham, Alabama, and are opposites in many ways, including obvious physical traits. Crane, impulsive, is six feet tall and heavyset; Hollowell, a retired schoolteacher, is sensible and barely over five feet. The sisters first appeared in a short story, based on a real incident that happened to George and a cousin (George 2000:12). In the story, the two sisters are arguing in an antique mall when a tornado arrives, and they end up continuing their argument while seeking shelter from the storm by hiding under a table. As George noted in her essay in *The Writer,* her novels are character driven (11), with an emphasis on a humorous voice (12). She also recounted her research approaches, which involved asking her veterinarian about how to "kill a woman with hair products" and checking with the officers at a sheriff's substation in a shopping mall about which law enforcement agency would be called to investigate a dead body on the beach (12–13).

In the first novel, Hollowell is drawn into a mystery when Crane buys a country-western music club. The two sisters get involved in solving a number of crimes throughout the series, including solving a murder during a wedding, solving the murder of a neighbor, and solving the disappearance of a daughter-in-law.

In addition to her mysteries and her works of poetry, George also published one non-mystery novel entitled *The One and Magic Life,* which follows a Southern family that is dealing with life and death.

CRITICAL RECEPTION

Her first novel won an Agatha Award and was also nominated for a Macavity. Critical response was favorable. Her first novel was praised for its "refreshingly different heroine," "sprightly dialogue," and "humorous eye for detail" (Steinberg 66).

The second novel, *Murder Runs in the Family,* was critiqued for weak plotting, but the "wonderful dialogue" and strong character development and descriptions were praised (Simson 71). *Murder Makes Waves* received a similar review, with praise for "enjoyable characters and light humor [that] compensate for a plot that's hardly unique" (Klett 130), as did *Murder Gets a Life,* with a reviewer noting that "the down-home humor, sisterly squabbling and a zany supporting cast will likely make up for the fragile plot" (Brainard 81).

In a review of *Murder Shoots the Bull,* George was praised for having "a sure touch for creating comedic dialogue and believable characters" in creating an "amusing romp of a mystery that makes good use of the tradition of Southern eccentricity, exuding a properly cozy atmosphere and a nifty web of subplots and domestic complications" (Zaleski 1999: 71).

A reviewer of *Murder Carries a Torch* found the sisters to be "great company" and noted that they had "grow[n] in depth and delight" (DeCandido 1616). Another reviewer called it "genuinely funny," with "hilarious dialogue and small details [that] enrich a plot that's spread thin" (Zaleski 2000:63). Her final novel was praised for having "dialogue so true and natural that it could go straight to stage or film" (Cannon 51).

BIBLIOGRAPHY

Works by Anne George

Southern Sisters Series

Murder on a Girls' Night Out. New York: Avon, 1996.
Murder on a Bad Hair Day. New York: Avon, 1996.
Murder Runs in the Family. New York: Avon, 1997.
Murder Makes Waves. New York: Avon, 1997.
Murder Gets a Life. New York: Avon, 1998.
Murder Shoots the Bull. New York: Morrow, 1999.
Murder Carries a Torch. New York: Morrow, 2000.
Murder Boogies with Elvis. New York: Morrow, 2001.

Other Works

Dreamer, Dreaming Me. Birmingham: University of Alabama in Birmingham, 1980.
Wild Goose Chase. Birmingham: Druid Press, 1982.
Spraying Under the Bed for Wolves. Birmingham: Druid Press, 1985.
Editor, with Jerri Beck. *A Baker's Dozen: Contemporary Women Poets of Alabama*. Birmingham: Druid Press, 1988.
Some of It Is True: Poems. Carrollton, GA: Curbow Publications, 1993.
This One and Magic Life: A Novel of a Southern Family. New York: Avon, 1999.
The Map That Lies between Us: New and Collected Poems, 1980–2000. Montgomery: Black Belt Press, 2000.
"Stress-Free Turkeys and Murder." *The Writer* June 2000: 10–13.

Works about Anne George

"Anne Carroll George." *Contemporary Authors*. New Revision Series, Vol. 130. Ed. Tracey Watson. Detroit: Gale, 2006. 158–60.

Brainard, Dulcy. *"Murder Gets a Life."* *Publishers Weekly* 23 March 1998: 81.
Cannon, Peter. *"Murder Boogies With Elvis."* *Publishers Weekly* 9 July 2001: 51.
DeCandido, GraceAnne A. *"Murder Carries a Torch"* *Booklist* 1 May 2000: 1616.
Klett, Rex E. *"Murder Makes Waves."* *Library Journal* July 1997: 130.
Simson, Maria. *"Murder Runs in the Family."* *Publishers Weekly* 14 April 1997: 71.
Steinberg, Sybil S. *"Murder on a Girls' Night Out."* *Publishers Weekly* 22 January 1996: 66.
Zaleski, Jeff. *"Murder Shoots the Bull."* *Publishers Weekly* 24 May 1999: 71.
———. *Murder Carries a Torch.* *Publishers Weekly* 19 June 2000: 63.

Elizabeth George (1949–)

BIOGRAPHY

Many readers have been surprised to learn that Susan Elizabeth George was born in Warren, Ohio, rather than in the United Kingdom, on February 26, 1949. Her father, Robert Edwin George, worked as a salesman for a conveyor company and her mother, Anne Rivelle George, was a nurse. She has one older brother. At a young age, the family moved to San Francisco, partially because her father "hated the Midwestern weather" and also because he "wanted to get his wife away from her large Italian family" (Stenger 133). George notes that she missed not having an extended family nearby while growing up.

Her parents encouraged creative and imaginative activities and endowed her with a love of reading. She began writing at a young age, telling one interviewer she "knew from the age of seven that [she] was meant to be a writer" and at age 12, she turned out her first novel, a Nancy Drew-like story called "The Mystery of Horseshoe Lake" (Fryxell 32).

She became interested in British literature and pop culture in the 1960s, during the pop music "British Invasion," and she first went to London in 1966 for a summer course in Shakespeare (Stenger 133). This experience solidified her love for all things English, and she studied English literature in college, graduating with a bachelor's degree and secondary teaching credentials from the University of California, Riverside in 1970. She married a fellow student named Ira Jay Toibin in 1971; they divorced in 1995.

George's teaching career got off to a rocky start, as she was fired from her first job for taking part in union activities (Stenger 133). Soon hired by another school, she taught high school English there until 1987. She also earned a master's degree in counseling and psychology in 1979, and was honored in 1981 as the Orange County Teacher of the Year.

When her husband bought a computer in 1983, she realized she should stop thinking about writing a novel and use the new tool to actually do it. Her first novel was written in two months and focused on the Simon St. James character. She began traveling to England during summer vacations to do research and completed another manuscript about St. James. Both of these were rejected, but she persevered, and her third novel was accepted by Bantam. She quit teaching full-time in 1987, but she continues to teach creative writing courses and seminars. Her papers and manuscripts, except for the manuscript of the first novel, are held by Boston University's Mugar Library. She resides in Huntington Beach, California, and spends a great deal of time each year in England.

MAJOR WORKS AND THEMES

George has characterized her work as "whydunits" rather than "whodunits, noting that her interests lie in the "psychology of her characters and the dynamics of dysfunctional families" rather than solving the mystery (Stenger 133). As Carl D. Malmgren puts it, the solution to the case, "cannot be revealed by the cool calculation of an armchair detective" but rather "must be wrung from the parties involved in a face-to-face confrontation that leads to the most heart-wrenching kind of exposure" (51).

George is credited with writing books in British English, successfully capturing the tone and vocabulary, although she notes that critics who know she isn't British "generally try to pick at something" (Kreck I1). Carol Kreck noted that George has accomplished her mastery of the "slang and mannerisms of two disparate English classes" with a great deal of research and work (I1). George's series deals directly with issues of those two classes as portrayed in her two protagonists, Thomas Lynley and Barbara Havers. Tommy Lynley often obscures, or attempts to obscure, the fact that he is also known as Lord Asherton, whereas Havers comes from a working-class background. The differences in their families, upbringing, and general outlook on life often factor into their professional work. Lynley has not had an easy life by some measures, but the privilege he enjoys makes his problems seem less severe than the ones Havers has faced in her life.

In their first case together, Havers and Lynley uncover the secrets behind a patricide, exposing a family history of molestation. In the follow-up, *Payment in Blood,* a true crime writer is murdered in a country house setting that evokes the traditional British mystery and certainly provides a number of suspects. Lynley's old friend, forensic scientist Simon Allcourt-St. James, takes part in the investigation, as he does throughout the series. The three tackle a murder case at Lynley's old school in *Well-Schooled in Murder,* uncovering pedophilia and blackmail in the process. Academia also provides the setting in *For the Sake of Elena,* where they solve the murder of a female university student.

As the series continues, the novels become more and more complex. As George admits, she wrote *A Great Deliverance* in less than a month, but the research and rough draft for *In Pursuit of the Proper Sinner* took 15 months (Kreck I1). Karl L. Stenger sees her "concern for the psychology of her characters" increase with the size of the novels, noting that in *Playing for the Ashes,* only one murder takes place, Lynley doesn't appear until page 204 of the 517-page novel, and the "psychological development and tangled relationships" of all the characters are the focus (139). In describing her writing process, George relates that "each character gets a physical description, a family history and a 'pathology,' a particular psychological maneuver that he engages in when he's under stress" (Fryxell 33).

Havers's character is strongly developed throughout the series and readers see more of her life, particularly her relationship to her Pakistani neighbors. In *Deception on His Mind,* Havers follows Taymullah Azhar and his daughter to their vacation spot in Essex when a Pakistani is murdered there and violence erupts. Events at the conclusion of that story lead to Havers's demotion. *In Pursuit of the Proper Sinner* centers around Lynley's distancing himself from Havers. They become engrossed in a case involving murder and prostitution, and Lynley is faced with a situation similar to the one Havers had faced, where he must choose between what he thinks is right and what follows protocol.

George has also written a guide to writing entitled *Write Away.* The work covers the basics of the craft of writing, such as plot, character, setting, and dialogue, and also outlines her philosophies of teaching writing and being a writer. She does not subscribe to the well-known piece of writing advice regarding writing about what one knows, noting that limiting oneself only to what one knows can limit one's learning (Kreck I1). She also dismisses the notion that writing cannot be taught, and she thinks that American fiction is "alive and well" because American novelists are willing to teach the craft of writing (Kreck I1).

CRITICAL RECEPTION

Reception to her first novel was quite favorable, and *A Great Deliverance* won Anthony and Agatha awards for best first novel in 1989. Her work has been steadily popular and well received ever since, although the tragic plot twist in *With No One as Witness* angered many fans and readers, who have been vocal on email lists and in online chat rooms that they will never read her work again (O'Briant G1; Fox D22). George was "surprised by the intensity of the criticism," noting that her intentions are always to grow as a writer (O'Briant G1).

George is renowned for her solid character development, providing portraits of interesting, well-rounded human characters. P. G. Koch has noted that she "grants even seemingly peripheral characters their rich and complete due" (23). *In Pursuit of a Proper Sinner* also brought accolades for her "rich and complex British mystery, masterfully plotted, thoughtful and bursting with clever complications" (Zvirin 1894). In a review of the same novel, Margo Kaufman stated that George "is a genius at drawing psychological revelations from an act as casual as choosing wallpaper" (3). Kaufman noted an abundance of red herrings and a dense plot with a number of characters readers are expected to know, but cited Havers's search for redemption and the "moving climax" as effective (3).

A Traitor to Memory was deemed to be a "masterly performance" which "embrace[s] the narrative depth and reflective pace of the 19th-century novel" (Koch 23). *A Place of Hiding,* which focused on Simon Allcourt-St. James and his wife, brought recognition of George's achievement in complex plotting, along with her carefully detailed settings, this time in Guernsey (Kelly D4).

BIBLIOGRAPHY

Works by Elizabeth George

Thomas Lynley and Barbara Havers Series

A Great Deliverance. New York: Bantam, 1988.
Payment in Blood. New York: Bantam, 1989.
Well-Schooled in Murder. New York: Bantam, 1990.
A Suitable Vengeance New York: Bantam, 1991.
For the Sake of Elena. New York: Bantam, 1992.
Missing Joseph. New York: Bantam, 1993.
Playing for the Ashes. New York: Bantam, 1994.
In the Presence of the Enemy. New York: Bantam, 1996.
Deception on His Mind. New York: Bantam, 1997.
In Pursuit of the Proper Sinner. New York: Bantam, 1999.
A Traitor to Memory. New York: Bantam, 2001.
A Place of Hiding. New York: Bantam, 2003.
With No One as Witness. New York: Bantam, 2005.
What Came Before He Shot Her. New York: HarperCollins, 2006.

Other Works by Elizabeth George

The Evidence Exposed. London: Hodder & Stoughton, 1999.

I, Richard: Stories of Suspense. New York: Bantam, 2002.

Write Away: One Novelist's Approach to Fiction and the Writing Life. New York: HarperCollins, 2004.

Works about Elizabeth George

Bakerman, Jane S. "Elizabeth George." *St. James Guide to Crime & Mystery Writers.* 4th ed. Ed. Jay P. Pederson. Detroit: St. James Press, 1996. 407–408.

"Elizabeth George." *Contemporary* Authors. Vol. 112, New Revision Series. Ed. Scot Peacock. Detroit: Gale, 2003. 119–22.

Fox, Ben. "George Fans Take Umbrage." *Vancouver Sun* 7 May 2005: D22.

Fryxell, David A. "The Core Need of Elizabeth George." *Writers Digest* February 2002: v32–33, 60.

Kaufman, Margo. "Insight into Complex Characters in *Sinner's Salvation*." *Los Angeles Times* 22 September 1999: 3.

Kelly, Susan. "*Place of Hiding* Is a Murder Most Interesting." *USA Today* 21 August 2003: D4.

Koch, P. G. "Elizabeth George's New Winner." *Houston Chronicle* 1 July 2001: 23.

Kreck, Carol. "How to Speak British: No. 1 Writer of English Mysteries is a Californian." *Denver Post* 12 September 1999: I1.

Malmgren, Carl D. "Truth, Justice and the American Way: Martha Grimes and Elizabeth George." *Clues* 21.2 (2000): 47–56.

O'Briant, Don. "Novel's Dark Ending Stirs Readers' Fury." *Atlanta Journal-Constitution* 8 April 2005: G1.

Stenger, Karl L. "Elizabeth George." *Dictionary of Literary Biography.* Vol. 306. Ed. George Parker Anderson. Detroit: Gale, 2005. 132–43.

Zvirin, Stephanie. "*In Pursuit of the Proper Sinner*." *Booklist* July 1999: 1893–94.

Sue Grafton (1940–)

BIOGRAPHY

Sue Grafton was born April 24, 1940, to Vivian Harnsberger and Cornelius Warren "Chip" Grafton. She grew up in Louisville, Kentucky. Her mother had taught chemistry and her father was an attorney who also had written several mystery novels. She and her sister Ann grew up in a home filled with books, but both parents were alcoholics. Grafton was "left to her own devices" much of the time, but she notes that it was good training for being a writer (Kay 177). She has given extensive interviews about her childhood, and in "*G*" *Is for Grafton,* Natalie Hevener Kaufman and Carol McGinnis Kay draw a number of parallels between Grafton's childhood and the history she created for Kinsey Millhone.

Grafton was a voracious reader as a child, and she credits her parents with providing her with access to books and instilling a love for reading. She studied English at the University of Kentucky, earning a bachelor's degree in 1961.

Grafton married soon after college and had two children. The marriage ended in divorce, as did her second marriage, during which she had a third child. After another failed relationship, she met Stephen Humphrey in 1974, and they have been married since 1978.

MAJOR WORKS AND THEMES

During the 1960s, Grafton wrote seven novels, five of which remain unpublished. Two of them were published, and one of them, *The Lolly-Madonna Wars,* was made into a movie by MGM. During the 1970s, Grafton worked steadily as a television writer, working for shows such as "Rhoda" and adapting numerous novels into teleplays. She grew tired of the politics in Hollywood, realized she worked better alone than writing in committee, and in 1977 began brainstorming ideas for a female hard-boiled private eye, in the tradition of Philip Marlowe or Sam Spade.

In 1982, her first mystery novel was published, and she has continued writing in the genre ever since. Beginning with *A Is for Alibi,* the series features Kinsey Millhone, a private investigator in the fictionalized setting of Santa Teresa, California (a tribute to Ross MacDonald who used the name for his version of Santa Barbara). Millhone is as tough as traditional male hard-boiled heroes, unafraid to use her weapon or enter into dangerous situations, although she prides herself on conducting research and interviews to gain the necessary background information (Reynolds 135). On the personal side, Millhone also resembles the traditional male private investigators. She is an orphan, with few ties and few possessions, or as Moira Davison Reynolds puts it, "a woman without children, pets or house plants" (135), although she is quite attached to her octogenarian landlord, Henry. Grafton believes that women readers are "looking for a mirror rather than an escape," and Millhone therefore "reflects the complicated lives of women," although tough, she is not lacking in sentiment, she is independent-minded, and she juggles demands of her work and her personal life (DuBose 387). Millhone also represents typical human contradictions: she loves junk food buts gets up every morning to run, no matter what.

The novels are styled as reports about her cases, with introductory material about herself and the case, and a closing phrase: Respectfully submitted, Kinsey Millhone. (*"P" Is for Peril* omitted the closing line, and numerous discussions about that took place on email lists and in chat rooms.) Grafton has been careful to make clear what year it is in the novels; Millhone does not age in accordance with the publication dates of the books. In *"R" is for Ricochet,* published in 2004, the series timeline has reached 1987, still long before cell phones, the Internet, and other tools frequently used by present-day detectives. Throughout the series, Millhone tackles a variety of cases, including missing persons, fraud, and murder that allow her to explore various social issues including family, domestic violence, child abuse, prostitution, discrimination, and the justice system. Her personal life also develops throughout, with her learning more about her family and meeting distant cousins in *"J" Is for Judgment.* In *"O" Is for Outlaw,* she investigates the death of her ex-husband, which leads her to reevaluate their relationship and her own life. *"Q" Is for Quarry* marked the first time Grafton used a real case as a basis. At the end of the book are included several reconstructed portraits of a woman killed in 1969, who remains unidentified. Grafton's plot is a fictionalized account of what might have happened to her, but Grafton wanted to raise awareness of how many unidentified victims there are and hoped that the forensic reconstruction work would help close that part of the case. In *"R" Is for Ricochet,* Millhone also accepts help from a sidekick character for the first time, sharing aspects of the investigation with an amateur in ways she had not done before.

CRITICAL RECEPTION

Although some reviews of the early novels were less favorable, and most reviewers and readers agreed that *"L" Is for Lawless* is a weaker entry in the series, Grafton's works since

"*F*" *Is for Fugitive* has been widely praised and commercially successful. In addition to Anthony and Macavity awards, she was the first woman to win a Shamus Award. Most reviewers think "*J*" *Is for Judgment* is the best in the series, and it is Grafton's own favorite (Kay 184).

Most recent reviews note the growth and sustained excellence of the series. For example, a review of "*P*" *Is for Peril* stated that "as the alphabet mystery series has progressed, so has Sue Grafton's writing style," further noting that Millhone "has developed from a one-dimensional female version of the hard-boiled private eye into a complex and thoroughly likeable character whose eccentricities only add to her subversive charm" ("P" 57). Another review noted that "Grafton writes with assurance, and her ability to mix this stew of self-important medical people, rebellious teens, and good-natured neighbors speaks to her ability to create a satisfying read" (Hennrikus D8). A third review stated that even when Grafton's works are not "perfect," she shows her "genius in molding a character who lingers in your memory long after the novel is finished" (Smith L1).

Given Grafton's status as one of the first women writers to introduce a woman detective in the hard-boiled style, numerous works of literary criticism have appeared, including the book-length study, "*G*" *Is for Grafton.* The book is fascinating for Grafton fans, looking at all aspects of Millhone's life and cases, with charts, quotes, and photographs from places in Santa Barbara that are featured in the books. Other examples of critical essays include Scott Christianson's exploration of the Grafton novels as they challenge patriarchy and assert feminine autonomy, looking specifically at Millhone's use of language and violence. Priscilla L. Walton and Manina Jones looked at women's detective novels and their treatment of clothing in an examination of gender roles in various novels. Millhone's famous black dress, all purpose, polyester, often carried in her bag for occasions where she needs to wear something other than jeans, was discussed. That the dress becomes a running joke, surviving Millhone's wearing it underwater, as well as the bomb that damages her apartment in "*E*" *Is for Evidence,* is for Walton and Jones perhaps a symbol of "the embattled status of conventions of femininity" in Grafton's works (101). Peter J. Rabinowitz explored Grafton's first novel in terms of its narrative structure, looking at possible readings of the work within and outside of the convention of the genre.

BIBLIOGRAPHY

Works by Sue Grafton

Kinsey Millhone Series

"*A*" *Is for Alibi.* New York: Holt, 1982.
"*B*" *Is for Burglar.* New York: Holt, 1985.
"*C*" *Is for Corpse.* New York: Holt, 1986.
"*D*" *Is for Deadbeat.* New York: Holt, 1987.
"*E*" *Is for Evidence.* New York: Holt, 1988.
"*F*" *Is for Fugitive.* New York: Holt, 1989.
"*G*" *Is for Gumshoe.* New York: Holt, 1990.
"*H*" *Is for Homicide.* New York: Holt, 1991.
"*I*" *Is for Innocent.* New York: Holt, 1992.
Kinsey and Me. Columbia, SC: Bench Press, 1992.
"*J*" *Is for Judgment.* New York: Holt, 1993.
"*K*" *Is for Killer.* New York: Holt, 1994.
"*L*" *Is for Lawless.* New York: Holt, 1995.
"*M*" *Is for Malice.* New York: Holt, 1996.

"N" Is for Noose. New York: Holt, 1998.
"O" Is for Outlaw. New York: Holt, 1999.
"P" Is for Peril. New York: Putnam, 2001.
"Q" Is for Quarry. New York: Putnam, 2002.
"R" Is for Ricochet. New York: Putnam, 2004.
"S" Is for Silence. New York: Putnam, 2005.

Other Works

Keziah Dane. New York: Macmillan, 1967.
The Lolly-Madonna War. New York: P. Owen, 1969.

Works about Sue Grafton

Christianson, Scott. "Talkin' Trash and Kickin' Butt: Sue Grafton's Hard-boiled Feminism." *Feminism in Women's Detective Fiction.* Ed. Glenwood Irons. Toronto: U Toronto P, 1995. 127–47.
DuBose, Martha Hailey. "Sue Grafton: An Ornery Original." *Women of Mystery: The Lives and Works of Notable Women Crime Novelists.* New York: Thomas Dunne/St. Martin's Minotaur, 2000. 386–92.
Hennrikus, Kathleen. "To the Letter, Grafton Has Mystery Solved." *Boston Globe* 17 August 2001: D8.
Kaufman, Natalie Hevener and Carol McGinnis Kay. *G Is for Grafton: The World of Kinsey Millhone.* Rev. ed. New York: Holt, 2000.
Kay, Carol McGinnis. "Sue Grafton." *Dictionary of Literary Biography,* Vol. 226. *American Hard-Boiled Crime Writers.* Eds. George Parker Anderson and Julie B. Anderson. Detroit: Gale, 2000. 175–87.
""*P* is for Peril." *Virginia Quarterly Review* 78.2 (Spring 2002): 57.
Rabinowitz, Peter J. "'Reader, I blew him away': Convention and Transgression in Sue Grafton." *Famous Last Words: Changes in Gender and Narrative Closure.* Ed. Alison Booth. Charlottesville: U of Virginia P, 1993. 326–44.
Reynolds, Moira Davison. "Sue Grafton." *Women Authors of Detective Series: Twenty-One American and British Writers, 1900–2000.* Jefferson, NC: McFarland, 2001. 132–38.
Smith, Edward P. "*P Is for Profit*: Popular Detective Kinsey Propels Another Grafton Mystery." *Denver Post* 10 June 2001: L1.
"Sue Grafton." *Contemporary Authors.* Vol. 134, New Revision Series. Ed. Tracey L. Matthews. Detroit: Gale, 2005. 74–78.
Swanson, Jean. "Sue Grafton." *Mystery and Suspense Writers: The Literature of Crime, Detection and Espionage.* Eds. Maureen Corrigan and Robin Winks. New York: Scribner's, 1998. 439–48.
Walton, Priscilla L. and Manina Jones. *Detective Agency: Women Rewriting the Hard-Boiled Tradition.* Berkeley: U California P, 1999.

Martha Grimes

BIOGRAPHY

Martha Grimes was born in Pittsburgh, Pennsylvania. Her father, D. W. Grimes, was an attorney and her mother, June Dunnington Grimes, owned a resort hotel, where Grimes grew up. Grimes is divorced with one son.

She earned bachelor's and master's degrees from the University of Maryland and has taught English at Montgomery College, Frostburg State University, and the University of Iowa. She resides in Washington, D.C.

MAJOR WORKS AND THEMES

Although her works are often compared to British masters such as Dorothy L. Sayers, Margery Allingham, and Agatha Christie, Grimes is not British. Like Elizabeth George and Deborah Crombie, Grimes is an American writer who sets her work in England. To fully appreciate Grimes's work, Richard C. Carpenter and Dean James note that readers need "to have a grasp of English topography, customs, modes of expression, the class system, cuisine … and the center of a great deal of English life, the pub," all of which is even more remarkable given her nationality (461). The first novel's title is the name of a pub, and she has continued to use the name of a British pub as the title and/or a setting for each novel. Grimes notes that she was looking at a book about English pub names in 1977, and when she saw the segment about the pub called The Man with a Load of Mischief, she "suddenly knew that's what [she] wanted to do: write books set in English pubs" (qtd in Conroy).

The bulk of Grimes's work comprises the long-running series featuring Richard Jury, a Scotland Yard detective, his aristocratic friend and sidekick Melrose Plant, the solid but hypochondriac Sergeant Wiggins, and a wide array of eccentric characters. Jury is reminiscent of other protagonists in British mysteries: a tall, handsome, cultured, sensitive man with a sharp mind. Grimes noted that neither character was consciously modeled on anyone or any other characters, although she initially intended Melrose Plant to have an Oscar Wilde-style wit. She had to "dispense with this idea" since she herself didn't "have the wit of Oscar Wilde" and realized it "was going to be a little difficult to give him that particular characteristic" (Nolan 61). Her settings also evoke other British mysteries, including village settings a la Agatha Christie, but as Carpenter and James point out, Grimes takes literary allusions and "echoes of the classic mystery" and creates something new and varied in each book (461). She does not consider her works to be in the cozy genre and finds the comparisons to Christie inaccurate (Pate E5).

In addition to the British settings, Grimes also occasionally takes the characters to the United States. In The Horse You Came In On, Jury, Plant, and Wiggins go to Baltimore to solve three "seemingly unrelated murders" that include elements of plagiarism, forgery, Edgar Allan Poe, professional football, genealogy, greed, and love (Melton 1652).

In later works, social issues increasingly underpin the mysteries, with Jury and Plant uncovering pedophilia rings in The Winds of Change, fighting mistreatment of race horses in The Grave Maurice, and exposing corporate greed, along with solving various kidnapping, assault, and murder cases. In some cases, the actual history of the pub plays a role in its namesake novel. In The Blue Last, Jury investigates bodies found in an excavation. The real Blue Last was destroyed in 1940 and the ruins of the pub—with its uncovered skeletons—was the last war-era bomb site cleared in Britain. In the novel, Grimes uses this as a lever to include a parallel story set during wartime and to explore Jury's own memories of his childhood during the Blitz. In The Lamorna Wink, Plant takes center stage solving a case in Cornwall and Devon, away from the usual settings. Grimes gives readers a much fuller portrait of Plant and also plays with some gothic and ghost story elements throughout the plot.

In addition to the Jury series, Grimes has written several stand-alone novels and a set of four novels that focus on the same characters and settings. The stand-alone works include Foul Matter, The Train Now Departing, and Biting the Moon. Foul Matter satirizes the cutthroat nature of the publishing industry, takes on the competitive nature of the publishing business, with writers hiring hit men to clear the way for winning a lucrative contract. Biting the Moon explores issues related to animal rights. Grimes, a vegetarian, donated a portion of her royalties from that book to organizations fighting animal abuse (Silet; Zipp).

The four works that focus on the town of LaPorte are *End of the Pier, Hotel Paradise, Cold Flat Junction*, and *Belle Ruin. End of the Pier* was the first departure from the Jury/Plant series and is set at a later time than the other novels. *Hotel Paradise* introduces a 12-year-old protagonist named Emma Graham, who lives at the hotel run by her parents. Emma becomes obsessed with a drowning that occurred 40 years ago and with some mysteries in her own family history. Although there are parallels between Emma's life and Grimes' childhood, Grimes is clear that the setting is autobiographical but the plot is not (Pate E5). She has stated in several interviews that she is dismayed that critics and readers do not want her to write outside the mystery genre and outside the Jury series. In addition to her novels, Grimes published a book of poetry, which has been called a mystery in verse, featuring a detective named Bygraves (Zipp; Pate E5).

CRITICAL RECEPTION

Grimes's work can evoke the spirit and sensibility of the classic British mystery, but her works are definitely modern and beyond the cozy genre. As Carl D. Malmgren noted, Grimes "presents[s] us with a grittier version of reality" than the classic British mysteries, with treatment of unemployment, alcoholism, treatment of the elderly, and other social issues that are more often seen in hard-boiled fiction than in English village mysteries (48). In addition, a number of plots involve children or young people who are exposed to the violence in the world. Grimes's work often includes a "precocious but forlorn child" who joins the story ("Cold" 135). Yet, Grimes's use of humor is also heralded by critics. In one of her reviews, Emily Melton stated that Grimes may be the "funniest of all mystery writers" given her "delicious, dry wit, wonderfully understated sense of humor and eclectic, eccentric characters" (1993:1652).

One critic examined her recently reissued earlier works and noted that *The Old Fox Deceiv'd* offered an intricate plot, natural humor, and a "denouement [that] is arresting" (Pais 26). This critic also reviewed *Help the Poor Struggler,* heralding "excellent pacing, superb plotting and a revealing climax" (Pais 26). These sentiments match other reviews of her work.

Typical praise for Grimes was seen in a review for *The Lamorna Wink.* Jeff Zaleski acclaimed her "richly portrayed characters and stunningly described settings" along with "a tangled plot strewn with a host of genuine clues, as well as red herrings that beguile as effectively as they mislead" (63). Grimes' use of humor is also widely viewed as effective. Bill Ott and Brad Hooper wrote that the series is "distinguished by the pub settings … and by the eccentric flair of the leading characters," but that she "can be a very funny writer as well" as demonstrated by her portrayal of the "hilariously inept" brothers who run the pub in *I Am the Only Running Footman* (1457). Another review of *I Am the Only Running Footman* called Grimes an "artist in plotting" who concludes her "knife-edge thriller with a double twist" (Steinberg 1986:81). A review of *Rainbow's End* stated that "it's hard to say what makes Grimes's mysteries such a delight," noting that possible reasons include her "hilariously eccentric characters or her imaginative and cleverly convoluted plots" and her "wry humor" or "intelligence and humanity" (Melton 1995:1530).

In addition to the mysteries, Sybil S. Steinberg wrote that Grimes has "also successfully produced character-driven psychological fiction," specifically praising *Cold Flat Junction* as "smartly written" (2001:46). Steinberg found that the plot unwinds slowly, with 12-year-old Emma leading the investigation and the plotting, but that the effect is "surprisingly satisfying" (2001:46). Alan Paul Curtis and Susan Kelly both noted that *Foul Matter* could be a bit of revenge; although the publicity materials stress that this work is not based on real characters or situations ("*Foul Matter*" 55), Grimes was dropped from Knopf before the Jury novels became best sellers (Curtis; Kelly D4). Kelly began her review by noting that Grimes is not only "biting the hand that feeds her" but also "making a delicious meal of it" (D4). Another review praised its "quirky plot, atmospheric settings and dry sense of humor" ("*Foul Matter*" 55).

BIBLIOGRAPHY

Works by Martha Grimes

Richard Jury Series

The Man with a Load of Mischief. Boston: Little, Brown, 1981.
The Old Fox Deceiv'd. Boston: Little, Brown, 1982.
The Anodyne Necklace. Boston: Little, Brown, 1983.
The Dirty Duck. Boston: Little, Brown, 1984.
The Jerusalem Inn. Boston: Little, Brown, 1984.
Help the Poor Struggler. Boston: Little, Brown, 1985.
The Deer Leap. Boston: Little, Brown, 1985.
I Am the Only Running Footman. Boston: Little, Brown, 1986.
The Five Bells and Bladebone. Boston: Little, Brown, 1987.
The Old Silent. Boston: Little, Brown, 1989.
The Old Contemptibles. Boston: Little, Brown, 1991.
The Horse You Came in On. New York: Knopf, 1993.
Rainbow's End. New York: Knopf, 1995.
The Case Has Altered. New York: Holt, 1997.
The Stargazey. New York: Holt, 1998.
The Larmorna Wink. New York: Viking, 1999.
The Blue Last. New York: Viking, 2001.
The Grave Maurice. New York: Viking, 2002.
The Winds of Change. New York: Viking, 2004.
The Old Wine Shades. New York: Viking, 2006.

Other Works

Send Bygraves. New York: Putnam, 1989.
The End of the Pier. New York: Random House, 1992.
Hotel Paradise. New York: Knopf, 1996.
Biting the Moon. New York: Holt, 1999.
The Train Now Departing. New York: Viking, 2000.
Cold Flat Junction. New York: Viking, 2001.
Foul Matter. New York: Viking, 2003.
Belle Ruin. New York: Penguin, 2005.

Works about Martha Grimes

The Book Reporter. "Interview with Martha Grimes." October 5, 2001. http://www.marthagrimes.com/html/int_aol.htlml May 4, 2005.
Carpenter, Richard C. and Dean James. "Martha Grimes." *St. James Guide to Crime & Mystery Writers.* 4th ed. Ed. Jay P. Pederson. Detroit: St. James Press, 1996. 460–62.
"*Cold Flat Junction.*" *Virginia Quarterly Review* 77.4 (2001): 135.
Curtis, Alan Paul. "Foul Matter by Martha Grimes." Who Dunnit. http://www.who-dunnit.com/reviews/49/ May 4, 2005.
"*Foul Matter.*" *Publishers Weekly* 14 July 2003: 55.

Kelly, Susan. "Greed, Indeed, Is a Foul Matter." *USA Today* 3 September 2003: D4.

Malmgren, Carl D. "Truth, Justice and the American Way: Martha Grimes and Elizabeth George." *Clues* 21.2 (2000): 47–56.

"Martha Grimes." *Contemporary* Authors. Vol. 109, New Revision Series. Ed. Scot Peacock. Detroit: Gale, 2002. 104–10.

Melton, Emily. "*The Horse You Rode In On.*" *Booklist* 15 May 1993: 1652.

———. "*Rainbow's End.*" *Booklist* 1 May 1995: 1530.

Nolan, Tom. "Martha Grimes." *Mystery Scene* 73 (2001): 61–62.

Ott, Bill and Brad Hooper. "*I Am the Only Running Footman.*" *Booklist* 15 April 1999: 1457.

Pais, Arthur. "First Time Lucky: Deborah Crombie and Martha Grimes' Early Novels Make for Compelling Reading." *India in New York* 12 September 2003: 26.

Pate, Nancy. "Martha Grimes: As British as Apple Pie." *Ottowa Citizen* 16 November 1998: E5.

Silet, Charles L.P. "Martha Grimes, Author Interview." MysteryNet.com. http://www.mysterynet.com/books/testimony/grimes.shtm May 4, 2005.

Steinberg, Sybil S. "*I Am the Only Running Footman.*" *Publishers Weekly* 10 October 1986: 78; 81.

———. "*Cold Flat Junction.*" *Publishers Weekly* 8 January 2001: 46.

Zaleski, Jeff. "*The Lamorna Wink.*" *Publishers Weekly* 13 September 1999: 63.

Zipp, Yvonne. "Ms. Grimes, in the Parlor, with a Pen." *Christian Science Monitor* 13 January 2000. 4 May 2005. http://www.csmonitor.com/atcsmonitor/specials/women/lit/lit011300.html

Patricia Hall (1940–)

BIOGRAPHY

Patricia Hall is the pseudonym used by journalist Maureen O'Connor. She was born in Bradford, West Yorkshire, England, the daughter of a Latin teacher. She had two younger sisters whom she recalls "escaping from … with my latest read" (homepage). She was interested in writing and storytelling from a young age, but during school became interested in politics and decided to become a journalist. She worked for a newspaper for a year when she was 18 years old before being "persuaded reluctantly" to study English at Birmingham University (homepage). She gained experience with the school newspaper and after graduation began an internship with the *Guardian*.

After marrying, she worked for the *Evening Standard,* the BBC, and the *Guardian*. She created, edited, and wrote for the education section of the *Guardian* for 16 years before turning to freelance journalism and trying her hand at fiction (homepage).

She and her husband have two sons and live in Oxford.

MAJOR WORKS AND THEMES

Hall's first novel featured a case that brings together a police inspector named Alex Sinclair and a social worker named Kate Weston when a mentally impaired young man is accused of a crime. Her second novel features a detective chief inspector who investigates a possible racially motivated murder. The bulk of Hall's work consists of a series featuring a police detective named Michael Thackeray and a reporter named Laura Ackroyd. Thackeray is new to Bradford when the series begins and appears to have a secret past. Ackroyd, like Hall herself, is vitally concerned with a number of social issues and she brings issues of class and social justice to light in the cases they collaborate on.

The series tackles issues of environmentalism, class and race discrimination, violence against immigrants, and other issues, along with having the team solve cases of corruption, fraud, and murder. *Death by Election* takes place in the political milieu, with blackmail, sexual politics, and murder resulting. In *The Dead of Winter* Thackeray must return to his hometown to assist his elderly parents and face the demons of his past. *The Italian Girl* leads Thackeray and Ackroyd into a case involving World War II history and an old murder recently uncovered. *Deep Freeze* addresses issues of family planning, including abortion laws and a fertility doctor who may be going beyond ethical boundaries with his genetics research.

Secondary characters are well developed in the series. Among the various detectives who work for Thackeray are Kevin Mower, Val Ridley, and Rita Desai. Ackroyd's grandmother Joyce, who continues her Socialist leanings and activism into her retirement years, is also a key figure. The novels are richer for their involvement.

She recently departed from Ackroyd and Hall with *The Masks of Darkness,* a novel of suspense about a woman who returns to her hometown and begins working for the historical society to set up a new museum. During her work, she uncovers a mystery that reaches back to her childhood.

CRITICAL RECEPTION

Reception to her work has been positive from the first novel, which was heralded as an "auspicious debut" with an "action-filled plot" (Brainard 1993:66) and as "promis[ing] good things to come" (Klett 152). *Death by Election* was called a "thoughtful procedural" that "planted the seeds of a complex, involving series" to come (Carroll 27).

In a review of *Dead of Winter,* Hall was heralded for her "remarkable balancing of the professional and personal lives of her characters," in a novel described as "an insightful, well-paced tale of lives infected by greed and ambition" (Brainard 1997:68).

Perils of the Night was called "yet another darkly compelling mystery from Hall, memorable particularly for its well-detailed setting, intelligent, vital lead characters and dark-hued plotting" (Zaleski 1998:54). Another review of this novel concluded that the "real mystery here may be why Hall does not yet enjoy the best-seller status of some of her peers" (McLarin 572).

According to one reviewer, *The Italian Girl* had a "sinuous style and moody tone" evoking the Yorkshire moors without romanticizing the setting (Stasio 32). Another reviewer praised Hall's "careful attention to psychology and skillful plotting" (Zaleski 2000:65). *Skeleton at the Feast* was noted for its "excellent pacing and nicely textured characters [that] carry the reader along for a very pleasant ride" (Cannon 46).

BIBLIOGRAPHY

Works by Patricia Hall

Michael Thackeray and Laura Ackroyd Series

Death by Election. London: Little, Brown, 1993; New York: St. Martin's, 1994.
Dying Fall. London: Little, Brown, 1994; New York: St. Martin's, 1995.
In the Bleak Midwinter. London: Little, Brown, 1997. Also published as *Dead of Winter.* New York: St. Martin's, 1997.
Perils of the Night. New York: St. Martin's, 1999.
The Italian Girl. New York: St. Martin's, 2000.
Dead on Arrival. London: Constable, 1999; New York: St. Martin's, 2001.

Skeleton at the Feast. London: Allison & Busby, 2000; New York: St. Martin's, 2002.
Deep Freeze. London: Allison & Busby, 2001; New York: St. Martin's, 2003.
Death in Dark Waters. London: Allison & Busby, 2002; New York: St. Martin's, 2004.
Dead Reckoning. London: Allison & Busby, 2004.
False Witness. London: Allison & Busby, 2004.
Sins of the Father. London: Allison & Busby, 2005.

Other Novels

The Coldness of Killers. London: Collins, 1992.
The Poison Pool. London: Crime Club, 1991; New York: St. Martin's, 1993.
The Masks of Darkness. London: Allison & Busby, 2004.

Works about Patricia Hall

Brainard, Dulcy. "*The Poison Pool.*" *Publishers Weekly* 4 October 1993: 66.
———. "*Dead of Winter.*" *Publishers Weekly* 6 January 1997: 68.
Cannon, Peter. "*Skeleton at the Feast.*" *Publishers Weekly* 24 December 2001: 46.
Carroll, Mary. "*Death by Election.*" *Booklist* 1 September 1994: 26–27.
Klett, Rex E. "*The Poison Pool.*" *Library Journal* 1 November 1993: 152.
McLarin, Jenny. "*Perils of the Night.*" *Booklist* 15 November 1998: 572.
Patricia Hall. Homepage. n.d. 10 November 2004. http://www.patriciahall.co.uk "Patricia Hall."
    Contemporary Authors. Vol. 181. Scot Peacock, ed. Detroit: Gale, 2000. 155–56.
Stasio, Marilyn. "Crime." *New York Times Book Review* 11 June 2000: 32.
Zaleski, Jeff. "*Perils of the Night.*" *Publishers Weekly* 7 December 1998: 54–55.
———. "*The Italian Girl.*" *Publishers Weekly* 3 April 2000: 65.

Charlaine Harris (1951–)

BIOGRAPHY

Charlaine Harris was born November 25, 1951, in Tunica, Mississippi, the daughter of Robert Ashley Harris, a school principal, and Jean Balentine Harris, a librarian. She and her brother grew up in a family of readers, leading to her lifelong interest in books and writing. Harris has stated that she knew she wanted to be a writer from an early age, noting that as soon as she could "hold a pencil and form the words" she knew writing was all she wanted to do in life (Ward).

Harris earned a bachelor's degree at Southwestern at Memphis (now called Rhodes College) in 1973. She worked throughout the 1970s as a typesetter. A first marriage ended in divorce and in 1978, she married Hal Schulz, a chemical engineer, who encouraged her to try writing professionally. She began writing full-time in 1978, and her first novel was published in 1980.

She and her husband have two sons and one daughter, and the family lives in Magnolia, Arkansas.

MAJOR WORKS AND THEMES

Her first two published novels are stand-alone works. *Sweet and Deadly* follows a young woman who solves the murder of her parents in a small Southern town, and *A Secret Rage* is a mystery that deals with the rape of a young woman.

She introduced her first series character, Aurora "Roe" Teagarden, in *Real Murders*. Teagarden is the town librarian and becomes an amateur sleuth. In the first novel in the series, a group of true crime buffs become the center of a murder investigation. Although this series is light in tone, the books do address serious issues. Harris calls this series "cozies with teeth" (Ward).

Her second series returns to the more serious tone and themes of her first two novels. Lily Bard was brutally raped, and the event left her emotionally and physically scarred. She returns to rural Arkansas, settling in the small town of Shakespeare, where she runs a housecleaning service and spends most of her free time in martial arts training. Harris herself is a rape survivor (Ward; Bookhaunts). Through Bard, Harris can write about "how it feels to live with that terrible inner conflict," allowing those who have not been victimized to gain understanding (Bookhaunts).

In 2002, Harris introduced a third mystery series, which is considerably different from any of her previous writings. In this series, Sookie Stackhouse works as a cocktail waitress in Bon Temps, a small town in Louisiana. Stackhouse has an unusual characteristic: she is psychic and can hear people's thoughts. Her otherwise boring and lonely life changes when vampires come to town. Initially, her agent was not thrilled with the work, and it took almost two years to find a publisher for it (Ward; Stabbert; McCune). As it turned out, though, *Dead Until Dark,* the first in the Stackhouse series, was nominated for an Agatha Award and won the Anthony Award for Best Paperback Original. Harris has continued to write about Stackhouse and her boyfriend, The Vampire Bill, who solve mysteries together. Stackhouse is initially attracted to Bill because her psychic powers don't work with him. Harris jokes that she has "cornered the market on southern vampire romantic mystery adventures" (Sheridan).

Harris has summed up her three heroines in this way: "The Aurora Teagarden books are about a woman who is perfectly conventional in many ways, yet nothing ever goes right for her. The Lily Bard books are about a very unconventional woman who really wants conventional things without knowing it, and they happen for her. And then we've got Sookie, who just wants to have a nice date that she can't hear in her head" (Ward).

Harris recently introduced a fourth character in her novel *Grave Sight.* This new series focuses on Harper Connelly, who was left with clairvoyant powers after being struck by lightning at age 14. She is able to locate dead people and can often see their last moments. She travels with her brother, working as a consultant for people who are seeking the truth about their deceased friends and family members. The novel features Harris's strong sense of humor and dialogue, blended with an unusual heroine presented in a realistic manner.

CRITICAL RECEPTION

In a review of *Dead Over Heels,* Rex E. Klett praised Teagarden's "likable, indomitable fashion" of investigation and Harris' "infectious prose, engaging characters, [and] crafty plotting" (213). *Three Bedrooms, One Corpse* was heralded as a "high-spirited" mystery (Brainard 1994:237), and in *The Julius House,* Harris's "brisk, upbeat style keeps tension simmering under the everyday surface" (Brainard 1995:58).

In *Shakespeare's Christmas,* Harris "tells a forceful story with a complex, flawed heroine who is wary of emotional attachments," with a "memorable gallery of secondary characters" (Brainard 89). The reviewer, perhaps expecting another series like Harris' first, notes that the "blend of cozy style with more hard-boiled elements isn't always smooth" but concludes that "it's interesting to see her working toward a deeper complexity" (Brainard 1998:89).

Odile Cogdill praised *Shakespeare's Landlord* as "a well-constructed psychological study that moves at a steady pace" and "also takes a look at how society often views victims of violent crimes" (9D).

Critics love the Stackhouse series. A review of the first Stackhouse adventure praised Harris for her "knack for fusing together elements of chick lit, gothic horror and detective fiction into a whimsical, often racy and occasionally horrifying thriller," also highlighting her strong sense of humor and avoidance of the "detailed pseudo-mythologies" most writers of vampire stories adhere to vigorously (Ng 6). In a review of *Dead as a Doornail,* Jeff Zaleski noted that "Harris does an admirable job of creating a heroine who's not only interesting but completely believable in a world of the strange and the different" (47). Peter Cannon states that the series offers "consistent, well-built characters and a strong, action-packed plot that will keep readers guessing to the end distinguish this frothy fusion of romance, mystery and fantasy" (46).

BIBLIOGRAPHY

Works by Charlaine Harris

Aurora Teagarden Series

Real Murders. New York: Walker, 1990.
A Bone to Pick. New York: Walker, 1992.
Three Bedrooms, One Corpse. New York: Scribner, 1994.
The Julius House. New York: Scribner, 1995.
Dead over Heels. New York: Scribner, 1996.
A Fool and His Honey. New York: St. Martin's, 1999.
Last Scene Alive. New York: St. Martin's, 2002.
Poppy Done to Death. New York: St. Martin's, 2003.

Lily Bard Series

Shakespeare's Landlord. New York: St. Martin's, 1996.
Shakespeare's Champion. New York: St. Martin's, 1997.
Shakespeare's Christmas. New York: St. Martin's, 1998.
Shakespeare's Trollop. New York: St. Martin's, 2000.
Shakespeare's Counselor. New York: St. Martin's, 2001.

Sookie Stackhouse Series

Dead Until Dark. New York: Ace, 2001.
Living Dead in Dallas. New York: Ace, 2002.
Club Dead. New York: Ace, 2003.
Dead to the World. New York: Ace, 2004.
Dead as a Doornail. New York: Ace, 2005.
Definitely Dead. New York: Ace, 2006.

Harper Connelly Series

Grave Sight. New York: Berkley, 2005.

Other Novels

Sweet and Deadly. Boston: Houghton, 1980.
A Secret Rage. Boston: Houghton, 1984.

Works about Charlaine Harris

Bookhaunt.net. "Charlaine Harris: Q&As." 2003. 22 May 2005. http://www.webrighter.co.uk/bookhaunts/charnsQA.htm

Brainard, Dulcy. "*Three Bedrooms, One Corpse.*" *Publishers Weekly* 21 February 1994: 237.

———. "*The Julius House.*" *Publishers Weekly* 9 January 1995: 58.

———. "*Shakespeare's Christmas.*" *Publishers Weekly* 7 September 1998: 88–89.

Cannon, Peter. "*Dead to the World.*" *Publishers Weekly* 5 April 2004: 46.

Charlaine Harris. Home page. 2005. 22 May 2005. http://www.charlaineharris.com

"Charlaine Harris." *Contemporary Authors.* Vol. 99, New Revision Series. Ed. Scot Peacock. Detroit: Gale, 2002. 160–61.

Cogdill, Odile. "Alas, Poor Lily, We Know Her Not At All." *Sun Sentinel* 28 July 1996: 9D.

Klett, Rex E. " *Dead Over Heels.*" *Library Journal* 1 September 1996: 213.

McCune, Alisa. "A Conversation with Charlaine Harris." April 2004. 22 May 2005. http://www.sfsite.com/05a/ch175.htm

Ng, U-En. "Saving the Dead from the Living." *New Straits Times* 14 July 2004: 6.

Sheridan, Barbara. "Meet Charlaine Harris." April 2002. 23 May 2005. http://paranormalromance.writerspace.com/CharlaineHarris.htm

Stabbert, Jonette. "Interview with Charlaine Harris." Sisters in Crime Internet Chapter. May 2003. 22 May 2005. http://www.sinc-ic.org/spot0603.shtml

Ward, Jean Marie. "Charlaine Harris: Putting the Bite on Cozy Mysteries." Crescent Blues. 2001. 22 May 2005. http://www.crescentblues.com/4_4issue/int_charlaine_harris.shtml

Zaleski, Jeff. "*Dead as a Doornail.*" *Publishers Weekly* 4 April 2005: 47.

Cynthia Harrod-Eagles (1948–)

BIOGRAPHY

Cynthia Harrod-Eagles was born August 13, 1948, in Shepherd's Bush, London. She was educated at Burlington School, and at the University of Edinburgh and University College London, where she studied English, history, and philosophy.

She wrote her first novel, *The Waiting Game,* while she was in college, and it won the Young Writers' Award in 1972 in the United Kingdom. After she finished her degree, she worked as a sales manager for Coca Cola in Edinburgh and later as a pension officer for the BBC in London. She continued writing during her free time. After beginning the Morland Dynasty series, she was able to turn to writing full-time in 1979. The Morland series was originally set to be 12 volumes, but as a result of its popularity, it now has 30 volumes planned.

Harrod-Eagles lives in London with her husband. They have three children, Hannah, Jane, and Michael. In addition to her writing, she performs with several amateur orchestras.

MAJOR WORKS AND THEMES

Most of Harrod-Eagles's works are historical fiction, including several elaborate series of family sagas. She also wrote historical romances in the 1970s and 1980s under the pseudonyms of Emma Woodhouse and Elizabeth Bennett. She notes that "when [she] originally embarked on the first of the Bill Slider books, [she] was just doing it for fun, as a relaxation between other books," with no plans of publishing it (homepage).

She does meticulous research for her historical fiction, particularly the Morland Dynasty series, which traces a family from the time of the War of the Roses through the Napoleonic era. She also does research for the Slider series, noting that she spends time with police detectives to understand their attitudes, concerns and language, reads police trade magazines, does legal research, and studies forensic science guides (Zollo).

Her mystery series features Detective Inspector Bill Slider, a sensitive man who is an excellent police detective. Slider has less success with his personal life, though, as he feels trapped in an unhappy marriage. His partner, Jim Atherton, is well educated, urbane, and a natty dresser. A highlight of the novels is their wordplay, including a wide array of puns and allusions.

In the first novel, Slider investigates the death of a musician and falls in love with the victim's friend, violist Joanna Marshall. Marshall assists Slider and Atherton occasionally with subsequent cases. Harrod-Eagles presents cases that seem to be typical mystery fare at first, but then have a twist. A number of the cases also have connections to music, allowing Marshall to take part in many plots. In *Grave Music,* Slider must find who shot and killed a conductor during a rehearsal, and in *Blood Lines,* a nasty music critic falls victim. Harrod-Eagles also enjoys creating victims with many possible murderers, presenting tricky cases for Slider and Atherton.

CRITICAL RECEPTION

Critical reception has been positive, recognizing Harrod-Eagles' excellent writing and her skills in developing characters and plots. *Orchestrated Death* was praised for its "nicely detailed prose" and "approachable characters" (Klett 1992:181). It was also termed a "masterful debut" with "a sophisticated ending [that] whets readers' interest in the further adventures of these strong players" (Brainard 1992b:51). The follow-up, *Death Watch,* was called a "fine example of the British police procedural," with a "simmering narrative" and "plenty of quick wit," in a "skillfully written and solidly plotted" novel (Miller 881) and was praised for its "realistic characters, dry wit, and surprising plot twists" (Klett 1993:169). Another review of *Death Watch* noted that Harrod-Eagles offered "unerring characterization, droll copper dialogue and a gritty London setting" with a plot that "slyly sifts various strata of society" (Brainard 1992a:55).

Death to Go was billed as a "witty, intricate puzzle" (Brainard 1993:73). Another reviewer found that besides the murder plot, the novel is "an examination of love, love lost and the ways in which people cope with both" (Lukowsky 740). *Grave Music* was hailed as "confirm[ing] Slider's place among those intelligent fictional British coppers whose presence guarantees a satisfying read" (Brainard 1995:62).

Bill Ott noted that "as Slider and Atherton slog toward a solution" in *Shallow Grave,* "they both struggle with their ever-muddled personal lives, giving Harrod-Eagles the opportunity to do what she does best: build character from the bootstraps up" (2034). Ott stated that the "the plot here [may] seem a shade predictable, [but] Harrod-Eagles's ability to plumb the pathos from the depths of daily life remains razor sharp" (Ott 2034).

Publishers Weekly praised "the emotional complexity and intelligent dialogue that have marked" the series (Zaleski 56). The reviewer further noted that "alert readers will identify the murderer before Harrod-Eagles allows her hero to, but time spent in the company of this literate crew is always worthwhile" (Zaleski 57). Another testament to Harrod-Eagles's character development was seen in a comment from *Booklist* that "Slider's ability to see the complexity in the people around him is both his strength and his weakness" (Hooper 1457).

Character development is also praised in *Killing Time,* with one review noting that "Harrod-Eagles affectionately portrays a colorful London of warmhearted prostitutes and cabbies speaking in Cockney slang" (Brainard 1997:58). The reviewer also acclaimed "the witty wordplay between Atherton and Joanna and Slider's complicated relationships with Joanna and Irene" in producing "another solid addition to an outstanding, highly literate series" (Brainard 1997:58).

Peter Cannon noted that "although Slider and Atherton often overanalyze, their attention to detail pays off" and he found *Gone Tomorrow* to be a satisfying and compelling novel (Cannon 46). Marilyn Stasio stated that "plots and graceful writing count for a lot in the English police procedural" and called Harrod-Eagles an admirable practitioner (22). Stasio continued that Harrod-Eagles is "just as admirable when she plays it straight, [and] has a discerning eye and sympathetic ear for the criminals" (22).

BIBLIOGRAPHY

Works by Cynthia Harrod-Eagles

Bill Slider Series

Orchestrated Death. New York: Scribner, 1991.
Death Watch. New York: Scribner, 1992.
Death to Go. New York: Scribner, 1993. (Also published as *Necrochip*).
Dead End: A Bill Slider Mystery. Boston: Little, Brown, 1994.
Grave Music: An Inspector Bill Slider Mystery. New York: Scribner, 1995.
Blood Lines: A Bill Slider Mystery. Boston: Little, Brown, 1996.
Killing Time: An Inspector Bill Slider Mystery. New York: Scribner, 1998.
Shallow Grave: A Bill Slider Mystery. New York: Simon & Schuster, 1999.
Gone Tomorrow. New York: St. Martin's, 2002.
Dear Departed. New York: St. Martin's, 2005.

Other Works

The Waiting Game. New York: New American Library, 1972.
Hollow Night. London: Methuen, 1980.
Deadfall. London: Methuen, 1982.
The Orange Tree Plot. London: Pan, 1989.
Anna. New York: St. Martin's, 1990.
Fleur. New York: St. Martin's, 1991.
Emily. New York: St. Martin's, 1992.
The Enchanted Isle. Sutton: Severn House, 1992.
I, Victoria. New York: St. Martin's, 1994.
Real Life. Sutton: Severn House, 1999.
The Longest Dance. Sutton: Severn House, 2000.
The Horsemasters. Sutton: Severn House, 2001.
Julia. Sutton: Severn House, 2003.
The Colonel's Daughter. Sutton: Severn House, 2006.

Morland Dynasty Series

The Founding. New York: Dell, 1980.
The Dark Rose. New York: Dell, 1981.
The Distant Wood. New York: Dell, 1981. (Also published as *The Princeling.* London: Macdonald, 1981.)
The Crystal Crown. New York: Dell, 1982. (Also published *The Oak-Apple.* London: Macdonald, 1982.)
The Black Pearl. New York: Dell, 1982.

The Long Shadow. New York: Dell, 1983.
The Chevalier. London: Macdonald, 1984.
The Maiden. London: Macdonald, 1985.
The Flood-Tide. London: Macdonald, 1986.
The Tangled Thread. London: Macdonald, 1987.
The Emperor. London: Macdonald, 1988.
The Victory. London: Macdonald, 1989.
The Regency. London: Macdonald, 1990.
The Campaigners. London: Macdonald, 1991.
The Reckoning. London: Macdonald, 1992.
The Devil's Horse. London: Warner, 1993.
The Poison Tree. London: Little, Brown, 1994.
The Abyss. London: Little, Brown, 1995.
The Hidden Shore. London: Little, Brown, 1996.
The Winter Journey. London: Little, Brown, 1997.
The Outcast. London: Little, Brown, 1998.
The Mirage. London: Little, Brown, 1999.
The Cause. London: Little, Brown, 2000.
The Homecoming. London: Little, Brown, 2001.
The Question. London: Little, Brown, 2002.
The Dream Kingdom. London: Little, Brown, 2003.

Works about Cynthia Harrod-Eagles

Brainard, Dulcy. "*Death Watch.*" *Publishers Weekly* 23 November 1992a: 55.
———. "*Orchestrated Death.*" *Publishers Weekly* 6 January 1992b: 51.
———. "*Death to Go.*" *Publishers Weekly* 15 November 1993: 73.
———. "*Grave Music.*" *Publishers Weekly* 13 March 1995: 62.
———. "*Killing Time.*" *Publishers Weekly* 10 November 1997: 58.
Cannon, Peter. "*Gone Tomorrow: A Bill Slider Mystery.*" *Publishers Weekly* 25 November 2002: 46.
Cynthia Harrod-Eagles. Homepage. 25 May 2005. http://www.cynthiaharrodeagles.com/index.html
"Cynthia Harrod-Eagles." *Contemporary Authors.* Vol. 85, New Revision Series. Ed. Scot Peacock. Detroit: Gale, 2000. 88–90.
Hooper, Brad. "*Killing Time.*" *Booklist* 15 April 1999: 1457.
Klett, Rex E. "*Orchestrated Death.*" *Library Journal* January 1992: 181.
———. "*Death Watch.*" *Library Journal* January 1993: 169.
Lukowsky, Wes. "*Death to Go.*" *Booklist* 15 December 1993: 740.
Miller, Stuart. "*Death Watch.*" *Booklist* 15 January 1993: 881.
Ott, Bill. "*Shallow Grave.*" *Booklist* August 1999: 2034.
Stasio, Marilyn. "Crime." *New York Times Book Review* 1 December 2002: 22.
Zaleski, Jeff. "*Shallow Grave.*" *Publishers Weekly* 28 June 1999: 56–57.
Zollo, Wendy. "Morlands and Mysteries with Cynthia Harrod-Eagles." 2003. 25 May 2005. http://www.triviumpublishing.com/articles/cynthiaharrodeagles.html

Carolyn G. Hart (1936–)

BIOGRAPHY

Carolyn Gimpel Hart was born August 25, 1936, in Oklahoma City to Roy William and Doris Akin Gimpel. Her father worked as an organ builder. She married Philip Donnell

Hart in 1958, and also earned a degree in journalism from the University of Oklahoma that same year. She worked as a newspaper reporter and as a magazine writer for several years before they began their family. They have two children, Philip and Sarah.

She pursued fiction writing instead of journalistic work, and in 1964, she won a contest that led to the publication of her mystery novel for young girls called *The Secrets of the Cellar.* She wrote several other books for young adult readers before turning to writing for adults. On the advice of an agent, she even tried her hand at romance and sold one novel she views as a suspense novel "disguised as a romance" to Harlequin for their "gothic" line before she became successful with writing in the mystery and suspense genre (Andrews).

Hart is one of the founding members of Sisters in Crime. She and her husband live in Oklahoma City.

MAJOR WORKS AND THEMES

In the 1970s and 1980s, Hart wrote a number of suspense and mystery novels, as well as two works of historical fiction, both set during World War II. A number of these novels were reprinted in 2000.

In 1987, she introduced her first series characters, Annie Laurence and Max Darling. Set on the fictional island of Broward's Rock, South Carolina, Laurence owns a mystery bookstore called Death on Demand, which is inhabited by a cat named Agatha and is visited daily by a cast of locals. The store also has a contest during each novel. A painting is unveiled in the store, showing scenes from five different mystery novels. The denouement of each novel includes not only solving the crime at hand, but also solving the clues shown in the paintings to reveal the five books depicted. In the first novel, the no-nonsense, frugal Laurence meets Darling, a rich aristocratic type, and the pair fall in love. They join forces throughout the series to solve various crimes, many of them related to mystery writers, mystery fan conventions, literary workshops, and other scenarios related to the publishing business. As one review of *The Christie Caper* noted, "What better setting" for the novel than an Agatha Christie fan convention (Cooper 2033). The novel is filled with trivia and allusions for Christie fans, and the ending features everyone in one room for the unveiling of the murder. Darling is an unofficial, unlicensed investigator who takes on a variety of cases, in addition to the ones his wife finds herself involved in.

Hart's second mystery series features Henrietta O'Dwyer Collins, called Henrie O. Collins is a retired newspaper reporter and widow who remains very active in life and finds herself serving as an amateur sleuth. Hart has called this character "a braver, idealized" version of herself (Carolyn 186). Troubled by negative images of older women in fiction, Hart created Collins as a woman "who deserved respect because she has lived a challenging life, known joy and sorrow, achievement and failure" (Andrews) and who is an older woman, not "cute" or "dithery" (James 54). Early in the series, Collins lives in Missouri and teaches at a local college, but the novels take place in various locales, including San Antonio, South Carolina, Bermuda, and Hawaii. Several of the novels feature Collins visiting a friend or relative and stumbling into a murder; in *Death in Paradise* Collins receives an anonymous phone call and launches an investigation into the death of her husband, which had been ruled as an accident years before.

Hart describes her recent novel, *Letter from Home,* as mostly dealing with the effects of World War II but also the effect of a crime on people, without a focus on the solving of the crime (Brundige). Set partly during World War II, the era of Hart's childhood, the novel centers on Gretchen Grace Gilman, who was featured in two earlier short stories published by Hart. The novel begins with Gilman, a respected journalist reaching the end of her career, receiving a letter that takes her back to when she was 13 and got her first shot at reporting for her hometown newspaper during the war. The novel does include a mystery element, but it is also a strong study of friendship and the choices Gilman made personally and professionally.

CRITICAL RECEPTION

Hart has won two Agatha Awards, two Anthony Awards, and a Macavity Award for novels in the Death on Demand series. She also garnered additional nominations for novels in both of her mystery series. Her recent stand-alone novel, *Letter from Home,* also won an Agatha Award.

The Death on Demand series has gained critical acclaim. *Southern Ghost* was praised as a "southern gothic mystery" with a "wealth of suspects, a generous scattering of literary allusions" and ghost stories, and a "chain of intriguing flashbacks that will leave readers puzzled until the end" (Duree 36). Another reviewer also praised the flashbacks, noting that the "segues to the dark night 22 years ago are chillingly effective and tantalizingly brief" (Brainard 1992:54). *Mint Julep Murder* was praised for "combin[ing] genteel ambience, southern charm, a likeable heroine and some wonderfully nasty characters" into an "entertaining mystery" (Melton 1995:1932). *Yankee Doodle Dead* was praised for its "rich Southern atmosphere," "diverse and engaging cast," and a "charming and gripping" plot (Brainard 1998:57). A review of *April Fool Dead* noted that the banter between the Darlings "evokes classic screwball comedy" (Cannon 2002:81). *Death Walks the Plank* was seen to "reinforce Hart's high standing among the cozy mystery cognoscenti" (Cannon 2004:40). The most recent entry in the series was heralded as a "feel-good" cozy mystery with numerous suspects and "intriguing clues, another murder and just enough red herrings to keep readers guessing" ("*Death of the Party*" 54).

The first Henrie O novel was lauded as an "action packed series launch" with a "feisty and incisive" heroine who solves the case in a "tumultuous resolution" (Brainard1993:60). *Scandal in Fair Haven* was described as "look[ing] at the feelings, emotions and passions of real-life people in real-life situations" with a "compelling plot, potpourri of fascinating characters and revealing insights into what makes us humans tick" (Melton 1994:2027). One review of *Death in Lovers' Lane* noted that "more than a little of [Agatha] Christie's gift for plotting and suspense can be found in this intricately wrought tale" (Moores 825). A review of *Death in Paradise* praised Hart for bringing the setting "vividly alive," further noting that "the plot is suspenseful from first page to last" (Havens 164). Another reviewer noted that if she were to teach a course on mystery writing, *Death in Paradise* would be a required text, further noting that the strong descriptions of the settings made her "want to call [her] travel agent" (Kaufman 2). Although one reviewer found the plot of *Death on the River Walk* to be "slender," the novel is recommended because of the development of the character of Henrie O as "sturdy, relentless yet compassionate" (Zaleski 75). A review of *Resort to Murder* noted that the Henrie O series "has a deeper and darker emotional texture" than the Death on Demand novels, but that readers would "enjoy the complex plot, local color and vivid characters" (Cannon 2001:66).

Letter from Home won particularly strong praise. One review praised the evidence of "obviously well-researched history" in addition to the characters being "Steinbeck vivid" as Hart "masterfully portrays an American small town during WWII" ("*Letter from Home*" 58).

BIBLIOGRAPHY

Works by Carolyn Hart

Annie and Max Darling Series

Death on Demand. New York: Bantam, 1987.
Design for Murder. New York: Bantam, 1988.
Something Wicked. New York: Bantam, 1988.
Honeymoon with Murder. New York: Bantam, 1989.
A Little Class on Murder. New York: Doubleday, 1989.
Deadly Valentine. New York: Doubleday, 1990.
The Christie Caper. New York: Bantam, 1991.
Southern Ghost. New York: Bantam, 1992.
Mint Julep Murder. New York: Bantam, 1995.
Yankee Doodle Dead. New York: Avon, 1998.
White Elephant Dead. New York: Avon, 1999.
Sugarplum Dead. New York: Morrow, 2000.
April Fool Dead. New York: Morrow, 2002.
Engaged to Die. New York: Morrow, 2003.
Murder Walks the Plank. New York: Morrow, 2004.
Death of the Party. New York: Morrow, 2005.
Dead Days of Summer. New York: Morrow, 2006.

Henrietta O'Collins Dwyer Series

Dead Man's Island. New York: Bantam, 1993.
Scandal in Fair Haven. New York: Bantam, 1994.
Death in Lovers' Lane. New York: Avon, 1997.
Death in Paradise. New York: Avon, 1998.
Death on the River Walk. New York: Avon, 1999.
Resort to Murder. New York: Morrow, 2001.

Other Novels

Flee from the Past. New York: Bantam, 1975.
A Settling of Accounts. New York: Doubleday, 1976.
Escape from Paris. London: R. Hale, 1982; New York: St. Martin's Press, 1983.
The Rich Die Young. London: R. Hale, 1983.
Death by Surprise. London: R. Hale, 1983.
Castle Rock. London: R. Hale, 1983.
Skulduggery. London: R. Hale, 1984.
Brave Hearts. New York: Pocket Books, 1987.
Letter from Home. New York: Berkley, 2003.

Works about Carolyn Hart

Andrews, Donna. "Carolyn Hart: Justice on Demand." *Crescent Blues* 3.4 (1999). 30 January 2006. http://www.crescentblues.com/2_4issue/hart.shtml
Brainard, Dulcy. "*Southern Ghost.*" *Publishers Weekly* 29 June 1992: 54.
———. "*Dead Man's Island.*" *Publishers Weekly* 28 June 1993: 60.
———. "*Yankee Doodle Dead.*" *Publishers Weekly* 27 July 1998: 56–57.
Brundige, Kay. "PW Interviews Carolyn Hart." n.d. 31 January 2006. http://www.carolynhart.com/pw.htm

Cannon, Peter. "*Resort to Murder.*" *Publishers Weekly* 12 March 2001: 66.

———. "*April Fool Dead.*" *Publishers Weekly* 18 March 2002: 81.

———. "*Murder Walks the Plank.*" *Publishers Weekly* 12 January 2004: 40.

"Carolyn G(impel) Hart." *Contemporary Authors.* New Revision Series, Vol. 126. Ed. Tracey Watson. Detroit: Gale, 2001. 184–88.

Cooper, Ilene. "*The Christie Caper.*" *Booklist* July 1991: 2033.

"*Death of the Party.*" *Publishers Weekly* 7 March 2005: 54.

Duree, Barbara. "*Southern Ghost.*" *Booklist* 1 September 1992: 36.

Havens, Shirley E. "*Hawaiian Caper.*" *Library Journal* July 1998: 164.

James, Dean. "Interviews: Carolyn G. Hart." *Mystery Scene* 43 (1994): 38+.

Kaufman, Margo. "Sunday Brunch Book Shelf." *Los Angeles Times* 29 March 1998: 2.

"*Letter from Home.*" *Publishers Weekly* 8 September 2003: 58.

Melton, Emily. "*Scandal in Fair Haven.*" *Booklist* August 1994: 2027.

———. "*Mint Julep Murder.*" *Booklist* August 1995: 1931–32.

Moores, Alan. "*Death in Lovers' Lane.*" *Booklist* 1–15 January 1997: 825.

Zaleski, Jeff. "*Death on the River Walk.*" *Publishers Weekly* 25 January 1999: 75.

Sue Henry (1940–)

BIOGRAPHY

Born in 1940, Sue Henry has lived in Alaska since the 1970s. When she's not traveling in her RV, she lives in Anchorage. She worked as a instructor and administrator at the University of Alaska and also held other jobs, including driving the bookmobile for the Fairbanks library in the 1970s, before trying her hand at writing fiction.

MAJOR WORKS AND THEMES

Her first series introduced Jessie Arnold, a musher who also works as a guide, taking others out in dog sleds, and a police detective named Alex Jensen. In the first novel, a string of accidents during the Iditarod race turns out to be murder. With her insider knowledge of the race and the players involved, Arnold assists Jensen with the investigation. They begin a relationship that lasts through several novels, during which Arnold either gets involved with Jensen's cases or stumbles into cases linked to her work. Their personal relationship was dissolved in *Beneath the Ashes,* but Arnold continues to solve various mysteries. It is interesting that early reviews of the series focused on Jensen, some even neglecting to name Arnold as a character or referring to her only as Jensen's girlfriend.

In *Dead North,* Henry introduced a new character, Maxine McNab. McNab is retired and travels in her RV when she meets Arnold, who is driving a friend's RV from Idaho back to Colorado for him. They become fast friends and plan to meet each evening. When Arnold gives a young hitchhiker a ride, and then learns the police were looking for him in connection with a murder, Arnold and McNab join forces to prove the young man's innocence. McNab has been featured in two subsequent novels of her own. The first features McNab finding out the truth behind the recent death of a friend.

Henry's novels are set mostly or partly in Alaska. The vivid descriptions of the settings and the connections between the plots and the natural environment make Alaska seem like a character in many of them.

CRITICAL RECEPTION

Henry won Macavity and Anthony awards for her first novel. Critical reception has been positive throughout her career. Her first work was praised as an "enthralling debut," with "suspense and excitement" and a "powerful Alaskan landscape" (Steinberg 51). Another reviewer called it a "polished action mystery" with a cast of "intrepid daredevils" that are well developed, with a "strong sense of individuality" (Stasio 33). The review also highlights Henry's "smooth, uncluttered prose" and "breath-catching" descriptions (Stasio 33). Another review noted the "incredible descriptions of scenery" and "in-depth knowledge of the sport" as contributing to "an absorbing read" (Klett 1991:157).

Termination Dust was predicted to "duplicate the success" of the first novel, with its "pristine scenery, in-depth characterization and historical" subplot (Klett 1995:136). *Sleeping Lady* was heralded as a "hymn" to Alaska, with "textured characterization" and "attentive depiction of the wilderness" (Brainard 1996:229). Another reviewer praised the novel as a "captivating mystery" with "straightforward writing, engaging characters and an inventive plot" (Melton 1996:67).

Death Take Passage was praised for its blend of "classic" devices, such as locked rooms and missing passengers, with a "well-paced" plot and depiction of the "great beauty of Alaska" (Rowen 1997:1802). Another reviewer critiqued the dialogue as sometimes "wooden," but praised the novel's portrayal of "Alaska's spectacular scenery," inclusion of "intriguing history," and a "well-engineered showdown" (Brainard 1997:49).

One reviewer found *Deadfall* to be "more psychological thriller than whodunit," with a "solid plot with a cliff-hanger ending, beautiful settings, and realistic human and canine characters" (Rowen 1998:1733). Another review praised the novel's "riveting suspense, wildly beautiful and dangerous setting and gutsy heroine" (Brainard 1998:39).

Murder on the Yukon Quest has a "slow start," but "when the action kicks in, the story hurtles along agreeably to a surprising ending" (Melton 1999:1800). Another reviewer found the plot "thin," but praised Henry for "beautiful writing" and for "decorat[ing] her novel with glorious evocations of Alaska, believable characters, interesting mushing lore and deft explanations of dogsledding mechanics" (Zaleski 77). *Beneath the Ashes* was noted for its "jittery, nail-biting pace [that] hooks readers early on," and although the reviewer found the ending "disappointing," the novel was praised overall as a being "as entertaining as it is compelling" (Rowen 2000:1618).

In *Dead North,* the "talented Henry shows her love of the Alaskan wilderness with vivid descriptions of its spectacular beauty, using it as the backdrop for several heart-stopping chases" in "one of her best—if not the best—because characters drive the plot" Cannon 2001:64). In a review of *Cold Company,* it is noted that "one of the hallmarks of Henry's series is the beautiful and rugged Alaskan landscape, and she has never used it more effectively than she does here" (Cannon 2002:40). Although that reviewer found *Death Trap* to "rarely achieve her usual level of suspense" (Cannon 2003:51), another review of the novel praised Henry's "excellent job of building suspense" that include "nail-biting scenes" (Deegan 2).

BIBLIOGRAPHY

Works by Sue Henry

Jessie Arnold Series

Murder on the Iditarod Trail. New York: Atlantic Monthly Press, 1991.
Termination Dust. New York: Morrow, 1995.

Sleeping Lady. New York: Morrow, 1996.
Death Takes Passage. New York: Avon, 1997.
Deadfall. New York: Morrow, 1998.
Murder on Yukon Quest. New York: Avon, 1999.
Beneath the Ashes. New York: Morrow, 2000.
Dead North. New York: Morrow, 2001.
Cold Company. New York: Avon, 2002.
Death Trap. New York: Morrow, 2003.
Murder At Five Finger Light. New York: NAL, 2005.

Maxine "Maxie" McNab Series

The Serpent's Trail. New York: NAL, 2004.
The Tooth of Time. New York: NAL, 2006.

Works about Sue Henry

Brainard, Dulcy. "*Sleeping Lady.*" *Publishers Weekly* 22 July 1996: 229.
———. "*Death Takes Passage.*" *Publishers Weekly* 16 June 1997: 49.
———. "*Deadfall.*" *Publishers Weekly* 29 June 1998: 39.
Cannon, Peter. "*Dead North.*" *Publishers Weekly* 11 June 2001: 64.
———. "*Cold Company.*" *Publishers Weekly* 27 May 2002: 40.
———. "*Death Trap.*" *Publishers Weekly* 28 April 2003: 51.
Deegan, Carol. "Sue Henry's *Death Trap* a Nail-Biter." *Chicago Tribune* 22 August 2003: 2.
Hall, Jaimie. "Writing on the Road: Novelist Sue Henry." Roadtrip America.com. 10 October 2004.
    15 February 2006. http://www.roadtripamerica.com/rv/Sue-Henry-Writing-on-the-Road.htm
Klett, Rex E. "*Murder on the Iditarod Trail.*" *Library Journal* 1 April 1991: 157.
———. "*Termination Dust.*" *Library Journal* 1 May 1995: 136.
Melton, Emily. "*Sleeping Lady.*" *Booklist* 1 September 1996: 67.
———. "*Murder on the Yukon Quest.*" *Booklist* 1–15 June 1999: 1800.
Rowen, John. "*Death Takes Passage.*" *Booklist* July 1997: 1802.
———. "*Deadfall.*" *Booklist* 1–15 June 1998: 1733.
———. "*Beneath the Ashes.*" *Booklist* 1 May 2000: 1618.
Stasio, Marilyn. "Crime." *New York Times Book Review* 7 April 1991: 33.
Steinberg, Sybil. "*Murder on the Iditarod Trail.*" *Publishers Weekly* 8 February 1991: 51.
"Sue Henry." *Contemporary Authors.* Vol. 199. Ed. Scot Peacock. Detroit: Gale, 2002. 202–203.
Zaleski, Jeff. "*Murder on the Yukon Quest.*" *Publishers Weekly* 7 June 1999: 77.

Patricia Highsmith (1921–1995)

BIOGRAPHY

Patricia Highsmith once noted that one of her proudest achievements was having the *Times Literary Supplement* refer to her as "the crime writer who comes closest to giving crime writing a good name" (Highsmith 1966:viii). She was born Mary Patricia Plangman on January 19, 1921, in Fort Worth, Texas. Her parents, Jay Bernard Plangman and Mary Coates, were divorced shortly before her birth. She spent a good deal of time with her grandparents during her childhood. In 1924, her mother married Stanley Highsmith, and the family relocated to New York. She did not get along well with her stepfather, and she spoke of her childhood in various negative ways over the years. One positive aspect of her early years was her love of writing. She wrote a number of stories during high school while growing up in Manhattan, and she won prizes for several of them.

She attended Barnard College, earning a bachelor's degree there in 1942. She studied English, Latin, and Greek, and continued writing short stories, with many appearing in the *Barnard Quarterly.* A story written in 1941 was later published in *Harper's Bazaar* and was included in *O. Henry's Best Short Stories of 1946* (Stenger 146).

After college, she worked in New York and continued writing. Before her first novel was published, she wrote for popular media, including comic books. Based on recommendations from Truman Capote and others, she won a place at Yaddo, a writers' colony in Saratoga Springs, and there she was able to rework and finish her first novel (Stenger 147). While there, she met and became engaged to a novelist named Marc Brandel, but she had also experienced a number of affairs with women. In 1949, she underwent psychoanalysis in an attempt to change her sexuality (Wilson 153–54). She left New York for a trip to Europe later that year and ultimately decided that she was not interested in marriage and children. She concentrated on her writing and scored a breakout success with *Strangers on a Train,* published in 1950, with the film rights soon purchased by Alfred Hitchcock.

She continued to travel extensively and moved to Europe permanently in 1963, including 13 years living in France and the final 15 years of her life in Switzerland. She suffered several serious illnesses, including lung cancer and anemia, and her health continued to decline in the 1990s. Highsmith died on February 4, 1995, in Locarno, Switzerland. She died with no survivors and left $3 million in a bequest to Yaddo.

MAJOR WORKS AND THEMES

Highsmith is known as a master of psychological fiction. Many of her works deal with the psychological motivations and effects of murder. Her first novel featured a plot between two men to commit murder for each other to avoid blame for the killing. Made popular by Hitchcock's film, the plot device has also been used by many other writers and filmmakers, sometimes even for comic effect.

Most of her works were stand-alone novels, but throughout her career, Highsmith returned several times to the character of Tom Ripley. First introduced in 1955, Ripley is a psychopathic murderer whom Highsmith treats in such a way as to make "shocked but fascinated readers find themselves cheering for the amoral Mr. Ripley" (Thomas 331). A master of forgery and disguise, Ripley seeks a better life for himself, which he believes he deserves. Some critics find that Ripley is not entirely immoral or insane, that he has a "strong sense" and an "intense desire to change his lifestyle and himself" (Klein 189). Highsmith herself noted that she found Ripley to be sane, with the distinction that he "doesn't feel guilt in a normal way" (Dupont 28). Another critic noted that the theme tying together the subsequent Ripley novels is domesticity, as he works to control his life in exile in France, living with his wife and their servant (Harrison 28).

Three of her works published from 1957 to 1962 solidified her reputation as more than a suspense novelist. *Deep Water, This Sweet Sickness* and *The Cry of the Owl* certainly have aspects of suspense and mystery fiction with crimes to be solved or analyzed, but the novels provide deeper portraits of small town life, relationships gone sour, and the desperation of the characters. As one critic puts it, Highsmith's early villains were "psychopathic and repulsive," but as her career continued, her characters were "more likely to be an ordinary sort with whom it is frighteningly easy for the reader to identify" (Thomas 336). Many of Highsmith's novels explore an ordinary person and his or her "capacity for violence and murder" (Klein 174). The characters are "so much like known and understood people in the everyday world that their decisions to kill are unanticipated, unpredicted and baffling" (Klein 195).

Her last novel, *Small g*, was published shortly after she died, and has some elements in common with one of her first works. A departure from her works of mystery and suspense, *Small g* depicts a group of people from different backgrounds and nationalities who are living in Switzerland, dealing with life, death, and other issues, including their sexuality. Many critics found its treatment of the characters and of the theme of homosexuality to be overly romanticized. In 1952, Highsmith's second novel, *The Price of Salt*, was published under a pseudonym, Claire Morgan. This novel focuses on a lesbian relationship, and unlike almost all other Highsmith works, features a happy ending. The work was republished under her own name as *Carol* in 1984.

In addition to her fiction, Highsmith wrote a book about writing mystery and suspense fiction. As she noted in the preface, it was not intended as a textbook or how-to book, but to "make people who want to write realize what is already within them" (1966:viii). The book also provides interesting insights into Highsmith's writing habits and style, as well as her philosophy. One of her statements in the book is often quoted, namely that she found "the public passion for justice quite boring and artificial, for neither life nor nature cares if justice is ever done or not" (Villalon B1; Corliss 159).

Since her death, there have been two collections of short stories, a lengthy biography, a memoir written by one of her former lovers, and a popular film version of *The Talented Mr. Ripley*, all of which have renewed interest in her work. Norton has also announced plans to reprint a number of her earlier novels.

CRITICAL RECEPTION

Highsmith's works drew a wide array of reviews over the years. Some found her works depressing and disgusting, others were drawn to the negative elements, and still others focused on the skillful impact of her writing. She gained more acclaim in Europe, and her books were often out of print in her native United States. Beyond the blurring of genre lines and acceptability in Europe, James Sallis points out that Highsmith's novels "also inflamed bare-rubbed spots of the American soul others had agreed to leave alone," with her work chronicling "a bursting of the blisters that develop when shoes of seem (the salesman measured and assured you they were perfect) don't fit the feet that be. She pushed things to the very borders of expectation, civility, civilization and reason—even of humanity" (Sallis).

Ripley drew attention from the start, with the reviewer for the *New Yorker* calling the novel "remarkably immoral" and Ripley "one of the most repellent and fascinating characters" (76). *Ripley Under Ground* was called a "sophisticated novel of crime," with Ripley "as charming as he is callous," and a "slightly ambiguous ending" so that readers "cannot help but hope to meet him again" (Johnston 69). *The Boy Who Followed Ripley* was seen as "engrossing and shiver packed" (Fletcher 1980:1344), with Highsmith praised for writing "cleanly, cleverly and dramatically" (Bannon 56). *Ripley Under Water* was praised for its display of Highsmith's trademark "chilling, knife-edge subtlety," with the reviewer noting that Highsmith "will make readers look closer at their neighbors, and at themselves" (Brainard 65). Another review found that Highsmith "is once again our unfaltering guide through these ambiguous nether regions of good and evil," with her writing playing brilliantly on readers' everyday fears" (Robertson 4).

Deep Water was called a "full-fleshed novel of pity and irony" by Anthony Boucher (1957:34). Boucher also praised *The Story-Teller* as a "curious and absorbing novel, almost unique in its fantastic and ironic tone" (1965:82). *Edith's Diary* was called "profoundly moving" by *Publishers Weekly* (74), while the *Booklist* reviewer praised Highsmith for "build[ing] a subtle tension as she quietly orchestrates the reader's understanding and sympathy toward Edith" (139). In *Found in the Street* Highsmith was praised for writing "compellingly" and as a "fine psychological ironist," with the novel praised as a "powerfully disturbing, resonant creation" (Burgin 24).

One collection of her stories, *The Snail Watcher and Other Stories,* was praised as "subtle, intelligent and imaginative tales," and a later collection, *Little Tales of Misogyny,* were deemed as "written with exemplary style," but the reviewer warned they would "make the flesh crawl, but not pleasurably, as reliable suspense fiction does" (Steinberg 1986:82). Another collection, *Mermaids on the Golf Course,* was seen as "more mood pieces and psychological studies than nicely plotted stories" and as well written, although "depressing and downbeat" (Steinberg 1988:78–79).

In addition, her works have been studied by numerous literary critics in the United States and Europe, with many scholars focusing on issues of homosexuality, masculinity, and sexual identity in her works. A number of her novels were adapted for film, and there is also a good deal of comparative criticism of the formats and treatments of her works. Two recent examples are William Cook's exploration of *Ripley's Game,* which starred John Malkovich, and Wim Wenders's *The American Friend,* which was also based on *Ripley's Game.* Another comparative work examines the novels and film versions of *The Talented Mr. Ripley* and Chuck Palahniuk's *Fight Club* (Tuss).

Kathleen Gregory Klein applies feminist criticism to Highsmith's work, noting her concern with how Highsmith "almost unconsciously validates the concept of women as appropriate victims of murder or violence" (174). Odette L'Henry Evans explores a number of Highsmith's works from a variety of feminist approaches, with a particular focus on the role of women characters as they interact with the more prevalent male characters.

As Russell Harrison noted, "it is hard to evaluate Highsmith's work by conventional standards. Her achievements cannot be easily categorized in traditional terms" (136). Russell expands his comments by reminding readers that Highsmith was not considered to be a "striking stylist," and that although her plots are "ingenious," her characters are not memorable for their characteristics, but for "the intensity of their problematic" concerns with control (136).

BIBLIOGRAPHY

Works by Patricia Highsmith

Tom Ripley Series

The Talented Mr. Ripley. New York: Coward-McCann, 1955.
Ripley under Ground. New York: Doubleday, 1970.
Ripley's Game. New York: Knopf, 1974.
The Boy Who Followed Ripley. New York: Crowell, 1980.
Ripley under Water. New York: Knopf, 1991.

Other Novels

Strangers on a Train. New York: Harper, 1950.
As Claire Morgan. *The Price of Salt.* New York: Coward-McCann, 1952. (Republished as *Carol.* Tallahassee: Naiad Press, 1984.)
The Blunderer. New York: Coward-McCann, 1954. (Also published as *Lament for a Lover.* New York: Popular Library, 1956.)

Deep Water. New York: Harper, 1957.

A Game for the Living. New York: Harper, 1958.

This Sweet Sickness. New York: Harper, 1960.

The Cry of the Owl. New York: Harper, 1962.

The Two Faces of January. New York: Doubleday, 1964.

The Glass Cell. New York: Doubleday, 1964.

The Story-Teller. New York: Doubleday, 1965. (Also published as *A Suspension of Mercy.* London: Heinemann, 1965.)

Those Who Walk Away. New York: Doubleday, 1967.

The Tremor of Forgery. New York: Doubleday, 1969.

Eleven. London: Penguin, 1972.

A Dog's Ransom. New York: Knopf, 1972.

Edith's Diary. New York: Simon & Schuster, 1977.

People Who Knock on the Door. London: Heinemann, 1983; New York: Mysterious Press, 1985.

Mermaids on the Golf Course. London: Heinemann, 1985; New York: Mysterious Press, 1988.

Found in the Street. London: Heinemann, 1986; New York: Atlantic Monthly Press, 1987.

Tales of Natural and Unnatural Catastrophes. London: Heinemann, 1987; New York: Atlantic Monthly Press, 1989.

Small g: A Summer Idyll. London: Bloomsbury, 1995.

The Selected Stories of Patricia Highsmith. Foreword, Graham Greene. New York: Norton, 2001.

Nothing That Meets the Eye: The Uncollected Stories of Patricia Highsmith. New York: Norton, 2002.

Nonfiction

Plotting and Writing Suspense Fiction. New York: Writers Inc., 1966. Rev. ed.: New York: Mysterious Press, 1981.

Works about Patricia Highsmith

Bannon, Barbara. "*The Boy Who Followed Ripley.*" *Publishers Weekly* 21 March 1980: 56.

Berch, Bettina. "Patricia Highsmith." *Belles Lettres* 10.3 (Summer 1995): 64.

Boucher, Anthony. "*Deep Water.*" *New York Times* 6 October 1957: 34.

———. "Criminals at Large." *New York Times Book Review* 31 October 1965: 81–82.

Brainard, Dulcy. "*Ripley Under Water.*" *Publishers Weekly* 24 August 1992: 65.

Burgin, Richard. "*Found in the Street.*" *New York Times Book Review* 1 November 1987: 24.

Cochran, David. "'Some Torture That Perversely Eased': Patricia Highsmith and the Everyday Schizophrenia of American Life." *Clues: A Journal of Detection* 18.2 (1997): 157–80.

Cook, William A. "*Ripley's Game* and The American Friend: A Modernist and Postmodernist Comparison." *Journal of Popular Culture* 37.3 (2004): 399–408.

Corliss, Richard. "The Talented Ms. Highsmith." *Time* 27 December 1999: 159.

Dupont, Joan. "The Poet of Apprehension: Patricia Highsmith's Furtive Generosities." *Village Voice* 30 May 1995: 27–29.

"*Edith's Diary.*" *Booklist* 15 September 1977: 139.

"*Edith's Diary.*" *Publishers Weekly* 11 April 1977: 74.

Evans, Odette L'Henry. "A Feminist Approach to Patricia Highsmith's Fiction." Ed. Brian Docherty. *American Horror Fiction: From Brockden Brown to Stephen King.* New York: St. Martin's, 1990. 107–19.

Fletcher, Connie. "*The Boy Who Followed Ripley.*" *Booklist* 15 May 1980: 1344.

Harrison, Russell. *Patricia Highsmith.* New York: Twayne, 1997.

Hesford, Victoria. "Patriotic Perversions: Patricia Highsmith's Queer Vision of Cold War America in The Price of Salt, The Blunderer, and Deep Water." *Women's Studies Quarterly* 33.3/4 (2005): 215–33.

Hilfer, Anthony Channell. "'Not Really Such a Monster': Highsmith's Ripley as Thriller Protagonist and Protean Man." *Midwest Quarterly: A Journal of Contemporary Thought* 25.4 (1984): 361–74.

Johnston, Albert. "*Ripley Under Ground*." *Publishers Weekly* 20 July 1970: 69.

Klein, Kathleen Gregory. "Patricia Highsmith." *And Then There Were Nine ... More Women of Mystery*. Ed. Jane S. Bakerman. Bowling Green: Bowling Green UP, 1985. 168–97.

Little, Craig. "PW Interviews: Patricia Highsmith." *Publishers Weekly* 2 November 1992: 46–47.

Meaker, Marijane. *Highsmith: A Romance of the 1950s*. San Francisco: Cleis, 2003.

Robertson, Peter. "*Ripley Under Water*." *Booklist* 1 September 1992: 4.

Sallis, James. "*The Selected Stories of Patricia Highsmith*." *Boston Review* 26.5 (2001). 31 March 2006. http://www.bostonreview.net/BR26.5/sallis.html

"*The Snail Watchers and Other Stories*." *Publishers Weekly* 20 April 1970: 56.

Steinberg, Sybil. "Little Tales of Misogyny." *Publishers Weekly* 7 March 1986: 82.

———. "*Mermaids on the Golf Course*." *Publishers Weekly* 28 August 1988: 78.

Stenger, Karl L. "Patricia Highsmith." *Dictionary of Literary Biography*, Vol. 306: American Mystery and Detective Writers. Ed. George Parker Anderson. Detroit: Gale, 2005. 144–61.

"*The Talented Mr. Ripley*." *New Yorker* 7 January 1956: 76.

Thomas, Margaret Caldwell. "Patricia Highsmith: Murder with a Twist." *Women of Mystery*. Ed. Martha Hailey Dubose. New York: St. Martin's, 2000. 326–39.

Tuss, Alex. "Masculine Identity and Success: A Critical Analysis of Patricia Highsmith's The Talented Mr. Ripley and Chuck Palahniuk's Fight Club." *Journal of Men's Studies: A Scholarly Journal about Men and Masculinities* 12.2 (2004): 93–102.

Villalon, Oscar C. "The Talented Ms. Highsmith—Ripley Author Transcended Crime Genre with Unsettling Insights into Evil." *San Francisco Chronicle* 11 January 2000: B1.

Wilson, Andrew. *Beautiful Shadow: A Life of Patricia Highsmith*. London: Bloomsbury, 2003.

P. D. James (1920–)

BIOGRAPHY

Phyllis Dorothy James was born on August 3, 1920, in Oxford, England, to Sidney Victor and Dorothy May Hone James. Her father was an officer of the Internal Revenue agency. She grew up with two younger siblings, Monica and Edward. The family lived in Ludlow before moving to Cambridge in 1931, and she attended Cambridge Girls' High School from 1931 to 1937. Unable to attend college because of financial reasons and the fact that her father was "not disposed to educate girls" (Siebenheller 1), James left school at age 16 and began working in a tax office. This did not keep her from reading widely and educating herself, particularly in literature and architecture. She also gained experience as assistant stage manager for Cambridge's Festival Theatre, work that she enjoyed more than the tax office (Gidez 1).

She married Ernest Conner Bantry White in August 1941. Her husband was a doctor and served in the Royal Army Medical Corps, and she worked as a Red Cross nurse during the war. White suffered from post-traumatic stress syndrome and never fully recovered. Often hospitalized, he was unable to maintain a regular medical practice. James returned to work full-time to support them and their two daughters, Clare and Jane. She was hired by the North West Regional Hospital Board in London, and she held the position of principal administrative assistant from 1949 to 1968.

She began writing an hour or two each day, hoping to fulfill her childhood dream of being a novelist and wanting to avoid being "one of those failed writers who never got down to it" (Gidez 2). She had always enjoyed reading mysteries, particularly Dorothy L. Sayers and Margery Allingham, and she turned to that genre when she began writing her first novel in earnest (Gidez 5; Joyner 109). She believed that detective fiction was "challenging," with its "inner tensions between plot and character and atmosphere," but also pragmatically determined that she might have better success becoming published by writing genre fiction (Joyner 108). *Cover Her Face,* her first novel, and the first to feature Adam Dalgliesh, was published in 1962. It was accepted by the first publisher who reviewed the work. She chose to use her initials to avoid being classified as a woman writer, and she used her maiden name to distance her writing from her professional life (Reynolds 86).

Her husband died in 1964, and in 1968, she moved in a civil service position as the principal administrative assistant for the police department, in the Department of Home Affairs in London. In 1972, she transferred to another position in the Criminal Policy Department. She retired in 1979 to devote herself fully to her writing. James has noted that knowledge gained from her work experience in the police department and in hospitals gave her valuable information for her writing..

She received the Order of the British Empire in 1983 and was named a Life Peer of the United Kingdom in 1991. She published a "fragment" of an autobiography entitled *Time to Be in Earnest* in 1999, which consists of journal entries on a wide range of topics. James resides in London.

MAJOR WORKS AND THEMES

Most of the novels written by James focus on police inspector Adam Dalgliesh. Two of her mystery novels, though, focus on a private investigator named Cordelia Gray, with Dalgliesh making cameo appearances. The Gray series is composed of *Unsuitable for a Woman* (1972) and *The Skull Beneath the Skin* (1982). In the first novel, Gray is working as an apprentice to a private detective, who formerly served in the police force under Dalgliesh. When he commits suicide, she learns she has inherited the firm and eagerly takes on her first case, hired by Sir Ronald Callender to discover why his son committed suicide. In the 10 years between the novels, James received numerous requests to write more novels about Gray and many letters asking if Gray and Dalgliesh would marry. James published an essay entitled "Ought Adam to Marry Cordelia?" in which she discussed the topic of married sleuths in the genre and noted that "the love interest complicates and confuses both the investigation and the hero's emotions" (69). Yet after the second novel, Gray did not return. Nicola Nixon's essay explores the differences between the first and second novels through the lens of feminist criticism, providing theories about why the series did not continue. However, James stated in her autobiography that the reason she did not write further novels featuring Gray was that a British television show based on the character had "violated" her concept of Gray by "saddling her with an unwanted pregnancy" (Breen 36).

The bulk of her work features Dalgliesh, an intelligent, sensitive widower who is a published poet in addition to his profession as a homicide investigator. The first novel features many classic elements of a Golden Age mystery, with a murder occurring at a country house filled with suspects, all of whom are harboring secrets. With James's second novel, though, Norma Siebenheller noted that the author "comes into her own as an innovative writer (12). Siebenheller also points out that James opens her third novel with a provocative opening line, immediately "plung[ing] into mayhem" (19).

Her next three novels included two Dalgliesh novels, both of which won Silver Dagger awards from the Crime Writers Association, and the often-studied *An Unsuitable Job for a Woman,* discussed previously. *A Shroud for a Nightingale* features a series of murders of student nurses, and *The Black Tower* finds Dalgliesh recuperating from a serious illness that had been misdiagnosed as a fatal one. Dalgliesh decides to visit an old friend in Dorset and reflect on his life while he recovers from both the illness and the shock of learning it was not after all terminal. When he arrives, he finds his friend has recently died and has already been cremated. Dalgliesh uncovers clues that the death may not have been natural.

The next three Dalgliesh novels, *Death of an Expert Witness, A Taste for Death,* and *Devices and Desires* were published over a span of 13 years. Since 1995, though, she has focused on the Dalgliesh series, publishing an entry in the series every two to three years. In *Original Sin,* James introduces a new detective inspector, Kate Miskin, who has overcome a disadvantaged background to rise through the ranks of the police force. She assists him with a tricky case involving a publishing firm. *A Certain Justice* and *Death in Holy Orders* focused on the murder of a most unlikable barrister and murder at a seminary, respectively. *The Murder Room* features a locked-room type mystery, with a corpse discovered in a museum that features historical crimes.

Harriet Waugh points out that since James's retirement from civil service, the typical resolution of her novels has shifted. As Waugh noted, none of the murderers in James's novels have had "to face a jury of his peers in a criminal court or sweat it out behind bars," and instead "die rather melodramatically" (1997: 48). Despite this note, critics have described the more recent Dalgliesh novels as deeply satisfying explorations of the justice system and contemporary society (Caldwell L1; Quackenbush 24).

In addition to her mystery novels, James has also written two stand-alone novels, *Innocent Blood* and *The Children of Men.* The former is a novel of suspense about a woman who searches for her biological parents and discovers an awful truth, and the latter features a futuristic dystopia where humans have lost the ability to reproduce. She also has several plays and numerous short stories and essays to her credit, along with a work of nonfiction that explored a nineteenth-century murder case.

CRITICAL RECEPTION

P. D. James has won numerous awards for her writing, including honors for individual works, along with the Diamond Dagger, the highest honor for lifetime achievement bestowed by the Crime Writers Association.

Richard B. Gidez catalogues some early critical responses to James in his monograph. Renowned critic Anthony Boucher, writing in the *New York Times Book Review* in July 1966, found *Cover Her Face* to be "a literate and not unpromising first novel"; Jacques Barzun called it "immensely pleasing and impressive" (Gidez 24–25). *A Mind to Murder* was noted for its "double-barreled ending that will keep you in great suspense" and its "nice touches of wit and deft personality sketches"(Bannon 71).

Publishers Weekly called *The Black Tower* "very realistic and honest" and praised it for its portrayal of people with disabilities in a nursing home ("*The Black Tower*" 64). The *Booklist* reviewer called it "one to savor" and noted that the "suspense builds with choice detail" ("*The Black Tower*" 118). One review of *Death of an Expert Witness* noted that "a disturbing perspective on crime combines brilliant plotting with the Scotland Yard's unrivaled Adam Dalgliesh" (666), and the *Publishers Weekly* reviewer stated that Dalgliesh's "sensitivity to the human condition is one of his greatest talents" ("*Death of an Expert Witness*" 143). This review also noted that "James's insights into sexual fears and needs ... is profound" and commented on her ability to create characters, even murderers, who can be pitied ("*Death of an Expert Witness*" 143).

Although *A Taste for Death* has erudite characters, "James's civilized digressions do not detract from the suspense of the plot" and her careful attention to detail "totally immerses readers in the investigation" (Steinberg 1986:90). Another review found Dalgliesh to be "painstakingly brilliant" and the novel to be "ambitious, powerful" and "almost Dickensian" ("*A Taste for Death*" 1633). *Devices and Desires* was called "dark, with deeply and sympathetically plumbed characters" and was heralded as an "intricate, layered mystery [which] may be read as parable: we can escape the consequences of our choices no more than we can shed our personal histories" (Steinberg 1989:48).

Original Sin was called "well written and literate," with the "unraveling of the mystery beautifully done" (Bowen F5). Another reviewer found that James gave "pride of place" to "lush, leisurely descriptions of waterside London" (Brainard 48). James was noted for paying "careful attention to the rigors of the formula" in *Original Sin*, but the reviewer stressed that the novel is more than just "building scenarios and detecting red herrings," featuring extensive, realistic character development (Ott 779).

One review of *A Certain Justice* praised James's "virtuoso ingenuity" and praised the novel as "thought-provoking" and "gripping" (Kemp 23). Another found it "deeply satisfying" with a "meticulously crafted momentum" (Caldwell L1), with another noting James's "keen eye for detail and character" and her interest in the "mysteries of the human condition" in addition to the details of the detective work (Quackenbush 24).

Death in Holy Orders was heralded as demonstrating "impressive mastery over the complex plotting" (O'Donoghue 21), and another reviewer noted that James used a "defiantly traditional form" in creating a "serious, sombre novel about guilt, remorse, responsibility and death" (Mann 55). Reviews of the recent *The Murder Room* were somewhat mixed, with some praising her return to more classic plots, and others criticizing her return to less action-packed plots (Waugh 2003:59). Even those who thought the novel had weaknesses, however, reminded the reader of James's excellence in "characterization and basic human psychology" ("*The Murder Room*" 47).

In the introduction to her book, Siebenheller noted that little had been written about James at that time. In the ensuing 25 years, literary scholarship focusing on James has grown immensely. James has been widely studied by international literary scholars taking numerous approaches. In addition to British and American critics, James has been examined by scholars writing in German, Spanish, Italian, Finnish, Swedish, and other languages.

Mary Hadley sees James as a "bridge" between Golden Age writers like Agatha Christie and later feminist writers (17). For Hadley, James's focus on the psychological aspects of the victims and murderers is a key element, with her introspection and "concern with justice" making her a "far more profound and serious writer" than Christie (17). Throughout her chapter on James, Hadley examines the character of Cordelia Gray, analyzing her place within feminist writing. Joan G. Kotker also focuses on Gray, contrasting her characterization in the two novels that feature her. Jane S. Bakerman analyzed the first novel as a *bildungsroman* of Gray's development.

Susan Rowland explores the use of the gothic in a modern sense in James's work, particularly focusing on her settings, such as the castle that Gray visits in *The Skull Beneath the Skin*, and the various plots that are linked to the atrocities of World War II (137–140). Christine Wick Sizemore also focuses on the importance of setting in James's works. Sizemore's book looks at London as written by James, Doris Lessing, Margaret Drabble, Iris Murdoch, and

Maureen Duffy. Her chapter on James's work explores the connections between urban and rural settings in her novels. It is not surprising that setting has been the focus of several critical studies. James has stated that the settings are most important to her as she begins writing a new novel, that "the inspiration usually comes from a place" (Krangle D7).

James F. Maxfield analyzed *An Unsuitable Job for a Woman* by looking at psychological elements in the novel, including the impact of characters taking on father figure roles for Gray. Eric Nelson also focuses on psychological aspects of James's work, also focusing on the Gray novels. Nelson explores the level of dispassion or dissociation in the works of James, with parallels drawn to Edgar Allan Poe, Willkie Collins, and Arthur Conan Doyle.

Although literary critic Martin Priestman cannot accept James as an author of true, highbrow literary fiction, Betty Richardson describes how James's work, with its lengthiness, lack of graphic sex and violence, allusions to mythology and art, and literary style, succeeds as both literary and bestselling fiction. Richardson also provides a comparative study of James and T. S. Eliot. Delphine Kresge-Cingal also explores links between James's writings and various masters of British literature, including Shakespeare, Marlowe, and others.

BIBLIOGRAPHY

Works by P. D. James

Adam Dalgliesh Series

Cover Her Face. London: Faber & Faber, 1962; New York: Scribners, 1966.
A Mind to Murder. London: Faber & Faber, 1963; New York: Scribners, 1967.
*Unnatural Cause*s. New York: Scribners, 1967.
Shroud for a Nightingale. New York: Scribners, 1971.
The Black Tower. New York: Scribners, 1975.
Death of an Expert Witness. New York: Scribners, 1977.
A Taste for Death. New York: Knopf, 1986.
Devices and Desires. New York: Knopf, 1990.
Original Sin. New York: Knopf, 1995.
A Certain Justice. New York: Knopf, 1997.
Death in Holy Orders. New York: Knopf, 2001.
The Murder Room. New York: Knopf, 2003.
The Lighthouse. New York: Knopf, 2005.

Cordelia Gray Series

An Unsuitable Job for a Woman. London: Faber & Faber, 1972; New York: Scribners, 1973.
The Skull Beneath the Skin. New York: Scribners, 1982.

Other Novels

Innocent Blood. New York: Scribners, 1980.
The Children of Men. New York: Knopf, 1993.

Selected Nonfiction Works

"Ought Adam to Marry Cordelia?" *Murder Ink.* Ed. Dilys Winn. New York: Workman, 1977. 68–69.
With T. A. Critchley. *The Maul and the Pear Tree: The Ratcliffe Highway Murders, 1811.* London: Constable, 1971. Reprinted by Mysterious Press (New York), 1986.

"The Art of the Detective Novel." *New Welsh Review* II.1 (1989): 4–9.
Time to Be in Earnest: A Fragment of Autobiography. London: Faber & Faber, 1999.

Works about P. D. James

Bakerman, Jane S. "Cordelia Gray: Apprentice and Archetype." *Clues* 5.1 (1984): 101–14.
Bannon, B. A. "*A Mind to Murder.*" *Publishers Weekly* 6 February 1967: 71.
Barber, Lynn. "The Cautious Heart of P. D. James." *Vanity Fair* March 1993: 80–94.
"*The Black Tower.*" *Booklist* 15 September 1975: 118.
"*The Black Tower.*" *Publishers Weekly* 18 August 1975: 64.
Bowen, Jill. "P. D. James Delights Fans with Her Latest Mystery." *Roanoke Times & World News* 21 May 1995: F5.
Brainard, Dulcy. "*Original Sin.*" *Publishers Weekly* 19 December 1994: 48.
Breen, Jon. "Murder Most British." *Weekly Standard* 8 December 2003: 36.
Caldwell, Gail. "Laying Down the Law." *Boston Globe* 16 November 1997: L1.
"*Death of an Expert Witness.*" *Booklist* 15 December 1977: 666.
"*Death of an Expert Witness.*" *Publishers Weekly* 19 September 1977: 143.
Gidez, Richard B. *P. D. James.* Boston: Twayne, 1986.
Goddard, Donald. "The Unmysterious P. D. James." *New York Times Book Review* 27 April 1980: 26.
Hadley, Mary. *British Women Mystery Writers.* Jefferson; London: McFarland, 2002.
Joyner, Nancy Carol. "P. D. James." *10 Women of Mystery.* Ed. Earl F. Bargainnier. Bowling Green: Bowling Green State UP, 1981. 107–23.
Kemp, Peter. "Baroque Decease." *Times Literary Supplement* 2 October 1997: 23.
Kotker, Joan G. "The Re-Imagining of Cordelia Gray." *Women Times Three.* Ed. Kathleen Gregory Klein. Bowling Green: Bowling Green State UP, 1995. 53–64.
Krangle, Karenn. "Interview with the Author: P. D. James Knows How to Get Inside a Character." *Vancouver Sun* 26 November 1994: D7.
Kresge-Cingal, Delphine. "Intertextuality in the Detective Fiction of P. D. James: Literary Game or Strategic Choice?" *Clues* 22.2 (2001): 141–52.
Macdonald, Andrew F. "P. D. James." *Dictionary of Literary Biography,* Vol. 276: *British Mystery and Thriller Writers Since 1960.* Ed. Gina Macdonald. Detroit: Gale, 2003. 217–28.
Mann, Jessica. "Dalgliesh Must Score." *New Statesman* 5 March 2001: 55.
Maxfield, James F. "The Unfinished Detective: The Work of P. D. James." *Critique* 28 (Summer 1987): 211–23.
"*The Murder Room.*" *Publishers Weekly* 15 September 2003: 47.
Nelson, Eric. "P. D. James and the Dissociation of Sensibility." *British Women Writing Fiction.* Ed. Abby H. P. Werlock. Tuscaloosa: U Alabama P, 2000. 56–69.
Nixon, Nicola. "Gray Areas: P. D. James's Unsuiting of Cordelia." Ed. Glenwood Irons. *Feminism in Women's Detective Fiction.* Toronto: U Toronto P, 1995. 29–45.
O'Donoghue, Heather. "Bells and Smells." *Times Literary Supplement* 2 March 2001: 21.
Ott, Bill. "*Original Sin.*" *Booklist* 1 January 1995: 779.
Priestman, Martin. "P. D. James and the Distinguished Thing." *On Modern British Fiction.* Ed. Zachary Leader. Oxford: Oxford UP, 2002. 234–57.
Quackenbush, Rich. "Disorder in the Court." *Houston Chronicle* 14 December 1997: 24.
Reynolds, Moira Davidson. *Women Authors of Detective Series.* Jefferson; London: McFarland, 2001.
Richardson, Betty. "'Sweet Thames, Run Softly': P. D. James's Waste Land in *A Taste for Death.*" *Clues* 9.2 (1988): 105–18.
Rowland, Susan. "The Horror of Modernity and the Utopian Sublime: Gothic Villainy in P. D. James and Ruth Rendell." *The Devil Himself: Villainy in Detective Fiction and Film.* Westport: Greenwood, 2002. 135–46.
Siebenheller, Norma. *P.D. James.* New York: Ungar, 1981.
Steinberg, Sybil. "*A Taste for Death.*" *Publishers Weekly* 5 September 1986: 90.
———. "*Devices and Desires.*" *Publishers Weekly* 1 December 1989: 48.

"*A Taste for Death.*" *Booklist* August 1986: 1633.

Waugh, Harriet. "Who Caused the Deaths and What the Deaths Caused." *The Spectator* 18 October 1997: 48.

———. "Trouble at the Mill." *The Spectator* 21 June 2003: 59.

J. A. Jance (1944–)

BIOGRAPHY

Judith Ann Busk was born on October 27, 1944, in Watertown, South Dakota, to Norman and Evelyn Anderson Busk. Her father was an insurance salesman. The family moved to Arizona when she was young, and she grew up in Bisbee. She describes herself as the third child in a large family, but she was four years younger than the second child and four years older than the fourth, which she says left her "alone in a crowd" and helped her grow into a reader and excellent student (homepage).

She earned a scholarship for college and was the first in her family to attend university. Jance had wanted to be a writer from an early age. She was introduced to Frank Baum's *Wizard of Oz* series in the second grade and wanted to be the person "who had put the words on those pages" ("One Book" F11). At the University of Arizona, she was refused admittance to creative writing courses because of the professor's gender bias. She noted that "being excluded from that class may have slowed me down, but it didn't stop me," and that her favorite book of the many she has published is *Hour of the Hunter,* in which the villain is a creative writing professor from the University of Arizona ("One Book" F11, Wigod E21).

She earned a bachelor's degree in English and secondary education in 1966 and a master's degree in library science in 1970 from the University of Arizona. The university also awarded her an honorary doctorate in 2000. She taught English at a Tucson high school and also worked as a librarian for the Indian Oasis Schools in Sells, Arizona. From 1974 to 1984, she lived in New York and worked as a district manager for an insurance company. In 1985, she turned to writing mysteries full-time after producing a true crime manuscript that didn't sell and several children's books that were published.

She married Jerry Joseph Teale Jance in 1967; they divorced in 1980. She was married again in 1985, to a widower named William Alan Schilb. She has a daughter and son from her first marriage and three stepchildren and lives in Bellevue, Washington.

MAJOR WORKS AND THEMES

Jance writes two different mystery series and she also writes thrillers. One of her series features a recovered alcoholic homicide detective in Seattle named J. P. Beaumont; the other series focuses on Joanna Brady, a woman sheriff in Arizona.

Beaumont is a prickly loner who is a successful homicide detective but is never really part of the team. His drinking becomes increasingly problematic in the series; he enters a treatment program in the seventh book. In the first book, he falls in love and marries a woman who turns out to be a killer; however, she leaves him her substantial fortune. Like John Sandford's independently wealthy police detective Lucas Davenport, Beaumont has financial freedom that his colleagues do not enjoy.

Jance uses experiences from her life in her writing. She grew up in Arizona, and she lives in Seattle, and she uses those two places as settings for her books. She also uses her experiences for character development. Her first husband was an alcoholic, who died two years after she divorced him. Her experiences of living with him for many years allows her to portray Beaumont's problems, and supporting their children alone after the divorce gave her experience to create the Joanna Brady character.

Joanna Brady is introduced to readers as the daughter of a former sheriff and the wife of the current sheriff. Her husband is killed early in the first book, and Brady takes it upon herself to solve his murder. She is subsequently elected sheriff to replace him. Family life is important in the series, as Brady juggles her new job responsibilities with raising their daughter alone. She is close to her in-laws, and her mother also lives nearby. Friction with her mother provides some comic relief in the series. Bill Farley points out that, perhaps ironically, the Beaumont novels are written in first person, but the Brady series is told in third person (567). In 2002's *Partner in Crime,* Beaumont travels to Arizona for a case and joins forces with Brady. That novel alternates between them, using first and third person as appropriate. Farley also noted that both series are action oriented, but are above all, "stories about conflicts between people" and are solved through the detectives' "observation of human nature [rather] than from police science" (567).

In interviews and on her Web site, Jance has rated her mystery series as "PG-13" but warns readers that her thrillers are "R"-rated. The three thrillers, which focus on some of the same characters and cover a wide range of time, are certainly grittier and more graphic than the two series. In 1970, Jance's first husband unwittingly got a ride home from a man who had just committed murder. Her husband was then involved as a witness, and the case was covered in Jance's true crime manuscript that was never published. This experience eventually became the basis for the plot in *Hour of the Hunter,* although all details are fictionalized. *Hour of the Hunter* is set in 1970 and includes a great deal of information about Native American customs. The plot is complex, tying together a number of disparate characters who are terrorized by a crazed killer. *Kiss of the Bees* revisits two of those characters years later. Writer Diana Ladd and sheriff Brandon Walker have married since the first book and are living with their adopted daughter, when the murderer's new disciple gains release from prison and returns to finish what they started in 1970. *Day of the Dead* finds Ladd and Walker struggling with a new evil that arises from a cold case Walker investigates.

In 2004, the University of Arizona Press released a revised edition of *After the Fire;* the original version was a chapbook of poems Jance wrote about her life with her alcoholic husband. The revised edition includes additional narrative to provide background information about the poems.

CRITICAL RECEPTION

Reviews of the thrillers often mention the increased gore and violence as compared to the Brady and Beaumont books, but these novels tend to rate more highly among reviewers. Jance's incorporation of Native American lore is also touted by most reviewers. *Kiss of the Bees* was acclaimed as a "fine thriller" in which Jance "skillfully interweave[s] Native American legend and the magic of the Southwest with a riveting tale of psychological suspense" (Melton 580). In a review of *Day of the Dead,* Stephanie Zvirin noted that "suspense builds gradually in the multilayered novel, which is filtered through multiple perspectives, each person adding a piece to a textured puzzle that tracks a pair of serial killers whose crimes extend backward across three decades. As in Jance's two series, the action is intermixed with well-placed social commentary" (1670).

In a review of *Paradise Lost,* Peter Cannon noted that "With more than two dozen mysteries to her credit, the author has learned a great deal about pacing and it's evident in this page-turner, which nicely builds suspense and throws in some nifty surprises as well. Jance's sense of place remains strong, whether here in the beautifully rendered rural Arizona setting or in the rainy Seattle of her J. P. Beaumont mysteries" (54). A review of *Breach of Duty* describes the complex plot, noting that "throughout all this, one gets the sense that things are not as they seem, that there's an undercurrent of evil at work—and that would be an accurate intuition. As both cases escalate and personal lives become more complicated, one can only surmise there will be surprises at the end. Jance doesn't disappoint" (DuVal 3).

Marilyn Rye takes up a common critical pursuit, which explores the notion of whether detective fiction written by women about women characters can be feminist. Kathleen Gregory Klein and others "have concluded that genre conventions inevitably lead authors to subvert or sabotage female heroines" (Rye 105). Rye compared Jance's portrayals of male and female protagonists to see whether gender issues influence the character development and plots of the novels. Rye concludes that Jance uses a "repetition of the heroic plot" in the Beaumont series, whereas the Brady series "demonstrates the progressive professional and moral development of her female detective character" (118).

BIBLIOGRAPHY

Works by J. A. Jance

J. P. Beaumont Series

Until Proven Guilty. New York: Avon, 1985.
Injustice for All. New York: Avon, 1986.
Trial by Fury. New York: Avon, 1987.
Improbable Cause. New York: Avon, 1987.
A More Perfect Union. New York: Avon, 1988.
Dismissed with Prejudice. New York: Avon, 1989.
Minor in Possession. New York: Avon, 1990.
Payment in Kind. New York: Avon, 1991.
Without Due Process. New York: Morrow, 1992.
Failure to Appear. New York: Morrow, 1993.
Lying in Wait. New York: Morrow, 1994.
Name Withheld. New York: Morrow, 1995.
Breach of Duty. New York: Morrow, 1999.
Birds of Prey. New York: Morrow, 2001.
Partner in Crime. New York: Morrow, 2002.
Long Time Gone. New York: Morrow, 2005.

Joanna Brady Series

Desert Heat. New York: Avon, 1993.
Tombstone Courage. New York: Morrow, 1994.
Shoot/Don't Shoot. New York: Avon, 1995.
Dead to Rights. New York: Avon, 1997.
Skeleton Canyon. New York: Avon, 1997.
Rattlesnake Crossing. New York: Avon, 1998.
Outlaw Mountain. New York: Avon, 1999.

Devil's Claw. New York: Morrow, 2000.
Paradise Lost. New York: Morrow, 2001.
Partner in Crime. New York: Morrow, 2002.
Exit Wounds. New York: Morrow, 2003.
Dead Wrong. New York: Morrow, 2006.

Other Works

Hour of the Hunter. New York: Morrow, 1991.
Kiss of the Bees. New York: Avon, 2000.
Day of the Dead. New York: Morrow, 2004.
After the Fire. Rev. ed. Tucson: U Arizona P, 2004.
Edge of Evil. New York: Avon, 2006.

Works about J. A. Jance

Cannon, Peter. "*Paradise Lost.*" *Publishers Weekly* 23 July 2001: 53–54.
DuVal, Linda. "*Breach of Duty.*" *Chicago Tribune* 4 February 1999: 3.
Farley, Bill. "J. A. Jance." *St. James Guide to Crime & Mystery Writers.* 4th ed. Ed. Jay P. Pederson. Detroit: St. James Press, 1996. 566–68.
J. A. Jance. Homepage. 2005. 20 May 2005. http://jajance.com/index.htm
"J(udith) A(nn) Jance." *Contemporary Authors.* Vol. 105, New Revision Series. Ed. Scot Peacock. Detroit: Gale, 2002. 272–74.
Melton, Emily. "*Kiss of the Bees.*" *Booklist* 15 November 1999: 580.
"One Book that Changed Your Life: J. A. Jance." *The Oregonian* 23 July 2000: F11.
Rye, Marilyn. "Changing Gender Conventions and the Detective Formula: J. A. Jance's Beaumont and Brady Series." *Journal of Popular Culture* 37.1 (2003): 105–19.
Wigod, Rebecca. "This Writer Makes a Killing: Rebuffed by Academe, J. A Jance Had No Trouble Finding Readers for Her Thrillers." *The Vancouver Sun* 17 February 2001: E21.
Zvirin, Stephanie. "*Day of the Dead.*" *Booklist* June 2004: 1670.

Faye Kellerman (1952–)

BIOGRAPHY

Faye Kellerman was born on July 31, 1952, in St. Louis, Missouri, to Oscar and Anne Steinberg Marder. Her father was a retailer. When she was five years old, her parents packed up their three children to move to Arizona, although they settled in Los Angeles instead.

She married Jonathan Seth Kellerman, who is a psychologist and also a novelist, on July 23, 1972. They have four children, Jesse Oren, Rachel Diana, Ilana Judith, and Aliza Celeste. Jesse Kellerman is following is his parents' footsteps and has published a mystery novel.

Kellerman earned her bachelor's degree in mathematics in 1974 from the University of California-Los Angeles, and in 1978, she earned a D.D.S. degree from UCLA. She was pregnant with her first child when she finished her degree, and so she didn't begin practicing dentistry immediately; "no great loss for the American Dental Association," Kellerman has joked (Reynolds 64). After her child was born, she felt the need to write, and wrote a number of romances, which remain unpublished. She eventually turned to mystery fiction, never returned to dentistry, and her first mystery novel *The Ritual Bath* was published in 1986.

MAJOR WORKS AND THEMES

Most of Kellerman's work features Peter Decker, a police detective, and Rina Lazarus, who is a young Orthodox Jewish widow when they first meet. Decker investigates a rape that occurred at Lazarus' synagogue. The series combines graphic depictions of serious crimes with sensitive portrayals of Decker, Lazarus, and their families.

Judaism plays a major role in the novels. Kellerman is a practicing modern Orthodox Jew and she noted that she has "a great deal of love for the religion" and wanted to "transmit some of that feeling and emotion" through her writing (Kornbluth). Kellerman enjoys learning about other cultures and religions and thought her readers might also enjoy learning about Orthodox Judaism (Kornbluth).

As the series progresses, Decker and Lazarus begin a romantic relationship, made difficult because of their different backgrounds. This prompts Decker's family to tell him that he was adopted at birth and was born to a Jewish woman. Learning about his heritage strengthens Decker's interest in Judaism, and he fully converts before he and Lazarus marry.

During their honeymoon trip to New York, they are drawn into investigating the disappearance of Lazarus's nephew in *Day of Atonement.* Lazarus stays home with her new baby during most of *Grievous Sin,* as Decker solves a kidnapping case, but is back in the forefront in *Sanctuary.* Decker and Lazarus go to Israel together to investigate a case involving diamonds. *Justice* differs from the other novels in that part of the story is told in first person by a young woman whose friend is accused of murder. In addition to crimes of murder and missing persons, Decker is drawn into a case involving a cult in *Jupiter's Bones.* Two of the recent novels prominently feature Decker's daughter from his first marriage, Cindy, who has joined the police force. In *Street Dreams* and *Stalker,* Cindy Decker takes the lead, with her cases at the focus of the novels.

In addition to the Decker and Lazarus series, Kellerman has written two stand-alone novels. The first, *The Quality of Mercy,* features William Shakespeare as an amateur detective. Shakespeare is in love with a Spanish Jewish woman whose father was the physician of Elizabeth I. The second nonseries novel, *Moon Music,* tells the story of twins, one of whom is a near giant, and the other normally proportioned and who works as a detective. In addition, she and her husband collaborated for the first time in 2004's *Double Homicide,* which features two novellas, both with distinct settings and detectives. The book was manufactured in a "flip" style with two covers for the two stories, one of which takes place in Boston and the other in Sante Fe.

CRITICAL RECEPTION

Kellerman won a Macavity Award for her first novel, *The Ritual Bath.* The early novels in the series were well received, with critics praising Kellerman's blending of Judaism with Decker's secular world and the skillful portrayal of the growing relationship between Decker and Lazarus.

Criticism of later works has also been uniformly positive. In a review of *Stalker,* which features Cindy Decker prominently, Jeff Zaleski praised how Kellerman deals "realistically with the problems women face in a male police world" (47). Zaleski also noted that "her development of the tense father-daughter relationship is wise and honest: Decker is torn between his inability to accept Cindy as an independent adult and his pride in her accomplishments" (47).

A review of *The Forgotten* applauds how "Kellerman again adroitly balances Rina Lazarus's consuming Orthodox Judaism with the broader societal issues faced by her husband,

L.A. homicide detective Peter Decker," also noting that Kellerman "seamlessly weaves her themes of religious belief and familial respect into a multilayered thriller, with finely realized characters and a tangible sense of place" (Cannon 2001:161).

Oline H. Cogdill notes that "Kellerman has shown how religious beliefs affect every aspect of life—from family relations to the methodical investigation of a murder" (7F). In comparing Lazarus's work with her husband's, Cogdill states that "Faye Kellerman's mysteries are more personal, with multidimensional characters realistically constructed and action quick and plausible" (7F).

In a review of *Stone Kiss,* which features a return of the young criminal from *Justice,* Peter Cannon noted that "whether Kellerman is depicting the ultra-Orthodox Jewish community or a pornographer's studio, she is utterly convincing" (2002:57). Cannon continues that, "amid the wreckage of lives taken or thrown away, Kellerman's heroes find glimmers of hope and enough moral ambiguity to make even her most evil villain look less than totally black" (2002:57).

In addition to commercial reviews, several literary scholars have studied Kellerman's works. In an examination of the first four novels, Ellen Serlen Uffen points out that detective fiction is "the most orthodox literary form," in that it follows conventions and "organizes closely the movements" of the good and evil characters (196). Carmen Birkle explores how Lazarus negotiates the expectations of her as an Orthodox wife with her contributions to Decker's work (63–67), in addition to addressing issues of gender roles in the novels. Laurence Roth also studies Kellerman's series in his book *Inspecting Jews: American Jewish Detective Stories.* Roth carefully describes the two characters and looks at the impact of the marriage on their identities and work. Diana Arbin Ben-Merre explores the role of Judaism in several mystery writers' works. Although many works focus on the Lazarus character, she looks specifically at Decker's conversion and his relationship to the religion.

BIBLIOGRAPHY

Works by Faye Kellerman

Peter Decker and Rina Lazarus Series

The Ritual Bath. New York: Arbor House, 1986.
Sacred and Profane. New York: Arbor House, 1987.
Milk and Honey. New York: Morrow, 1990.
Day of Atonement. New York: Morrow, 1991.
False Prophet. New York: Morrow, 1992.
Grievous Sin. New York: Morrow, 1993.
Sanctuary. New York: Morrow, 1994.
Justice. New York: Morrow, 1995.
Prayers for the Dead. New York: Morrow, 1996.
Serpent's Tooth. New York: Morrow, 1997.
Jupiter's Bones. New York: Morrow, 1999.
Stalker. New York: Morrow, 2000.
The Forgotten. New York: Morrow, 2001.
Stone Kiss. New York: Warner, 2002.
Street Dreams. New York: Warner, 2003.

Other Works

The Quality of Mercy. New York: Morrow, 1988.
Moon Music. New York: Morrow, 1998.

Double Homicide. With Jonathan Kellerman. New York: Warner, 2004.
Straight into Darkness. New York: Warner, 2005.
The Garden of Eden and Other Criminal Delights. New York: Warner, 2006.

Works about Faye Kellerman

Ben-Merre, Diana Arbin. "Murdering Traditional Assumptions: The Jewish-American Mystery." *The Detective in American Fiction, Film and Television.* Eds. Jerome H. Delamater and Ruth Prigozy. Westport: Greenwood, 1998. 57–69.

Birkle, Carmen. "Of Sherlocks, Shylocks, and the Shoah: Ethnicity in Jewish American Detective Fiction." *Sleuthing Ethnicity: The Detective in Multiethnic Crime Fiction.* Eds. Dorothea Fischer-Hornung and Monika Mueller. Madison: Fairleigh Dickinson UP, 2003. 53–80.

Cannon, Peter. "*The Forgotten: A Peter Decker/Rina Lazarus Novel.*" *Publishers Weekly* 16 July 2001: 161.

————. "*Stone Kiss: A Peter Decker/Rina Lazarus Novel.*" *Publishers Weekly* 1 July 2002: 57.

Cogdill, Oline H. "Faith Helps Solve the Crime." *Sun Sentinel* 31 August 1997: 7F.

"Faye Kellerman." *Contemporary Authors.* Vol. 60, New Revision Series. Eds. Daniel Jones and John D. Jorgensen. Detroit: Gale, 1998. 200–203.

Kornbluth, Jesse and Jennifer Levitsky. Book Report. 2 October 1996. 25 May 2005. http://www.bookreporter.com/authors/au-kellerman-faye.asp

Reynolds, Susan Salter. "Faye Kellerman: Murder on Her Mind." *Publishers Weekly* 18 August 1997: 64–65.

Roth, Laurence. *Inspecting Jews: American Jewish Detective Stories.* New Brunswick: Rutgers UP, 2004.

Uffen, Ellen Serlen. "The Orthodox Detective Novels of Faye Kellerman." *Studies in American Jewish Literature* 11.2 (1992): 195–203.

Zaleski, Jeff. "*Stalker: A Peter Decker/Rina Lazarus Novel.*" *Publishers Weekly* 10 July 2000: 47.

Laurie R. King (1952–)

BIOGRAPHY

Notable for having a longstanding email listserv dedicated to one of her characters, Laurie R. King was born September 19, 1952, in Oakland, California. Her father Roger Richardson was a furniture restorer, and her mother, Mary Dickson Richardson, worked as a librarian and curator. King earned a bachelor's degree in comparative religion at the University of California Santa Cruz in 1977 and married Noel King, a professor, that same year. She also earned a master's degree in theology from the Graduate Theological Union in 1984.

She began writing in 1987 when her children, Nathan and Zoe, had both reached school age. She began using her mornings to write, and she recounts that it was an "extraordinary and apparently unrepeatable experience" when she began by writing 300 pages of what became *The Beekeeper's Apprentice* in less than a month (Oleksiw 603).

She enjoys travel and posts information about her journeys and other topics on her Web site and her Web log. She and her family live in Watsonsville, California.

MAJOR WORKS AND THEMES

King writes two series and also has several stand-alone novels to her credit. The two series could not be any more different on the surface: in one, Kate Martinelli is a lesbian police detective in the present day San Francisco Bay area, and the other series begins in 1915 in England and features Mary Russell, apprentice and eventually professional partner and wife to Sherlock Holmes. The series explore some common themes, however, and both feature strong female characters.

Martinelli and Alfonzo Hawkin are homicide detectives who tackle a variety of cases that involve various social issues. Martinelli's partner, Leonora Cooper, is a psychologist, who becomes involved in some of the cases. When asked why she chose to portray Martinelli as a lesbian, King noted that it was not a deliberate decision but allowed her to depict the relationship with her male detective partner without "erotic overtones" (Silet 148).

King has said that with the Russell and Holmes series, she was able to "free Holmes from Conan Doyle's preconceptions," noting that as a result of the changes in the world after the World War I, that Holmes would have been quite different than he was during the Victorian era (Hahn 78). King has also noted that she has also been able to pit Holmes against "an equal mind," perhaps answering the question of what it would have been like if Watson had been Holmes' "intellectual equal" (Hahn 78). King sees herself as being able to more fully develop the "characteristics and idiosyncrasies that Conan Doyle introduced" in Holmes (Schechter).

Her stand-alone novels are loosely connected, with some overlapping characters. These novels are extremely suspenseful and deal with psychological studies of people in trouble. In *A Darker Place,* a religious studies professor moonlights as an FBI agent. She was involved with a cult earlier in her life, and left, but lost her husband and daughter to a mass suicide. She infiltrates the cult years later during an investigation. In *Folly,* a woman carpenter goes to a secluded spot in the San Juan Islands to rebuild a house and try to put her past behind her. In *Keeping Watch,* a Vietnam veteran who helps abused women and children faces a perilous situation.

King also has published one science fiction novel under the name Leigh Richards, which can be described as a postapocalyptic novel depicting a society controlled by women, who survived at a greater rate than the men. King began the work as a "refutation" of Margaret Atwood's *The Handmaid's Tale,* a novel that King did not find to be empowering or feminist (homepage, "Mutterings on Feminism").

Her academic background in theology is apparent in many of her works. In *Monstrous Regiment of Women,* Russell helps an old friend who has turned to a cultlike religious group. *To Play the Fool* offers an erudite study of the concept of the holy fool in a contemporary setting; in *Night Work,* King explores issues from Hinduism. *A Darker Place* portrays a contemporary professor of theology who during her research becomes dangerously close to a cult. The novels also address issues of gender and class, throughout their wide span of place and time. As Susan Oleksiw noted, King "often focuses on the intellectual aspect" of feminism, rather than the overtly political (604). Oleksiw noted how King's use of epigrams from male writers in *A Monstrous Regiment of Women,* which "sound as absurd as nonsense verse," provide more resounding arguments about the equality of women than could a more direct approach (604).

CRITICAL RECEPTION

Apart from the Holmes "purists" who speak against King's works, critics and readers have responded favorably from her first novel, which won American and British mystery awards; King won both an Edgar and a John Creasey Dagger for *A Grave Talent.* She has been nominated for Agatha, Nero, and Edgar awards for other books in both of her series.

A review of *A Grave Talent* mentions an "uncertain start" but praised the "appealing detective"(Brainard 1992:59–60); another reviewer found it to be "well crafted, prickling with excitement, [and] full of intriguing characters" (Kuda 972). The novel was also praised for its "strong psychological undertones, compelling urgency and dramatic action"

(Klett 1993:169). The next novel, *To Play the Fool,* was heralded for the way King portrayed homeless characters with "honesty and compassion" (Klett 1995:102). *Night Work* was praised for "King's ability to turn esoteric religious concepts into key narrative points" and offering a "highly unusual—and memorable—novel" (Zaleski 47). A review of *With Child* noted that although readers may solve the crime before Martinelli, "the pleasure of her company and the accelerating suspense" make the novel " a compelling read" (Brainard 1995b:55).

The Beekeeper's Apprentice was called a "delightful and well-wrought addition to the master detective's casework" (Brainard 1994:73). Another reviewer found it "a wonderfully original and entertaining story" that is "funny, heartwarming, and full of intrigue" (Melton 997). It was also praised for being an "elegantly written, enjoyable book [which] features a spirited female protagonist, a whimsical Holmes, unusual mysteries, and plenty of historic detail and humor" (Rosenfeld 1609). A review of the second Russell and Holmes novel focuses on King's "riveting plot" based on feminism and class issues, noting that it "lives up to all the accomplished promise of the first" novel in the series (Brainard 1995a:46). Another reviewer noted that the Holmes character had been "much used and even abused," and that King's work is "a delight" as she is "able to make profound changes while hewing so closely to the spirit of the original" (Cannon 78).

In addition, literary scholars have begun to explore King's works. Alanna Preussner wrote about the Mary Russell series in terms of revisioning or rewriting history and the intertextuality of King's fiction.

BIBLIOGRAPHY

Works by Laurie R. King

Kate Martinelli Series

A Grave Talent. New York: St. Martin's Press, 1993.
To Play the Fool. New York: St. Martin's Press, 1995.
With Child. New York: St. Martin's Press, 1996.
Night Work. New York: Bantam, 2000.
The Art of Detection. New York: Bantam, 2006.

Mary Russell Series

The Beekeeper's Apprentice; or, *On the Segregation of the Queen.* New York: St. Martin's Press, 1994.
A Monstrous Regiment of Women. New York: St. Martin's Press, 1995.
A Letter of Mary. New York: St. Martin's Press, 1997.
The Moor. New York: St. Martin's Press, 1998.
O Jerusalem. New York: Bantam, 1999.
Justice Hall. New York: Bantam, 2002.
The Game. New York: Bantam, 2004.
Locked Rooms. New York: Bantam, 2005.

Other Works

A Darker Place. New York: Bantam, 1999. (Also published as *Birth of a New Moon*). *Folly.* New York: Bantam, 2001.
Keeping Watch. New York: Bantam, 2003.
As Leigh Richards. *Califia's Daughter.* New York: Bantam, 2004.

Works about Laurie R. King

Anderson, R. J. *The Beekeeper's Holmes Page.* 11 August 2004. 4 May 2005. http://www3.sympatico. ca/mudthehut/beekeepr.html

Brainard, Dulcy. "*A Grave Talent.*" *Publishers Weekly* 28 December 1992: 59–60.

———. "*The Beekeeper's Apprentice.*" *Publishers Weekly* 3 January 1994: 73.

———. "*A Monstrous Regiment of Women.*" *Publishers Weekly* 10 July 1995a: 46.

———. "*With Child.*" *Publishers Weekly* 4 December 1995b: 55.

Cannon, Peter. "*Justice Hall.*" *Publishers Weekly* 18 Feb 2002: 78–79.

Hahn, Robert C. "PW Talks with Laurie R. King." *Publishers Weekly* 18 February 2002: 78.

Klett, Rex E. "*A Grave Talent.*" *Library Journal* January 1993: 169.

———. "*To Play the Fool.*" *Library Journal* 1 February 1995: 102.

Kuda, Marie. "*A Grave Talent.*" *Booklist* 1 February 1993: 972.

"Laurie R. King." *Contemporary Authors.* Vol. 105, New Revision Series. Ed. Scot Peacock. Detroit: Gale, 2002. 285–88.

Laurie R. King. Homepage. 2004. 10 November 2004. http://www.laurieking.com

Melton, Emily. "*The Beekeeper's Apprentice.*" *Booklist* 1 February 1994: 997.

Oleksiw, Susan. "Laurie R. King." *St. James Guide to Crime & Mystery Writers.* 4th ed. Ed. Jay P. Pederson. Detroit: St. James Press, 1996. 603–604.

Preussner, Alanna. "The Nouveau Sherlock Holmes: Rewriting History and Implying Audience." *Publications of the Missouri Philological Association* 27 (2002): 92–102.

Rosenfeld, Shelle. "*The Beekeeper's Apprentice.*" *Booklist* 1 May 2000: 1609.

Schechter, Andi and Wiley Saicheck. "Interview with Laurie R. King." Bookreporter.com. 5 March 2004. 10 November 2004. http://www.bookreporter.com/authors/au-king-laurie.asp

Silet, Charles L. P. "Beekeepers, Fools, and Sherlock Holmes' Wife." *Talking Murder: Interviews with 20 Mystery Writers.* Princeton: Ontario Review Press, 1999. 142–54.

Zaleski, Jeff. "*Night Work.*" *Publishers Weekly* 17 January 2000: 46–47.

Rochelle Majer Krich (1947–)

BIOGRAPHY

Rochelle Majer Krich was born in Bayreuth, Germany, in 1947. Her family immigrated to the United States in 1951, living in Brooklyn, and Lakewood, New Jersey, before moving to Los Angeles in 1960. Her parents were Holocaust survivors who met after the war. Her father had lost his first wife and daughters in the camps, and Krich never met her grandparents or other relatives.

She graduated from Stern College, a women's college associated with Yeshiva University in New York, earning a degree in English. She met her husband while she was working on her master's degree in English. Married with six children, she taught English at an orthodox Jewish high school in Los Angeles, serving as department chair for many years.

When asked why she writes mysteries, Krich noted that she has been addicted to them since childhood, an avid reader who loved Nancy Drew and continued reading mysteries as an adult (Andrus). Further, she loves "the puzzle aspect," but more than that, she loves reading and writing about "a world in which justice has been restored" (Andrus). For Krich, writing is a way for her to practice *tikkun olam* (repairing the world) by illuminating important social topics in her novels (Harris 28).

MAJOR WORKS AND THEMES

Although not present in all her earlier works, Judaism plays a major role in her novels. She has stated that she writes about Judaism in her mysteries because she wants to share her traditions with the readers while not "reinforce[ing] stereotypes or creat[ing] characters with whom readers can't identify." Ellen Harris noted that Krich's writing is "distinguish[ed] [by] her ability to weave information about Judaism or compelling contemporary issues into her stories without disturbing their literary flow" (28).

In her first series, Krich writes about Jessie Drake, a divorced homicide detective in Los Angeles who has difficult relationships with her mother and sister. In the first novel, she solves a serial killing case, and in the second, Drake is involved in a complicated murder case. Laurence Roth explores the character of Jessie Drake and other Jewish fictional detectives, looking specifically at novels where anti-Semitism plays a role. In the third novel, *Angel of Death,* Drake unexpectedly learns that not only is her mother Jewish, but that family members were lost in the Holocaust. Drake is in the middle of a case involving neo-Nazis and a Jewish lawyer being murdered, and the revelation about her family history changes her outlook on the case. In the follow-up novel, *Blood Money,* Drake takes part in an investigation that involves the attempts to claim Swiss bank accounts containing Holocaust victim and survivor assets.

Her second series features Molly Blume, a crime reporter who plays amateur sleuth. Blume comes from an Orthodox Jewish family, and family members, particularly her grandmother, play key supporting roles. Blume is a bit rebellious about certain aspects of Orthodox Judaism, which causes some conflict when she falls in love with a rabbi. Blume's cases involve solving a hit and run, where the victim had killed her son, possibly as a result of postpartum depression. Another case involves a missing person and real estate fraud. Perhaps her most poignant case comes in *Grave Endings,* where she finally finds the truth about the murder of her best friend years before.

Her stand-alone novels are also in the mystery and suspense realm, with *Fertile Ground* covering crimes surrounding a fertility clinic, and a legal thriller involving date rape called *Speak No Evil.*

CRITICAL RECEPTION

Krich won the Anthony Award for best paperback original for *Where's Mommy Now?* She has been nominated for an Agatha Award twice, for *Fair Game* and *Angel of Death,* two of the Jessie Drake novels. She also won the Mary Higgins Clark Award in 2005, a new award from the Mystery Writers of America. Reviews of the Drake series in mainstream publications have at times pointed out flaws, but have been overall positive. Reviews in Jewish publications have criticized the Drake series, seeing Drake's reaction to learning she is really Jewish as lacking passion or realism (Raphael 13).

Critical acclaim for the Blume novels includes Zaleski's view that "Krich never misses a beat as her heroine unravels the dark tangle of the senseless crime, … once again expertly mixes Orthodox Jewish faith with crisp whodunit plotting" (231). Harris noted that *Blues in the Night* is "written in a crisp, fast-paced style, the plot has more twists than a braided challah and keeps the reader guessing until the very end" (28). Cannon writes that "the affectionate portrait of a large, boisterous Jewish family" is particularly effective, and praised the work for its "fascinating look inside the culture and rituals of Orthodox Judaism" (46).

Priscilla L. Walton compared the Drake character to Ana Grey in April Smith's *North of Montana,* showing how both characters are initially resistant to their discovered multicultural identities. In *Angel of Death,* before Drake learns that her mother is Jewish, she is less than sensitive to the people involved in case she is assigned to that involves anti-Semitism. Walton noted that both novels she discusses end with the "characters resolving their conflicting identifications" although both novels serve to "highlight the problematics of multiculturalism" (142), making the issues of identity politics "immediate and accessible" to readers (143).

BIBLIOGRAPHY

Works by Rochelle Majer Krich

Jessie Drake Series

Fair Game. New York: Mysterious Press, 1993.
Angel of Death. New York: Mysterious Press, 1994.
Blood Money. New York: Avon, 1999.
Dead Air. New York: Avon, 2000.
Shadows of Sin. New York: Morrow, 2001.

Molly Blume Series

Blues in the Night. New York: Ballantine, 2002.
Dream House. New York: Ballantine, 2003.
Grave Endings. New York: Ballantine, 2004.
Now You See Me. New York: Ballantine, 2005.

Other Novels

Where's Mommy Now? New York: Zebra/Pinnacle, 1990.
Till Death Do Us Part. New York: Avon, 1992.
Nowhere to Run. New York: Avon, 1994.
Speak No Evil. New York: Mysterious Press, 1996.
Fertile Ground. New York: Avon, 1998.

Works about Rochelle Majer Krich

Andrus, Reed. "The Holocaust in Her Soul, Romantic Comedy in Her Heart: An Interview with Rochelle Majer Krich." 2000. 20 May 2005. www.rochellekrich.com
Cannon, Peter. "*Blues in the Night.*" *Publishers Weekly* 26 August 2002: 46.
Harris, Ellen. "Writer Takes Clue from Real Life: *Blues in the Night.*" *Cleveland Jewish News* 1 November 2002: 28.
Raphael, Lev. "Drawing on Swiss Banks for a Mystery: Rochelle Krich Weaves Holocaust History into a Police Procedural." *Forward* 25 June 1999: 13.
"Rochelle Majer Krich." *Contemporary Authors.* Vol. 110, New Revision Series. Ed. Scot Peacock. Detroit: Gale, 2002. 232–35.
Roth, Laurence. *Inspecting Jews: American Jewish Detective Stories.* New Brunswick: Rutgers UP, 2004.
Walton, Priscilla L. "Identity Politics: April Smith's *North of Montana* and Rochelle Majer Krich's *Angel of Death.*" *Diversity and Detective Fiction.* Ed. Kathleen Gregory Klein. Bowling Green: Bowling Green State UP, 1999. 130–43.
Zaleski, Jeff. "*Grave Endings.*" *Publishers Weekly* 9 August 2004: 230–31.

Virginia Lanier (1930–2003)

BIOGRAPHY

Virginia Rudd Lanier was born October 28, 1930, in Madison County, Florida, and was adopted by Ira and Mary Holt Rudd. She married Robert "Hoss" Lanier and they raised five sons. Her husband was in the military, which took them to a number of different states over the years. She worked at a variety of jobs, including as a bookkeeper and store manager. After her husband's retirement in 1974, they settled in Fargo, Georgia.

In 1993, she threw a book across the room and proclaimed she could write a better one. Her husband encouraged her to try and bought her a typewriter, dictionary, and desk. Within five months, she had written an 857-page manuscript, which she sold to a regional publisher, Pineapple Press. The novel was well received, and she signed a contract with a national publisher for additional books in the series.

From 1996 onward, she and her husband both suffered from a number of health problems. Her husband died in November 2001, and Virginia Lanier died on October 27, 2003.

MAJOR WORKS AND THEMES

Lanier's series features a bloodhound trainer named JoBeth Sidden who, along with her dogs, works with search-and-rescue teams. Sidden is fiercely independent and security conscious because of the value of her canine partners and an abusive ex-husband. In the first novel, she is involved with several search-and-rescue operations while dealing with personal issues. As one reviewer noted, Sidden "appears abrasive and outspoken, qualities that mask her fear" her ex-husband. The second novel finds her hosting a training seminar for law enforcement and being asked to investigate one of the officers who is suspected of drug abuse. In subsequent novels, Sidden and the hounds find a missing child, help a young woman claim her rightful inheritance, and track down the truth about a decades-old murder. In *Ten Little Bloodhounds,* she joins a search-and-rescue effort that turns out to be for a missing cat, but she uncovers a murder.

The novels contain a great deal of interesting information about bloodhounds and their training, and Sidden and the other characters are well drawn. Lanier noted that she "made JoBeth a feminist because I've always wanted to be a feminist, but I had to stay in the closet.... I enjoy JoBeth having the freedom to do and say what she wants to" (Virginia 234).

CRITICAL RECEPTION

Her first novel won the Anthony Award for Best First Mystery, and it was also nominated for Agatha and Macavity awards. Critical response was favorable to the series. One review of her first novel heralded it as a "very appealing first novel," with "literate, well-modulated prose, satisfyingly detailed descriptions" and a "leisurely pace punctuated by thrilling moments of action" (Klett 103). Another reviewer noted that Lanier gave readers a "thorough, insider's look at a unique profession," along with a "detailed view of Southern life near the swamp" (Brainard 1995:199).

Although one reviewer found the plot of *The House on Bloodhound Lane* to be "fragmented," Lanier was praised for "Jo Beth's brash ingenuity and wry sense of humor" (Brainard 1996:51). *A Brace of Bloodhounds* was "cram[med].... with plots and subplots, characters and dogs and encyclopedic bloodhound lore," with the reviewer noting that the novel was "fun" and "folksy" (Brainard 1997:201).

Blind Bloodhound Justice was praised for Lanier's "grandness, humor, and eye for detail," along with her "unstereotyped southerners and vivid Georgia landscape" (Rowen 1988:1733), and another reviewer found that it "lives up to the promise of her debut," with Lanier showing "an increasing mastery of plot and pacing to complement the established sass-appeal of the endearingly ornery Jo Beth" (Brainard 1998:57–58).

In *Ten Little Bloodhounds*, Lanier offered "sympathetic characters and vivid southern settings" while "skillfully juggl[ing] multiple mysteries" (Rowen 1999:1481).

Another reviewer commented on how well Lanier "combines fascinating bloodhound lore and detection with dead-on perceptions of her Georgia friends and neighbors," noting that "she just keeps getting better and better" (Fialkoff 149). Although the ending was criticized as weak, another reviewer noted that "the novel is witty and brisk and so lovingly detailed with the fine qualities of bloodhounds that even the most avid dog-hater will be brought to heel" (Zaleski 54).

In *A Bloodhound to Die For,* her final work, Lanier was praised for "min[ing] the situation's comic possibilities nicely without straying into farce and, as usual, turns an expert eye on bloodhounds and their care and training in this warmly entertaining concoction" ("*A Bloodhound to Die For*" 56).

BIBLIOGRAPHY

Works by Virginia Lanier

Death in Bloodhound Red. Sarasota: Pineapple Press, 1995.
The House on Bloodhound Lane. New York: HarperCollins, 1996.
A Brace of Bloodhounds. New York: HarperCollins, 1997.
Blind Bloodhound Justice. New York: HarperCollins, 1998.
Ten Little Bloodhounds. New York: HarperCollins, 1999.
A Bloodhound to Die For. New York: HarperCollins, 2003.

Works about Virginia Lanier

"*A Bloodhound to Die For.*" *Publishers Weekly* 7 July 2003: 56.
Brainard, Dulcy. "*Death in Bloodhound Red.*" *Publishers Weekly* 20 February 1995: 199.
———. "*The House on Bloodhound Lane.*" *Publishers Weekly* 17 June 1996: 50–51.
———. "*A Brace of Bloodhounds.*" *Publishers Weekly* 5 May 1997: 201.
———. "*Blind Bloodhound Justice.*" *Publishers Weekly* 1 June 1998: 57–58.
Fialkoff, Francine. "*Ten Little Bloodhounds.*" *Library Journal* 15 April 1999: 149.
Klett, Rex E. "*Death in Bloodhound Red.*" *Library Journal* 1 February 1995: 103.
Official Virginia Lanier Mystery Page. n.d. 17 March 2006. http://www.geocities.com/ripleygold/vlanier.htm
Rowen, John. "*Blind Bloodhound Justice.*" *Booklist* 1–15 June 1998: 1733–34.
———. "*Ten Little Bloodhounds.*" *Booklist* 15 April 1999: 1481.
"Virginia Lanier." *Contemporary Authors. New Revision Series*, Vol. 144. Ed. Tracey L. Matthews. Detroit: Gale, 2006. 233–35.
Zaleski, Jeff. "*Ten Little Bloodhounds.*" *Publishers Weekly* 14 June 1999: 54.

Emma Lathen

BIOGRAPHY

Emma Lathen was the pseudonym used by a pair of writers named Martha Hennisart and Mary Jane Latsis. The pseudonym was a combination of their real names, with M from Mary and "Ma" from Martha, and the first letters of their last names providing Lathen. The pair also wrote several novels under another pseudonym, R. B. Dominic.

Martha Hennisart was born June 4, 1929, in Manhattan, and was the daughter of a French parfumier (Dinneen 197). She earned a bachelor's degree in physics from Mount Holyoke College in 1950 and then attended law school at Harvard University. She worked for Raytheon in the 1950s and then practiced corporate law in Boston and New York until 1973.

Mary Jane Latsis was born July 12, 1927, in Oak Park, Illinois. Her parents were immigrants from Greece, and her father was a pharmacist. She graduated from Wellesley College in 1949, earning a degree in economics. After college, she worked for the government, both in Washington, D.C. and in international postings, including a position with the Central Intelligence Agency during the Korean War (Dinneen 197). Latsis attended Harvard in the early 1950s, earning a master's of public affairs (MPA) degree. She continued her work for the government before becoming an agricultural economist for the United Nations. She also taught economics at Wellesley College (Dinneen 197).

Hennisart and Latsis met at Harvard in 1952 and found they had a shared love of reading mystery novels. When Henissart took a position in Boston in 1960, she and Latsis renewed their friendship. Given that there was a lack of mysteries in the style they preferred that they had not already read, they decided to write one together. Like Carolyn Heilbrun writing as Amanda Cross, Latsis and Henissart kept their identities secret for many years so as not to jeopardize their status in their respective professions.

Latsis died from a heart attack and stroke on October 27, 1999, and was survived by her companion of 40 years, Walter Frank.

MAJOR WORKS AND THEMES

Under the Lathen name, Hennisart and Latsis wrote a series of novels featuring John Putnam Thatcher, a Wall Street banker. As Vice President of Sloane Guaranty Trust, Thatcher is in a position to become involved in a wide variety of cases. All of the plots have some tie to the world of finance, including a case of travelers check fraud during the 1980 Winter Olympics in *Going for the Gold*, a scandal involving government contracts for oil production in *Double, Double, Oil and Trouble*, and an intellectual property battle between two agribusiness firms in *Green Grow the Dollars. Murder Without Icing* looks at the world of professional hockey, and events in *Picking Up Sticks* take place during Thatcher's vacation to the Appalachian Trail.

International politics are taken on in *When in Greece;* with her Greek heritage, Latsis was particularly outraged by political events in Greece in the late 1960s, and they used the political unrest as a plot device. *The Longer the Thread* tackles the issue of Puerto Rican statehood, with labor issues in the garment industry as a backdrop. Later, *A Shark Out of Water* is set in Poland, with themes of modernization and international finance surrounding

---

Also writing as R. B. Dominic

a canal project. As they told John C. Carr, any industry besides publishing and higher education were fair game for them (189–90). At the time of Latsis's death, they were writing another Thatcher novel, and Henissart said she planned to complete it, but the novel has not yet appeared in print.

From 1968 to 1984, they published novels in a second series under another pseudonym, R. B. Dominic. This series featured a congressman from Ohio named Ben Safford. Safford plays the role of amateur sleuth in various cases involving bribery and corruption. For example, in *Attending Physician,* Lathen takes on Medicaid fraud.

CRITICAL RECEPTION

Lathen won a number of awards, including Gold and Silver Dagger Awards from the Crime Writers Association (CWA), which is quite notable, as the CWA tends to focus their awards on British writers. *When in Greece* was nominated for an Edgar Award, and in 1983, the Mystery Writers Association presented the pair with the inaugural Ellery Queen Award. They also won the Agatha Award for Lifetime Achievement in 1997.

Critical reception was positive throughout their career. Their writing style was appreciated, as was their insider knowledge of business and finance and their inclusion of "solid novel information" on a variety of wide-ranging topics ("*Murder Without Icing*" 562). *Come to Dust* was noted for its "quiet and often delicious" wit (1431). A reviewer said of *When in Greece* that "one would gladly say that this novel is one of Miss Lathen's best if only one hadn't said it so often before" (333). Another reviewer praised the novel as "crisp humorous entertainment with good characterization" (39).

A review of *Sweet and Low* noted that Lathen was "probably now the only competent proponent" of the "true, intelligent detective story," further praising the "drily comical" writing (1437). Noting that the plot of *Double, Double, Oil and Trouble* would not have worked in less skilled hands, one reviewer praised Lathen for "keeping her novels from becoming bogged down by excess verbiage and unnecessary violence" (1719).

Right on the Money was heralded as a "bright-as-a-penny" entry in their "bankable financial-mystery series" (Stasio 1993:A17). Another reviewer found this novel to be "smoothly done, well put together, and very appealing: just as the title indicates" (Klett 112). Another reviewer, after registering the hope that Thatcher would never retire, noted that Lathen's strength "lies in dialogue that reveals character while never failing to push the plot forward," further praising how they "write with an underlying stylish humor" and have solid plotting (Waugh 31).

Brewing Up a Storm was critiqued for stiff dialogue and overuse of fancy vocabulary, but the reviewer was mostly positive, noting that "the premise here is wonderfully plausible, and the details about brewing and business are well-rendered" (Stead F9). Their last novel, *A Shark out of Water,* won praise for how they "enlivened their latest cerebral puzzle with a satiric take on international organizations and a comic portrait of Poland adapting to capitalism" (Brainard 1997:55). Another reviewer called it an "entertaining, intellectually stimulating read that will delight" readers (Melton 456).

BIBLIOGRAPHY

Works by Emma Lathen

John Putnam Thatcher Series

Banking on Death. New York: Macmillan, 1961.
A Place for Murder. New York: Macmillan, 1963.

Accounting for Murder. New York: Macmillan, 1964.
Death Shall Overcome. New York: Macmillan, 1966.
Murder Makes the Wheels Go 'Round. New York: Macmillan, 1966.
Murder against the Grain. New York: Macmillan, 1967.
Come to Dust. New York: Simon & Schuster, 1968.
A Stitch in Time. New York: Macmillan, 1968.
Murder to Go. New York: Simon & Schuster, 1969.
When in Greece. New York: Simon & Schuster, 1969.
Pick Up Sticks. New York: Simon & Schuster, 1970.
The Longer the Thread. New York: Simon & Schuster, 1971.
Ashes to Ashes. New York: Simon & Schuster, 1971.
Murder Without Icing. New York: Simon & Schuster, 1972.
Sweet and Low. New York: Simon & Schuster, 1974.
By Hook or by Crook. New York: Simon & Schuster, 1975.
Double, Double, Oil and Trouble. New York: Simon & Schuster, 1978.
Going for the Gold. New York: Simon & Schuster, 1981.
Green Grow the Dollars. New York: Simon & Schuster, 1982.
Something in the Air. New York: Simon & Schuster, 1988.
East Is East. New York: Simon & Schuster, 1991.
Right on the Money. New York: Simon & Schuster, 1993.
Brewing Up a Storm. New York: St. Martin's, 1996.
A Shark Out of Water. New York: St. Martin's, 1997.

Works by R. B. Dominic

Ben Safford Series

Murder, Sunny Side Up. New York: Abelard-Schuman, 1968.
Murder in High Places. New York: Doubleday, 1970.
There Is No Justice. New York: Doubleday, 1971.
Epitaph for a Lobbyist. New York: Doubleday, 1974.
Murder Out of Commission. New York: Doubleday, 1976.
The Attending Physician. New York: Harper, 1980.
A Flaw in the System. London: Macmillan, 1983.
Unexpected Developments. New York: St. Martin's, 1984.

Works about Emma Lathen

Bedell, Jeanne F. "Emma Lathen." *Ten Women of Mystery.* Ed. Earl F. Bargainnier. Bowling Green: Bowling Green UP, 1983. 248–67.

Brainard, Dulcy. "*A Shark Out of Water.*" *Publishers Weekly* 15 September 1997: 55.

Carr, John C. "Emma Lathen." *The Craft of Crime: Conversations with Crime Writers.* Boston: Houghton Mifflin, 1983.

"*Come to Dust.*" *Times Literary Supplement* 11 December 1969: 1431.

Dinneen, Marcia B. "Emma Lathen." *Dictionary of Literary Biography,* Vol. 306: *American Mystery and Detective Writers.* Ed. George Parker Anderson. Detroit: Gale, 2005. 196–205.

"*Double, Double, Oil and Trouble.*" *Booklist* 15 July 1978: 1719.

Klett, Rex. E. "*Right on the Money.*" *Library Journal* 1 March 1993: 112.

Mahoney, Mary Kay. "Wall Street Broker John Putnam Thatcher." *Clues* 22.2 (2001): 73–82.

"Martha Hennissart." *Contemporary Authors.* New Revision Series, Vol. 64. Eds. Daniel Jones and John D. Jorgensen. Detroit: Gale, 1998. 178–80.

"Mary Jane Latsis." *Contemporary Authors.* Vol. 162. Ed. Scot Peacock. Detroit: Gale, 1998. 221–22.

Melton, Emily. "*A Shark Out of Water.*" *Booklist* 1 November 1997: 456.

"*Murder Without Icing.*" *Times Literary Supplement* 18 May 1973: 562.

Sarjeant, William. "Crime on Wall Street." *Armchair Detective* 21.2 (1988): 128–32.

Stasio, Marilyn. "Crime." *New York Times* 4 April 1993: A17.

Stead, Deborah. "Mischief Afoot: Murder with an MBA." *New York Times* 2 February 1997: F9.

"Sweet and Low." Times Literary Supplement 20 December 1974: 1437.

Thomas, Robert M. "Mary Jane Latsis, 70, Emma Lathen Writing Team Collaborator." *New York Times* 31 October 1997: D23.

Waugh, Harriet. "Recent Crime Novels." *The Spectator* 15 January 1994: 31.

"When in Greece." Times Literary Supplement 27 March 1969: 333.

"When in Greece." Booklist 1 September 1970: 39.

Donna Leon (1942–)

BIOGRAPHY

Donna Leon was born September 28, 1942, and was raised in New Jersey. In 1966, she left the United States to continue her education in Italy. She moved around Europe and the Middle East for various positions teaching at American schools, including Switzerland, Saudi Arabia, England, Iran, and China. She lived in Iran at the time of the Islamic Revolution. She was working on her dissertation at the time, and all of her papers and books were confiscated. She chose to stop her master's degree rather than begin rewriting her dissertation (Freeman F19).

Leon settled in Italy in 1981, where she found a teaching job with a university who had a satellite campus at the American military base, and she has remained there since. She turned to writing full-time after the publication of her first novel. In addition to her fictional work, she reviews opera and writes liner notes for opera recordings (Keyes 214; Freeman F19). She also writes occasional book reviews for the *Sunday Times*.

MAJOR WORKS AND THEMES

Leon first had the idea of writing a mystery when she attended a concert at La Fenice. While chatting with the conductor and some friends, conversation turned to another conductor some felt deserved to suffer a terrible fate (Petrocelli; Freeman F19). She tried her hand at writing a mystery, and the novel was published after it won the Sundory Prize, a contest for first novels in Japan (Petrocelli). All of her novels are set in Venice and feature Commissario Guido Brunetti. Leon captures the bureaucracy and corruption that Brunetti deals with and complicates his life by making his wife, Paola, the daughter of a powerful man. Throughout the series, Brunetti is faced with various choices and, in the pursuit of justice, often goes against the wishes of his superiors. As John T. D. Keyes noted, Brunetti "[keeps] his fingers crossed that he'll never have to arrest his father-in-law and his boss for the same scam" (213).

The novels feature lush descriptions of life in Venice, including the surroundings, the food, and other aspects of the culture there. Food is so important in the novels that Dick Adler wrote an article focused on the various restaurant scenes throughout the novels (28–29). Brunetti's early cases include an investigation of the drowning of an American soldier and the murder of a transvestite, who turns out to have been dressed in that manner as subterfuge. Brunetti also deals with a human smuggling ring and an art forgery ring. As the series progresses, Leon pays more attention to political aspects, such as in *Uniform Justice,* in which Brunetti investigates the possible suicide of a military cadet who is also the son of a powerful politician, and in *A Noble Radiance*, which features a case that leads back to World War II. Her most recent novel deals with the death of an illegal alien, one of the African vendors so present in Venice. Leon notes that her motivation for this novel was the moment she suddenly took notice of the vendors and realized that they were "here but invisible" (Freeman F19).

In an interview, Leon was asked about her avoidance of what the interviewer called "neat, pseudo-justice" endings that mark some mystery novels. Leon replied that "books that offer justice and punishment to the evildoer at the end should be confined to the children's section," further noting that "in a world where the abuse of political and national power has become so outrageous, it's difficult to interest readers in the happy solution as to who killed Lord Farnsworthy in the library with the Balinese kris" (Anable 58).

Although the novels are not translated into Italian by her choice, they are translated into 20 other languages, and Leon enjoys a particularly strong following in Germany, Switzerland, and Austria (Petrocelli). She chooses not to have the novels published in Italy so that she can attempt to maintain her anonymity (Kingston 11). After several years of not having a publisher in the United States, Atlantic Monthly Press has begun publishing her works so that her new novels are readily available in the U.S. market.

CRITICAL RECEPTION

In addition to Japan's Suntory Prize, which she won for her first novel, she won a Crime Writers Association Silver Dagger for *Friends in High Places*. Critical reception has been favorable for the series.

A review of *Dressed for Death* praised the series for being "richly evocative mysteries" and noted that in this entry, "Venice takes on a deep noir tint in Leon's well crafted work" (Brainard 1994:53). The next novel in the series, *Death and Judgment,* was described as written "with consummate skill" and was noted for its "heady atmosphere of Venice and a galaxy of fully realized characters" and an "intriguing and finally, horrifying tale" (Brainard 1995: 55).

Acqua Alta was called an "agreeably readable novel full of intriguing contrasts" with "credible" plotting (Cooper 1996:21). Another reviewer praised its "intricate and intimate descriptions of Venetian life" combined with a "high-stakes mystery in which the setting vibrates with life" (Yamashita 2004:48).

A review of *A Noble Radiance* was praised as a "culturally rich" and "gripping intellectual mystery" and an "atmospheric tale" (Yamashita 2003:45). Another reviewer found *A Noble Radiance* to be "an impressive addition to the series" and praised Leon's portrayal of Venice as "an ideal backdrop to her explorations of cruelty and deceit, ravishing on the surface and yet subject to breathtaking corruption" (Cooper 1998:24).

A Sea of Troubles was heralded as a "skillful evocation of life in Venice" and according to the reviewer, compared to other novels set in Venice, "Brunetti is hard to beat"(Latimer 24). The "superb" *Uniform Justice* was noted for its flowing plot and strong character development ("*Uniform Justice*" 58). Although the plot in *Doctored Evidence* unfolded too slowly for Peter Cannon, he noted that the novel "offers many pleasures, including a clever puzzle" and "evokes the real Venice, not the place of romantic novels or glitzy travel guides" (54).

Blood from a Stone was heralded as "stunning" with an "engrossing, complex plot" and a cast of secondary characters who "balance this dark cynical tale of widespread secrecy, violence and corruption" ("*Blood from a Stone*" 38). In her review, Marilyn Stasio noted that although Brunetti "takes neither pride nor pleasure in his cloak-and-dagger activities, readers will enjoy the paradoxical way that justice is served" (21).

Leon's works have also drawn attention from literary scholars. Indira Ghose's essay compared Leon's treatment of Venice to that of Michael Dibdin, who also writes a mystery series set in Venice. Elizabeth Glass explores Leon, Dibdin, and Magdalen Nabb.

BIBLIOGRAPHY
Works by Donna Leon
Guido Brunetti Series

Death at La Fenice. New York: HarperCollins, 1992.
Death in a Strange Country. New York: HarperCollins 1993.
Dressed for Death. New York: HarperCollins, 1994.
Death and Judgment. New York: HarperCollins, 1996.
Acqua Alta. New York: HarperCollins, 1996.
The Death of Faith. London: Macmillan, 1997.
A Noble Radiance. London: Heinemann, 1998.
Fatal Remedies. London: Heinemann, 1999.
Friends in High Places. London: Heinemann, 2000.
A Sea of Troubles. London: Heinemann, 2001.
Wilful Behaviour. London: Heinemann, 2002.
Uniform Justice. London: Heinemann; New York: Atlantic Monthly Press, 2003.
Doctored Evidence. London: Heinemann; New York: Atlantic Monthly Press, 2004.
Blood from a Stone. London: Heinemann; New York: Atlantic Monthly Press, 2005.
Through a Glass, Darkly. New York: Atlantic Monthly Press, 2006.

Works about Donna Leon

Adler, Dick. "Culinary Escapades in Venice." *Harper's Bazaar* October 2000: 28–29.
Anable, Stephen. "PW Talks with Donna Leon." *Publishers Weekly* 4 August 2003: 58.
"*Blood from a Stone.*" *Publishers Weekly* 21 March 2005: 38.
Brainard, Dulcy. "*Dressed for Death.*" *Publishers Weekly* 16 May 1994: 53.
———. "*Death and Judgment.*" *Publishers Weekly* 10 April 1995: 55.
Cannon, Peter. "*Doctored Evidence.*" *Publishers Weekly* 23 February 2004: 54.
Cooper, Natasha. "*Acqua Alta.*" *Times Literary Supplement* 26 April 1996: 21.
———. "*A Noble Radiance.*" *Times Literary Supplement* 8 May 1998: 24.
"Donna Leon." *Contemporary Authors.* Vol. 183. Ed. Scot Peacock. Detroit: Gale, 2000. 219–21.
Freeman, John. "An American in Venice." *Vancouver Sun* 11 June 2005: F19.
Ghose, Indira. "Venice Confidential." *Venetian Views, Venetian Blinds: English Fantasies of Venice.* Eds. Manfred Pfister and Barbara Schaff. Amsterdam: Rodopi, 1999. 213–24.
Glass, Elizabeth. "Cosi fan tutti: The Pessimism of Place." *Textus: English Studies in Italy* 14.1 (2001): 29–52.
Keyes, John T. D. "Life and Death in Venice." *Armchair Detective* 30.2 (1997): 212–14.
Kingston, Peter. "Going Incognito in Italy: Donna Leon Tells Peter Kingston Why She Prefers to Bask in Anonymity." *The Guardian* 7 April 2001: 11.
Latimer, Karen. "*A Sea of Troubles.*" *Times Literary Supplement* 1 June 2001: 24.
Petrocelli, Elaine. "At Lunch with Donna Leon." Donna Leon homepage. 2005. 11 January 2006. http://www.groveatlantic.com/leon/author.htm
Stasio, Marilyn. "Dead Merchant of Venice." *New York Times Book Review* 22 May 2005: 21.
"*Uniform Justice.*" *Publishers Weekly* 4 August 2003: 58.
Yamashita, Brianna. "*A Noble Radiance.*" *Publishers Weekly* 25 August 2003: 45.
———. "*Acqua Alta.*" *Publishers Weekly* 16 August 2004: 48.

Gillian Linscott (1949–)

BIOGRAPHY

Gillian Linscott was born September 27, 1944, in Windsor, England. Her father, Thomas Snow Linscott, managed a shoe store, and her mother, Muriel Rosaline Fountain Linscott, worked as a shop assistant. She earned a degree in English language and literature from Oxford in 1966. She worked as a journalist for the *Liverpool Daily Post* from 1967 to 1970, for the *Birmingham Post* from 1970 to 1972, and for the *Guardian* from 1972 to 1979. At that time, she joined the British Broadcasting Corporation, and wrote radio plays for them, among other duties. She has noted that she "can't remember a time when [she] wasn't trying to write" (Gillian 251). She married the writer Anthony Joseph Vincent Geraghty in 1988, and they reside in Herefordshire, England.

MAJOR WORKS AND THEMES

Linscott has written novels in two distinctly different series, along with several stand-alone novels. Her first series features Birdie Linnet, who Linscott describes as "remarkable chiefly for getting the point later than anybody else on the page. He's well-meaning, none too intelligent, and frequently hit on the head" (Gillian 251). Linnet is a former police officer who works as a fitness trainer and becomes involved in various cases linked to his clients. In one novel, he is leading an adventure tour on a remote island in the Caribbean when murder interrupts the schedule.

Linscott's other series portrays Nell Bray, an Oxford-trained freelance translator and suffragette in early twentieth-century Britain. *Sister Beneath the Sheet* introduces Bray as a member of the Women's Social and Political Union, a suffrage organization. Fresh out of jail for vandalism at the prime minister's house, Bray becomes entangled in a case involving a woman whose apparent suicide may have been murder. The second novel finds Bray being called to volunteer at a clinic where World War I veterans with shell shock are being treated. Bray has to investigate a suspicious death there, and in *Stage Fright*, Bray is hired by George Bernard Shaw to protect the star of his new play. Bray's next adventure takes place in France while Bray is on a vacation trip and is pressed into duty to solve a murder. In *Crown Witness* Bray assists with a case involving a murder that occurred during a parade for the new king. Other cases involve politics, post-World War I issues in England, and in *Absent Friends*, Bray stands for Parliament.

CRITICAL RECEPTION

In addition to other recognition, Linscott won a Crime Writers Association Ellis Peters Historical Dagger Award in 2000 for *Absent Friends*. Her work has received consistently strong critical acclaim. A review of the third Birdie Linnett novel called it "particularly felicitous and engaging," with an effective combination of an "exotic setting and deft plotting, odd characters and poignancy" (Steinberg 1988:47). One of Linscott's stand-alone novels, *Murder, I Presume,* was noted for its "deft touch with characterization and an authoritative feel for Victorian society" (Steinberg 1990:49).

The Nell Bray series was won similar acclaim. The debut novel was praised for Bray's "smart and feisty" character and how Linscott "shows off her historical and political backdrop to good effect and leavens her mystery with well-measured wit" (Steinberg 1991:49). Another reviewer found it to be a "deft combination of history and mystery," with a "plucky" heroine and a cast of "delightfully varied suspects" (Flanagan 33).

Reviews for subsequent novels praise Linscott for "deftly combin[ing] period details and psychological elements in a suspenseful plot" (Brainard 1992:56) and herald Bray as "an admirably liberated and intelligent heroine" (Melton 1993:678). *Stage Fright* was also noted for the "interesting commentary on the sociopolitical climate" of the time, as well as for "nice touches of humor" (Melton 1993:678). *An Easy Day for a Lady* praised the sleuth and setting as "unique" but not overpowering the plot, which has "sufficient twists and turns to keep even the most inveterate puzzle solvers happy" (Cooper 1063). *Crown Witness* was noted for being a "fascinating read filled with abundant political detail, historical ambience, romance and intrigue" (Melton 1995:688.) The award-winning *Absent Friends* was described as "loaded with interesting history, unique characters, and vivid descriptions of the English countryside" and exploring a "surprising murder case while weaving in sobering thoughts on the cost of World War I and a realistic, witty view of politics" (Rowen 1481). Another reviewer praised the effective "blend of social and cultural history with artful mystery" and Linscott's skill in "captur[ing] the bustling activity of political work as well as the intricacies of" detective work (Zaleski 225). *Blood on the Wood* was noted for Linscott's "adept characterizations and understated use of the mores, customs, fads and manners of early 20th-century Britain [which] make for an engrossing read" (Cannon 53).

BIBLIOGRAPHY

Works by Gillian Linscott

Nell Bray Series

Sister Beneath the Sheet. New York: St. Martin's, 1991.
Hanging on the Wire. New York: St. Martin's, 1993.
Stage Fright. New York: St. Martin's, 1993.
Crown Witness. New York: St. Martin's, 1995.
Widow's Peak. London: Little, Brown, 1994. Also published as *An Easy Day for a Lady*. New York: St. Martin's, 1995.
Dead Man's Sweetheart. New York: St. Martin's, 1996.
Dance on Blood. New York: St. Martin's, 1998.
Absent Friends. New York: St. Martin's, 1999.
The Perfect Daughter. New York: St. Martin's, 2001.
Dead Man Riding. New York: St. Martin's, 2002.
Blood on the Wood. New York: St. Martin's, 2004.

Birdie Linnet Series

A Healthy Body. New York: St. Martin's, 1984.
Murder Makes Tracks. New York: St. Martin's, 1985.
A Whiff of Sulphur. New York: St. Martin's, 1987.

Other Mystery Novels

Knightfall. New York: Macmillan, 1986.
Unknown Hand. New York: Macmillan, 1988.
Murder, I Presume. New York: St. Martin's, 1990.

Works about Gillian Linscott

Brainard, Dulcy. "*Hanging on the Wire.*" *Publishers Weekly* 23 November 1992: 55–56.
Cannon, Peter. "*Blood on the Wood.*" *Publishers Weekly* 8 March 2004: 53.
Cooper, Ilene. "*An Easy Day for a Lady.*" *Booklist* 15 February 1995: 1063.
Flanagan, Margaret. "*Sister Beneath the Sheet.*" *Booklist* 1 September 1991: 33.
"Gillian Linscott." *Contemporary Authors.* New Revision Series, Vol. 107. Ed. Scot Peacock. Detroit: Gale, 2002. 250–51.
Melton, Emily. "*Stage Fright.*" *Booklist* 1 December 1993: 678.
———. "*Crown Witness.*" *Booklist* 15 December 1995: 688.
Rowen, John. "*Absent Friends.*" *Booklist* 15 April 1999: 1481.
Steinberg, Sybil. "*A Whiff of Sulphur.*" *Publishers Weekly* 29 January 1988: 417.
———. "*Murder, I Presume.*" *Publishers Weekly* 12 October 1990: 49.
———. "*Sister Beneath the Sheet.*" *Publishers Weekly* 19 July 1991: 49.
Zaleski, Jeff. "*Absent Friends.*" *Publishers Weekly* 5 April 1999: 225.

Laura Lippman (1959–)

BIOGRAPHY

Laura Lippman was born in Atlanta, Georgia, in 1959. Her father was a journalist and her mother was a children's librarian. Her family moved to the Washington, D.C. area when she was two years old, and eventually settled in Baltimore. She grew up in a Baltimore mill village called Dickeyville, which is now a national historical site. Lippman noted that her southern relatives thought of them as Yankees, but the Maryland natives always thought of her and her sister as true southerners (homepage).

After graduating from Wilde Lake High School, she studied journalism at Northwestern University. She worked as a reporter for several newspapers in Waco and San Antonio during the 1980s, and returned home to Maryland in 1989 when she landed a position at the *Baltimore Evening Sun*. After the paper folded in 1992, she worked for the *Morning Sun* until 2001. Part of her work was serving as the poverty reporter. She notes that she "was the last poverty reporter" at the newspaper because "the editors decided that poverty was really a downer. It wasn't helping them to sell papers in the suburbs" ("Give" 87).

She tried writing fiction when she was in her twenties, but she characterizes that effort as "a typical autobiographical first novel" (Lanham 18) and as "drivel" (Silet 20). She turned to mystery writing after an editor suggested that she would get better assignments if she were a better writer. She decided the way to answer that critique was by writing a novel, and she completed the manuscript of her first mystery within one year (Lanham 18). After the novel was published, she continued to work on her novels in the mornings before going to her regular job at the newspaper for several years, eventually turning to fiction full-time. She resides in Baltimore.

MAJOR WORKS AND THEMES

Most of Lippman's novels feature Tess Monaghan. Like Lippman, Monaghan is a journalist, but unlike Lippman, Monaghan finds herself investigating a number of crimes and becomes a licensed private investigator. Lippman has said that Monaghan is "brave and principled" and "gets to say the rude or funny things I would never dare say out loud" (Healy) and also that "Tess is someone I might have been if I'd lost my job and been forced to reinvent myself" (Quinn 32). Monaghan has a quirky extended family and an unusual on-again, off-again boyfriend, all of whom play major roles in the books. Although some of the crimes are serious and there is some degree of violence in the books, there is also a great deal of humor. Unlike other private investigators who use their weapons in every novel, Monaghan does not kill anyone until the seventh book in the series.

Monaghan has taken on a number of issues in the novels, including bulimia, accidental shootings, and domestic violence. In *The Sugar House,* Monaghan tries to find the identity of a murdered young woman. *The Last Place* begins with Monaghan exacting revenge on a man trolling for young girls on the Internet, but her scheme backfires. She later becomes involved in a complex case involving domestic violence, and in the novel Lippman "takes an unconventional look at the anger and maliciousness behind domestic violence" (Cogdill 2002:11G). In *By a Spider's Thread,* Monaghan, who is half-Jewish, finds herself involved in a case involving an Orthodox man whose wife has disappeared. Carol Memmott noted that Lippman "uses his beliefs and cultural touchstones to highlight the disintegration of a family and the issue of identity" (D7). Most of the novels take place in the Baltimore area, but *In Big Trouble* finds Monaghan in Texas tracking down her boyfriend, Crow.

Baltimore and its history play an important role in the series. Phyllis Levin finds Baltimore "the most indelibly drawn character" in her review of Lippman's work (54). *In a Strange City* takes on a mystery surrounding Edgar Allan Poe fans. When asked what attracted her to the Poe story, Lippman replied that it was "inevitable" for her to be interested, being a "journalist working in Baltimore" (Koch 61). She notes that most of her novels have been "inspired by real events" (Jordan).

Her first nonseries novel, *Every Secret Thing,* moves away from the humorous, amateur sleuth model that works well for her in the Monaghan series. The story deals with two young girls who abduct and kill a baby. The bulk of the novel takes place in present day when the girls turn 18 years old and are released from custody in juvenile detention centers. Lippman was motivated by several true crime cases of children killing other children, including the 1968 case of Mary Bell in England. A journalist contacted Mary Bell as an adult and wrote her story. Lippman "was struck by the hole at the heart" of that story, noting that "Mary Bell is almost inarticulate" when she tries to answer why she did it (Lanham 18). Although her agent was concerned about possible reactions to the plot, Lippman wanted to explore "the limits of empathy" and the issue of whether people can be rehabilitated or forgiven (Lanham 18).

CRITICAL RECEPTION

Lippman's work has been well received from the start. Her first novel, *Baltimore Blues,* was nominated for a Shamus Award. Her second novel, *Charm City,* won both Edgar and Shamus awards, in addition to an Anthony nomination, and her third novel, *Butcher's Hill,* won an Agatha and an Anthony and was nominated for the Shamus, Macavity and Edgar awards.

Reviews of the first novel noted some unevenness, but saw potential in the series. A review of *Charm City* praised its "shrewd observation, on-target descriptions, believable characters and hilarious one-liners" and noted that *Baltimore Blues* showed "promise after a faltering start, and here Lippman displays a far surer, more even, hand" (Simson 1997:89). In reviewing *Butchers Hill,* Maria Simson noted that "dialogue is on the mark, accompanied by lively observations about female entrepreneurship, adoption, foster home rackets, and quirky Baltimore natives and neighborhoods" (1998:59).

A review of *The Sugar House* noted that although it "may not be the first mystery to explore eating disorders," the novel is "the only one to really explore this problem, to make it understandable and to elicit sympathy even from readers who feel little connection" (Cogdill 2000:9F). Another reviewer noted that Lippman's works are "effective thrillers, because they are stories about wanting to know what happens next" (Kaveney 21). *In a Strange City* was acclaimed as "an engrossing detective novel and a look at contemporary life through an unconventional heroine" (Cogdill 2001:8). Another reviewer found the novel to be proof "that she's indeed deserving of all the kudos she's received" (Cannon 60).

Every Secret Thing garnered a great deal of attention, being so different from the Monaghan series. It was nominated for a Hammett Award. In addition to the weighty subject matter, it is also Lippman's first use of multiple, third-person narrators. Lippman noted that using multiple point-of-view was "much more challenging" than she thought it would be, but that it made writing "jumps in time and space seem effortless" (Abbott). One review noted that with this work "Lippman shows she is an author willing to take risks in both writing and storytelling" and praised "her deft handling of this disturbing material" ("Every" 49).

BIBLIOGRAPHY

Works by Laura Lippman

Tess Monaghan Series

Baltimore Blues. New York: Avon, 1997.
Charm City. New York: Avon, 1997.
Butcher's Hill. New York: Avon, 1998.
In Big Trouble. New York: Avon, 1999.
The Sugar House. New York: Morrow, 2000.
In a Strange City. New York: Morrow, 2002.
The Last Place. New York: Morrow, 2003.
By a Spider's Thread. New York: Morrow, 2004.
No Good Deeds. New York: Morrow, 2006.

Other Novels

Every Secret Thing. New York: Morrow, 2003.
To the Power of Three. New York: Morrow, 2005.

Works about Laura Lippman

Abbott, Jeff. "Writer 2 Writer: Laura Lippman." n.d. http://www.jeffabbott.com/writer_lippman.html
Cannon, Peter. "*In a Strange City.*" *Publishers Weekly* 20 August 2001: 60.
Cogdill, Oline H. "Sugar House Hits the Sweet Spot." *South Florida Sun Sentinel* 3 September 2000: 9F.
————. "Poe, Baltimore and a Midnight Caller Add up to Intriguing 'Strange City'." *Chicago Tribune* 5 October 2001: 8.
————. "Last Place is First-Rate Baltimore Noir." *South Florida Sun Sentinel* 27 October 2002: 11G.
"*Every Secret Thing.*" *Publishers Weekly* 7 July 2003: 49.
"Give My Love to Baltimore." *Economist* 12 May 2001: 87.
Healy, Ellen. "Meet the Author: In Big Trouble with Baltimore Mystery Author Laura Lippman." MysteryNet.com. 18 May 2005. http://www.mysterynet.com/lippman/author.shtml

Jordan, Jon. "Interview with Laura Lippman." Books 'n' Bytes. n.d. http://www.booksnbytescom/auth_interviews/laura_lippman.htm

Kaveney, Roz. "*The Sugar House*." *Times Literary Supplement* 5 January 2001: 21.

Koch, Pat. "PW Talks to Laura Lippman." *Publishers Weekly* 20 August 2001: 61.

Lanham, Fritz. "Gambling with Fiction: Author Deviates from Series to Delve into Deeper Mystery." *Houston Chronicle* 7 December 2003: 18.

"Laura Lippman." Ed. Scot Peacock. *Contemporary Authors*. Vol. 207. Ed. Scot Peacock. Detroit: Gale, 2003. 237–38.

Laura Lippman. Homepage. 2004. 20 March 2005. http://www.lauralippman.com

Levin, Phyllis. "*Every Secret Thing*." *Baltimore Jewish Times* 17 December 2004: 54.

Memmott, Carol. "It's No Mystery Why We Love These Women." *USA Today* 22 July 2004: D7.

Quinn, Judy. "No Mystery to Laura Lippman's Leap." *Publishers Weekly* 29 November 1999: 32–33.

Silet, Charles L. P." An Interview with Laura Lippman." *Mystery Scene* 81 (2003): 19–22.

Simson, Maria. "*Charm City*." *Publishers Weekly* 18 August 1997: 89.

———. "*Butchers Hill*." *Publishers Weekly* 1 June 1998: 59.

Summers, K. C. "Baltimore, Wrapped in Mystery." *Washington Post* 18 January 2004: O1.

Charlotte MacLeod
(1922–2005)

BIOGRAPHY

Charlotte MacLeod was born on November 12, 1922, in Bath, New Brunswick, Canada. Her parents, Edward Phillips MacLeod and Mabel Maude Hayward MacLeod, immigrated to the United States when she was very young, and she and her siblings grew up in the Boston area. She studied art at the school now known as the Art Institute of Boston and then worked as a writer and artist for Stop and Shop Supermarkets. In 1952, she took a position with an advertising firm, and she worked there for 30 years, retiring in 1982 as a vice-president.

MacLeod was an avid reader from a young age and also began writing as a child. She noted that she decided to become a writer at age six, when one of her uncles gave her a children's book that was written by a distant relative (Long C21). She won a writing contest at age 10 and had a story published in the newspaper (Oliver B9). She began publishing fiction during the 1960s, producing a number of juvenile mysteries and other children's books, published under her own name and also under the pseudonym of Matilda Hughes. She began writing mysteries for adult readers in 1978.

She died January 14, 2005, in Lewiston, Maine, and is survived by her sister and brother, and two nieces.

MAJOR WORKS AND THEMES

In addition to her juvenile fiction and numerous short stories, MacLeod wrote four mystery series, two under her own name and two under the pseudonym of Alisa Craig. All

---

Also writing as Alisa Craig

of her works were in the "cozy" genre; as her sister Alexandria Baxter, who typed MacLeod's manuscripts, put it, MacLeod "wrote specifically for people who didn't want a lot of blood and guts" and produced novels that featured "a lot of tea drinkers" (Long C21; Oliver B9). It was often thought that she was the model for the Jessica Fletcher character on the television series "Murder, She Wrote," but MacLeod always rejected that notion, and had also rejected an offer to write for the show (Edwardsen D6; Oliver B9; Long C21). MacLeod herself noted that she followed Dorothy L. Sayers's definition of a traditional mystery as a "novel of manners in which crime is committed" (Gorner F1).

Her first series featured Peter Shandy, a professor at the Balaclava Agricultural College. The college was well known for having developed a special rutabaga called the Balaclava Buster. Shandy teams up with Helen Marsh, a librarian, to solve a case.

Her second series featured Sarah Kelling, a young widow who gets involved in a case involving art fraud. Kelling is down on her luck and runs a boarding house in the family mansion. The tenants are an eclectic bunch, only slightly more wacky than Kelling's family. She meets Max Bittersohn, who investigates the case, and the two join forces personally and as a crime-solving team.

The novels published under the Alisa Craig name are set in Canada. The first series featured Madoc Rhys, a Royal Canadian Mounted Police officer. The other Craig series is set in a fictional small town in Ontario and features Dittany Henbit Monk and her husband Osbert, along with a number of local citizens who are part of the "Grub-and-Stakers" gardening club.

In addition to her fictional works, MacLeod wrote a biography of Mary Roberts Rinehart. Rinehart was one of her favorite writers, and MacLeod felt Rinehart had always been overshadowed by her contemporary Agatha Christie.

CRITICAL RECEPTION

She received a Nero Wolfe award in 1987, had several Edgar and Agatha nominations throughout her career, and was also presented with the Agatha Award for Lifetime Achievement in 1998 at the Malice Domestic convention. Critics of all four of her series have praised her works for the strong use of humor, casts of eccentric characters, and literate prose, while often noting that her plotting tends to be thin.

A review of the first Shandy and Marsh novel, *Rest You Merry,* expressed a hope that MacLeod would have "many more stories up her talented sleeve" ("*Rest You Merry*" 104). *The Curse of the Giant Hogweed* included fantasy elements, which one reviewer found "bizarre, offbeat and fascinating" and "very satisfying" (Fletcher 1985:823). *The Corpse in Oozak's Pond* was praised as a "funny, endlessly inventive mystery" ("*Corpse*" 1252). Another reviewer found it "lucid and humorous" (Steinberg 1987a:71). *An Owl Too Many* was noted for its "piquant puns, suitably silly nomenclature, and audacious adventures" (Donavin 1991:1179). In *Exit the Milkman,* one reviewer found that MacLeod "again demonstrates her skill and with incomparable whimsy makes her bucolic puzzles great fun" (Steinberg 1996:45).

The Kelling series also gained praise over the years. The second in the series was lauded as being in the style of Agatha Christie (Fletcher 1980:506), and *The Bilbao Looking Glass* was praised as "winning" with its "combination of a traditional whodunit with a very funny look at Bostonians" (Steinberg 1982:56). A review of *The Recycled Citizen* pointed out a particularly "hilarious scene" that finds the whole cast of characters, including a pregnant Kelling, in disguise (Steinberg 1987b:62); a reviewer of *The Gladstone Bag* noted that

MacLeod always "serves up unalloyed pleasure" in her tales of Kelling (Steinberg 1990:65). One review of *The Resurrection Man* praised MacLeod for her "sure touch with the cheerily eccentric and her keen eye for the often strange social habits of apparently staid society" (Brainard 1992:50) Her final novel, *The Balloon Man,* which was the twelfth to feature Kelling and Bittersohn, was praised as a "delightful mystery" with "Max and Sarah mak[ing] a strong claim to be the Nick and Nora Charles of the 1990s, urbane, witty and thoroughly appealing" (Zaleski 1998:73). Another reviewer noted that "it isn't the plots that keep readers buying her books, but the polished charm and humor of her writing, the delight in depicting some of the zaniest characters of the mystery genre" (Roach 1). A third reviewer quipped that "the tone in this madcap mystery is so arch that even the corpses seem to have their tongues firmly in their lifeless cheeks" (DeCandido 203).

Several scholars wrote about MacLeod's works, with Richard Carpenter exploring her use of the "comically bizarre" (110) in constructing her plots along the rules of traditional mysteries. Uwe Baumann wrote about the Shandy and Marsh series, comparing it with two other writers who set mysteries on college campuses, and Neysa Chouteau looks at MacLeod's use of romance in her plotting.

BIBLIOGRAPHY

Works by Charlotte MacLeod

Peter Shandy and Helen Marsh Series

Rest You Merry. New York: Doubleday, 1978.
The Luck Runs Out. New York: Doubleday, 1979.
Wrack and Rune. New York: Doubleday, 1982.
Something the Cat Dragged In. New York: Avon, 1984.
The Curse of the Giant Hogweed. New York: Doubleday, 1985.
The Corpse in Oozak's Pond. New York: Mysterious Press, 1987.
Vane Pursuit. New York: Mysterious Press, 1989.
An Owl Too Many. New York: Mysterious Press, 1991.
Something in the Water. New York: Mysterious Press, 1994.
Exit the Milkman. New York: Mysterious Press, 1996.

Sarah Kelling and Max Bittersohn Series

The Family Vault. New York: Doubleday, 1979.
The Withdrawing Room. New York: Doubleday, 1980.
The Palace Guard. New York: Doubleday, 1981.
The Bilbao Looking Glass. New York: Doubleday, 1983.
The Convivial Codfish. New York: Doubleday, 1984.
The Plain Old Man. New York: Doubleday, 1985.
The Recycled Citizen. New York: Mysterious Press, 1988.
The Silver Ghost. New York: Mysterious Press, 1988.
The Gladstone Bag. New York: Mysterious Press, 1990.
The Resurrection Man. New York: Mysterious Press, 1992.
The Odd Job. New York: Mysterious Press, 1995.
The Balloon Man. New York: Mysterious Press, 1998.

Nonfiction

Had She But Known: A Biography of Mary Roberts Rinehart. New York: Mysterious Press, 1994.

Works as Alisa Craig

The Terrible Tide. New York: Doubleday, 1983.

Madoc Rhys Series

A Pint of Murder. New York: Doubleday, 1980.
Murder Goes Mumming. New York: Doubleday, 1981.
A Dismal Thing to Do. New York: Doubleday, 1986.
Trouble in the Brasses. New York: Avon, 1989.
The Wrong Rite. New York: Morrow, 1992.

Grub-and-Stakers Series

The Grub-and-Stakers Move a Mountain. New York: Doubleday, 1981.
The Grub-and-Stakers Quilt a Bee. New York: Doubleday, 1985.
The Grub-and-Stakers Pinch a Poke. New York: Avon, 1988.
The Grub-and-Stakers Spin a Yarn. New York: Avon, 1990.
The Grub-and-Stakers House a Haunt. New York: Morrow, 1993.

Works about Charlotte MacLeod

Bakerman, Jane S. and Helen M. Francini. "Charlotte MacLeod." *St. James Guide to Crime & Mystery Writers.* 4th ed. Ed. Jay P. Pederson. Detroit: St. James Press, 1996. 682–84.

Baumann, Uwe. "The Campus: A Cozy Place Where Comedy Meets Crime." Ed. Peter Nover. *The Great Good Place? A Collection of Essays on American and British College Mystery Novels.* Frankfurt: Peter Lang, 1999. 115–41.

Brainard, Dulcy. "*The Resurrection Man.*" *Publishers Weekly* 17 February 1992: 50.

Carpenter, Richard C. "The Antic Imagination of Charlotte MacLeod." *Clues* 14.2 (1993): 107–33.

"Charlotte (Matilda) MacLeod." *Contemporary Authors.* New Revision Vol. 141. Tracey L. Matthews, ed. Detroit: Gale, 2005. 289–91.

Chouteau, Neysa. "Hanky-Panky in the Middle Ages and Older: Charlotte MacLeod's Use of Romance as a Subplot." *Clues* 6.2 (1985): 53–59.

"*The Corpse in Oozak's Pond.*" *Booklist* 15 April 1987: 1252.

DeCandido, GraceAnne A. "*The Balloon Man.*" *Booklist* 15 September 1998: 203.

Donavin, Denise Perry. "*An Owl Too Many.*" *Booklist* 15 February 1991: 1179.

Edwardsen, Elizabeth. "Murder She Writes, But She's Not Jessica." *Greensboro News Record* 5 June 1994: D6.

Fletcher, Connie. "*The Withdrawing Room.*" *Booklist* 11 December 1980: 506.

———. "*The Curse of the Giant Hogweed.*" *Booklist* 15 February 1985: 823.

Gorner, Peter. "MacLeod: Mysteries, She Writes." *Orlando Sentinel* 6 March 1988: F1.

James, Dean. "The Charlotte MacLeod Interview." *Mystery Scene* 44 (1994): 19+.

Long, Tom. "Charlotte MacLeod, Author of More than 30 Mysteries." *Boston Globe* 21 January 2005: C21.

Oliver, Myrna. "Charlotte MacLeod, 82." *Los Angeles Times* 19 January 2005: B9.

"*Rest You Merry.*" *Publishers Weekly* 4 September 1978: 104.

Roach, Bill. "Balloon Man, A Whimsical Whirl." *Bangor Daily News* 13 February 1999: 1.

Steinberg, Sybil. "*The Bilbao Looking Glass.*" *Publishers Weekly* 26 November 1982: 56.

———. "*The Corpse in Oozak's Pond.*" *Publishers Weekly* 20 March 1987a: 71.

———. "*The Recycled Citizen.*" *Publishers Weekly* 20 November 1987b: 62.

———. "*The Gladstone Bag.*" *Publishers Weekly* 5 January 1990: 65.

———. "*Exit the Milkman.*" *Publishers Weekly* 1 July 1996: 45.

Zaleski, Jeff. "*The Balloon Man.*" *Publishers Weekly* 2 November 1998: 73.

Margaret Maron

BIOGRAPHY

Born in Greensboro, North Carolina, Margaret Maron is the daughter of C. O. and Claudia Stephenson Brown. When she was young, the family moved to a farm her grandfather had purchased southeast of Raleigh. When she was 11 years old, she decided that "even a kid in the Johnston County tobacco fields could be a writer;" and after reading work published by Edna St. Vincent Millay at age 19, Maron came to the decision that she had "eight years to write as good a poem as *Renascence*" (Taylor 1994b:63).

She married Joseph J. Maron, an artist, on June 20, 1959. While he was serving in the Navy, they were stationed in Italy. While living abroad, she taught school. After returning to the United States, they lived in New York for 10 years. Her husband was on the faculty at Brooklyn College, and she also taught there part-time before beginning her writing career. They have one son, John, and live in North Carolina.

Although she started out writing poetry, she found that market difficult to break into, and she tried her hand at short stories. She sold her first mystery short story in 1968. She wrote a few non-mystery stories that were published in women's magazines such as *Redbook,* but most of her work was in the mystery genre. Many of her stories have been collected and republished in two recent anthologies.

Maron enjoys doing research for the books and has taken criminology and paralegal courses. She also interviews people who live in the areas where she sets her novels and does research into the history and culture of the region. When writing about areas she is less familiar with, she often subscribes to the local newspapers and obtains phone books to avoid using real people's names (Taylor 1994b: 61, 65).

She was a founding member of Sisters in Crime and has taken the work of that organization seriously, noting that she is "so proud" of what they have accomplished (Carroll 1605). In addition to numerous nominations, she has won two Agatha Awards, an Anthony, a Macavity and an Edgar. One of her Agatha Awards is for *Up Jumps the Devil.* The other four awards were all for *Bootlegger's Daughter,* making her the first to win all four awards for one book.

MAJOR WORKS AND THEMES

Maron's first series is composed of eight books that take place over the course of one year in the life of New York homicide detective Sigrid Harald. Maron planned for the series to cover the one year, as Harald would make a "journey from the intellect to the emotions" (Carroll 1604). Harald is the daughter of a policeman who died in the line of duty. She is a loner, a quiet, plain woman who takes her career very seriously, although she is often dismissed as the "token" female by her colleagues. In the first novel, *One Coffee With,* she is called to investigate the death of an art professor at a local university. During her investigation, she meets a painter named Oscar Naumann, and her life is drastically changed when they fall in love. Throughout the series, Harald takes on various cases involving fraud, murder, and police corruption. Many cases have a link to the art world and feature Naumann assisting unofficially. Her personality, appearance, and general outlook on life go through a subtle transformation as her relationship with Naumann grows. Harriette C. Buchanan traced this aspect of the series, noting that in addition to the superficial or outward changes in appearance, Harald's investigative techniques also change, as Harald "comes out of her self-imposed shell of isolation into the world of vulnerable human beings" (41).

Maron's second series is set in North Carolina and focuses on Deborah Knott, a lawyer who is standing for election to district judge in the first novel, *Bootlegger's Daughter*. Knott comes from a large southern family, and a family tree often accompanies the novels. Knott's mother is the second wife of patriarch Keziah Knott. Between the first wife who died and Deborah's mother, there are 12 children in the family: 11 sons and Deborah, the youngest and only girl. Maron has stated that Knott was "deliberately conceived to be Sigrid's polar opposite" (Silet 312). In this series, Knott is involved in solving serious crimes, but her relationships with family and friends are crucial and are fully explored. Maron has addressed numerous social issues, such as racism and conflicts over development, in the series. Maron believes "the mystery genre is just as respectable as books generally labeled "literary," and thinks that mysteries "have the added benefit of being well-plotted and entertaining" (Nicholson). She further notes that she hates that mystery fiction "has been shunted over into a separate genre" and she resents that it is often viewed as "less valid," further nothing that "there's nothing you can't say in a mystery" (Nicholson).

CRITICAL RECEPTION

Maron's Sigrid Harald series had been well received, but Maron made history when *Bootlegger's Daughter* took all four major mystery awards in the United States. Michele Ross reviewed that work and noted that Maron's "dialogue is wonderfully accurate and funny, the emotions she conveys are poignant and realistic," summing up that the book was "so good you feel deprived when you finish" reading it (N8).

In a review of *Home Fires*, Carolyn Nizzi Warmbold noted that "Southern social fabric is part and parcel of the fine Knott series, but this time Maron has outdone herself ... not only present[ing] a long list of suspects but cleverly interrogat[ing] readers' own racial codes in the exploration of who might have done it" (K10). Jeff Zaleski found that in *Home Fires* "Maron lays the groundwork [of the plot] with subtlety, and she brings much more depth to her portrait of small-town doings than do most mystery writers" (84). Peter Cannon noted a similar sentiment in his review of *Uncommon Clay*, praising "Maron's mastery of jurisprudence, her well-researched depiction of the potting world but especially her sensitive portrayal of human relationships raise this novel far above the ordinary run of mysteries" (54).

Even when a reviewer thinks the plot is less compelling, as in the case of *Storm Track*, Maron is still praised for her "convincing" characters and her success in "detailing how the old South is giving way to the new, the rural to the urban, and the inevitable problems that arise" (Pate 3). Another reviewer found that the "real subject" in *Storm Track* is community, its abiding pleasures and its inevitable complexities, and this novel treats both with great sensitivity (Ott 1089).

BIBLIOGRAPHY

Works by Margaret Maron

Sigrid Harald Series

One Coffee With. New York: Raven House, 1981.
Death of a Butterfly. New York: Doubleday, 1984.

Death in Blue Folders. New York: Doubleday, 1985.
The Right Jack. New York: Bantam, 1987.
Baby Doll Games. New York: Bantam, 1988.
Corpus Christmas. New York: Doubleday, 1988.
Past Imperfect. New York: Doubleday, 1991.
Fugitive Colors. New York: Mysterious Press, 1995.

Deborah Knott Series

Bootlegger's Daughter. New York: Mysterious Press, 1992.
Southern Discomfort. New York: Mysterious Press, 1993.
Shooting at Loons. New York: Mysterious Press, 1994.
Up Jumps the Devil. New York: Mysterious Press, 1996.
Killer Market. New York: Mysterious Press, 1997.
Home Fires. New York: Mysterious Press, 1999.
Storm Track. New York: Mysterious Press, 2000.
Uncommon Clay. New York: Mysterious Press, 2001.
Slow Dollar. New York: Mysterious Press, 2002.
High Country Fall. New York: Mysterious Press, 2004.
Rituals of the Season. New York: Mysterious Press, 2005.
Winter's Child. New York: Mysterious Press, 2006.

Other Works

Bloody Kin. New York: Doubleday, 1985.
Shoveling Smoke: Selected Mystery Stories. Norfolk: Crippen and Landru, 1997.
Last Lessons of Summer. New York: Mysterious Press, 2003.
Suitable for Hanging: Selected Mystery Stories. Norfolk: Crippen and Landru, 2004.

Works about Margaret Maron

Buchanan, Harriette. C. "Sigrid's Saga: Text, Subtext, and Supertext in Margaret Maron's Sigrid Harald Novels." *Clues* 17.2 (1996): 33–42.
Cannon, Peter. "*Uncommon Clay.*" *Publishers Weekly* 9 April 2001: 53–54.
Carroll, Mary. "The *Booklist* Interview: Margaret Maron." *Booklist* 1 May 2001: 1604–605.
"Margaret Maron." *Contemporary Authors.* Vol. 66, New Revision Series. Eds. Daniel Jones and John R. Jorgensen. Detroit: Gale, 1998. 308–309.
Nicholson, Scott. "Margaret Maron: Bootlegger Belle." N.d. 22 May 2005. http://www.hauntedcomputer.com/ghostwr28.htm
Ott, Bill. "*Storm Track.*" *Booklist* 15 February 2000: 1089.
Pate, Nancy. "Mystery at Eye of Storm, from the Carolinas to Massachusetts." *Chicago Tribune* 26 April 2000: 3.
Ross, Michele. "Spotlight: Margaret Maron and Sharyn McCrumb." *Atlanta Constitution* 24 May 1992: N8.
Silet, Charles L. P. "Knotty Problems: An Interview with Margaret Maron." *The Armchair Detective* 30.3 (1997): 308–15.
Taylor, Art. "Blood Kin and *Bloody Kin:* Villainy and Family in the Works of Margaret Maron." *The Armchair Detective* 27.1 (1994a): 20–25.
———. "Sister in Crime: An Interview with Margaret Maron." *North Carolina Literary Review* 2.1 (1994b) 61–68.
Warmbold, Carolyn Nizzi. "Maron's Latest Homes in on More-than-Skin-Deep Truths." *The Atlanta Journal-Constitution* 13 December 1998: K10.
Zaleski, Jeff. "Home Fries." *Publishers Weekly* 5 October 1998: 84.

Sujata Massey (1964–)

BIOGRAPHY

Sujata Banerjee Massey was born in Sussex, England, in 1964, to an Indian father and a German mother. On her Web page, she explains that she was named for a woman who served the Buddha a bowl of rice. At the age of five, her parents immigrated to the United States. The family lived in Philadelphia, Berkeley, and St. Paul, but often returned to England. She is a legal resident of the United States but retains her United Kingdom citizenship. Being exposed to many cultures has affected her in many ways. She notes that when she moved to the United States as a child, it was hard for her "to decide which culture [she] wanted to belong to" (Pais 31).

She attended college at Johns Hopkins University and graduated in 1986. She began working as a food, fashion, and culture reporter for the *Baltimore Evening Sun.* She married Tony Massey, who was an officer in the U.S. Navy and was about to be stationed in Japan. The couple lived in Japan from 1991 to 1993, and during this time, Massey became interested in the culture and history of the country. She combined her interests and knowledge of Japan with her desire to write mystery novels and created the character of Rei Shimura, the main character of Massey's mystery series.

She and her husband have adopted two children from India, and they live in Baltimore. She returns to Japan each year to research her novels.

MAJOR WORKS AND THEMES

Massey began her mystery series with 1997's *The Salaryman's Wife,* which won the Agatha Award for Best First Novel. The series features Rei Shimura, the daughter of a Japanese father and American mother who chooses to reside in Japan. When the series begins, she is teaching English and attempting to begin an antiques business. As the series progresses, the antiques business becomes her primary work.

Each novel focuses on an aspect of Japanese culture. The first novel has extensive information about the culture of business in Japan. In *The Flower Master,* Shimura begins taking an *ikebana* class to please her aunt, and ends up embroiled in a mystery surrounding the school's owner. The novel is a primer on the art of *ikebana. The Floating Girl* has a mystery plot that involves *anime,* animated film, and *manga,* a popular form of comics; *The Bride's Kimono* has Shimura involved with an exhibition of antique kimono. *The Samurai's Daughter* tackles historical issues, looking at the continued effects of events from World War II. The most recent novel, *The Pearl Diver,* has Shimura once again living in the United States, but the mystery Shimura helps solve in this book involves a decades-old disappearance of a Japanese woman who had married an American soldier. Massey includes a great deal of information about Japanese cultural reactions to such mixed marriages, as well as the cultural history of the women from the missing woman's homeland who worked as pearl divers. In addition, Shimura is consulting as a designer for a new Japanese restaurant, and Massey provides interesting information about *kaseki* cuisine.

Massey is a strong advocate of gun control and has "pledged that there will be no guns" in her books (qtd in Potts 1B). Japan's stringent gun laws help her keep that pledge while writing realistic settings. Although there are murders and other violent events in the books, most of them happen off-stage and are never gratuitous or gory.

Massey also explores issues related to her own multicultural identity through her character. Shimura is of two cultures and often deals with the clashes between them. Her relationships with her parents and her Japanese relatives often convey the conflicts she finds herself facing. In addition, Shimura has an ongoing romantic relationship with a Scottish lawyer whose specialty in international law brings him to Japan, introducing another layer of culture clash. Massey notes that the mystery portion of the novels come later, that she begins with "a cultural phenomenon or historical topic" she wants to consider (Klug).

CRITICAL RECEPTION

As might be expected of a writer whose first novel won a major writing award, the critical reception of Massey's work has been positive overall. In a review of *The Salaryman's Wife*, Robert J. Collins noted that Massey had "hit the nail of the cross-cultural, multi-national circus that is so much a part of our lives in this society squarely on the head. Better yet, she has created a character who we want to know" (qtd in Potts 1B). Another reviewer called it an "unusual" mystery with "universal appeal" and a "riveting, page-turning style that will make readers late for work" (Noe 77).

Nakasha Ahmad recognizes that Massey's works provide interesting insights into Japanese culture and multicultural identities, but she thinks Massey's key talent is "creating characters the reader actually cares about" (Ahmad). She finds the romantic relationships realistically portrayed and noted that readers can be "both surprised by and occasionally frustrated with Rei" (Ahmad).

Zen Attitude was noted for combining a "very entertaining mystery with lessons in Japanese culture" (Simson 72). The third novel, *The Flower Master*, the first to be published in hardcover, gained praise for its "appealing sleuth" and "volatile yet harmonious mix of ancient Eastern traditions [and] modern American chutzpah" (Zaleski 1999:225). Jenny McLarin praised it for its "unique plot" and "exceptional protagonist" (1999:1482).

Praise has continued along with the series. *The Floating Girl* was viewed as taking readers on "a thoughtful tour of contemporary Japanese youth culture" within an "accomplished murder mystery" (Zaleski 2000:54) which succeeds in "captivating and educating" readers (McLarin 2000:1622). *The Bride's Kimono* was acclaimed as an "absorbing, sophisticated mystery" with interesting "multicultural details of customs and attitudes of East and West" (Cannon 2001: 66). Peter Cannon has reviewed several of Massey's novels. In *The Samurai's Daughter* he noted that Massey "poses some deeply resonating questions about guilt and responsibility" (Cannon 2003: 56), and in his review of *The Pearl Diver* remarks that Massey is "adept at crafting dead-on dialogue and juggling serious issues with humor" (Cannon 2004:148).

BIBLIOGRAPHY

Works by Sujata Massey

Rei Shimura Series

The Salaryman's Wife. New York: HarperCollins, 1997.
Zen Attitude. New York: HarperCollins, 1998.
The Flower Master. New York: HarperCollins, 1999.
The Floating Girl. New York: HarperCollins, 2000.
The Bride's Kimono. New York: HarperCollins, 2001.

The Samurai's Daughter. New York: HarperCollins, 2003.
The Pearl Diver. New York: HarperCollins, 2004.
The Typhoon Lover. New York: HarperCollins, 2005.
Girl in a Box. New York: HarperCollins, 2006.

Works about Sujata Massey

Ahmad, Nakasha. "Mysterious Ways." *Nirali Magazine* 2 (October 2004). Online edition. 11 October 2004. http://www.niralimagazine.com/arts/0409_sujata.html

Cannon, Peter. "*The Bride's Kimono.*" *Publishers Weekly* 6 August 2001: 66.

———. "The Samurai's Daughter." *Publishers Weekly* 24 February 2003: 56.

———. "The Pearl Diver." *Publishers Weekly* 19 July 2004: 148.

Klug, Foster. "Mystery Writer Looks to Japan's Quirks." *The Japan Times* 14 April 2003. Online edition. 11 October 2004. http://www.japantimes.co.jp/cgi-bin/getarticle.p15?nn20030414b3.htm

McLarin, Jenny. "*The Flower Master.*" *Booklist* 15 April 1999: 1482.

———. "*The Floating Girl.*" *Booklist* 1 May 2000: 1622.

Noe, N. Rain. "The Accidental Sleuth." *A. Magazine.* 30 November 1997: 77.

Pais, Arthur J. "'I Have Started Discovering My Family in India': Writer Sujata Massey Discusses Her Life and Novels." *India in New York* 5.42 (25 April 2003): 31.

Potts, Michel W. "Sujata Massey: Unique Among Indian Novelists." *India West* 15 October 1999: 1B.

Simson, Maria. "*Zen Attitude.*" *Publishers Weekly* 13 April 1998: 72.

"Sujata Massey." *Contemporary Authors.* Vol. 215. Ed. Scot Peacock. Detroit: Gale, 2004. 272–4.

Sujata Massey. 2004. 11 October 2004. http://interbridge.com/sujata/

Zaleski, Jeff. "*The Flower Master.*" *Publishers Weekly* 5 April 1999: 225.

———. "*The Floating Girl.*" *Publishers Weekly* 17 April 2000: 54.

Francine Mathews (1963–)

BIOGRAPHY

Francine Stephanie Barron was born in Binghamton, New York in 1963, the youngest of six sisters. Her father was an Air Force general who died when she was a freshman in high school (homepage). She grew up in Washington, D.C., and the family spent many summers at Cape Cod.

After graduating from Georgetown Visitation Preparatory School, she attended Princeton University. Although she did not major in journalism, one of her extracurricular interests was writing for the university newspaper, which led to later jobs with *The Miami Herald* and *The San Jose Mercury News.* She earned her degree in European history in 1984, and won a prestigious Arthur W. Mellon Foundation Fellowship in the Humanities in her senior year. She notes that her best memories come from a course called The Literature of Fact, which was taught by John McPhee (homepage). She studied history as a graduate student at Stanford, with a focus on international finance and law, but didn't complete her doctorate degree. After leaving Stanford with a master's degree in history, she applied for a position

---

Also writing as Stephanie Barron

with the CIA. She was employed by the CIA for several years as an intelligence analyst, working on such high-profile cases as the bombing of Pan Am Flight 103.

She decided she really wanted to try writing as a career, and she chose mystery fiction because she thought "it would be helpful to write what [she] loved to read" ("Francine" 69). She notes that Elizabeth George was a particular influence. After writing and selling her first book, she soon turned to writing fiction full-time. She lives in Golden, Colorado, with her husband and children.

MAJOR WORKS AND THEMES

Mathews writes three series, two under the name Francine Mathews and one under the name Stephanie Barron. As Mathews, she wrote four books set on Nantucket featuring police officer Meredith "Merry" Folger. In this series, Folger is the latest in a long line of police officers in her family. Family and genealogy play a large role in the novels, as they do generally on Nantucket. In this series Mathews aimed to "capture the difficult life in New England today," looking at the "bitter and embedded economic issues" that have plagued the fishing industry ("Francine" 70). Folger tackles cases involving drug use, child neglect, corruption, and environmental protection issues and proves herself as a police detective to her boss, who is also her father. Throughout the series, Mathews portrays the culture of Nantucket as well, with its year-round population that needs the tourist trade to survive and the very different settings that occur with and without the seasonal inhabitants.

As Barron, she writes a historical mystery series featuring the British writer Jane Austen, who plays amateur sleuth. Her academic training in European history is highlighted in this series (Shindler 2001:F3). She notes that she has heavily researched the lives of Austen and her family, using Austen's correspondence as a key source, and that she "look[s] for holes in key events in her life that are compelling" and uses those to launch the plot ("Francine" 70). She rereads Austen's work almost every winter, and in February 1994, she writes that she "had read Austen to such an extent that her syntax and oddities of speech had infiltrated my own.... I reveled in Austen's speech. I adopted it as my own. I was, I am convinced, channeling Jane. I sat down to write what she told me" ("Detective"). When she was finished, she had the draft manuscript for the first Jane Austen mystery. The books are presented as Austen's lost diaries that Barron merely edits (Wales 16). In addition to solving various crimes, the books include accounts of various events in Austen's life, as well as the history of England. For example, the second novel, *Jane and the Man of the Cloth,* focuses on a seaside vacation that we know Austen and her family took in 1804. As Dulcy Brainard points out, the trip happened but is "sparsely enough documented to allow Barron great latitude in creating a tale that makes the most of the period when the Napoleonic Wars raged and the coast was rife with smugglers" (1996:59).

In addition to these two series, Mathews has also published novels that have come out of her own experiences with the CIA. She notes that she wanted to write a spy thriller for many years, but that she hesitated because of a secrecy agreement with the CIA that required her to "submit anything work-related for review" (Shindler 2001: F3). *The Cutout* features Caroline Carmichael, a CIA analyst described as "an intellectual, a high priestess of reason, a master of disguises" (Bowers 20). Carmichael leads an antiterrorism unit and is determined to find those who killed her husband. When another attack occurs, she learns that he isn't really dead, and the couple becomes caught up in an international plot. Mathews returns to the Carmichael character in *Blown.* Another thriller, *The Secret Agent,* is a fictionalized account of the life of the first CIA intelligence chief in Bangkok (Shindler 2002: E3).

CRITICAL RECEPTION

Reviews of the Merry Folger series were quite positive. A review of *Death in a Mood Indigo* spoke of strong characters and realistic plotting, with "all loose ends tied up in a way that makes sense" (DuVal 1997:3). Another reviewer found that novel to exhibit "vivid description, good interrogative technique, psychological undercurrents, and island atmosphere" (Klett 1997:156). Coverage of *Death in a Cold Hard Light* called the work appealing, with "human, fallible and thoughtful" characters in a believable plot (DiNizo 167). Another reviewer noted that the novel "advances the distinctive characterization and deft plotting that mark this series" (Brainard 1998:72). John Rowen found *Death in a Cold Hard Light* to be " dark, taut, and unsettling" with dialogue that "crackles" and a "nail-biting pace" (1389).

Reviews of the Jane Austen series praise her for the voice in the novels, noting that she "masterfully imitates Austen's voice" ("*Jane and His Lordship's Legacy*" 57) and "catches Austen's tone amazingly well" (Zaleski 178). She also is widely praised for getting the details right. Another review noted that "her research is so meticulous and detailed, it's almost as if one were reading a book from Austen's era, not our own" (DuVal 1999:3). *Jane and the Man of the Cloth* was deemed to be "worthy of its origins" (Brainard 1996:59) and as "historical fiction at its best" (Klett 1996:151).

Reviews of her espionage titles have been more mixed, with critics preferring the two novels that feature Caroline Carmichael to the stand-alone *The Secret Agent*. *The Cutout* praised Mathews for her knowledge of the field, which allowed her to create "a vivid tale of seduction, betrayal, revenge and international political intrigue" (Bowers 20). Another reviewer found a few flaws with the novel, but noted that Mathews "makes up for these small flaws by avoiding an obvious formula ending" (Steinberg 53). *Blown* was praised for "dexterously serv[ing] up strong suspense and crisp espionage maneuvers" ("*Blown*" 33).

BIBLIOGRAPHY

Works by Francine Mathews

Merry Folger Series

Death in the Off-Season. New York: Morrow, 1994.
Death in Rough Water. New York: Morrow, 1995.
Death in a Mood Indigo. New York: Bantam, 1997.
Death in a Cold Hard Light. New York: Bantam, 1998.

Espionage Novels

The Cutout. New York: Bantam, 2001.
The Secret Agent. New York: Bantam, 2002.
Blown. New York: Bantam, 2005.

Works by Stephanie Barron

Jane Austen Series

Jane and the Unpleasantness at Scargrave Manor. New York: Bantam, 1997.
Jane and the Man of the Cloth. New York: Bantam, 1997.
Jane and the Wandering Eye. New York: Bantam, 1998.
Jane and the Genius of the Place. New York: Bantam, 1999.
Jane and the Stillroom Maid. New York: Bantam, 2000.

Jane and the Prisoner of Wool House. New York: Bantam, 2001.
Jane and the Ghosts of Netley. New York: Bantam, 2003.
Jane and His Lordship's Legacy. New York: Bantam, 2005.
Jane and the Barque of Frailty. New York: Bantam, 2006.

Works about Mathews/Barron

"*Blown*." *Publishers Weekly* 11 April 2005: 33.
Bowers, Faye. "Tinker, Seamstress, Soldier, Spy." *Christian Science Monitor* 15 February 2001: 20.
Brainard, Dulcy. "*Jane and the Man of the Cloth*." *Publishers Weekly* 11 November 1996: 59.
———. "*Death in a Cold Hard Light*." *Publishers Weekly* 30 March 1998: 72.
"Detective Jane Austen." n.d. 18 May 2005. http://www.stephaniebarron.com/books.html
DiNizo, Alice. "*Death in a Cold Hard Light*." *Library Journal* 1 June 1998: 167.
DuVal, Linda. "Mathews' *Mood Indigo* More Than Just a Good Mystery." *Chicago Tribune* 26 August 1997: 3.
———. "As Fact or Fiction, Author Remains True to Jane Austen." *Chicago Tribune* 23 February 1999: 3.
"Francine Mathews." *Mystery Scene* 61 (1998): 69–70.
Francine Mathews. Homepage. n.d. 18 May 2005. www.francinemathews.com
"*Jane and His Lordship's Legacy*." *Publishers Weekly* 14 February 2005: 57.
Klett, Rex E. "*Jane and the Man of the Cloth*." *Library Journal* December 1996: 151.
———. "*Death in a Mood Indigo*." *Library Journal* 1 June 1997: 156.
Rowen, John. "*Death in a Cold Hard Light*." *Booklist* 15 April 1998: 1389.
Shindler, Dorman T. "There's No Mystery to Mathews' Success." *Denver Post* 4 March 2001: F3.
———. "Too Many Twists, Turns, Flashbacks." *Denver Post* 14 July 2002: E3.
Steinberg, Sybil. "*The Cutout*." *Publishers Weekly* 27 November 2000: 53.
Wales, Ruth Johnstone. "The Author, in the Parlor, with the Fountain Pen." *Christian Science Monitor* 31 August 2000: 16.
Zaleski, Jeff. "*Jane and the Stillroom Maid*." *Publishers Weekly* 17 July 2000: 178.

Sharyn McCrumb (1948–)

BIOGRAPHY

Sharyn Arrowood McCrumb was born in North Carolina and grew up near Chapel Hill. From an early age, she was an avid reader and knew at the age of seven that she wanted to be a writer. She grew up in a family with storytellers that passed down the family history; her father's family was Scots-Irish from the mountain region, and her mother's people came from what McCrumb calls the Flatland South (homepage). She describes it as a "mixed marriage" and often recounts the story of her father's first dinner with her mother's family, where he made waves by pouring cream and sugar, not gravy, on his rice (Silet 369). Her great-grandfathers were circuit preachers, and the family's Scottish ancestors have roots in the Smoky Mountain region back to the 1700s.

She wanted to major in English at the University of North Carolina at Chapel Hill, but on her father's advice instead took degrees in communications and Spanish. She jokes that she could have been "a Cuban disk jockey" but instead wrote for a small newspaper and did "all those sorts of things that liberal arts majors do while they're trying to figure out what they want to be" (Silet 370). She returned to graduate school at Virginia Tech, earning a master's degree in English. She taught journalism and Appalachian Studies courses at Virginia Tech before turning to writing full-time in 1988. In addition to her writing, she also lectures widely on Appalachian history and culture.

She and her husband David have two children, Spencer and Laura, and they live in Virginia.

MAJOR WORKS AND THEMES

McCrumb writes novels in three series that are quite distinct in style and tone. One series deals with an engineering professor named James Owens Mega who also writes science fiction novels as Jay Omega. This satirical, humorous series features Omega solving crimes at science fiction fan conventions and other settings with a group of quirky friends.

The Elizabeth MacPherson novels also are in light in tone and highlight McCrumb's sense of humor. Part mystery, part comedy of manners, and part social satire, the novels feature Elizabeth MacPherson, an American who marries a Scotsman and lives in the United Kingdom. MacPherson is drawn into solving a variety of crimes, often related to her career as a forensic anthropologist. One of the most interesting in the series is in *Missing Susan,* which finds MacPherson taking a guided tour of famous crime scenes in Britain. One of the people in the tour group is plotting the murder of another, and MacPherson unwittingly becomes involved.

The novels known as the "Ballad" series highlight McCrumb's expertise in Appalachian history and tackle more serious issues in a more serious way. As the series progresses, McCrumb moves further from mystery conventions, and although some of the novels do not feature the two key characters from the first four books, McCrumb refers to them all as the Ballad novels. McCrumb compares her novels to Appalachian quilts, noting that she takes "brightly colored scraps of legends, ballads, fragments of rural life, and local tragedy, and piece[s] them together into a complex whole that tells not only a story, but also a deeper truth about the culture of the mountain South" (homepage). She also has stated that the Ballad novels "are mysteries in the same way that *To Kill a Mockingbird* is a legal thriller," further noting that as with "any of the best books in the mystery field, you can read them as formula or read them with your brains in gear and get something more out of them" (Baker C1).

In the first five novels, local sheriff Spencer Arrowood, named in honor of McCrumb's grandfather, solves crimes, often with input from Nora Bonesteel, a local woman who is clairvoyant. Themes include losing land that has been passed down through generations, environmental degradation, and dealing with the aftermath of past events, including the Vietnam War. In the fifth novel, *The Ballad of Frankie Silver,* Arrowood is haunted by his role in a capital murder case and he begins to study another case that never seemed right, the real case of Frankie Silver. As Arrowood recalls the case he was involved with, McCrumb also brings in the story of Silver, who in 1833 was the first woman hanged for murder in North Carolina. McCrumb artfully blends Arrowood's anguished search into a possible miscarriage of justice with a historical account of Silver's life and the possible miscarriage of justice she suffered in the 1800s.

The next two Ballad novels move away from mystery plots and themes into the realm of historical fiction. *The Song Catcher* portrays the story of a search for a ballad. Lark McCourry, a folk singer and the descendant of a man from Scotland who came to America before the Revolution, traces her family history through a ballad that has been passed down. As McCourry recalls parts of the song, the novel jumps back in time to trace the family through various stages of American history. *Ghost Riders* also combines a story from the past with one from the present, first tracing how Appalachia was split by the Civil War, through fictionalized accounts of two real figures, Governor Zebulon Vance and Malinda Blalock, who dressed as a man and followed her husband to war. The second part of the novel follows present day Civil War reenactors.

Her recent novel returns to her earlier comic style, but does not return to the mystery or detective genre. *St. Dale* has been described as a "contemporary take on Chaucer's *Canterbury Tales* set in the world of stock-car racing" (Williams 50), although readers who are "blissfully unaware of the author's designs still will enjoy" the tale (Shindler F14). She knew nothing of NASCAR; the idea about reworking the *Canterbury Tales* with a more modern saint had been percolating in her mind for some time. In the outpouring of public grief that occurred when Dale Earnhardt died, she realized he was the modern "homeboy" secular saint she had been looking for (Wicker 37; Williams 50). In the novel, a down-and-out driver takes a motley crew on a tour of race tracks in the South where Earnhardt had raced.

CRITICAL RECEPTION

McCrumb's writing has received numerous nominations and awards. She has won awards for works in all three of her series, including an Edgar Award for *Bimbos of the Death Sun;* a Macavity Award for *If Ever I Return, Pretty Peggy-O;* Nero, Agatha, Anthony, and Macavity awards for *She Walks These Hills;* and another Agatha for *If I'd Killed Him When I Met Him.*

Critical acclaim has been consistent for her works. *The Hangman's Beautiful Daughter* was seen as a successful mystery, but a reviewer noted that "it works even better as a meditative novel in the grand southern tradition" (Robertson 1340). *She Walks These Hills* was praised for its blend of "mystery with the supernatural, folklore, and history" and how McCrumb explores "the importance of family and place ... and the possibility or impossibility of escaping your roots" (Pearl 140). A review of *The Ballad of Frankie Silver* noted that "as is her wont, McCrumb asks topical and controversial questions in the deftly entwined tales," including how the justice system treats the poor and whether capital punishment can be administered fairly (Earle J2). The reviewer also noted that "the many intertwining stories in *Frankie Silver* do not confuse. Instead, they build, one on the other, and eventually take us to a logical, satisfying, if not happy, ending" (Earle J2).

Hal Jacobs praised McCrumb's ability to "perfectly capture the rhythms, magic and characters of whatever era she's describing. [*Songcatcher*] is a ballad in itself to the Appalachians and the history of the people who have settled it" (D5). Another review pointed out that "McCrumb writes high-spirited historical fiction, [with] her lush, dense narratives shored up by thorough research and convincing period detail. [*Ghost Riders*] is another harmonious, folksy blend of history and backwoods lore" ("*Ghost Riders*" 49).

Another review of *Ghost Riders* draws attention to McCrumb's "gritty descriptions of this hills-and-hollows feuding, reflecting the author's fine ear for colloquial language and thought," which "add up to the best kind of historical realism" (Hebert E3). Using McCrumb's own quilt metaphor, the reviewer continues that "in this particular quilt, she culls, juxtaposes and sews with almost magical skill, leaving Americans of all ancestries with a patchwork creation that both haunts and throws light into unfamiliar places," which are "worth visiting" (Hebert E3).

A review of the latest Elizabeth MacPherson novel praised McCrumb's humorous, snappy dialogue, noting that "McCrumb excels at flawless characterization in which characters tell their own stories, "calling her "smart, funny writer with something better to put in her character's mouths than clichés dipped in bile" (Doucette E3). Dorman Shindler praised *St. Dale* as a "present-day, blue-collar comedy dealing with spirituality, stock cars and shaky lives" that marks "new territory for McCrumb, and she treads the ground with admirable sure-footedness" (F14).

Meredith Sue Willis analyzed the first four Ballad novels in an essay for *Appalachian Journal* in 1998, noting that McCrumb has particularly strong female characters. Willis writes that "women in McCrumb's novels, as in life, are central to most of the action, and they are good, bad, ugly, and legendary…. Even the weak and despicable women are interesting" (323). Willis also criticizes McCrumb's work in terms of detective fiction conventions, positing that the genre "is not what McCrumb wants to be writing" (326). McCrumb has indeed resisted being classified as a genre writer from the start, stating clearly as early as 1995 that she wanted to write novels, works beyond any genre classifications, and that above all, she sees herself as a storyteller (Silet 370, 380).

Gwen McNeill Ashburn looked at McCrumb's use of language and the discourse of law and power in *The Ballad of Frankie Silver*. The Ballad novels appear to be the most interesting to literary scholars, and a collection of critical essays about them was published in 2003 (Holloway). These essays provide a variety of approaches in studying the themes, narrative structure and use of history in the novels. Several address aspects of McCrumb's use of music, something she finds crucial to the process and content of her works.

BIBLIOGRAPHY

Works by Sharyn McCrumb

Ballad Novels

If Ever I Return, Pretty Peggy-O. New York: Scribner, 1990.
The Hangman's Beautiful Daughter. New York: Scribner, 1992.
She Walks These Hills. New York: Scribner, 1994.
The Rosewood Casket. New York: Dutton, 1996.
The Ballad of Frankie Silver. New York: Dutton, 1998.
The Song Catcher. New York: Dutton, 2001.
Ghost Riders. New York: Dutton, 2003.
St. Dale. New York: Kensington, 2005.

Elizabeth MacPherson Series

Sick of Shadows. New York: Avon, 1984.
Lovely in Her Bones. New York: Avon, 1985.
Highland Laddie Gone. New York: Avon, 1986.
Paying the Piper. New York: Avon, 1988.
The Windsor Knot. New York: Ballantine, 1990.
Missing Susan. New York: Ballantine, 1991.
MacPherson's Lament. New York: Ballantine, 1992.
If I'd Killed Him When I Met Him. New York: Ballantine, 1995.
PMS Outlaws. New York: Ballantine, 2000.

Jay Omega Series

Bimbos of the Death Sun. New York: TSR Books, 1987.
Zombies of the Gene Pool. New York: Simon and Schuster, 1992.

Other Works

Foggy Mountain Breakdown and Other Stories. New York: Ballantine, 1997.

Works about Sharyn McCrumb

Ashburn, Gwen McNeill. "Silence in the Courtroom: Language, Literature, and Law in *The Ballad of Frankie Silver*." Ed. Michael J. Meyer. *Literature and Law*. Amsterdam: Rodopi, 2004. 67–81.

Baker, Jeff. "She Walks Those Hills." *The Oregonian* 20 May 1996: C1.

Doucette, John-Henry. "Writer Turns out a Smartly Written Plot with Tough Characters." *Virginian – Pilot* 19 November 2000: E3.

Earle, Peggy Deans. "Mountain Ballad of Entwined Murders Sung in Minor Key." *Virginian – Pilot* 28 June 1998: J2.

"*Ghost Riders*." *Publishers Weekly* 19 May 2003: 49.

Goodwin, B. Lynn. "Literary Quilts: An Interview with Sharyn McCrumb." N.d. 25 May 2005. http://www.writeradvice.com/download.html

Hebert, George. "A Patchwork that Haunts and Illuminates." *Virginian – Pilot* 20 July 2003: E3.

Holloway, Kimberley M., Ed. *From a Race of Storytellers: Essays on the Ballad Novels by Sharyn McCrumb*. Macon: Mercer UP, 2003.

Jacobs, Hal. "Reading the South: A Ballad Spans Generations, Lands in *Songcatcher*." *The Atlanta Journal-Constitution* 19 August 2001: D5.

James, Dean. "Sharyn McCrumb." *St. James Guide to Crime & Mystery Writers*. 4th ed. Ed. Jay P. Pederson. Detroit: St. James Press, 1996. 724–25.

Pearl, Nancy and Rachel Singer Gordon. "*She Walks These Hills*." *Library Journal* 15 September 2001: 140.

Robertson, Peter. "The *Booklist* Interview: Sharyn McCrumb." *Booklist* 15 March 1992: 1341.

"Sharyn McCrumb." *Contemporary Authors*. Vol. 168. Ed. Scot Peacock. Detroit: Gale, 1999. 238–41.

Sharyn McCrumb. Homepage. 2005. 25 May 2005. http://www.sharynmccrumb.com

Shindler, Dorman T. "If Chaucer Had Written Tales about NASCAR." *Denver Post* 13 March 2005: F14.

Silet, Charles L.P. "*She Walks These Hills*: An Interview with Sharyn McCrumb." *Armchair Detective* 28.4 (1995): 368–80.

Stankard, Linda. "Song of the South: Sharyn McCrumb Adds Another Verse to Her Ballad Series." Bookpage.com. 2003. 25 May 2005. http://www.bookpage.com/0307bp/sharyn_mccrumb.html

Wicker, Ann. "Ghost Racers." *Creative Loafing* 20 October 2004: 37–39. http://charlotte.creativeloafing.com/2004–10–20-arts_feature.html

Williams, Wilda. "Q&A: Sharyn McCrumb." *Library Journal* 15 November 2004: 50.

Willis, Meredith Sue. "The Ballads of Sharyn McCrumb." *Appalachian Journal* 25.3 (1998): 320–29.

Val McDermid (1955–)

BIOGRAPHY

Val McDermid was born June 4, 1955, in Kircaldy, Scotland, which she describes on her homepage as being a large producer of linoleum and the birthplace of Adam Smith. She also spent a lot of time with her grandparents in East Wemyss, a mining village, also in Fife. She recalls that there wasn't a lot of extra money in her working-class family, but her parents recognized the importance of education. The best thing that happened to her as a child, she notes, is when the family moved to a house across the street from the central library (Aldrich 2).

She was one of the youngest students ever admitted to Oxford University and the first from a Scottish state school (homepage). She received her degree in English from St. Hilda's College in 1975. On her Web site, she notes that she "had always wanted to write, ever since [she] realized that real people actually produced all those books in the library" (homepage). Since people told her she would never make a living from being a writer, she chose journalism as a career. From 1975 to 1977, she trained as a journalist in Devon and then went on to a career in newspaper writing and managing in Manchester and Glasgow, including four years as the crime reporter for the *Manchester Evening News.*

Her interest in writing fiction didn't wane, though, and she did continue with creative writing projects. After reading a number of the detective fiction novels written by American women that emerged in 1980s, she decided that mystery fiction would be her focus. Her first mystery novel was published in 1987, and since 1991, she has been writing fiction full-time.

She and her partner have one son and they live in England.

MAJOR WORKS AND THEMES

McDermid has written several stand-alone novels in addition to works in three distinct series. Her first series features a "cynical lesbian socialist journalist" named Lindsay Gordon who is McDermid's alter ego but with a personality "that is pure fiction" (Val 268). Gordon uncovers various crimes through her work as a journalist. Through the series, McDermid takes on a number of issues, including class, race, and gender inequalities.

Another series featuring a private investigator named Kate Brannigan was published under the name V. L. McDermid. McDermid had noted in interviews that she would like to write another in the Brannigan series, but that the thrillers take a great deal of time and energy (Jordan); after a 10-year hiatus, Brannigan returned to print in 2006. The Brannigan series was a more traditional approach to the genre, as McDermid knew that lesbian amateur sleuth novels would not sell well (Hadley 77).

Her third series features a forensic psychologist and profiler named Tony Hill, who collaborates with a detective inspector named Carol Jordan. These novels are much darker in tone, include much more graphic violence than the Gordon and Brannigan books, and are best labeled as psychological thrillers.

She also has written several stand-alone thrillers. *A Place of Execution* is set at the time of the infamous Myra Hindley and Ian Brady murders. A young girl has gone missing, but this case seems different from the others that are plaguing the police. A new detective tackles the case and solves it. The second half of the novel takes place 25 years later and explores the lives of the victim's family, the police, and others who were touched by the case. *The Distant Echo* also follows that structure. In the first part, set in 1978, four young men find a body and are then suspected of her rape and murder, although there is not enough evidence to charge them. In 2003, the case is reopened by a cold case squad to use modern forensic techniques to review the evidence. The victim's brothers remain convinced the four are guilty and seek revenge, while suspicion grows among the four friends as well.

CRITICAL RECEPTION

The Lindsay Gordon and Kate Brannigan series have not been as popular in the United States, although critics responded positively to the works. Her novels about the criminal profilers Tony Hill and Carol Jordan have been more visible on both sides of the Atlantic. The first Hill and Jordan novel, *The Mermaids Singing,* won the Gold Dagger Award from the

Crime Writers Association. Her stand-alone thrillers have also done well commercially and critically. *A Place of Execution* won McDermid an Anthony Award, a Barry Award, a Macavity Award, a Dilys Award from the Independent Mystery Booksellers Association, as well as Book of the Year and Notable Book citations from the *Los Angeles Times* and the *New York Times*.

In a review of *A Place of Execution,* Jeff Zaleski noted that "McDermid spins a haunting tale whose complexity never masks her adroitness at creating memorable characters and scenes. Her narrative spell is such that the reader is immersed immediately in the rural Britain of the early '60s" (91). Zaleski also recognizes McDermid's "extensive research on how police work was done at the time," noting that this work "paid off beautifully" (91). Another review deemed it McDermid's best work, praising the novel as "brilliantly organized and immensely engrossing" and "written with a sure feeling for place and time" (Raine 33).

The first novel in the Hill and Jordan series features explicit descriptions of torture and killing, as represented in the killer's journal. This aspect, noted Dulcy Brainard, "makes this graphic, psychologically terrifying tale almost as off-putting as it is impossible to put down" (61). Natasha Cooper felt that *The Mermaids Singing* was "spoiled" by the graphic descriptions and found the follow-up novel, *The Wire in the Blood,* "quite restrained" in comparison, although still quite graphic (1997:24). Cooper noted that the technique of switching between the point of view of the killer and the detective can be "dangerous in lesser hands" but that McDermid "handles it extremely well" (24). Cooper praised McDermid's strong character development and skillful portrayals of the "credible relationships" between characters (24).

In a review of *The Distant Echo* Cooper noted that McDermid writes "without flinching from the pain inflicted on murder victims and their families" and "has used the crime genre to write a novel that, above everything else, celebrates life and loyalty" (2003:24). *Publishers Weekly* called this an "absorbing psychological novel of revenge [that] shows McDermid at the top of her form," with praise for her "outstanding pacing, character and plot development, plus evocative place descriptions" (59).

Samantha Hume writes about issues of gender and ethnic identity as borne out in the Gordon series. Her use of feminist theory illuminates the larger social themes in McDermid's works. Mary Hadley also explores Gordon's relationships and emotional issues, particularly in her journalistic detachment to the crimes she writes about or works to solve (80–81). Hadley also traces innovations in setting, plot and character throughout McDermid's three series of novels.

BIBLIOGRAPHY

Works by Val McDermid

Carol Jordan and Tony Hill Series

The Mermaids Singing. New York: HarperCollins, 1996.
The Wire in the Blood. New York: HarperCollins, 1997.
The Last Temptation. New York: St. Martin's Press, 2002.
The Torment of Others. New York: St. Martin's Press, 2005.

Lindsay Gordon Series

Report for Murder. New York: St. Martin's Press, 1987.
Common Murder. London: Women's Press, 1989; Duluth: Spinsters Ink, 1995.
Final Edition. London: Women's Press, 1991. (Also published as *Open and Shut.* New York: St. Martin's Press, 1991 and also published as *Deadline for Murder.* Duluth: Spinsters Ink, 1997.)

Union Jack. London: Women's Press, 1993. (Also published as *Conferences Are Murder.* Duluth: Spinsters Ink, 1999.)
Booked for Murder. Duluth: Spinsters Ink, 2000.
Hostage to Murder. London: HarperCollins, 2003.

Other Works

A Suitable Job for a Woman: Inside the World of Women Private Eyes. London: HarperCollins, 1995.
A Place of Execution. New York: HarperCollins, 1999.
Killing the Shadows. New York: St. Martin's Press, 2001.
The Distant Echo. New York: St. Martin's Press, 2003.

Works Published as V. L. McDermid

Kate Brannigan Series

Dead Beat. New York: St. Martin's Press, 1993.
Kickback. New York: St. Martin's Press, 1993.
Crack Down. New York: Scribner, 1994.
Clean Break. New York: Scribner, 1996.
Blue Genes. New York: Scribner, 1996.
Stranded. New York: St. Martin's, 2006.

Works about Val McDermid

Aldrich, Chris. "Val McDermid: A Working Class Lassie." *Mystery News* 19.5 (2001): 1–3.
Brainard, Dulcy. "*The Mermaids Singing.*" *Publishers Weekly* 28 October 1996: 61.
Cooper, Natasha. "*The Wire in the Blood.*" *Times Literary Supplement* 14 November 1997: 24.
———. "New Ways with Old Crimes." *Times Literary Supplement* 23 May 2003: 24.
"*The Distant Echo.*" *Publishers Weekly* 8 September 2003: 59.
Hadley, Mary. "Val McDermid." *British Women Mystery Writers: Authors of Detective Fiction with Female Sleuths.* Jefferson, NC: McFarland, 2002. 77–96.
Hume, Samantha. "'Here's tae Us, Wha's Like Us': Val McDermid's Lindsay Gordon Mysteries." *Sleuthing Ethnicity: The Detective in Multiethnic Crime Fiction.* Eds. Dorothea Fischer-Hornung and Monika Mueller. Madison: Fairleigh Dickinson UP, 2003. 227–39.
Jordan, Jon. "Jon Jordan Talks to Val McDermid." 9 September 2001. 25 May 2005. http://www.valmcdermid.com/pages/interviews3.html
Raine, Pat. "A Place of Execution." *Times Literary Supplement* 5 November 1999: 33.
"Val McDermid." *Contemporary Authors.* Vol. 228. Ed. Julie Keppen. Detroit: Gale, 2005. 266–70.
Val McDermid. Homepage. 2005. 25 May 2005. http://www.valmcdermid.com
Zaleski, Jeff. "*A Place of Execution.*" *Publishers Weekly* 18 September 2000: 91.

Jill McGown (1947–)

BIOGRAPHY

Born August 9, 1947, in Campbeltown, Argyll, Scotland, Jill McGown and her family emigrated to Corby, Northamptonshire, England, in 1957. Her father was a fisherman in Campbeltown, but had to seek new work when the fishing industry was at a low. Her mother was originally from Glasgow and worked as a secretary.

McGown attended Kettering Technical College and worked as a secretary and administrative assistant for several companies, including the British Steel Corporation, from 1964 to 1980. In 1980, after spending months processing paperwork for those who chose a voluntary early retirement plan, she herself was downsized, and, given the poor economy in Britain at that time, she decided to try writing on a full-time basis.

Her Web site features monthly newsletters that highlight her sense of humor. There is also an "interview" in which she talks with Lloyd and Judy Hill, her two protagonists. She also provides an article that explains the rank system in the British police, and as further testament to her sense of humor, provides another form of her writing, song lyric parodies. She resides in Corby in her childhood home.

MAJOR WORKS AND THEMES

McGown tackles tough issues in her mysteries without dwelling on the gory aspects. Her detectives solve murder and rape cases, as well as spouse abuse and kidnapping. The plots are always complex and multifaceted, with plenty of possible suspects and red herrings galore. McGown is truly a master of the red herring, always offering readers a twisted path toward the plot resolution.

Character development is strong in the series. McGown's two protagonists are professional colleagues and personal partners. Lloyd, whose first name remains a mystery, doesn't look dashing like many of his fictional counterparts. He is bald, obsessed with grammar, but has a great wit. Judy Hill is competent and independent-minded. Hill takes a logical approach to solving cases, where Lloyd often constructs scenarios that help him see all the pieces of the puzzle.

As revealed in the first book, they were attracted to each other when they first met when she first joined the force, but he was married then. As the first novel opens, years have passed, he's divorced, and they are again assigned together. Their personal relationship progresses over the series, as her career also advances.

Gone to Her Death finds Lloyd and Hill solving a rape and murder at a public school. Their progress is hindered by one of the suspects, who supplies numerous false leads in an attempt to implicate an old enemy. In *The Murders of Mrs. Austin and Mrs. Beale,* Lloyd and Hill tackle a case where two women with no discernible connection are murdered at the same time in two different places while on the telephone with each other. *Murder...Now and Then* combines an older unsolved case with a new crime, teasing out the connections between the two murders. *Verdict Unsafe* places Hill at risk when a rapist she helped convict is set free on a legal technicality. In *Picture of Innocence,* a brutal farmer is killed, and possible suspects include, among others, his abused wife, his daughter, and a builder who wanted his land. The media's involvement in cases is covered in *Unlucky for Some,* where Lloyd and Hill have to deal with a reporter who once solved a case the police had bungled. Although someone had already been convicted, the real murderer was still at large. This reporter becomes involved in their new case as well.

She wrote several stand-alone novels of suspense before beginning the Lloyd and Hill series, and also has published one pseudonymous novel, *Hostage to Fortune,* which studies a failing marriage.

CRITICAL RECEPTION

B. A. Pike laments that McGown has not received the level of acclaim she deserves. Her books have not won awards, although she "makes much of the competition look feeble"

(Pike 735). Pike noted that her writing has depth and substance, and "her gift for contrivance is altogether remarkable" (735). Although she is not as well known in the United States as other British writers, her works have received acclaim from major American reviewers.

With *Gone to Her Death,* reviewers found that McGown had "produced another top-notch police procedural" (Steinberg 65). One reviewer praised *Murder...Now and Then* for its "complex but rewarding case" (Brainard 1993:90) and also noted the "devious, cunning, charming [and] truly, truly wicked" characters that populate *A Shred of Evidence,* a novel that features Lloyd and Hill "at the top of their form" (Brainard 1996: 72). Another review of *A Shred of Evidence* heralded its "well-cadenced prose," which "increases tension, establishes emotional complicity, and layers the plot with subtle complexity" (Klett 155).

Marilyn Stasio finds McGown's character development to be her strong suit in *Verdict Unsafe,* noting that she "delivers strong studies of the deep mental scars that rape victims carry in places where pity can't reach" (22). One reviewer noted that *A Picture of Innocence* "possesses a wealth of psychological nuance and narrative depth, all the way through to the resolution, a masterpiece of controlled complexity" (Brainard 1998:206). *Death in the Family* provides an "expertly crafted, fast-moving plot" with "enough red herrings to keep even the most astute readers on their toes" (Cannon 43). A review of *Unlucky for Some* praised the way McGown "blend[s] police procedural and twisty whodunit tropes with sardonic humor and byplay between members of the police force" ("Unlucky" 48). Another review found McGown's "wry, deftly written drama and head-scratching red herrings" to be "irresistibly addictive" (Barr 89).

BIBLIOGRAPHY

Works by Jill McGown

Judy Hill & Lloyd Series

A Perfect Match. New York: St. Martin's Press, 1983.
Murder at the Old Vicarage. New York: St. Martin's Press, 1988. (Also published as *Redemption*)
Gone to Her Death. New York: St. Martin's Press, 1990. (Also published as *Death of a Dancer*)
The Murders of Mrs. Austin and Mrs. Beale. New York: St. Martin's Press, 1991.
The Other Woman. New York: St. Martin's Press, 1992.
Murder...Now and Then. New York: St. Martin's Press, 1993.
A Shred of Evidence. New York: Fawcett Columbine, 1996.
Verdict Unsafe. New York: Fawcett Columbine, 1997.
Picture of Innocence. New York: Ballantine, 1998.
Plots and Errors. New York: Ballantine, 1999.
Scene of Crime. New York: Ballantine, 2001.
Death in the Family. New York: Ballantine, 2003.
Unlucky for Some. New York: Ballantine, 2005.

Other Novels

Record of Sin. London: Macmillan, 1985.
An Evil Hour. New York: St. Martin's Press, 1986.
The Stalking Horse. New York: St. Martin's Press, 1988.
Murder Movie. New York: St. Martin's Press, 1990.
Published as Elizabeth Chaplin *Hostage to Fortune.* New York: Scribner, 1992.

Works about Jill McGown

Barr, Karyn. "*Unlucky for Some.*" *Entertainment Weekly* 28 January 2005: 89.

Brainard, Dulcy. "Murder ... Now and Then." *Publishers Weekly* 16 August 1993: 90.
———. "*A Shred of Evidence.*" *Publishers Weekly* 6 May 1996: 72.
———. "*Picture of Innocence.*" *Publishers Weekly* 4 May 1998: 206.
Cannon, Peter. "*Death in the Family.*" *Publishers Weekly* 6 January 2003: 43.
Jill McGown. Homepage. May 2005. 2 May 2005. http://www.jillmcgown.com
"Jill McGown." *Contemporary Authors.* Vol. 221. Ed. Lisa Kumar. Detroit: Gale, 2004. 318–21.
Klett, Rex E. "*A Shred of Evidence.*" *Library Journal* 1 June 1996: 155.
Pike, B. A. "Jill McGown." *St. James Guide to Crime & Mystery Writers.* 4th ed. Ed. Jay P. Pederson. Detroit: St. James Press, 1996. 734–36.
Stasio, Marilyn. "Crime." *New York Times Book Review* 29 June 1997: 22.
Steinberg, Sybil. "Gone to Her Death." *Publishers Weekly* 5 January 1990: 65.
"*Unlucky for Some.*" *Publishers Weekly* 13 December 2004: 48.

Margaret Millar (1915–1994)

BIOGRAPHY

Margaret Ellis Sturm was born on February 5, 1915 in Kitchener, Ontario, and was raised in Canada in a comfortable, happy family setting. Her father, Henry William Sturm, was a businessman who twice served as mayor, and her mother, Lavinia Ferrier Sturm, was the daughter of a high school principal (DeFord 270). In 1949, she said that her life was "remarkable only for its omissions. I have never broken a limb, been divorced or arrested, had anything stolen" (DeFord 270). She studied piano as a child and during adolescence was quite serious about music as a career, but her interest in archeology and classical studies, along with her talent in creative writing, led her down a different path. During high school, she met future husband Kenneth Millar; they were both involved in the debate team and were also both published in a student literary magazine (Marks 8).

After studies at the Kitchener-Waterloo Collegiate Institute (1929–1933), Millar received a scholarship to attend the University of Toronto. From 1933 to 1936, she studied classics and also developed her interest in psychology and psychiatry while at the university. She became reacquainted with Kenneth Millar while studying in Toronto, and she left the university before graduating to marry him. The marriage has been characterized as rocky from the start (Nolan 1999:47), but they had a strong partnership, particularly in terms of supporting each other's creative works (Marks 11).

After the birth of their daughter Linda in 1939, Millar became seriously ill around 1940 and passed the time of her mandated bed rest by reading scores of mystery novels for entertainment. The works she read inspired her to begin writing her own, and she published at least a book a year from 1941 to 1945. She published steadily throughout the 1940s, 1950s, and mid-1960s, and continued writing through the mid-1980s. Better known as Ross MacDonald, Kenneth Millar surpassed Margaret Millar in commercial success as a mystery writer, but she preceded him in working in the genre. She won a number of awards before he even began his writing career, including the prestigious Edgar Award, an honor he never achieved.

After their marriage, the Millars moved to Ann Arbor, Michigan, where Kenneth Millar was enrolled in graduate school. During World War II, he served with the Naval Reserves, and they moved to California. Millar published steadily after his first novel in 1944, but he did finish his degree in 1951. The Millars settled in Santa Barbara, California, with their daughter, Linda. Little is written about her in most sources about Margaret Millar except that she predeceased her mother, but a recent biography of Ross MacDonald contains a great deal of information about the family, including details of Linda's troubled adolescence and her death in November 1970 at the age of 31 (Nolan 1999:204–13; 302–303; Marks 20–21; 26–27). Ross MacDonald suffered from Alzheimer's disease and died in 1983, and Millar remained in Santa Barbara until her death from a heart attack on March 26, 1994.

MAJOR WORKS AND THEMES

Millar's works dealt with a number of social issues and themes. As Virginia S. Hale noted, Millar may have been "ahead of her time" in her treatment of issues such as pedophilia and race relations during the 1960s (225). Millar wrote several series, as well as a number of non-series or stand-alone works.

Her first three novels make up the Paul Prye series, which featured a psychiatrist who solved crimes. These novels were light in tone, even considered farce by some. The plots focus on Dr. Prye stumbling into cases as an amateur sleuth and feature settings reminiscent of classic mysteries.

Two of her next three novels feature Inspector Sands, a detective with the Toronto Police Department who had appeared briefly in the third Paul Prye novel. The Sands novels feature a combination of psychological suspense and a police procedural style, and they were much more serious in tone and style. In *The Iron Gates,* a woman is haunted by nightmares about her husband's first wife's murder. Given other problems she is having with her stepchildren, she flees. After she is located by Inspector Sands, details begin to emerge that may indicate someone is trying to drive her mad. The case of the first wife's murder also comes under new scrutiny.

Throughout the 1950s and 1960s, Millar wrote a number of novels but did not return to Prye or Sands. Some of her novels went outside the mystery or suspense genres, but most dealt with crime, murder, and suspense. She often alternated between serious crime novels, with psychological aspects, and lighter, more humorous mysteries. For example, as Jeffrey Marks points out, *Do Evil in Return,* published in 1950, features a doctor who is having an affair with the husband of one of her patients. After refusing an abortion to a young woman, she seeks out the woman, who has disappeared. She becomes involved in solving several murders stemming from this event. Millar followed that with *Rose's Last Summer,* a black comedy of sorts, which some see as less effective than her earlier humorous writing (Marks 18).

She began a third series in the 1970s, which featured Tom Aragon, a Latino lawyer. John M. Reilly noted that her portrayals of discrimination and other social issues "are not patently didactic" as compared to other mystery series of the time that featured ethnically diverse sleuths (229). Reilly analyzes the first Aragon novel, *Ask for Me Tomorrow* in some depth. This is another example in which Millar employs a surprise ending, but in this case, the results are much darker than in some of her earlier works. In this case, Aragon is hired to find a woman's first husband. During his investigation in Mexico, several key witnesses are killed before he can interview them. When Aragon locates the missing man, he realizes that he has been used, that the client was seeking the man for criminal intent (228–29).

She wrote one work of nonfiction, *The Birds and the Beasts Were There,* an account of her passionate hobby of birding. Published in 1967, the work includes elements of memoir, travelogue, and bird-watching manuals, while also serving as a commentary of the lives and habits of all the birds and beasts she knew. The book often highlights her sense of humor and provides a number of insights into her life and philosophies. In one of the first chapters, Millar notes:

> Occasionally I am asked what difference bird watching has made in my life. I can only repeat, the days don't begin quickly enough, and never last long enough, and the years go by too soon. (18)

Millar also wrote the occasional short story. Kenneth Millar's biographer, Tom Nolan, uncovered some unpublished short stories that Margaret Millar left behind. These and other stories, which had been published but never anthologized, were published in 2004 in a collection called *The Couple Next Door*. Included is a novella featuring Paul Prye that was published in a magazine in 1942 but had not been reprinted since.

CRITICAL RECEPTION

Millar's contemporary critics rarely failed to praise her work, and many current critics hail her as a master of the genre. John M. Reilly catalogues the positive reviews given Millar from her earliest work onward (224). After *A Beast in View* won the 1956 Edgar Award, eminent critic Anthony Boucher wrote that Millar's work was "so detailedly convincing" and "so admirably written" that even "the most bitter antagonist of mystery fiction may be forced to acknowledge it as a work of art" (qtd in Reilly 224). *A Beast in View* is often heralded for its surprising plot twist involving a character with a split personality. As Edward D. Hoch points out, the use of the plot twist became more commonly used "but rarely has it been done as effectively" (749).

Millar herself noted her love for writing dialogue and her disdain for writing action scenes. She told Tom Nolan:

> I hate writing action. When somebody has to go someplace, I say: 'He went somewhere.' That's the most action I want to write. Because to me, it's irrelevant; what's relevant are the words—the mood, and the words that are exchanged. Because you can be driving a Chrysler or a Jeep—who in the hell cares? What matters is what you say, when you get there! (qtd in Nolan 2004:61)

The mystery genre has gained ground in literary studies as a topic worthy of analysis and discussion. Articles appear in mainstream journals and dissertations on mystery writers are produced with some regularity. Surprisingly, there is little scholarly output in regard to Millar's works beyond literary encyclopedias and reference guides. Reilly noted this in his critical essay published in 1981 (225), and since then, it appears that only one collection of essays that includes an analysis of Millar's work has been published.

Reilly examines Millar's work, positing that she fits into no single mold, with a body of work that includes detective fiction, gothic romances, puzzle mysteries, and farces. Reilly portrays Millar as a genre revisionist, noting her originality and depth of plotting (228–29). Reilly compares Millar with other writers, illustrating her skill in character development and use of generic conventions.

Jeffrey Marks's book about women mystery writers from the 1940s and 1950s includes a chapter on Millar. Marks links her interests in psychology to plots, and also shows connections between her personal life and her writings. Marks explores many of Millar's novels, providing interesting literary analysis of Millar's technical uses of humor and suspense, as well as her character development and dialogue. Marks, like Reilly, discusses Millar's use of various generic types, such as the private investigator novel, the black comedy, or the courtroom drama, showing how she often included elements that twisted the genre into something beyond what the reader might expect.

Although Millar's work was widely hailed as superior by critics and writers alike, extensive literary analysis is currently unavailable. Perhaps as serious study of the genre continues to grow, and attention is paid to the recent collection of her short stories, her work will become more widely discussed and receive the further recognition it deserves. An announcement in May 2005 that the spring 2007 issue of *Clues: A Journal of Detection* will be devoted to Millar is welcome news.

BIBLIOGRAPHY

Works by Margaret Millar

Paul Prye Series

The Invisible Worm. New York: Doubleday, 1941.
The Weak-Eyed Bat. New York: Doubleday, 1942.
The Devil Loves Me. New York: Doubleday, 1942.

Inspector Sands Series

Wall of Eyes. New York: Random House, 1943.
The Iron Gates. New York: Random House, 1945.

Tom Aragon Series

Ask for Me Tomorrow. New York: Random House, 1976.
The Murder of Miranda. New York: Random House, 1979.
Mermaid. New York: Morrow, 1982.

Other Works by Margaret Millar

Fire Will Freeze. New York: Random House, 1944.
Experiment in Springtime. New York: Random House, 1947.
It's All in the Family. New York: Random House, 1948.
The Cannibal Heart. New York: Random House, 1949.
Do Evil in Return. New York: Random House, 1950.
Vanish in an Instant. New York: Random House, 1952.
Rose's Last Summer. New York: Random House, 1952.
Wives and Lovers. New York: Random House, 1954.
Beast in View. New York: Random House, 1955.
An Air That Kills. New York: Random House, 1957.
The Listening Walls. New York: Random House, 1959.
A Stranger in My Grave. New York: Random House, 1961.
How Like an Angel. New York: Random House, 1961.
The Fiend. New York: Random House, 1964.
The Birds and Beasts Were There. New York: Random House, 1967.
Beyond This Point Are Monsters. New York: Random House, 1970.
Banshee. New York: Morrow, 1983.

Spider Webs. New York: Morrow, 1986.
The Couple Next Door: Collected Short Mysteries. Ed. Tom Nolan. Norfolk: Crippen & Landru, 2004.

Works about Margaret Millar

DeFord, Miriam Allen. "Margaret Millar." *Wilson Library Bulletin* 21.4 (December 1949): 270.

DeMarr, Mary Jean. "Margaret Millar." Eds. Maureen Corrigan and Robin Winks. *Mystery and Suspense Writers: The Literature of Crime, Detection and Espionage.* New York: Scribner's, 1998. 679–87.

Hale, Virginia S. "Margaret Millar." Ed. Kathleen Gregory Klein. *Great Women Mystery Writers.* 1st ed. Westport: Greenwood, 1994. 225–28.

Hoch, Edward D. "Margaret Millar." *St. James Guide to Crime & Mystery Writers.* 4th ed. Ed. Jay P. Pederson. Detroit: St. James Press, 1996. 749–50.

"Margaret Millar." Ed. Scot Peacock. *Contemporary Authors* . New Revision Series, Vol. 81. Detroit: Gale, 1999. 264–67.

Marks, Jeffrey. *Atomic Renaissance: Women Mystery Writers of the 1940s and 1950s.* Lee's Summit, MO: Delphi Books, 2003.

Nolan, Tom. *Ross MacDonald: A Biography.* New York: Scribner's, 1999.

———. "Stop the Presses! A New Collection of Margaret Millar's Stories Unearths Hidden Treasures." *Mystery Scene* 87 (2004): 60–61.

Reilly, John M. "Margaret Millar." Ed. Earl F. Bargainnier. *10 Women of Mystery.* Bowling Green: Bowling Green State UP, 1981. 223–46.

Denise Mina (1966–)

BIOGRAPHY

Denise Mina was born in 1966, in Glasgow, Scotland. Her father was an oil engineer whose work caused the family to move often. On her Web site, she notes that the family relocated 20 times as she grew up, living in France, the Netherlands, Norway, and London. Although born in Glasgow, she did not live there until she was 19 years old. She left school at age 16 and took on a number of jobs including working in a meat factory and as a hospice nurse. At age 21, she returned to school and earned a law degree from Glasgow University. She then began a doctoral program at Strathclyde University in criminal justice, focusing on mental illness in women prisoners, and also taught courses in criminology there. While working on her coursework, she began writing her first novel and sent sample chapters to agents who were listed in the phone book (McGinty 4). One agent wanted to see the complete work, and she soon turned to writing fiction full-time. She and her partner Stephen Evans, who is a forensic psychologist, have a son named Fergus. They live in Glasgow.

MAJOR WORKS AND THEMES

Her first three novels are a trilogy about Maureen O'Donnell, a sexual abuse survivor with a drinking problem who has recently spent time in a mental institution. The first novel, *Garnethill,* which won the John Creasey Award, opens eight months after her release, when she finds the body of one of her doctors, Douglas Brady, with whom she had been having an affair, murdered in her living room. Given her background, she is a prime suspect. Her own mother even thinks she could be guilty. To clear her name, she works to solve the case. In *Exile,* she is working in a shelter for abused women and solves the murder of one of the shelter residents. In addition, the murderer she uncovered in the first novel is threatening her. *Resolution* finds O'Donnell concerned about her testimony against Brady's murderer and dealing with another case that is closer to home. All three novels are dark in tone, and although the portrayed physical violence is minimal, the books are disturbing, difficult reads with their depictions of victimized characters. Her fourth novel, a stand-alone work, explores the case of a psychiatrist, Susan Harriot, who is accused of murdering a serial killer, who was her patient. The novel uses an intriguing framing device: a prologue signed by Mina herself explaining how she came to be in possession of the diaries of Lachlan Harriot. Through his diaries, the novel recounts his attempts to clear her name, tracing his increasingly complex and troubling investigation into his wife's work and life. The tone and style of the novel are vastly different than the *Garnethill* trilogy, which portrays a brutal, urban life in unflinching terms. Although *Deception* lays out a suspenseful tale that deals with upper-class professionals in comfortable suburbia, at the heart of Mina's work is an exploration of the psyche of the characters. O'Donnell is certainly a troubled character, but *Deception* features an unreliable narrator who deceives himself as he works to uncover the truth about his wife, building suspense in a different style than the trilogy.

Her recent work, *The Field of Blood,* is the first in a planned series of five books about a young journalist named Patricia "Paddy" Meehan, not to be confused with the Scottish safecracker Paddy Meehan, who was wrongly convicted of murder and pardoned in a famous case. The series begins in 1981 and is slated to follow Meehan's career, while serving as a chronicle of the events that took place in Scotland during the 1980s and 1990s. In the first novel, Meehan is a copy clerk at a newspaper who dreams of becoming a journalist. She is obsessed with a child abduction case that has captured the public's attention; Mina uses a real case, the 1993 incident in which two young boys killed a 3-year old, as a basis for her tale. When her fiancé's young cousin and his friend are charged with the crime, she begins her own investigation, unwittingly causing more tragedy, but uncovering the truth and solidifying her entree into the profession. Mina has also written a number of short stories and was recently commissioned to write a new entry in the *Hellblazer* series of graphic novels that will feature detective John Constantine in Glasgow.

CRITICAL RECEPTION

Mina burst onto to the scene in 1998, winning two awards from the British Crime Writers Association, one for her first novel and another for a short story. In addition, the critics have praised her works from the start.

Reviews of *Garnethill* praised the work for its strong, bold writing. One reviewer noted that Mina brought a "world of drug dealers, broken families, sanctimonious health-care workers and debilitated victims to startling life" and that O'Donnell's "valiant struggle to act sane in an insane world will leave readers seeing sex abuse victims in a new light" (Zaleski 1999:63). Another review noted that the novel "crackles with mordant Scottish wit and throbs with the pain of badly treated mental illness" (Adler 2). Reviews of her second novel hailed Mina as a "writer of stunning talent and accomplishment" (Zaleski 2001:71) and noted her "enhanced reputation as gripping chronicler of the dark side of Glasgow" (MacLaren 13). Another reviewer noted that "Mina is a distinctly gifted writer, able to convey the intimate feel and sound of Glasgow, from the icy rain to the working-class lilt," while also offering "a wonderfully solid and convincing background for her edgy heroine" (Koch 11). The final novel of the trilogy was called a "powerful, disturbing, wrenching" work that "culminates in a startling crescendo of violence, vengeance and resolution" (Cannon 45).

One review of *Deception* (published in Britain as *Sanctum*) noted that Mina uses the diary format "to her advantage," prompting a comparison to Minette Walters, and noting that the novel is an "intense psychological study that careens along a collision course on which Mina has total control" (Cogdill 20). Another reviewer noted that readers may think they know where the plot is heading, only to be surprised, as their "suspicions turn to sympathy, then back again" (Ross J10). The review also praised Mina's depiction of a "complex, unappealing" yet "compelling" narrator (Ross J10).

Reviews of her latest novel have also been positive. One review noted that if it were a movie, it would be the "one to beat" at the Oscars ("*Field of Blood*" 37). The review also praised Mina as "brilliant" with writing that is "unsparing of brutal details, but unfailingly elegant in her humanity" ("*Field of Blood*" 37). Another reviewer discussed Mina's research into the time period, using newspapers and other primary materials to accurately depict Glasgow in the 1980s (Clydesdale 19). Another review outlines her deft portrayal of Meehan, her ambition and her ethics, noting that it is "clear that she is something more than a crime writer," and compared her work to Dennis Lehane's *Mystic River*, observing that Mina "describes a close-knit, secretive community in a substantial novel that happens to be centered on a crime" (Maslin E6).

BIBLIOGRAPHY

Works by Denise Mina

Maureen O'Donnell Series

Garnethill. New York: Carroll & Graf, 1999.
Exile. New York: Carroll & Graf, 2001.
Resolution. New York: Carroll & Graf, 2002.

Paddy Meehan Series

Field of Blood. London: Bantam, 2005.
The Dead Hour. London: Bantam, 2006.

Other Works

Deception. Boston: Little, Brown, 2004. Also published as *Sanctum* (London: Bantam, 2002).

Works about Denise Mina

Adler, Dick. "Euromayhem: Tracking Killers and Other Criminals on Both Sides of the English Channel." *Chicago Tribune* 4 April 1999: 2.
Cannon, Peter. "*Resolution.*" *Publishers Weekly* 29 April 2002: 45.
Clydesdale, Lindsay. "Murder through the Eyes of a Child." *Daily Record* (Glasgow) 1 March 2005: 18–19.
Cogdill, Oline H. "Diarist Tells Lies Even to Himself." *South Florida Sun-Sentinel* 5 September 2004: 20.
"Denise Mina." *Contemporary Authors.* Vol. 228 Ed. Julie Keppen. Detroit: Gale, 2005. 280–81.
"*Field of Blood.*" *Publishers Weekly* 9 May 2005: 37.
Koch, P. G. "Some Deadly Aftereffects: Mina Follows Up on Debut Novel." *Houston Chronicle* 4 March 2001: 11.
MacLaren, Lorna. "Out to Make a Killing; Why is the Fair Sex Hooked on Crime?" *Herald* (Glasgow) 21 February 2001: 13.

Maslin, Janet. "Glasgow and Nashville Color Two Portraits of Crime." *New York Times* 7 July 2005:E6.

McGinty, Stephen. "From Flirting to Feminism." *Sunday Times* (London) 19 April 1998: 4.

Ross, Michele. "It Can Be So Delightful to Be Left in the Dark." *Plain Dealer* 26 September 2004: J10.

Zaleski, Jeff. "*Garnethill.*" *Publishers Weekly* 1 March 1999: 63.

————. "*Exile.*" *Publishers Weekly* 1 January 2001: 70–71.

Marcia Muller (1944–)

BIOGRAPHY

If Marcia Muller hadn't moved to northern California, Sharon McCone might not have been born. Muller is credited with being the first American woman to write a hardboiled detective novel featuring a female investigator, and many other writers, including Sue Grafton and Sara Paretsky, acknowledge that their works might not have come along without Muller to lead the way. Muller deflects that praise, though, noting that she was "just trying to make a living" and "had little to do with other people entering the field"; it is her belief that many were working toward writing strong female characters in the mystery genre (Martin 270).

Marcia Muller was born in Detroit, Michigan, on September 28, 1944, to Henry J. and Kathryn Minke Muller. Her father was a marketing executive. She grew up in Birmingham, Michigan, the youngest sibling of a brother and two sisters. She was an avid reader as a child, and particularly enjoyed mystery novels, including the Judy Bolton series (Martin 269). Long before creating McCone, Muller first wrote an illustrated novel about her dog, completed at age 12 (Martin 269; Martelle E1). Muller has noted that her "relatives are holding" copies of that work "for ransom" (Bibel 1596).

She enjoyed literature and writing, and majored in English at the University of Michigan. She took a creative writing course during college and was told by the instructor that "she would never be a writer because she had nothing to say" (Martin 269; Brainard 1994:361). This led her to move into journalism as a career option, although she has noted many times that she was not very good at it, because she had a tendency to embellish. She earned her bachelor's degree in English in 1966 and also earned a master's degree in journalism there in 1971.

She married Frederick T. Gilson, Jr., in 1967, and although that marriage ended in divorce in 1981, it was with him that she moved to California. He was an officer in the U.S. Navy and was posted in the San Francisco Bay area for several years, while Muller worked for *Sunset* magazine. They returned to Ann Arbor, and she studied journalism during this time. They returned to California in 1971, choosing to live in a more rural area instead of the city, and it was there that Muller began writing about McCone to combat her boredom. She had begun reading detective fiction in the late 1960s, when she discovered the work of Ross MacDonald.

Muller has a notable hobby that is connected to her writing: she builds and decorates miniature houses, replicas of the places where McCone has lived and worked. There are pictures of the interiors available on her Web site, and she is also shown working on the exterior of McCone's house in the documentary, *Women of Mystery: Three Writers Who Forever Changed Detective Fiction.*

She married Bill Pronzini, who writes the "Nameless Detective" series, in 1992. They have worked on numerous projects as co-writers and co-editors since the 1980s and live in Sonoma County, California.

MAJOR WORKS AND THEMES

The bulk of Muller's work is in the Sharon McCone series, although she has written novels in three other mystery series and has also produced a number of short stories in the mystery and western genres. The first McCone novel, *Edwin of the Iron Shoes,* was published in 1977 and introduced a professional female private investigator character in the hard-boiled tradition.

Sharon McCone is introduced as a private investigator who has office space, such as it is, in a building that houses a legal cooperative called All Souls. In addition to sharing this space, some of McCone's cases come from their referrals. After several novels, McCone is able to move from her closet into a larger space in All Souls, and in *The Broken Promise Land* opens her own offices with several staff members, including her assistant from All Souls and her nephew.

Throughout the series, McCone tackles a number of cases that touch on a number of themes. Early cases find McCone delving into the world of antiques dealers to solve a murder and into real estate to find an arsonist, in addition to various disappearances and murders. She finds herself involved in cases that touch on the plight of Vietnam veterans and immigrants, as well as race, class, and urban development concerns. As her practice grows and incorporates new staff, her investigative methods also grow, particularly with the technological savvy that her nephew and other younger investigators bring to the firm.

In the 1990s, McCone begins a relationship with Hy Ripinsky, a man with past experience with the CIA who is affiliated with a security and antiterrorism agency. Cases involving ethics become more important to the case, merging with environmental concerns or cases involving pharmaceutical corporations. As Rebecca E. Martin points out, the ties between McCone and Ripinsky allow Muller to "expand her plots into the international arena," while bringing new focus to a recurring theme, namely "the role of ethical behavior in the pursuit of justice" (279).

The series also shows growth in McCone's character, particularly in *The Broken Promise Land* and *Listen to the Silence,* which feature cases that involve McCone's family members and her heritage. The first finds McCone involved in a case helping her brother-in-law, and in the second example, McCone begins investigating her own family history after finding some papers among her recently deceased father's belongings. As Dean James points out, Muller introduced a new aspect to the solitary private investigator model in adding not only family members, but also deep relationships with co-workers, having her colleagues at All Souls serve as "a family of her own making" (James 6).

Two series written during the 1980s focused on amateur sleuths. The Elena Oliverez series featured an art museum curator, and the Joanna Stark series followed the director of a security firm that specialized in museums. Clearly showing an interest in the arts with these works, Muller has nonetheless noted that it was "restrictive coming up with convincing plot lines" involving museums (Taylor 262).

Her fourth series is set in Soledad County, a fictional area in California that Muller has created in between Mendocino and Humboldt counties. This series is more loosely connected in terms of characterization, with different protagonists in each outing. Recurring characters working in law enforcement, including Deputy Rhoda Swift, often play a more minor role in the plots. In the first novel in the series, Swift is working to put her career back on track. One night she drives by a woman with a disabled car, turns back, but is suddenly called to an emergency elsewhere. Later, when she tries to follow up, she becomes involved in a web of murders from the past and present. *Cyanide Wells* tells the story of a man who was accused of killing his wife, who was never found. Fourteen years later, he receives an anonymous call informing him his wife is alive, and he returns to Soledad County to track her down. *Cape Perdido* features a bitter environmental dispute that rips a town apart and brings to light a past crime.

CRITICAL RECEPTION

Muller has won a number of awards throughout her career, including Shamus awards in 1991 and 1993 and Anthony Awards in 1994 and 1996. In 2005, the Mystery Writers of America bestowed their highest honor on Muller, naming her Grand Master during the 2005 Edgar Awards ceremony.

The reviews of her early works were positive. Newgate Callendar noted that although *Edwin of the Iron Shoes* didn't break "new ground," the "plotting [was] competent and the writing lively" (36). Callendar also noted that McCone was a "bright girl" who "handles herself very well" (36). Another review of the first novel found it an "entertaining puzzle" ("*Edwin*" 60), and a third review praised Muller's "considerable savvy" in her "high-powered first novel" (Fletcher 1978:1166). Subsequent reviews praised McCone's combination of "brassiness and braininess" (Fletcher 1982:1510) and Muller's plotting and "witty dialogue" (Fletcher 1984:192). Others admired the presence of a "self-sufficient female sleuth" (Herbert 511) and the "vivid sociological detail" and "affecting characterizations" (Fletcher 1985:1635).

Her work garnered consistently positive reviews throughout the 1990s, with comments including praise for "a suspenseful and fully fashioned tale" (Steinberg 1991:49) and notice of her "finely tuned secondary cast, well-drawn settings and satisfyingly intricate plot" (Steinberg 1993:68). Others have praised Muller's "fine writing" and creation of "original plots with plenty of unusual twists and rapid-fire action" in her portrayal of McCone's "ingenuity, sparkle, grit and very human vulnerability" (Melton 1486). Other reviews have praised Muller's "exemplary high standards" in her writing (Klett 133) and have noted that she "surpasses herself" with a "vigorous and trenchant mystery thriller" that is "meticulously plotted" and "absorbing" (Brainard 1996:61).

Reviews of the Soledad County series have been mixed, with some reviewers commenting that the plots are less complicated and the villains more obvious, although the strong sense of setting has been praised. Peter Cannon states that readers will "taste the fog and smell the seaweed" in *Point Deception* (53), but another review noted that *Cape Perdido* offers "less than compelling characters and a pat ending," characterizing the book as "an uncharacteristic lapse for Muller" ("*Cape*" 45).

In addition to strong critical reception, Muller's works have been considered by numerous scholars. Most studies of women crime fiction authors explore Muller, Grafton, and Paretsky as the three most important writers in the development of the female private investigator in American mystery fiction, although much more literature is available on Paretsky and Grafton. A forthcoming collection devoted to Muller will be welcome. An interesting article about Muller appeared in the *Irish Journal of American Studies* in 1997. In this article, Alan Bairner explores the role of San Francisco in the McCone series. As with Paretsky's writing about Chicago, Muller's portrayal of San Francisco is central to the books, and Bairner looks at how crime writers like Muller approach their settings.

BIBLIOGRAPHY

Works by Marcia Muller

Sharon McCone Series

Edwin of the Iron Shoes. New York: McKay, 1977.
Ask the Cards a Question. New York: St. Martin's, 1982.
The Cheshire Cat's Eye. New York: St. Martin's, 1983.
Games to Keep the Dark Away. New York: St. Martin's, 1984.

Leave A Message for Willie. New York: St. Martin's, 1984.
Double. With Bill Pronzini. New York: St. Martin's, 1984.
There's Nothing to Be Afraid Of. New York: St. Martin's, 1985.
Eye of the Storm. With Bill Pronzini. New York: Mysterious Press, 1988.
The Shape of Dread. New York: Mysterious Press, 1989.
There's Something in a Sunday. New York: Mysterious Press, 1989.
Trophies and Dead Things. New York: Mysterious Press, 1990.
Where Echoes Live. New York: Mysterious Press, 1991.
Pennies on a Dead Woman's Eyes. New York: Mysterious Press, 1992.
Wolf in the Shadows. New York: Mysterious Press, 1993.
Till the Butchers Cut Him Down. New York: Mysterious Press, 1994.
A Wild and Lonely Place. New York: Mysterious Press, 1995.
The McCone Files: The Complete Sharon McCone Stories. Norfolk: Crippen & Landru, 1995.
The Broken Promise Land. New York: Mysterious Press, 1996.
Both Ends of the Night. New York: Mysterious Press, 1997.
While Other People Sleep. New York: Mysterious Press, 1998.
Duo. With Bill Pronzini. Unity, ME: Five Star, 1998.
A Walk through the Fire. New York: Mysterious Press, 1999.
Listen to the Silence. New York: Mysterious Press, 2000.
McCone and Friends. Norfolk: Crippen & Landau, 2000.
Dead Midnight. New York: Mysterious Press, 2002.
The Dangerous Hour. New York: Mysterious Press, 2004.
The Vanishing Point. New York: Mysterious Press, 2006.

Soledad County Series

Point Deception. New York: Mysterious Press, 2001.
Cyanide Wells. New York: Mysterious Press, 2003.
Cape Perdido. New York: Mysterious Press, 2005.

Elena Oliverez Series

The Tree of Death. New York: Walker & Company, 1983.
The Legend of Slain Soldiers. New York: Walker & Company, 1985.
Beyond the Grave. With Bill Pronzini. New York: Walker & Company, 1986.

Joanna Stark Series

The Cavalier in White. New York: St. Martin's, 1986.
There Hangs the Knife. New York: St. Martin's, 1988.
Dark Star. New York: St. Martin's, 1989.

Other Novels

The Lighthouse: A Novel of Terror. With Bill Pronzini. New York: St. Martin's, 1987.

Works about Marcia Muller

Bairner, Alan. "Sharon McCone's San Francisco: The Role of the City in the Work of Marcia Muller." *Irish Journal of American Studies* 6 (1997): 117–38.
Bibel, Barbara. "The *Booklist* Interview: Marcia Muller." *Booklist* 1 May 2000: 1596.
Brainard, Dulcy. "Marcia Muller: The Time Was Ripe." *Publishers Weekly* 8 August 1994: 361–62.
———. "*The Broken Promise Land*." *Publishers Weekly* 22 April 1996: 61.
Callendar, Newgate. "Crime." *New York Times Book Review* 27 November 1977: 36.
Cannon, Peter. "*Point Deception*." *Publishers Weekly* 25 June 2001: 53.
"*Cape Perdido*." *Publishers Weekly* 27 June 2005: 45.

"*Edwin of the Iron Shoes.*" *Publishers Weekly* 10 October 1977: 60.

Fletcher, Connie. "*Edwin of the Iron Shoes.*" *Booklist* 15 March 1978: 1166.

———. "*Ask the Cards a Question.*" *Booklist* August 1982: 1510.

———. "*Leave a Message for Willie.*" *Booklist* 1 October 1984: 192.

———. "*There's Nothing to Be Afraid Of.*" *Booklist* August 1985: 1635.

Herbert, Rosemary. "*Games to the Keep the Dark Away.*" *Library Journal* 1 March 1984: 511.

Jackson, Christine and Alexander Howe, eds. *Echoes from a Wild and Lonely Place: Marcia Muller and American Literature.* Forthcoming, 2007.

James, Dean. "Marcia Muller is MWA's Newest Grand Master." *The 3rd Degree: Official Newsletter of the Mystery Writers of America* December 2004: 1, 6.

Klett, Rex. "*Till the Butchers Cut Him Down.*" *Library Journal* July 1994:133.

"Marcia Muller." *Contemporary Authors.* New Revision Series, Vol. 97. Ed. Scot Peacock. Detroit: Gale, 2001. 302–306.

Marcia Muller. Homepage. n.d. 18 August 2005. http://www.marciamuller.com/

Martelle, Scott. "One Tough Cookie Made Mystery Fans Want More." *Los Angeles Times* 25 April 2005: E1.

Martin, Rebecca E. "Marcia Muller." *Dictionary of Literary Biography,* Vol. 226: American Hard-Boiled Crime Writers. Eds. George Parker Anderson and Julie B. Anderson. Detroit: Gale Group, 2000. 267–82.

Melton, Emily. "*Till the Butchers Cut Him Down.*" *Booklist* 15 April 1994: 1486.

Steinberg, Sybil. "*Where Echoes Live.*" *Publishers Weekly* 24 May 1991: 49.

———. "*Wolf in the Shadows.*" *Publishers Weekly* 17 May 1993: 68.

Taylor, Bruce. "The Real McCone." *The Armchair Detective* 23.3. (1990): 260–66.

Women of Mystery: Three Women Who Forever Changed Detective Fiction. Prod. and Dir. Pamela Beere Briggs and William McDonald. Videocassette. New Day Films, 2000.

Janet Neel (1940–)

BIOGRAPHY

Janet Neel was born July 4, 1940, in Oxford. Her father was an architect and her mother was a social worker. In 1971, she married James Lionel Cohen, a businessman, and they have three children, Henry, Richard, and Isobel.

Neel studied law at Cambridge, earning a degree from Newnham College in 1962. She worked in the United States designing war games before returning to England. Neel worked as a solicitor and has experience with the Board of Trade, the Charterhouse Bank, the London Stock Exchange, and the Ministry of Defense. She also is Baroness Cohen of Pimlico and holds a seat in the House of Lords. She lives in north London with her husband.

MAJOR WORKS AND THEMES

After her first two novels, Neel turned to writing more traditional mysteries, focusing on a series featuring Francesca Wilson and Detective John MacLeish. Wilson works for the Department of Trade and Industry and also comes from a prolifically talented musical family. Her path crosses with MacLeish in the first novel when a businessman her agency was working with is murdered. She wrangles her way into the investigation, and they end up paired romantically as well. In *Death on Site,* a murder at a construction site takes their attention, while in *Death of a Partner* the murder of a cabinet minister's young fiancée is juxtaposed with Wilson and MacLeish's personal difficulties.

In *Death among the Dons,* Wilson has returned to work part-time after the birth of their first child. She becomes a part-time administrator at a private girls' school that is in turmoil. When events turn murderous, Wilson uses her inside position to assist with the investigation. *A Timely Death* deals with spousal abuse and adultery, with Wilson becoming embroiled in a case through her volunteer work at a women's shelter. In *O Gentle Death,* a distraught young woman has committed suicide, but Wilson and MacLeish uncover that it was murder.

Along with various social themes, many subplots revolve around Wilson and her four brothers, and the world of professional musicians. While one brother has gained fame as a pop singer, another is making a career as an operatic tenor. Neel's knowledge of music is substantial, and Dean James compared her use of music to Ellis Peters's use of music as "an effective counterpoint to crime" (784). Her background in restaurant management comes into play in *To Die For,* which features a case involving a fancy restaurant.

Except for *Children of a Harsh Winter,* her other novels are in the suspense or thriller genre. *The Highest Bidder* is set in the financial world. Her latest novel, *Ticket to Ride,* is a stand-alone political thriller featuring a lawyer with a troubled past who is drawn into a case involving Serbian asylum seekers.

CRITICAL RECEPTION

Neel's first mystery novel won the John Creasey Prize from the Crime Writers Association, and two other novels have been considered for Golden Dagger awards. Critical reception has been solid for her works.

A review of her first novel in the series states that "side plots add piquancy to the suspense," also praising Neel's "fresh approach," which combines "delicious humor" with "a hair-raising tale of dark deeds" (Steinberg 1988:47). According to one critic, Neel "skillfully untangles her plot while reflecting thoughtfully on the complexities of two-career marriages" in *Death of a Partner* (Miller 1625). Another reviewer noted that power structures are "crisply explored in this stylish mystery" and that Neel adds "keen observation of human nature to a suspenseful plot" (Steinberg 1990:47).

One reviewer called *A Timely Death* a "sophisticated and cerebral mystery with dark overtones and plenty of dark twists" (Melton 1997:825). Neel was also praised for writing about a "spectrum of intimate relations … with admirable nuance, carving psychological texture" into the "skillfully plotted" novel (Brainard 1996:60). Although another reviewer of this novel found fault with its editing, she called it a "thoroughly lively and interesting book," further noting that Neel "writes well and with confident authority" (Cooper 25).

Death among the Dons was called a "byzantinely plotted whodunnit" set in "a seething cauldron of motive and opportunity" with "real characters who could easily exist" (Lukowsky 810). Another reviewer noted that "by firmly establishing each character as a believable individual, Neel effectively and with plenty of humor draws the reader in the complex and often secret dynamics" of the school (Brainard 1993:51).

A review of *O Gentle Death* noted that there is a large cast of secondary characters to keep track of, but that Neel puts "more life in them than the protagonists" have in other series (Schantz F2). Another reviewer also praised Neel's "subtle" character development and "burnished prose," noting that she "adroitly renders the adolescent students and is no less successful in depicting the members of the teaching staff" (Cannon 62). Marilyn Stasio found the characters to be "difficult people" but noted that "Neel's compassionate character work" makes the reader "really care" about them, even to the point of hoping none of them are guilty of the crime (26).

BIBLIOGRAPHY

Works by Janet Neel

Francesca Wilson and John McLeish Series

Death's Bright Angel. New York: St. Martin's Press, 1988.
Death on Site. London: Constable, 1989; New York: St. Martin's Press, 1990.
Death of a Partner. New York: St. Martin's Press, 1991.
Death among the Dons. London: Constable, 1993; New York: St. Martin's Press, 1994.
A Timely Death. New York: St. Martin's Press, 1997.
To Die For: A Mystery. New York: St. Martin's Press, 1999.
O Gentle Death. New York: St. Martin's Press, 2001.

Other Novels

As Janet Cohen. *The Highest Bidder.* London: Michael Joseph, 1992.
As Janet Cohen. *Children of a Harsh Winter.* London: Michael Joseph, 1994.
Ticket to Ride. London: Allison & Busby, 2005.

Works about Janet Neel

Brainard, Dulcy. "*Death among the Dons.*" *Publishers Weekly* 22 November 1993: 51.
———. "*A Timely Death.*" *Publishers Weekly* 11 November 1996: 60.
Cannon, Peter. "*O Gentle Death.*" *Publishers Weekly* 18 June 2001: 62.
Cooper, Natasha. "*A Timely Death.*" *Times Literary Supplement* 5 July 1996: 25.
James, Dean. "Janet Neel." *St. James Guide to Crime and Mystery Fiction.* 4th ed. Ed. Jay P. Pederson. Detroit: St. James Press, 1996. 783–84.
"Janet Cohen." *Contemporary Authors.* New Revision Vol. 89. Ed. Scot Peacock. Detroit: Gale, 2000. 59–61.
Lukowsky, Wes. "*Death among the Dons.*" *Booklist* 1 January 1994: 810.
Melton, Emily. "*A Timely Death.*" *Booklist* 1 January 1997: 825.
Miller, Stuart. "*Death of a Partner.*" *Booklist* 15 April 1991: 1625.
Schantz, Tom and Enid. "Reporter Puts Face on Grim 'Jasmine Trade'." *Denver Post* 5 August 2001: F2.
Stasio, Marilyn. "Crime." *New York Times Book Review* 9 September 2001: 26.
Steinberg, Sybil. "Fiction-Mysteries." *Publishers Weekly* 2 December 1988: 47.
———. "*Death of a Partner.*" *Publishers Weekly* 21 December 1990: 47.

Barbara Neely (1941–)

BIOGRAPHY

Barbara Neely was born in 1941 in Lebanon, Pennsylvania, to Bernard and Ann Neely. She earned a master's degree from the University of Pittsburgh and lives in Jamaica Plain,

Massachusetts. Neely has held a number of administrative positions in community service organizations, including a community-based corrections facility for women and the YWCA, and she ran a consulting firm for nonprofit organizations. She also has experience with producing radio programs and serves as the host of "Commonwealth Justice," a radio program on WUMB in Boston.

MAJOR WORKS AND THEMES

Neely's novels focus on Blanche White, an African American domestic worker who becomes embroiled in mystery cases. When readers first meet White, she is contemplating running away from the courthouse in North Carolina where she has just been convicted of bouncing checks. She was overdrawn by less than $50, caused by several of her employers leaving town on vacation without paying her. She does go "on the lam," and while hiding from the authorities, she ends up solving a murder case.

Neely has stated that she wanted to write a book that was about race and class but that also was humorous (Goeller 301), addressing race, class, and color consciousness in an accessible, entertaining way (qtd in Bailey 186). As Neely notes, "If you don't get that this is a book about race, let me give you this big black woman whose name means white— twice" (Goeller 301). Neely also wanted White to have adopted children, but not to be married and have children of her own, and not to be dependent on a man. Neely notes that she set out to write against the standards she still sees in society that say women should be married and bearing children to be complete (Goeller 302). Neely does not view herself as a mystery writer, but rather as a writer who "examine[s] issues of race and class in America" while "pok[ing] fun at the absurdity of it all" (Stanton C1). Neely's works have found an audience outside of the African American community. She posits that "it's the class part that gets lots of non-Black people … I think Blanche strikes a chord with people who do invisible work … She doesn't let people mess with her and she finds ways to get justice. I think that attracts people across race, age and class" (qtd in Stanton C1). Kathy Phillips indicated that this invisibility gives White an edge as an investigator; as an African American maid, she can "stroll across most domestic scenes without inhibiting" those who employ her (42).

The second novel, *Blanche Among the Talented Tenth,* features White visiting an exclusive vacation resort for African Americans in Maine. Her young charges have made wealthy friends at their private school and are invited to the resort. White goes along, offering to provide childcare for her niece and nephew and their friends. While *Blanche on the Lam* explored issues of class and race relations between African Americans and white Americans, this novel deals with class and race issues among African Americans. The third installment in the series looks at politics and corruption. White has taken a temporary position working for a renowned family, whose patriarch is running for governor. She uncovers some unpleasant secrets and must solve the case to keep herself, her niece, and her nephew safe from the villains.

In the fourth novel, *Blanche Passes Go,* White returns to North Carolina to work with a friend who has started a catering business. White finds herself pulled into a case involving the sister of a man who raped her years before. In this novel, White must face her past "in a New South that clings to racist ways" in order to solve the case and "settl[e] old scores and heal deep wounds" (Coleman D5). Throughout the novel, Neely explores issues of race and class, but as Sandy Coleman notes, "it is never a one-sided attack. She gets in just as many licks against black folks who discriminate within their own race because of skin tone as she does against white bigots" (D5).

CRITICAL RECEPTION

Neely scored major accolades with her first novel, winning the Agatha, Anthony, and Macavity Awards for *Blanche on the Lam*. She also received an award from the Black Women's Reading Club for the book. Her subsequent books have also received critical acclaim, and a number of scholarly writings about detective fiction have explored her work. One critic noted her "remarkable" facility with descriptions and portraying quirky characters (Coleman D5), and another praised her ability as a "phrase-maker" and highlighted the character development of White and her family members (Zaleski 55). A review of the first novel in *The Black Scholar* noted that her style was "straightforward and familiar"; White was seen as "believable and likable" (Lockhart 56). In a review of *Blanche Cleans Up,* Neely was praised as a "skilled and pleasing writer," with "sharp-tongued" White named as "one of the best fictional detectives conjured up in years" (DiNizo 95). Another review concurred, calling White "direct, endlessly entertaining and nobody's fool" as she solves a "sizzling mystery" (Brainard 73).

Literary criticism of Neely's work focuses on the class and race issues that Neely sees as central to her writing. Shirley Tolliver Geiger and Natalie Hevener Kaufman point out that Neely "defies the norms for detective novels" in having Blanche White be an African American working-class woman who has children in her care (95). Although many novels have broken away from white male loners as protagonist, Geiger and Kaufman are correct to note that Neely also rejects the traditional role of the detective. In many novels, the detective restores the status quo by solving the case, but in Neely's works, the status quo is what needs to be disrupted (95). Neely's work succeeds for Geiger and Kaufman in its challenge of stereotypes about detectives, African American women and domestic workers (103). Nancy Tolson agrees, noting that Neely "replaces [the media image of the Black female domestic] with a literate, logical and liberated woman" (76).

BIBLIOGRAPHY

Works by Barbara Neely

Blanche on the Lam. New York: St. Martin's Press, 1992.
Blanche Among the Talented Tenth. New York: St. Martin's Press, 1994.
Blanche Cleans Up. New York: Viking, 1998.
Blanche Passes Go. New York: Viking, 2000.

Works about Barbara Neely

Aldridge, Pearl G. "Barbara Neely." *St. James Guide to Crime & Mystery Writers*. 4th ed. Ed. Jay P. Pederson. Detroit: St. James Press, 1996. 784–86.

Bailey, Frankie Y. "*Blanche on the Lam,* or the Invisible Woman Speaks." Kathleen Gregory Klein, ed., *Diversity and Detective Fiction*. Bowling Green: Bowling Green State UP, 1999. 186–204.

"Barbara Neely." *Contemporary Authors*. Vol. 120, New Revision Series. Ed. Scot Peacock. Detroit: Gale, 2004. 247–49.

Brainard, Dulcy. "*Blanche Cleans Up*." *Publishers Weekly* 30 March 1998: 73.

Coleman, Sandy. "Humor Lightens Tale of Rape, Race and Revenge." *Boston Globe* 31 August 2000: D5.

DiNizo, Alice. "*Blanche Cleans Up*." *Library Journal* 15 March 1998: 95.

Geiger, Shirley Tolliver and Natalie Hevener Kaufman. "Barbara Neely's Blanche White Series." *Clues* 22.2 (2001): 95–108.

Goeller, Alison D. "Interview with Barbara Neely." *Sleuthing Ethnicity: The Detective in Multiethnic Crime Fiction.* Eds. Dorothea Fischer-Hornung and Monika Mueller. Madison: Fairleigh Dickinson UP, 2003. 299–307.

Lockhart, Leslie. "*Blanche on the Lam.*" *The Black Scholar* 23.2 (1993): 56.

Mueller, Monika. "A Cuban American 'Lady Dick' and an African American Miss Marple? The Female Detective in the Novels of Carolina García-Aguilera and Barbara Neely." *Sleuthing Ethnicity: The Detective in Multiethnic Crime Fiction.* Eds. Dorothea Fischer-Hornung and Monika Mueller. Madison: Fairleigh Dickinson UP, 2003. 114–32.

Phillips, Kathy. "Mystery Woman." *Women's Review of Books* July 2000: 42–43.

Stanton, Junious R. "Best Kept Secret: Barbara Neely Keeps Black Mystery Genre Alive." *Indianapolis Recorder* 20 October 2000: C1.

Tolson, Nancy D. "The Butler Didn't Do It So Now They're Blaming the Maid: Defining a Black Feminist Trickster through the Novels of Barbara Neely." *South Central Review* 18.3/4 (2001): 72–85.

Witt, Doris. "Detecting Bodies: Barbara Neely's Domestic Sleuth and the Trope of the (In)visible Woman." *Recovering the Black Female Body: Self-Representations by African American Women.* Eds. Michael Bennett and Vanessa D. Dickerson. New Brunswick: Rutgers UP, 2001. 165–84.

Zaleski, Jeff. "Blanche Passes Go." *Publishers Weekly* 29 May 2000: 55.

Zola, Nkenge. "Fun Reading, Deep Social Commentary: A Conversation with Barbara Neely." *Michigan Citizen* 20 June 1998: B1.

Sharan Newman (1949–)

BIOGRAPHY

Sharan Newman was born April 15, 1949, in Ann Arbor, Michigan. Her father, Charles William Hill, was a captain in the U.S. Air Force, and her mother, Betty Martin Hill, was a psychologist. She graduated from Antioch College in 1971, and in June of that year, she married Paul Richard Newman, a physicist. They have one daughter, Allison. In addition to her bachelor's degree, Newman earned a master's degree in medieval history in 1973 from Michigan State University. Newman lectures widely on topics related to women in history, Jewish communities in medieval times, and myths of medieval history. She resides in Newbury Park, California.

MAJOR WORKS AND THEMES

Newman's first works of fiction were a trilogy of novels about Guinevere. She became interested in Guinevere during graduate school, when she was researching Guinevere for one of her history courses. Newman found that Guinevere was "a very neglected part of the legend at that time," and after she left graduate school, she realized that what she "wanted to say about Guinevere would fit better in a novel than in a scholarly paper" (Thompson). She was particularly interested in writing against the tradition portrayals of Guinevere found in medieval literature, that Newman found to be misogynistic.

Later, Newman turned her focus toward medieval France and chose to write historical mysteries. She selected this time period because of her academic research interests (James 1996:22). When the series begins, Catherine LeVendeur is a novice at a convent run by Heloise. When the convent and its reputation are under attack, Heloise asks LeVendeur to seek out the truth. She undertakes the undercover and successfully solves the case with the assistance of a man called Edgar, who works for one of the players in the case. In the second novel, LeVendeur has chosen to leave the convent to marry Edgar, but before she leaves she is pulled into another case. As the series progresses, the couple are drawn into various cases, often working undercover to solve matters related to those with religious and political power in medieval Europe. LeVendeur's own heritage also frames several plots. Her father was Jewish, and when his family was killed, he was raised by a Christian family. He is portrayed as straddling both worlds, a position that became increasingly difficult during the twelfth century.

CRITICAL RECEPTION

Newman won the Macavity Award for *Death Comes as Epiphany* and has received other awards and nominations, including the Herotodus Award and the Bruce Alexander Award. Her novels about Guinevere have received treatment by literary scholars, although her mystery series has not received scholarly examination.

Her mystery series has been well received critically from the beginning. A review of *Death Comes as Epiphany* praised Newman for "skillfully depict[ing] historical figures and issues" and for "breath[ing] life and vigor into the scholastic debates and religious controversies" of the time (Brainard 1993:54). Another reviewer noted that Newman was "writing with assurance" and brought twelfth century France "vividly to life" (James 128). *The Devil's Door* was heralded as "meticulously prepared" and "adroitly craft[ed]," with an "engaging, lively cast" (Brainard 1994:60).

The Wandering Arm was called an "exquisitely crafted historical whodunit" with a "vividly rendered backdrop" and "another perplexing mystery" (Flanagan 1995:388). Another review praised Newman for her "sure hand with the period and her affecting cast in the deftly crafted tale" (Brainard 1995:47). In *Strong as Death,* Newman gained praise for an "extremely intelligent, highly suspenseful and richly textured" novel (Flanagan 1996:68). Another reviewer noted the "vibrant, often unexpected dynamics" and "emotional punch" of Newman's portrayal of LeVendeur and her family, along with the "vivid depiction of medieval life" (Brainard 1996:88). Another reviewer noted that "medieval history never was so enjoyable as in" *Strong as Death* (Havens 128).

Although *The Difficult Saint* "lean[ed] more heavily on history than mystery" for one reviewer, the novel was still praised as "an absorbing and entertaining narrative" (Zaleski 1999:67). *To Wear the White Cloak* was praised for "its attention to detail, depth of research and well-developed characters" and was noted for being "seasoned with wit and humor … a recommended read" (Zaleski 2000:90). Reviews of *Heresy* were also strong, with one reviewer predicting that "readers will love the total immersion into medieval history through character, surroundings, turbulent events, and culture" (Klett 182). A review of *The Outcast Dove* noted that "the author's intriguing picture of a crusade-laden world with its battles among Jew, Catholic and Muslim is all too relevant and recognizable" ("*The Outcast Dove*" 46).

BIBLIOGRAPHY

Works by Sharan Newman

Catherine LeVendeur Series

Death Comes as Epiphany. New York: Tor, 1993.
The Devil's Door. New York: Forge, 1994.
The Wandering Arm. New York: Forge, 1995.

Strong as Death. New York: Forge, 1996.
Cursed in the Blood. New York: Forge, 1998.
The Difficult Saint. New York: Forge, 1999.
To Wear the White Cloak. New York: Forge, 2000.
Heresy. New York: Forge, 2002.
The Outcast Dove. New York: Forge, 2003.

Other Fiction

Guinevere. New York: St. Martin's, 1981.
The Chessboard Queen. New York: St. Martin's, 1983.
Guinevere Evermore. New York: St. Martin's, 1985.

Works about Sharan Newman

Brainard, Dulcy. "Death Comes as Epiphany." *Publishers Weekly* 7 June 1993: 54.
———. "*The Devil's Door*." *Publishers Weekly* 25 April 1994: 60.
———. "*The Wandering Arm*." *Publishers Weekly* 25 September 1995: 46–47.
———. "Strong as Death." *Publishers Weekly* 10 June 1996: 88.
Flanagan, Margaret. "*The Wandering Arm*." *Booklist* 15 October 1995: 388.
———. "*Strong as Death*." *Booklist* 1 September 1996: 68.
Havens, Shirley E. "Medieval Murder." *Library Journal* 15 May 1997: 128.
James, Dean. "12th Century Mysteries." *Library Journal* 15 May 1994: 128.
———. "The Mystery Scene Interview with Sharan Newman." *Mystery Scene* 51 (January-February 1996): 22+.
Klett, Rex E. "*Heresy*." *Library Journal* December 2002: 182.
"*The Outcast Dove*." *Publishers Weekly* 10 November 2003: 46.
"Sharan Newman." *Contemporary Authors*. New Revision Series, Vol. 73. Eds. Daniel Jones and John D. Jorgensen. Detroit: Gale, 1999. 336–37.
Thompson, Raymond H. "Interview with Sharan Newman." Mythcon, Vancouver, B.C. 28 July 1989. 31 January 2006. http://www.lib.rochester.edu/camelot/intrvws/newman.htm
Zaleski, Jeff. "*The Difficult Saint*." *Publishers Weekly* 4 October 1999: 67.
———. "*To Wear the White Cloak*." *Publishers Weekly* 18 September 2000: 90.

Carol O'Connell (1947–)

BIOGRAPHY

As she was growing up, Carol O'Connell's family moved frequently because of her father's work. She was born May 26, 1947, in New York, the daughter of Norman and Berta O'Connell. She lived there only six days after she was born, but since her return in 1983, she has been a faithful resident of the city (Feldman 24).

Writing was an early interest for O'Connell, and some of her poems appeared in school publications, but her main interest was in art (Shindler 1995:441). She attended Arizona State University, earning a B.F.A. in painting. Her career in art was ultimately unsuccessful, and after returning to New York, she made a living with various jobs, including waitressing, graphic design, and copy editing. After realizing that the mystery and thriller genre was "fascinating," she began writing novels in her spare time and during her "painter's blocks," although her first works were unpublished (Feldman 24; Melton 1998:1371).

After numerous rejections from New York publishers, O'Connell decided to send a novel to Ruth Rendell's publisher in England. Although the first novel was rejected, Hutchinson was encouraging, and when she sent them *Mallory's Oracle,* the work was accepted (Smith). That she received a rather lucrative book deal from a British publisher who then sold the rights to an American publisher—and did so without having an agent—made a splash in the American publishing world (Feldman 24).

MAJOR WORKS AND THEMES

Except for one stand-alone mystery, all of O'Connell's works feature Kathleen Mallory. Mallory was an orphan, living alone on the streets and surviving by stealing, when she was taken in by a New York police detective and his wife. Although she never entirely overcomes her past and claims to have been diagnosed as a sociopath at a young age, she grows up, receives an educated in computer technology, and follows in her adoptive father's footsteps, joining the police force. As Andrew Vachss puts it, Mallory's "religion is pragmatism and she's a practicing fundamentalist" (33).

As the series begins, she is a sergeant with a special unit that allows her to use her computer expertise. Early in the book, her adoptive father is found dead with another murder victim. Mallory is familiar with the case he was working and is convinced she knows the identity of the killer. Given a bereavement leave of absence, she uses the time to solve the case as unofficial private investigator.

In the next book, she investigates the murder of a woman who is initially identified as Mallory. She does not work alone; her cases involve her mentor, Detective Riker, and her friend, Charles Butler, a psychiatrist who is quietly in love with her. *Killing Critics* involves the death of an artist and draws on O'Connell's insider knowledge of the New York art scene. *Stone Angel* finds Mallory in Louisiana exploring the mystery of her mother's murder. The revenge she plots for her mother has been described as both "brilliantly calculated and utterly terrifying" (Melton 1997:1620).

Shell Game features a case involving the death of a magician, and *Crime School* has Mallory on the trail of a serial killer. *Dead Famous* turns its focus to Riker's character, who is recovering from a shooting. Mallory takes on a case involving a radio personality, while also working to help Riker back from his physical and psychic wounds. In *Winter House,* Mallory is called to a house where a burglar lies dead. The owner of the house has a past history that may relate to the present case.

Although the novels are realistic and gritty, even drawing comparisons to nineteenth-century realistic fiction (Kelleghan 798), O'Connell uses "generous dashes of surrealism, hints of the occult and a touch of horror" (Vachss 33). She uses an omniscient narrator that shifts point of view among human characters, but also sometimes, in Fiona Kelleghan's opinion, "bizarrely speaks from the point of view" of various animals (798). For example, in *The Man Who Cast Two Shadows,* the cat who belonged to the murder victim becomes attached to Mallory, and at times, the narration shifts to the cat's perceptions and observations about Mallory. Another interesting case is that *Stone Angel,* the story of Mallory's revenge on her mother's killers, is told almost exclusively from Butler's point of view. Kelleghan also noted O'Connell's "jarring technique" of having "characters' traded looks" translated "into entire sentences or conversations" (798).

In addition to the Mallory novels, O'Connell wrote *Judas Child,* a novel featuring an investigator named Rouge Kendall. A case involving the murder of twin girls reminds Kendall of the unsolved murder of his own twin sister 15 years prior.

CRITICAL RECEPTION

Several of O'Connell's novels have been nominated for major awards, including an Edgar nomination for her first novel. According to a review of the first novel, it offers "excellent scene-setting, some clever plot twists" and is a "fast-moving [story] with quirky characters" (*Mallory's Oracle* E6). Although the *Publishers Weekly* review found the novel lacking in character and depth (Steinberg 1994:55), Emily Melton praised the novel lavishly, noting that it featured "writing [that] is stunning in its luminosity, originality, simplicity and power" and an "ingenious, inventive, enigmatic" plot (1994:1894). She further noted that "there may not be enough superlatives to describe O'Connell's book" (Melton 1994:1894). The *Publishers Weekly* review of the second Mallory novel was much more positive, praising its "intelligent plot," "crisp dialogue," and "supple prose" (Steinberg 1995:38). Melton again praised O'Connell strongly, noting that O'Connell had succeeded in producing "another book that's just as intense, powerful and affecting" as the debut (1995:1140). Melton also noted its "highly original and intensely gripping" plot and "unique" characters (1995:1140). Another review noted that "few mysteries embody the intensity" of this novel (Klett 136).

One reviewer deemed *Killing Critics* too gory (Leon 1), but another found that it demonstrates O'Connell's "creative plotting plus mastery of prose and style plus vivid characterization" to deliver a "great reading experience" (Woods C7). Melton praised its "well-nigh flawless plotting and incandescent writing" and "heart-stopping devastating ending"(1996:1077). The novel was also praised for its "driven and sharp-edged detective," with O'Connell offering a "narrative force and character development [that] are irresistible" (Brainard 1996:52).

Stone Angel is seen as having "rich, southern traditions and scenery as a framework," with O'Connell "paint[ing] a dark, Gothic tale of suspense, mystery and romance with just a touch of horror" (Shindler 1997:13). Another review called it "a chilling, terrifying revenge story" with insights into the "cold, cold soul of a genre hero like no other" (Ott 1361). Another noted that the novel could be read as horror or as a gothic romance, "but from any angle, [this] is a stunningly original mystery" (Brainard 1997:42).

Shell Game was heralded as a "rich, complex, memorable tale" (Melton 1999:1483). Another reviewer noted that her "tough realism and hypnotic prose" would leave readers anxious for the next Mallory adventure (Zaleski 1999:54). *Crime School* was heralded as "gripping" and "gritty, streetwise, and funny" (Zaleski 2002:67). A review of *Dead Famous* saw O'Connell as "set[ting] the standard in crime fiction" with her "sharp, gritty and street-wise prose" (Zaleski 2003:55). A review of *Winter House* proclaimed that "brilliant storytelling and vivid characterization are rarely as perfectly combined as they are here" (Ephron D6). A review that compared several works found *Winter House* to be "by far the most ambitious" compared to its peers, with its aspects of a "densely plotted modern gothic and police procedural in one" (Bernas).

A review of *Judas Child* noted that, although O'Connell "succeeds on all levels," such as plot, character and setting, "it's her characters you'll remember" (Johnson D1). The review also finds the novel to be beyond an "ordinary" mystery, finding it "a beautifully written thriller that is also a moving story of reconciliation and redemption" (Johnson D1). Another reviewer was not sure about the plot's supernatural aspects, but found that O'Connell's "subtle characterization of people who face tragedy with resilience and spirit makes for a moving novel" (Steinberg 1998:42). Her works have also drawn attention from literary scholars. Donatella Izzo's essay about the Mallory novels explores their portrayal of urban themes and denizens.

BIBLIOGRAPHY

Works by Carol O'Connell

Kathleen Mallory Series

Mallory's Oracle. New York: Putnam, 1994.
The Man Who Cast Two Shadows. New York: Putnam, 1995.
Killing Critics. New York: Putnam, 1996.
Stone Angel. New York: Putnam, 1997.
Shell Game. New York: Putnam, 1999.
Crime School. New York: Putnam, 2002.
Dead Famous. New York: Putnam, 2003.
Winter House. New York: Putnam, 2004.
Find Me. New York: Putnam, 2006.

Other Novel

Judas Child. New York: Putnam, 1998.

Works about Carol O'Connell

Bernas, Ron. "Winter House by Carol O'Connell." *Knight Ridder Tribune News Service* 27 October 2004.

Brainard, Dulcy. "Killing Critics." *Publishers Weekly* 15 April 1996: 52.

———. "Stone Angel." *Publishers Weekly* 9 June 1997: 41–42.

"Carol O'Connell." *Contemporary Authors. New Revision Series*, Vol. 121. Ed. Scot Peacock. Detroit: Gale, 2004. 321–23.

Ephron, Hallie. "Women who Sleuth, and the Perps who Fear Them." *Boston Globe* 28 November 2004: D6.

Feldman, Gayle. "*Mallory's Oracle* Predicts Megabucks for First Novelist." *Publishers Weekly* 31 January 1994: 24–25.

Izzo, Donatella. "Investigating the Labyrinth: Homeless, Freaks and Cyberwomen in Carol O'Connell's Detective Fiction." *America Today: Highways and Labyrinths*. Ed. Gigliola Nocera. Siracusa: Grafia, 2003. 574–81.

Johnson, Sharon. "Judas Child a Spine-tingling Thriller." *Patriot News* (Harrisburg) 1 November 1999: D1.

Kelleghan, Fiona. "Carol O'Connell." *St. James Guide to Crime & Mystery Writers*. 4th ed. Ed. Jay P. Pederson. Detroit: St. James Press, 1996. 797–98.

Klett, Rex E. "The Man Who Cast Two Shadows." *Library Journal* 1 May 1995: 136.

Leon, Donna. "Plenty of Blood and Thunder." *Sunday Times* (London) 28 July 1996: 1.

"Mallory's Oracle." *Oregonian* 21 August 1994: E6.

Melton, Emily. "*Mallory's Oracle.*" *Booklist* July 1994: 1894.

———. "*The Man Who Cast Two Shadows.*" *Booklist* 1 March 1995: 1140.

———. "*Killing Critics.*" *Booklist* 1 March 1996: 1077.

———. "*Stone Angel.*" *Booklist* 1/15 June 1997: 1620.

———. "The Booklist Interview: Carol O'Connell." *Booklist* 15 April 1998: 1370–71.

———. "*Shell Game.*" *Booklist* 15 April 1999: 1483.

Ott, Bill. "*Stone Angel.*" *Booklist* 15 April 1998: 1361.

Shindler, Dorman T. "Mallory's True Oracle: An Interview with Carol O'Connell." *Armchair Detective* 28.4 (1995): 440–43.

———. "Mallory off on a Dark, Romantic Adventure." *Milwaukee Journal Sentinel* 27 July 1997: 13.

Smith, Julia Llewellyn. "Prime Time for a Crime Writer." *The Times* (London) 11 May 1994: n.p.

Steinberg, Sybil. "*Mallory's Oracle.*" *Publishers Weekly* 27 June 1994: 55.

———. "*The Man Who Cast Two Shadows*." *Publishers Weekly* 17 April 1995: 38.
———. "*Judas Child*." *Publishers Weekly* 27 April 1998: 42.
Vachss, Andrew. "Never Kill a Cop's Father." *New York Times Book Review* 2 October 1994: 33.
Woods, Larry D. "No Threats Needed: Critics Adds Up as Fine Fiction." *Nashville Banner* 15 August
    1996: C7.
Zaleski, Jeff. "*Shell Game*." *Publishers Weekly* 14 June 1999: 53–54.
———. "*Crime School*." *Publishers Weekly* 19 August 2002: 67.
———. "*Dead Famous*." *Publishers Weekly* 4 August 2003: 55.

Abigail Padgett (1942–)

BIOGRAPHY

Mary Abigail Padgett was born May 13, 1942, in Vincennes, Indiana. Her father, William Ludington Padgett, worked in construction and the home improvement business, and her mother, Martha Virginia Moore Padgett, was a teacher. Her first publication credit came at age six, when she wrote a letter to the editor suggesting that new puppies be covered in the newspaper along with the news of human births (Salm 6).

She attended college at Indiana University, Bloomington, and earned her bachelor's degree in education in 1964. She married Robert Michael Dolgin on December 26, 1965. They had one son and divorced in 1982. Padgett also earned a master's degree in counseling from the University of Missouri in 1969, and completed coursework toward a doctorate at Washington University in St. Louis.

Padgett taught high school English in St. Louis from 1964 to 1969. During the 1970s and 1980s, she held various positions as a vocational rehabilitation specialist, an adjunct professor, the director of the American Civil Liberties Union office in Houston, and as an indexer and abstracter for Sociological Abstracts. In 1986, she began working as a court investigator for Child Protective Services in San Diego.

Since leaving that post in 1988, Padgett has focused on writing and her advocacy work for children and the mentally ill. When she first decided to give writing a try as a career, she attended a workshop on writing romance novels. When she named her first hero Cade Stanton, the instructor was not amused and suggested she try another genre (Salm 6). She turned to mystery writing, using her experiences and interests to develop the characters.

MAJOR WORKS AND THEMES

Padgett's first series features Barbara "Bo" Bradley, who works as a child protection advocate investigator in San Diego. Bradley also suffers from bipolar disorder, or manic depression, and much attention is paid to how she deals with her illness. Padgett told *Contemporary Authors* that "recognizing the pervasive contribution to psychiatric stigma by popular fiction and its legion of 'psycho' killers, I determined to drain the stereotype by creating a mystery series in which the good guy, not the villain, has the psychiatric illness" (Abigail 3511).

The novels focus on various cases that Bradley is involved with that turn complex. In the first novel, she is called in to assist when a deaf child is found abandoned at a reservation. When she and the child are threatened, she delves deeper to solve the mystery surrounding the child. In *Strawgirl,* a young girl is assigned to Bradley after her younger sister is molested and killed by her mother's boyfriend. Bradley approves her placement with her grandmother, but when it is learned that the grandmother is involved with a religious cult, Bradley is pulled into a case that goes beyond the initial appearances. All the novels in the series feature Bradley working with children in peril and solving the crimes that the adults around them are involved in.

Her second series follows Blue McCarron, a lesbian social psychologist who lives as a recluse. In the first novel, a frozen corpse is found at an elderly woman's home; she claims she killed the person in self-defense and hid the body out of fear. Her son hires McCarron to do a psychological analysis, and McCarron ends up solving the mystery. In the second novel, McCarron becomes involved in the hunt for a serial killer who is attacking women politicians in the San Diego area.

CRITICAL RECEPTION

Padgett's first novel was viewed as "ambitious" and "promising," with an "action packed climax" and "well-drawn" characters, including an "intelligent and appealing" protagonist (Melton 1992:651). *Strawgirl* was noted for being "stirring, insightful" with a "corker of an ending," but also praised for its "taboo-shattering frankness" about Bradley's manic depression (Brainard 1993:65). *Turtle Baby* was praised as "timely," with its treatment of issues including immigration and child abuse, but also was called a "fine mystery" with a "compelling" protagonist (Lukowsky 1182). Another reviewer noted that "Padgett expertly crafts this mystery," but that "what sets her story apart is her description of the workings of public child protection and her convincing portrayal" of Bradley's struggle with her mental illness (Brainard 1995:62). *Moonbird Boy* was lauded for its "complex, well-orchestrated" plot, which made it a "gripping novel" (Brainard 1996:87).

The McCarron series was praised for a "great new character" who is "sassy, tough, scared, vulnerable, and funny" (Anderson 139). The second novel in the series was noted for its "funny, idiosyncratic cast of characters and a cunningly developed series of murders," although the reviewer pointed out that the ending was flat and that some readers might not appreciate the feminist politics that are present in the novel (Cannon 72).

BIBLIOGRAPHY

Works by Abigail Padgett

Bo Bradley Series

Child of Silence. New York: Mysterious Press, 1993.
Strawgirl. New York: Mysterious Press, 1994.
Turtle Baby. New York: Mysterious Press, 1995.
Moonbird Boy. New York: Mysterious Press, 1996.
The Dollmaker's Daughters. New York: Mysterious Press, 1997.

Blue McCarron Series

Blue. New York: Mysterious Press, 1998.
The Last Blue Plate Special. New York: Mysterious Press, 2001.

Works about Abigail Padgett

"Abigail Padgett." *Contemporary Authors.* New Revision Series, Vol. 104. Ed. Scot Peacock. Detroit: Gale, 2003. 3510–12.

Anderson, Karen. "*Blue.*" *Library Journal* 1 October 1998: 139.

Brainard, Dulcy. "*Strawgirl.*" *Publishers Weekly* 13 December 1993: 65.

———. "*Turtle Baby.*" *Publishers Weekly* 2 January 1995: 62.

———. "*Moonbird Boy.*" *Publishers Weekly* 26 February 1996: 87.

Cannon, Peter. "*The Last Blue Plate Special.*" *Publishers Weekly* 19 February 2001: 72.

Lukowsky, Wes. "*Turtle Baby.*" *Booklist* 1 March 1995: 1182.

Melton, Emily. "*Child of Silence.*" *Booklist* 1 December 1992: 651.

Salm, Arthur. "It's No Mystery Why She Fell under Genre's Romantic Spell." *San Diego Union-Tribune* 30 January 2000: 6.

Sara Paretsky (1947–)

BIOGRAPHY

Sara Paretsky was born June 8, 1947, in Ames, Iowa, to David and Mary Edwards Paretsky. Her father was a college professor and her mother was a librarian. The only daughter of five children, Paretsky grew up in a family she has described as one "where girls became secretaries and wives, and boys became professionals" (qtd in Shapiro 67).

She wrote constantly during high school and college, but she never felt encouraged to attempt to publish any of her works (Rozan 44); the gender bias she felt in her family life spilled over into her education. In discussing her desire to write a strong female character, she recalls only one book written by a woman, George Eliot's *Silas Marner,* as being included in her secondary school curriculum (qtd in Ross 336). After earning a bachelor's degree from the University of Kansas in 1967, Paretsky studied history at the University of Chicago. The study of history was not her top priority, however, as she comments that she read 24 mysteries in the month before her oral examinations for the doctoral degree (Shapiro 67).

Also during this period in her life, she married S. Courtenay Wright, a widowed father of three who is a professor of physics at the University of Chicago. She finished her Ph.D. in 1977, but she decided against a career in academia. She enrolled in the MBA program at the University of Chicago and soon entered the business world. She was quite successful as a marketing manager in the insurance industry, but reading and writing remained her true loves. After her first novel was published, she stayed with her job for several years before turning to writing full-time.

She had always read and enjoyed mystery fiction, and the decision to write a detective novel was an easy one. She was most interested in writing about a female detective and worked on a manuscript for several years. As a New Year's resolution, she set a goal to complete the novel in 1979. She wanted to write a novel about a female working in the Raymond Chandler tradition, a woman would be "a success in a field traditionally dominated by men" (qtd in Ross 335), and in 1979, V. I. Warshawski emerged. Paretsky has said that Warshawski was born while she was saying one thing to her boss but thinking another (Evans G1). To help achieve her goal, she enrolled in a continuing education course in mystery writing taught by Stuart Kaminsky; this experience helped her hone the manuscript and gain access to the publishing world. Within 18 months of her New Year's resolution, she finished *Indemnity Only* and began searching for a publisher, eventually signing with Dial Press, which published the novel in 1982.

Social issues have long been a concern of Paretsky's, and her character, V. I. Warshawski, shares these concerns. Paretsky's grandparents met on a union picket line, and although the gender-based inequities of her parents were problematic, the family was quite liberal politically (Rozan 44). Her first experiences in Chicago were as a college student volunteering for community service projects during a summer. As for the gender bias she suffered, Paretsky says that "the women's movement of the '60's changed my life," allowing her to move beyond doubts she had about herself and "make a difference in the public sphere" (Rozan 45).

In addition to being a prolific participant in the mystery genre, Paretsky also is one of the founding members of Sisters in Crime, a group organized in 1986 to increase the visibility and status of women writing in the mystery field with reviewers, readers, and publishers. Paretsky served as the first president of the group. The group is also concerned with graphic violence toward women in crime fiction and works to correct imbalances in the treatment of women (Herbert 31). Paretsky recently noted that her first novel was published in 1982, the same year that women were first allowed to be full officers, not "matrons," with the Chicago Police Department (Martelle E1).

Paretsky was selected as *Ms Magazine*'s Woman of the Year in 1987 and also won an award from the Friends of American Writers for Deadlock and a Crime Writers Association Silver Dagger Award for *Blood Shot.*

MAJOR WORKS AND THEMES

Except for one novel, *Ghost Country,* Paretsky's body of work consists of a detective series featuring the female investigator Victoria Iphigenia Warshawski. Known as V. I. to most people, she is a lawyer turned private investigator who was born and raised, and lives and works, in Chicago. The only child of a Polish police officer and an Italian opera singer, Warshawski represents a unique blend of cultures, languages, and religions. Her mother died when she was 15 years old, her father 10 years later, and these events have greatly shaped Warshawski. The novels are best described as hard-boiled and do feature a good amount of violence, both meted out and received by Warshawski. The cases draw on Warshawski's expertise in finance and law, often involving fraud in various industries and political settings.

Indemnity Only, the first Warshawski novel and one of the first detective novels written by a woman about a woman investigator, features Warshawski tracking down a missing woman and becoming entangled with a fraudulent scheme involving union leaders, gangsters, and crooked insurance executives. In *Deadlock,* Warshawski takes on the investigation of the death of her cousin, again uncovering corruption and fraud, this time in the shipping business. The third Warshawski novel, *Killing Orders,* tackles fraud and corruption among the powerful elite of the Catholic Church.

With *Bitter Medicine,* Paretsky begins to tackle even more social issues. *Bitter Medicine* involves the death of a young woman mistreated at a hospital owing to her race. Medical malpractice is the major area of fraudulent activities uncovered by Warshawski, but there is an extra layer of social commentary presented here. *Blood Shot* involves a chemical company that covered up evidence that its products were harming the workers, and *Burn Marks* centers on arson and corruption in the building industry and also features Warshawski's aunt, who is alcoholic and semi-homeless. *Guardian Angel* looks at the plight of elderly persons and focuses on corrupt schemes involving bankers and lawyers who prey on this population. *Tunnel Vision* draws attention to the homeless, child abuse, and racially motivated funding decisions regarding social services.

A year after *Tunnel Vision*, Paretsky published *Windy City Blues,* a collection of short stories featuring Warshawski, and the stand-alone *Ghost Country* followed. Some reviewers and critics thought that *Tunnel Vision,* with its ambiguity about the aging Warshawski's situation, might be the last novel of the series (Porsdam 145), but Paretsky herself invited readers to visit her Web site and share speculations about Warshawski's future (Evans G1). Four years after *Tunnel Vision, Hard Time* appeared, with Warshawski returning to active investigations. *Hard Time* focuses on the exploitation and experience of immigrants and brings to light a corrupt prison system. *Total Recall* tells the story of Warshawski's friend, psychologist Lotty Herschel, and also finds Warshawski tangled up in a case involving Holocaust survivors and Chicago politics. *Blacklist* takes place post-9/11, with Warshawski tackling another case involving politics, prejudice, and terrorism. *Fire Sale* finds Warshawski investigating sabotage at a local factory and looking for a missing teen, while Paretsky deals with larger issues of globalization and religious fanaticism.

Elaine Budd noted that "the 'whydunnit' in Ms. Paretsky's books is often embedded in the fabric of problems that confront us all…this extra dimension adds an immediacy that is not found in many private eye novels" (qtd in "Paretsky" 443). Some readers do not appreciate such themes; Paretsky received an angry letter from a reader who wanted to know why the Warshawski novels were "infested" with social and political issues (Paretsky "Storyteller" E1). Paretsky's response is that mysteries are by definition political (E1). Paretsky notes that she does not intend to write social or political commentary, that what matters is the story, but the fact is that the stories that matter most to her are those of people who are powerless and voiceless (E1). She has echoed these themes in numerous interviews. She notes that all of her books are "driven by themes of helplessness and powerlessness," and further notes that her own lack of empowerment led her to create the series (Lee). Along with attention to issues of class, feminism is a driving force in Paretsky's work. As Alice Yeager Kaplan noted, Paretsky writes fiction in which "a woman claims her right to the city, her right to her body, her right to feel" (28).

Among the key themes of the Warshawski novels is Chicago itself. Paretsky has said that she often begins with the idea for the crime plot, but that the setting is crucial, noting that "when you live in a place and it really gets into your blood, it takes over your imagination. The reason I write about Chicago is because I know and I love this city really passionately" (qtd in Herbert 31). Margaret Kinsman also explores the presence and importance of Chicago in Paretsky's novels, noting that the city "provides a geographical, moral and ethical landscape" for Warshawski, "against which she defines her purpose as a detective" (1998: 709). Ralph Willett further analyzes the use of Chicago area settings as informative of Warshawski's history and actions (110–115).

In addition to the Warshawski series, Paretsky has published one non-mystery novel entitled *Ghost Country.* In this work, Paretsky tackles similar themes of corruption, homelessness, and life in Chicago. This novel interweaves the stories of several characters, including an alcoholic, washed-up opera singer, a young woman who chooses to live on the street, a homeless woman who sees a miraculous vision of the Virgin Mary, and a psychologist assigned to treat that woman. Use of multiple points of view allows all of these characters to serve as narrators at various points in the novel. Of interest, Paretsky has said that before writing *Ghost Country*, she would not have called herself a writer, but the accomplishments and the process of writing this novel have rejuvenated her attitude toward writing and toward herself as a writer (Rozan 45).

CRITICAL RECEPTION

In addition to a huge array of favorable book reviews, Paretsky's works have been examined by scholars in publications ranging from *Journal of Popular Culture* to *Yale French Studies*. *Clues: A Journal of Detection* has announced the intent to publish a special issue devoted to Paretsky in early 2007, which will add even more selections to the wide array of literary criticism available on Paretsky's work.

Patricia E. Johnson examines Paretsky's *Bitter Medicine* in conjunction with Sue Grafton's *A is for Alibi,* novels that share the plot device of having the female detective become sexually involved with a man who becomes implicated in the crime. Johnson addresses the debate in feminist criticism regarding female hard-boiled detectives, the concern that in writing female characters who function in a stereotypically male world, more harm than good is done. Kathleen Gregory Klein is one of the most often cited sources for this, positing that "adopting the hard-boiled formula traps their authors" (qtd in Johnson 98). On the other hand, Jane S. Bakerman and Maureen T. Reddy see female hard-boiled detective fiction as a rewriting and powerful transformation of the traditional genre (Johnson 98). As Bakerman puts it, "Sara Paretsky has reformulated and reenergized an old literary pattern by recognizing the value of combining the hard-boiled detective novel with feminist fiction" (135).

Helle Porsdam focuses on feminism and legal issues in her study of Paretsky's works and other feminist detective fiction. She also examines the issue of whether fiction involving violence and victimization can advance a feminist agenda (131–32). Richard Goodkin's ambitious article compared *Killing Orders* with Racine's *Iphigénie.* Goodkin starts by contrasting two critics, one who views the Oedipus story as a "classical analytical detective story" and another who makes a strong distinction between "mythic crime" and "profane crime" (81). Goodkin examines intertextual links between Racine's work and Paretsky's; it should be noted that Warshawski's middle name of Iphigenia is revealed in *Killing Orders.* Goodkin contends that the two works are both readings of Euripides's *Iphigenia in Aulis,* focusing on the attempt to blind Warshawksi and the recurring images of fire throughout the novel (88–91).

Margaret Kinsman brings a mix of personal and academic outlooks to her study of Paretsky. A Chicago native who has lived in London for many years, Kinsman recognizes the coping mechanisms Warshawski uses in managing her environment as similar to ones Kinsman herself uses (1995:16). Kinsman examines Warshawski as a feminist character and Paretsky as a feminist writer via a brief historiography of Chicago, literary history and sociology (18–22). In addition, Kinsman explores two prevalent symbols in the works: cars and restaurants. Cars are important to Warshawski, and, like her, her cars take a lot of physical abuse. Also, as Kinsman points out, the automobiles allow her to go places she should not go (23). Warshawski is always able to find a restaurant, no matter where she is, and she never hesitates to dine alone, which Kinsman finds interesting as a feminist action against traditional expectations and roles (24–25).

BIBLIOGRAPHY

Works by Sara Paretsky

Indemnity Only. New York: Dial, 1982.
Deadlock. New York: Dial, 1984.
Killing Orders. New York: Morrow, 1985.
Bitter Medicine. New York: Morrow, 1987.
Blood Shot. New York: Delacorte, 1988.

Burn Marks. New York: Delacorte, 1990.
Guardian Angel. New York: Delacorte, 1992.
Tunnel Vision. New York: Delacorte, 1994.
Windy City Blues. New York: Delacorte, 1995.
Ghost Country. New York: Delacorte, 1998.
Hard Time. New York: Delacorte, 1999.
"A Storyteller Stands Where Justice Confronts Basic Human Needs: Mysteries, Like Life, Have to be Political." *New York Times* 25 September 2000: E1.
Total Recall. New York: Delacorte, 2001.
Blacklist. New York: Putnam, 2003.
Fire Sale. New York: Putnam, 2005.

Works about Sara Paretsky

Bakerman, Jane S. "Living 'Openly and with Dignity': Sara Paretsky's New-Boiled Feminist Fiction." *Midamerica: The Yearbook of the Society for the Study of Midwestern Literature* 12 (1985): 120–35.

Crawford, Brad. "Sara Paretsky's Immortal Character." *Writer's Digest* September 1999: 8–9.

Decure, Nicole. "V. I. Warshawski, a 'Lady with Guts': Feminist Crime Fiction by Sara Paretsky." *Women's Studies International Forum* 12.2 (1989): 227–38.

Evans, Judith. "V. I. Warshawski Goes Behind Bars in Sara Paretsky's Latest Novel." *St. Louis Post-Dispatch* 9 September 1999: G1.

Ford, Susan Allen. "Detecting (and Teaching) the Gothic." *Studies in Popular Culture* 24.1 (October 2001): 47–57.

Goodkin, Richard E. "Killing Order(s): Iphigenia and the Detection of Tragic Intertextuality." *Yale French Studies* 76 (1989): 81–107.

Green, Michelle. "Sara Paretsky's Cult Heroine is a Woman's Woman—V. I. Warshawski, the Funky, Feminist Private Eye." *People's Weekly* 14 May 1990: 132–34.

Herbert, Rosemary. "Aiming Higher." *Publishers Weekly* 13 April 1990: 30–32.

Johnson, Patricia E. "Sex and Betrayal in the Detective Fiction of Sue Grafton and Sara Paretsky." *Journal of Popular Culture* 27.4 (1994): 97–106.

Jones, Louise Conley. "Feminism and the P. I. Code: Or, Is a Hard-Boiled Warshawski Unsuitable to Be Called a Feminist?" *Clues: A Journal of Detection* 16.1 (1995): 77–87.

Kaplan, Alice Yaeger. "Critical Fictions: The New Hard-Boiled Woman." *Artforum* January 1990: 26–28.

Kinsman, Margaret. "A Question of Visibility: Paretsky and Chicago." Ed. Kathleen Gregory Klein. *Women Times Three: Writers, Detectives, Readers.* Bowling Green: Bowling Green State University Popular Press, 1995. 15–27.

———. "Sara Paretsky." Eds. Maureen Corrigan and Robin Winks. *Mystery and Suspense Writers: The Literature of Crime, Detection and Espionage.* New York: Scribner's, 1998. 699–713.

Klein, Kathleen Gregory. "Watching Warshawski." Eds. William Reynolds and Elizabeth Trembley. *It's a Print!: Detective Fiction from Page to Screen.* Bowling Green: Bowling Green State University Popular Press, 1994. 145–56.

Lee, Adam. "Mystery Writer Returns to Kansas City Roots." *Johnson County Sun* 23 June 2005. 9 July 2005. http://www.zwire.com/site/news.cfm?newsid = 14739564&BRD = 1459&PAG = 461&dept_id = 155725&rfi = 6

Martelle, Scott. "One Tough Cookie Made Mystery Fans Want More." *Los Angeles Times* 25 April 2005: E1.

"Paretsky, Sara." Ed. Judith Graham. *1992 Current Biography Yearbook.* New York: H. W. Wilson, 1992. 441–44.

Pope, Rebecca A. "'Friends Is a Weak Word for It': Female Friendship and the Spectre of Lesbianism in Sara Paretsky." Ed. Glenwood Irons. *Feminism in Women's Detective Fiction.* Toronto: University of Toronto Press, 1995. 157–70.

Porsdam, Helle. "Embedding Rights within Relationships: Gender, Law and Sara Paretsky." *American Studies* 39.3 (1998): 131–51.

Reddy, Maureen T. *Sisters in Crime: Feminism and the Crime Novel*. New York: Continuum, 1988.

Ross, Jean W. "*CA* Interview: Sara Paretsky." Ed. Susan M. Trosky. *Contemporary Authors* Vol. 129. Detroit: Gale, 1990. 335–38.

Rozan, S. J. "Sara Paretsky: A Gun of One's Own." *Publishers Weekly* 25 October 1999: 44–45.

"Sara Paretsky." Eds. Daniel Jones and John D. Jorgenson. *Contemporary Authors New Revision Series*, Vol. 59. Detroit: Gale, 1998. 306–10.

Sara Paretsky. 2004. 11 October 2004. http://www.saraparetsky.com/

Shapiro, Laura. "Interview with Sara Paretsky." *Ms.* January 1988: 66–67+.

Shepherdson, Nancy. "The Writer Behind Warshawski." *Writer's Digest* September 1992: 38–41.

Szuberla, Guy. "The Ties That Bind: V. I. Warshawski and the Burdens of Family." *Armchair Detective* 27.2 (1994): 146–53.

Willett, Ralph. *The Naked City: Urban Crime Fiction in the USA*. Manchester: Manchester UP, 1996.

P. J. Parrish

BIOGRAPHY

P. J. Parrish is a pseudonym used by two sisters, Kelly Montee and Kristy Montee, who were born and raised in Detroit. According to their Web site, Kristy Montee attended college at Eastern Michigan University, earning a degree in education. Instead of teaching, though, she went into journalism and worked as a reporter in Michigan before moving to Fort Lauderdale, Florida, in 1973. She held several positions at the *Sun-Sentinel,* including reporter, editor, and assistant managing editor, before leaving to devote her time to fiction writing in 1985. She published four novels before beginning to collaborate with her sister. She lives in Fort Lauderdale with her husband Daniel, who is the managing editor for the *Sun-Sentinel.*

Their Web site also notes that Kelly Montee attended college at Northern Michigan University and moved to Arizona after college. She later lived in Nevada for 15 years, working in the gaming industry, and moved to Philadelphia, Mississippi, to take a position as a human resources manager at a casino. She now lives outside Memphis. She has three children and three grandchildren. She always wanted to write and was struggling with a mystery novel manuscript. Her sister was bored with the romantic fiction she had been writing, so the two joined forces.

MAJOR WORKS AND THEMES

Parrish writes a series set in the 1980s, featuring a biracial police detective named Louis Kincaid. The first novel finds Kincaid returning to his hometown of Black Pool, Mississippi, owing to the terminal illness of his mother, whom he has not seen in years. His status as a policeman in Michigan allows him to take a temporary position in Black Pool, where he faces racism among his new colleagues. The bias deepens as remains of a lynching victim are discovered, and, against the wishes of the department, Kincaid insists on investigating the case.

In *Dead of Winter,* Kincaid returns to Michigan, having secured a position with a force in a resort area. When he discovers that his predecessor, also an African American, was killed mysteriously, Kincaid must uncover the truth. In subsequent novels, Kincaid is drawn to Florida by a job offer, and after again working to solve a case against the wishes of his superiors, gets his license to work as a private investigator. He takes on a number of cases throughout the series, including solving a string of decades-old murders and finding the truth about a murder the wrong man served 20 years for committing.

Given the timeline of the series, some common contemporary investigative techniques are not yet available. The series also focuses a great deal on Kincaid's identity, his past, and the discrimination he deals with in society.

CRITICAL RECEPTION

P. J. Parrish's first novel won acclaim as filled with "plenty of action," with Parrish "vividly creat[ing] a divided community with a violent secret and a determined investigator whose shaky self-concept and inability to trust contribute nearly as much to his difficulties in solving the case as the vicious bigotry and arrogance he encounters" (Zvirin 965). Another reviewer found it "tense but predictable," but deemed the debut novel as "promising" (Zaleski 63–64).

For *Dead of Winter* Parrish was praised for "deftly depict[ing] the empty winter landscape and the relentless intensity of the killer's pursuit," producing a "fast-paced thriller" and "suspenseful tale of a man who must question his principles and loyalties" (Rotella 73).

Thicker Than Water was lauded for its "crisp prose and evocative descriptions of southern Florida [which] set the tone for this grim mystery" and the "sympathetic characters and sudden twists" that will draw readers in (Yamashita 2002:49). *Island of Bones* was praised for plotting and characterization, along with "Parrish's crisp dialogue and skill at stringing out the suspense … [that] make this carefully constructed mystery so absorbing" (Yamashita 2003:46).

The plot twists in *A Killing Rain* were criticized, but the novel was praised overall as a "lean, fast-paced yarn" featuring Kincaid in a "brisk race against time" ("*A Killing Rain*" 44). The review of *An Unquiet Grave* compared Parrish to Dennis Lehane and noted that Parrish "manages to make what could be a formulaic plot fresh, both through her gift at creating sympathetic main and secondary characters and through her skill at creating suspense and sustaining a mood," praising their "ability to raise goose bumps" ("*An Unquiet Grave*" 37).

BIBLIOGRAPHY

Works by P. J. Parrish

Dark of the Moon. New York: Kensington, 1999.
Dead of Winter. New York: Kensington, 2001.
Paint It Black. New York: Kensington, 2002.
Thicker Than Water. New York: Kensington, 2003.
Island of Bones. New York: Kensington, 2004.
A Killing Rain. New York: Kensington, 2005.
An Unquiet Grave. New York: Kensington, 2006.

Works about P. J. Parrish

"A Killing Rain." *Publishers Weekly* 10 January 2005: 44.
P. J. Parrish. Homepage. 18 March 2006. http://www.pjparrish.com
Rotella, Mark. "*Dead of Winter*." *Publishers Weekly* 1 January 2001: 73.

"*An Unquiet Grave.*" *Publishers Weekly* 5 December 2005: 37.

White, Pamela. "An Interview with P. J. Parrish." *Over My Dead Body: The Mystery Magazine* Online. n.d. 18 March 2006. http://overmydeadbody.com/pjparrish.htm

Yamashita, Brianna. "*Thicker Than Water.*" *Publishers Weekly* 25 November 2002: 49.

———. "*Island of Bones.*" *Publishers Weekly* 1 December 2003: 46.

Zaleski, Jeff. "*Dark of the Moon.*" *Publishers Weekly* 1 March 1999: 63–64.

Zvirin, Stephanie. "*Dark of the Moon.*" *Booklist* 1 February 1999: 965.

Rebecca Pawel (1977–)

BIOGRAPHY

Born in 1977, Rebecca Pawel grew up in New York. She attended the New York public schools and earned a bachelor's degree in Spanish at Columbia University. She began learning about Spain when she studied dance during junior high school, and she studied in Madrid in the summer of 1994. She earned a master's degree from Columbia in 2000, and she currently teaches English and journalism at the High School for Enterprise, Business and Technology in Brooklyn.

MAJOR WORKS AND THEMES

Pawel's works are set in the time after the Civil War in Spain and focus on Carlos Tejada Alonso y Leon, a sergeant in the Guardia Civil and a fierce Nationalist. The first novel opens in 1939, as Madrid is reeling in the final days of the Civil War. Tejada makes an incorrect assumption about the identity of the killer of one of his comrades and kills an innocent woman. He is then driven to find the real killer. The second novel in the series finds Tejada in a new post in Salamanca, and addresses the issue of Jewish intellectuals being deported from Spain to Nazi Germany. He meets Elena, a woman from a family of leftists, and they fall in love and marry, even though the political gulf between them is wide. In the third novel, Tejada and Elena, now pregnant, have been sent to Potes, a city destroyed during the war. In his first command position, Tejada has problems with his new subordinates, and on the home front, Tejada and his in-laws clash. When Elena and their newborn son are kidnapped, Tejada uncovers a number of related crimes, including the murder of his predecessor at the post.

CRITICAL RECEPTION

Her first novel won an Edgar Award, but critics have had a mixed response to her works, particularly to Tejada's negative characterization. Many have difficulty referring to him as an antihero, which is what Pawel herself calls him (homepage). One reviewer found Pawel taking a "risky course" in showing Tejada "commit an act of swift and brutal street justice" (Koch 19). The review also discusses how "the fact that Tejada's self-exasperation when he realizes he executed an innocent woman doesn't satisfy the repulsed reader is ironic testament to Pawel's own success at evoking a time and place of nearly exhausted humanity" (Koch 19). On the other hand, another review found Pawel "unsparing in her depiction of the casual brutalities spawned by the war," but saw the novel as showing "evidence of the power of little civilities and kindnesses" ("*Death of a Nationalist*" 36). Another review praised her as a "gutsy writer and a risk-taker," naming Pawel "the best new mystery author … in a long time" (Dunn).

Marietta Dunn recounts the brutality of the first novel and compared it to the portrayal of Tejada in the second novel, noting that the fact "that Pawel is able to turn Tejada into the hero of her series is an astonishing achievement in writing and psychological development" (Dunn). Dunn finds this "a more conventional mystery than the first," but noted that it is "a finely thought-out examination of the 'other victims' of war … poignantly captur[ing] the sense of isolation, humiliation and defeat of those who dared to question the regime" (Dunn). Lev Raphael found *Law of Return* to be "a colorful, thrilling story about loyalty and love making people do things they could never have imagined," with Pawel "weav[ing] together her characters' fates with a deft and cunning hand" (Raphael). Her third novel was heralded for its effective mix of "history, relationships and Spanish culture" that offer a "thought-provoking and entertaining novel" (Bibel 712). Another reviewer praised her "low-key, bare-bones prose" that "belies the complex layers of her story" (Woog L7).

Some critics also warn readers that Pawel's work is not within expected models of detective fiction. One reviewer praised how Pawel "captures the anomie of postwar Spain while eschewing excess bloodshed" but is concerned that "the deliberate pace and relative inaction will frustrate readers expecting a more conventional crime novel" (Cannon 40). A review of the third novel finds it "well-researched if austere," with a complex plot and "richness of detail," but noted that "the lack of narrative drive and flatness of tone may disappoint fans of more conventional mystery fare" ("*The Watcher in the Pine*" 26). Other reviewers, however, see Pawel's work as having broader appeal. One review noted that Pawel's first novel "easily transcends the formulaic crime story" ("*Death of a Nationalist*" 36), and a review of *The Watcher in the Pine* noted that the work would appeal to readers outside the mystery genre (Bibel 712).

BIBLIOGRAPHY

Works by Rebecca Pawel

Carlos Tejada Series

Death of a Nationalist. New York: Soho Press, 2003.
Law of Return. New York: Soho Press, 2004.
The Watcher in the Pine. New York: Soho Press, 2004.
The Summer Snow. New York: Soho Press, 2006.

Works about Rebecca Pawel

Bibel, Barbara. "*The Watcher in the Pine*." *Booklist* 15 December 2004: 712.
Cannon, Peter. "*Law of Return*." *Publishers Weekly* 12 January 2004: 40.
"Death of a Nationalist." *Publishers Weekly* 2 December 2002: 36.
Dunn, Marietta. "*Law of Return* by Rebecca Pawel is a Treat." *Messenger-Inquirer* 16 May 2004. 16 June 2005. http://www.messenger-inquirer.com/features/lifestyle/7159928.htm
Koch, P. G. "Shades of Gray/Nominal Hero Seen in Terrifying Light." *Houston Chronicle* 4 May 2003: 19.
Raphael, Lev. "*Law of Return* by Rebecca Pawel." *Detroit Free Press* 8 February 2004. 16 June 2005. http://www.freep.com/features/books/myst8_20040208.htm
Rebecca Pawel. Homepage. 2 April 2005. 13 June 2005. http://www.rebeccapawel.com/
"Rebecca Pawel." *Contemporary Authors*. Vol. 222. Ed. Lisa Kumar. Detroit: Gale, 2004. 371–72.
"*The Watcher in the Pine*." *Publishers Weekly* 29 November 2004: 26.
Woog, Adam. "Scene of the Crime; What's New." *Seattle Times* 13 February 2005: L7.

Anne Perry (1938–)

BIOGRAPHY

Anne Perry was born Juliet Marion Hulme on October 28, 1938, in Blackheath, London. Her father, Henry Hulme, was a mathematician, and her mother, Hilda Marion Reavley Hulme, was a teacher. They moved often for her father's work and also because of Perry's poor health. They lived in the Bahamas for some time, and later her father became rector of Christchurch University College, allowing them to move to New Zealand, again seeking a better climate for Perry's respiratory problems. It was while living in Christchurch that she was involved in the incident that she successfully hid from the public for years, until the 1954 murder of Pauline Parker's mother. Perry's role in the crime was portrayed in the 1994 movie *Heavenly Creatures*. After her release from the juvenile detention center at age 21, she returned to England, and changed her name, taking the surname of her mother's new husband, Walter Perry. She worked at a variety of jobs, including serving as a flight attendant and as an assistant buyer, although her goal since childhood had been to write. She went to California in 1967 and worked for an insurance firm until 1972. During her time in California, she converted to the Mormon faith. She has worked full-time as a writer since 1972, and she currently lives in Portmahomack, Scotland.

MAJOR WORKS AND THEMES

Perry's first works were historical novels, but she is best known for her three different mystery series, all of which take place in England during different historical periods. The first series is set beginning in 1881 and features a Victorian-era police detective named Thomas Pitt, who meets his wife Charlotte during his investigation. Charlotte is of a higher social class than her husband, and she also fancies herself an amateur sleuth. Along with her sister Emily, the pair infiltrates his cases, often assisting him when the crimes reach into the higher social classes that they can easily move within. Their different backgrounds also allow Perry to explore a number of issues related to class conflicts during the Victorian era. As the series progresses, Perry also deals with imperialism, Darwinism, and other issues from the era.

The Cater Street Hangman, the first novel to feature the Pitts, features him investigating a crime that Charlotte's family may be involved in. Subsequent cases involve child abuse, incest, infanticide, and abortion, and serve as a grounds for critically exploring the legal rights of women during the era. Although these topics are intense, the series has a light tone, with many details of their lives and surroundings. One critic called the second novel "as much a novel of manners as a mystery story" (Callendar 33). As Bill Ott suggests, the series "set a standard for historical mysteries by using the past for more than ambience. Victorian mores drive the plots in these novels, setting context for the crimes and providing the psychological underpinnings for the characters' motivations" (997).

Her second series debuted in 1990, featuring a police inspector named William Monk This series is set earlier than the Pitt novels, beginning in 1856, and is darker in tone. As the series begins, Monk is recovering from an attack that has left him with amnesia. As he struggles to regain his memory and identity, and deals with the fact that the person he cannot remember himself being was apparently disliked and disrespected, he continues with his caseload, including a murder investigation. As he essentially reinvestigates the case, he finds himself wondering if his earlier progress had been impeded because he himself is the culprit. The novel is a fascinating portrait of an identity crisis, with deep explorations of what actions are possible. After the disclosure of her juvenile crime, the themes take on an even darker tone as explorations of her own actions and redemption. Perry's answers to questions posed during a 1992 interview about the violence in her novels and whether she believes all humans are capable of killing are quite interesting in retrospect (Clark). Throughout the series, Monk works together with Hester Latterly, a nurse who served in the Crimean War, and a lawyer named Oliver Rathbone. Early in the series, Monk leaves the police force to become a private "enquiry agent," and later in the series, he and Latterly marry.

Her third series is set as World War I begins and features Joseph Reavley, a professor and scholar of Biblical languages, a character based on her maternal grandfather (Menconi 60). Reavley was first featured in an Edgar-winning short story. In the first novel, his parents are killed in a car accident right after Duke Franz Ferdinand is assassinated, but his brother Matthew, who works as a Secret Service agent, is convinced it was not an accident. Along with their sister Judith, the brothers investigate the deaths of their parents and uncover dangerous political intrigue. As the series continues, the siblings are all off at war, Judith as a volunteer driver, Joseph as a chaplain, and Matthew continuing his career as an intelligence agent.

Perry has written a novel or novella for the past few Christmas seasons, which feature minor characters from her series in their own adventures, set during the Christmas season. For example, *A Christmas Visitor* features Rathbone, and *A Christmas Guest* features Charlotte Pitt's grandmother. She has also edited numerous short story anthologies. For example, *Thou Shall Not Kill,* which includes a variety of authors using Bible stories as a frame for their tales, was particularly well received.

CRITICAL RECEPTION

From the start, the Pitt novels have received favorable critical acclaim. A review of *The Cater Street Hangman* praised aspects of Pitt's character and noted that Perry's "steamy climax goes right to the heart of Victorian prudery and repression" (Steinberg 1979:113). The second novel, *Callander Square,* was praised as "lively" and as a "story no mystery fan should miss" (Steinberg 1979:60). *Paragon Walk* was heralded as a "complex thriller" that provides a "searing tour of the self-enclosed world of the very wealthy" (Fletcher 1981:1079). A review of *Bluegate Fields* noted that Perry "excels in recreating the atmosphere of hypocrisy and corruption" of the era (Steinberg 1984:132). One review of *Death in the Devil's Acre* praised the "splendid Victorian London atmosphere" as enhancing Perry's "natural dialogue" and "suspenseful tale" (Fletcher 1985:195). Another reviewer found the dialogue in the novel to be "stilted," but praised how Perry "skillfully evokes the atmosphere of 19th century London and its sharp social contrasts" (Steinberg 1985:417). A review of *Cardington Crescent* stated that Perry "brings the era to life not just by period detail, but with sure-handed characterization and a compelling, timeless plot" (Steinberg 1987:87).

Highgate Rise was noted for one of its secondary characters, thought to be "Perry's most dynamic character to date" (Steinberg 1991:138). A reviewer of *Farrier's Lane* praised Perry for writing "characters [which] are authentically and appealingly drawn, and her plot [which] is sinister, gripping, and intense, with a surprising but satisfying ending" (Melton 1993:1300). A review of *Pentecost Alley* noted that "as Perry edges toward her surprise ending, she crafts her tale with elegance, narrative depth and gratifying scope" (Steinberg 1996:62). In a review of *Bedford Square,* Marilyn Stasio praised Perry for her "generous" nature with "colorful period details about daily life," and noted that she is "even more remarkable at shaping historical events into a piece of fiction that offers both a satisfactory mystery to solve and a grave social injustice to get all worked up about" (1999:28).

The Whitechapel Conspiracy was praised as "a mesmerizing and suspenseful tale, rich in period detail, rife with articulate and believable characters" (Zaleski 2000:73), and *Long Spoon Lane* was noted for how "Perry manages to paint a convincing historical backdrop with echoes of modern-day fears of urban terrorism" (Long 57). *Southampton Row* was particularly praised for Perry's treatment of women characters, noting that Perry's "proto-feminists" are always "shrewd of wit and quick of tongue," as well as possessing the "kind of intellectual radiance that eludes their spouses" (Stasio 2002:25).

The first novel to feature Monk won praise for its "rich, unpredictable plot" and its "pronounced and satisfying psychological dimension" (Steinberg 1990:113). Although criticized for going on too long, *Defend and Betray* won praise for its "historical flavor, characterization and provocative and surprising ending" (Cooper 37). *The Sins of the Wolf* was lauded for a plot that is "taut, compelling and ringing with verisimilitude" (Brainard 36).

Cain His Brother was praised for its "superb plotting, fine writing, intriguing characters, and outstanding historical detail" (Melton 1995:1911). *The Silent Cry* was praised for Perry's ability to "bring a rank sense of reality to the wretched living conditions of the working poor" with her "grimly detailed descriptions" (Stasio 1997:36) and also received notice for its "suspenseful plot filled with quirky twists," and its dramatic courtroom scene (Melton 1997:1776). *The Twisted Root* was noted for "strong characterization" and "a compelling subplot [that] adds emotional depth to the story," which follows Perry's "proven formula [of] a desperate and impassioned effort to save someone who is wrongfully accused" (Bliss 139). Another reviewer praised the novel's as "suffused with period details, many of which focus on the conventions of gender and class that so marked the times," particularly highlighting the "denouement, when the guilty party and the meaning of the title are dramatically unveiled in a packed London courtroom" (Zvirin 1988).

A Breach of Promise "reaffirms" for one reviewer why the "supremely talented Perry [is] a perennial favorite," noting that she "makes Victorian London come brilliantly alive with authentic period details; her plot is stunningly original; and she has a knack for making her characters both real and genuine" (Melton 1998:7). Although recent novels in the Pitt series receive consistently positive reviews, with, for example, *Bedford Square,* the nineteenth in the series, being praised as "fresh as if it were her first effort," later novels in the Monk series have received mixed reviews (Melton 1999:793) A representative example is found in a review that begins by noting that "the strain of publishing two major novels a year continues to show" in her work (Cannon 2004:42). This reviewer also noted that *Death of a Stranger* "offers an ingenious and baffling plot, compelling characters, both major and minor, plus plenty of courtroom drama, but is something of a diamond in the rough" (Cannon 2002:46).

Her new series was welcomed by some critics for its freshness. According to one reviewer, *No Graves as Yet* "marks a powerful start" to the series, providing a "gripping" plot and an "absorbing" thriller (Cannon 2003:59), while in *Shoulder the Sky* "she does a superb job of bringing the grimness and waste to life, in a nice shift of gears from her two 19th-century historical series" (Cannon 2004:41).

Perry's works have also received a great deal of attention from literary scholars. Caren J. Town explores issues of sexuality and desire, particularly representations of homosexuality, in Perry's works about Thomas and Charlotte Pitt. Jennifer S. Tuttle concentrates on the Monk series, exploring Hester Latterly's femininity and masculinity in her roles as war nurse and amateur sleuth. Elizabeth Foxwell also explored the Latterly character in her article, which looks at her work in both roles and how that expresses the roles available to women in their public and private lives. Mary Hadley also examines Perry's works in terms of their portrayal of social injustices.

BIBLIOGRAPHY

Works by Anne Perry

Charlotte and Thomas Pitt Series

The Cater Street Hangman. New York: St. Martin's, 1979.
Callander Square. New York: St. Martin's, 1980.
Paragon Walk. New York: St. Martin's, 1981.
Resurrection Row. New York: St. Martin's, 1982.
Rutland Place. New York: St. Martin's, 1983.
Bluegate Field. New York: St. Martin's, 1984.
Death in the Devil's Acre. New York: St. Martin's, 1985.
Cardington Crescent. New York: St. Martin's, 1987.
Silence in Hanover Close. New York: St. Martin's, 1988.
Bethlehem Road. New York: St. Martin's, 1990.
Highgate Rise. New York: Fawcett Columbine, 1991.
Belgrave Square. New York: Fawcett Columbine, 1992.
Farriers' Lane. New York: Fawcett Columbine, 1993.
The Hyde Park Headsman. New York: Fawcett Columbine, 1994.
Traitors Gate. New York: Fawcett Columbine, 1995.
Pentecost Alley. New York: Fawcett Columbine, 1996.
Ashworth Hall. New York: Fawcett, 1997.
Brunswick Gardens. New York: Fawcett, 1998.
Bedford Square. New York: Ballantine, 1999.
Half Moon Street. New York: Ballantine, 2000.
Southampton Row. New York: Ballantine, 2002.
Seven Dials. New York: Ballantine, 2003.
Long Spoon Lane. New York: Ballantine, 2005.

William Monk and Hester Latterly Series

The Face of a Stranger. New York: Fawcett Columbine, 1990.
A Dangerous Mourning. New York: Fawcett Columbine, 1991.
Defend and Betray. New York: Fawcett Columbine, 1992.
A Sudden, Fearful Death. New York: Fawcett Columbine, 1993.
The Sins of the Wolf. New York: Fawcett Columbine, 1994.
Cain His Brother. New York: Fawcett Columbine, 1995.
Weighed in the Balance. New York: Fawcett Columbine, 1996.
The Silent Cry. New York: Fawcett Columbine, 1997.
A Breach of Promise. New York: Fawcett, 1998.
The Twisted Root. New York: Ballantine, 1999.
Slaves of Obsession. New York: Ballantine, 2000.
Funeral in Blue. New York: Ballantine, 2001.
Death of a Stranger. New York: Ballantine, 2002.
The Shifting Tide. New York: Ballantine, 2004.
Dark Assassin. New York: Ballantine, 2006.

Matthew, Joseph, and Judith Reavley Series

No Graves as Yet: A Novel of World War I. New York: Ballantine, 2003.
Shoulder the Sky. New York: Ballantine, 2004.
Angels in the Gloom. New York: Ballantine, 2005.
At Some Disputed Barricade. New York: Ballantine, 2006.
We Shall Not Sleep. New York: Ballantine, 2007.

Other Fiction

Tathea. Salt Lake City: Shadow Mountain, 1999.
A Dish Taken Cold. London: Caroll & Graf, 2001.
Come Armageddon. New York: Ace, 2003.
A Christmas Journey. New York: Ballantine, 2003.
A Christmas Visitor. New York: Ballantine, 2004.
A Christmas Guest. New York: Ballantine, 2005.

Works about Anne Perry

"Anne Perry." *Contemporary Authors.* New Revision Series, Vol. 84. Ed. Scot Peacock. Detroit: Gale, 2000. 381–83.

Anne Perry. Homepage. 2005. 21 February 2006. http://www.anneperry.net/index.html

Bliss, Laurel. "*The Twisted Root.*" *Library Journal* 1 October 1999: 139.

Brainard, Dulcy. "*The Sins of the Wolf.*" *Publishers Weekly* 25 July 1994: 36.

Callander, Newgate. "Crime." *New York Times Book Review* 23 March 1980: 33.

Cannon, Peter. "*Death of a Stranger.*" *Publishers Weekly* 9 September 2002: 46.

———. "*No Graves as Yet.*" *Publishers Weekly* 30 June 2003: 59.

———. "*The Shifting Tide.*" *Publishers Weekly* 29 March 2004: 42.

———. "*Shoulder the Sky.*" *Publishers Weekly* 26 July 2004: 41.

Clark, Diana Cooper. "Interview with Anne Perry." *Clues* 3.2 (1992): 52–65.

Cooper, Ilene. "*Defend and Betray.*" *Booklist* 1 September 1992: 37.

Fletcher, Connie. "*Paragon Walk.*" *Booklist* 1 April 1981: 1079.

———. "*Death in the Devil's Acre.*" *Booklist* 1 October 1985: 195.

Foxwell, Elizabeth. "Anne Perry's Hester Latterly." *Clues* 22.2 (2001): 63–72.

Hadley, Mary. "Social Injustices in Anne Perry's Victorian England." *Clues* 20.2 (1999): 1–12.

"*Long Spoon Lane.*" *Publishers Weekly* 14 February 2005: 57.

Melton, Emily. "*Farrier's Lane.*" *Booklist* 15 March 1993: 1300.

———. "*Cain His Brother.*" *Booklist* August 1995: 1911.

———. "*The Silent Cry.*" *Booklist* July 1997: 1776.

———. "*A Breach of Promise.*" *Booklist* 1 September 1998: 7.

———. "*Bedford Square.*" *Booklist* 1–15 January 1999: 793.

Menconi, Ralph. "Murder on the Eve of War." *Publishers Weekly* 30 June 2003: 60.

Ott, Bill. "*Half Moon Street.*" *Booklist* 1 February 2000: 997.

Rye, Marilyn. "Anne Perry." *Dictionary of Literary Biography,* Vol. 276: *British Mystery and Thriller Writers Since 1960.* Ed. Gina Macdonald. Detroit: Gale, 2003. 269–83.

Stasio, Marilyn. "Crime." *New York Times Book Review* 19 October 1997: 36.

———. "Crime." *New York Times Book Review* 2 May 1999: 28.

———. "Crime." *New York Times Book Review* 7 April 2002: 25.

Steinberg, Sybil. "*Callendar Square.*" *Publishers Weekly* 10 December 1979: 60.

———. "*The Cater Street Hangman.*" *Publishers Weekly* 25 June 1979: 113.

———. "*Bluegate Fields.*" *Publishers Weekly* 14 September 1984: 132.

———. "*Death in the Devil's Acre.*" *Publishers Weekly* 30 August 1985: 416–7.

———. "*Cardington Crescent.*" *Publishers Weekly* 6 February 1987: 87.

———. "*The Face of a Stranger.*" *Publishers Weekly* 14 September 1990: 113.

———. "*Highgate* Rise." *Publishers Weekly* 5 April 1991: 138.

———. "*Pentecost Alley.*" *Publishers Weekly* 22 January 1996: 62.

Town, Caren J. "'Naked into the World's Gaze': The Dark Secret in Anne Perry's Novels." *Studies in Popular Culture* 27.1 (2004): 45–60.

Tuttle, Jennifer S. "Liminality in Women's 'History-Mystery': The Case of Anne Perry." *Popular Culture Review* 11.1 (2000): 85–97.

Zaleski, Jeff. "*The Whitechapel Conspiracy.*" *Publishers Weekly* 6 November 2000: 73.

Zvirin, Stephanie. "*The Twisted Root.*" *Booklist* August 1999: 1988.

Elizabeth Peters (1927–)

BIOGRAPHY

Barbara Louise Gross was born September 29, 1927, in Canton, Illinois. Her father, Earl D. Gross, was a printer, and her mother, Grace Tregellas Gross, was a teacher. During elementary school, the family moved to a suburb of Chicago. She was an avid reader as a child and began writing during high school.

She earned a bachelor's degree in history from the University of Chicago in 1947. She had been encouraged to train as a teacher, but she has stated that she did not enjoy the education courses she took. She wanted to be an archaeologist and continued her education at Chicago, also earning a master's degree in 1950 and her Ph.D. in 1952. She married Richard R. Mertz in 1950 and had two children, Elizabeth Ellen and Peter William; they were divorced in 1969.

She found that academic positions for women in Egyptology were rare in the 1950s, and she focused on her family. They lived in Germany for several years in the 1960s, and she began focusing on her writing during that time. While trying to break into the fiction publishing world, she wrote two books about Egypt and archeology, which were published under her real name. She has noted that her degree "had finally paid off in a way [she] never expected" (MPM). The books have remained in print and were re-released in new editions in 1990. She serves on the editorial advisory board of *KMT: A Modern Journal of Ancient Egypt* and on the Board of Governors of the American Research Center in Egypt.

She lives near Frederick, Maryland.

MAJOR WORKS AND THEMES

Her first mystery novel was published in 1966 under the Barbara Michaels pseudonym. Under the Michaels name, she publishes novels of romantic suspense, many of which have a supernatural element. These are mostly stand-alone novels, but there are three Michaels works that all involve the same house: *Ammie, Come Home; Shattered Silk;* and *Stitches in Time.* The latter two also have recurring characters. The first novels by Michaels were reminiscent of writers like Phyllis A. Whitney or Victoria Holt; Mertz herself calls those works "derivative" (Rose). Dean James points out that while the first novel was "conventional," Michaels "very quickly began experimenting with the form," bringing "subversive notions" to her "outwardly conventional gothics" (25). Elizabeth Foxwell also argues that Michaels's novels have become more complex over the years, using the supernatural elements to "emphasize that the past is always with us" (1996: 332). Foxwell noted that Michaels "firmly ties the past to present, showing how individuals can learn from the past to reshape the present and redirect their futures" (1996:333).

As Elizabeth Peters, Mertz has published three series, along with stand-alone mysteries. The longest-running series features Amelia Peabody, an archaeologist. The series begins in 1884, as Peabody travels to Egypt and is drawn into helping solve a mystery. As the series progresses, she marries fellow archaeologist Radcliffe Emerson and they have a "frighteningly precocious" son named Walter, whose nickname is Ramses (Mussell 837). The plots of the novels often connect to historical events, with a number taking place during World War I.

Also writing as Barbara Michaels

Peabody and Emerson work together to save the "treasures of Egypt form the depredations of vandals and grave robbers" (Mussell 837).

Another series features Vicki Bliss, an American art historian who lives and works in Germany. Bliss becomes involved in various cases involving art theft or fraud, and she often travels throughout Europe to seek clues to the mysteries. The series also features the problematic relationship Bliss has with Sir John Smythe, who is an art thief.

The third series features Jacqueline Kirby, a librarian who gets involved in crime-solving. During the series, Kirby becomes a successful romance novelist, and continues as an amateur sleuth. *Die for Love* takes place at a romance fiction convention, where Kirby gets her book contract and solves a crime, giving Peters a chance to satirize the publishing industry, conventions, and writers.

CRITICAL RECEPTION

Her works have been nominated for all major awards. She won an Agatha Award in 1989 and has also received two awards for her body of work, the Grand Master Award from the Mystery Writers of America, and the Malice Domestic Lifetime Achievement Award. The Malice Domestic award not only recognized her for her writing but also for her key role in the founding of the convention (Foxwell 2001:26). Critical reception has been consistently solid.

A review of 1972's *Greengallows* praised Michaels's work as having a "few new twists" that raised it above the typical Gothic novel (Greygallows 73). In *Shattered Silk,* she was commended for how she "cleverly manipulates motive and suspects while contriving equally delightful twists to the romantic subplot;" the reviewer called it an "engaging suspense tale imbued with believable emotions and actions" (Donavin 1986:1634). Another reviewer found the novel to have "engrossing" descriptions and praised Michaels for "adroitly keep[ing] the suspense mounting until the surprising, action-filled conclusion" (Steinberg 1986:70). *Search the Shadows* was praised for being "packed with archaeological details" and having suspense that "lingers until the final pages" (Donavin 1987:1718). *Houses of Stone* was heralded as "one of her best," with a plot that is "brimming with suspense" (Donavin 1993:418). Another reviewer found the novel to start well, "with vivid descriptive writing and convincing dialogue," but to "falter" at the end (Steinberg 1993:62).

Reviews of the Bliss and Kirby novels have also been positive. *The Street of the Five Moons* was noted for its "snappy dialogue, a touch of romance and well-paced action and suspense [that] add up to a winning combination" (1325). *Trojan Gold* was called a "delectable blend of humor, romance and suspense" by one reviewer (Flanagan 1252), while another found that "the author's clever mix of frights, comedy and sexy doings makes this another of her can't-fail diversions" (Steinberg 1987:70). *Night Train to Memphis* was complimented for its "clever plot," "exotic setting," and use of humor (Melton 1992). Another reviewer praised it as a "quirky, light-hearted novel" (Brainard 1994:89). *The Murders of Richard III* was called "lively, often whimsical" and was noted for its appeal to "both English history and Gothic enthusiasts"(93). Another reviewer commended the "nice touches of humor throughout" and noted that Kirby "turns detective and comes up with a most ingenious answer just in time to stop a 20th century killing" (73). Peters was acclaimed for "satiriz[ing] both the mystery and romance genres while displaying perfect mastery of each" in a review of *Die for Love* (1009). *Naked Once More* was praised not only for its mystery elements but for its success as a "wonderfully comic moral fable about an author's life" (Donavin 1989:1850).

One review of the first Amelia Peabody novel called it "romantic suspense with the flavor of a nineteenth-century personal narrative," with praise for its "well-realized setting and archaeological detail [that] add to a delightful story" (Crocodile 908); the *Publishers Weekly* reviewer found it to show Peters "at her best in this exciting, romantic and unusual novel" ("*Crocodile on the Sandbank*" 72). With *The Mummy Case* Peters was seen to "score again with a riotously witty, tense and cunningly constructed tale" ("*The Mummy Case*" 64). Another reviewer found the novel to be a "witty mystery featuring fast-paced action in a romantic setting" (Fletcher 1984:530). *Lion in the Valley* was praised as a "captivating entry in the witty series" ("*Lion*" 1118). In a review of *The Last Camel Died at Noon*, Peabody was named as an "immensely likable heroine" noted for "combining a fierce affection for her family with indefatigable independence" (Steinberg 1991:91).

In *The Ape Who Guards the Balance,* Peters presented "a lively assortment of characters" and "plenty of period flavor," as well as "poking great fun at the social conventions of the early 1900s" and "incorporat[ing] some terrific action and a nice bit of romantic tension" (Zvirin 1988:1670). Another reviewer referred to Peters's winning the Mystery Writers of America Grand Master Award, and proclaimed that this novel "validates her peers' high regard" (Brainard 1998:49). A review of *The Falcon at the Portal* praised Peters for doing "an admirable job of keeping its many subplots in balance" and for her "dialogue and rapid pacing [which] make for high suspense," concluding that "Peters has never written with more assurance or passion than she does in this latest chronicle of a superb series" (Zaleski 1999:69). Another reviewer found that "details of the dig hold attention as always, but it's the way Peters mines the previous books for personal history that makes this adventure such a standout" (Cooper 1484). *He Shall Thunder in the Sky* was called "the latest superb installment in this renowned series ... one of Peters's best" (Zaleski 2000:53). The reviewer also praised the novel as "a deeply satisfying story that combines elements of espionage, mystery and romance" (Zaleski 2000:53). Another reviewer also praised the work, particularly noting how Peters "works in drama galore, plus the usual shots of wry humor and local color" (Zvirin 2000:1623).

Reviews of recent books in the series show that Peters has not lost her touch. One review noted that "a fast-moving, intrigue-filled plot propels" *The Children of the Storm* (Cannon 2003:57), while a review of *The Guardian on the Horizon* praised her expertise in Egyptology and the "authentic trappings that add greatly to the enjoyment" and noted that the book, the 16th in the series, has "particular appeal for fans" (Cannon 2004:54). The *Publishers Weekly* review of *The Serpent on the Crown* commended Peters for keeping the plot "hopping," and her "droll sense of humor and picture of a leisurely and less complicated age add to the appeal" (53). Their review of *The Tomb of the Golden Bird* summed up that "once again Peters delivers an irresistible mix of archeology, action, humor and a mystery that only the redoubtable Amelia can solve" (64–65).

BIBLIOGRAPHY

Works by Elizabeth Peters

Amelia Peabody Series

Crocodile on the Sandbank. New York: Dodd, 1975.
The Curse of the Pharaohs. New York: Dodd, 1981.
The Mummy Case. New York: Congdon & Weed, 1985.
Lion in the Valley. New York: Atheneum, 1986.
Deeds of the Disturber. New York: Atheneum, 1988.

The Last Camel Died at Noon. New York: Warner Books, 1991.
The Snake, the Crocodile, and the Dog. New York: Warner Books, 1992.
The Hippopotamus Pool. New York: Warner Books, 1996.
Seeing a Large Cat. New York: Warner Books, 1997.
The Ape Who Guards the Balance. New York: Avon, 1998.
The Falcon at the Portal. New York: Avon, 1999.
He Shall Thunder in the Sky. New York: Avon, 2000.
Lord of the Silent. New York: Morrow, 2001.
The Golden One. New York: Morrow, 2002.
Children of the Storm. New York: Morrow, 2003.
With Kristen Whitbread. Amelia Peabody's Egypt: A Compendium to Her Journals. New York: Morrow, 2003.
Guardian of the Horizon. New York: Morrow, 2004.
The Serpent on the Crown. New York: Morrow, 2005.
The Tomb of the Golden Bird. New York: Morrow, 2006.

Jacqueline Kirby Series

The Seventh Sinner. New York: Dodd, 1972.
The Murders of Richard III. New York: Dodd, 1974.
Die for Love. New York: Congdon & Weed, 1984.
Naked Once More. New York: Warner Books, 1989.

Vicki Bliss Series

The Camelot Caper. New York: Meredith Press, 1969.
Borrower of the Night. New York: Dodd, 1973.
Street of the Five Moons. New York: Dodd, 1978.
Silhouette in Scarlet. New York: Congdon & Weed, 1983.
Trojan Gold. New York: Atheneum, 1987.
Night Train to Memphis. New York: Warner Books, 1994.

Other Mystery Fiction

The Jackal's Head. New York: Meredith Press, 1968.
The Dead Sea Cipher. New York: Dodd, 1970.
The Night of 400 Rabbits. New York: Dodd, 1971. (Also published as *Shadows in the Moonlight*. London: Coronet, 1975.)
Legend in Green Velvet. New York: Dodd, 1976. (Also published as *Ghost in Green Velvet*. London: Cassell, 1977.)
Devil-May-Care. New York: Dodd, 1977.
Summer of the Dragon. New York: Dodd, 1979.
The Love Talker. New York: Dodd, 1980.
The Copenhagen Connection. New York: Congdon & Lattes, 1982.

Works by Barbara Michaels

The Master of Blacktower. New York: Appleton, 1966.
Sons of the Wolf. New York: Meredith Press, 1967. (Also published as *Mystery on the Moors*. New York: Paperback Library, 1968.)
Ammie, Come Home. New York: Meredith Press, 1968.
Prince of Darkness. New York: Meredith Press, 1969.
Dark on the Other Side. New York: Dodd, 1970.
The Crying Child. New York: Dodd, 1971.
Greygallows. New York: Dodd, 1972.
Witch. New York: Dodd, 1973.

House of Many Shadows. New York: Dodd, 1974.
The Sea King's Daughter. New York: Dodd, 1975.
Patriot's Dream. New York: Dodd, 1976.
Wings of the Falcon. New York: Dodd, 1977.
Wait for What Will Come. New York: Dodd, 1978.
The Walker in the Shadows. New York: Dodd, 1979.
The Wizard's Daughter. New York: Dodd, 1980.
Someone in the House. New York: Dodd, 1981.
Black Rainbow. New York: Congdon & Weed, 1982.
Here I Stay. New York: Congdon & Weed, 1983.
Dark Duet. New York: Congdon & Weed, 1983.
The Grey Beginning. New York: Congdon & Weed, 1984.
Be Buried in the Rain. New York: Atheneum, 1985.
Shattered Silk. New York: Atheneum, 1986.
Search the Shadows. New York: Atheneum, 1987.
Smoke and Mirrors. New York: Simon & Schuster, 1989.
Into the Darkness. New York: Simon & Schuster, 1990.
Vanish with the Rose. New York: Simon & Schuster, 1992.
Houses of Stone. New York: Simon & Schuster, 1993.
Stitches in Time. New York: HarperCollins, 1995.
The Dancing Floor. New York: HarperCollins, 1997.
Other Worlds. New York: HarperCollins, 1999.

Nonfiction Works

Mertz, Barbara. *Temples, Tombs, and Hieroglyphs: The Story of Egyptology.* New York: Coward, 1964.
   (Revised edition: New York: Peter Bedrick, 1990.)
Mertz, Barbara. *Red Land, Black Land: The World of the Ancient Egyptians.* New York: Coward, 1966.
   (Revised edition: New York: Peter Bedrick, 1990.)
Mertz, Barbara and Richard R. Mertz. *Two Thousand Years in Rome.* New York: Coward, 1968.

Works about Elizabeth Peters/Barbara Michaels

"Barbara Gross Mertz." *Contemporary Authors. New Revision Series*, Vol. 135. Ed. Tracey L. Matthews.
   Detroit: Gale, 2005. 277–82.
Brainard, Dulcy. "*The Ape Who Guards the Balance.*" *Publishers Weekly* 8 June 1998: 49.
Cannon, Peter. "*Children of the Storm.*" *Publishers Weekly* 3 March 2003: 57.
———. "*Guardian of the Horizon.*" *Publishers Weekly* 1 March 2004: 54.
Cooper, Ilene. "*The Falcon at the Portal.*" *Booklist* 15 April 1999: 1484.
"*Crocodile on the Sandbank.*" *Booklist* 1 May 1975: 908.
"*Crocodile on the Sandbank.*" *Publishers Weekly* 17 February 1975: 72.
"*Die for Love.*" *Booklist* 15 March 1984: 1009.
Donavin, Denise Perry. "*Shattered Silk.*" *Booklist* August 1986: 1634.
———. "*Search the Shadows.*" *Booklist* August 1987: 1718.
———. "*Naked Once More.*" *Booklist* July 1989: 1850.
———. "*Houses of Stone.*" *Booklist* 15 October 1993: 418.
Flanagan, Margaret. "*Trojan Gold.*" *Booklist* 15 April 1987: 1252.
Fletcher, Connie. "*The Mummy Case.*" *Booklist* 15 December 1984: 530.
Foxwell, Elizabeth. "Novels of Many Shadows: The Messages of Barbara Michaels." *The Armchair Detective* 29.3 (1996): 330–33.
———. "With Malice Aforethought: Barbara Mertz and the Birth of a Mystery Convention." *Mystery Scene* 71 (2001): 26+.
"*Greygallows.*" *Publishers Weekly* 21 August 1972: 73.
James, Dean. "The Gothic World of Barbara Michaels." *Mystery Scene* 71 (2001): 24–26.

"*Lion in the Valley.*" *Booklist* 1 April 1986: 1118.

Melton, Emily. "*Night Train to Memphis.*" *Booklist* August 1994: 1992.

MPM: Barbara Mertz / Elizabeth Peters / Barbara Michaels. Biography: In Her Own Words. n.d. 12 March 2006. http://www.mpmbooks.com/MPMBIO.HTM

"*The Mummy Case.*" *Publishers Weekly* 18 January 1985: 64.

"*The Murders of Richard III.*" *Booklist* 15 September 1974: 93.

"*The Murders of Richard III.*" *Publishers Weekly* 22 April 1974: 73.

Mussell, Kay. "Elizabeth Peters." *St. James Guide to Crime & Mystery Writers.* 4th ed. Ed. Jay P. Pederson. Detroit: St. James Press, 1996. 835–37.

Rose, Mark. "Queen of the Novel." *Archaeology* 58.2 (2005). 12 March 2006. http://www.archaeology.org/0503/abstracts/mertz.html

"*The Serpent on the Crown.*" *Publishers Weekly* 7 March 2005: 53.

Steinberg, Sybil. "*Shattered Silk.*" *Publishers Weekly* 1 August 1986: 70.

———. "*Trojan Gold.*" *Publishers Weekly* 20 March 1987: 70.

———. "*The Last Camel Died at Noon.*" *Publishers Weekly* 28 June 1991: 90–91.

———. "*Houses of Stone.*" *Publishers Weekly* 20 September 1993: 62.

"*Street of the Five Moons.*" *Booklist* 15 April 1978: 1325.

Swanson, Jean. "PW Talks with Elizabeth Peters." *Publishers Weekly* 23 April 2001: 53.

"*Tomb of the Golden Bird.*" *Publishers Weekly* 13 February 2006: 64–65.

Zaleski, Jeff. "*The Falcon at the Portal.*" *Publishers Weekly* 3 May 1999: 69.

———. "*He Shall Thunder in the Sky.*" *Publishers Weekly* 1 May 2000: 53.

Zvirin, Stephanie. "*The Ape Who Guards the Balance.*" *Booklist* 1–15 June 1998: 1670.

———. "*He Shall Thunder in the Sky.*" *Booklist* 1 May 2000: 1623.

Nancy Pickard (1945–)

BIOGRAPHY

Nancy Pickard was born September 19, 1945, in Kansas City, Missouri, to Clint and Mary Wolfe. She studied journalism at the University of Missouri, earning her bachelor's degree in 1967. She was married to Guy Pickard in 1976. They have one son and are divorced. She lives in Prairie Village, Kansas.

Before turning to fiction writing, she worked as a reporter in Overland Park, Kansas, and also worked as a technical writer. She also spent 15 years as a freelance writer before trying her hand at mystery fiction (Shindler 48).

As one interviewer noted, Pickard "stays out of the limelight" (McBride), although she did disclose to another interviewer that she "loves dogs, chocolate and popcorn," and owes everything to her mother, stating that without her, she would not have been a reader, and without that, she could not have been a writer (Randisi 44).

MAJOR WORKS AND THEMES

Her first series features Jenny Cain, who works as the director of a civic foundation in a fictional New England town, Port Frederick, Massachusetts. Cain becomes involved in a number of cases as an amateur sleuth, which brings her into contact with the local police detective, Geof Bushfield, whom she eventually marries. The novels feature humor, but some of the themes are serious, such as when Cain uncovers a funeral home scam or gets involved with domestic violence cases.

She writes two other series, as well. One features true crime writer Marie Lightfoot, whose own writings are interspersed with the narratives. Lightfoot becomes involved in several cases that connect to her research, and she also has mysteries in her personal life to solve. Her parents died when she was young, and in the third novel, she searches for the truth about them and their deaths.

The third series is actually a continuation of an earlier series by another author, Virginia Rich. Before her death in 1984, Rich had begun outlining *The 27-Ingredient Chili Con Carne Murder*, and Pickard was chosen to take on the project in 1993 (Nancy 312). On her homepage, Pickard relates that she had written Rich a fan letter in 1983. Pickard has also written two more novels in the series, which features Eugenia Potter, a 64-year-old rancher and retired chef who lives in Arizona and finds herself involved in various mysteries.

Her most recent work is a stand-alone novel about a long unsolved murder of an unidentified woman in a small community in Kansas. When a young man who left town at the time of the murder returns, questions about the past resurface.

CRITICAL RECEPTION

Pickard has won numerous awards for her short stories and novels; her novels have won an Anthony, two Macavity and two Agatha awards. She has been nominated for Edgar awards several times and was also a finalist for the Mary Higgins Clark Award.

Generous Death, reviewed on its re-release in hardcover in 1992, was noted for a combination of "fast-paced action, appealing characters, suspenseful plot, and clever dialogue" (Melton 1992:718). *No Body* was acclaimed as "fast-moving, sparked by humor and an unusual plot" (Steinberg 1986:72). *Marriage Is Murder* was kept "moving at a fast clip" by an "energetic array of friends and co-workers" and a "fine mix of romance, violence and sleuthing" (Steinberg 1987:87). A review of *Bum Steer* praised Cain as an "appealing detective" who "displays warmth, intelligence and a social conscious" (Steinberg 1990:49).

One reviewer found *I.O.U.* to be a "brave and downright uneasy" turn into darker subject matter, with Pickard "wad[ing] through swamplike emotional backwaters with sure-footed precision," avoiding becoming melodramatic (Robertson 1179). The novel won Agatha and Macavity awards. *But I Wouldn't Want to Die There* was commended as "a pleasure from start to finish" (Brainard 1993:65) and as "thoroughly entertaining" (Melton 1993:1919). A review of *Confession* noted that Pickard "just gets better and better" (Melton 1994:1645); *Twilight* gained notice for the "telling observations on love and marriage, family and friendships, and small-town politics" that "add texture to this well-wrought puzzle" (Brainard 1995:53).

The Whole Truth was nominated for four major mystery awards, and the series has won critical praise. One reviewer highlighted "the frightening climax to this stunning synthesis of psychological suspense and commentary on our culture of celebrity" (Zaleski 84). In *Ring of Truth,* Pickard is praised for "construct[ing] an intricate, perfectly timed double mystery. The dastardly plot she reveals at last is satisfyingly grotesque, and Lightfoot is a down-to-earth heroine, plagued with all the convincing problems of a real-life writer" (Cannon 2001:62). In a review of *The Truth Hurts,* Pickard is noted to "succeed with the daring Marie Lightfoot, attractive secondary characters, vivid Florida setting, a keen sense of history and a singular plot device" (Cannon 2002:43).

BIBLIOGRAPHY

Works by Nancy Pickard

Jenny Cain Series

Generous Death. New York: Avon 1984.
Say No to Murder. New York: Avon, 1985.
No Body. New York: Scribner, 1986.
Marriage Is Murder. New York: Scribner, 1987.
Dead Crazy. New York: Scribner, 1988.
Bum Steer. New York: Pocket, 1990.
I.O.U. New York: Pocket, 1991.
But I Wouldn't Want to Die There. New York: Pocket, 1993.
Confession. New York: Pocket, 1994.
Twilight. New York: Pocket, 1995.

Marie Lightfoot Series

The Whole Truth. New York: Atria, 2000.
Ring of Truth. New York: Atria, 2001.
The Truth Hurts. New York: Atria, 2002.

Eugenia Potter Series

The 27-Ingredient Chili Con Carne Murders. New York: Delacorte, 1993.
The Blue Corn Murders. New York: Delacorte, 1998.
The Secret Ingredient Murders. New York: Delacorte, 2001.

Other Fiction

The Virgin of Small Plains. New York: Ballantine, 2006.

Nonfiction

With Lynn Lott. *Seven Steps on the Writer's Path.* New York: Ballantine, 2003.

Works about Nancy Pickard

Brainard, Dulcy. "*But I Wouldn't Want to Die There.*" *Publishers Weekly* 5 July 1993: 65.
————. "*Twilight.*" *Publishers Weekly* 4 September 1995: 53.
Cannon, Peter. "*Ring of Truth.*" *Publishers Weekly* 4 June 2001: 61–2.
————. "*The Truth Hurts.*" *Publishers Weekly* 24 June 2002: 43.
McBride, Susan. "Nothing But the Truth: An Interview with Nancy Pickard." Between the Pages. July 2001. 1 March 2006. http://www.myshelf.com/betweenthepages/01/pickard.html
Melton, Emily. "*Generous Death.*" *Booklist* 15 December 1992: 718.
————. "*But I Wouldn't Want to Die There.*" *Booklist* July 1993: 1918–19.
————. "*Confession.*" *Booklist* 15 May 1994: 1645.
"Nancy Pickard." *Contemporary Authors.* Vol. 153. Eds. Terrie M. Rooney ad Jennifer Gariepy. Detroit: Gale, 1997. 311–12.
Randisi, Robert. "Nancy Pickard." *Mystery Scene* 57 (1997): 41–44.
Robertson, Peter. "*I.O.U.*" *Booklist* 15 February 1991: 1179.
Shindler, Dorman T. "The Third Stage of Evolution." *Publishers Weekly* 5 August 2002: 48–49.
Steinberg, Sybil. "*No Body.*" *Publishers Weekly* 15 August 1986: 72.
————. "*Marriage Is Murder.*" *Publishers Weekly* 11 August 1987: 87.
————. "*Bum Steer.*" *Publishers Weekly* 12 January 1990: 49.

Wallace, Marilyn. "Nancy Pickard." *St. James Guide to Crime & Mystery Writers*. 4th ed. Ed. Jay P. Pederson. Detroit: St. James Press, 1996. 842–43.

Zaleski, Jeff. "*The Whole Truth*." *Publishers Weekly* 31 January 2000: 84.

Ruth Rendell (1930–)

BIOGRAPHY

Born Ruth Barbara Graseman in London on February 17, 1930, she was the only child of Arthur and Elba Kruse Graseman. Her parents were both teachers. Rendell does not speak of her childhood frequently but has occasionally alluded to it being unhappy. Her mother suffered from multiple sclerosis in a time when little was known of the disease (DuBose 364). Rendell was an avid reader and began writing at a young age, completing a novel in verse at age 15 (Reynolds 111).

After graduating from Loughton County High School in 1948, she worked at local newspapers. In 1950, she married a fellow journalist, Donald Rendell, and later left the newspaper to care for their son Simon. She preferred fiction to journalism and turned her focus to publishing short stories. After a period of drought, she broke into the market with a mystery novel that she had written "for fun" (Reynolds 112).

Rendell and her husband were divorced in 1975 but remarried in 1977, staying together until his death from cancer in 1999. Their son is a psychiatric social worker, and he lives in the United States. Rendell was named Commander of the British Empire in 1996 and also was given a life peerage in the House of Lords, where she sits as Baroness Rendell of Babergh. She lives in London.

MAJOR WORKS AND THEMES

Rendell is a prolific writer, with almost 60 books to her credit as of 2006. Under the Rendell name, she has written a number of stand-alone mystery novels, as well as a long-running series featuring a police detective named Reginald Wexford. In 1986, she also began publishing under the name Barbara Vine, which is a combination of her middle name and her grandmother's family name. The pseudonym was never intended to hide her identity. She has noted that the subject matter of *A Dark Adapted Eye* led to the need to set it in the past, and she wanted to let her readers "know that it was going to be different than anything [she] had written before" (Robertson 1992:126). The Vine novels tend to feature historical settings and often have supernatural elements that make them quite different than the realistic, contemporary Rendell mysteries.

Jane S. Bakerman discussed Rendell's use of "skillful and individualistic" approaches to questions of life and fate, while noting that although "her plots stem from violence, Rendell never substitutes blood or sensationalism for development" (1981:127–28). Her strength in character development was explored by Bakerman as well; she quotes Rendell herself talking about the importance of it, noting that what she is "really interested in" is the study

Also writing as Barbara Vine

of the people and the pressures put upon them that can "drive them to murder" (1981:128). Character development is often noted as Rendell's key strength.

The Wexford series has 20 entries in it as of 2006, although it was unclear whether it would ever reach such a quantity. Even before 1992, Rendell had begun warning people that there would be no more Wexford books. In response to a question of why there had been a four-year gap between *The Veiled One* and *Kissing the Gunner's Daughter,* Rendell replied that she had not "meant to write [*Kissing the Gunner's Daughter*], but [she] had an idea for it," adding that she was "not really planning on" having any further ideas for other Wexford books (Robertson 1992:126). Since 1992, though, Rendell has published five more in the series, and in 2002, in answer to the question about Wexford's future, she replied that the one she was then writing "may be the last, and it may not" (Anable 275). Three of those, *Simisola, Road Rage,* and *Harm Done,* have gained great notice as comprising her first "political" Wexford novels, with their treatment of racism, domestic violence, environmentalism and other social issues that she had not dealt with as directly in previous works (Rowland 193).

The series features not only Reginald Wexford, but also his wife and daughters and his police partner Mike Burden. Bakerman commented on the strong relationship between Wexford and his wife Dora, noting that his "personal family is as interesting as his professional crew" (1981:141). Throughout the series, Rendell traces Wexford's family as his daughters grow up and also Wexford's career as he solves a variety of cases. Wexford and Burden are a study in contrasts as well, with their differences in age, background, and politics.

Rendell has also published a number of novels that do not deal with Wexford. In these, the focus shifts away from a crime-solving team to the characters who are involved in various problems. A recent novel, *Adam and Eve and Pinch Me,* Rendell "manages to blend the titillation of political scandal with the suspense of a ghost story" (Gabilondo 329). Readers meet a con man with three different names who victimizes three different women, a single mother in the working-class, a professional woman, and a mentally ill woman who works in a laundry. He fakes his death and Rendell studies the effects of that on the women, as well as a subsequent murder.

The Vine novels are in the suspense genre and cover a wide array of topics and settings. The first, *A Dark-Adapted Eye,* deals with the attempts of a young woman to find out the truth about her sister's murder when they were children. Her aunt was accused of the crime. *The Chimney Sweeper's Boy* follows the aftermath of the death of a famous author. One of his daughters begins work on a biography of her famous father, only to learn that he had assumed his identity years before. *The Blood Doctor* depicts a man who is looking into his family's past. His great-grandfather was a doctor who researched hemophilia, particularly in the royal family during Victorian times. During his research, he uncovers a terrible secret about his family. Rendell has noted that the Vine novels allow her to pursue one of her particular interests in writing, exploring "guilt and the fictional process of moving back and forward in time" (Gabilondo 332).

CRITICAL RECEPTION

Rendell has won numerous awards and nominations for her writing, and she has achieved two major lifetime achievement awards, the Crime Writers Association Diamond Dagger and the Mystery Writers of America Grand Master award.

Praise for the Wexford series has been consistent throughout the years. A review of *From Doon with Death* noted that the novel featured "meticulous detective work" that uncovers the truth behind the murder (From 95). A review of the second novel referred to the first Wexford book as "excellent" and noted that in *A New Lease on Death* Rendell "stirs up a fascinating little brew of nastiness" and praised Rendell for her "excellent delineation of the characters" and sustained suspense (Bannon 1967:75). Anthony Boucher also reviewed *A New Lease on Death*. He wrote that he hoped readers who enjoy British mysteries had discovered Rendell, and called the novel "her best yet" with its "strong characters, clever use of British law, nice observation of middle aged passion and admirable plotting" (Boucher 18).

A Speaker of Mandarin was lauded as "an intricate and tantalizing case with a number of unexpected twists" (Bannon 1983:56), while *An Unkindness of Ravens* was called "an elegant, leisurely police procedural" and "a brilliant tapestry of motive and modus operandi"(Fletcher 1985:1475). Another review noted that Rendell is "renowned for her remarkably literate novels," and that *An Unkindness of Ravens* was deemed to be "arguably her best" (Steinberg 1985:58). The reviewer also stated that "the reader can only marvel at Rendell's artistry and sharp perceptions of human nature that inform this outstanding work" (Steinberg 1985:58). This novel was not universally praised, though. As Patricia A. Gabilondo noted, a review of the novel in *Ms* called Rendell "the biggest anti-feminist there is," and scholar Sally R. Munt has called it Rendell's most feminist text, although she critiques Rendell for her hostility against the feminist movement (324).

Kissing the Gunner's Daughter was noted for its graphic opening scene and for being more than just a novel of solving a crime, with Rendell providing a "morbid reflection on the fragility of flesh and of the social structures that we build to disguise our mortality" (Kimberley 41). Another reviewer called this Wexford novel a "superbly characterized, deftly plotted puzzler that explores the dark side of family life" (Brainard 1992:62). *Simisola* was praised for its "freshness," with the reviewer remarking that her "long acquaintance with her characters" has not diminished it or her "consummate storytelling" (Knight 30). *Road Rage* was heralded for Rendell's "eloquent" portrayal of the "natural environment and its threatened life-forms" (Stasio 34). *Harm Done* showed Rendell's skills as a storyteller and "experienced entertainer" who "cannot fail to keep her audiences engrossed," even in this novel, which goes beyond a typical murder mystery to "evoking one kind of abuse after another," with a detailed accounting of the plight of the poor and the effects of abuse (Craig 1999:21).

Along with the Wexford novels, Rendell has earned praise for her stand-alone fiction. *Live Flesh* was noted for being a "subtly told tale [that] builds to a devastating climax" (Fletcher 1986:1634) and was also praised as an "original and mesmerizing novel," that features Rendell's "penetrating insights" into her characters (Steinberg 1986:53). One reviewer found faults with both *The Veiled One* and *The Bridesmaid*, noting that the plots were "mechanically contrived" (Waugh 1988:40) and stretching too much (Waugh 1989:31), although both were praised overall, as "an extremely pleasant way of passing a day" (Waugh 1988:40) and as being so "gripping" the reader would be "unlikely to put it down" (Waugh 1989:31). Another reviewer called *The Bridesmaid* "characteristically stringent and ingenious" (Craig 1989:39). In *The Copper Peacock and Other Stories*, Rendell is praised for a collection of "crisp and intriguing" stories that take risks that "pay off" in their "effect on our imagination" (Craig 1991:19). Another reviewer noted that the collection "delights with its fine-tuned psychological effects," with Rendell's "signature" being "the malevolence of the day-to-day, shot through with currents of wit and whimsy" (Steinberg 1991:49).

The Vine novels have also received consistent praise, although reviews of her recent novels have been increasingly mixed. *Grasshopper* was praised as "another of her intriguing, multifaceted psychological suspense novels" (Steinberg 2000:50). One reviewer of *The*

Blood Doctor called it a "rich, labyrinthine book" with vivid characters who are "at once repellent and compelling" (Cannon 2002:43). A review of *The Minotaur* noted that it was "less elegantly written than" her previous novel, but that it "delivers a more palpable, and thus satisfying, crime" ("*The Minotaur*" 40).

Many scholars and critics have explored Rendell's works. Among them are Nicola King, who studied Rendell, Margaret Atwood, Toni Morrison and others in her work *Memory, Narrative, Identity: Remembering the Self*. In one chapter, King compared two of Rendell's works published as Vine, exploring the use of memory within psychological fiction. Susan Rowland has done an extensive comparison of Rendell, P. D. James, Agatha Christie, Dorothy L. Sayers, Ngaio Marsh, and Margery Allingham. Rowland explores various themes, such as class, race, and gender, as well as psychological aspects and elements of the gothic, with illustrative examples from works by all six women.

Other scholars have touched on a wide range of topics, including the representation of China in Rendell and another mystery writer, Dorothy Gilman. Tony Giffone applies Edward Said's theories of Orientalism in a critique of *A Speaker of Mandarin*. Lidia Kyzlinkova also examines Rendell's portrayal of class and ethnicity in several novels that do not feature Wexford, namely *A Demon in My View, A Fatal Inversion,* and *The Crocodile Bird*.

Barbara Fass Leavy explores the use of folkloric plots and motifs in *Some Lie and Some Die*. In 1978, Bakerman published an essay about the first six Wexford novels, outlining the role of love in the plots, including friendship, sexual love, and familial love. Thomas M. Leitch uses critical works by Julian Symons in offering a study of whether Rendell's works illustrate a subversion of the classic mystery formula.

Several of Rendell's novels have been made into films, including those by directors Pedro Almodovar, Claude Chabrol, and Claude Miller. A number of scholars have contributed to the literature studies of those films and also comparative works dealing with the formats and adaptations of Rendell's writings.

BIBLIOGRAPHY

Books by Ruth Rendell

Reginald Wexford Series

From Doon with Death. London: John Long, 1964; Garden City: Doubleday, 1965.

Wolf to the Slaughter. London: John Long, 1967; Garden City, Doubleday, 1968.

A New Lease of Death. Garden City: Doubleday, 1967. Republished as *Sins of the Fathers*. New York: Ballantine, 1970.

The Best Man to Die. London: John Long, 1969; Garden City: Doubleday, 1970.

A Guilty Thing Surprised. London: Hutchinson; Garden City: Doubleday, 1970.

No More Dying Then. London: Hutchinson, 1971; Garden City: Doubleday, 1972.

Murder Being Once Done. London: Hutchinson; Garden City: Doubleday, 1972.

Some Lie and Some Die. London: Hutchinson; Garden City: Doubleday, 1973.

Shake Hands Forever. London: Hutchinson; Garden City: Doubleday, 1975.

A Sleeping Life. London: Hutchinson; Garden City: Doubleday, 1978.

Means of Evil. London: Hutchinson, 1979; Garden City: Doubleday, 1980.

Put On by Cunning. London: Hutchinson, 1981. Also published as *Death Notes*. New York: Pantheon, 1981.

The Speaker of Mandarin. London: Hutchinson; New York: Pantheon, 1983.

An Unkindness of Ravens. London: Hutchinson; New York: Pantheon, 1985.

The Veiled One. London: Hutchinson; New York: Pantheon, 1988.

Kissing the Gunner's Daughter. London: Hutchinson; New York: Mysterious Press, 1992.
Simisola. London: Hutchinson, 1994; New York: Random House, 1995.
Road Rage. New York: Crown, 1997.
Harm Done. New York: Crown, 1999.
The Babes in the Wood. New York: Crown, 2002.
End in Tears. London: Hutchison, 2005; New York: Crown, 2006.

Other Works

To Fear a Painted Devil. London: John Long; Garden City: Doubleday, 1965.
Vanity Dies Hard. London: John Long, 1966; New York: Beagle, 1970. Also published as *In Sickness and in Health.* Garden City: Doubleday, 1966.
The Secret House of Death. London: John Long, 1968; Garden City: Doubleday, 1969.
One Across, Two Down. London: Hutchinson; Garden City: Doubleday, 1971.
The Face of Trespass. London: Hutchinson; Garden City: Doubleday, 1974.
A Demon in My View. London: Hutchinson, 1976; Garden City: Doubleday, 1977.
A Judgment in Stone. London: Hutchinson, 1977; Garden City: Doubleday, 1978.
Make Death Love Me. London: Hutchinson; Garden City: Doubleday, 1979.
The Lake of Darkness. London: Hutchinson; Garden City: Doubleday, 1980.
Master of the Moor. London: Hutchinson; New York: Pantheon, 1982.
The Killing Doll. London: Hutchinson; New York: Pantheon, 1984.
The Tree of Hands. London: Hutchinson; New York: Pantheon, 1985.
The New Girl Friend and Other Stories of Suspense. London: Hutchinson, 1985; New York: Pantheon, 1986.
Live Flesh. London: Hutchinson; New York: Pantheon, 1986.
Heartstones. London: Hutchinson; New York: Harper, 1987.
Talking to Strangers. London: Hutchinson, 1987. Also published as *Talking to Strange Men.* New York: Pantheon, 1987.
The Bridesmaid. London: Hutchinson; New York: Mysterious Press, 1989.
Going Wrong. London: Hutchinson; New York: Mysterious Press, 1990.
The Crocodile Bird. London: Hutchinson; New York: Crown, 1993.
Ginger and the Kingsmarkham Chalk Circle. London: Phoenix, 1996.
The Keys to the Street. London: Hutchinson; New York: Random House, 1996.
Bloodlines. Rockland, MA: Wheeler, 1997.
Thornapple. London: Travelman, 1998.
A Sight for Sore Eyes. London: Hutchinson, 1998; New York: Crown, 1999.
Piranha to Scurfy and Other Stories. London: Hutchinson, 2000; New York: Crown, 2001.
Adam and Eve and Pinch Me. London: Hutchinson; New York: Crown, 2001.
The Rottweiler. London: Hutchinson; New York: Crown, 2004.
Thirteen Steps Down. London: Hutchinson; New York: Crown, 2005.

Books by Barbara Vine

A Dark-Adapted Eye. New York: Viking, 1985.
A Fatal Inversion. New York: Bantam, 1987.
The House of Stairs. New York: Harmony Books, 1989.
Gallowglass. New York: Harmony Books, 1990.
King Solomon's Carpet. New York: Harmony Books, 1992.
Anna's Book. New York: Harmony Books, 1993.
No Night Is Too Long. New York: Harmony Books, 1994.
The Brimstone Wedding. New York: Harmony Books, 1996.
The Chimney Sweeper's Boy. New York: Harmony Books, 1998.
Grasshopper. New York: Harmony Books, 2000.

The Blood Doctor. New York: Shaye Areheart Books, 2002.
The Minotaur. London: Viking, 2005; New York: Shaye Areheart Books, 2006.

Works about Ruth Rendell and Barbara Vine

Anable, Stephen. "PW Talks with Ruth Rendell." *Publishers Weekly* 28 January 2002: 275.

Bakerman, Jane S. "Explorations of Love: An Examination of Some Novels by Ruth Rendell." *Armchair Detective* 11 (1978): 139–44.

———. "Ruth Rendell." Ed. Earl F. Bargainnier. *10 Women of Mystery.* Bowling Green: Bowling Green State UP, 1981. 124–49.

Bannon, Barbara. "*A New Lease on Death.*" *Publishers Weekly* 6 March 1967: 75.

———. "*A Speaker of Mandarin.*" *Publishers Weekly* 12 August 1983: 56.

Boucher, Anthony. "Criminals at Large." *New York Times Book Review* 25 June 1967: 18.

Brainard, Dulcy "*Kissing the Gunner's Daughter.*" *Publishers Weekly* 23 March 1992: 62.

Cannon, Peter. "*The Blood Doctor.*" *Publishers Weekly* 24 June 2002: 43.

Craig, Patricia. "The Allure of Unreality." *New Statesman & Society* 21 April 1989: 39.

———. "*The Copper Peacock and Other Stories.*" *Times Literary Supplement* 12 April 1991: 19.

———. "A Strange Use for Wexford's Raincoat." *Times Literary Supplement* 1 October 1999: 21.

DuBose, Martha Hailey. *Women of Mystery: The Lives and Works of Notable Women Crime Novelists.* New York: St. Martin's Minotaur, 2000.

Fletcher, Connie. "*An Unkindness of Ravens.*" *Booklist* July 1985: 1475.

———. "*Live Flesh.*" *Booklist* August 1986: 1634.

"*From Doon with Death.*" *Publishers Weekly* 10 January 1966: 95.

Gabilondo, Patricia A. "Ruth Rendell." *Dictionary of Literary Biography,* Vol. 276: *British Mystery and Thriller Writers Since 1960.* Ed. Gina Macdonald. Detroit: Gale, 2003. 315–32.

Giffone, Tony. "Disoriented in the Orient: The Representation of the Chinese in Two Contemporary Mystery Novels." Ed. Bonnie Braendlin. *Cultural Power/Cultural Literacy.* Tallahassee: Florida State UP, 1991.143–51.

Kimberley, Nick. "Laws of Life." *New Statesman & Society* 7 February 1992: 41.

King, Nicola. *Memory, Narrative, Identity: Remembering the Self.* Edinburgh: Edinburgh UP, 2000.

Knight, Lynn. "*Simisola.*" *Times Literary Supplement* 7 October 1994: 30.

Kyzlinkova, Lidia. "Ruth Rendell/Barbara Vine: Racial Otherness and Conservative Englishness." *Brno Studies in English* 29.9 (2003): 123–31.

Leavy, Barbara Fass. "A Folklore Plot in Ruth Rendell's Wexford Series." *Clues* 20.2 (1999): 49–62.

Leitch, Thomas M. "Not Just Another Whodunit: Disavowal as Evolution in Detective Fiction." *Clues* 20.1 (1999): 63–76.

"*The Minotaur.*" *Publishers Weekly* 16 January 2006: 39–40.

Reynolds, Moira Davison. "Ruth Rendell." *Women Writers of Detective Series: Twenty-One American and British Writers, 1900–2000.* Jefferson, NC: McFarland, 2001. 111–18.

Robertson, Peter. "The Booklist Interview: Ruth Rendell." *Booklist* 15 September 1992: 126–27.

Rowland, Susan. *From Agatha Christie to Ruth Rendell: British Women Writers in Detective and Crime Fiction.* Hampshire; New York: Palgrave, 2001.

Stasio, Marilyn. "Crime." *New York Times Book Review* 7 September 1997: 34.

Steinberg, Sybil. "*An Unkindness of Ravens.*" *Publishers Weekly* 5 July 1985: 58.

———. "*Live Flesh.*" *Publishers Weekly* 11 July 1986: 53.

———. "*The Copper Peacock and Other Stories.*" *Publishers Weekly* 16 August 1991: 49.

———. "*Grasshopper.*" *Publishers Weekly* 28 August 2000: 50.

Waugh, Harriet. "Thrills on a Wet Afternoon." *The Spectator* 24 September 1988: 40.

———. "Murders of Quality." *The Spectator* 15 April 1989: 31.

Willem, Linda M. "Rewriting Rendell: Pedro Almodovar's *Carne tremula.*" *Literature/Film Quarterly* 30.2 (2002): 115–18.

Kate Ross (1956–1998)

BIOGRAPHY

Katherine Ross was raised in Massachusetts and attended Wellesley College, earning a bachelor's degree in Greek language and literature; she then earned her law degree from Yale. She had always loved reading and planned to be an English major, but she became more interested in the classics after taking a course featuring Greek literature in translation and decided to major in Greek so that she could read Euripides in the original (homepage). She called studying the law a "great refuge" for people with humanities degrees (homepage). She noted that during law school, she had the opportunity to study English legal history with a prominent visiting professor, and it was then that she became interested in the Regency period, particularly its primitive law enforcement system.

She began her legal career in 1981 with the firm of Sullivan and Worcester in Boston and continued her work as a trial lawyer after she began writing fiction. She resided in Brookline, Massachusetts. Ross died of cancer on March 12, 1998, cutting short not only her legal career, but also a well-researched historical mystery series.

MAJOR WORKS AND THEMES

All four of her novels are set in the Regency period in England in the 1820s. The series features Julian Kestrel, a self-made man who is comfortable among the aristocracy, although he does not have a title or a privileged background. Helen M. Francini called Kestrel the "precursor to and successor of Dorothy L. Sayers's Lord Peter Wimsey" (904). Kestrel's sidekick Dipper, a somewhat reformed thief, acts as his valet when they need to visit with the upper classes. In the first novel, Kestrel is asked to serve as best man at a friend's wedding. When a murder occurs, Dipper is accused and Kestrel begins to investigate. The major theme of the work is family honor, which hinders the investigation to a great extent.

Although Ross's works feature a male protagonist, women characters are also strongly present in the novels. The second novel in the series, *A Broken Vessel,* features a case that involves prostitutes and the nineteenth-century reformation societies that worked to help women leave that profession. A murder occurs in one of the homes run by a society, and Kestrel enlists the assistance of Dipper's sister, Sally Stokes, to go undercover in the home.

In the third novel, Kestrel is asked to investigate the murder of an aristocrat and finds links to another murder that took place in a seedier part of London. The fourth novel moves to Italy, as Kestrel travels through Europe with a friend. He reads about an unsolved murder and decides to test his investigational skills. During his investigation, he uncovers links to a disappearance and to political problems of the time.

CRITICAL RECEPTION

Her works were well received by critics and readers, and Ross won an Agatha Award for Best Novel for *The Devil in Music.* Francini offered praise for her plotting, but particularly noted Ross's strong characterizations. As Francini explains, even the female secondary characters are quite strong (904). Francini also praised Ross for paying "minute attention" to details, including vocabulary from that period, references to popular culture, and correct descriptions of legal matters (905).

Susanna Yager praised *For Whom the Gods Love* for its "enjoyable and not over-intrusive historical background," along with its more traditional investigative techniques (14). Reviews for Ross's final novel were also strong. One noted that Ross "adeptly fashions a mystery" with a cast, plot and setting of "operatic proportions," resulting in "an elegant and finely tuned performance" (Brainard 1997:68). Another review praised its "densely plotted" and "well-research[ed]" content, along with Ross's "finely manicured writing" (Pierce). One review thought the mystery elements were lacking but still described it as "very diverting" (Stasio 34).

Francini concluded her essay about Ross by noting that it would be "most interesting" to see what future adventures Kestrel would have. It is indeed unfortunate that his adventures were cut short by Ross's untimely death. Readers still lament her passing; there are numerous recent blog postings about her work, including one at a site called "Risky Regencies" that generated a great deal of discussion.

BIBLIOGRAPHY

Works by Kate Ross

Cut to the Quick. New York: Viking, 1993.
A Broken Vessel. New York: Viking, 1994.
Whom the Gods Love. New York: Viking, 1995.
The Devil in Music. New York: Viking, 1997.

Works about Kate Ross

Brainard, Dulcy. "*The Devil in Music.*" *Publishers Weekly* 14 July 1997: 68.
Francini, Helen M. "Kate Ross." *St. James Guide to Crime & Mystery Writers.* 4th ed. Ed. Jay P. Pederson. Detroit: St. James Press, 1996. 904–905.
Kate Ross. Homepage. http://www.iwillfollow.com/kjr/whoami.html n.d. 23 October 2005.
"Kate Ross, Mystery Book Writer, Award Recipient, Attorney; At 41." *Boston Globe* 16 March 1998: B5.
Mullany, Janet. "Kate Ross." Risky Regencies. http://riskyregencies.blogspot.com/2005/09/kate-ross.html 29 September 2005. 10 November 2005.
Pierce, J. Kingston. "Minor Offenses." *January Magazine* http://epe.lac-bac.gc.ca/100/202/300/january/1999/01/nonfiction/minor.html 24 August 1998. 10 November 2005.
Stasio, Marilyn. "Crime." *New York Times Review of Books* 7 September 1997: 34.
Yager, Susanna. "Books: Crime Thrives in Court." *Sunday Telegraph* 21 January 1996: 14.

S. J. Rozan

BIOGRAPHY

S. J. Rozan is an architect and serious basketball fan. Born in the Bronx, New York, she grew up with a brother and two sisters. Rozan earned a bachelor's degree from Oberlin College and a master's degree in architecture from the State University of New York at Buffalo. In addition to her career as an architect, she has also worked as a janitor, instructor for self-defense classes, photographer, and salesperson. Her architectural firm specializes in public buildings, such as police stations, firehouses, and zoos. She now writes full-time and lives in lower Manhattan.

Once asked what makes her unusual as a writer, she responded that as an architect, she is "used to creativity being an iterative process" involving revision and rethinking ("*Reflecting the Sky*").

MAJOR WORKS AND THEMES

The bulk of Rozan's work is composed of a series featuring two private investigators, Lydia Chin and Bill Smith. Chin and Smith take turns at narrating the books, which gives the series an interesting twist. Many of Rozan's readers love to discuss which narrator they prefer. Rozan has noted in interviews that she began the first novel with Smith as the central character and Chin as a sidekick, as someone opposite Smith in every way possible (Xialolong). As she was writing, Chin's character seemed strong and interesting, so she tried a short story to see if Chin "really emerged as a full-bodied character" ("*Reflecting the Sky*"). After finishing the first book, she wrote another from Chin's point of view, which became *China Trade,* the first published in the series.

Chin and Smith are quite different, and the cases they take on and narrate tend to be different as well. Chin, the dutiful daughter of Chinese immigrants, lives at home and tries to reconcile her choice of career with her mother's expectations. Smith is older, a veteran and a loner, a tough man with a sensitive streak. They grow closer as friends with each novel, and the sexual tension grows too. Rozan has said that the award she is most proud of is her "Nevermore." The Nevermore Awards are given the night before the Edgar Award ceremonies by Partners in Crime, an independent mystery bookstore in New York; Rozan won the "Hauled Ashes Award" for having the fictional couple "most in need of getting it on" ("*Reflecting the Sky*").

Chin narrates cases that tend to be referred to her by family. In *Mandarin Plaid,* for example, her brother asks her to help a fashion designer whose work has been stolen by a rival. Nothing is as easy as it seems, and as Chin and Smith deliver a ransom for the sketches, shots ring out. They become involved in a case mired in sweatshops, drugs, and prostitution. In *A Bitter Feast,* Chin and Smith take on a case involving the illegal importation of people and drugs, murder, and more in Chinatown. *Reflecting the Sky* takes Chin and Smith to Hong Kong at the request of her grandfather. They intend to deliver an heirloom to a relative, but end up involved in a case there that they did not anticipate when that relative has been kidnapped.

Smith's cases involve going undercover at a construction site (*No Colder Place*) and at a home for the elderly (*Concourse*). Smith tries to get away to a cabin in the country in *Stone Quarry* but is pulled into two local cases there. In *Winter and Night,* readers learn more about Smith's family and past, when his nephew calls him for help. This novel also takes on the issue of troubled youth, the obsession with sports, and school violence.

Her first stand-alone novel was the poignant *Absent Friends,* which was set in October and November 2001. As a writer, she knew she had to write about 9–11, but she felt that having Chin and Smith face it would be inappropriate, as they live in what she considers a "fictional universe" (Aldrich 2). It is a multilayered novel, told partially in flashbacks, as a group of characters are traced through childhood, young adulthood, and present day. One of them becomes a heroic firefighter, who dies during the attacks. Another plot line involves two reporters, one young and ambitious, the other older and alcoholic, who are lovers.

Before 9–11, the older reporter had been investigating the firefighter, who was possibly involved in criminal activity. In addition to the mysteries surrounding these characters, the book also is an intense portrait of a city recovering from a devastating attack. Although she considers it a crime novel, Rozan was "thrilled" that *Publishers Weekly* reviewed it in their fiction section, not with the mysteries (Aldrich 3).

She is writing another stand-alone novel, tentatively titled *In This Rain,* which she describes as a novel about real estate and civil service investigators. With even more points of view than *Absent Friends,* it will focus on "questions of honor" (Aldrich 3). The next Chin and Smith book is tentatively titled *Nothing is Lovely,* and will be set in the world of gems with Chin narrating (Aldrich 3).

CRITICAL RECEPTION

Rozan has won numerous awards for her writing, including Edgar, Anthony, Nero, and Macavity awards. Rozan also has won Shamus Awards for *Concourse* and *Reflecting the Sky.* Sue Grafton, Carolina García-Aguilera, and Rozan are the only women writers to have won the Shamus Award for best novel, although other women have won Shamus Awards in other categories, for best paperback original novel or best first novel.

Mandarin Plaid was criticized for "too many red herrings" but was lauded for the way in which Rozan "creates a fully realized Manhattan populated with memorable characters" (Steinberg 74). A review of *No Colder Place* praised Rozan's plotting and suspense, while noting that "best of all are Bill and Lydia, originals who are strong enough to carry emotional baggage from other books without weakening their credibility" (Brainard 1997:57).

Stuart Miller wrote of *A Bitter Feast* that Rozan's writing shows "skill and verve in the most complex plot she has yet written," and he noted that "Lydia and Bill's relationship provides the intriguing subplot in what may be the best of this uniformly excellent, well written, and entertaining series" (1998:1976). Another reviewer noted that "lots of amazing things happen" in the novel, with a story "that manages to satisfy all the senses" (Brainard 1998:38).

Stone Quarry was viewed as a "first-rate mystery" with an "invigorating pace" and an exploration of the "myriad ways in which violence can warp human relationships" (Zaleski 76). Miller's review noted that Rozan "demonstrates again the superior plotting, deft characterizations, and beautiful use of setting" (1999:73). Peter Cannon praised *Reflecting the Sky,* stating that "every bit of humor and evocative description serves the action; there's not a smidgen of clunky exposition as the Chin-Smith relationship continues to grow and fascinate" (56). Miller found this novel in the series to have "great characters, intricate plotting, and an exotic locale, beautifully described" (2000:791).

Absent Friends was widely regarded as excellent, with novelist and reviewer Hallie Ephron calling it "an eloquent and profoundly sad story about heroes who are flawed in a world that needs all the heroes it can get" and having an "ending [that] left me stunned and staring into my lap for minutes on end, then paging back to reread the beginning" (E6). Dick Adler noted that Rozan "knows how to balance the [characters'] pasts and their presents without trivializing anything that happened on 9/11. Her performance—a dance in front of the burning towers—takes guts, brains and heart, and all are present in abundance" (6). Another reviewer called it a "well-told suspenseful tale with fully developed characters," which offers a "haunting examination of the nature of friendship, truth and heroism" (Foyt 50).

BIBLIOGRAPHY

Works by S. J. Rozan

Lydia Chin and Bill Smith Series

China Trade. New York: St. Martin's, 1994.
Concourse. New York: St. Martin's, 1995.
Mandarin Plaid. New York: St. Martin's, 1996.
No Colder Place. New York: St. Martin's, 1997.
A Bitter Feast. New York: St. Martin's, 1998.
Stone Quarry. New York: St. Martin's, 1999.
Reflecting the Sky. New York: St. Martin's, 2001.
Winter and Night. New York: St. Martin's, 2002.

Other Works

The Gift of the Magi: A Christmas Story. New York: Mysterious Bookshop, 2000.
Absent Friends. New York: Delacorte, 2004.

Works about S. J. Rozan

Adler, Dick. "Terrorism, Treachery and Some Terrific Writing." *Chicago Tribune* 3 October 2004: 6.
Aldrich, Chris. "S. J. Rozan: Telling Everyone's Story." *Mystery News* 22.5 (October/November 2004): 1–3.
Brainard, Dulcy. "*No Colder Place.*" *Publishers Weekly* 28 July 1997: 57.
———. "*A Bitter Feast.*" *Publishers Weekly* 29 June 1998: 38.
Cannon, Peter. "*Reflecting the Sky.*" *Publishers Weekly* 15 January 2001: 55–56.
Ephron, Hallie. "Heroes with Flaws, Scottish Secrets and One Very Cold Case." *Boston Globe* 31 October 2004: E6.
Foyt, Michelle. "*Absent Friends.*" *Library Journal* 15 September 2004: 50.
Matter, Paula J. "S. J. Rozan." *Mystery Scene* 72 (2001): 57–59.
Miller, Stuart. "*A Bitter Feast.*" *Booklist.* August 1998: 1976.
———. "*Stone Quarry.*" *Booklist* 1 September 1999: 73.
———. "*Reflecting the Sky.*" *Booklist* 15 December 2000: 791.
"Reflecting the Sky: An Interview with S. J. Rozan." 2004. 18 May 2005. http://www.sjrozan.com/rozan/interviewarchive.html
"S. J. Rozan." *Contemporary Authors.* Vol. 104, New Revision Series. Ed. Scot Peacock. Detroit: Gale, 2002. 376–78.
S. J. Rozan. 2004. 4 November 2004. http://www.sjrozan.com
Steinberg, Sybil. "*Mandarin Plaid.*" *Publishers Weekly* 29 July 1996: 74.
Xiaolong, Qui. "At Home Online: S. J. Rozan." *Mystery Readers International.* 4 November 2004. http://www.mysteryreaders.org/athomerozan.html
Zaleski, Jeff. "*Stone Quarry.*" *Publishers Weekly* 2 August 1999: 76.

Lisa Scottoline (1955–)

BIOGRAPHY

Lisa Scottoline was born in July 1955 in Philadelphia into an Italian-American family. Her heritage is important to her, and it has played a crucial role in her fictional works, as well as in her civic service.

She graduated from the University of Pennsylvania twice, first in 1976 with a magna cum laude bachelor's degree in English and then with a law degree, also with honors, in 1981. She worked as a clerk for a state appellate court judge after law school and later with a large firm in Philadelphia. Although her career was going well, her marriage dissolved shortly after the birth of her daughter, and she left the firm in 1986 to stay home to care for her. As noted on her Web site, Scottoline decided to try writing and gave herself a limit of how much debt she would accrue to live while writing her first novel. She reached the limit of indebtedness and had taken a part-time position as a law clerk when her first novel was accepted by Harper.

She is a lifelong citizen of Philadelphia and remains active in her community and in the legal community. Among other activities, she is a contributing editor to *Justice* magazine, serves on the board of directors of the National Italian American Foundation, and plans to teach a course on "Justice and Fiction" at the University of Pennsylvania in 2006.

MAJOR WORKS AND THEMES

All of Scottoline's novels are legal thrillers, with most of them focusing on three women lawyers who work together, Bennie Rosato, Judy Carrier, and Mary DiNunzio. DiNunzio and Carrier are introduced in Scottoline's first novel, which is set before they meet Rosato. In that work, DiNunzio, a young widow who is close to her family, is being stalked. Colleague Carrier helps her solve the case.

Scottoline's second and third novels are stand-alone works that feature women lawyers who did not later join Rosato's firm, although many fans would have liked to have seen Rita Morrone and Grace Rossi reappear. In *Final Appeal,* Rossi, a single mother, begins an affair with a judge, who is found dead the morning after their first evening together. She cannot accept the verdict of suicide and begins investigating his death. In *Running from the Law,* Morrone defends her boyfriend's father on a sexual harassment charge and is thrust in a case that is turns into involving murder.

Scottoline's fourth novel introduced Benedetta "Bennie" Rosato, whose legal partner and ex-boyfriend turns up murdered. Accused of the crime, she must find the truth to clear her name. During her quest for the truth, Rosato uses a number of disguises while she goes undercover in her own city. In the fifth novel, Rosato returns, having opened a new firm of her own, which will employ women lawyers exclusively. DiNunzio and Carrier join the firm, and the novel highlights their first big case. A prominent defense attorney, whom Marilyn Stasio describes as having "the ethical code of a cobra" (34), has hired them to assist her with the aftermath of a case she won for a man accused of murder.

Subsequent novels have unique twists, including *Mistaken Identity,* in which Rosato finds out she has a long-lost half sister who is impersonating her, and *Killer Smile,* which involves the little-known history of the forced registration and internment of Italian-Americans during World War II. Scottoline learned about this when she found her grandparents' registration cards among their effects and conducted research into the government practices during the war.

Her recent novels have departed from the Rosato series, introducing two new protagonists, assistant U.S. Attorney Vicki Allegretti and federal judge Cate Fante. In *Devil's Corner,* Allegretti is thrust into a complex case involving drug smuggling. In *Dirty Blonde,* the judge balances her work with a secret sex life that is exposed when a high profile case leads to a murder-suicide. In all her works, Scottoline deftly mixes courtroom drama with a great sense of humor and strongly developed characters. As Oline Cogdill stated, Scottoline has recreated the legal thriller to include humor, noting that "no matter how serious the topic, Scottoline manages to leaven it with a wide swath of humor. Her protagonists face their challenges in part with a ready, dry wit and tart remark" (2).

CRITICAL RECEPTION

Her first novel was nominated for an Edgar award, and the second won an Edgar. Her works have received acclaim from critics and readers. Her first novel was called "engaging" with humor in "just the right proportions" (Kaganoff 59). Another reviewer praised how Scottoline "knows her milieu and recreates it flawlessly" (Joyce 38). A review of the second novel, *Final Appeal,* stated that Scottoline "has again pulled together an intriguing cast of characters and a smart mystery" that added up to an "exciting, action-packed read" (Simpson 65). The plot of her third novel was commended for Scottoline's "expert design," with "an intelligent sense of irony at work" (Steinberg 101). Praise for her work has continued throughout her career. Even when there are criticisms of the way a plot resolves, or in the case of *Courting Trouble,* complaints of too much humor, reviewers consistently praise her strong dialogue and character development.

A review of *Killer Smile* called the characters "immensely human," within a "complex, perceptive story that moves briskly to its surprising ending" (Cogdill 2). Another review noted that Scottoline is even more effective than normal, given the personal nature of the story, with the plot line about the treatment of Italian-Americans during World War II. (Zaleski 58). The reviewer further stated that she "skillfully weaves a complicated, gripping and fast-paced tale, at turns comical, nerve-wracking and enlightening" (Zaleski 58).

BIBLIOGRAPHY

Works by Lisa Scottoline

Rosato & Associates Series

Everywhere That Mary Went. New York: Harper, 1993.
Legal Tender. New York: HarperCollins, 1996.
Rough Justice. New York: HarperCollins, 1997.
Mistaken Identity. New York: HarperCollins, 1999.
Moment of Truth. New York: HarperCollins, 2000.
The Vendetta Defense. New York: HarperCollins, 2001.
Courting Trouble. New York: HarperCollins, 2002.
Dead Ringer. New York: HarperCollins, 2003.
Killer Smile. New York: HarperCollins, 2004.

Other Novels

Final Appeal. New York: Harper, 1994.
Running from the Law. New York: Harper, 1996.
Devil's Corner. New York: HarperCollins, 2005.
Dirty Blonde. New York: HarperCollins, 2006.

Works about Lisa Scottoline

All About Lisa. Lisa Scottoline.com. 2005. 8 November 2005. http://scottoline.com/Site/About/
Cogdill, Oline H. "Humor Sets the Tone in *Killer Smile.*" *Chicago Tribune* 22 June 2004: 2.
Joyce, Alice. "*Everywhere That Mary Went.*" *Booklist* 1 September 1993: 38.

Kaganoff, Penny. "*Everywhere That Mary Went.*" *Publishers Weekly* 27 September 1993: 59.

"Lisa Scottoline." *Contemporary Authors* Vol. 186. Scot Peacock, ed. Detroit: Gale, 2000. 320–24.

Pierleoni, Allen. "A Paper Trail—Bee Book Club." *Sacramento Bee* 15 June 2005: E1.

Simpson, Maria. "*Final Appeal.*" *Publishers Weekly* 3 October 1994: 65.

Stasio, Marilyn. "Crime." *New York Times Book Review* 7 September 1997: 34.

Steinberg, Sybil. "*Running from the Law.*" *Publishers Weekly* 28 August 1995: 101.

Zaleski, Jeff. "*Killer Smile.*" *Publishers Weekly* 22 March 2004: 58.

Dorothy Simpson (1933–)

BIOGRAPHY

Dorothy Preece Simpson was born in Blaenavon, Monmouthshire, Wales on June 20, 1933. Her father, Robert Wilfrid Preece, was a civil servant and her mother, Gladys Jones Preece, was an elocution teacher.

She attended the University of Bristol, earning a bachelor's degree with honors and a teaching diploma. She taught English and French at various grammar schools from 1955–1962. She worked as a marriage guidance counselor from 1969–1982, and began her writing career in 1975. Unfortunately, severe repetitive stress injury caused her to cease writing in 2000. Although she recently reported that her health has improved, she does not plan to write any more novels (Skupin 80).

She married Keith Taylor Simpson, a barrister, on July 22, 1961. They have three children, Mark Taylor, Ian Robert, and Emma Morag. She and her husband live in Maidstone, Kent, England.

MAJOR WORKS AND THEMES

Her first novel, *Harbingers of Fear,* was published in 1977. She notes that her husband had encouraged her for years to try writing a novel, but she felt "uninspired" to do so (Dorothy 415). After a lengthy illness, she began to write, having "plenty of time for reflection and reassessment" (Dorothy 415). She notes that she was lucky, finding an agent and having the book published by the first house that considered it.

After her original success, though, Simpson's next three manuscripts were rejected. Although it was "disheartening," Simpson reflected on her writing skills and strengths, and "realized the crime novel is of such diversity that it offers enormous scope to the writer" (Bakerman 935). She decided to "devote her next efforts to creating an intriguing murder mystery staged around an engaging sleuth" (Dorothy 415). She created Inspector Luke Thanet and his colleague Sergeant Michael Lineham and wrote *The Night She Died,* which introduced Thanet and his professional detecting skills but also introduced Thanet as a human character, concerned about his wife and children, and suffering from a bad back. Her "chief interest is in character" and she thinks her books might better be labeled "Whydunnits" than "Whodunnits" (Bakerman 935). Her setting is fictional but is an amalgam of various places in her home county of Kent. She recalls one review that claimed a specific town to be the setting and her amusement that she had never even been there (Skupin 80).

CRITICAL RECEPTION

Simpson won the Silver Dagger Award from the Crime Writers Association of Great Britain for the fifth Thanet novel, *Last Seen Alive.* Critical reception to her work before and after that has been positive overall.

In a review of *Dead on Arrival* Sybil Steinberg noted that Thanet's "methodical habits lead him to question" other possible solutions, with Simpson providing "a triple twist in the solution" (1986:65). Steinberg also examined *Element of Doubt,* again praising Thanet's work in "probing gently into every aspect, carefully gleaning leads from the most recalcitrant suspect" in a plot that provides a "thoughtful, logically perused course of action" (1988:417). Steinberg's review of *Dead by Morning* heralded it as a "skillfully plotted" mystery "replete with vivid characters," and noted that "yet once more it's the likable and humane inspector, and the glimpse into his family life, that gives the novel its rewarding texture" (1989:53).

A review of *Doomed to Die* warned that "confirmed clue-sniffers" should be "ready for a surprise," noting that "the solution and the sinner are shockers, though eminently fair ones" (Robertson 415). Emily Melton praised the "eminently readable story with a strong cast of characters and compelling plot" found in *Wake the Dead,* but noted that Simpson's "real strength lies in her ability" to provide "intimate glimpses of her characters' foibles and weaknesses" (406). Although many reviewers find this aspect of Simpson's work admirable or interesting, at least one disagreed, finding that Simpson's interest in the "detective's domestic problems" is "to the detriment of her story" (Craig 22).

Simpson was heralded for *Once Too Often,* an example of how she "tailors her plot with skill and care, nicely dovetailing all the clues and reserving a special twist for the end" (Klett 131). Another review found it "cleverly and intricately plotted" with Simpson "adroitly explor[ing] the fragile web of loves and loyalties that bind as well as blind" with "the result [being] another satisfying mystery in which Thanet operates more like a surgeon with a scalpel than a policeman with a truncheon" (Brainard 73). Another reviewer noted this novel, "about the steady, exacting, and slightly dull Inspector Luke Thanet," proves how "Dorothy Simpson is dependably pleasing, even at her most acerbic," writing a series that is "all of a high order" (Winks F2).

One review of *Dead and Gone* noted that "the closely woven British mystery is alive and well in the hands of Dorothy Simpson," who "has found a niche, and her readers are grateful she's content to stay in it" (Campbell 3). Another review found that this entry in the "well-respected British series gets off to a fast start," with Simpson "build[ing] the tension carefully to a satisfying conclusion worthy of Agatha Christie. Her Thanet is a compassionate man for whom the why is every bit as important as the how" (Zaleski 296).

In addition, William Reynolds wrote about the series for *Clues: A Journal of Detection.* He analyzes her works as being "soft" procedurals, meaning that each book deals with one case and that the evidence can never completely solve the crime, that the detective always pulls the pieces together for the solution (40). Reynolds also highlights the social themes Simpson explores and looks at her extensive character development, which adds depth to the novels.

BIBLIOGRAPHY

Works by Dorothy Simpson

Inspector Luke Thanet Series

The Night She Died. New York: Scribner, 1981.
Six Feet Under. New York: Scribner, 1982.

Puppet for a Corpse. New York: Scribner, 1983.
Close Her Eyes. New York: Scribner, 1984.
Last Seen Alive. New York: Scribner, 1985.
Dead on Arrival. New York: Scribner, 1987.
Element of Doubt. New York: Scribner, 1988.
Suspicious Death. New York: Scribner, 1988.
Dead by Morning. New York: Scribner, 1989.
Doomed to Die. New York: Scribner, 1991.
Wake the Dead. New York: Scribner, 1992.
No Laughing Matter. New York: Scribner, 1993.
A Day for Dying. New York: Scribner, 1996.
Once Too Often. New York: Scribner, 1998.
Dead and Gone. New York: Scribner, 2000.

Other Works

Harbingers of Fear. London: Macdonald & Janes, 1977.

Works about Dorothy Simpson

Bakerman, Jane S. "Dorothy Simpson." *St. James Guide to Crime & Mystery Writers.* 4th ed. Ed. Jay P. Pederson. Detroit: St. James Press, 1996. 934–36.
Brainard, Dulcy. "*Once Too Often.*" *Publishers Weekly* 26 January 1998: 73.
Campbell, Mary. "*Dead and Gone* Fits Nicely in the British Mystery Niche." *Chicago Tribune* 4 April 2000: 3.
Craig, Patricia. "*Wake the Dead.*" *Times Literary Supplement* 26 June 1992: 22.
"Dorothy Simpson." *Contemporary Authors.* Vol. 95, New Revision Series. Ed. Scot Peacock. Detroit: Gale, 2001. 414–17.
Klett, Rex E. "*Once Too Often.*" *Library Journal* 1 March 1998: 130–31.
Melton, Emily. "*Wake the Dead.*" *Booklist* 15 October 1992: 406.
Reynolds, William. "Second Best, But Not Second-Rate: Dorothy Simpson's Luke Thanet Series." *Clues* 19.1 (1998): 39–46.
Robertson, Peter. "*Doomed to Die.*" *Booklist* 15 October 1991: 415.
Skupin, Brian. "What's Happening with Dorothy Simpson." *Mystery Scene* 90 (Summer 2005): 80.
Steinberg, Sybil. "*Dead on Arrival.*" *Publishers Weekly* 5 December 1986: 65.
———. "*Element of Doubt.*" *Publishers Weekly* 29 January 1988: 417.
———. "*Dead by Morning.*" *Publishers Weekly* 21 July 1989: 53.
Winks, Robin W. "The Brits Who Do Not Induce—Nor Disturb—His Slumbers." *Boston Globe* 25 January 1998: F2.
Zaleski, Jeff. "*Dead and Gone.*" *Publishers Weekly* 24 January 2000: 296.

Karin Slaughter (1971–)

BIOGRAPHY

Born in Georgia, Karin Slaughter lives in Atlanta. She grew up in a small town in southern Georgia and had planned to be a lawyer. She enjoyed school and credits her ninth grade teacher with showing her how to revise and enhance her work (New Mystery Reader). Instead of going to law school, she owned a sign business before turning to writing full-time.

MAJOR WORKS AND THEMES

Most reviews and marketing materials stress that Slaughter's works are not for faint-hearted readers. Slaughter writes a forensically descriptive series of novels featuring Sara Linton, a pediatrician who serves as medical examiner, and her police chief ex-husband, Jeffrey Tolliver. Slaughter herself doesn't think her novels "are any more graphic than what is out there," noting that she thinks she may be getting attention for this aspect because she is a woman (Patrick). At least one reviewer has made a distinction, noting that while Slaughter's work is "unflinchingly graphic," she "never stoops to gratuitous violence" (Cogdill 2002:9G). There are an increasing number of women writing forensic thrillers and when asked why she thinks this area is gaining in popularity, Slaughter replied that it may just be something that interests the writer. She noted that she once dated a mortician and had lots of questions for him (Dunn 54).

Her interest in and knowledge of legal matters plays a role in the novels, and she attended a mini-medical school seminar at Emory University, a four-week training course for people interested in an overview of medicine (Dunn 54). In addition, she enjoys doing research and has explored a number of cases and studies that provide her with information for her novels.

The series setting of Heartsdale, in Grant County, Georgia, is fictional, but is based on her hometown. She notes that most small towns anywhere have similar "casts of background characters," including good and bad families, the town gossip, and the "old guys" who sit and talk at the hardware store (Patrick). By placing her stories in this setting, she hopes to "honor the South" and show "appreciation for the lives" of the people who inhabit such small towns (Patrick). In *Blindsighted,* a blind professor is murdered in a public restroom, and the small town is rocked by the presence of evil. The victim's sister, Lena Adams, is a police detective in town. Adams is a complex character who struggles to deal with the death of her sister, the fact that she plays an official role in investigation due to the small size of the police force, and the horror of being targeted by her sister's killer. *Kisscut* deals with violence against children, as Linton and Tolliver uncover a child pornography ring. In *A Faint Cold Fear,* Adams is working at the local college as a security guard when Linton is called there to investigate a possible suicide. Linton's sister is attacked, and the case becomes quite complex. *Indelible* combines a present day hostage situation with a prequel, providing flashbacks to when Linton and Tolliver first met. The two mystery plot lines tie together, although the flashback sections are much more interesting in terms of character development and learning more about the personal histories of the protagonists.

CRITICAL RECEPTION

For Oline H. Cogdill, *Blindsighted* explored what happens to a small town when "evil wears a familiar face of a neighbor," noting that Slaughter "veers into the Southern gothic tradition complete with the brooding atmosphere" while offering "an engaging story" (2001:11G). Slaughter's character development is also praised, in terms of her "cadre of believable characters who ... immediately take form and emerge as complete persons" (Cogdill 2001:11G). Cogdill also reviewed *Kisscut,* again noting Slaughter's strengths in character development and plotting, noting an unpredictable, suspenseful plot composed of "an obstacle course of unflinching twists and turns that are anything but routine" (2002:9G). Jabari Asim praised the character development in *Kisscut,* noting how Linton's "failure to detect signs of abuse makes [her] doubt herself and increases her dedication to finding the responsible parties" (C3).

In his review of *A Faint Cold Fear,* Jeff Zaleski stated that "readers who can stomach gruesome details and like fitting together multiple stories of physical and psychological abuse will savor the way Slaughter can evoke sympathy for perverse, even criminal, behavior by tracing its origins" and alerted readers that they "will be rewarded with a satisfyingly chilling ending" (35).

Dennis Drabelle noted that in *Indelible,* "Slaughter excels at pitting one strong character against another," citing a particularly effective scene with Linton and her mother (T9). Another reviewer praised how Slaughter "skillfully maintains the tension in the parallel stories as she switches back and forth, but midway through the novel the hostage scene becomes much less compelling than the buried secrets Sara uncovers about a murder from Jeffrey's childhood" (O'Briant B1).

BIBLIOGRAPHY

Works by Karin Slaughter

Sara Linton and Jeffrey Tolliver Series

Blindsighted. New York: Morrow, 2001.
Kisscut. New York: Morrow, 2002.
A Faint Cold Fear. New York: Morrow, 2003.
Indelible. New York: Morrow, 2004.
Faithless. New York: Morrow, 2005.

Other Novel

Triptych. New York: Delacorte, 2006.

Works about Karin Slaughter

Asim, Jabari. "Devil Down in Georgia." *Washington Post* 3 September 2002: C3.
Cogdill, Oline H. "When Evil Comes from a Neighbor." *South Florida Sun Sentinel* 21 October 2001: 11G.
———. "Small Town's Secrets Chillingly Exposed." *South Florida Sun Sentinel* 15 September 2002: 9G.
Drabelle, Dennis. "In Thrall to Slick." *Washington Post* 1 August 2004: T9.
Dunn, Adam. "PW Talks with Karin Slaughter." *Publishers Weekly* 5 August 2002: 54.
"Karin Slaughter." *Contemporary Authors.* Vol. 216. Ed. Scot Peacock. Detroit: Gale, 2004. 342–43.
"Karin Slaughter—Q & A's." Bookhaunts.net. 2002. 10 November 2004. http://www.webrighter. co.uk/bookhaunts/slaughter/slaughterQA.htm
Karin Slaughter. 10 November 2004. http://www.karinslaughter.com
Lippman, Laura. "Interview." http://www.karinslaughter.com/interview.html
Newmysteryreader.com. Karin Slaughter: Featured Author. n.d. 10 November 2004. http://www. newmysteryreader.com/karin_slaughter.htm
O'Briant, Don. "Atlanta Author Hones Dark Edge in Prequel." *Atlanta Journal-Constitution* 6 August 2004: B1.
Patrick, Bethanne Kelly. "Karin Slaughter." Bookreporter.com. 2004. 10 November 2004. http:// www.bookreporter.com/authors/au-slaughter-karin.asp
Zaleski, Jeff. "*A Faint Cold Fear.*" *Publishers Weekly* 25 August 2003: 35.

Julie Smith (1944–)

BIOGRAPHY

Born November 25, 1944, in Annapolis, Maryland, Julie Smith is the daughter of Malberry and Claire Tanner Smith. Her father was a lawyer and her mother was a school counselor. She grew up in Savannah, Georgia, with two younger siblings.

After graduating from the University of Mississippi in 1965, she worked as a reporter for the *Times-Picayune* in New Orleans, and in 1967, she moved to San Francisco and worked as a reporter for the *Chronicle*. She notes that she liked to substitute for the crime reporter and eventually was assigned many stories on murders and other crimes (Eckinger O1). One of her most memorable assignments was to cover the activities of the Reverend Jim Jones in the early 1970s. She left the newspaper in 1979 to start Invisible Ink with Marcia Muller; the company did freelance writing and editing work. In the 1980s, she turned to writing mystery novels.

Smith moved back to New Orleans permanently in 1995 (Eckinger O1). She also married that year, and her husband Lee Pryor moved with her to New Orleans ("Julie Smith" 400). When she began writing about a character who wanted to become a private investigator, she did research into the requirements and decided to take the course herself. She became a licensed investigator in 2001, although she did not complete the requirement of working for a licensed investigator who would sponsor her. After extracting a promise that she would never work as a P.I., her instructor agreed to be her sponsor so that she could be officially licensed (Eckinger O1).

According to a posting at the New Orleans Literary Institute Web site, Smith and her husband were safely evacuated during Hurricane Katrina and returned home in October 2005 (KARES).

MAJOR WORKS AND THEMES

Smith has written novels about four different sleuths, ranging from lawyers and amateur detectives to police officers and private investigators. Her first series featured Rebecca Schwartz and was set in San Francisco. Schwartz was a feminist lawyer who became involved in various cases. The series also featured her law partner and a friend who was a mystery writer. The writer friend, Paul McDonald, was featured in two novels of his own, where he took on the role of amateur sleuth.

With the Skip Langdon series, Smith turned to New Orleans for her setting. Langdon is the daughter of a wealthy, prominent family in New Orleans society who rejects her expected roles and responsibilities to become a city police officer. Langdon deals with cases that highlight aspects of New Orleans, including links to jazz musicians, race and class issues in the city, historical events, and political figures, including the evil evangelist Errol Jacomine, who serves as Langdon's nemesis in several novels. The character is based on Smith's own experiences with being investigated by Jim Jones while writing her profile of him (Jordan).

Talba Willis is introduced as a character in *82 Desire,* one of the Langdon novels. She is seen in her own series, beginning with *Louisiana Hotshot.* Willis is an African American poet and performance artist who is also a computer expert. After being involved in a few cases, her continued interest and talents in investigative work leads her to seek work with a private investigator and to begin training to be a private investigator. Her mentor, Eddie Valentine, is 65 years old, a former police officer, and still wed to old-fashioned investigative approaches. Smith contrasts their strengths and personalities in an effective, humorous way.

CRITICAL RECEPTION

Smith won an Edgar award for her first Langdon novel. Critical acclaim for her works has been strong. *New Orleans Mourning* was praised for its "careening" plot, "complex view-points of her fully formed characters," and a "psychological and emotional depth" (Steinberg 1990:100). The second Langdon novel, *The Axeman's Jazz,* was noted for Smith's "acute ear for New Orleans speech and a sharp eye for the city's social stratification" in a "mystery of unusual depth" (Steinberg 1991:55). *Jazz Funeral* was called "smooth, polished, tightly orchestrated and eminently readable," also noting that she "manipulates her plot skillfully" and raises her "troubled teen" character "above stereotype" (Ott 1677).

New Orleans Beat was called a "humorous, suspenseful mystery" that "evoke[s] the steamy, mysterious ambiance of New Orleans" (Melton 1994:1927), but another reviewer found it focused too keenly on Langdon's biography and not on the case (Brainard 1994:53). *House of Blues* was praised as "wickedly paced and haunting" with Smith giving Langdon a "credibly textured emotional life" (Brainard 1995:63).

A review of *The Kindness of Strangers* noted that "without sacrificing the eccentric but believable characters, the moody deep South exoticism and the careful plotting that have popularized her recent work," Smith "pushes her protagonist to the breaking point and the series to a new high water mark of suspense" (Lochte 8). Another reviewer noted that while the plot "occasionally strained credibility, its claustrophobic impact" on Langdon led to an "intriguing" exploration of Langdon's crisis (Brainard 1996:59). *Crescent City Kill* featured Smith "adroitly weaving" subplots and offering "colorful characterizations" and a suspenseful finale to "make this an excellent addition to the series" (Brainard 1997: 70).

82 Desire, the novel that introduces Talba Willis, was praised for being "intricately constructed" with "some nice little surprises" for readers (Pitt 1977). Another review noted that Smith "crams a full cast and plenty of plot twists into her complicated story, in which the New Orleans atmosphere and Talba, with her fierce wise poetry, shine brightest" (Brainard 1998:64). A review of *Louisiana Hotshot* commended Smith for "generat[ing] plenty of tension as the savvy veteran and the eager novice combine their talents," but that her "evocation of her beloved New Orleans and her deft exploration of her characters' intimate relationships" is what readers will appreciate (Cannon 54). The latest Willis novel was called a "spicy gumbo of steamy mystery, saucy humor and piquant social commentary [that] should appeal to discriminating crime fans" ("P.I." 62).

BIBLIOGRAPHY

Works by Julie Smith

Rebecca Schwartz Series

Death Turns a Trick. New York: Walker, 1982.
The Sourdough Wars. New York: Walker, 1984.
Tourist Trap. New York: Mysterious Press, 1986.
Dead in the Water. New York: Ivy, 1991.
Other People's Skeletons. New York: Ivy, 1993.

Paul McDonald Series

True-Life Adventure. New York: Mysterious Press, 1985.
Huckleberry Fiend. New York: Mysterious Press, 1987.

Skip Langdon Series

New Orleans Mourning. New York: St. Martin's Press, 1990.
The Axeman's Jazz. New York: St. Martin's Press, 1991.
Jazz Funeral. New York: Fawcett, 1993.
New Orleans Beat. New York: Fawcett, 1994.
House of Blues. New York: Fawcett, 1995.
The Kindness of Strangers. New York: Fawcett, 1996.
Crescent City Kill. New York: Fawcett, 1997.
82 Desire. New York: Fawcett Columbine, 1998.
Mean Woman Blues. New York: Forge, 2003.

Talba Willis Series

Louisiana Hotshot. New York: Forge, 2001.
Louisiana Bigshot. New York: Forge, 2002.
Louisiana Lament. New York: Forge, 2004.
P.I. on a Hot Tin Roof. New York: Forge, 2005.

Works about Julie Smith

Brainard, Dulcy. "*New Orleans Beat.*" *Publishers Weekly* 13 June 1994: 53.
———. "*House of Blues.*" *Publishers Weekly* 24 April 1995: 63.
———. "*The Kindness of Strangers.*" *Publishers Weekly* 13 May 1996: 58–59.
———. "*Crescent City Kill.*" *Publishers Weekly* 30 June 1997: 70.
———. "*82 Desire.*" *Publishers Weekly* 13 July 1998: 64.
Cannon, Peter. "*Louisiana Hotshot.*" *Publishers Weekly* 9 April 2001: 54.
Eckinger, Helen. "The Mystery Lady: Author Julie Smith Loves New Orleans Almost as Much as She Loves a Good Crime Story." *Times Picayune* 6 August 2005: O1.
Jordan, Jon. "Interview with Julie Smith." MysteryOne.com. May 2002. 31 January 2006. http://www.mysteryone.com/JulieSmithInterview.htm
"Julie Smith." *Contemporary Authors.* Vol. 230. Ed. Julie Keppen. Detroit: Gale, 2005. 383–401.
KARES: Katrina Arts Relief and Emergency Support. New Orleans Literary Institute. 22 November 2005. 6 February 2006. http://neworleansliteraryinstitute.com/article.php?story = smith.julie
Lochte, Dick. "Criminal Pursuits." *Los Angeles Times* 11 August 1996: 8.
Melton, Emily. " *New Orleans Beat.*" *Booklist* July 1994: 1927.
Ott, Bill. "*Jazz Funeral.*" *Booklist* 15 May 1993: 1677.
"*P.I. on a Hot Tin Roof.*" *Publishers Weekly* 23 May 2005: 62.
Pitt, David. "*82 Desire.*" *Booklist* August 1998: 1977.
Steinberg, Sybil. "*New Orleans Mourning.*" *Publishers Weekly* 19 January 1990: 100.
———. "*The Axeman's Jazz.*" *Publishers Weekly* 12 July 1991: 55.

Julia Spencer-Fleming (1961–)

BIOGRAPHY

Julia Spencer-Fleming was born in Plattsburgh, New York. Her father was an Air Force pilot who died in a crash when she was an infant. Her mother remarried another Air Force pilot, and Spencer-Fleming grew up in a number of places in the United States and abroad, including Mobile, Alabama; Syracuse, New York; Rome; and Stuttgart. She has earned degrees from Ithaca College, George Washington University, and the University of Maine School of Law. She married Ross Hugo-Vidal in 1987, and they have three children: Victoria, Spencer, and Virginia. Her husband was also a lawyer, but now works as a teacher. The family lives in Buxton, Maine.

She completed her first novel just days after the birth of her third child, and as she did not have time to find an agent at that point, she entered it into the St. Martin's Press "Best First Novel" contest. The novel won the competition and a contract with the press. She subsequently left her legal practice and turned to writing full-time.

MAJOR WORKS AND THEMES

Spencer-Fleming's series is set in Millers Kill, a fictional small town in upstate New York. The novels feature Clare Fergusson, who has come to Millers Kill as the new Episcopal priest, and Russ Van Alstyne, the local police chief. They first meet when an infant is abandoned at the rectory. Fergusson is compelled to get involved, and she and Van Alstyne work together to solve the case. The second novel tackles homophobia and violence against gays, and *Out of the Deep I Cry* deals with harmful side effects of vaccines and a community's response. *To Darkness and Death* touches on issues of environmental activism in relation to a kidnapping that may be related to a land sale. In addition to the social issues that underpin the crimes they solve, Fergusson and Van Alstyne struggle with their personal attraction to each other, made difficult by her status with the church and his being married, however unhappily.

Spencer-Fleming's family settled in the Adirondack region in the 1720s, and she also comes from an Episcopalian family. These factors both played a role in her selection of setting and career for her main character. She found her work in the legal profession to be unsatisfying and wanted to write about "someone who was different and exciting and knew things" that she did not know and could learn about through researching for the novels (Kaczmarek 1). Spencer-Fleming notes that the inclusion of the social issues in her works reflects her own interests and concerns (Kaczmarek 2). Not wanting to write legal mysteries, Spencer-Fleming also thought that a member of the clergy could be "expected to get involved in others' problems, the way the rest of us are not," making for a believable amateur sleuth (Ryan 13).

In addition to continuing the Fergusson series, she has plans for a stand-alone thriller that will feature a snowbound prison. Spencer-Fleming notes that living in New York and Maine "has given her an affinity for wintery murder and mayhem…The weather, like any well-written victim, is both fascinating and deadly" (homepage).

CRITICAL RECEPTION

In addition to winning the St. Martin's Press award, her first novel also won Anthony, Agatha, Macavity, and Dilys awards. *Out of the Deep I Cry,* the second novel in the series, was nominated for an Edgar Award.

In the Bleak Midwinter was heralded as a "freshly conceived and meticulously plotted whodunit" (Stasio 2002:20) and as "a riveting page turner" with a "fast-paced plot" and "vivid setting descriptions" (Cannon 2002:164). The second novel was noted for its "eloquent exposition and natural dialogue" with a "precisely constructed plot [that] moves effortlessly to its dramatic conclusion" (Cannon 2003:55). Further, the "poignant reflections" of Fergusson and Van Alstyne as they struggle with their attraction to each other "never detract from the crime solving" (Cannon 2003:55). Another review of *A Fountain Filled with Blood* noted that "serious issues … add depth to the story" and "an exciting mountain rescue keeps the pages turning as the pace picks up at the end" (O'Brien 1055).

Out of the Deep I Cry was praised for having "a well-constructed story line, sympathetic characters with believable relationships, and a strong sleuthing pair" (Klett 126). Another review of this novel noted that Spencer-Fleming "expertly portrays the power of grief, guilt, greed and love and their effect on good people" and praised the "subtle sense of humor [that] further enhances this poignant and provocative mystery" (Cannon 2004:54). According to Judy Harrison, Spencer-Fleming's knowledge and skill "gives the story a layered depth rare in the genre today" (7).

Marilyn Stasio described Millers Kill as a place written with a "grave and tender touch" that readers "want to visit and hate to leave" (2004:23). Betty Smartt Carter praised Spencer-Fleming for writing "with uncommon sensibility and depth" (25).

BIBLIOGRAPHY

Works by Julia Spencer-Fleming

In the Bleak Midwinter. New York: St. Martin's Minotaur, 2002.
A Fountain Filled with Blood. New York: St. Martin's Minotaur, 2003.
Out of the Deep I Cry. New York: St. Martin's Minotaur, 2004.
To Darkness and to Death. New York: St. Martin's Minotaur, 2005.
All Mortal Flesh. New York: St. Martin's Minotaur, 2006.

Works about Julia Spencer-Fleming

Brundige, Kay. "PW Talks with Julia Spencer-Fleming." *Publishers Weekly* 8 March 2004: 54.
Cannon, Peter. "*In The Bleak Midwinter.*" *Publishers Weekly* 11 February 2002: 164.
———. "*A Fountain Filled with Blood.*" *Publishers Weekly* 24 February 2003: 55.
———. "*Out of the Deep I Cry.*" *Publishers Weekly* 8 March 2004: 53–54.
Carter, Betty Smartt. "Mystery Women." *Christian Century* 19 October 2004: 24–31.
Harrison, Judy. "Spencer-Fleming Third Shot Hits Mark Masterfully." *Bangor Daily News* 24 May 2004: 7.
"Julia Spencer-Fleming." *Contemporary Authors.* Vol. 218. Ed. Jenai A. Mynatt. Detroit: Gale, 2004. 399.
Julia Spencer-Fleming. Homepage. 25 June 2004. 10 November 2004. http://www.juliaspencerfleming. com
Kaczmarek, Lynn. "Julia Spencer-Fleming: Committed." *Mystery News* April/May 2004: 1–3.
Klett, Rex. "*Out of the Deep I Cry.*" *Library Journal* 1 April 2004: 126.
"Maine Author Spotlight Interview." *Maine Bar Journal.* Fall 2002. 16 June 2005.
http://www.juliaspencerfleming.com/me-interview.html
O'Brien, Sue. "*A Fountain Filled with Blood.*" *Booklist* 15 February 2003: 1055.
Routhier, Ray. "Episcopal Priest/Sleuth Rides Again." *Portland Press Herald* 18 April 2004: 10E.
Ryan, Laura T. "She Did It: Whodunit Wins a Prize for Liverpool Grad." *The Post Standard* (Syracuse) 14 April 2002: 13.
Stasio, Marilyn. "Crime." *New York Times Book Review* 17 March 2002: 20.
———. "Crime." *New York Times Book Review* 25 April 2004: 23.
Wahlheim, Emily. "Contest Victory Puts Lawyer on a Different Career Path." *Pantagraph* 13 June 2004: C5.

Dana Stabenow (1952–)

BIOGRAPHY

Born on March 27, 1952, in Anchorage, Alaska, Dana Stabenow's father was a pilot, and her mother worked as a bookkeeper and a ground crew assistant for aviation services. She spent part of her childhood on a fishing boat after her parents separated. Her mother worked as a deck hand on a salmon tender, and they lived on board for five years. As she has noted in several interviews, when she wasn't seasick, she wrote stories about "normal children who lived on shore" and made her mother read them; she also claims this was probably some of her best work (White; Aldrich 950; homepage). Before she began writing these stories around age 10, she also was a voracious reader. She recalls her mother getting books for her from the Seldovia Public Library to take out on the boat with them; Nancy Drew was an early favorite (Mowery 89).

After graduating from high school, she worked at a seafood company to pay her way through college at the University of Alaska in Anchorage. She notes that she wasn't a stellar student, but she earned a bachelor's degree in journalism in 1973. After college, she backpacked through Europe with a college friend and returned to Alaska just as many jobs were becoming available with the construction of the TransAlaska Pipeline. Stabenow worked hard on the pipelines, earning excellent money and taking frequent vacations to Hawaii, but in 1982, she decided to return to school and focus on her writing. She earned an MFA degree in 1985.

She struggled for several years, trying to engage an agent and racking up a number of rejection slips for her work. She discovered just how remote Alaska was during her attempts to hire an agent. One of her queries netted a response that the agent loved the work but unfortunately only represented American authors ("Alaska").

Stabenow's first novel, a science fiction work called *Second Star*, was published in 1991, but was not a commercial or critical success. She had also tried her hand at mystery writing, and when her editor saw the manuscript for the first Kate Shugak novel, offered her a contract for three Shugak books.

The first in the series, *A Cold Day for Murder,* was nominated for an Edgar Award. Stabenow recalls that she had to ask her editor what that meant (homepage). The novel won the Edgar, and she has been writing mysteries full-time since then. She continues to reside in Alaska and writes a travel column for *Alaska* magazine.

MAJOR WORKS AND THEMES

Although Stabenow has produced three science fiction novels, all about a character named Star Svensdotter, her mystery series have been much more popular and widely acclaimed. Her first mystery series features Kate Shugak, a former investigator with the district attorney. In the first novel, Shugak has moved away from Anchorage and has given up her professional position. Her last case, investigating a child killer, ended in a violent confrontation. Badly wounded, with her throat cut, she killed him and survived, but chose to walk away from the city and her work. Her former boss comes to find her to ask for her assistance in solving a crime in the Park, the area of Alaska where Shugak now lives. Shugak's cases throughout the series deal with a number of issues, including crooked business dealings and murders. Stabenow brings out a number of other social issues through subplots and supporting characters, offering powerful commentaries on fetal alcohol syndrome, spouse abuse, child neglect, economic strife, and environmental concerns. Above all is a representation of Alaska, with its mix of traditional and outside cultures. As Pearl G. Aldrich noted, "tradition and assimilation are always at war within" Shugak (950). In *The Singing of the Dead,* Stabenow combines political campaigns with a scandal that happened during the Gold Rush. The novel "shifts effortlessly between the present and the past," offering a portrait of life in Alaska in the late 1800s and the "narrow choices offered women" at that time (Cannon 2001:43). Shugak's investigation circles around a contested political campaign, and the historical case has an impact on the modern-day political players. *Blood Will Tell* also deals with politics, as Shugak's grandmother convinces her to take part in the Alaskan Federation of Natives convention in Anchorage, where a number of key issues are discussed and political lobbying is pervasive.

Stabenow's writing features strong female characters and well-drawn supporting characters. She also has quite a sense of humor: one scene that is often cited by reviewers and critics takes place in *Play with Fire,* where an annoying French tourist's toy poodle is snatched by an eagle. The state of Alaska is central to the novels, with excellently portrayed settings. Shugak's cases take her all over the state, giving readers a full tour of Alaska, its people and its cultures, from the oil pipelines of Prudhoe Bay, to a convention held in Anchorage, from a coastal fishing village to a hunting trip in the forest, with settings taking place in all four seasons. *Breakup* is one of the most comic of the series, with the mystery plot taking the backseat to a portrayal of the intense spring fever that attacks the denizens of the Park as the ice melts.

Stabenow's second series also focuses on crime and law enforcement in Alaska. This series features Liam Campbell, an Alaskan state trooper who is involved in a scandal that costs him his family and his job in Anchorage. Exiled to the Bush, Campbell is sent to Newenham, a small post where crimes need solving, and also where his first love, pilot Wy Chouinard, lives. Chouinard is surprised to see him but ends up collaborating with Campbell on various cases and rebuilding a life together. Stabenow deals with similar themes in this series, including the treatment of children, societal and cultural clashes, and life in Alaska. In *Better to Rest,* the discovery of the wreckage of a World War II-era plane opens up a case that ties into modern controversies over fishing rights.

In addition to her mysteries and science fiction novels, Stabenow published a stand-alone thriller in 2006. *Blindfold Game* deals with international terrorists who threaten the United States by sea.

CRITICAL RECEPTION

As noted previously, her first Shugak novel was nominated for an Edgar award. Stabenow gained critical notice very early on, and her works have continued to earn critical acclaim. In a review of *Play with Fire,* Stabenow was praised for "endow[ing] her writing with admirable sensory descriptions" and for "provid[ing] unusual settings for her deceptively simple plot" (Klett 103). A review of *Killing Grounds* noted that "even though this is the eighth Kate Shugak novel, the series remains lively and suspenseful, with enjoyable characters. The case is challenging, the descriptions of the Alaskan landscape are compelling, and the passages on women hunters and on fishing compare favorably" to nonfiction works on those themes (Rowen 1998b: 989). *Hunter's Moon,* the follow-up to *Killing Grounds,* was hailed for its "razor-sharp suspense and gritty prose" (Zaleski 1999:64), and *Midnight Come Again* was praised for its "breathtaking descriptions of natural scenery and incisive depiction of Alaskan natives caught between traditional and modern cultures" (Zaleski 2000:78). A review of *A Fine and Bitter Snow* noted that the series "truly evolves rather than simply revisiting the same setting," although, as the reviewer stated, "the setting is a doozy: an austere and beautiful Alaskan outback, populated with eccentrics and wild creatures" (Cannon 2002: 40).

A review of the first Liam Campbell novel, *Fire and Ice,* found it "compelling reading" with a "mystery [that] is hard to solve," a fast-paced plot, a "stunning" depiction of the Alaskan setting, and "vivid and sympathetic" characters (Rowen 1998a: 72).

BIBLIOGRAPHY

Works by Dana Stabenow

Kate Shugak Series

A Cold Day for Murder. New York: Berkley, 1992.
Dead in the Water. New York: Berkley, 1993.
A Fatal Thaw. New York: Berkley, 1993.
A Cold-Blooded Business. New York: Berkley, 1994.
Play with Fire. New York: Berkley, 1995.
Blood Will Tell. New York: Berkley, 1996.
Breakup. New York: Putnam, 1997.
Killing Grounds. New York: Putnam, 1998.
Hunter's Moon. New York: Putnam, 1999.
Midnight Come Again. New York: Putnam, 2000.
The Singing of the Dead. New York: Putnam, 2001.
A Fine and Bitter Snow. New York: St. Martin's, 2002.
A Grave Denied. New York: St. Martin's, 2003.
A Taint in the Blood. New York: St. Martin's, 2004.
A Complement to Rage. New York: St. Martin's, 2007.

Liam Campbell Series

Fire and Ice: A Liam Campbell Mystery. New York: Dutton, 1998.
So Sure of Death: A Liam Campbell Mystery. New York: Dutton, 1999.
Nothing Gold Can Stay: A Liam Campbell Mystery. New York: Dutton, 2000.
Better to Rest: A Liam Campbell Mystery. New York: New American Library, 2002.

Star Svensdotter Series

Second Star. New York: Berkley/Ace, 1991.
A Handful of Stars. New York: Ace, 1991.
Red Planet Run. New York: Berkley/Ace, 1995.

Other Novel

Blindfold Game. New York: St. Martin's Minotaur, 2006.

Works about Dana Stabenow

"Alaska Mystery Writer Dana Stabenow Talks about Writing Mysteries." *MysteryNet.com.* n.d. 20 October 2004. http://www.mysterynet.com/books/testimony/writing-alaska-mysteries.shtml

Aldrich, Pearl G. "Dana Stabenow." *St. James Guide to Crime & Mystery Writers.* 4th ed. Ed. Jay P. Pederson. Detroit: St. James Press, 1996. 950–52.

Cannon, Peter. "The Singing of the Dead." *Publishers Weekly* 2 April 2001: 42–43.

———. "A Fine and Bitter Snow." *Publishers Weekly* 27 May 2002: 40.

"Dana Stabenow." *Contemporary Authors.* Vol. 98, New Revision Series. Ed. Scot Peacock. Detroit: Gale, 2001. 405–408.

Dana Stabenow. Home page. 2005. 20 October 2004. http://www.danastabenow.com

Klett, Rex E. "Play with Fire." *Library Journal* 1 February 1995: 103.

Mowery, Danielle. "A Cold-Blooded Business: An Interview with Alaskan Mystery Writer Dana Stabenow." *Armchair Detective: A Quarterly Journal Devoted to the Appreciation of Mystery, Detective, and Suspense Fiction* 27:1 (1994): 88–91.

Rowen, John. "*Fire and Ice.*" *Booklist* 1 September 1998a: 72.

———. "*Killing Grounds.*" *Booklist* 15 February 1998b: 989.

White, Claire E. "A Conversation with Dana Stabenow." *Writers Write: The Internet Writing Journal* February 2000. 20 October 2004. http://www.writerswrite.com/journal/feb00/stabenow.html

Zaleski, Jeff. "*Hunter's Moon.*" *Publishers Weekly* 19 April 1999: 64.

———. "*Midnight Come Again.*" *Publishers Weekly* 10 April 2000: 78.

Sarah Strohmeyer

BIOGRAPHY

Sarah Strohmeyer was born in Bethlehem, Pennsylvania. After graduating from high school, she worked at the local newspaper as a copy editor. Her parents both worked at the paper as well; her father is John Strohmeyer, winner of the 1972 Pulitzer for editorial writing. After earning a bachelor's degree in international relations from Tufts University in 1984, she went to work as a reporter for the *Home News* in New Brunswick, New Jersey.

She moved to Cleveland to work as a reporter for the *Plain Dealer*. In Cleveland, she met and married her husband, Charles Merriman. She left the *Plain Dealer* when she became pregnant with her first child. She then attended Case Western Reserve and earned a master's degree in English. The family moved to New Hampshire in 1992, and while her husband attended law school, she covered the crime beat for the *Valley News* in Lebanon, New Hampshire. They currently live near Montpelier, Vermont, and have two children, Anna and Sam.

An assignment interviewing Janet Evanovich led to Strohmeyer's successful turn to fiction writing. She has noted that she had plans to write a mystery set in Vermont, but that Evanovich's advice on the setting and other logistical matters of agents and publishing shaped the development of her series and her character, Bubbles Yablonsky (McBride; Jurgelski 1). Strohmeyer is well known for dressing in character for her book signings.

MAJOR WORKS AND THEMES

Her first book was nonfiction, a collaborative effort with photographer Geoff Hansen, entitled *Barbie Unbound: A Parody of the Barbie Obsession*. It was well received and gained a good deal of media coverage.

Her first mystery novel was published in 2001 and introduced readers to Bubble Yablonsky. Set in Lehigh, Pennsylvania, Yablonsky is a hairdresser who has taken courses at the local community college and is determined to become a journalist. Not taken seriously at first, because of her ditzy blonde appearance and lack of experience and credentials, she is sent to cover an event: someone is threatening to jump off a building. She not only engineers a rescue for the potential suicide, but then blunders into a murder case and solves it, while exposing corruption and power struggles among the denizens of Lehigh.

Subsequent cases involve going to Amish country to track down a friend who disappeared on her wedding day, and helping a woman she believes has been wrongly convicted of killing her husband, all handled while Yablonsky deals with her teenage daughter, her mother, her ex-husband, and her new love interest, photographer Steve Stiletto.

In 2005, she published a humorous work of fiction called *The Secret Lives of Fortunate Wives,* which takes place in a gated community outside Cleveland, Ohio. Former reporter Claire Stark marries a wealthy man after a whirlwind romance and finds herself in the gated community as an outsider, thrust into a world of infidelity and suburban intrigue.

CRITICAL RECEPTION

Strohmeyer won an Agatha Award for best first novel. A review of the first novel, *Bubbles Unbound,* tells readers that "a wild ride awaits" with Yablonsky in her Camaro, as she takes the world by storm, "armed with her certificate from Two Guys Community College, abetted by a quirky array of social castoffs and fueled by Doritos, Velveeta and Diet Pepsi" (Zaleski 71).

A review of *Bubbles in Trouble* noted that Strohmeyer "successfully navigates the fine line between humorous stereotype and sympathetic amateur investigator," while "Bubbles goes undercover, frantically (and hilariously) shifting between her role as a sexy reporter and her cover as an Amish widow" (Cannon 2002:67). Her undercover assignment in this novel also attracted notice from another reviewer, who stated that "as in a well-scripted Lucille Ball routine, Bubbles gets into trouble in both of her roles. However, with her gold toenail polish, her hot-oil treatments for cows and her abysmal cooking skills, it's a given that her adventures as an Amish woman have great comic rhythm" (Rabinovitz 21).

Bubbles Ablaze was seen to offer "lots of madcap fun" and "laugh-out-lines," including the often-cited scene where Yablonsky is asked if she knows who John Gotti is, and she replies that she's "almost positive he ran a pizza parlor in Allentown" (Cannon 2003:52). A review of *Bubbles A Broad* found Yablonsky to be "good-hearted, persistent and very, very funny" (Cannon 2004:41).

BIBLIOGRAPHY

Works by Sarah Strohmeyer

Bubbles Yablonsky Series

Bubbles Unbound. New York: Dutton, 2001.
Bubbles in Trouble. New York: Dutton, 2002.
Bubbles Ablaze. New York: Dutton, 2003.
Bubbles a Broad. New York: Dutton, 2004.
Bubbles Betrothed. New York: Dutton, 2005.

Other Novels

The Secret Lives of Fortunate Wives. New York: Dutton, 2005.
The Cinderella Pact. New York: Dutton, 2006.

Works about Sarah Strohmeyer

Cannon, Peter. "*Bubbles in Trouble.*" *Publishers Weekly* 3 June 2002: 67.
———. "*Bubbles Ablaze.*" *Publishers Weekly* 26 May 2003: 52.
———. "*Bubbles A Broad.*" *Publishers Weekly* 29 March 2004: 41.

Jurgelski, Susan. "World According to Bubbles is Complete with Spandex, Murder and Some Humor." *Lancaster New Era* 15 July 2003: 1.

McBride, Susan. "Sarah Unbound: An Interview with Sarah Strohmeyer." Between the Pages. June 2001. February 6, 2006. http://www.myshelf.com/betweenthepages/01/strohmeyer.html

Rabinovitz, Amy. "Double Bubbles: Sarah Strohmeyer Brings Heroine Back for Rollicking Good Read." *Houston Chronicle* 4 August 2002: 21.

Salter, Rosa. "Bethlehem Native Ablaze with Newest Bubbles." *Morning Call* 13 July 2003: E1.

"Sarah Strohmeyer." *Contemporary Authors.* Vol. 210. Ed. Scot Peacock. Detroit: Gale, 2003. 404–405.

Zaleski, Jeff. "*Bubbles Unbound.*" *Publishers Weekly* 1 January 2000: 71.

P. J. Tracy

BIOGRAPHY

P. J. Tracy is the pseudonym of a pair of writers: Patricia J. Lambrecht and her daughter Traci Lambrecht. Traci lives in California, far from her mother in their native Minnesota, but the team is able to collaborate easily. In all their interviews, it is clear that they have always had an extremely close relationship that allows them to successfully work as partners (Scott 13; Tillotson 1F; Dunn 52).

Among other sources, an article in the St. Olaf College alumni magazine provides some background information about the writers. P. J. attended the college before leaving to marry Phillip Lambrecht, who graduated in 1965. They divorced when Traci was eight (Scott 13). P. J. later remarried Ted Platz, and they live near Chisago City, Minnesota. P. J. notes that she "has absolutely no qualifications" as a writer except for "a penchant for lying" (Engblom 12). Traci graduated from St. Olaf's in 1989, with a degree in Russian studies. She also studied opera during college, and was the lead singer for a rock band in St. Paul for a short time after graduation. She currently lives in Santa Monica, California, and Aspen, Colorado, with Dale Launer, a screenwriter.

Before turning to writing mystery fiction with her daughter, P. J. had years of experience as a writer, with many short stories to her credit. Her first story was published in the *Saturday Evening Post* when Traci was eight years old (Engblom 12). She published a number of short stories and also wrote nonfiction magazine articles and stories for romance fiction magazines (Kaczmarek 1). When Traci decided to give up her musical career, she and her mother joined forces and collaborated on writing romance novels (Kaczmarek 1). P. J. notes that they wrote for Harlequin under the name Melinda Cross, and earned good money, but she eventually tired of the genre and "as menopause drew near, [her] thoughts began to move from romance to murder" (Scott 13). They saved enough money to live for a year, and devoted themselves completely to writing their first mystery novel (Scott 13).

MAJOR WORKS AND THEMES

All of Tracy's novels feature the same cast of characters from the Minneapolis police force, a rural Wisconsin sheriff's office, and a computer software company called Monkeewrench, combining elements of police procedurals with a cast of amateur sleuths and aspects of techno-thrillers. In the first novel, a game created by the company is being used by a serial killer. The game featured a detective tracking down killers, and someone is killing people to match the scenarios in the game. When the police turn their investigation toward the company, a number of red flags appear for Detective Leo Magozzi. The Monkeewrench crew, consisting of Grace MacBride, Annie Belinksi, Harley Davidson, and Roadrunner, all turn out to have abbreviated backgrounds, having starting over after a major trauma in their past. Their reticence to reveal all the facts about their backgrounds makes Magozzi suspicious. Another case also ties in, bringing the programmers together with Magozzi and his partner from Minneapolis, and with a sheriff and deputy team from rural Wisconsin to solve the case. The Monkeewrench team continues to work with the police on future cases, sometimes for their computer expertise, and sometimes because they end up inadvertently involved.

The second novel, *Live Bait,* finds Sherifff Michael Halloran and Deputy Sharon Mueller puzzling over a series of murders of local senior citizens. MacBride's new computer program is called into service, and the case turns out to be much more than the surface appeared. *Dead Run* takes place in a small town that MacBride, Belinksi, and Mueller are stranded in when their car breaks down. The town is completely deserted and the trio uncovers a shocking event. The Lambrechts note that their imagination was piqued when they drove through a deserted town on their way to visit relatives. P. J.'s husband theorizes that every-one was inside watching the Packers, but the Lambrechts prefer their more sinister take on the situation (Steinberg F6).

CRITICAL RECEPTION

P. J. Tracy has enjoyed an extremely positive critical reception, with an Anthony Award nomination for *Live Bait.* One review of the debut novel noted that readers may think that "serial killers have been done to death," but that the "smart, stylish, suspenseful, surprisingly funny and wholly satisfying" novel will change their minds (Pate). Another reviewer felt the novel was so well written that the fact it was a debut was surprising, and that even more surprising was that it was a collaborative work, noting that "most collaborative novels are about as well stitched together as an autopsied corpse"; but *Monkeewrench* is a rare exception, sewn as seamlessly as the work of a master tailor."(Montgomery D6). Jeff Zaleski called it a "a soundly plotted thriller that fires on all cylinders" (2003:52) and noted that the work "covers all the bases in this debut thriller: an accelerating, unpredictable plot that combines police procedural with techno-geekspeak, an array of well-drawn characters and, most importantly, witty repartee" (2003:53). The second novel also received lavish praise. One review noted the "fresh plot delivers a new surprise with each twist of the tale" and "simmers with believable characters, crisp dialogue, an authentic look at police work and dark humor" (Cogdill) Another review praised the "sharp, satisfying thriller" for its "generous doses of humor and suspense" (Zaleski 2004:60).

BIBLIOGRAPHY

Works by P. J. Tracy

Monkeewrench. New York: Putnam, 2003. Also published as *Want to Play?* London: Michael Joseph, 2003.
Live Bait. New York: Putnam, 2004.
Dead Run. New York: Putnam, 2005.
Snow Blind. New York: Putnam, 2006.

Works about P. J. Tracy

Cogdill, Oline H. "*Live Bait* by P.J Tracy." *Knight Ridder Tribune News Service* 12 May 2004. www.proquest.com 5 November 2005.

"*Dead Run.*" *Publishers Weekly* 21 February 2005: 157.

Dunn, Adam. "PW Talks with P. J. Tracy." *Publishers Weekly* 3 March 2003: 52.

Engblom, Carole Leigh. "Portrait: P.J. and Traci Lambrecht." *St. Olaf Magazine* Fall 2003: 12–13. http://www.stolaf.edu/offices/communications/magazine/2003fall/lambrechts.pdf 5 November 2005.

Kaczmarek, Lynn. "P. J. Tracy: It's in the Genes." *Mystery News* 23.2 (April/May 2005): 1–3.

Montgomery, David. "Debut Mysteries Are on the Case." *USA Today* 20 May 2003: D6.

Pate, Nancy. "*Monkeewrench* by P.J. Tracy." *Knight Ridder Tribune News Service* 31 March 2004. www.proquest.com 5 November 2005.

"P(atricia) J. Lambrecht." *Contemporary Authors.* Vol. 230. Ed. Julie Keppen. Detroit: Gale, 2005. 247–48.

Scott, Caroline. "Relative Values." *Sunday Times* (London) 24 July 2005: 13.

Steinberg, David. "Mom and Daughter Turn Out Second Mystery." *Albuquerque Journal* 16 May 2004: F6.

Tillotson, Kristin. "Blood Ties." *Star Tribune* 29 August 2004: 1F.

"Traci Lambrecht." *Contemporary Authors.* Vol. 230. Ed. Julie Keppen. Detroit: Gale, 2005. 248–49.

Zaleski, Jeff. "*Monkeewrench.*" *Publishers Weekly* 3 March 2003: 52–53.

———. "*Live Bait.*" *Publishers Weekly* 22 March 2004: 60.

Kathy Hogan Trocheck (1954–)

BIOGRAPHY

Born in St. Petersburg, Florida, in 1954, Kathy Hogan Trocheck grew up in a family with four siblings. Her mother managed a restaurant in a residential hotel but made sure there was time for reading and books. Trocheck recalls her mother taking all five children regularly to the bookmobile and that her mother or older sister often read to them before they could read themselves (Morris).

She earned a degree in journalism at the University of Georgia and worked as a reporter for the *Atlanta Constitution-Journal* before turning to fictional works. Among her numerous assignments was a murder trial in Savannah that become widely known when John Berendt wrote about it later in *Midnight in the Garden of Good and Evil.*

Trocheck had not planned to leave journalism, but she became disillusioned with the changes in the newspaper business, with the "emphasis on shorter stories" rather than "a long story in which a reporter can examine why things happen" (Morris). In 1990, with one novel finished but unsold and a new idea for another novel, she attended a writers' workshop at Antioch College and had the opportunity to consult with Sue Grafton. Grafton encouraged her to focus on editing the novel she had brought with her to the workshop, but when Grafton heard Trocheck read from the other project, Grafton changed her mind and told Trocheck to focus on the new project after all (Bookreporter). That new project was soon published as the first in her Callahan Garrity series.

Also writing as Mary Kay Andrews

She and her husband Tom, described as her high school sweetheart on her Web page, have two children, Mary Kathleen and Andrew. After years of living in Atlanta, they now live in Raleigh, North Carolina. In addition to her writing, she teaches at various workshops across the country.

MAJOR WORKS AND THEMES

Under her real name, Trocheck has written two different mystery series. She also has written several novels under the pseudonym Mary Kay Andrews. Her first series features Julia Callahan Garrity, a former police officer who runs a cleaning service called House Mouse. Her employees are a cast of quirky characters, and she also has regular interactions with her mother, her boyfriend, and her former police partner, Bucky Deavers. Given her background, she is approached by various people for assistance, and she and her crew also stumble into various mysteries. The novels tackle a number of issues, such as race relations, gentrification, homelessness, and other issues specifically sensitive in Atlanta (O'Briant T1). Although the books deal with serious crimes and issues, Trocheck's strong sense of humor comes through in the series.

Her second series consists of two novels featuring Truman Kicklighter, a retired journalist who lives in St. Petersburg in a residential hotel. He is bored with his retired life and becomes involved in various cases as an amateur sleuth.

Her Mary Kay Andrews novels are best classified as comedic fiction. She takes on the mores of Southern suburban culture, while writing about contemporary women and their choices. Several of the works, including *Savannah Blues,* have a mystery or suspense element, drawing comparisons to the works of Susan Isaacs. The main character is in the antiques business and discovers a body in a house. Trocheck will return to Savannah with *Savannah Breeze,* but a minor character from the first novel will be in the spotlight in the novel. Other works deal more directly with issues of relationships, but with her strong sense of humor. For example, in *Little Bitty Lies,* a woman is busy helping her friends cope with their divorces when her own husband leaves her and cleans out the bank accounts on his way out of town. She decides to fake his death to collect the insurance money, but then has to deal with a number of complications, such as discovering her husband was under investigation for business fraud and the fact that she is attracted to the investigator.

CRITICAL RECEPTION

Trocheck has been nominated for Agatha, Macavity, and Edgar awards for her mystery novels. The first Garrity novel won rave reviews from a variety of sources. *The Virginia Quarterly Review,* often tough on popular or genre fiction, even praised Trocheck as a "fresh voice on the mystery scene" and noted that Garrity's targets, "the pretentious, the pompous and the powerful," were "pretty good targets for a detective story" ("*Every Crooked Nanny*" 21). *Publishers Weekly* heralded it as a "high-caliber debut" with "vivid, captivating characters," summing up that the novel was a "clever, colorful page turner, not to be missed" (Brainard 1992:57). Another called it a "quick-paced thriller [that] provides an intriguing introduction to a delightfully down-to-earth sleuth"(Flanagan 1924).

A review of *Happy Never After* noted that it was "spiced with personal drama plus music biz nostalgia" and ended with a "tense confrontations with a very ruthless killer"(Carroll 1555). *Heart Trouble* was praised for its "trademark laugh-out-loud humor, an intriguing plot, and a cast of eccentric by charming characters," all of which made this "another winning entry" in the series for critic Emily Melton (1681). For another reviewer, it was a "sure winner," narrated with "zesty enthusiasm" and providing a "thrilling climax" (Brainard 1996:59).

In a review of *Midnight Clear,* Trocheck was praised for her "good ear for regional dialect and a fine eye for detail," as well as strong, realistic portrayals of family relationships (English D8). *Irish Eyes* was praised for how well "Trocheck skillfully blends family, generational, ethnic, racial, medical and criminal conflicts," with Garrity as "an appealing heroine, hard-working and principled" (Zaleski 2000:68). Another review of this novel called it "an entertaining, suspenseful romp" with a plot that "zips along but not too fast to blur the exceptional characters" (McLarin 1090).

The Kicklighter series and her Mary Kay Andrews novels have also been well received. A review of *Crash Course* praised its "lively wit, memorable characters, and cutting prose" (Klett 106). One critic noted that "her eye for social satire and ear for colorful speech turn every novel into an entertainment" (Morris). A review of *Hissy Fit* noted that the "winning read" features "lush and appealing" descriptions of furniture and interiors that will "seduce even the decorating-challenged," in addition to an "idyllic southern setting and the humorous, often-scintillating banter" (Wilkinson 1895). Another review of *Hissy Fit* noted that the novel is "darker than [its] fluffy title suggests" and is a "black comedy riven with shocking secrets" (Zaleski 2004:36).

BIBLIOGRAPHY

Works by Kathy Hogan Trocheck

Callahan Garrity Series

Every Crooked Nanny. New York: HarperCollins, 1992.
To Live and Die in Dixie. New York: HarperCollins, 1993.
Homemade Sin. New York: HarperCollins, 1994.
Happy Never After. New York: HarperCollins, 1995.
Heart Trouble. New York: HarperCollins, 1996.
Strange Brew. New York: HarperCollins, 1997.
Midnight Clear. New York: HarperCollins, 1998.
Irish Eyes. New York: HarperCollins, 2000.

Truman Kicklighter Series

Lickety-Split. New York: HarperCollins, 1996.
Crash Course. New York: HarperCollins, 1997.

Works by Mary Kay Andrews

Savannah Blues. New York: HarperCollins, 2002.
Little Bitty Lies. New York: HarperCollins, 2003.
Hissy Fit. New York: HarperCollins, 2004.
Savannah Breeze. New York: HarperCollins, 2006.

Works about Kathy Hogan Trocheck/Mary Kay Andrews

Bookreporter.com. Interview with Mary Kay Andrews. February 15, 2002. 31 January 2006. http://www.bookreporter.com/authors/au-andrews-mary-kay.asp
Brainard, Dulcy. "*Every Crooked Nanny.*" *Publishers Weekly* 11 May 1992: 57.
———. "*Heart Trouble.*" *Publishers Weekly* 13 May 1996: 59.
Carroll, Mary. "*Happy Never After.*" *Booklist* 1 May 1995: 1555.
English, Bella. "A Southern-Fried Christmas Mystery." *Boston Globe* 18 December 1998: D8.
"*Every Crooked Nanny.*" *Virginia Quarterly Review* 69.1 (Winter 1993): 21.

Flanagan, Margaret. "*Every Crooked Nanny.*" *Booklist* July 1992: 1924.

"Kathy Hogan Trocheck." *Contemporary Authors.* Vol. 184. Ed. Scot Peacock. Detroit: Gale, 2000. 415–17.

Klett, Rex E. "*Crash Course.*" *Library Journal* 1 March 1997: 106.

MaryKayAndrews.com Homepage. 2005. 31 January 2006. http://www.marykayandrews.com

McLarin, Jenny. "*Irish Eyes.*" *Booklist* 15 February 2000: 1090.

Melton, Emily. "*Heart Trouble.*" *Booklist* 1–15 June 1996: 1680–81.

Morris, Anne. "Behind Closed Doors: Mary Kay Andrews Spoofs the Secrets and Lies of Suburbia." Bookpage.com. 2003. 31 January 2006. http://www.bookpage.com/0308bp/mary_kay_andrews. html

O'Briant, Don. "Scenes of the Crimes." *Atlanta Journal-Constitution* 23 April 2000: T1.

Wilkinson, Joanne. "*Hissy Fit.*" *Booklist* August 2004: 1895.

Zaleski, Jeff. "*Irish Eyes.*" *Publishers Weekly* 21 February 2000: 68.

———. "*Hissy Fit.*" *Publishers Weekly* 5 July 2004: 36.

Mary Willis Walker (1942–)

BIOGRAPHY

Mary Willis Walker was born May 24, 1942, in Foxpoint, Wisconsin, to Ralph and Marjorie Schultz Willis. She graduated from Duke University with a degree in English in 1964. She was married in 1967 to Lee Walker, who became president of Dell Computers; they divorced in 1993. They have two daughters, Amanda and Susannah, and lived in New York and Virginia before moving to Austin. She taught high school English before beginning her writing career. She noted that she had "always kept a journal" and in 1988, "just sat down and started to write fiction" (Morris 90). She lives in Austin, Texas.

MAJOR WORKS AND THEMES

Willis Walker's first novel, *Zero at the Bone,* featured a dog trainer and kennel owner named Kate Driscoll. After her father is killed, Driscoll becomes involved in investigating the case.

Her second novel, *The Red Scream,* introduced a new character, Molly Cates. Cates is a true crime writer who has written about a serial killer named Louie Bronk. When a murder is committed in a strikingly similar way, Cates must question whether there is a copycat or if Bronk was convicted for a murder he did not commit. Willis Walker wrote *Under the Beetle's Cellar* after the Branch Davidian incident at Waco, Texas. In this novel, Cates investigates a charismatic cult leader who takes children hostage. These two novels provide hints about Cates's difficult life, with her mother having died when she was a child and her father's suicide when she was 16 years old. She has never been convinced he took his own life, and in *All the Dead Lie Down,* she has finally discovered evidence to back up her conviction that he was murdered.

Willis Walker has not published since 1998, but the Random House Web site indicates she is still working on her next novel. An online mystery newsletter from 2002 reported that she was suffering from writer's block. Other Web sites show that she has been reviewing mystery novels and has been active in Austin's literary scene over the past few years, including

254 Mary Willis Walker

serving as a judge in a short story contest and serving on the board of the Texas Institute of Letters.

CRITICAL RECEPTION

Willis Walker's first novel won Macavity and Agatha awards, and her second scored an Edgar Award. *Under the Beetle's Cellar* won Anthony and Hammett awards. Critical acclaim was also strong for her four novels. *Publishers Weekly* called her first novel a "gripping debut," further noting that "the very believable players make the resolution all the more harrowing" ("*Zero at the Bone*" 47).

The Red Scream was praised as a "very well-written and plausibly plotted" novel (Klett 1994:168). Another review noted that Willis Walker is a "masterly writer, weaving horror, humor and suspense" into a "gripping, provocative" novel (Melton 1994:2029). Further praise is given for Cates's character development, describing her as "full of vinegar, a wonderfully appealing heroine with a lot of guts" (Melton 1994: 2029).

One review of *Under the Beetle's Cellar* noted that "if there can be such a thing as a heart-warming suspense thriller, then Mary Willis Walker has written a nifty one" (Stasio 28). Another reviewer called it a "dynamite" successor, praising Willis Walker as a "master at building suspense to a well-nigh unbearable level" and highlighting the "spellbinding plot, outstanding writing, and one-of-a-kind characters" (Melton 1995:1911). Another review warned that the novel is "not for the claustrophobic" with Willis Walker bringing readers into the underground lair of the villain with "terrifying immediacy" (Pate F7).

All the Dead Lie Down was heralded as a "superb tale" that "delivers an irresistible mix of laughter, tears, fear, heartache and, of course, suspense" (Melton 1998:1394). Another reviewer praised its "literate prose, in-depth characterization, and a cleverly manipulated plot" (Klett 1998:127).

BIBLIOGRAPHY

Works by Mary Willis Walker

Zero at the Bone. New York: St. Martin's Press, 1991.
The Red Scream. New York: Doubleday, 1994.
Under the Beetle's Cellar. New York: Doubleday, 1995.
All the Dead Lie Down. New York: Doubleday, 1998.

Works about Mary Willis Walker

Klett, Rex E. "*The Red Scream.*" *Library Journal* 1 June 1994: 168.
———.. "*All the Dead Lie Down.*" *Library Journal* 1 April 1998: 127.
"Mary Willis Walker." *Contemporary Authors.* Vol. 161. Ed. Scot Peacock. Detroit: Gale, 1998. 296–97.
Melton, Emily. "*The Red Scream.*" *Booklist* August 1994: 2029.
———. "*Under the Beetle's Cellar.*" *Booklist* August 1995: 1911.
———. "*All the Dead Lie Down.*" *Booklist* 15 April 1998:1394.
Morris, Anne. "Mary Willis Walker: 'I Follow My Obsessions'." *Publishers Weekly* 28 August 1995: 90–91.
Pate, Nancy. "Dig into New Puzzlers." *Orlando Sentinel* 3 September 1995: F7.
Stasio, Marilyn. "Crime." *New York Times Book Review* 1 October 1995: 28.
"*Zero at the Bone.*" *Publishers Weekly* 25 October 1991: 47.

Minette Walters (1949–)

BIOGRAPHY

Minette Caroline Mary Jebb was born September 26, 1949, in Bishop's Stortford, Hertfordshire, England. Her father, Samuel, was an army captain, and her mother, Colleen, was an artist. She has two brothers. Her father died when she was young, and she has stated that not having been able to know him is her greatest regret (Greenstreet 10). She became an avid reader and was given a collection of Agatha Christie novels at age 11, which "hooked [her] into the crime and thriller genres for life" ("When" 8). She attended Goldophin School and Durham University, where she earned a bachelor's degree in French. After school, she worked as an editor in London for IPC Magazines, which specialized in romance fiction. Her work was excellent training for seeing "what could go wrong and how to construct a good, tight plot" (Silet 183). She also began writing stories for the magazine, under what are termed "well-guarded pen names" (East 102). She married businessman Alexander Walters in 1978 and they have two sons, Roland and Philip. She began writing again when her children were both in school. She and her husband currently reside on a farm in Dorset, where they report they have become do-it-yourself experts.

MAJOR WORKS AND THEMES

All of Walters's works are stand-alone novels, usually labeled as psychological suspense. Stylistically, her works include fictionalized reports, diaries, newspaper articles, and other items that are skillfully blended into the narrative. Her first novel, *The Ice House,* deals with the discovery of a corpse at an estate. Suspected of the murder of her husband when he disappeared 10 years earlier, the body brings new police attention to Phoebe Maybury and her housemates.

Many of Walters's novels have a darker tone than the first novel, which featured humorous dialogue and quirky characters. In *The Sculptress,* for example, a journalist named Rosalind Leigh is assigned to write a biography of a woman serving a life sentence for brutally murdering her mother and sister. As Leigh discovers more and more about Olive Martin and the case, she becomes less certain that justice was served. *The Scold's Bridle* also features a brutal murder of a woman with a medieval contraption that was designed to quiet women. The victim's doctor suspects murder but comes under suspicion herself when she is revealed as the beneficiary of the victim's wealth. Both of these novels are noted for their suspense and "cat and mouse interchanges" between characters (East 102).

The Dark Room features a woman who wakes up in a mental hospital, unable to remember the crimes she is accused of. In *The Echo,* a homeless man who starves to death is discovered to have been a fugitive, a banker who had disappeared with a great deal of money years before. A journalist is fascinated by the case and begins an investigation into the man, his wife, and the circumstances of his death, all of which contribute to a suspenseful plot. *The Breaker* uses a similar motif. A woman's body washes ashore in Dorset, and her young daughter is found alone in the streets in a nearby town. Once she is identified and the cause of death is known, three suspects emerge, as does an unflattering portrait of the victim.

The Shape of Snakes addresses issues of race and class. In this novel, a woman named Mrs. Sam Ranelagh, only identified as "M," has insisted for 20 years that the apparent accidental death of a neighbor, a woman called "Mad Annie" Butts, was a racially motivated murder. With Walters's trademark assortment of articles, reports, and other documents, Mrs. Ranelagh lays out her case, seeking justice for Annie. As the story unfolds, though, it becomes unclear whether Mrs. Ranelagh is seeking justice or revenge, and on whose behalf. *Acid Row,* the story of a violent outburst in council housing, was notable in that all the action takes place in one day. A man who has been falsely accused of child molestation is placed in a housing unit. When a girl disappears, he comes under attack from neighbors who believe the original story. The pace was much quicker than her other novels, but the suspense and the detail of the story were as strong as in other works. *Fox Evil* offered a complex plot involving a man whose wife died in an apparent accident. Neighbors believe murder has been committed. In the meantime, the town deals with the intrusion of a group of squatters, with a charismatic leader, who are trying to claim land.

Disoriented Minds continues Walters's examination of race and class issues. In this work, the racial identity of Dr. Jonathan Hughes, and his assumptions about other people's racist views, is a stumbling block for him and the investigation. Hughes has written a book about miscarriages of justice and he is asked to consider another case. As he becomes more comfortable with his new ally, Georgina "George" Gardiner, they are able to tackle the case of Howard Stamp. Stamp was accused of killing his aunt and later committed suicide in prison. Stamp was mentally impaired and Gardiner, Hughes and others believe he was not guilty of the crime. While working to uncover the truth, the team also addresses other crimes from the past, allowing Walters to explore a number of issues related to class and violence against women.

CRITICAL RECEPTION

Walters has won a number of awards for her work, including the John Creasey Award for *The Ice House,* the Macavity and Edgar awards for *The Sculptress,* and two Gold Dagger awards from the British Crime Writers' Association, one for *The Scold's Bridle* and one for *Fox Evil.* *The Ice House* was well received as an "intelligent mystery, full of twists and turns" and as an "excellent tale rich with characterizations and unique surprises" (Grimes 136). Another reviewer called it a "zinger of a debut" that "skillfully brings together" the characters into a "complicated but believable puzzle," which Walters "solves with panache" (Brainard 1992:40). A review of *The Sculptress* heralded it as a "sleek, exciting tale" which would readers would find "mesmerizing" and "stunning" (Melton 1993:257). Although another reviewer found fault with the characters in the novel, it was nevertheless praised it as a "gripping read" (Brainard 1993:48). Similar praise met Walters's third novel, *The Scold's Bridle,* with reviewers calling it "well-written, provocative, intelligent" (Melton 1994:244) and "articulate, sophisticated, imaginative" (Klett 118).

With *The Dark Room,* one reviewer posited that Walters "sets a new standard for British mysteries," praising the "fine characterizations and intelligent prose" in a "riveting, intricately woven tale" (Leber 100). Another reviewer found that "the quest for truth is punctuated by touches of humanity that lift this novel way above others of its genre" (Scott 32). Although other reviewers felt that the plot lost its momentum (Melton 1996:749) and was overplotted (Steinberg 1995:65), both still found room to praise the original premise of the novel (Steinberg 1995:65) and its "psyche-probing character analyses" (Melton 1996:749).

A review of *The Echo* praised Walters as "a superior storyteller who plumbs psychological depths with an acuity that here, as before, will have readers enthralled" (Steinberg 1997:93). *The Breaker* was heralded as a "wonderfully convoluted whodunit that will perplex even expert villain spotters" (Pitt 1105) and as "psychological suspense at its best, engendered in a novel whose sinuous plot and enigmatic characters will captivate readers" (Zaleski

1999:57). A review of *The Shape of Snakes* praised Walters as "a master storyteller," who writes "with an immediacy that draws the reader personally into the tragedy," further noting that the inclusion of letters and articles add "verisimilitude …[that] illuminate and advance the plot" (Croan G10). Marilyn Stasio confessed that she had "learned never to trust the narrators" in Walters' works, noting that the "complex characters can be cunning, deceitful, even mad—which is exactly what makes them such absorbing company" (2001:22).

Reviewers praised the suspense of *Acid Row*, noting that "although the myriad scenes are short, *Acid Row* is rich with details about characters" (Cogdill 9G). Another reviewer stated that Walters "demonstrates her eye for the sociological and psychological avalanche provoked by human temptation and people living in cramped quarters" (Zaleski 2002:42). Reviewers tended to dislike the plot of *Fox Evil*, but again, those critiques were tempered with praise. One reviewer noted that "even when the narrative loses momentum … Walters' characters vibrate with the envy and spite of their pent-up grievances" (Stasio 2003:33). *Disordered Minds* was heralded as a "very enjoyable, sophisticated affair," with a complex plot and characters (Waugh 57) and as "an enigma wrapped in social commentary, tied up with a measure of psychoanalysis" (Krangle F20). Not light recreational reading, the novel is also viewed as "an intense look at family relations, including abuse, both mental and sexual, as well as discrimination" (Krangle F20).

Literary scholars have addressed Walters's work. Jill Lebihan applies psychoanalytic and feminist critical theory to *The Ice House*, exploring the roles of the women characters and the development of their identities within the narrative. M. D. Fletcher and R. J. Whip also explore feminist themes in Walters's work, examining her use of various themes, such as incest, rape, domestic abuse, and body image issues, within the format of the amateur sleuth subgenre. Tilda Maria Forselius focused on *The Shape of Snakes*, examining the role of memory and the motives of the narrator in the construction of the novel.

BIBLIOGRAPHY

Works by Minette Walters

The Ice House. New York: St. Martin's Press, 1992.
The Sculptress. New York: St. Martin's Press, 1993.
The Scold's Bridle. New York: St. Martin's Press, 1994.
The Dark Room. New York: Putnam, 1995.
The Echo. New York: Putnam, 1997.
The Breaker. New York: Putnam, 1999.
The Shape of Snakes. New York: Putnam, 2001.
Acid Row. New York: Macmillan, 2002.
Fox Evil. New York: Putnam, 2003.
Disoriented Minds. New York: Berkley, 2004.
The Tinder Box. 1999. London: Pan Macmillan, 2005.
The Devil's Feather. London: Macmillan, 2005.
Chickenfeed. London: Pan, 2006.

Works about Minette Walters

Brainard, Dulcy. "*The Ice House*." *Publishers Weekly* 25 May 1992: 40.
———. "*The Sculptress*." *Publishers Weekly* 27 September 1993: 48.
Cogdill, Oline H. "24 Hours in the Grip of a Rioting Mob." *South Florida Sun-Sentinel* 1 September 2002: 9G.
Croan, Robert. "Walters Plots Twisted Tale of Revenge." *Pittsburgh Post-Gazette* 9 September 2001: G10.

East, George. "Minette Walters." *St. James Guide to Crime & Mystery Writers.* 4th ed. Ed. Jay P. Pederson. Detroit: St. James Press, 1996. 101–102.

Fletcher, M. D. and R. J. Whip. "Minette Walters's Feminist Detective Fiction." *Clues* 18.1 (1997): 101–112.

Forselius, Tilda Maria. "The Impenetrable M and the Mysteries of Narration: Narrative in Minette Walters's *The Shape of Snakes.*" *Clues* 24.2 (2006): 47–61.

Greenstreet, Rosanna. "Q&A: Minette Walters." *The Guardian* 8 September 2001: 10.

Grimes, Tim. "Word of Mouth." *Library Journal* 15 September 1993: 136.

Klett, Rex E. "*The Scold's Bridle.*" *Library Journal* 1 October 1994: 118.

Krangle, Karen. "Minette Walters Crafts Another Terrific Puzzle." *The Vancouver Sun* 14 February 2004: F20.

Leber, Michele. "*The Dark Room.*" *Library Journal* 1 February 1996: 100.

Lebihan, Jill. "Tearing the Heart out of Secrets: Inside and Outside a Murder Mystery." *Journal of Gender Studies* 10.3 (2001): 287–95.

Melton, Emily. "*The Sculptress.*" *Booklist* 1 October 1993: 257.

———. "*The Scold's Bridle.*" *Booklist* 1 October 1994: 244.

———. "*The Dark Room.*" *Booklist* 1–15 January 1996: 749.

Minette Walters. Homepage. 2005. 9 September 2005. http://www.minettewalters.co.uk/

"Minette Walters." *Contemporary Authors.* Vol. 160. Ed. Scot Peacock. Detroit: Gale, 1998. 415–16.

Pitt, David. "*The Breaker.*" *Booklist* 1 March 1999: 1105.

Scott, Mary. "The Knives Are Out: *From Potter's Field* by Patricia Cornwell and *The Dark Room* by Minette Walters." *New Statesman & Society* 13 October 1995: 32.

Silet, Charles L. P. "An Interview with Minette Walters." *The Armchair Detective* 27.2 (1994): 182–85.

Stasio, Marilyn. "Crime." *New York Times Book Review* 22 July 2001: 22.

———. "Crime." *New York Times Book Review* 18 May 2003: 33.

Steinberg, Sybil. "*The Dark Room.*" *Publishers Weekly* 20 November 1995: 65.

———. "*The Echo.*" *Publishers Weekly* 3 February 1997: 93.

Waugh, Harriet. "*Disordered Minds.*" *The Spectator* 22 November 2003: 57.

"When We Were 10: Minette Walters Escaped into Adventure and Crime." *Daily Telegraph* 10 April 2004: 8.

Zaleski, Jeff. "*The Breaker.*" *Publishers Weekly* 12 April 1999: 57.

———. "*Acid Row.*" *Publishers Weekly* 10 June 2002: 42.

Valerie Wilson Wesley (1947–)

BIOGRAPHY

Valerie Wilson Wesley was born November 22, 1947, and grew up in Ashford, Connecticut. Her father was in the Air Force and they lived overseas for several periods of time. She is married to Richard Wesley, a screenwriter and playwright, whom she met during college. They have two daughters and live in New Jersey.

She earned a bachelor's degree in 1970 from Howard University and also earned master's degrees from the Bank Street College of Education and the Graduate School of Journalism, Columbia University.

Wesley worked as an associate editor for *Scholastic News* from 1970 to 1972 before beginning work with *Essence.* She began as travel editor in 1972, working her way up to senior and executive editorships. In 1994, she became a contributing editor.

Wesley began writing as a child "when she would make up stories and plays for her dolls to act out" (Washington 8A). Wesley chose to work in journalism owing to the tough market for fiction in the 1970s. She has loved the mystery genre since she read Edgar Allan Poe as a child (Valentine 83), noting that mysteries appeal to her because "plot and character are very important" and "justice always wins" (Valentine 83). She is a former board member of Sisters in Crime and is active in other organizations in New Jersey.

She enjoys teaching and served as an artist-in residence at Columbia College in Chicago during spring 2005. Although it "leaves her less time to write," Wesley wants to teach more in the future, noting that "she feels that she is learning as much from her students as they are from her, and it will only enhance her next work" (Edmonds 1D).

MAJOR WORKS AND THEMES

In addition to her mystery series, Wesley writes fiction for adults and books for children. Her mystery series features Tamara Hayle, an African American single mother, who was formerly a police officer and is a private investigator, working for herself. The series is set in Newark, New Jersey, and takes on a number of issues that African Americans face in urban America.

She has read and loved mysteries since she was a child, and her choice in writing in the genre came from that love but also from "her desire to fill a void in the mystery market-place" and provide another African American heroine (Washington 8A). Wesley noted that she "wanted to write a novel for contemporary Black women" with the "central character to be very now … not set in the sixties, for instance" (Washington 8A).

In the first novel, Hayle is approached by her ex-husband for assistance and must investigate a matter with personal ramifications. Sons of her ex-husband are being killed, the police are not able to find the killer, and she fears for the life of her own son, Jamal. In other cases in the series, she is hired to find missing children and look into unsolved murders. Throughout the series, Wesley focuses on family concerns, developing Hayle's relationship with her son and her own unresolved issues with her brother's suicide.

Wesley has also written a number of books for children and several novels for adults. Her adult fiction deals with romantic relationships and the concerns of modern African American families. In *Always True to You in My Fashion,* a woman finally leaves her womanizing boyfriend, even though she is pregnant with his child. *Blues for My Mother* features a complex plot and extensive character development, with four different voices telling parts of the story. Two sisters, their mother, and the aunt who raised them recount the events of their lives, from the 1970s to present day, when the mother has been released from prison after 18 years, and the family is brought back together.

CRITICAL RECEPTION

The first Tamara Hayle novel was nominated for a Shamus Award. Wesley has also won awards from the National Association of Black Journalists and the American Library Association for her adult fiction and children's books.

A review of the first novel noted that "Valerie Wilson Wesley has created a smart, sexy, knowing heroine unlike any readers have met before" ("*When Death Comes Stealing*" 12). The review also praised Wesley's "wry humor and a keen sense of urban life" and her development of Hayle's character, predicting that readers will "eagerly await" more novels in the series (("*When Death Comes Stealing*" 12).

One review of *Easier to Kill* criticized Wesley's "meandering" dialogue, but noted that "she's a standout in her ability to weave important social issues into her story, considering in this tale the rise of a black professional class from the old Newark housing projects, the desperation of teenage mothers, the bond of fathers and daughters" (Brainard 65).

In *The Devil Riding,* one reviewer found that "Wesley's first-person narrative skills are solid, gripping the reader with her down-to-earth realism and winning them with her wise, sometimes poetic insights into the soul" (Thomas 70). Another reviewer thought the plot "occasionally strays too far into melodrama" but praised Wesley's "solid characterizations (especially the captivating Tamara), well realized setting, and authentic depiction of teenage runaways" (Miller 1625).

The recent Hayle mystery, *Dying in the Dark,* was hailed as "a well-written, fast-paced whodunit" with a story that "is compelling without being too graphic or gory, and plot twists [that] are believable" (Olouyne 48). The reviewer also found that Wesley adds "a good dose of intelligence, sensitivity and humor," making the novel "thoroughly satisfying" (Olouyne 48).

BIBLIOGRAPHY

Works by Valerie Wilson Wesley

Tamara Hayle Series

When Death Comes Stealing. New York: Putnam, 1994.
Devil's Gonna Get Him. New York: Putnam, 1995.
Where Evil Sleeps. New York: Putnam, 1996.
No Hiding Place. New York: Putnam, 1997.
Easier to Kill. New York: Putnam, 1998.
The Devil Riding. New York: Putnam, 2000.
Dying in the Dark. New York: Ballantine, 2004.

Other Works

Ain't Nobody's Business If I Do. New York: Avon, 1999.
Always True to You in My Fashion. New York: Morrow, 2002.
Playing My Mother's Blues. New York: Morrow, 2005.

Works about Valerie Wilson Wesley

Brainard, Dulcy. "*Easier to Kill.*" *Publishers Weekly* 13 July 1998: 64–65.
Edmonds, Arlene. "*Blues* Unravels Family Passions, Murder." *Philadelphia Tribune* 18 March 2005: 1D.
Miller, Stuart. "*The Devil Riding.*" *Booklist* 1 May 2000: 1625.
Olouyne, Mary. "*Dying in the Dark: A Tamara Hayle Mystery.*" *Black Issues Book Review* 7.2 (2005): 48.
Thomas, Sheree R. "A Mystery's Gripping Cast of Potential Devils." *Emerge* June 2000: 70.
Valentine, Victoria. "Valerie Wilson Wesley Has Hayle Back on the Case." *Emerge* September 1997: 83.
"Valerie Wilson Wesley." *Contemporary Authors*. Vol. 167. Ed. Scot Peacock. Detroit: Gale, 1999. 422–24.
Valerie Wilson Wesley. Homepage. 2005. 22 May 2005. http://www.TamaraHayle.com
Washington, Linn. "Author Finds Profit in Mystery: Essence Editor's Novel Fills Void in the Mystery Genre." *Philadelphia Tribune* 2 August 1994: 8A.
"*When Death Comes Stealing*: A Tamara Hayle Mystery." *Call & Post* 14 July 1994: 12.

Kate Wilhelm (1928–)

BIOGRAPHY

Kate Wilhelm was born Katie Gertrude Meredith on June 8, 1928, in Toledo, Ohio, the daughter of Jesse Thomas and Ann (McDowell) Meredith. She graduated from high school in Louisville, Kentucky. She married Joseph B. Wilhelm on May 24, 1947, had two sons, Douglas and Richard, and divorced in 1962. On February 23, 1963, she married Damon Knight, a science fiction writer and editor, and they had a son named Jonathan. She and Knight, who died in 2002, were part of the Clarion Science Fiction and Fantasy Workshop, a writers' workshop held at Michigan State University. Wilhelm taught there each year between 1968 and 1996.

She had a number of jobs in the service sector, such as telephone operator, sales clerk, and insurance company underwriter, before turning to writing full-time in 1956.

Wilhelm resides in Eugene, Oregon.

MAJOR WORKS AND THEMES

Wilhelm has been a prolific contributor to the science fiction and mystery genres, and has also written a number of works often labeled as psychological fiction. She has also written plays and one work of nonfiction, a collaboration with her son Richard, a nature photographer. Wilhelm prefers to be labeled only as a writer, not within any particular genres ("Katie" 1986:482).

Wilhelm has written two mystery series along with a number of stand-alone mystery novels. Her first series features Charlie Mieklejohn and Constance Leidl, retired arson investigator and psychiatrist, respectively. The characters are also married and solve crimes together. The novels involve murders, art thefts, and other crimes. Wilhelm has also written short stories and novellas featuring the duo that veer back into science fiction territory at times.

Her second series features lawyer Barbara Holloway, who works with her father, Frank, also a lawyer, and several investigators who assist her. The series is set in Eugene, Oregon. Holloway is a defense attorney, who spends a good deal of her time running an informal free legal clinic out of a friend's restaurant. The first novel in the series, *Death Qualified,* has roots to her science fiction work. The plot of the mystery involves a computer program and chaos theory being used in nefarious ways, and was reviewed across many sources as a mystery novel and as science fiction. The rest of the series has been more mainstream in terms of focusing on legal cases without otherworldly aspects, although Wilhelm does introduce a number of interesting characters along the way. The novels have explored a number of social issues connected to the murder cases Holloway and her team get involved in, including spouse abuse and mentally impaired people accused of crimes.

Her stand-alone mystery novels have dealt with a range of topics. *Justice for Some* features a judge who returns home to visit family and discovers her father has been murdered. When a private investigator that he had hired is also murdered, she decides to investigate on her own. A woman solves her father's murder in *The Deepest Water.* In *Skeletons,* a young woman discovers her grandfather's past connection to a racially motivated crime. *The Price of Silence* features a reporter, new to a small town, who uncovers the fact that many young girls have disappeared over the years but that no real investigation has occurred.

CRITICAL RECEPTION

Wilhelm has won Nebula, Jupiter, and Hugo awards for her science fiction novels. Critical acclaim for her mysteries has also been strong.

Sweet, Sweet Poison was lauded as a "fresh, entertaining mystery" with an appealing "blend of suspense and humor" (Steinberg 1990:48). A review of *A Flush of Shadows* found the work "imaginative," noting that the detective duo was in top form and that their authors also showed "no signs of a flagging imagination" (Brainard 51).

Reviews of the Holloway series have been positive. *Death Qualified* was noted for its "arresting first paragraph" and sustained "intensity until the final page" (Sorci 108). Another reviewer praised Wilhelm for "sensitively depict[ing] her characters and their relationships," providing a "thought-provoking" novel (Steinberg 1991:46). *The Best Defense* was praised for Holloway's development as a "complex and appealing woman" and for an "ambitious" plot and subplots that weave together a number of social issues (Pendleton 140). *Malice Prepense* was called a "riveting tale" that features a "corker of a trial" that makes the legal system "comprehensible and compelling" for readers (Steinberg 1996:66). Another reviewer also praised this "courtroom thriller," noting the presence of "nail-biting courtroom tension" (Clifford 94). *No Defense* was labeled as a "riveting story" that includes a "labyrinth of legal intricacies and tiny shreds of evidence," with believable characters and "perfectly crafted and intertwined" subplots (Braun 164). Another reviewer found that the novel highlighted Wilhelm's "multiple skills" of "outstanding characterization, a keen ear for dialogue, and expert plot construction" (Needham 761). A review of *Desperate Measures* stated that the novel "sustains her reputation as a fine stylist who is able to craft compelling plots and characters" (Zaleski 50).

Although her mysteries have not been studied academically, a number of literary scholars have explored Wilhelm's science fiction works, examining her female characters and feminist approaches to the novels.

BIBLIOGRAPHY

Works by Kate Wilhelm

Mystery Fiction

More Bitter Than Death. New York: Simon & Schuster, 1962.
Justice for Some. New York: St. Martin's, 1993.
The Good Children. New York: St. Martin's, 1998.
The Deepest Water. New York: St. Martin's, 2000.
Skeletons. New York: St. Martin's, 2002.
The Price of Silence. Toronto: Mira, 2005.

Constance Leidl and Charlie Meiklejohn Series

The Hamlet Trap. New York: St. Martin's, 1987.
The Dark Door. New York: St. Martin's, 1988.
Smart House. New York: St. Martin's, 1989.
Sweet, Sweet Poison. New York: St. Martin's, 1990.
Seven Kinds of Death. New York: St. Martin's, 1992.
A Flush of Shadows: Five Short Novels Featuring Constance Leidl and Charlie Meiklejohn. New York: St. Martin's, 1995.
The Casebook of Constance and Charlie. New York: St. Martin's, 2000.

Barbara Holloway Series

Death Qualified: A Mystery of Chaos. New York: St. Martin's, 1991.
The Best Defense. New York: St. Martin's, 1994.
Malice Prepense. New York: St. Martin's, 1996.
Defense for the Devil. New York: St. Martin's, 1999.
No Defense. New York: St. Martin's, 2000.
Desperate Measures. New York: St. Martin's, 2001.
Clear and Convincing Proof. Toronto: Mira, 2003.
Unbidden Truth. Toronto: Mira, 2004.

Science Fiction Works

The Mile-long Spaceship. New York: Berkley, 1963. Also published as *Andover and the Android* (London: Dobson, 1966).
With Theodore L. Thomas. *The Clone.* New York: Berkley, 1965.
The Nevermore Affair. New York: Doubleday, 1966.
The Killer Thing. New York: Doubleday, 1967. Also published as *The Killing Thing* (London: Jenkins, 1967).
The Downstairs Room, and Other Speculative Fiction. New York: Doubleday, 1968.
Let the Fire Fall. New York: Doubleday, 1969.
With Theodore L. Thomas. *The Year of the Cloud.* New York: Doubleday, 1970.
Abyss: Two Novellas. New York: Doubleday, 1971.
City of Cain. Boston: Little, Brown, 1973.
The Clewiston Test. New York: Farrar, Straus, 1976.
Where Late the Sweet Birds Sang. New York: Harper, 1976.
The Infinity Box: A Collection of Speculative Fiction. New York: Harper, 1976.
Somerset Dreams and Other Fictions. New York: Harper, 1978.
Juniper Time: A Novel. New York: Harper, 1979.
With Damon Knight. *Better than One.* Boston: New England Science Fiction Association, 1980.
Listen, Listen. Boston: Houghton, Mifflin, 1981.
A Sense of Shadow. Boston: Houghton, Mifflin, 1981.
Welcome Chaos. Boston: Houghton, Mifflin, 1983.
Huysman's Pets. New York: Bluejay Books, 1986.
Crazy Time. New York: St. Martin's, 1988.
Children of the Wind. New York: St. Martin's, 1989.
State of Grace. Eugene: Pulphouse, 1991.
And the Angels Sing. New York: St. Martin's, 1992.

Other Novels

Margaret and I. Boston: Little, Brown, 1971.
Fault Lines: A Novel. New York: Harper, 1976.
Oh, Susannah!: A Novel. Boston: Houghton, Mifflin, 1982.
Cambio Bay. New York: St. Martin's, 1990.

Plays

Axotl. First produced in Eugene, Oregon, in 1979.
The Hindenberg Effect. First produced in Ashland, Oregon, in 1985.

Nonfiction

With Richard Wilhelm. *The Hills Are Dancing.* Minneapolis: Corroboree, 1986.

Works about Kate Wilhelm

Brainard, Dulcy. "*A Flush of Shadows.*" *Publishers Weekly* 22 May 1995: 51.
Braun, Susan Clifford. "*No Defense.*" *Library Journal* January 2000: 164.
Clifford, Susan. "*Malice Prepense.*" *Library Journal* 15 June 1996: 94.
"Katie Gertrude Wilhelm." *Contemporary Authors.* New Revision Series Vol. 17. Linda Metzger and Deborah A. Straub, eds. Detroit: Gale, 1986. 478–83.
"Katie Gertrude Wilhelm." *Contemporary Authors.* New Revision Series Vol. 94. Scot Peacock, ed. Detroit: Gale, 2001. 425–29.
Needham, George. "*No Defense.*" *Booklist* 15 December 1999: 761.
Pendleton, Elsa. "*The Best Defense.*" *Library Journal* 1 May 1994: 140.
Sorci, Kathy Armendt. "*Death Qualified.*" *Library Journal* 15 June 1991: 108.
Steinberg, Sybil. "*Sweet, Sweet Poison.*" *Publishers Weekly* 22 June 1990: 48.
———. "*Death Qualified.*" *Publishers Weekly* 24 May 1991: 46.
———. "*Malice Prepense.*" *Publishers Weekly* 27 May 1996: 66.
Zaleski, Jeff. "*Desperate Measures.*" *Publishers Weekly* 25 June 2001: 50.

Jacqueline Winspear (1955–)

BIOGRAPHY

Jacqueline Winspear was born in 1955, in Kent, England. She studied at the University of London's Institute of Education and then worked in publishing, education, and marketing communications in London. She has written a number of articles on international education issues.

She emigrated to California in 1990 and operated a coaching business there, consulting with individuals and companies. She began writing fiction in earnest in 2000 when Maisie Dobbs appeared in her mind while she was stuck in traffic (Solimini 16). Winspear focused on writing the novel while recovering from a horse-riding accident in 2001. She and her husband live in San Francisco and Ojai, California.

MAJOR WORKS AND THEMES

Winspear's works are set in Britain after World War I. The protagonist, Maisie Dobbs, went into service at a young age, but her employer recognized her intellectual skills and provided her with educational opportunities. After excelling at her studies at Oxford, Dobbs volunteers as a nurse during the war. In addition to seeing great suffering and violence, her fiancé, a doctor, is gravely wounded and never recovers mentally. When she returns from the war, she continues her training with her mentor so that she can earn a living helping others.

The series opens in 1929, as Dobbs has opened for business as a "Psychologist and Investigator," but the background story of Dobbs's life is told through extensive flashbacks. Her first case leads her to an investigation of abuse at a veterans' home, and her second case involves the disappearance of a woman who had earlier been part of a group that worked to persuade men to volunteer for the war. *Pardonable Lies* also features a wartime theme, with Dobbs assisting a man whose wife never accepted that their son died during the war. Dobbs must return to France, facing her demons while in pursuit of knowledge about several interlocking cases.

The novels are certainly mysteries in terms of their plots, but they also contain extensive historical details and a strong portrayal of class issues in England. The war and its aftermath play a large role in the lives of Dobbs, her investigative assistant Billy Beale, who was gravely wounded, and her clients, all of whom lost loved ones in the war. As Judith Maas noted, Winspear portrays the time and place but also "the collective mood of the era, the 'shared grief' lurking just beneath the surface of everyday life" (C12).

Winspear's grandfather was wounded in 1916 in France and suffered from shellshock. As a child, Winspear became interested in the war because of the impact it had on her family, and as an adult she continued her interest in the war's social and cultural effects. She found herself reading and researching the war extensively, although she noted that her main interest was not in the politics or the military history, but in "the experiences of ordinary men and women, boys and girls, not only on the battlefield, but on the home front" (Witts). Winspear notes that the war provides "fertile ground for a mystery," given the "great social upheaval [which] allows for the strange and unusual to emerge," providing "ample fodder for a compelling story, especially one concerning criminal acts and issues of guilt and innocence" (homepage).

CRITICAL RECEPTION

Winspear's works have been very well received. *Maisie Dobbs* was nominated for an Edgar Award for Best Novel, marking only the second time that a first novel was nominated for the best novel category. The novel won both the Agatha and Macavity awards for best first novel. Winspear's second novel followed that success by winning an Agatha Award for best novel. Critical reception has been solid.

Called an "inspired debut," one review of *Maisie Dobbs* heralded it as a "delightful mix of mystery, war story and romance" with "a refreshing heroine, appealing secondary characters and an absorbing plot" (Zaleski 55). Another reviewer noted that "there isn't a lot of room for originality" in mystery fiction, but that Winspear had delivered "something surprisingly fresh" (Lazarus M4). This review also praised Winspear for making Dobbs's "progression from domestic staff to college student to wartime nurse to private investigator both believable and compelling" (Lazarus M4).

Peter Cannon noted that Dobbs "continues to beguile in [the] chilling, suspenseful sequel" (174). He praised Winspear for giving "an intelligent and absorbing picture of the period, providing plentiful details for the history buff without detracting from the riveting mystery" (Cannon 174). Another review also praised Winspear's continuing excellence, claiming that there is "no sophomore jinx" with *Birds of a Feather*, with its stronger mystery plot that is "cleverly and fairly laid out" (Schantz F14). The review further noted that Winspear "skillfully and gradually peels back the layers, eventually revealing the murderer who was there all the time" (Schantz F14).

BIBLIOGRAPHY

Works by Jacqueline Winspear

Maisie Dobbs Series

Maisie Dobbs. New York: Soho Press, 2003.
Birds of a Feather. New York: Soho Press, 2004.
Pardonable Lies. New York: Holt, 2005.
Messenger of Truth. New York: Holt, 2006.

Works about Jacqueline Winspear

Cannon, Peter. "Birds of a Feather." *Publishers Weekly* 3 May 2004: 174.

"Jacqueline Winspear." *Contemporary Authors*. Vol. 229. Ed. Julie Keppen. Detroit: Gale, 2005. 436–37.

Jacqueline Winspear. Homepage. 2005. 13 June 2005. http://www.jacquelinewinspear.com

Lazarus, David. "Upstairs Investigator Was Downstairs Staff." *San Francisco Chronicle* 6 July 2003: M4.

Maas, Judith. "A Sleuth Finds Her Calling in Wilds of World War I." *Boston Globe* 22 July 2004: C12.

Schantz, Tom and Enid. "*Birds of a Feather*." *Denver Post* 6 June 2004: F14.

Solimini, Cheryl. "Echoes from a Great War: A Conversation with Jacqueline Winspear." *Mystery Scene* 91 (2005): 16–19.

Witts, Davina. "Author Interview: Jacqueline Winspear." Bookbrowse. 2005. 15 August 2005. http://bookbrowse.com/author_interviews/full/index.cfm?author_number = 1028

Zaleski, Jeff. "*Maisie Dobbs*." *Publishers Weekly* 16 June 2003: 55.

Paula L. Woods (1953–)

BIOGRAPHY

Paula L. Woods was born in Los Angeles and grew up as an only child. As a young girl, she was extremely close to her parents, who supported her love of reading and books. Her mother died when she was a senior at the University of Southern California, and she left school (Cain 1771). Before returning to finish her bachelor's degree, she worked as a telephone operator at a hospital and became interested in inner-city trauma centers (Cain 1771). She later earned a master's degree in hospital administration, and she and her husband, Felix Liddell, began a consulting firm (Cain 1771).

Woods is a member of the National Book Critics Circle and frequently publishes reviews in the *Los Angeles Times* and other newspapers and magazines. She and her husband have collaborated on two nonfiction books about African Americans, in addition to their business partnership.

MAJOR WORKS AND THEMES

In the early 1990s, Woods undertook a project of anthologizing and studying African American detective fiction. After completing this work, *Spooks, Spies and Private Eyes,* Woods realized there was a need for more books about a "savvy black female who was a law enforcement professional but who was also sexy and hip and culturally grounded" ("A Conversation"), and she decided to turn to fiction writing.

Woods's series features Charlotte Justice, an African American police officer. The series is set in Los Angeles and begins in 1991, shortly after Rodney King was beaten by police officers. Woods chose these details deliberately, noting that Justice's status as an African American woman homicide detective in Los Angeles "places her at ground zero in an important era in law enforcement, a vantage point I use as a writer to explore sexism, racism, and the role of women in policing" ("Paula L. Woods" 443).

In addition to issues on the job, Justice has personal baggage. Her husband, who was also a police officer, and their daughter were killed in a drive-by shooting in 1979. The gang member responsible was never brought to justice. In *Inner City Blues* the gang murder is found murdered, and Justice investigates his death, while also finding more facts about her own loss.

Stormy Weather involves the death of a documentary filmmaker who was chronicling the history of African Americans in Hollywood. Although he was dying of cancer, his home health worker is accused of hastening his death. Justice finds that the truth behind his murder is linked to the victim's project and past secrets that someone does not want revealed.

Dirty Laundry finds Justice investigating the death of a Korean woman who was active in city politics, and in *Strange Bedfellows,* set in 1993, a suspect from an old case reappears, prompting a reinvestigation of a complex case that also leads to her learning secrets from her own family's past. In this novel, Woods explores Muslim American characters and also looks at the toy industry and its effects on minorities in the United States.

CRITICAL RECEPTION

Woods's first novel won a Macavity Award, along with other awards. She has received nominations for Macavity, Edgar and Anthony awards for her fiction and nonfiction work. *Inner City Blues* was praised for its mystery content, as well as for "the rich portrait Woods paints of the multifaceted black community in Los Angeles" and for "her marvelous sense of humor and keen eye for detail put readers exactly where she wants them to be, without the use of stereotypes or clichés" (Dretzka 12). Another reviewer proclaimed that from the first page, the novel "hits the reader right between the eyes with her sharp prose and on target dialogue," praised the pacing as "even with never a dull moment" and noted that the character development "sparkles, with her secondary characters giving outstanding performances" (Hill 32).

A reviewer noted that in *Stormy Weather,* "Woods masterfully juggles all her plot elements, seamlessly incorporating the riveting historical material on blacks in Hollywood with an all-too-contemporary story of wrongdoing within the LAPD" (Ott 1643). Another reviewer found that "the family banter and office politics balance nicely with the sleuthing and social commentary in this charming but pointed police procedural" (Nolan A16).

In her review of *Dirty Laundry,* Jacquelin Thomas praised Woods for her "well-drawn character" and "intense, gripping suspense" combined with a "realistic" portrayal of power struggles and racial issues (24). Another reviewer found that Woods "redefines L.A. urban noir as an explosive blend of race relations, politics and murder" in this "satisfying, fast-paced police procedural"(Zaleski 33). Woods was also praised for giving readers a "convincing portrayal of a grieving widow and mother without stooping to an easy, formulaic use of Justice's tragedy" (Fletcher 1751).

Although some aspects of plotting were critiqued, a reviewer of *Strange Bedfellows* concluded that her "unique mix of moral outrage, social commentary, and therapy definitely has an audience" (Graff 31). Another reviewer found it "searing" and predicted that readers "will appreciate its stunning conclusion as well as its rich portrait of LAPD politics and of the African-American community" ("*Strange Bedfellows*" 56).

BIBLIOGRAPHY
Works by Paula L. Woods
Charlotte Justice Series

Inner City Blues. New York: Norton, 1999.
Stormy Weather. New York: Norton, 2001.

Dirty Laundry. New York: One World/Ballantine, 2003.
Strange Bedfellows. New York: One World/Ballantine, 2006.

Nonfiction

With Felix H. Liddell. *I, Too, Sing America: The African American Book of Days.* New York: Workman, 1992.
Edited with Felix H. Liddell. *I Hear a Symphony: African Americans Celebrate Love.* New York: Anchor Press, 1994.
Spooks, Spies, and Private Eyes: Black Mystery and Suspense Fiction. New York: Doubleday, 1995.

Works about Paula L. Woods

Cain, Joy Duckett. "Paula L. Woods." *Encyclopedia of African American Literature.* Eds. David Macey and Hans Ostrom. Westport: Greenwood Press, 2005. 1770–71.
"A Conversation with Paula." Woods on the Web. 6 December 2005. 31 January 2006. http://www.woodsontheweb.com/Bio/a_conversation_with_paula.htm
Dretzka, Gary. "Short Takes from the South Seas to the North Shore." *Chicago Tribune* 7 March 1999: 12.
Fletcher, Connie. "*Dirty Laundry.*" *Booklist* 1–15 June 2003: 1751.
Graff, Keir. "*Strange Bedfellows.*" *Booklist* 15 November 2005: 30–31.
Hill, Donna. "*Inner City Blues.*" *Mosaic Literary Magazine* 2.1 (1999): 32.
Nolan, Tom. "Thrillers with a Social Context." *Wall Street Journal* 31 July 2000: A16.
Ott, Bill. "*Stormy Weather.*" *Booklist* 1 May 2001: 1643.
"Paula L. Woods." *Contemporary Authors.* New Revision Series, Vol. 96. Ed. Scot Peacock. Detroit: Gale, 2001. 442–43.
"*Strange Bedfellows.*" *Publishers Weekly* 7 November 2005: 56.
Thomas, Jacquelin. "*Dirty Laundry.*" *Black Book Review* 10.5 (31 October 2003): 24.
Zaleski, Jeff. "*Dirty Laundry.*" *Publishers Weekly* 2 June 2003: 33.

Margaret Yorke (1924–)

BIOGRAPHY

Born Margaret Beda Larminie in Surrey, England, on January 30, 1924, Yorke was the daughter of John Peel Alexander Larminie and Alison Yorke Lyle Larminie. The family lived in Dublin when she was young, returning to England in 1937. After school, she was a driver in the Women's Royal Naval Service during World War II and married Basil Nicholson in 1945. They had two children, Diana Margaret and Ian Basil, before divorcing in 1957.

She wanted to be a novelist from a young age, "from when [she] was old enough to know what such a thing was" (Doherty). Her first novel was published in 1957. She worked at Oxford University from 1959 to 1965, serving as an assistant librarian in St. Hilda's College and a library cataloguer at Christ Church. She was the first woman to work in the library in the college of Christ Church (Tangled Web). In 1965, she turned to writing full-time.

She served as chairperson of the Crime Writers Association during 1979–1980, and she lives in Buckinghamshire, England.

MAJOR WORKS AND THEMES

Yorke's first 11 novels were romantic novels, but as Karl G. Frederiksson stresses, not the Harlequin or Mills and Boon type of book (1085). Yorke herself described them as "family problem" novels, and noted that she was "always tempted to stir up their quiet plots with some violent action" (qtd in Frederiksson 1084). Frederiksson also noted that marriage and relationship often serve as a "catalyst" in Yorke's crime novels, as he draws connections between her earlier works and the bulk of her writings (1085).

Her first mystery novels featured an Oxford don named Patrick Grant, who taught art history and solved crimes. As Yorke notes, when she began writing mysteries she knew nothing about the way police departments functioned, so she wrote about an amateur sleuth (Doherty). The Grant series has been described as "rather conventional" (Frederiksson 1084). In *Dead in the Morning,* Grant's neighbor's maid is poisoned. The matriarch was the intended victim, and there is no shortage of suspects or motives. Grant steps in to solve the case. In *Mortal Remains,* Grant is on vacation in Greece and becomes embroiled in a case involving politics and smuggling.

With *No Medals for the Major,* she turned to writing stand-alone novels. Her work is often described as being in the suspense genre or as a psychological thriller. In some of her works, people find themselves in extraordinary situations, often involving miscarriages of justice. For example, in *Intimate Kill,* an innocent man is accused and convicted of killing his wife. After his release from prison, he sets out to find her real killer. In *A Question of Belief,* a man is falsely accused of rape. By the time he is acquitted, both his professional and personal lives have been irreparably tainted. He fakes his own death to escape for a new life, and finds himself embroiled in a group of animal rights activists.

In many of her other novels, people find evil and danger within their daily lives, often close to home. *Speak for the Dead* features a man who killed his wife and later remarries a woman, having told her he was divorced. He learns that she also omitted an important detail of her life. In *Criminal Damage,* a widow's son and daughter are wrapped up in their own lives and do not notice that the woman next door "seems curiously determined to strike up an acquaintance" with their mother (Brainard 1992:59). In *A Case to Answer,* a widow searches for her missing granddaughter, setting off a tragic chain of events.

Yorke also has studied the effects of random, senseless violence in her novels. In *Act of Violence,* four adolescents break into a home to vandalize it. The occupants are home, and the event turns deadly. The novel deals with the effects of the event on the community and the role played by a grief counselor, who has her own secret past. In *Almost the Truth,* a man plans revenge on those who attacked him and raped his daughter.

CRITICAL RECEPTION

Yorke has won various awards and recognitions throughout her career, culminating in the Crime Writers Association's highest honor, the Diamond Dagger, which she was awarded in 1999.

A review of *A Small Deceit* noted that "only a writer with Yorke's smooth cunning and deceptively simplistic narrative technique" could produce such a "taut climax and cathartic emotional release" from the "disciplined" prose (Robertson 2108). Another reviewer found the work to have a "shattering climax" and to be a "riveting tale" (Steinberg 60). Another reviewer called it "one of Yorke's most accomplished thrillers ... written with authority and consistent appeal" (Craig 19).

Dangerous to Know was called an "elegantly simple, cleverly paced" novel, "guaranteed to keep readers on the edge of their seats" (Mills 58). Another review noted that Yorke "deftly explores the darker side of the lives of characters" who appear to be the "folks next door" (Brainard 1993:58).

In *Almost the Truth* Yorke was seen as demonstrating her "command of suspense writing" and was praised for an "absorbing, utterly unsentimental narrative" that reminds readers of the real people behind the news stories of crimes (Brainard 1995:87). The same reviewer called *Serious Intent* a "subtle psychological study of bad behavior," with a plot that lent a "strong emotional dimension" (Brainard 1996:88).

With its mix of mystery and social commentary, *A Question of Belief* was viewed as having "carve(d) out a place for itself both within and beyond the conventional crime-story framework" (Pitt 1997:310). This reviewer also gave high praise to Yorke's *The Price of Guilt*. He describes the plot as seemingly simple, but noted that "Yorke's stories are never simple," showing an understanding that "the key to a really good mystery isn't plot" but character (Pitt 2000:1090). He also states that "Yorke's characters are so realistic that we find ourselves looking at them very closely, trying to figure out what's going on behind their eyes, and that's usually when we realize we're not reading the story as much as living it" (Pitt 2000:1090).

A Case to Answer was viewed as a "very light mystery" but also "well weighted with superb plotting and in-depth personalities" (Cannon 2001:42). *Cause for Concern* was described as "another leisurely, psychological suspense thriller in which ordinary folks go about their business while danger hums quietly underneath" (Cannon 2002:44).

BIBLIOGRAPHY

Works by Margaret Yorke

Patrick Grant Series

Dead in the Morning. London: Bles, 1970.
Silent Witness. New York: Walker, 1973.
Grave Matters. London: Bles, 1973; New York: Bantam, 1983.
Mortal Remains. London: Bles, 1974.
Cast for Death. New York: Walker, 1976.

Mystery Fiction

No Medals for the Major. London: Bles, 1974.
The Small Hours of the Morning. New York: Walker, 1975.
The Cost of Silence. London: Hutchinson, 1977.
The Point of Murder. London: Hutchinson, 1978. Also published as *The Come-On* (New York: Harper, 1979).
Death on Account. London: Hutchinson, 1979.
The Scent of Fear. London: Hutchinson, 1980; New York: St. Martin's, 1981.
The Hand of Death. London: Hutchinson, 1981; New York: St. Martin's, 1982.
Devil's Work. New York: St. Martin's, 1982.
Find Me a Villain. New York: St. Martin's, 1983.
The Smooth Face of Evil. New York: St. Martin's, 1984.
Intimate Kill. New York: St. Martin's, 1985.
Safely to the Grave. New York: St. Martin's, 1986.

Evidence to Destroy. New York: Viking, 1987.
Speak for the Dead. New York: Viking, 1988.
Crime in Question. New York: Viking, 1989.
Admit to Murder. New York: Mysterious Press, 1990.
A Small Deceit. New York: Mysterious Press, 1992.
Criminal Damage. New York: Mysterious Press, 1992.
Dangerous to Know. New York: Mysterious Press, 1993.
Almost the Truth. New York: Mysterious Press, 1994.
Pieces of Justice. London: Warner Futura, 1994.
Serious Intent. New York: Mysterious Press, 1995.
A Question of Belief. New York: Mysterious Press, 1996.
Act of Violence. New York: St. Martin's Press, 1998.
False Pretences. New York: St. Martin's Press, 1999.
The Price of Guilt. New York: St. Martin's Press, 1999.
A Case to Answer. New York: St. Martin's Press, 2001.
Cause for Concern. New York: St. Martin's Press, 2002.

Other Works

Summer Flight. London: R. Hale, 1957.
Pray, Love, Remember. London: R. Hale, 1958.
Christopher. London: R. Hale, 1959.
Deceiving Mirror. London: R. Hale, 1960.
The China Doll. London: R. Hale, 1961.
Once a Stranger. London: Hurst & Blackett, 1962.
The Birthday. London: Hurst & Blackett, 1963.
Full Circle. London: Hurst & Blackett, 1965.
No Fury. London: Hurst & Blackett, 1967.
The Apricot Bed. London: Hurst & Blackett, 1968.
The Limbo Ladies. London: Hurst & Blackett, 1969.

Works about Margaret Yorke

Brainard, Dulcy. "Criminal Damage." *Publishers Weekly* 26 October 1992: 59.
———. " *Dangerous to Know.*" *Publishers Weekly* 6 December 1993: 58–59.
———. "*Almost the Truth.*" *Publishers Weekly* 30 January 1995: 87–88.
———. "*Serious Intent.*" *Publishers Weekly* 26 February 1996: 88.
Cannon, Peter. "*A Case to Answer.*" *Publishers Weekly* 26 November 2001: 42.
———. "*A Cause for Concern.*" *Publishers Weekly* 11 November 2002: 44.
Craig, Patricia. "*A Small Deceit.*" *Times Literary Supplement* 12 April 1991: 19.
Doherty, Harry. "The Bookends Interview: Margaret Yorke." Bookends: The Bookplace Magazine. n.d. December 13, 2005. http://www.bookplace.co.uk/bookends/chat/yorke.asp?TAG = &CID = emrfaber
Frederiksson, Karl G. "Margaret Yorke." *St. James Guide to Crime and Mystery Fiction.* Ed. Jay P. Pederson. Detroit: Gale, 1996. 1083–85.
"Margaret Beda Larminie." *Contemporary Authors.* New Revision Vol. 89. Scot Peacock, ed. Detroit: Gale, 2000. 217–19.
Mills, Beth Ann. "*Dangerous to Know.*" *Library Journal* January 1994: 166.
Pitt, David. "*A Question of Belief.*" *Booklist* 1 October 1997: 310.
———. "*The Price of Guilt.*" *Booklist* 15 February 2000: 1090.
Robertson, Peter. "*A Small Deceit.*" *Booklist* August 1991: 2108.
Steinberg, Sybil. "*A Small Deceit.*" *Publishers Weekly* 5 July 1991: 60.
Tangled Web UK. "Margaret Yorke." June 6, 2003. November 14, 2005. http://www.twbooks.co.uk/authors/margaretyorke.html

Appendix A
Author/Character
Series Master Index

Arranged by author, this chart shows character names, setting, and the profession of the characters in the series. Fictional locations are marked with an asterisk (*). Unless noted, settings are contemporary to publication.

Author Name	Main Character(s) Name	Series Location	Profession
Albert, Susan Wittig	China Bayles	Pecan Springs,* Texas	Former lawyer; herb store owner
	Ruby Wilcox		New age store owner
	Mike McQuaid		Police Detective
	Beatrix Potter	England	Writer
Andrews, Donna	Meg Langslow	Yorktown, Virginia	Blacksmith
	Michael Waterston		Actor / Professor
	Turing Hopper	Washington, DC	Artificial Intelligence Personality
	Maude Graham		Secretary
	Tim Pincoski		Library clerk
Bannister, Jo	Liz Graham	Castlemere,* The Fens, England	Police Detective
	Frank Shapiro		Police Detective
	Cal Donovan		Police Detective
	Brodie Farrell	Dimmock,* England	Owner of an investigative service
	Daniel Hood		Schoolteacher

Author Name	Main Character(s) Name	Series Location	Profession
	Jack Deacon	Police Detective	
	Primrose Holland	Skipley, England	Retired pathologist
	Clio Rees	England	Physician, mystery novelist
	Harry Marsh		Police Detective
Barnes, Linda	Michael Spraggue	Boston, Massachusetts	Actor
	Carlotta Carlyle	Boston, Massachusetts	Private Investigator
Barr, Nevada	Anna Pigeon	U.S. National Parks	Park ranger
Barron, Stephanie (Francine Mathews)	Jane Austen	Georgian England	Writer
Black, Cara	Aimee Leduc	Paris, France	Private Investigator
Bland, Eleanor Taylor	Marti MacAllister	Lincoln Heights,* Illinois	Police officer
Bowen, Rhys	Evan Evans	Llanfair,* Wales	Police officer
	Molly Murphy	1900–1910's New York City	Private Investigator
Buchanan, Edna	Britt Montero	Miami, Florida	Investigative reporter
	K. C. Riley	Miami, Florida	Police Detective
Burke, Jan	Irene Kelly	Las Piernas,* California	Investigative reporter
	Frank Harriman		Police Detective
Caudwell, Sarah	Hilary Tamar	Oxford, England	Oxford don, barrister
Churchill, Jill	Jane Jeffry	Chicago, Illinois	Stay at home mom
	Shelley Nowack		Stay at home mom
	Mel VanDyne		Police detective
	Lily and Robert Brewster	Great Depression-era New York	Formerly wealthy siblings
Cody, Liza	Anna Lee	London	Private Investigator
	Eva Wylie	London	Wrestler, security guard
Coel, Margaret	Fr. John O'Malley	Wind River Reservation, Wyoming	Priest
	Vicki Holden		Lawyer
Cornwell, Patricia	Kay Scarpetta	Richmond, Virginia	Medical Examiner
	Lucy Farinelli		FBI Agent

Author Name	Main Character(s) Name	Series Location	Profession
	Pete Marino		Police Detective
	Benton Wesley		FBI Profiler
	Judy Hammer	Charlotte, North Carolina	Police Chief
	Andy Brazil		Reporter
Craig, Alisa (Charlotte MacLeod)	Madoc Rhys	New Brunswick, Canada	Royal Canadian Mounted Police
	Osbert Monk	Lobelia Falls,* Ontario, Canada	Author of western fiction
	Dittany Henbit Monk		Gardening enthusiast
Crombie, Deborah	Gemma James	London	Police Detective
	Duncan Kincaid		Police Detective
Cross, Amanda	Kate Fansler	New York City	English professor
Davis, Lindsey	Marcus Didius Falco	Ancient Rome	Government detective
Day, Marele	Claudia Valentine	Sydney, Australia	Private Investigator
Dobson, Joanne	Karen Pelletier	Enfield,* Massachusetts	English professor
	Charlie Piotrowski		Police detective
Dunant, Sarah	Hannah Wolfe	London	Private Investigator
Evanovich, Janet	Stephanie Plum	Trenton, New Jersey	Bounty hunter
	Joe Morelli		Police detective
	Ranger		Bounty hunter
	Alexandra Barnaby	Baltimore; Miami	Mechanic
Fairstein, Linda	Alex Cooper	New York City	Assistant District Attorney
	Mike Chapman		Police detective
	Mercer Wallace		Police detective
Farmer, Jerrilyn	Madeline Bean	Hollywood, California	Caterer
Fowler, Earlene	Benni Harper	San Celina,* California	Folk art museum curator
	Gabe Ortiz		Police Chief
Fyfield, Frances	Helen West	London	Crown Prosecutor
	Geoffrey Bailey		Police Detective
	Sarah Fortune	London	Attorney
Garcia-Aguilera, Carolina	Lupe Solano	Miami, Florida	Private Investigator

Author Name	Main Character(s) Name	Series Location	Profession
George, Anne	Patricia Anne Hollowell	Birmingham, Alabama	Retired schoolteacher
	Mary Alice Crane		Bar owner
George, Elizabeth	Thomas Lynley	London	Police Detective
	Barbara Havers		Police Detective
Grafton , Sue	Kinsey Millhone	1970s–80s Santa Teresa,* California	Private Investigator
Grimes, Martha	Richard Jury	London; Long Piddleston,* England	Detective Inspector
	Melrose Plant		Reluctant aristocrat
	Emma Graham	LaPorte, New York	12-year-old daughter of an innkeeper
Hall, Patricia	Michael Thackeray	Bradfield, * Yorkshire, England	Police Detective
	Laura Ackroyd		Investigative reporter
Harrod-Eagles, Cynthia	Bill Slider	London	Police Detective
	Jim Atherton		Police Detective
	Joanna Marshall		Professional Musician
Harris, Charlaine	Aurora Teagarden	Lawrenceton,* Georgia	Librarian
	Lily Bard	Shakespeare,* Arkansas	House cleaner
	Sookie Stackhouse	Bon Temps,* Louisiana	Waitress/ Clairvoyant
	Harper Connelly	various	Clairvoyant
Hart, Carolyn	Annie Laurence Darling	Broward's Rock,* South Carolina	Bookseller
	Max Darling		Owner of an investigative service
	Henrietta O'Dwyer Collins	Various	Retired journalist
Henry, Sue	Jessie Arnold	Alaska	Dog sled trainer
	Maxine McNab	Alaska	Retired
James, P.D.	Adam Dalgliesh	London	Scotland Yard inspector/poet

Author Name	Main Character(s) Name	Series Location	Profession
	Cordelia Gray	London	Private Investigator
Jance, J. A.	J. P. Beaumont	Seattle, Washington	Police detective turned private investigator
	Joanna Brady	Bisbee, Arizona	Sheriff
Kellerman, Faye	Peter Decker	Los Angeles	Police Detective
	Rina Lazarus		Stay at home mom
King, Laurie R.	Kate Martinelli	San Francisco	Police Detective
	Mary Russell	England	Scholar
	Sherlock Holmes		Detective
Krich, Rochelle	Jessie Drake	Los Angeles	Police Detective
	Molly Blume	Los Angeles	Investigative reporter
Lanier, Virginia	JoBeth Sidden	Balsa City,* Georgia	Bloodhound trainer/search and rescue worker
Lathen, Emma	John Thatcher Putnam	New York City	Banker
	Ben Safford	Ohio	Senator
Linscott, Gillian	Birdie Linnett	Various	Police officer turned fitness trainer
	Nell Bray	Edwardian London	Suffragette
Lippman, Laura	Tess Monaghan	Baltimore, Maryland	Reporter/private investigator
MacLeod, Charlotte	Helen Marsh	Balaclava,* Massachusetts	Librarian
	Peter Shandy		Professor
	Sarah Kelling	Boston, Massachusetts	Boarding house manager
	Max Bittersohn		Art theft investigator
Maron, Margaret	Sigrid Harald	New York City	Police Detective
	Deborah Knott	Colleton County,* North Carolina	Judge
Massey, Sujata	Rei Shimura	Japan; Washington, D.C.; California	Antiques dealer
Matthews, Francine	Merry Folger	Nantucket, Massachusetts	Police Detective

Author Name	Main Character(s) Name	Series Location	Profession
	Caroline Carmichael	Various	CIA agent
McCrumb, Sharyn	Elizabeth MacPherson	Tennessee, various	Forensic anthropologist
	Jay Omega aka Dr. James Owens Mega	Various	Engineering Professor and Science Fiction Novelist
	Spencer Arrowood	Hamelin,* Tennessee	Sheriff
	Nora Bonesteel		Herbalist/ Clairvoyant
McDermid, Val	Kate Brannigan	Manchester, England	Private Investigator
	Tony Hill	Bradfield,* England	Psychologist
	Carol Jordan		Police Detective
	Lindsay Gordon	Various	Journalist
McGown, Jill	Lloyd	Bartonshire,* Northamptonshire,	Police Detective
	Judy Hill	England	Police Detective
Millar, Margaret	Paul Prye	Toronto	Psychologist
	Tom Aragon	Los Angeles	Lawyer
	Inspector Sands	Toronto	Police Detective
Mina, Denise	Maureen O'Donnell	Glasgow	Underemployed
	Paddy Meehan	1980s Glasgow	Newspaper clerk turned reporter
Muller, Marcia	Sharon McCone	San Francisco	Private Investigator
	Joanna Stark	San Francisco	Museum security specialist
	Elena Oliverez	Santa Barbara, California	Museum curator
Neel, Janet	John MacLeish	London	Police Detective
	Francesca Wilson		Musician, school official
Neely, Barbara	Blanche White	Boston	Domestic worker
Newman, Sharan	Catherine LeVendeur	Medieval France	Former novice
O'Connell, Carol	Kathleen Mallory	New York City	Police Detective
	Charles Butler		Psychologist
Padgett, Abigail	Barbara Joan "Bo" Bradley	San Diego, California	Social worker

Author Name	Main Character(s) Name	Series Location	Profession
	Blue McCarron	San Diego, California	Social psychologist
Paige, Robin	Charles Sheridan	Late Victorian/Edwardian England	Aristocrat, scientist
(Susan Wittig Albert)	Katherine Ardleigh		Writer
Paretsky, Sara	V. I. Warshawski	Chicago	Private Investigator
Parrish, P. J.	Louis Kincaid	1980s Mississippi, Michigan, Florida	Police detective turned private investigator
Pawel, Rebecca	Carlos Tejada Alonso	Civil War era Spain	Guardia Civil officer
Perry, Anne	Thomas Pitt	Victorian era London	Police Detective
	Charlotte Pitt		Homemaker
	William Monk	Victorian era London	Police Detective
	Hester Latterly		Nurse
	Joseph Reavley	WWI era England	Professor
Peters, Elizabeth	Amelia Peabody	Victorian era England and Egypt	Archaeologist
	Jacqueline Kirby	Coldwater,* Nebraska	Librarian turned novelist
	Vicki Bliss	Germany, Italy, Sweden, Egypt	Art historian
Pickard, Nancy	Jenny Cain	Port Frederick,* Massachusetts	Civic foundation director
	Eugenia Potter	Arizona	Rancher/cook
	Marie Lightfoot	Bahia Beach,* Florida	True crime writer
Rendell, Ruth	Reginald Wexford	Kingsmarkham,* Sussex, England	Police Detective
Ross, Kate	Julian Kestrel	Regency era England	Dandy
Rozan, S. J.	Lydia Chin	New York City	Private Investigator
	Bill Smith		Private Investigator
Scottoline, Lisa	Bennie Rosato	Philadelphia	Lawyer
	Mary DiNunzio		Lawyer
	Judy Carrier		Lawyer
Simpson, Dorothy	Luke Thanet	Sturrenden,* Kent, England	Police Detective
Slaughter, Karin	Sara Linton	Heartsdale,* Georgia	Pediatrician/ Coroner

Author Name	Main Character(s) Name	Series Location	Profession
	Jeffrey Tolliver		Police Chief
Smith, Julie	Rebecca Schwartz	San Francisco	Lawyer
	Paul McDonald	San Francisco	Mystery writer
	Skip Langdon	New Orleans	Police officer
	Talba Willis	New Orleans	Private Investigator / Poet
Spencer-Fleming, Julia	Clare Fergusson	Millers Kill,* New York	Episcopal priest
	Russ Van Alstyne		Police Chief
Stabenow, Dana	Kate Shugak	Alaska	District attorney turned private investigator
	Liam Campbell	Alaska	Police Detective
Strohmeyer, Sarah	Bubbles Yablonsky	Lehigh, Pennsylvania	Hairdresser turned journalist
Tracy, P. J.	Grace MacBride	Minneapolis-St. Paul and Kingsford County,* Wisconsin	Computer programmer
	Annie Belinski		Computer programmer
	Harley Davidson		Computer programmer
	Roadrunner		Computer programmer
	Michael Halloran		Sheriff
	Sharon Mueller		Deputy Sheriff
	Leo Magozzi		Police Detective
	Gino Rolseth		Police Detective
Trocheck, Kathy Hogan	Callahan Garrity	Atlanta, Georgia	Former police officer, cleaning service owner
	Truman Kicklighter	St. Petersburg, Florida	Retired journalist
Walker, Mary Willis	Molly Cates	Austin, Texas	True crime writer
Wesley, Valerie Wilson	Tamara Hayle	Newark, New Jersey	Police officer turned private investigator
Wilhelm, Kate	Barbara Holloway	Eugene, Oregon	Lawyer

Author Name	Main Character(s) Name	Series Location	Profession
Winspear, Jacqueline	Maisie Dobbs	Post WWI London	Private Investigator
Woods, Paula L.	Charlotte Justice	1990s Los Angeles	Police detective
Yorke, Margaret	Patrick Grant	Oxford, England	Oxford don

Appendix B
Series Character
Name Index

Arranged by characters, this list provides listings of character names alphabetized by last name and by first name, with the appropriate author name provided for reference. For example, readers can locate Linda Fairstein's Alexandra Cooper series under Alexandra and under Cooper.

Character Name	Author Name
Ackroyd, Laura	Patricia Hall
Aimee Leduc	Cara Black
Alexandra Barnaby	Janet Evanovich
Alexandra (Alex) Cooper	Linda Fairstein
Alonso y Leon, Carlos Tejada	Rebecca Pawel
Amelia Peabody	Elizabeth Peters
Andy Brazil	Patricia Cornwell
Anna Lee	Liza Cody
Anna Pigeon	Nevada Barr
Annie Laurence Darling	Carolyn Hart
Aragon, Tom	Margaret Millar
Ardleigh, Katherine	Robin Paige
Arnold, Jessie	Sue Henry
Arrowood, Spencer	Sharyn McCrumb
Atherton, Jim	Cynthia Harrod-Eagles
Aurora Teagarden	Charlaine Harris
Austen, Jane	Stephanie Barron (Francine Mathews)
Bailey, Geoffrey	Frances Fyfield
Barbara Joan "Bo" Bradley	Abigail Padgett
Barbara Holloway	Kate Wilhelm

Character Name	Author Name
Barbara Havers	Elizabeth George
Bard, Lily	Charlaine Harris
Barnaby, Alexandra	Janet Evanovich
Bayles, China	Susan Wittig Albert
Beatrix Potter	Susan Wittig Albert
Bean, Madeline	Jerrilyn Farmer
Benni Harper	Earlene Fowler
Bennie Rosato	Lisa Scottoline
Benton Wesley	Patricia Cornwell
Bill Slider	Cynthia Harrod-Eagles
Bill Smith	S. J. Rozan
Blanche White	Barbara Neely
Bliss, Vicki	Elizabeth Peters
Blue McCarron	Abigail Padgett
Bonesteel, Nora	Sharyn McCrumb
Bradley, Barbara Joan "Bo"	Abigail Padgett
Brannigan, Kate	Val McDermid
Brazil, Andy	Patricia Cornwell
Brewster, Lily	Jill Churchill
Brewster, Robert	Jill Churchill
Britt Montero	Edna Buchanan
Brodie Farrell	Jo Bannister
Bubbles Yablonsky	Sarah Strohmeyer
Cain, Jenny	Nancy Pickard
Cal Donovan	Jo Bannister
Callahan Garrity	Kathy Hogan Trocheck
Campbell, Liam	Dana Stabenow
Carlos Tejada Alonso y Leon	Rebecca Pawel
Carlotta Carlyle	Linda Barnes
Carlyle, Carlotta	Linda Barnes
Carmichael, Caroline	Francine Mathews
Carol Hill	Val McDermid
Caroline Carmichael	Francine Mathews
Carrier, Judy	Lisa Scottoline
Cates, Molly	Mary Willis Walker
Catherine LeVendeur	Sharan Newman
Chapman, Mike	Linda Fairstein

Character Name	Author Name
Charlie Piotrowski	Joanne Dobson
Charles Sheridan	Robin Paige
Charlotte Justice	Paula L. Woods
Charlotte Pitt	Anne Perry
Chin, Lydia	S. J. Rozan
China Bayles	Susan Wittig Albert
Clare Fergusson	Julia Spencer-Fleming
Claudia Valentine	Marele Day
Clio Rees	Jo Bannister
Collins, Henrietta O'Dwyer (Henrie O)	Carolyn Hart
Connelly, Harper	Charlaine Harris
Cooper, Alexandra	Linda Fairstein
Crane, Mary Alice	Anne George
Daniel Hood	Jo Bannister
Darling, Annie Laurence	Carolyn Hart
Darling, Max	Carolyn Hart
Davidson, Harley	P. J. Tracy
Deacon, Jack	Jo Bannister
Deborah Knott	Margaret Maron
DiNunzio, Mary	Lisa Scottoline
Dittany Henbit Monk	Alisa Craig (Charlotte MacLeod)
Dobbs, Maisie	Jacqueline Winspear
Donovan, Cal	Jo Bannister
Duncan Kincaid	Deborah Crombie
Elena Oliverez	Marcia Muller
Elizabeth MacPherson	Sharyn McCrumb
Emma Graham	Martha Grimes
Eugenia Potter	Nancy Pickard
Eva Wylie	Liza Cody
Evan Evans	Rhys Bowen
Evans, Evan	Rhys Bowen
Falco, Marcus Didius	Lindsey Davis
Fansler, Kate	Amanda Cross
Farinelli, Lucy	Patricia Cornwell
Farrell, Brodie	Jo Bannister
Fergusson, Clare	Julia Spencer-Fleming
Folger, Merry	Francine Mathews

Character Name	Author Name
Fortune, Sarah	Frances Fyfield
Francesca Wilson	Janet Neel
Frank Harriman	Jan Burke
Frank Shapiro	Jo Bannister
Gabe Ortiz	Earlene Fowler
Garrity, Callahan	Kathy Hogan Trocheck
Gemma James	Deborah Crombie
Geoffrey Bailey	Frances Fyfield
Gino Rolseth	P. J. Tracy
Gordon, Lindsay	Val McDermid
Grace MacBride	P. J. Tracy
Graham, Emma	Martha Grimes
Graham, Liz	Jo Bannister
Graham, Maude	Donna Andrews
Grant, Patrick	Margaret Yorke
Hammer, Judy	Patricia Cornwell
Hannah Wolfe	Sarah Dunant
Halloran, Michael	P. J. Tracy
Harald, Sigrid	Margaret Maron
Harper, Benni	Earlene Fowler
Harper Connelly	Charlaine Harris
Harley Davidson	P. J. Tracy
Harriman, Frank	Jan Burke
Harry Marsh	Jo Bannister
Havers, Barbara	Elizabeth George
Hayle, Tamara	Valerie Wilson Wesley
Helen West	Frances Fyfield
Henrie O (Henrietta O'Dwyer Collins)	Carolyn Hart
Hester Latterly	Anne Perry
Hilary Tamar	Sarah Caudwell
Hill, Judy	Jill McGown
Hill, Tony	Val McDermid
Holden, Vicky	Margaret Coel
Holland, Primrose	Jo Bannister
Holloway, Barbara	Kate Wilhelm
Hollowell, Patricia Anne	Anne George
Holmes, Sherlock	Laurie R. King

Character Name	Author Name
Hood, Daniel	Jo Bannister
Hopper, Turing	Donna Andrews
Irene Kelly	Jan Burke
Jack Deacon	Jo Bannister
Jacqueline Kirby	Elizabeth Peters
James, Gemma	Deborah Crombie
James Owens Mega	Sharyn McCrumb
Jane Austen	Stephanie Barron (Francine Mathews)
Jane Jeffry	Jill Churchill
Jay Omega	Sharyn McCrumb
Jenny Cain	Nancy Pickard
Jeffrey Tolliver	Karin Slaughter
Jeffry, Jane	Jill Churchill
Jessie Arnold	Sue Henry
Jim Atherton	Cynthia Harrod-Eagles
Joanna Marshall	Cynthia Harrod-Eagles
Joanna Stark	Marcia Muller
Joe Morelli	Janet Evanovich
John MacLeish	Janet Neel
John O'Malley	Margaret Coel
Jordan, Carol	Val McDermid
Joseph Reavley	Anne Perry
Judy Carrier	Lisa Scottoline
Judy Hill	Jill McGown
Julian Kestrel	Kate Ross
Jury, Richard	Martha Grimes
Justice, Charlotte	Paula L. Woods
Karen Pelletier	Joanne Dobson
Kate Fansler	Amanda Cross
Kate Shugak	Dana Stabenow
Katherine Ardleigh	Robin Paige
Kathleen Mallory	Carol O'Connell
Kay Scarpetta	Patricia Cornwell
K. C. Riley	Edna Buchanan
Kelly, Irene	Jan Burke
Kestrel, Julian	Kate Ross
Kicklighter, Truman	Kathy Hogan Trocheck

Character Name	Author Name
Kincaid, Duncan	Deborah Crombie
Kincaid, Louis	P. J. Parrish
Kinsey Millhone	Sue Grafton
Kirby, Jacqueline	Elizabeth Peters
Knott, Deborah	Margaret Maron
Langdon, Skip	Julie Smith
Langslow, Meg	Donna Andrews
Latterly, Hester	Anne Perry
Laura Ackroyd	Patricia Hall
Leduc, Aimee	Cara Black
Lee, Anna	Liza Cody
Leo Magozzi	P. J. Tracy
LeVendeur, Catherine	Sharan Newman
Liam Campbell	Dana Stabenow
Lightfoot, Marie	Nancy Pickard
Lily Bard	Charlaine Harris
Lily Brewster	Jill Churchill
Lindsay Gordon	Val McDermid
Linton, Sara	Karin Slaughter
Liz Graham	Jo Bannister
Lloyd	Jill McGown
Louis Kincaid	P. J. Parrish
Lucy Farinelli	Patricia Cornwell
Luke Thanet	Dorothy Simpson
Lupe Solano	Carolina Garcia-Aguilera
Lydia Chin	S. J. Rozan
Lynley, Thomas	Elizabeth George
MacAlister, Marti	Eleanor Taylor Bland
MacBride, Grace	P. J. Tracy
MacLeish, John	Janet Neel
MacPherson, Elizabeth	Sharyn McCrumb
Madeline Bean	Jerrilyn Farmer
Madoc Rhys	Alisa Craig (Charlotte MacLeod)
Magozzi, Leo	P. J. Tracy
Maisie Dobbs	Jacqueline Winspear
Mallory, Kathleen	Carol O'Connell
Marcus Didius Falco	Lindsey Davis

Character Name	Author Name
Marie Lightfoot	Nancy Pickard
Marino, Pete	Patricia Cornwell
Marsh, Harry	Jo Bannister
Marshall, Joanna	Cynthia Harrod-Eagles
Marti MacAlister	Eleanor Taylor Bland
Mary Alice Crane	Anne George
Mary DiNunzio	Lisa Scottoline
Maude Graham	Donna Andrews
Maureen O'Donnell	Denise Mina
Maxine McNab	Sue Henry
McCarron, Blue	Abigail Padgett
McCone, Sharon	Marcia Muller
McDonald, Paul	Julie Smith
McNab, Maxine	Sue Henry
McQuaid, Mike	Susan Wittig Albert
Meehan, Paddy	Denise Mina
Meg Langslow	Donna Andrews
Mega, James Owens	Sharyn McCrumb
Mel Van Dyne	Jill Churchill
Melrose Plant	Martha Grimes
Mercer Wallace	Linda Fairstein
Merry Folger	Francine Mathews
Michael Halloran	P. J. Tracy
Michael Spraggue	Linda Barnes
Michael Thackeray	Patricia Hall
Michael Waterston	Donna Andrews
Mike Chapman	Linda Fairstein
Mike McQuaid	Susan Wittig Albert
Millhone, Kinsey	Sue Grafton
Molly Cates	Mary Willis Walker
Molly Murphy	Rhys Bowen
Monk, Dittany Henbit	Alisa Craig (Charlotte MacLeod)
Monk, Osbert	Alisa Craig (Charlotte MacLeod)
Monk, William	Anne Perry
Montero, Britt	Edna Buchanan
Morelli, Joe	Janet Evanovich
Mueller, Sharon	P. J. Tracy

Character Name	Author Name
Murphy, Molly	Rhys Bowen
Nora Bonesteel	Sharyn McCrumb
Nowack, Shelley	Jill Churchill
O'Donnell, Maureen	Denise Mina
Oliverez, Elena	Marcia Muller
O'Malley, John	Margaret Coel
Omega, Jay	Sharyn McCrumb
Ortiz, Gabe	Earlene Fowler
Osbert Monk	Alisa Craig (Charlotte MacLeod)
Paddy Meehan	Denise Mina
Patricia Anne Hollowell	Anne George
Patrick Grant	Margaret Yorke
Paul McDonald	Julie Smith
Paul Prye	Margaret Millar
Peabody, Amelia	Elizabeth Peters
Pelletier, Karen	Joanne Dobson
Pete Marino	Patricia Cornwell
Pigeon, Anna	Nevada Barr
Pincoski, Tim	Donna Andrews
Piotrowski, Charlie	Joanne Dobson
Pitt, Charlotte	Anne Perry
Pitt, Thomas	Anne Perry
Plant, Melrose	Martha Grimes
Plum, Stephanie	Janet Evanovich
Potter, Beatrix	Susan Wittig Albert
Potter, Eugenia	Nancy Pickard
Primrose Holland	Jo Bannister
Prye, Paul	Margaret Millar
Ranger	Janet Evanovich
Reavley, Joseph	Anne Perry
Rebecca Schwartz	Julie Smith
Rees, Clio	Jo Bannister
Reginald Wexford	Ruth Rendell
Rei Shimura	Sujata Massey
Richard Jury	Martha Grimes
Rhys, Madoc	Alisa Craig (Charlotte MacLeod)
Riley, K. C.	Edna Buchanan

Character Name	Author Name
Robert Brewster	Jill Churchill
Rolseth, Gino	P. J. Tracy
Rosato, Bennie	Lisa Scottoline
Ruby Wilcox	Susan Wittig Albert
Russ Van Alstyne	Julia Spencer-Fleming
Sands	Margaret Millar
Sara Linton	Karin Slaughter
Sarah Fortune	Frances Fyfield
Scarpetta, Kay	Patricia Cornwell
Schwartz, Rebecca	Julie Smith
Shapiro, Frank	Jo Bannister
Sharon McCone	Marcia Muller
Sharon Mueller	P. J. Tracy
Shelley Nowack	Jill Churchill
Sheridan, Charles	Robin Paige
Sherlock Holmes	Laurie R. King
Shimura, Rei	Sujata Massey
Shugak, Kate	Dana Stabenow
Sigrid Harald	Margaret Maron
Skip Langdon	Julie Smith
Slider, Bill	Cynthia Harrod-Eagles
Smith, Bill	S. J. Rozan
Solano, Lupe	Carolina Garcia-Aguilera
Sookie Stackhouse	Charlaine Harris
Spencer Arrowood	Sharyn McCrumb
Spraggue, Michael	Linda Barnes
Stackhouse, Sookie	Charlaine Harris
Stark, Joanna	Marcia Muller
Stephanie Plum	Janet Evanovich
Talba Willis	Julie Smith
Tamar, Hilary	Sarah Caudwell
Tamara Hayle	Valerie Wilson Wesley
Teagarden, Aurora	Charlaine Harris
Tejada Alonso y Leon, Carlos	Rebecca Pawel
Thackeray, Michael	Patricia Hall
Thanet, Luke	Dorothy Simpson
Thomas Lynley	Elizabeth George

Appendix C
Series Setting Index

Unless noted, settings are contemporary with date of publication. Series names are noted for authors with multiple series in different locations, but no notation is added if all of the author's works are set in the same location.

United States

Alabama
  Anne George

Alaska
  Sue Henry
  Dana Stabenow

Arkansas
  Charlaine Harris (Bard series)

Arizona
  J. A. Jance (Brady series)
  Nancy Pickard (Potter series)

California
  Nevada Barr
  Jan Burke
  Jerrilyn Farmer
  Earlene Fowler
  Sue Grafton (1970s–1980s)
  Faye Kellerman
  Laurie R. King (Martinelli series)
  Rochelle Krich
  Sujata Massey
  Margaret Millar (Aragon series)
  Marcia Muller
  Julie Smith (Schwartz series, McDonald series)
  Paula L. Woods (1990s)

Colorado
  Nevada Barr

Florida
  Nevada Barr
  Edna Buchanan
  Janet Evanovich (Barnaby series)
  Carolina Garcia-Aguilera
  P. J. Parrish (1980s)
  Nancy Pickard (Lightfoot series)
  Kathy Hogan Trocheck (Kicklighter series)

Georgia
  Nevada Barr
  Virginia Lanier
  Karin Slaughter
  Kathy Hogan Trocheck (Garrity series)

Illinois
  Eleanor Taylor Bland
  Jill Churchill (Jeffry series)
  Sara Paretsky

Louisiana
  Charlaine Harris (Stackhouse series)
  Julie Smith (Langton series, Willis series)

Maryland
  Janet Evanovich (Barnaby series)
  Laura Lippman

Laurie R. King (Russell series)
Gillian Linscott (Edwardian period)
Val McDermid
Jill McGown
Janet Neel
Robin Paige (Susan Wittig Albert) (Victorian era)
Anne Perry (Pitt series, Monk series: Victorian era; Reavley series: World War I era)
Elizabeth Peters (Peabody series: Victorian era)
Ruth Rendell
Kate Ross (Regency era)
Dorothy Simpson
Jacqueline Winspear (World War I era)
Margaret Yorke

Egypt
Elizabeth Peters (Peabody series: Victorian era)

France
Cara Black
Sharan Newman (Medieval era)

Germany
Elizabeth Peters (Bliss series)

Italy
Lindsey Davis (ancient Rome)

Japan
Sujata Massey

Scotland
Denise Mina (Meehan series: 1980s)

Spain
Rebecca Pawel (1930s)

Wales
Rhys Bowen (Evans series)

Appendix D
Sleuth Type Index

This appendix provides a listing of characters and authors by type of detective. Professional detectives, including law enforcement officers, police detectives, sheriffs, and licensed private investigators, are listed first, followed by the amateur sleuths' occupations.

Type of Sleuth	Character Name	Author Name
Police Officers/Detectives, Professional Law Enforcement & Sheriffs	Liz Graham	Jo Bannister
	Marti MacAllister	Eleanor Taylor Brand
	Evan Evans	Rhys Bowen
	K. C. Riley	Edna Buchanan
	Mel Van Dyne	Jill Churchill
	Lucy Farinelli	Patricia Cornwell
	Judy Hammer	Patricia Cornwell
	Pete Marino	Patricia Cornwell
	Benton Wesley	Patricia Cornwell
	Madoc Rhys	Alisa Craig
	Gemma James	Deborah Crombie
	Duncaid Kincaid	Deborah Crombie
	Marcus Didius Falco	Lindsey Davis
	Charlie Piotrowski	Joanne Dobson
	Joe Morelli	Janet Evanovich
	Mike Chapman	Linda Fairstein
	Mercer Wallace	Linda Fairstein
	Geoffrey Bailey	Frances Fyfield
	Thomas Lynley	Elizabeth George
	Barbara Havers	Elizabeth George

Type of Sleuth	Character Name	Author Name
	Richard Jury	Martha Grimes
	Michael Thackeray	Patricia Hall
	Bill Slider	Cynthia Harrod-Eagles
	Jim Atherton	Cynthia Harrod-Eagles
	Adam Dalgliesh	P. D. James
	J.P. Beaumont	J. A. Jance
	Joanna Brady	J. A. Jance
	Peter Decker	Faye Kellerman
	Kate Martinelli	Laurie R. King
	Jessie Drake	Rochelle Krich
	Max Bittersohn	Charlotte MacLeod
	Sigrid Harald	Margaret Maron
	Merry Folger	Francine Mathews
	Spencer Arrowood	Sharyn McCrumb
	Carol Jordan	Val McDermid
	Lloyd	Jill McGown
	Judy Hill	Jill McGown
	Inspector Sands	Margaret Millar
	John MacLeish	Janet Neel
	Kathleen Mallory	Carol O'Connell
	Louis Kincaid	P. J. Parrish
	Carlos Tejada Alonso	Rebecca Pawel
	Thomas Pitt	Anne Perry
	William Monk	Anne Perry
	Reginald Wexford	Ruth Rendell
	Liam Campbell	Kate Shugak
	Luke Thanet	Dorothy Simpson
	Jeffrey Tolliver	Karin Slaughter
	Skip Langdon	Julie Smith
	Russ Van Alstyne	Julia Spencer-Fleming
	Michael Halloran	P. J. Tracy
	Leo Magozzi	P. J. Tracy
	Sharon Mueller	P. J. Tracy
	Gino Rolseth	P. J. Tracy
	Charlotte Justice	Paula L. Woods
Private Investigators	Carlotta Carlyle	Linda Barnes
	Aimee Leduc	Cara Black

Type of Sleuth	Character Name	Author Name
Civic Foundation Director	Jenny Cain	Nancy Pickard
Clairvoyant	Harper Connelly	Charlaine Harris
	Sookie Stackhouse	Charlaine Harris
	Nora Bonesteel	Sharyn McCrumb
Computer Programmers	Grace MacBride	P. J. Tracy
	Annie Belinksi	P. J. Tracy
	Harley Davidson	P. J. Tracy
	Roadrunner	P. J. Tracy
Cooks/Caterers	Madeline Bean	Jerrilyn Farmer
	Eugenia Potter	Nancy Pickard
Dog Trainers	Jessie Arnold	Sue Henry
	JoBeth Sidden	Virginia Lanier
Forensic Anthropologist	Elizabeth MacPherson	Sharyn McCrumb
Gardener	Dittany Henbit Monk	Alisa Craig (Charlotte MacLeod)
Hairdresser	Bubbles Yablonsky	Sarah Strohmeyer
Herbalists	China Bayles	Susan Wittig Albert
	Nora Bonesteel	Sharyn McCrumb
House Cleaners	Lily Bard	Charlaine Harris
	Blanche White	Barbara Neely
	Callahan Garrity	Kathy Hogan Trocheck
Lawyers and Judges	China Bayles	Susan Wittig Albert
	Hilary Tamar	Sarah Caudwell
	Alex Cooper	Linda Fairstein
	Sarah Fortune	Frances Fyfield
	Helen West	Frances Fyfield
	Deborah Knott	Margaret Maron
	Tom Aragon	Margaret Millar
	Bennie Rosato	Lisa Scottoline
	Mary DiNunzio	Lisa Scottoline
	Judy Carrier	Lisa Scottoline
	Rebecca Schwartz	Julie Smith
	Kate Shugak	Dana Stabenow
	Barbara Holloway	Kate Wilhelm
Librarians and Library Workers	Tim Pincoski	Donna Andrews
	Aurora Teagarden	Charlaine Harris

Type of Sleuth	Character Name	Author Name
	Helen Marsh	Charlotte MacLeod
	J Jacqueline Kirby	Elizabeth Peters
Mechanics	Alexandra Barnaby	Janet Evanovich
Museum curators/Museum security	Benni Harper	Earlene Fowler
	Elena Oliverez	Marcia Muller
	Joanna Stark	Marcia Muller
	Vicki Bliss	Elizabeth Peters
Novelists and Poets	Beatrix Potter	Susan Wittig Albert
	Jane Austen	Stephanie Barron
	Osbert Monk	Alisa Craig (Charlotte MacLeod)
	Adam Dalgliesh	P. D. James
	Jay Omega	Sharyn McCrumb
	Katherine Ardleigh	Robin Paige
	Jacqueline Kirby	Elizabeth Peters
	Paul McDonald	Julie Smith
	Talba Willis	Julie Smith
Owner-Operators of Unlicensed Investigative Services Firms	Brodie Farrell	Jo Bannister
	Max Darling	Carolyn Hart
	Maisie Dobbs	Jacqueline Winspear
Park Ranger	Anna Pigeon	Nevada Barr
Politicians and Political Activists	Nell Bray	Gillian Linscott
	Ben Safford	Emma Lathen
Physicians and Medical Examiners	Primrose Holland	Jo Bannister
	Clio Rees	Jo Bannister
	Kay Scarpetta	Patricia Cornwell
	Sara Linton	Karin Slaughter
Priests/Religious	John O'Malley	Margaret Coel
	Catherine LeVendeur	Sharan Newman
	Clare Fergusson	Julia Spencer-Fleming
Professors and Teachers	Michael Waterston	Donna Andrews
	Daniel Hood	Brodie Farrell
	Hilary Tamar	Sarah Caudwell

Type of Sleuth	Character Name	Author Name
	Kate Fansler	Amanda Cross
	Karen Pelletier	Joanne Dobson
	Patricia Anne Hollowell	Anne George
	James Owens Mega	Sharyn McCrumb
	Peter Shandy	Charlotte MacLeod
	Patrick Grant	Margaret Yorke
Psychologists and Social Workers	Tony Hill	Val McDermid
	Paul Prye	Margaret Millar
	Charles Butler	Carol O'Connell
	Bo Bradley	Abigail Padgett
	Blue McCarron	Abigail Padgett
Reporters and Investigative Journalists	Britt Montero	Edna Buchanan
	Laura Ackroyd	Patricia Hall
	Henrietta O'Dwyer Collins	Carolyn Hart
	Molly Blume	Rochelle Krich
	Lindsay Gordon	Val McDermid
	Paddy Meehan	Denise Mina
	Bubbles Yablonsky	Sarah Strohmeyer
	Truman Kicklighter	Kathy Hogan Trocheck
Secretary	Maude Graham	Donna Andrews
Shopkeepers	China Bayles	Susan Wittig Albert
	Ruby Wilcox	Susan Wittig Albert
	Annie Laurence Darling	Carolyn Hart
Sports Related	Eva Wylie	Liza Cody
	Birdie Linnett	Gillian Linscott
Stay-at-Home Moms/ Homemakers	Jane Jeffry	Jill Churchill
	Shelley Nowack	Jill Churchill
	Rina Lazarus Decker	Faye Kellerman
	Charlotte Pitt	Anne Perry
True Crime Writers	Marie Lightfoot	Nancy Pickard
	Molly Cates	Mary Willis Walker
Waitress	Sookie Stackhouse	Charlaine Harris

Appendix E
In Memoriam

Listed here are the birth and death dates of writers who were included in the first edition of *Great Women Mystery Writers* who have passed away since 1994. The information in the first edition entries remains current.

Anna Clarke 1919–2004
S. T. Haymon 1918–1995
Lucille Kallen 1926–1999
Elizabeth Lemarchand 1906–2000
Patricia Moyes 1923–2000
Ellis Peters 1913–1995

Several other authors have died since the first edition, but there was additional information to warrant an updated entry. Those writers are:

Sarah Caudwell 1939–2000
Amanda Cross (Carolyn Heilbrun) 1926–2003
Patricia Highsmith 1921–1995
Mary Jane Latsis (half of Emma Lathen) 1927–1999
Charlotte MacLeod (Alisa Craig) 1922–2005
Margaret Millar 1915–1994

In addition, entries are provided for three deceased writers whose mystery writing careers emerged after the first edition. They are:

Anne George d. 2001
Virginia Lanier 1930–2003
Kate Ross 1956–1998

Appendix F
The Edgar Awards

Known as the Academy Awards of mystery fiction, the Edgars, named for Edgar Allan Poe, are bestowed by the Mystery Writers of America (MWA). Although sponsored by an American group, the awards have often been given to writers outside the United States. The MWA was founded in 1945, and some Edgar awards were first presented at the first banquet in 1946. For the first few years, they did not offer a Best Novel award for reasons ranging from the concern that writers who did not win would be offended and resign from the organization to the sense that no one felt competent to judge the award (Zeman). They decided to offer the Best Novel award for the first time in 1954, and the first winner was a woman writer, Charlotte Jay.

There are several Edgar Awards given each year, including Best Novel, Best First Mystery Novel, Best Original Paperback, and Best Short Story. The Best First Novel award is exclusively reserved for American writers. The Best Original Paperback award was begun in 1970. Over the years, Edgar Awards have also been introduced for Best True Crime, Best Critical/Biographical Study, Best Juvenile Mystery, and Best Motion Picture. From 1954 to 1973, they awarded a prize to the Best Dust Jacket; the goal was to bring attention to the cover art and promotional aspects of the packaging of mystery novels (Zeman).

A Grand Master is also named each year, which is a lifetime achievement award. The first Grand Master was Agatha Christie, who earned the honor in 1954. Other women Grand Master winners are Mignon C. Eberhart (1971), Ngaio Marsh (1978), Dorothy B. Hughes (1978), Daphne du Maurier (1978), Margaret Millar (1983), Dorothy Salisbury Davis (1985), Phyllis A. Whitney (1988), Helen McCloy (1990), Ruth Rendell (1997), Barbara Mertz/Elizabeth Peters/Barbara Michaels (1998), P. D. James (1999), Mary Higgins Clark (2000), and Marcia Muller (2005).

There are also several awards in honor of various writers. The Ellery Queen Award was instituted in 1983; Emma Lathen was named the first recipient. In 1984, the Robert L. Fish Memorial Award was begun, and more recently, the MWA has administered the Mary Higgins Clark Award. Sponsored by Simon & Schuster, the award is given to the novel that best meets criteria set forth by Clark. These criteria involve a young, independent female protagonist who is minding her own business when her life is suddenly disrupted. Along with no violence, swearing or explicit sex, the character must solve the problem with courage and intelligence. The winners of the award for 2001–2006 are Barbara D'Amato, for *Authorized Personnel Only,* Judith Kelman, for *Summer of Storms,* Rose Conners, for *Absolute Certainty,* M. K. Preston, for *Song of the Bones,* Rochelle Krich, for *Grave Endings,* and Karen Harper for *Dark Angel.*

The MWA forms committees to select the prizes. Authors, editors, and publishers submit copies of books for consideration. After various rounds of deliberation, the committee members decide on finalists and the prizewinner for each category. Since the third year of the ceremonies, the award-winners receive a ceramic statuette of Poe.

The following list provides information about women nominees for Edgar awards over the years. Winners are marked with an asterisk (*). The MWA tracks the awards by the year it is presented; works are published in the year prior.

Year	Category	Nominee
1947	Best First Novel	*Helen Eustis, *The Horizontal Man*
1949	Best First Novel	*Mildred Davis, *The Room Upstairs*
1950	Best First Novel	Evelyn Piper, *The Innocent*
1951	Best First Novel	Patricia Highsmith, *Strangers on a Train*
1952	Best First Novel	*Mary McMullen, *Strangle Hold*
1953	Best First Novel	Peggy Bacon, *The Inward Eye*
1954	Best Novel	*Charlotte Jay, *Beat Not the Bones*
1955	Best First Novel	*Jean Potts, *Go, Lovely Rose*
1956	Best Novel	Patricia Highsmith, *The Talented Mr. Ripley*
	Best Novel	*Margaret Millar, *Beast in View*
1957	Best Novel	*Charlotte Armstrong, *A Dram of Poison*
	Best Novel	Margot Bennett, *The Man Who Didn't Fly*
1958	Best Novel	Marjorie Carleton, *The Night of the Good Children*
1959	Best Novel	Dorothy Salisbury Davis, *A Gentleman Called*
	Best First Novel	Frances Duncombe, *Death of a Spinster*
1960	Best Novel	*Celia Fremlin, *The Hours Before Dawn*
	Best First Novel	Mary O. Rank, *A Dream of Falling*
1962	Best Novel	Anne Blaisdell, *Nightmare*
	Best Novel	Suzanne Blanc, *The Green Stone*
	Best First Novel	*Suzanne Blanc, *The Green Stone*
	Best First Novel	Olivia Dwight, *Close to His Eyes*
	Best First Novel	Breni James, *Night of the Kill*
	Best First Novel	Winifred Van Atta, *Shock Treatment*
1963	Best Novel	*Ellis Peters, *Death and the Joyful Woman*
	Best Novel	Shelley Smith, *The Ballad of the Running Man*
	Best Novel	Jean Potts, *The Evil Wish*
1964	Best Novel	Elizabeth Fenwick, *The Make-Believe Man*
	Best Novel	Dorothy B. Hughes, *The Expendable Man*
	Best First Novel	Frances Rickett, *The Prowler*
1965	Best First	Margaret Millar, *The Fiend*
	Best First	Mary Stewart, *This Rough Magic*
	Best First Novel	Amanda Cross, *In the Last Analysis*

1966	Best Novel	Mary Stewart, *Airs Above the Ground*
	Best Novel	Dorothy Salisbury Davis, *The Pale Betrayer*
	Best First Novel	Alexandra Roudybush, *Before the Ball Was Over*
1967	Best Novel	Ngaio Marsh, *Killer Dolphin*
	Best First Novel	Babs Deal, *Fancy's Knell*
1968	Best Novel	Charlotte Armstrong, *Lemon in the Basket*
	Best Novel	Charlotte Armstrong, *The Gift Shop*
1969	Best Novel	Dorothy Salisbury Davis and Jerome Ross, *God Speed the Night*
	Best First Novel	*Dorothy Uhnak, *The Bait*
1970	Best Novel	Dorothy Salisbury Davis, *Where the Dark Streets Go*
	Best Novel	Emma Lathen, *When in Greece*
	Best First Novel	Naomi Hintze, *You'll Like My Mother*
	Best Paperback Original	Elsie Cromwell, *The Governess*
1971	Best Novel	Margaret Millar, *Beyond This Point Are Monsters*
	Best Novel	Patricia Moyes, *Many Deadly Returns*
	Best Novel	*Maj Stowell and Per Wahloo, *The Laughing Policeman*
1972	Best Novel	P. D. James, *Shroud for a Nightingale*
	Best First Novel	Hildegarde Dolson, *To Spite Her Face*
	Best Paperback Original	Alicen White, *Nor Spell, Nor Charm*
1973	Best Novel	Ngaio Marsh, *Tied Up in Tinsel*
1974	Best Novel	P. D. James, *An Unsuitable Job for a Woman*
	Best Novel	Jean Stubbs, *Dear Laura*
	Best Paperback Original	Dinah Palmtag, *Starling Street*
1976	Best First Novel	Lynn Meyer, *Paperback Thriller*
	Best Paperback Original	Jacqueline Park, *Charlie's Back in Town*
1977	Best First Novel	Janice Law, *The Big Pay-Off*
1979	Best Novel	Ruth Rendell, *A Sleeping Life*
1980	Best Novel	Ruth Rendell, *Make Death Love Me*
1981	Best Novel	B. M. Gill, *Death Drop*
	Best First Novel	Betsy Aswald, *Winds of the Old Days*
	Best First Novel	Susanne Jaffe, *The Other Ann Fletcher*
1982	Best Novel	Liza Cody, *Dupe*

1983	Best Paperback Original	Teri White, *Triangle*
1984	Best First Novel	Carolyn Wheat, *Dead Man's Thoughts*
	Best Paperback Original	Margaret Tracy, *Mrs. White*
1985	Best Novel	B. M. Gill, *The Twelfth Juror*
	Best Novel	Jane Langton, *Emily Dickinson is Dead*
	Best First Novel	Orania Papazouglou, *Sweet, Savage Death*
	Best First Novel	Alison Smith, *Someone Else's Grave*
1986	Best Novel	Ruth Rendell, *The Tree of Hands*
	Best Novel	Ruth Rendell, *An Unkindness of Ravens*
	Best Novel	*L. R. Wright, *The Suspect*
	Best First Novel	Tony Fennelly, *The Glory Hole Murders*
1987	Best Novel	P. D. James, *A Taste of Death*
	Best Novel	*Barbara Vine, *A Dark-Adapted Eye*
	Best Paperback Original	Lillian Jackson Braun, *The Cat Who Saw Red*
	Best Paperback Original	Kate Green, *Shattered Moon*
1988	Best Novel	Linda Barnes, *A Trouble of Fools*
	Best Novel	B. M. Gill, *Nursery Crimes*
	Best Novel	Charlotte MacLeod, *The Corpse in Oozak's Pond*
	Best First Novel	*Deidre S. Laiken, *Death Among Strangers*
	Best Paperback Original	*Sharyn McCrumb, *Bimbos of the Death Sun*
1989	Best First Novel	Mary Lou Bennett, *Murder Once Done*
	Best First Novel	Elizabeth George, *A Great Deliverance*
	Best First Novel	Shelley Reuben, *Julian Solo*
	Best Paperback Original	Lia Matera, *A Radical Departure*
1990	Best Novel	Frances Fyfield, *A Question of Guilt*
	Best First Novel	Susan Taylor Chehak, *The Story of Annie D.*
	Best First Novel	Melodie Johnson Howe, *The Mother Shadow*
	Best First Novel	*Susan Wolfe, *The Last Billable Hour*
	Best Paperback Original	Deborah Valentine, *A Collector of Photographs*
1991	Best Novel	*Julie Smith, *New Orleans Mourning*
	Best First Novel	Edna Buchanan, *Nobody Lives Forever*

	Best First Novel	*Patricia Cornwell, *Postmortem*
	Best Paperback Original	Jane Haddam, *Not a Creature Was Stirring*
	Best Paperback Original	B. J. Oliphant, *Dead in the Scrub*
1992	Best Novel	Lia Matera, *Prior Convictions*
	Best Novel	Nancy Pickard, *I.O.U.*
	Best First Novel	Marcy Heidish, *Deadline*
	Best First Novel	Mary Willis Walker, *Zero at the Bone*
	Best Paperback Original	P. M. Carlson, *Murder in the Dog Days*
	Best Paperback Original	Deborah Valentine, *Fine Distinctions*
1993	Best Novel	Liza Cody, *Backhand*
	Best Novel	*Margaret Maron, *Bootlegger's Daughter*
	Best First Novel	Jane Stanton Hitchcock, *Trick of the Eye*
	Best Paperback Original	Gini Hartzmark, *Principal Defense*
	Best Paperback Original	Billie Sue Mosiman, *Night Cruise*
	Best Paperback Original	*Dana Stabenow, *A Cold Day for Murder*
1994	Best Novel	Marcia Muller, *Wolf in the Shadow*
	Best Novel	*Minette Walters, *The Sculptress*
	Best First Novel	*Laurie R. King, *A Grave Talent*
	Best Paperback Original	Margaret Frazer, *The Servant's Tale*
	Best Paperback Original	Lisa Scottoline, *Everywhere That Mary Went*
1995	Best Novel	Edna Buchanan, *Miami, It's Murder*
	Best Novel	*Mary Willis Walker, *The Red Scream*
	Best First Novel	Janet Evanovich, *One for the Money*
	Best First Novel	Carol O'Connell, *Mallory's Oracle*
	Best First Novel	Barbara Parker, *Suspicion of Innocence*
	Best Paperback Original	*Lisa Scottoline, *Final Appeal*
	Best Paperback Original	Chassie West, *Sunrise*
1996	Best First Novel	Martha C. Lawrence, *Murder in Scorpio*
	Best Paperback Original	Gloria White, *Charged with Guilt*

1997	Best Novel	Laurie R. King, *With Child*
	Best Novel	Margaret Lawrence, *Hearts and Bones*
	Best Novel	Anne Perry, *Pentecost Alley*
	Best Novel	Carolyn Wheat, *Mean Streak*
	Best First Novel	Margaret Moseley, *Bonita Faye*
	Best First Novel	Sharon Kay Penman, *The Queen's Man*
	Best Paperback Original	Joan M. Drury, *Silent Words*
	Best Paperback Original	Teri Holbrook, *The Grass Widow*
	Best Paperback Original	Susan Wade, *Walking Rain*
1998	Best Novel	Deborah Crombie, *Dreaming of the Bones*
	Best First Novel	Suzanne Berne, *A Crime in the Neighborhood*
	Best First Novel	Lisa See, *Flower Net*
	Best Paperback Original	Susan Rogers Cooper, *Home Again, Home Again*
	Best Paperback Original	Margaret Frazer, *The Prioress' Tale*
	Best Paperback Original	*Laura Lippman, *Charm City*
	Best Paperback Original	Gloria White, *Sunset and Santiago*
1999	Best First Novel	Jen Sachs, *Nice*
	Best Paperback Original	Laura Lippman, *Butchers Hill*
	Best Paperback Original	Sujata Massey, *Zen Attitude*
2000	Best Novel	*Jan Burke, *Bones*
	Best First Novel	Paula L. Woods, *Inner City Blues*
	Best Paperback Original	Laura Lippman, *In Big Trouble*
2001	Best Novel	Val McDermid, *A Place of Execution*
	Best Novel	Kris Nelscott, *A Dangerous Road*
	Best Novel	Nancy Pickard, *The Whole Truth*
	Best First Novel	Marcia Simpson, *Crow in Stolen Colors*
	Best Paperback Original	Victoria Thompson, *Murder on St. Mark's Place*
	Best Paperback Original	Chassie West, *Killing Kin*

	Best Paperback Original	Sally S. Wright, *Pursuit and Persuasion*
2002	Best Novel	S. J. Rozan, *Reflecting the Sky*
	Best First Novel	Denise Hamilton, *The Jasmine Trade*
	Best Paperback Original	Teri Holbrook, *The Mother Tongue*
	Best Paperback Original	P. J. Parrish, *Dead of Winter*
2003	Best Novel	Mary Kay Andrews, *Savannah Blues*
	Best Novel	*S. J. Rozan, *Winter and Night*
	Best Novel	Manda Scott, *No Good Deed*
	Best Paperback Original	Anna Salter, *Prison Blues*
2004	Best Novel	Natsuo Kirino, *Out*
	Best Novel	Jacqueline Winspear, *Maisie Dobbs*
	Best First Novel	Martha Conway, *12 Bliss Street*
	Best First Novel	*Rebecca C. Pawel, *Death of a Nationalist*
	Best Paperback Original	Nina Revoyr, *Southland*
	Best Paperback Original	*Sylvia Maultash Warsh, *Find Me Again*
2005	Best Novel	Rhys Bowen, *Evan's Gate*
	Best Novel	Laura Lippman, *By a Spider's Thread*
	Best Novel	Julia Spencer-Fleming, *Out of the Deep I Cry*
2006	Best Novel	Tess Gerritsen, *Vanish*
	Best First Novel	Megan Abbott, *Die A Little*
	Best First Novel	Alison Gaylin, *Hide Your Eyes*
	Best First Novel	*Theresa Schwegel, *Officer Down*
	Best Paperback Original	Anne Argula, *Homicide My Own*

BIBLIOGRAPHY

Edgar Awards. Mystery Writers of America. 2006. 28 April 2006. http://www.mysterywriters.org/pages/awards/index.htm

Zeman, Barry and Angela. "Mystery Writers of America: A Historical Survey." *Mystery Writers of America.* 3 April 2000. 17 March 2006. http://www.mysterywriters.org/pages/about/history.htm

Appendix G
The Agatha Awards

Malice Domestic began their awards in 1989, the first year they held a convention. Their convention is typically held in April or May, always in Washington, D.C. The mission of Malice Domestic is to honor and promote "mysteries of manners," novels in the style of Agatha Christie. Often called "cozy" mysteries, the novels that win Agatha Awards feature an amateur sleuth, no gory violence, and attention to character and setting. Books that feature police detectives as characters may qualify, but novels considered to be "hard-boiled" do not.

An awards committee reviews nominations and prepares a ballot of eligible items published during the previous year, and those who attend the convention vote for the winners in the various categories. In addition to Best Novel and Best First Novel, Agatha Awards are also given for the best short story and nonfiction work. Winners receive a teapot with the Malice Domestic skull and crossbones logo.

Malice Domestic presents Lifetime Achievement Awards, as well, although they do not give one each year. The awards have been given to Phyllis A. Whitney (1990), Mignon G. Eberhart (1994), Mary Stewart (1996), Emma Lathen (1997), Charlotte MacLeod (1998), Patricia Moyes (1999), Mildred Wirt Benson (2001), Barbara Mertz/Elizabeth Peters/ Barbara Michaels (2003), and Marian Babson (2004).

Listed next are women novelists nominated for Agatha Awards. Winners are marked with an asterisk. Note that these awards are tracked by the year of publication, not the year they are bestowed.

1988
Best Novel

Dorothy Cannell, *The Widow's Club*
*Carolyn Hart, *Something Wicked*
Joan Hess, *Mischief In Maggody*
Sharyn McCrumb, *Paying The Piper*
Nancy Pickard, *Dead Crazy*

Best First Novel

*Elizabeth George, *A Great Deliverance*
Caroline Graham, *The Killings at Badger's Drift*
Corinne Holt Sawyer, *The J. Alfred Prufrock Murders*
Susannah Stacey, *Goodbye, Nanny Grey*
Dorothy Sucher, *Dead Men Don't Give Seminars*

1989

Best Novel

Sarah Caudwell, *The Sirens Sang of Murder*
Carolyn Hart, *A Little Class on Murder*
Margaret Maron, *Corpus Christmas*
*Elizabeth Peters, *Naked Once More*
Gillian Roberts, *Philly Stakes*

Best First Novel

Eleanor Boylan, *Working Murder*
*Jill Churchill, *Grime and Punishment*
Frances Fyfield, *A Question of Guilt*
Melanie Johnson Howe, *The Mother Shadow*
Edith Skom, *The Mark Twain Murders*

1990

Best Novel

Charlaine Harris, *Real Murders*
Carolyn Hart, *Deadly Valentine*
Anne Perry, *The Face of a Strange*
Ellis Peters, *The Potter's Field*
*Nancy Pickard, *Bum Steer*

Best First Novel

Pat Burden, *Screaming Bones*
Diane Mott Davidson, *Catering To Nobody*
*Katherine Hall Page, *The Body in the Belfry*
Janet L. Smith, *Sea of Troubles*

1991

Best Novel

Carolyn Hart, The Christie Caper
Charlotte MacLeod, *An Owl Too Many*
Elizabeth Peters, *The Last Camel Died at Noon*
*Nancy Pickard, *I.O.U.*

Best First Novel

Mary Cahill, *Carpool*
Mary Daheim, *Just Desserts*
Rebecca Rothenberg, *The Bulrush Murders*
*Mary Willis Walker, *Zero at the Bone*
Ann Williams, *Flowers for the Dead*

1992

Best Novel

Carolyn Hart, *Southern Ghost*
*Margaret Maron, *Bootlegger's Daughter*
Sharyn McCrumb, *The Hangman's Beautiful Daughter*

Anne Perry, *Defend and Betray*
Elizabeth Peters, *The Snake, the Crocodile and the Dog*

Best First Novel

Deborah Adams, *All the Great Pretenders*
Susan Wittig Albert, *Thyme of Death*
Carol Higgins Clark, *Decked*
Miriam Grace Monfredo, *The Seneca Falls Inheritance*
*Barbara Neely, *Blanche on the Lam*

1993
Best Novel

*Carolyn Hart, *Dead Man's Island*
Joan Hess, *O Little Town of Maggody*
Rochelle Majer Krich, *Fair Game*
Margaret Maron, *Southern Discomfort*
Kathy Hogan Trocheck, *To Live and Die in Dixie*

Best First Novel

*Nevada Barr, *Track of the Cat*
Jan Burke, *Goodnight, Irene*
Deborah Crombie, *A Share in Death*
Sharan Newman, *Death Comes as Epiphany*
Abigail Padgett, *Child of Silence*

1994
Best Novel

Carolyn Hart, *Scandal in Fair Haven*
Laurie R. King, *The Beekeeper's Apprentice*
Rochelle Majer Krich, *Angel of Death*
*Sharyn McCrumb, *She Walks These Hills*
Elizabeth Peters, *Night Train to Memphis*

Best First Novel

Janet Evanovich, *One For The Money*
Earlene Fowler, *Fool's Puzzle*
Barbara Burnett Smith, *Writers of the Purple Sage*
Polly Whitney, *Until Death*

1995
Best Novel

Joan Hess, *Miracles In Maggody*
*Sharyn McCrumb, *If I'd Killed Him When I Met Him*
Sharan Newman, *The Wandering Arm*
Nancy Pickard, *Twilight*

Best First Novel

*Jeanne M. Dams, *The Body in the Transept*
Teri Holbrook, *A Far and Deadly Cry*

Jody Jaffe, *Horse of a Different Killer*
Virginia Lanier, *Death in Bloodhound Red*
Martha C. Lawrence, *Murder in Scorpio*

1996
Best Novel

Earlene Fowler, *Kansas Troubles*
Teri Holbrook, *Grass Widow*
Margaret Lawrence, *Hearts and Bones*
*Margaret Maron, *Up Jumps the Devil*
Sharan Newman, *Strong as Death*

Best First Novel

Nancy Bell, *Biggie and the Poisoned Politician*
*Anne George, *Murder on a Girls' Night Out*
Terris McMahan Grimes, *Somebody Else's Child*
Lillian Roberts, *Riding for a Fall*

1997
Best Novel

Jan Burke, *Hocus*
Deborah Crombie, *Dreaming of the Bones*
Earlene Fowler, *Goose in the Pond*
Elizabeth Peters, *Seeing a Large Cat*
*Kate Ross, *The Devil in Music*

Best First Novel

Joanne Dobson, *Quieter Than Sleep*
*Sujata Massey, *The Salaryman's Wife*
Phyllis Richman, *The Butter Did It*
Penny Warner, *Dead Body Language*
Barbara Jaye Wilson, *Death Brims Over*

1998
Best Novel

Jan Burke, *Liar*
Earlene Fowler, *Dove in the Window*
Virginia Lanier, *Blind Bloodhound Justice*
*Laura Lippman, *Butchers Hill*
Margaret Maron, *Home Fires*
Elizabeth Peters, *The Ape Who Guards the Balance*

Best First Novel

Jerrilyn Farmer, *Sympathy for the Devil*
Jacqueline Fiedler, *Tiger's Palette*
Judy Fitzwater, *Dying to Get Published*
*Robin Hathaway, *The Doctor Digs a Grave*
Sharon Kahn, *Fax Me a Bagel*

1999
Best Novel

Jerrilyn Farmer, *Immaculate Reception*
*Earlene Fowler, *Mariner's Compass*
Carolyn Hart, *Death on the River Walk*
Laura Lippman, *In Big Trouble*
Sujata Massey, *The Flower Master*

Best First Novel

*Donna Andrews, *Murder with Peacocks*
April Henry, *Circles of Confusion*
Kris Neri, *Revenge of the Gypsy Queen*
Elena Santangelo, *By Blood Possessed*
Marcia Talley, *Sing It to Her Bones*

2000
Best Novel

Taffy Cannon, *Guns and Roses*
Jerrilyn Farmer, *Killer Wedding*
*Margaret Maron, *Storm Track*
Sujata Massey, *The Floating Girl*
Elizabeth Peters, *He Shall Thunder in the Sky*

Best First Novel

Kate Grilley, *Death Dances to a Reggae Beat*
Julie Wray Herman, *Three Dirty Women and the Garden of Death*
Irene Marcuse, *Death of an Amiable Child*
*Rosemary Stevens, *Death on a Silver Tray*
Denise Swanson, *Murder of a Small Town Honey*

2001
Best Novel

*Rhys Bowen, *Murphy's Law*
Earlene Fowler, *Arkansas Traveler*
Charlaine Harris, *Dead Until Dark*
Rochelle Krich, *Shadows of Sin*
Sujata Massey, *The Bride's Kimono*

Best First Novel

*Sarah Strohmeyer, *Bubbles Unbound*
Anne White, *An Affinity for Murder*

2002
Best Novel

*Donna Andrews, *You've Got Murder*
Rhys Bowen, *Death of Riley*
Rochelle Krich, *Blues in the Night*

Katherine Hall Page, *The Body in the Bonfire*
Elizabeth Peters, *The Golden One*

Best First Novel

Pip Granger, *Not All Tarts Are Apple*
Roberta Isleib, *Six Strokes Under*
Claire M. Johnson, *Beat Until Stiff*
Nancy Martin, *How to Murder a Millionaire*
*Julia Spencer-Fleming, *In the Bleak Midwinter*
Lea Wait, *Shadows at the Fair*

2003
Best Novel

Donna Andrews, *Crouching Buzzard, Leaping Loon*
Jerrilyn Farmer, *Mumbo Gumbo*
*Carolyn Hart, *Letter from Home*
Rochelle Krich, *Dream House*
Margaret Maron, *Last Lessons of Summer*
Elaine Viets, *Shop till You Drop*

Best First Novel

Elaine Flinn, *Dealing in Murder*
Erin Hart, *Haunted Ground*
S. W. Hubbard, *Take the Bait*
Maddy Hunter, *Alpine for You*
Joyce Krieg, *Murder Off Mike*
Sarah Stewart Taylor, *O' Artful Death*
*Jacqueline Winspear, *Maisie Dobbs*

2004
Best Novel

Donna Andrews, *We'll Always Have Parrots*
Laura Lippman, *By a Spider's Thread*
Margaret Maron, *High Country Fall*
Sujata Massey, *The Pearl Diver*
*Jacqueline Winspear, *Birds of a Feather*

Best First Novel

Judy Clemens, *Till the Cows Come Home*
Patricia Harwin, *Arson and Old Lace*
Susan Kandel, *I Dreamed I Married Perry Mason*
*Harley Jane Kozak, *Dating Dead Men*
Pari Noskin Taichert, *The Clovis Incident*

2005
Best Novel

Donna Andrews, *Owls Well That Ends Well*
Margaret Maron, *Rituals of the Season*

*Katherine Hall Page, *The Body in the Snowdrift*
Pari Noskin Taichert, *The Belen Hitch*
Heather Webber, *Trouble in Spades*
Jacqueline Winspear, *Pardonable Lies*

Best First Novel

Laura Bradford, *Jury of One*
Shirley Damsgaard, *Witch Way to Murder*
*Laura Durham, *Better Off Wed*
Maggie Sefton, *Knit One, Kill Two*
Lisa Tillman, *Blood Relations*

BIBLIOGRAPHY

Agatha Awards. Malice Domestic Ltd. 2006. 28 April 2006. http://www.malicedomestic.org/
    agatha.htm

Appendix H
The Anthony Awards

The Anthony Awards are presented at one of the largest and well-known mystery conventions, Bouchercon. The award and the convention are named for Anthony Boucher, prominent mystery critic and fan. After Boucher's death in 1968, several mystery fans banded together to form a mystery convention to be held in his honor. Since 1970, the convention has been held annually, often in the United States, but at several international sites as well. The convention is run by unpaid volunteer mystery fans for other mystery fans, and is widely attended by writers and editors in addition to readers.

The Anthony Awards were first presented at the 1986 Bouchercon. Like other awards, Anthony Awards are given for best novel, best first mystery novel, best paperback original, best short story, and best critical work. Other awards have been given irregularly, including best critical/nonfiction work, best young adult mystery, best historical mystery, and best cover art. Nominees and winners are chosen by convention attendees. The awards are unique, designed by each convention program committee.

A listing of women who have been nominated for the Anthony Award is presented here. Information about all nominees is unavailable for 1986 through 1996. Winners are marked with an asterisk (*). The awards are tracked by the year presented and are for works published in the previous year.

1986	Best Novel	*Sue Grafton, *B is for Burglar*
	Best Paperback Original	*Nancy Pickard, *Say No to Murder*
1987	Best Novel	*Sue Grafton, *C is for Corpse*
1988	Best First Mystery	*Gillian Roberts, *Caught Dead in Philadelphia*
1989	Best First Mystery	*Elizabeth George, *A Great Deliverance*
	Best Paperback Original	*Carolyn Hart, *Something Wicked*
1990	Best Novel	*Sarah Caudwell, *The Sirens Sang of Murder*
	Best First Mystery	*Karen Kijewski, *Katwalk*
	Best Paperback Original	*Carolyn Hart, *Honeymoon for Murder*
1991	Best Novel	*Sue Grafton, *G is for Gumshoe*

	Best First Mystery	*Patricia Cornwell, *Postmortem*
	Best Paperback Original	*Rochelle Krich, *Where's Mommy Now?*
1992	Best First Mystery	*Sue Henry, *Murder on the Iditarod Trail*
1993	Best Novel	*Margaret Maron, *Bootlegger's Daughter*
	Best First Mystery	*Barbara Neely, *Blanche on the Lam*
1994	Best Novel	*Marcia Muller, *Wolf in the Shadows*
	Best First Mystery	*Nevada Barr, *Track of the Cat*
1995	Best Novel	*Sharyn McCrumb, *She Walks These Hills*
1996	Best Novel	*Mary Willis Walker, *Under the Beetle's Cellar*
	Best First Mystery	*Virginia Lanier, *Death in Bloodhound Red*
1997	Best Novel	Nevada Barr, *Firestorm*
	Best Novel	Linda Grant, *Lethal Genes*
	Best Novel	Margaret Lawrence, *Hearts and Bones*
1998	Best Novel	*S. J. Rozan, *No Colder Place*
1999	Best Novel	Nevada Barr, *Blind Descent*
	Best Novel	Aileen Schumacher, *Framework for Death*
	Best Paperback Original	*Laura Lippman, *Butcher's Hill*
2000	Best Novel	Jan Burke, *Bones*
	Best Novel	Janet Evanovich, *High Five*
	Best First Mystery	*Donna Andrews, *Murder with Peacocks*
	Best First Mystery	Cara Black, *Murder in the Marais*
	Best First Mystery	April Henry, *Circles of Confusion*
	Best First Mystery	Kris Neri, *Revenge of the Gypsy Queen*
	Best First Mystery	Paula L. Woods, *Inner City Blues*
	Best Paperback Original	Robin Burcell, *Every Move She Makes*
	Best Paperback Original	*Laura Lippman, *In Big Trouble*
	Best Paperback Original	Caroline Roe, *An Antidote for Avarice*
2001	Best Novel	Nevada Barr, *Deep South*
	Best Novel	*Val McDermid, *A Place of Execution*
	Best Novel	Marcia Muller, *Listen to the Silence*
	Best Novel	Elizabeth Peters, *He Shall Thunder in the Sky*
	Best Paperback Original	*Kate Grilley, *Death Dances to a Reggae Beat*
2002	Best Novel	Jan Burke, *Flight*
	Best Novel	S. J. Rozan, *Reflecting the Sky*
	Best First Mystery	Jan Grape, *Austin City Blue*
	Best First Mystery	Denise Hamilton, *The Jasmine Trade*

	Best First Mystery	K. J. Erickson, *Third Person Singular*
	Best Paperback Original	*Charlaine Harris, *Dead until Dark*
2003	Best Novel	Cara Black, *Murder in the Sentier*
	Best Novel	S. J. Rozan, *Winter and Night*
	Best First Mystery	*Julia Spencer-Fleming, *In the Bleak Midwinter*
	Best First Mystery	Libby Fisher Hellman, *An Eye for Murder*
	Best Paperback Original	*Robin Burcell, *Fatal Truth*
	Best Paperback Original	Roberta Isleib, *Six Strokes Under*
	Best Paperback Original	P. J. Parrish, *Paint It Black*
2004	Best Novel	*Laura Lippman, *Every Secret Thing*
	Best First Mystery	*P. J. Tracy, *Monkeewrench*
	Best First Mystery	Erin Hart, *Haunted Ground*
	Best First Mystery	Rebecca C. Pawel, *Death of a Nationalist*
	Best First Mystery	Jacqueline Winspear, *Maisie Dobbs*
	Best Paperback Original	*Robin Burcell, *Deadly Legacy*
	Best Paperback Original	Ealine Flinn, *Dealing in Murder*
	Best Paperback Original	P. J. Parrish, *Thicker than Water*
	Best Paperback Original	Sylvia Maultash Warsh, *Find Me Again*
2005	Best Novel	Laura Lippman, *By a Spider's Thread*
	Best Novel	Julia Spencer-Fleming, *Out of the Deep I Cry*
	Best First Mystery	Sandra Balzo, *Uncommon Grounds*
	Best First Mystery	Judy Clemens, *Till the Cows Come Home*
	Best First Mystery	Jillianne Hoffman, *Retribution*
	Best First Mystery	*Harley Jane Kozak, *Dating Dead Men*
	Best Paperback Original	Robin Burcell, *Cold Case*
	Best Paperback Original	Roberta Isleib, *Putt to Death*
	Best Paperback Original	Susan McBride, *Blue Blood*
	Best Paperback Original	M. J. Rose, *The Halo Effect*

BIBLIOGRAPHY

Anthony Award Winners. MostlyFiction.com. 2006. 17 March 2006. http://mostlyfiction.com/news/anthony2004.htm

Anthony Awards—Best Mystery Novel. Christchurch City Libraries. n.d. 17 March 2006. http://library.christchurch.org.nz/LiteraryPrizes/Anthony/

Bouchercon 2006. 2006. 16 March 2006. http://www.bouchercon.com

Appendix I
The Dagger Awards

The Dagger Awards began in 1955 and are given by the Crime Writers' Association (CWA) of Great Britain. From 1955 until 1969, the best novel of the year was awarded the Gold Dagger, with runner-up writers receiving notice. In 1969, the CWA began awarding a Silver Dagger for the second place book. In 1973, it added the John Creasey Memorial Dagger, which is given for best first novel; and in 1978, it began rewarding nonfiction works as well, with its own gold and silver daggers. In 1986, it introduced the Diamond Dagger, its lifetime achievement award. After the death of Ellis Peters, CWA began presenting a dagger in her honor, the Ellis Peters Historical Dagger. New in 2002 was the Ian Fleming Steel Dagger, given for best thriller writing, and in 2006, the first Duncan Lawrie International Dagger was awarded for best crime fiction translated into English.

Listed below are women writers who have won the major Dagger Awards

Gold Dagger

1961	Mary Kelly, *The Spoilt Kill*
1962	Joan Fleming, *When I Grow Rich*
1967	Emma Lathen, *Murder Against the Grain*
1970	Joan Fleming, *Young Man, I Think You're Dying*
1976	Ruth Rendell, *A Demon in My View*
1984	B. M. Gill, *The Twelfth Juror*
1985	Paula Gosling, *Monkey Puzzle*
1986	Ruth Rendell, *Live Flesh*
1987	Barbara Vine, *A Fatal Inversion*
1991	Barbara Vine, *King Solomon's Carpet*
1993	Patricia Cornwell, *Cruel and Unusual*
1994	Minette Walters, *The Scold's Bridle*
1995	Val McDermid, *The Mermaids Singing*
2003	Minette Walters, *Fox Evil*
2004	Sara Paretsky, *Blacklist*

Silver Dagger

1971	P. D. James, *Shroud for a Nightingale*
1973	Gwendoline Butler, *A Coffin for Pandora*
1975	P. D. James, *The Black Tower*
1980	Ellis Peters, *Monk's Hood*
1984	Ruth Rendell, *The Tree of Hands*
1985	Dorothy Simpson, *Last Seen Alive*
1986	P. D. James, *A Taste for Death*
1988	Sara Paretsky, *Blood Shot* (*Toxic Shock*)
1991	Frances Fyfield, *Deep Sleep*
1992	Liza Cody, *Bucket Nut*
1993	Susan Dunant, *Fatlands*
1997	Janet Evanovich, *Three to Get Deadly*
2000	Donna Leon, *Friends in High Places*
2003	Morag Joss, *Half-Broken Things*
2005	Barbara Nadel, *Deadly Web*

John Creasey Memorial Dagger

1975	Sara George, *Acid Drop*
1978	Paula Gosling, *A Running Duck*
1980	Liza Cody, *Dupe*
1983	Carol Clemeau, *The Ariadne Clue*
1988	Janet Neel, *Death's Bright Angel*
1989	Annette Roome, *A Real Shot in the Arm*
1990	Patricia Cornwell, *Postmortem*
1991	Minette Walters, *The Ice House*
1995	Janet Evanovich, *One for the Money*
1998	Denise Mina, *Garnethill*
2001	Susanna Jones, *The Earthquake Bird*
2002	Louise Welsh, *The Cutting Room*
2005	Dreda Say Mitchell, *Running Hot*

Diamond Dagger

1987	P. D. James
1991	Ruth Rendell
1993	Ellis Peters
1999	Margaret Yorke
2002	Sara Paretsky

Ellis Peters Historical Dagger

| 1999 | Lindsey Davis, *Two for the Lions* |

2000	Gillian Linscott, *Absent Friends*
2002	Sarah Waters, *Fingersmith*
2004	Barbara Cleverly, *The Damascened Blade*

BIBLIOGRAPHY

The Crime Writers' Association. n.d. 16 March 2006. http://www.thecwa.co.uk/

Appendix J
The Macavity Awards

Mystery Readers International is an organization of readers, fans, critics, editors, writers, and publishers and was founded by Janet A. Rudolph. The group began bestowing awards in 1987. The award is named for Macavity, the "mystery cat" in T. S. Eliot's *Old Possum's Book of Practical Cats*. The members of the organization nominate and vote for the award winners each year. Macavity Awards are given in four categories, Best Novel, Best First Novel, Best Short Story, and Best Non-Fiction Work.

Listed below are women nominated for the Macavity Awards. Winners are marked with an asterisk (*). Information about all nominees is unavailable for 1987–1995. Note that the awards are tracked by the year given; the books were published in the prior year.

1987	Best Novel	*P. D. James, *A Taste for Death*
	Best First Novel	*Faye Kellerman, *The Ritual Bath* (tie)
		*Marilyn Wallace, *A Case of Loyalties* (tie)
1988	Best Novel	*Nancy Pickard, *Marriage Is Murder*
1989	Best First Novel	*Caroline Graham, *The Killings at Badger's Drift*
1990	Best Novel	*Carolyn Hart, *A Little Class on Murder*
	Best First Novel	*Jill Churchill, *Grime and Punishment*
1991	Best Novel	*Sharyn McCrumb, *If Ever I Return, Pretty Peggy-O*
	Best First Novel	*Patricia Cornwell, *Postmortem*
1992	Best Novel	*Nancy Pickard, *I.O.U.*
	Best First Novel	*Barbara Neely, *Blanche on the Lam*
1994	Best Novel	*Minette Walters, *The Sculptress*
	Best First Novel	*Sharan Newman, *Death Comes as Epiphany*
1995	Best Novel	*Sharyn McCrumb, *She Walks These Hills*
1996	Best Novel	Barbara D'Amato, *Hard Christmas*
	Best Novel	Marcia Muller, *A Wild and Lonely Place*
	Best Novel	*Mary Willis Walker, *Under the Beetle's Cellar*
	Best First Novel	Jeanne M. Dams, *The Body in the Transept*

	Best First Novel	*Dianne Day, *The Strange Files of Fremont Jones*
	Best First Novel	Teri Holbrook, *A Far and Deadly Cry*
	Best First Novel	Jody Jaffe, *Horse of a Different Killer*
	Best First Novel	Virginia Lanier, *Death in Bloodhound Red*
1997	Best Novel	Janet Evanovich, *Two for the Dough*
	Best Novel	Teri Holbrook, *Grass Widow*
	Best Novel	Margaret Lawrence, *Hearts and Bones*
	Best First Novel	Linda Fairstein, *Final Jeopardy*
	Best First Novel	Anne George, *Murder on a Girls' Night Out*
1998	Best Novel	*Deborah Crombie, *Dreaming of the Bones*
	Best First Novel	Aljean Harmetz, *Off the Face of the Earth*
	Best First Novel	Laura Lippman, *Charm City*
	Best First Novel	Sujata Massey, *The Salaryman's Wife*
	Best First Novel	*Penny Warner, *Dead Body Language*
1999	Best Novel	Nevada Barr, *Blind Descent*
	Best Novel	Laura Lippman, *Butchers Hill*
	Best Novel	Margaret Maron, *Home Fires*
	Best Novel	Abigail Padgett, *Blue*
	Best First Novel	*Jerrilyn Farmer, *Sympathy for the Devil*
	Best First Novel	Jacqueline Fiedler, *Tiger's Palette*
	Best First Novel	Robin Hathaway, *The Doctor Digs a Grave*
2000	Best Novel	*Sujata Massey, *The Flower Master*
	Best First Novel	Donna Andrews, *Murder with Peacocks*
	Best First Novel	Cara Black, *Murder in the Marais*
	Best First Novel	Kris Neri, *Revenge of the Gypsy Queen*
	Best First Novel	*Paula L. Woods, *Inner City Blues*
2001	Best Novel	Taffy Cannon, *Guns and Roses*
	Best Novel	*Val McDermid, *A Place of Execution*
	Best Novel	Anne Perry, *Half Moon Street*
	Best Novel	Nancy Pickard, *The Whole Truth*
	Best First Novel	Kate Grilley, *Death Dances to a Reggae Beat*
	Best First Novel	Julie Wray Herman, *Three Dirty Women and the Garden of Death*
	Best First Novel	Marcia Simpson, *Crow in Stolen Colors*
2002	Best Novel	Linda Fairstein, *The Deadhouse*
	Best Novel	*Laurie R. King, *Folly*
	Best First Novel	Denise Hamilton, *The Jasmine Trade*
	Best First Novel	M. K. Preston, *Perhaps She'll Die*
	Best First Novel	Karin Slaughter, *Blindsighted*

2003	Best Novel	Mary Kay Andrews, *Savannah Blues*
	Best Novel	Jan Burke, *Nine*
	Best First Novel	*S. J. Rozan, *Winter and Night*
	Best First Novel	Radine Trees Nehring, *A Valley to Die For*
	Best First Novel	*Julia Spencer-Fleming, *In the Bleak Midwinter*
2004	Best Novel	Rhys Bowen, *For the Love of Mike*
	Best First Novel	Rebecca C. Pawel, *Death of a Nationalist*
	Best First Novel	*Jacqueline Winspear, *Maisie Dobbs*
2005	Best Novel	Robin Burcell, *Cold Case*
	Best Novel	Margaret Maron, *High Country Fall*
	Best First Novel	Sandra Balzo, *Uncommon Grounds*
	Best First Novel	Naomi Hirahara, *Summer of the Big Bachi*
	Best First Novel	*Harley Jane Kozak, *Dating Dead Men*

BIBLIOGRAPHY

Macavity Awards. Mystery Readers International. 2006. 16 March 2006. http://www.mysteryreaders. org/macavity.html

Appendix K
The Nero Wolfe Awards

The Wolfe Pack, an organization for fans of Nero Wolfe, was begun in 1978. The group hosts a number of meetings and activities, including the Black Orchid Banquet. In 1979, they began presenting an annual award at the banquet. According to the group's Web site, the award is given to an author who "exhibits literary excellence in the mystery genre."

Women Writers Who Have Won the Nero Wolfe Award

1980	Helen McCloy, *Burn This*
1981	Amanda Cross, *Death in a Tenured Position*
1983	Martha Grimes, *The Anodyne Necklace*
1984	Jane Langton, *Emily Dickinson Is Dead*
1987	Charlotte MacLeod, *The Corpse in Oozak's Pond*
1995	Sharyn McCrumb, *She Walks These Hills*
1996	Laurie R. King, *A Monstrous Regiment of Women*
2001	Laura Lippman, *The Sugar House*
2002	Linda Fairstein, *The Deadhouse*
2003	S. J. Rozan, *Winter and Night*

BIBLIOGRAPHY

The Nero Award. The Wolfe Pack. 2005. 16 March 2006. http://www.nerowolfe.org/htm/neroaward/award.html

Appendix L
The Shamus Awards

The Shamus Awards are presented by the Private Eye Writers of America, an organization of writers, fans, and publishers, devoted to private investigator mystery fiction. The group defines private eyes as professional detectives who do not work for the police or government. First given in 1982, the Shamus Awards are given in several categories, including best novel, best first novel, best paperback original, and best short story. Special awards are given for best new writer and for lifetime achievement.

Four women have won the lifetime achievement awards, which are called The Eye. In 1993, Marcia Muller was the first woman to earn the award, followed by Maxine O'Callaghan in 1999, Sue Grafton in 2003, and Sara Paretsky in 2005.

Women writers who have been nominated for the Shamus Award appear below. Winners are marked with an asterisk (*).

1983	Best Novel	Sue Grafton, *A is for Alibi*
1986	Best Novel	*Sue Grafton, *B is for Burglar*
1987	Best Novel	Sue Grafton, *C is for Corpse*
1988	Best Novel	Linda Barnes, *A Trouble of Fools*
1989	Best Novel	Sara Paretsky, *Blood Shot*
1990	Best Novel	Marcia Muller, *The Shape of Dread*
	Best First Novel	*Karen Kijewski, *Katwalk*
	Best Original Paperback	Deborah Valentine, *A Collector of Photographs*
1991	Best Novel	*Sue Grafton, *G Is for Gumshoe*
	Best First Novel	Janet Dawson, *Kindred Crimes*
1992	Best Novel	Marcia Muller, *Where Echoes Live*
	Best Original Paperback	Kay Hooper, *House of Cards*
1993	Best Original Paperback	Catherine Dain, *Lay It on the Line*
	Best Original Paperback	*Marele Day, *The Last Tango of Dolores Delgado*
	Best First Novel	Phyllis Knight, *Switching the Odds*

1994	Best Novel	Marcia Muller, *Wolf in the Shadows*
	Best Novel	Judith Van Gieson, *The Lies That Bind*
	Best First Novel	*Lynn Hightower, *Satan's Lambs*
	Best First Novel	Randye Lordon, *Brotherly Love*
	Best First Novel	Sandra West Prowell, *By Evil Means*
1995	Best Novel	*Sue Grafton, *K Is for Killer*
	Best Novel	Sandra West Prowell, *The Killing of Monday Brown*
	Best First Novel	Janet Evanovich, *One for the Money*
	Best First Novel	Valerie Wilson Wesley, *When Death Comes Stealing*
	Best Original Paperback	Catherine Dain, *Lament for a Dead Cowboy*
	Best Original Paperback	Bridget McKenna, *Dead Ahead*
	Best Original Paperback	Patricia Wallace, *Deadly Devotion*
1996	Best Novel	*S. J. Rozan, *Concourse*
	Best Paperback Original	Shelley Singer, *Interview with Mattie*
	Best Paperback Original	Gloria White, *Charged with Guilt*
	Best First Novel	Ruthe Furie, *If Looks Could Kill*
1997	Best Novel	Sandra West Prowell, *When Wallflowers Die*
	Best Paperback Original	Ruthe Furie, *Natural Death*
	Best First Novel	*Carol Lea Benjamin, *This Dog for Hire*
1998	Best Novel	Maxine O'Callaghan, *Down for the Count*
	Best Novel	S. J. Rozan, *No Colder Place*
	Best Paperback Original	*Laura Lippman, *Charm City*
	Best Paperback Original	Randye Lordon, *Father Forgive Me*
	Best Paperback Original	Gloria White, *Sunset and Santiago*
	Best First Novel	Laura Lippman, *Baltimore Blues*
	Best First Novel	Katy Munger, *Legwork*
1999	Best First Novel	Elizabeth Cosin, *Zen and the Art of Murder*
	Best Paperback Original	Laura Lippman, *Butchers Hill*
2000	Best Novel	S. J. Rozan, *Stone Quarry*
	Best Paperback Original	Sinclair Browning, *The Last Song Dogs*
	Best Paperback Original	P. J. Grady, *Maximum Insecurity*
	Best Paperback Original	*Laura Lippman, *In Big Trouble*
2001	Best Novel	*Carolina Garcia-Aguilera, *Havana Heat*
	Best Novel	Marcia Muller, *Listen to the Silence*
	Best Paperback Original	Mary Jo Adamson, *The Blazing Tree*
	Best Paperback Original	Sinclair Browning, *The Sporting Club*

	Best Paperback Original	Katy Munger, *Bad to the Bone*
2002	Best Novel	Martha C. Lawrence, *Ashes of Aries*
	Best Novel	*S. J. Rozan, *Reflecting the Sky*
	Best Paperback Original	Janet LaPierre, *Keepers*
	Best Paperback Original	*Lyda Morehouse, *Archangel Protocol*
2003	Best Novel	Laura Lippman, *The Last Place*
	Best Novel	S. J. Rozan, *Winter and Night*
	Best Paperback Original	P. J. Parrish, *Paint It Black*
2004	Best Paperback Original	P. J. Parrish, *Thicker Than Water*
2005	Best Paperback Original	Sallie Bissell, *Call the Devil by His Oldest Name*
	Best Paperback Original	P. J. Parrish, *Island of Bones*
	Best First Novel	*Ingrid Black, *The Dead*

BIBLIOGRAPHY

Private Eye Writers of America. n.d.. 16 March 2006. http://hometown.aol.com/rrandisi/
Smith, Kevin Burton. "The Shamus Awards." *The Thrilling Detective*. n.d. 16 March 2006. http://www.thrillingdetective.com/trivia/triv72.html

Appendix M
Twenty Years of
Sisters in Crime

In the first edition of *Great Women Mystery Writers,* Sara Paretsky contributed a piece about the important group she helped found in 1986: Sisters in Crime. At the time of this second edition, Sisters in Crime is celebrating its twentieth anniversary. The original group was convened by Paretsky at the 1986 Bouchercon in Baltimore. Twenty-six women attended the first meeting, and by the spring of 1987, their numbers had grown to more than 100 (Paretsky 379). At that point, they chose their name and formed a steering committee. The original members of that committee, along with Paretsky, were Dorothy Salisbury Davis, Susan Dunlap, Betty Francis, Charlotte MacLeod, Kate Mattes, and Nancy Pickard.

The group was formed to be an advocacy group for women in the mystery field, and this mission is still in place 20 years later. The Web site provides the complete mission statement:

> To combat discrimination against women in the mystery field, educate publishers and the general public as to inequities in the treatment of female authors, raise the level of awareness of their contributions to the field, and promote the professional advancement of women who write mysteries. (homepage)

In addition to a newsletter, the group maintains a "books in print" database of writings by women, which is available to members. They have worked over the past two decades to bring positive attention to women in the mystery field, to help women promote their works, and to fight against stereotypes and discrimination in the publishing field. One of their first projects was to analyze whether books by women mystery writers were being reviewed less frequently than their male counterparts and to work to solve the problem (Reddy 1054–55).

Paretsky reported membership at 1,600 people in 1993 (279); according to the group's Web site, their membership in 2006 is more than 3,400 people who belong to 48 different chapters. In addition to chapters in many states in the United States, there are chapters in Australia and Canada, along with a chapter that covers Germany, Austria, and Switzerland. In addition, an Internet chapter was formed in 1994.

The group has published several booklets to help writers, including two editions of a booklet on marketing, entitled *Shameless Promotion for Brazen Hussies.* They also have sponsored a series of short story collections that offer many women writers their first publication opportunity and also bring "women's work to an ever-growing audience"

(Paretsky 380). The organization's homepage shows a full calendar of events, including conferences and trade shows throughout the year. The group also is currently sponsoring a writers' workshop.

For more information about the group and its services, events and projects, visit the organization online at http://www.sistersincrime.org.

BIBLIOGRAPHY

Paretsky, Sara. "Sisters in Crime." Ed. Kathleen Gregory Klein. *Great Women Mystery Writers.* Westport: Greenwood, 1994. 379–81.

Reddy, Maureen T. "The Female Detective: From Nancy Drew to Sue Grafton." *Mystery and Suspense Writers: The Literature of Crime, Detection, and Espionage.* Eds. Robin W. Winks and Maureen Corrigan. New York: Scribners, 1998. 1047–67.

Sisters in Crime. Homepage. 23 September 2005. 31 March 2006. http://www.sistersincrime.org

Sisters in Crime Internet Chapter. Homepage. 2006. 31 March 2006. http://www.sinc-ic.org/

Critical Bibliography

This bibliography provides a listing of monographs and collections that address women writers and their contributions to mystery and detective fiction. Works that address a single author are included with their entry; works included here may focus on a particular author but more broadly address the history of the genre. A few of these works also cover male writers, but make a substantial contribution to the study of women mystery writers.

Bakerman, Jane S., ed. *And Then There Were Nine… More Women of Mystery.* Bowling Green: Bowling Green State UP, 1985.

Bargainnier, Earl F., ed. *Ten Women of Mystery.* Bowling Green: Bowling Green State UP, 1981.

Craig, Patricia and Mary Cadogan. *The Lady Investigates: Women Detectives and Spies in Fiction.* New York: St. Martin's, 1981.

Craig-Odders, Renee W., Jacky Collins, and Glen S. Close. *Hispanic and Luso-Brazilian Detective Fiction: Essays on the Genero Negro Tradition.* Jefferson: McFarland, 2006.

Della Cava, Frances A. and Madeline H. Engel. *Female Detectives in American Novels: A Bibliography and Analysis of Serialized Female Sleuths.* New York: Garland, 1993.

Dilley, Kimberly. *Busybodies, Meddlers, and Snoops: The Female Hero in Contemporary Women's Mysteries.* Westport: Greenwood, 1998.

DuBose, Martha Hailey. *Women of Mystery: The Lives and Works of Notable Women Crime Novelists.* New York: Thomas Dunne/St. Martin's Minotaur, 2000.

Dyer, Carolyn Stewart and Nancy Tilman Romalov, eds. *Rediscovering Nancy Drew.* Iowa City: U Iowa P, 1995.

Fischer-Hornung, Dorothea and Monika Mueller, eds. *Sleuthing Ethnicity: The Detective in Multiethnic Crime Fiction.* Madison: Fairleigh Dickinson UP, 2003.

Gosselin, Adrienne Johnson, ed. *Multicultural Detective Fiction: Murder from the "Other" Side.* New York: Garland, 1999.

Hadley, Mary. *British Women Mystery Writers: Authors of Detective Fiction with Female Sleuths.* Jefferson: McFarland, 2002.

Irons, Glenwood, ed. *Feminism in Women's Detective Fiction.* Toronto: U Toronto P, 1995.

Jackson, Christine A. *Myth and Ritual in Women's Detective Fiction.* Jefferson, NC: McFarland, 2002.

Kestner, Joseph A. *Sherlock's Sisters: The British Female Detective, 1864–1913.* Aldershot; Burlington: Ashgate, 2003.

Klein, Kathleen Gregory, ed. *Great Women Mystery Writers.* Westport: Greenwood, 1994.

———. *Women Times Three: Writers, Detectives, Readers.* Bowling Green: Bowling Green UP, 1995.

———. *The Woman Detective: Gender and Genre.* 2nd ed. Urbana: U Illinois P, 1995.

———. *Diversity and Detective Fiction.* Bowling Green: Bowling Green State UP, 1999.

Knight, Stephen Thomas. *Crime Fiction, 1800–2000: Detection, Death, Diversity.* Hampshire; New York: Palgrave Macmillan, 2004.

Maida, Patricia D. *Mother of Detective Fiction: The Life and Works of Anna Katharine Green.* Bowling Green: Bowling Green State UP, 1989.

Mann, Jessica. *Deadlier than the Male: Why are Respectable English Women So Good at Murder?* New York: Macmillan, 1981.

Mason, Bobbie Ann. *The Girl Sleuth: A Feminist Guide.* Old Westbury, NY: Feminist Press, 1975; Athens: U Georgia P, 1995.

Mizejewski, Linda. *Hardboiled and High Heeled: The Woman Detective in Popular Culture.* New York: Routledge, 2004.

Morris, Virginia B. *Double Jeopardy: Women Who Kill in Victorian Fiction.* Lexington: UP Kentucky, 1990.

Munt, Sally R. *Murder by the Book? Feminism and the Crime Novel.* London: Routledge, 1994.

Nichols, Victoria. *Silk Stalkings: When Women Write of Murder.* Berkeley: Black Lizard, 1988.

Nickerson, Catherine. *The Web of Iniquity: Early Detective Fiction by American Women.* Durham: Duke UP, 1998.

Pepper, Andrew. *The Contemporary American Crime Novel: Race, Ethnicity, Gender, Class.* Edinburgh: Edinburgh UP, 2000.

Plain, Gill. *Twentieth-Century Crime Fiction: Gender, Sexuality, and the Body.* Edinburgh: Edinburgh UP, 2001.

Reddy, Maureen. *Sisters in Crime: Feminism and the Crime Novel.* New York: Continuum, 1988.

Rehak, Melanie. *Girl Sleuth: Nancy Drew and the Women Who Created Her.* Orlando: Harcourt, 2005.

Reynolds, Moira Davison. *Women Authors of Detective Series: Twenty-One American and British Writers, 1900–2000.* Jefferson, NC: McFarland, 2001.

Rowland, Susan. *From Agatha Christie to Ruth Rendell: British Women Writers in Detective and Crime Fiction.* New York: Palgrave, 2001.

Seaman, Amanda C. *Bodies of Evidence: Women, Society, and Detective Fiction in 1990s Japan.* Honolulu: U Hawaii P, 2004.

Shaw, Marion and Sabine Vanacker. *Reflecting on Miss Marple.* London: Routledge, 1991.

Silet, Charles L. P. *Talking Murder: Interviews with 20 Mystery Writers.* Princeton: Ontario Review Press, 1999.

Swanson, Jean and Dean James. *By a Woman's Hand: A Guide to Mystery Fiction by Women.* New York: Berkley, 1996.

Walton, Priscilla L. and Manina Jones. *Detective Agency: Women Rewriting the Hard-Boiled Tradition.* Berkeley: U California P, 1999.

Windrath, Helen, ed. *They Wrote the Book: Thirteen Women Mystery Writers Tell All.* Duluth: Spinsters Ink, 2000.

Winks, Robin W. and Maureen Corrigan, eds. *Mystery and Suspense Writers: The Literature of Crime, Detection, and Espionage.* New York: Scribners, 1998.

Index

About the Author

ELIZABETH BLAKESLEY LINDSAY is the Assistant Director for Public Services and Outreach at the Washington State University Libraries, where she formerly served as Head of Library Instruction. She previously worked in the libraries at Indiana State University and UMass Dartmouth. She earned a bachelor's degree with a double major in English and Spanish from the University of Dayton and earned both her MLS and her master's in comparative literature at Indiana University, Bloomington.

DISCARD